MCSA Guide to
Installing and Configuring
Microsoft® Windows Server®
2012/R2, Exam 70-410

Greg Tomsho

CENGAGE
Learning·

Australia • Brazil • Japan • Korea • Mexico • Singapore • Spain • United Kingdom • United States

CENGAGE
Learning·

MCSA Guide to Installing and Configuring Microsoft® Windows Server® 2012/R2, Exam 70-410
Greg Tomsho

Vice President, General Manager: Dawn Gerrain

Product Director: Kathleen McMahon

Product Team Manager: Nick Lombardi

Director, Development: Marah Bellegarde

Product Development Manager: Leigh Hefferon

Senior Content Developer:
  Michelle Ruelos Cannistraci

Developmental Editor: Lisa M. Lord

Product Assistant: Scott Finger

Marketing Manager: Eric La Scola

Senior Production Director: Wendy Troeger

Production Manager: Patty Stephan

Senior Content Project Manager:
  Brooke Greenhouse

Art Director: GEX Publishing Services

Cover image: ©iStockphoto.com/agsandrew

For product information and technology assistance, contact us at
Cengage Learning Customer & Sales Support, 1-800-354-9706.

For permission to use material from this text or product,
submit all requests online at **www.cengage.com/permissions.**
Further permissions questions can be e-mailed to
permissionrequest@cengage.com.

Library of Congress Control Number: 2014938413

ISBN-13: 978-1-285-86865-3

ISBN-10: 1-285-86865-X

Course Technology
20 Channel Center St.
Boston, MA 02210
USA

Cengage Learning is a leading provider of customized learning solutions with office locations around the globe, including Singapore, the United Kingdom, Australia, Mexico, Brazil, and Japan. Locate your local office at **www.cengage.com/global.**

Cengage Learning products are represented in Canada by Nelson Education, Ltd.

To learn more about Cengage Learning, visit **www.cengage.com**

Purchase any of our products at your local college store or at our preferred online store **www.cengagebrain.com.**

Printed in the United States of America
4 5 6 7 8 9 10 21 20 19 18 17

Brief Contents

Contents

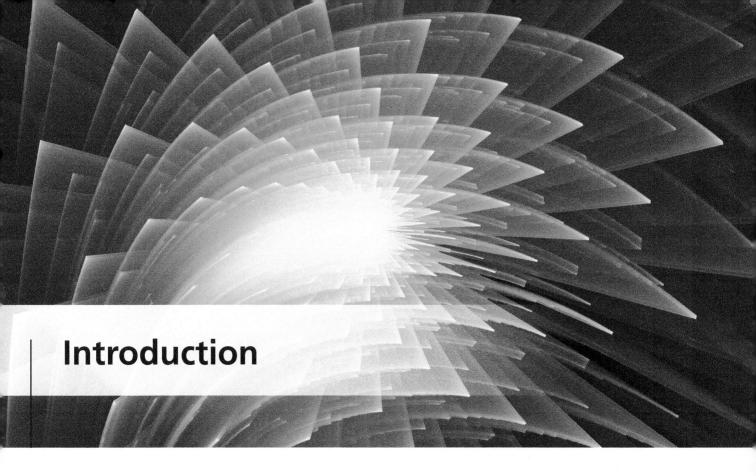

Introduction

MCSA Guide to Installing and Configuring Microsoft® Windows Server® 2012/R2, Exam 70-410, gives you in-depth coverage of the 70-410 certification exam objectives and focuses on the skills you need to install and configure Windows Server 2012/R2. With more than 130 hands-on activities and dozens of skill-reinforcing case projects, you'll be well prepared for the certification exam and learn valuable skills to perform on the job.

After you finish this book, you'll have an in-depth knowledge of Windows Server 2012/R2, including installation, local and remote management, file and storage services, Active Directory, group policies, TCP/IP, networking services, and Hyper-V virtualization. Both the original release of Windows Server 2012 and the R2 release are covered.

Intended Audience

MCSA Guide to Installing and Configuring Microsoft® Windows Server® 2012/R2, Exam 70-410, is intended for people who want to learn how to configure and manage a Windows Server 2012/R2 network and earn the Microsoft Certified Solutions Associate (MCSA) certification. This book covers in full the objectives of the first exam (70-410) needed to be MCSA: Windows Server 2012 certified. This book serves as an excellent tool for classroom teaching, but self-paced learners will also find that the clear explanations and challenging activities and case projects serve them equally well. Although this book doesn't assume previous experience with Windows servers, it does assume a familiarity with current Windows OSs, such as Windows 7 or Windows 8.x. Networking knowledge equivalent to an introductory networking course or Network+ is highly recommended.

What This Book Includes

- A lab setup guide is included in the "Before You Begin" section of this introduction to help you configure a physical or virtual (recommended) lab environment for doing the hands-on activities.

- Step-by-step hands-on activities walk you through tasks ranging from a basic Windows Server 2012 R2 installation to complex multiserver network configurations involving Active Directory, Group Policy, DNS, and many other services. All activities have been tested by a technical editor, reviewers, and validation experts.

- Extensive review and end-of-chapter materials reinforce your learning.
- Challenging case projects require you to apply the concepts and technologies learned throughout the book.
- Abundant screen captures and diagrams visually reinforce the text and hands-on activities.
- A list of 70-410 exam objectives is cross-referenced with chapters and sections that cover each objective.

About Microsoft Certification: MCSA/MCSE

This book prepares you to take the first exam in the Microsoft Certified Solutions Associate (MCSA) Windows Server 2012 certification. The MCSA Windows Server 2012 certification is made up of three exams, which should be taken in order as follows:

- Exam 70-410: Installing and Configuring Windows Server 2012
- Exam 70-411: Administering Windows Server 2012
- Exam 70-412: Configuring Advanced Windows Server 2012 Services

 Taking the exams in order is important because the objectives build on one another, with some topics introduced in an earlier exam and reinforced in subsequent exams.

Microsoft Certified Solutions Expert (MCSE): The Next Step

After achieving the MCSA Windows Server 2012 certification, you can move on to the MCSE certification. Microsoft offers three main options, and all require the three MCSA exams as a prerequisite:

- MCSE: Server Infrastructure
  - Exam 70-413: Designing and Implementing a Server Infrastructure
  - Exam 70-414: Implementing an Advanced Server Infrastructure
- MCSE: Desktop Infrastructure
  - Exam 70-415: Implementing a Desktop Infrastructure
  - Exam 70-416: Implementing Desktop Application Environments
- MCSE: Private Cloud
  - Exam 70-246: Monitoring and Operating a Private Cloud with System Center 2012
  - Exam 70-247: Configuring and Deploying a Private Cloud with System Center 2012

Chapter Descriptions

This book is organized to familiarize you with Windows Server 2012/R2 features and technologies and then provide in-depth coverage of Windows services. It wraps up by discussing Hyper-V virtualization, a technology that's the cornerstone of Microsoft's private cloud initiatives. The 70-410 exam objectives are covered throughout the book, and you can find a mapping of objectives and the chapters in which they're covered on the inside front cover, with a more detailed mapping in Appendix A. The following list describes this book's chapters:

- **Chapter 1**, "Introducing Windows Server 2012/R2," describes the role of a server operating system and compares the Windows Server 2012/R2 editions. Next, you're given an overview of Windows Server 2012/R2 core technologies, such as the NTFS file system, Active Directory, disk management, and networking. Finally, you learn about server roles and new features in Windows Server 2012/R2.

- **Chapter 2**, "Installing Windows Server 2012/R2," discusses the details of planning a Windows Server 2012/R2 installation, including installing the first server on a new network, expanding an existing network, and upgrading to Windows Server 2012/R2, including server role migration. The Server Core installation option is discussed next, followed by optimizing an installation by using Features on Demand.

- **Chapter 3**, "Local and Remote Server Management," explains how to work with server roles and features and how to configure server modes. Next, you learn how to manage servers remotely with new features in Server Manager. This chapter wraps up with a discussion on configuring services and NIC teaming and working with downlevel servers.

- **Chapter 4**, "Configuring Server Storage," describes the methods available for storage provisioning, including working with local and virtual disks and using disk partition and format options. You learn about the types of volumes you can create on a Windows server and how to use Storage Spaces, a new feature in Windows Server 2012/R2.

- **Chapter 5**, "File and Printer Services," discusses how Windows implements file and printer sharing. You learn how to secure access to files by using NTFS permissions and how permission inheritance works. This chapter also explains default and administrative shares and managing shared folders. Work Folders, a new feature in Windows Server 2012/R2, is discussed next, followed by details on configuring and managing Windows printing.

- **Chapter 6**, "Introducing Active Directory," describes the role of a directory service in a network and explains how to install Active Directory. Next, you learn about Active Directory components, such as the schema and Active Directory objects, and the Active Directory structure, including forests, trees, and domains. This chapter ends with an introduction to Group Policy.

- **Chapter 7**, "Managing OUs and Active Directory Accounts," gives you an in-depth look at the core organizing object in Active Directory: organizational units. Active Directory object permissions and delegation of control are discussed in detail. Next, you learn how to manage user accounts, group accounts, and computer accounts. Finally, you see how to use command-line tools to automate account management.

- **Chapter 8**, "Configuring Group Policies," gives you a detailed look at the architecture of Group Policy and Group Policy objects (GPOs). You learn how group policy replication works and how to create and link GPOs. You also learn about group policy inheritance and precedence, including local GPOs. Group policy nodes and some of their many settings are described, with particular attention to security settings and using security templates.

- **Chapter 9**, "Configuring TCP/IP," describes the TCP/IP protocol and its components. You learn how to configure TCP/IP addresses and calculate subnet masks for IPv4 addresses. Then you learn about IPv6 addresses and how to configure IPv6 autoconfiguration. Finally, you learn about IPv4-to-IPv6 transition technologies.

- **Chapter 10**, "Configuring DNS," gives you an overview of the Domain Name System and explains how to install DNS and create DNS zones. You learn about configuring zones, including Active Directory–integrated zones, zone replication, forward and reverse lookup zones, dynamic updates, and zone transfers. Finally, you explore advanced DNS server settings, such as forwarders and root hints, and see how to monitor and troubleshoot DNS.

- **Chapter 11**, "Configuring Dynamic Host Configuration Protocol," describes the DHCP protocol and the client address leasing process. You learn about installing and configuring a DHCP server, which includes scope configuration, DHCP reservations, and filters. This chapter ends with a discussion of DHCP server settings and how to configure a DHCP relay agent.

- **Chapter 12**, "Configuring Virtualization with Hyper-V," describes the Hyper-V server role installation and configuration. You learn how to create and configure virtual machines and virtual networks, including external, internal, and private virtual switches. You also learn about features such as checkpoints, dynamic memory, and types of virtual disks.

- **Appendix A**, "MCSA 70-410 Exam Objectives," maps each 70-410 exam objective to the chapter and section where you can find information on that objective.

Features

This book includes the following learning features to help you master the topics in this book and the 70-410 exam objectives:

- *Chapter objectives*—Each chapter begins with a detailed list of the concepts to be mastered. This list is a quick reference to the chapter's contents and a useful study aid.

- *Hands-on activities*—More than 130 hands-on activities are incorporated in this book, giving you practice in setting up, configuring, and managing a Windows Server 2012/R2 server. The activities give you a strong foundation for carrying out server installation and configuration tasks in production environments. Much of the learning about Windows Server 2012/R2 comes from doing the hands-on activities, and a lot of effort has been devoted to making the activities relevant and challenging.

- *A requirements table for hands-on activities*—A table at the beginning of each chapter lists the hands-on activities and what you need for each activity.

- *Screen captures, illustrations, and tables*—Numerous screen captures and illustrations of concepts help you visualize theories and concepts and see how to use tools and desktop features. In addition, tables are used often to give you details and comparisons of practical and theoretical information and can be used for a quick review.

- *Chapter summary*—Each chapter ends with a summary of the concepts introduced in the chapter. These summaries are a helpful way to recap and revisit the material covered in the chapter.

- *Key terms*—All terms in the chapter introduced with bold text are gathered together in the Key Terms list at the end of the chapter. This list gives you a way to check your understanding of all important terms.

- *Review questions*—The end-of-chapter assessment begins with review questions that reinforce the concepts and techniques covered in each chapter. Answering these questions helps ensure that you have mastered important topics.

- *Case projects*—Each chapter closes with one or more case projects. Many of the case projects build on one another, as you take a small startup company to a flourishing enterprise.

- *Trial Version Software*—To download the trial version software, go to https://www.microsoft.com/en-US/evalcenter/evaluate-windows-server-2012.

Text and Graphics Conventions

Additional information and exercises have been added to this book to help you better understand what's being discussed in the chapter. Icons throughout the book alert you to these additional materials:

 Tips offer extra information on resources, how to solve problems, and time-saving shortcuts.

 Notes present additional helpful material related to the subject being discussed.

 The Caution icon identifies important information about potential mistakes or hazards.

 Each hands-on activity in this book is preceded by the Activity icon.

 Case Project icons mark the end-of-chapter case projects, which are scenario-based assignments that ask you to apply what you have learned in the chapter.

CertBlaster Test Preparation Questions

MCSA Guide to Installing and Configuring Microsoft® Windows Server® 2012/R2, Exam 70-410 includes CertBlaster test preparation questions for the 70-410 MCSA exam. CertBlaster is a powerful online certification preparation tool from dti Publishing that mirrors the look and feel of the certification exam.

To log in and access the CertBlaster test preparation questions for *MCSA Guide to Installing and Configuring Microsoft® Windows Server® 2012/R2, Exam 70-410*, go to *www.certblaster. com/login/*. The CertBlaster user's online manual describes features and gives navigation instructions. Activate your CertBlaster license by entering your name, e-mail address, and access code (found on the card bound in this book) in their fields, and then click Submit. CertBlaster offers three practice modes and all the types of questions required to simulate the exams:

- *Assessment mode*—Used to determine the student's baseline level. In this mode, the timer is on, answers aren't available, and the student gets a list of questions answered incorrectly, along with a Personal Training Plan.

- *Study mode*—Helps the student understand questions and the logic behind answers by giving immediate feedback both during and after the test. Answers and explanations are available. The timer is optional, and the student gets a list of questions answered incorrectly, along with a Personal Training Plan.

- *Certification mode*—A simulation of the actual exam environment. The timer as well as the number and format of questions from the exam objectives are set according to the exam's format.

For more information about dti test prep products, visit the Web site at *www.dtipublishing.com*.

Instructor Companion Site

Everything you need for your course in one place! This collection of book-specific lecture and class tools is available online via *www.cengage.com/login*. Access and download PowerPoint presentations, images, the Instructor's Manual, and more.

- *Electronic Instructor's Manual*—The Instructor's Manual that accompanies this book includes additional instructional material to assist in class preparation, including suggestions for classroom activities, discussion topics, and additional quiz questions.

- *Solutions Manual*—The instructor's resources include solutions to all end-of-chapter material, including review questions and case projects.

- *Cengage Learning Testing Powered by Cognero*—This flexible, online system allows you to do the following:

   o Author, edit, and manage test bank content from multiple Cengage Learning solutions.

   o Create multiple test versions in an instant.

   o Deliver tests from your LMS, your classroom, or wherever you want.

- *PowerPoint presentations*—This book comes with Microsoft PowerPoint slides for each chapter. They're included as a teaching aid for classroom presentation, to make available to students on the network for chapter review, or to be printed for classroom distribution. Instructors, please feel free to add your own slides for additional topics you introduce to the class.

- *Figure files*—All the figures and tables in the book are reproduced in bitmap format. Similar to the PowerPoint presentations, they're included as a teaching aid for classroom presentation, to make available to students for review, or to be printed for classroom distribution.

Acknowledgments

I would like to thank Cengage Learning Product Manager Nick Lombardi for his confidence in asking me to undertake this challenging book project. In addition, thanks go out to Michelle Ruelos Cannistraci, the Senior Content Developer, who assembled an outstanding team to support this project. A special word of gratitude goes to Lisa Lord, the Development Editor, who has a knack for taking an unrefined product and turning it into a polished manuscript. Lisa's good humor and understanding as well as her commendable skills as an editor made my life considerably easier during the 8 months it took to complete this book. Serge Palladino, from the Manuscript Quality Assurance staff at Cengage Learning, tested chapter activities diligently to ensure that labs work as they were intended, and for that, I am grateful. I also want to include a shout-out to a student, Stephanie Garcia, who provided an extra layer of QA for hands-on activities.

Of course, this book wasn't written in a vacuum, and the peer reviewers offered thoughtful advice, constructive criticism, and much needed encouragement: Kara Brown, Sinclair College; Matt Halvorson, Yavapai College; Heith Hennel, Valencia College; and Michael Linkey, University of Illinois.

Finally, my family: My wife, Julie; daughters Camille and Sophia; and son, Michael, deserve special thanks and praise for going husbandless and fatherless 7 days a week, 14 hours a day, for the better part of a year. Without their patience and understanding and happy greetings when I did make an appearance, I could not have accomplished this.

About the Author

Greg Tomsho has more than 30 years of computer and networking experience and has earned the CCNA, MCTS, MCSA, A+, Security+, and Linux+ certifications. Greg is the director of the Computer Networking Technology Department and Cisco Academy at Yavapai College in Prescott, AZ. His other books include *MCSA Guide to Administering Windows Server 2012/R2, Exam 70-411, MCTS Guide to Microsoft Windows Server 2008 Active Directory Configuration, MCTS Guide to Microsoft Windows Server 2008 Applications Infrastructure Configuration, Guide to Networking Essentials, Guide to Network Support and Troubleshooting,* and *A+ CoursePrep ExamGuide.*

Contact the Author

I would like to hear from you. Please e-mail me at *w2k12@tomsho.com* with any problems, questions, suggestions, or corrections. I even accept compliments! Your comments and suggestions are invaluable for shaping the content of future books. You can also submit errata, lab suggestions, and comments via e-mail. I have set up a Web site to support my books at *http://books.tomsho. com*, where you'll find lab notes, errata, Web links, and helpful hints for using my books. If you're an instructor, you can register on the site to contribute articles and comment on articles.

Before You Begin

Windows Server has become more complex as Microsoft strives to satisfy the needs of enterprise networks. In years past, you could learn what you needed to manage a Windows Server-based network and pass the Microsoft certification exams with a single server, some good lab instructions, and a network connection. Today, as you work with advanced technologies—such as Hyper-V, Storage Spaces, and DirectAccess, just to name a few—your lab environment must be more complex, requiring two or even three servers and at least one client computer. Setting up this lab environment can be challenging, and this section was written to help you meet this challenge. Using virtual machines in VMware Workstation or VMware Player is highly recommended; other virtual environments work, too, but VMware allows you to install Hyper-V on a virtual machine. Hyper-V is used in Chapter 12.

If you can't set up a lab environment exactly as described in this section, you still have some options to help you gain the skills learned through hands-on activities:

- *Configure a partial lab*—If you have just one Windows Server 2012 R2 server available, you can still do many of the hands-on activities. Having one server and one client is even better, and having two servers and one client enables you to do the majority of the book's activities. If you can't do an activity, it's important to read the activity steps to learn important information about Windows Server 2012/R2.

- *Purchase the Web-Based Labs*—Cengage Learning offers Web-Based Labs for this book. This product gives you access to a real lab environment over the Internet by using a Web browser. Step-by-step lab instructions are taken directly from the hands-on activities in the book. See your sales representative or the Cengage Learning Web site for more information.

Lab Setup Guide

The lab equipment for hands-on activities consists of four computers (three of which are servers) and one client OS. One server with Windows Server 2012 R2 should be configured before doing the hands-on activities in Chapter 1. A client computer with Windows 8.1 Enterprise Edition should be available starting with Chapter 5. In Chapter 2, you install Windows Server 2012 R2 and Windows Server 2012 R2 Server Core on two additional servers. Figure 1 shows a diagram of the network.

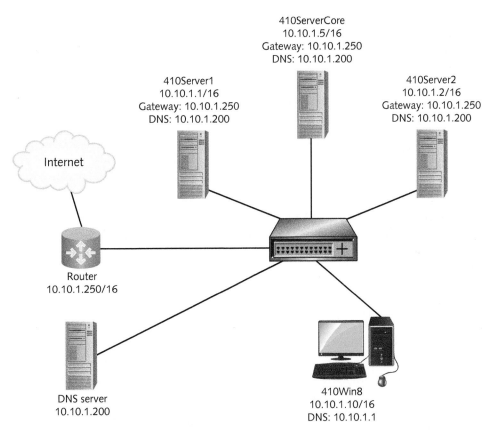

Figure 1 A diagram of the lab configuration

© 2015 Cengage Learning®

A few words about this diagram:

- The router address is suggested, but you can use a different address. You can do most activities without a router to the Internet, except those requiring Internet access.

- The DNS server address is suggested, but you can use a different address. The DNS server should have a zone named 410Server2012.local configured to accept unsecured updates. This DNS server is needed in only a few activities, mainly Chapter 3 when you're configuring server management. You can still do the activities without a DNS server but need to use IP addresses instead of server names when called for.

- Only 410Server1 must have an OS installed and configured before starting activities in Chapter 1.
- 410Server2 and 410ServerCore are installed and configured in Chapter 2.
- There's no activity to install Windows 8.1 on 410Win8, but it should be installed before Chapter 5, when it's first used.
- Specific installation requirements for each server are explained in the following sections.

410Server1

This server should be configured as follows before beginning the activities in Chapter 1:

- Windows Server 2012 R2 Standard or Datacenter
- Server name: 410Server1
- Administrator password: Password01
- Memory: 1 GB or more
- Hard disk 1: 60 GB or more
- Hard disk 2: 60 GB or more
- Network interface card
- Workgroup: 410Server2012
- Primary DNS suffix: 410Server2012.local (To set it, right-click Start, click System, click Change settings, click Change, and click More. Restart the server after changing the suffix.)
- Chapter 4 requires installing a third HDD. If you're using virtualization, you can just add the new virtual disk with the virtualization software. If you're using physical servers, you need another disk to install in the server.
- IP address: 10.10.1.1/16
- Default gateway: 10.10.1.250 (or an address supplied by the instructor)
- DNS: 10.10.1.200 or the address of a DNS server on your network that accepts unsecured dynamic updates and has a zone named 410Server2012.local
- Windows Update: Not configured
- The network location must be set to Private. To change the network location from Public to Private, if necessary, follow these steps:

1. Open Server Manager, and click **Tools, Local Security Policy** from the menu.
2. In the Local Security Policy console, click **Network List Manager Policies**. Double-click **All Networks**, and in the Network location section, click **User can change location**. Click **OK**.
3. Double-click the network you're connected to. (If you aren't sure, open the Network and Sharing Center, which shows the name of the network and whether it's configured as a Public, Private, or Domain network.)
4. In the Network Location tab, click the **Private** option button, and click **OK**.

- If you're using an evaluation version of Windows Server 2012 R2, you can rearm the evaluation up to five times. To do so, follow these steps:

1. Open a command prompt window as Administrator.
2. Type **slmgr -xpr** and press **Enter** to see the current status of your license. It shows how many days are left in the evaluation. If it says you're in notification mode, you need to rearm the evaluation immediately.
3. To rearm the evaluation, type **slmgr -rearm** and press **Enter**. You see a message telling you to restart the system for the changes to take effect. Click **OK** and restart the system.

410Server2

No OS is installed before beginning the activities. You install Windows Server 2012 R2 on 410Server2 in Chapter 2, Activity 2-1. Hyper-V is installed on this machine in Chapter 12, so it must meet the requirements for Hyper-V installation. You can install the Hyper-V role on VMs running in VMware Workstation 9 and later with the right hardware support, but it's not officially supported.

The configuration settings are done in the activities. They're listed here just for your information:

- Server name: 410Server2
- Administrator password: Password01
- Memory: 1 GB or more (4 GB or more for the Hyper-V activities in Chapter 12)
- Hard disk 1: 60 GB or more
- Hard disk 2: 60 GB or more
- Network interface card
- Workgroup: 410Server2012
- Primary DNS suffix: 410Server2012.local
- IP address: 10.10.1.2/16
- Default gateway: Same as for 410Server1
- DNS: Same as for 410Server1
- The network location must be set to Private. To change the network location from Public to Private, see the instructions for 410Server1.

410ServerCore

No OS is installed before beginning the activities. You install Windows Server 2012 R2 Server Core on this machine in Chapter 2, Activity 2-7.

The configuration settings are done in the activities. They're listed here just for your information:

- Server name: 410ServerCore
- Administrator password: Password01
- Memory: 1 GB or more
- Hard disk 1: 60 GB or more
- Network interface card
- Workgroup: 410Server2012
- Primary DNS suffix: 410Server2012.local
- IP address: 10.10.1.5/16
- Default gateway: Same as for 410Server1
- DNS: Same as for 410Server1
- The network location must be set to Private. To change the network location from Public to Private, see the instructions for 410Server1.

410Win8

This computer should be configured as follows before beginning Chapter 5:

- Windows 8.1 Enterprise Edition
- Machine name: 410Win8

- Local administrator account with the username Win8User and the password Password01
- Memory: 1 GB or more
- Hard disk 1: 60 GB or more
- Network interface card
- Workgroup: 410Server2012
- Settings: Express settings
- Sign in without a Microsoft account
- IPv4 address: 10.10.1.10/16
- Default gateway: Same as for 410Server1
- DNS: The IP address of 410Server1 (10.10.1.1)
- Windows Update: Not configured

Here are some additional recommended requirements:

- A router to the Internet. The recommended address is 10.10.1.250/16, but any address in this subnet will work.
- A DNS server with a zone named 410Server2012.local.

Deployment Recommendations

Using virtualization to configure your lab environment is recommended. If you're using physical computers, the requirements are much the same, but you need many more physical computers. If you're using physical computers, you can set up the network as shown previously in Figure 1 and configure the computers as described earlier.

Avoiding IP Address Conflicts

Whether you're using physical computers or virtual computers, you must have a method for avoiding IP address conflicts. There are two setups for working in a classroom environment:

- *All students computers are on the same physical subnet*—In this setup, IP addresses and computer names must be changed to avoid conflict. One strategy for avoiding IP address conflicts is using the third octet of the address. Each student is assigned a number, such as one from 1 to 50. When assigning IP addresses, simply change the third octet to the student-assigned number. For example, for student 15, address 10.10.1.1 becomes 10.10.15.1. Use the same number as a suffix for the computer and domain names. For example, 410Server1 becomes 410Server1-15, 410Server1-16, and so forth. The domain name also changes accordingly, such as 410Server2012-15.local, 410Server2012-16.local, and so on.

- *Each student works in a "sandbox" environment*—This setup is preferred, if it's possible. A router using NAT separates each student's sandboxed network environment, so there are no conflicts. This setup is easier to configure with virtualization. One possibility, as described later in the "Sample Configuration for Virtualization" section, is to configure an extra Windows Server 2012 VM as a NAT router with RRAS and as a DNS server. This machine can then route from the private network to the public Internet when needed. It also serves as the initial DNS server required for some activities, but its main purpose is to hide students' VMs from each other so that there are no address or name conflicts.

Using Virtualization

Using virtualization is highly recommended, and you have the following options for virtualization software:

- *VMware Workstation*—This sophisticated virtualization environment is a free download if your school or organization is a member of the VMware Academic Program (*http://vmapss .onthehub.com*). The advantage of VMware Workstation is that you can take periodic snapshots of VMs and revert to one if something goes wrong with a virtual machine. In addition, you can install Hyper-V in a virtual machine with just a few tweaks to the VM configuration if your host supports it. You can find instructions for installing Hyper-V in a VMware virtual machine at *http://4sysops.com/archives/how-to-run-hyper-v-under-vmware-workstation/*.

- *VMware Player*—This product is a free download from the VMware Web site. You can't take snapshots, but otherwise, it's an excellent virtual environment.

- *Hyper-V*—If you install Windows Server 2012 R2 or Windows 8.1 on your host computers, you can run Hyper-V as your virtual environment. The advantage of using Hyper-V is that you can do the Hyper-V activities in Chapter 12 without any additional configuration. The disadvantage of using Hyper-V is that you need Administrator access to your host computers to use Hyper-V Manager.

- *VirtualBox*—This excellent open-source virtualization product from Oracle has many advanced features, as VMware Workstation does, but it's free. However, it doesn't support running Hyper-V on a virtual machine.

Host Computer Requirements When Using Virtualization

The following are recommendations for the host computer when you're using virtualization:

- Dual-core or quad-core CPU with Intel-VT-x/EPT or AMD-V/RVI support. You can see a list of supported Intel processors at *http://ark.intel.com/products/virtualizationtechnology*.

Most activities can be done without a CPU that supports EPT, but you can't install Hyper-V on a VM if the host doesn't support EPT for Intel CPUs or RVI on AMD CPUs.

- 8 GB RAM.

Most activities can be done with 4 GB RAM installed on the host. Only those requiring three VMs running at the same time need more than 4 GB.

- 150 GB free disk space.

- Windows 7 or Windows 8/8.1 if you're using VMware Workstation, VMware Player, or VirtualBox.

- Windows Server 2012 R2 or Windows 8.1 Pro or Enterprise 64-bit if you're using Hyper-V.

Sample Configuration for Virtualization

Figure 2 shows a diagram of a setup that includes a virtual machine acting as a router and DNS server. The virtual networks are labeled for both a Hyper-V implementation and a VMware implementation. (The Server Core server isn't shown in this diagram.) The virtual machine set up as a router has two virtual NICs, one connected to the private network with lab computers and one connected to an external (Hyper-V) or bridged (VMware) network that connects to the physical network. The router VM is running RRAS and NAT for routing and DNS with the 410Server2012.local zone.

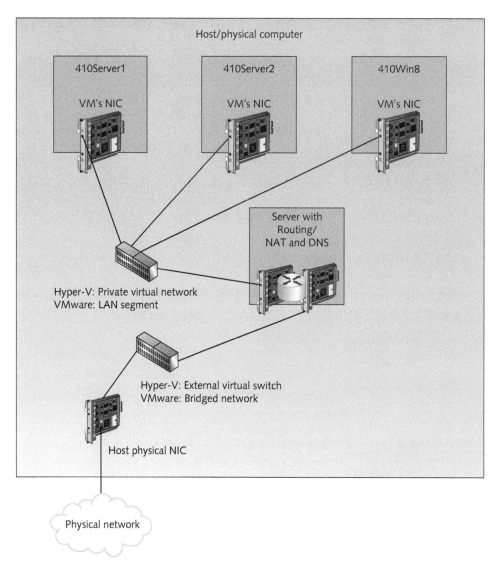

Figure 2   A sample virtual lab configuration

© 2015 Cengage Learning®

Where to Go for Help

Configuring a lab and keeping everything running correctly can be challenging. Even small configuration changes can prevent activities from running correctly. If you're using virtualization, use snapshots if possible so that you can revert virtual machines to an earlier working state in case something goes wrong. The author maintains a Web site that includes lab notes, suggestions, errata, and help articles that might be useful if you're having trouble, and you can contact the author at these addresses:

- Web site: *htttp://books.tomsho.com*
- E-mail: *w2k12@tomsho.com*

chapter 1

Introducing Windows Server 2012/R2

After reading this chapter and completing the exercises, you will be able to:

- Explain the function of a server operating system in a network
- Describe the editions of Windows Server 2012/R2
- Define private cloud terms and technologies
- Explain the core technologies of Windows Server 2012/R2
- Describe Windows Server 2012/R2 roles
- Summarize the new and enhanced features of Windows Server 2012/R2

Windows Server 2012/R2 is Microsoft's deep dive into the private cloud.
This new version is chock-full of new tools and features designed to help server administrators increase the availability of network services and limit security risks. Microsoft has also emphasized features that help datacenter operators deploy and manage a private cloud.

Most networks are set up so that the people using computers on them can communicate with one another easily. One of a server's functions is to facilitate communication between computers and, therefore, between people. The administrator of a computer network has the job of configuring servers and computers on the network to provide services that facilitate this communication. These services include, but aren't limited to, file sharing, device sharing (such as printers and storage), security, messaging, remote access, Web services, and services that work in the background to ensure a user-friendly and secure experience.

This chapter discusses the editions of Windows Server 2012/R2 and the requirements and uses for each. In addition, you learn about the roles a server operating system plays in a computer network and the many features in Windows Server 2012/R2 designed to fill these roles. With Microsoft's emphasis on Windows Server 2012's role in the private cloud, this chapter also defines cloud computing and some terms associated with this collection of technologies.

This book covers Windows Server 2012 and the newer Windows Server 2012 R2. When a topic or feature is relevant to both the original release of Windows Server 2012 and R2, the name Windows Server 2012/R2 is used. If a feature is particular to the R2 version, Windows Server 2012 R2 is used (without the "/" character). Microsoft has added a number of enhancements in Windows Server 2012 R2, and the new and modified features will have found their way into the Windows Server 2012 certification exams by the time this book is published.

About the Hands-On Activities

Be sure to read and complete the activities in the "Before You Begin" section of the Introduction. The hands-on activities in this chapter and all that follow require setting up your lab environment so that it's ready to go. The hands-on activities in this chapter use 410Server1, a Windows Server 2012 R2 Standard or Datacenter Edition computer that's already installed and initially configured. The "Before You Begin" section gives you step-by-step instructions on setting up your lab for use with all activities in this book.

Completing the hands-on activities in this book is important because they contain information about how Windows Server 2012/R2 works and the tools to manage it that's best understood by hands-on experience. If, for some reason, you can't do some of the activities, you should at least read through each one to make sure you don't miss important information. Table 1-1 summarizes the requirements of hands-on activities in this chapter.

Table 1-1   Activity requirements

Activity	Requirements	Notes
Activity 1-1: Reviewing System Properties	410Server1	Windows Server 2012 R2 Standard or Datacenter Edition installed according to instructions in "Before You Begin"
Activity 1-2: Exploring Server Manager	410Server1	
Activity 1-3: Examining NTFS Permissions and Attributes	410Server1	
Activity 1-4: Using a Prebuilt MMC	410Server1	
Activity 1-5: Creating a Custom MMC	410Server1	
Activity 1-6: Introducing the Disk Management Snap-in	410Server1	A second, uninitialized disk should already be installed in 410Server1
Activity 1-7: Comparing NTFS and FAT32 Volumes	410Server1	

(continues)

Activity	Requirements	Notes
Activity 1-8: Sharing a Folder in Windows Server 2012	410Server1	
Activity 1-9: Exploring Windows Networking Components	410Server1	

© 2015 Cengage Learning®

The Role of a Server Operating System

A server or collection of servers is usually at the center of most business networks. The functions a server performs depend on a number of factors, including the type of business using the server, size of the business, and extent to which the business has committed to using technology to aid operations. The latter factor is the crux of the matter. Technology is designed to help a person or an organization do things more efficiently or more effectively, and a server is used to provide services a business has deemed can help its operations. Before you explore these services in more detail, a few definitions are in order.

Server: Hardware or Software?

When most people hear the word "server," they conjure up visions of a large tower computer with lots of hard drives and memory. This image is merely a computer hardware configuration that may or may not be used as a server, however. In short, a computer becomes a server when software is installed on it that provides a network service to client computers. In other words, you could install certain software on an inexpensive laptop computer and make it act as a server. By the same token, a huge tower computer with six hard drives and 128 GB of RAM could be used as a workstation for a single user. So although some computer hardware configurations are packaged to function as a server, and others are packaged as desktop computers, what makes a computer a server or desktop computer is the software installed on it.

Of course, with modern operating systems (OSs), the lines between desktop and server computer are blurred. OSs such as Windows 8.1 and its predecessors are designed to be installed on desktop computers or workstations (and in the case of Windows 8.1, tablet computers); to run Web browser, word processing, spreadsheet, and other similar programs; and generally act as a personal computer. However, these OSs can perform server functions, such as file and printer sharing, and even act as a Web server. On the other hand, Windows Server 2012/R2 and its predecessors are designed as **server operating systems**, but there's nothing to stop you from installing a word processor or Web browser and using Windows Server 2012/R2 on your desktop computer. So what are the differences between a desktop OS, such as Windows 8.1, and a server OS, such as Windows Server 2012? The following section explains.

Server Operating Systems Versus Desktop Operating Systems

Both Windows Server 2012/R2 and Windows 8.1 can perform some server functions and some desktop functions, but important differences distinguish them. Windows 8.1 is configured to emphasize the user interface and is performance-tuned to run desktop applications. Windows Server 2012/R2, on the other hand, deemphasizes many of Windows 8.1's user interface bells and whistles in favor of a less flashy and less resource-intensive user interface. In addition, Windows vServer 2012/R2 is performance-tuned to run background processes so that client computers can access network services faster. Speaking of network services, most Windows Server 2012/R2 editions can run the following network services, among others:

- File and Printer Sharing
- Web Server
- Routing and Remote Access Services (RRAS)
- Domain Name System (DNS)
- Dynamic Host Configuration Protocol (DHCP)
- File Transfer Protocol (FTP) Server
- Active Directory

- Distributed File System (DFS)
- Hyper-V
- Fax Server

Of these services, Windows 8.1 supports only Hyper-V, File and Printer Sharing, Web Server, and FTP Server and in a limited capacity. In addition, Windows 8.1 is restricted to 20 logged-on network users, whereas on a Windows Server 2012/R2 computer running Standard or Datacenter Edition, logged-on users are limited only by the number of purchased licenses and available resources. In addition, because a server is such a critical device in a network, Windows Server 2012/R2 includes fault-tolerance features, such as redundant array of independent disks (RAID) 5 volumes, load balancing, and clustering, which aren't standard features in Windows 8.1 or other Windows desktop OSs. Windows Server 2012/R2 is also capable of supporting up to 64 processors; Windows 8.1 supports a maximum of 2.

Windows Server 2012/R2 Editions

In the realm of server OSs, Microsoft has an edition for all types of business, large and small. Businesses can choose the best solution for their size and the services they require. From a simple file-sharing server to a massive virtualization server, Windows Server 2012/R2 has it covered. The Windows Server 2012/R2 editions have been streamlined compared with Windows Server 2008:

- Datacenter
- Standard
- Essentials
- Foundation

Why the need for several editions? One size doesn't fit all is the short answer. For example, a small organization with a dozen users who mainly need a centralized network logon along with file and printer sharing can probably use Foundation Edition. A large company or one that needs a robust application server might opt for Standard Edition. A company with hundreds or thousands of users that's implementing a private cloud solution will likely opt for Datacenter Edition. As server virtualization has become an essential part of the Server 2012 family of products, there are important differences in editions for support of the Hyper-V role. The following sections review the features and requirements of the four Windows Server 2012/R2 editions.

Datacenter and Standard Editions

Both Datacenter and Standard editions are full-featured server OSs with only the virtual use limits setting them apart. For organizations using virtualization on a large scale, **Datacenter Edition** is clearly the best fit. A Datacenter Edition license allows you to install an unlimited number of virtual instances of the OS, meaning you can install Datacenter Edition with Hyper-V on a physical server and then install as many instances of Windows Server 2012/R2 Datacenter Edition in virtual machines as you need. You must purchase one Datacenter Edition license for every two physical processors installed on a server. So if you have a physical server with one or two populated CPU sockets, you need one Datacenter Edition license. If your server has three or four populated CPU sockets, you need two Datacenter Edition licenses, and so forth. The number of CPU cores is irrelevant in the licensing; only physical CPU sockets are counted. So, for example, if your server has two eight-core processors installed, you still need just one Datacenter Edition license.

Standard Edition has all the features of Datacenter Edition and the same processor licensing conditions. The only distinction (aside from price) is that a Standard Edition license permits only two virtual instances, so when you purchase Standard Edition, you can install it on a server with up to two populated CPU sockets, install the Hyper-V role, and then install Standard Edition on up to two virtual machines. If you want to install it on a server with more than two processors or on additional virtual machines, you must purchase additional licenses. Hyper-V is described later in this chapter in "Windows Server 2012/R2 Roles."

Both Datacenter and Standard editions support up to 4 TB of RAM, up to 64 physical processors, and server clusters with up to 64 nodes per cluster. When you install either edition of Windows Server 2012, you have an option to install it without the standard graphical user interface (GUI), a mode called Server Core. Server Core is now the default, and preferred, operating mode and is described later in this chapter in "New and Enhanced Features in Windows Server 2012/R2."

In addition, all Windows Server 2012/R2 server roles and features are supported in both editions, and either edition can be configured as a domain controller, member server, or stand-alone server. Both editions require **client access licenses (CALs)**, which are legally mandated for each user who logs on to the server.

 Datacenter Edition, as of this writing, costs about $3800, roughly five times the cost of Standard Edition, which can be purchased for around $750. CALs are about $125/license in small quantities.

Essentials Edition

Essentials Edition is aimed at small businesses with 25 or fewer users. It supports most of the roles and features in Standard and Datacenter editions, but some roles have restrictions or limited functions. In the original release of Windows Server 2012, the Hyper-V role couldn't be installed on Essentials Edition, but it's available in the R2 release. For the price of the license (typically around $500), you can install Essentials Edition one time on a physical server or a virtual machine, but not both. Essentials Edition is automatically configured as a **root domain controller**, which is the first domain controller installed in an Active Directory forest. During installation of Essentials Edition, you're asked for the domain name, and Active Directory is installed automatically. Several other services are configured automatically in this edition: Active Directory Certificate Services, DNS, File Services, Web Server (IIS), Network Policy Server, and Remote Desktop Services. In addition, Essentials Edition comes with a front-end management interface called Dashboard that serves as a simplified server manager. Other features particular to this edition include client backups and Remote Web Access. This edition supports up to two physical processors and 64 GB RAM and can't be installed in Server Core mode. No CALs are required. In the R2 release of this edition, Office 365 integration and touch-enabled Remote Web Access have been added.

 A new feature of Windows Server 2012 R2 that's not in the original release is the server role Windows Server Essentials Experience. Available in Standard and Datacenter editions, it includes the features and functions of Windows Server 2012 Essentials (such as automatic Active Directory configuration, the Dashboard view of Server Manager, client backup, and Remote Web Access), along with other preconfigured roles and features, and doesn't have the user and hardware limitations of Essentials Edition.

Foundation Edition

Foundation Edition, the entry-level Windows Server 2012/R2 edition, is suitable for small businesses that need to purchase a complete server solution for file and printer sharing, centralized control over user accounts and network resources, and common services used in most networks, such as Web services, DNS, and DHCP. Foundation Edition is available as an OEM version only, installed on a server by the manufacturer. The licensing is limited to 15 users, and like Essentials, no CALs are required.

Foundation Edition supports a single physical processor; like the other editions, the number of CPU cores is irrelevant. It supports up to 32 GB RAM and can be configured as a stand-alone server or a root domain controller. This edition can't be installed in Server Core mode, can't be installed in a virtual machine, and doesn't support Hyper-V.

Comparing Editions

Tables 1-2 and 1-3 summarize system requirements and compare features of the Windows Server 2012/R2 editions.

For an extensive comparison of Windows Server 2012/R2 editions, go to *www.microsoft.com/windowsserver2012/editions/overview.mspx.*

Table 1-2   Windows Server 2012/R2 minimum system requirements (all editions unless noted)

Component	Requirement
Processor	Minimum: 1.4 GHz 64-bit CPU Recommended: 3.1 GHz or faster 64-bit multicore
Memory	Minimum: 512 MB RAM (2 GB for Essentials) Recommended: 2 GB RAM or more (8 GB for Essentials)
Available disk space	Minimum: 32 GB (90 GB for Essentials) Recommended: 60 GB or more for the system partition
Additional drives	DVD drive
Network interface card	Gigabit (10/100/1000 BaseT) Ethernet Adapter
Display and peripherals	Super VGA or higher Keyboard and mouse Internet access

© 2015 Cengage Learning®

The minimum requirements for Essentials are higher than for the other editions because Essentials installs several network services automatically.

Roles not listed in Table 1-2 are fully supported by all editions.

Table 1-3   Comparing features in Windows Server 2012/R2 editions

Feature	Datacenter	Standard	Essentials	Foundation
Maximum RAM	4 TB	4 TB	64 GB	32 GB
Supported processor sockets	64	64	2	1
Virtual licenses	Can be a virtualization host Unlimited virtual instances	Can be a virtualization host 2 virtual instances	Can't be a virtualization host 1 virtual or 1 physical instance	Not available
Processor socket licensing	Each license supports two sockets	Each license supports two sockets	Maximum two sockets per system	Maximum one socket per system
Supported role limitations				
Active Directory Domain Services	No limitations	No limitations	Automatic/forest root only	Forest root only
Active Directory Certificate Services	No limitations	No limitations	Automatic/CA creation only	CA creation only
File and Storage Services	No limitations	No limitations	Data deduplication not available	Data deduplication not available
Hyper-V	No limitations	No limitations	No limitations	Not available
Read-only domain controller	No limitations	No limitations	Not available	Not available
Data deduplication	No limitations	No limitations	Not available	Not available
Failover clustering	No limitations	No limitations	Not available	Not available

(continues)

Feature	Datacenter	Standard	Essentials	Foundation
Hot add memory	No limitations	No limitations	Not available	Not available
Remote Access	No limitations	No limitations	Automatic/limited	Limited
Remote Desktop Services	No limitations	No limitations	Automatic/limited	Limited
Network Policy and Access Services	No limitations	No limitations	Automatic/limited	Limited
Windows Server Update Services	No limitations	No limitations	No limitations	Not available
Server Core mode	No limitations	No limitations	Not available	Not available

© 2015 Cengage Learning®

Windows Server 2012/R2 and the Private Cloud

With Microsoft's new emphasis on the private cloud and virtualization, it's probably a good idea to define some terms used when talking about the private cloud and cloud computing in general. Many of these terms and concepts are expanded on later as you learn about the technologies behind them, but this section should give you a running start.

So what exactly is cloud computing? This question isn't as easy to answer as it might seem, and you're likely to get different answers from different people. However, most networking professionals are likely to agree with this definition: **Cloud computing** is a collection of technologies for abstracting the details of how applications, storage, network, and other computing resources are delivered to users. Why the term "cloud"? It comes from network diagrams that included the Internet (see Figure 1-1), and because the Internet is a vast collection of different technologies, no single networking symbol could be used to represent it. So a cloud symbol conveys that a lot of complex stuff is going on, but the details are unimportant at this time. One goal of cloud computing is to abstract the details of how things get done so that people can get on with their work. For example, do users really care that the X drive is mapped to ServerA by using the SMB protocol over TCP/IP? No, they want to store their files in a place they know is reliable and secure and would rather not know the details of how this task is done.

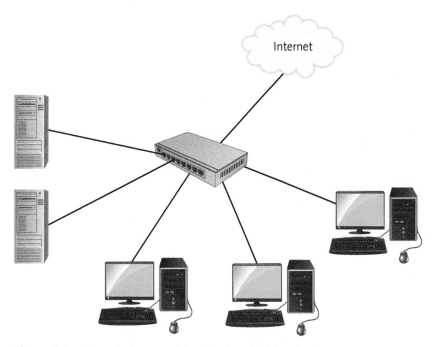

Figure 1-1   Network diagram with a cloud symbolizing the Internet
© 2015 Cengage Learning®

However, as an IT professional, you do need to know some details because setting up this technology is your job. A core technology of cloud computing is **virtualization**, which uses software (usually aided by specialized hardware) to emulate multiple hardware environments so that multiple operating systems can run on the same physical server simultaneously. Virtualization has its own terms for its operation and components. Some are defined in the following list:

- A **virtual machine (VM)** is the virtual environment that emulates a physical computer's hardware and BIOS. A **guest OS** is the operating system running in a VM.

- A **host computer** is the physical computer on which VM software is installed and VMs run.

- **Virtualization software** is the software for creating and managing VMs and creating the virtual environment in which a guest OS is installed. Microsoft Hyper-V Manager or VMware Workstation are examples of virtualization software.

- The **hypervisor** is the virtualization software component that creates and monitors the virtual hardware environment, which allows multiple VMs to share physical hardware resources. (In some software, this component is called Virtual Machine Monitor[VMM].) The hypervisor on a host computer acts in some ways like an OS kernel, but instead of scheduling processes for access to the CPU and other devices, it schedules VMs to have that access.

The preceding list is by no means exhaustive, and when you learn more about Hyper-V in Chapter 12, you run across more terms that are particular to virtualization.

Public Cloud Versus Private Cloud

There are two broad categories of cloud computing: public and private. The **public cloud** is a cloud computing service provided by a third party, whereas a **private cloud** is a cloud computing service provided by an internal IT department. Examples of public cloud computing are services such as DropBox and SkyDrive, which provide storage as a cloud service, or Google Apps and Office 365, which offer office applications as a cloud service. You don't have to do anything special to have access to these services (some of which are free) other than have access to the Internet.

With a private cloud, a company's IT department provides all services for employees and perhaps customers, but these services aren't generally open to the general public. Typical services include virtual desktops, storage, and applications. **Virtual desktop infrastructure (VDI)** is a rapidly growing sector of private cloud computing. With VDI, users don't run a standard desktop computer to access their data and applications. Instead, they connect to the private cloud with a Web browser or downloaded client software. They can then access their desktop and applications from wherever they happen to have an Internet connection, whether it's in their office, from a laptop in a local coffeeshop, or even from a tablet computer. The OS and applications run on servers in the company data center rather than on the local computer. Many of the new features and enhanced functions in Windows Server 2012/R2 are designed to make designing and building a private cloud easier and using cloud resources more efficient. The key feature for building private clouds in Windows Server 2012/R2 is Hyper-V 3.0, discussed later in this chapter in "New and Enhanced Features in Windows Server 2012/R2." All the core technologies in Windows Server 2012/R2, however, are necessary for running a cloud infrastructure. The following section explains these technologies.

Windows Server 2012/R2 Core Technologies

The new features and enhancements Microsoft added to Windows Server 2012/R2 command all the attention. Before you can understand and use these new features, however, you need a firm grasp of the technologies that form the foundation of a Windows Server OS. The following is a list of some of the technologies on which Windows Server 2012/R2 is built:

- Server Manager
- New Technology File System (NTFS)

- Active Directory
- Microsoft Management Console
- Disk Management
- File and printer sharing
- Windows networking

The following sections describe these technologies briefly, but most are covered in detail in later chapters.

Server Manager

Server Manager provides a single interface for installing, configuring, and removing a variety of server roles and features on your Windows server. It also summarizes your server's status and configuration and includes tools to diagnose problems, manage storage, and perform general configuration tasks. Server Manager has been substantially updated since its debut in Windows Server 2008. It can now be used to manage all servers in your network and access all the server administration tools from a single console.

When you start Server Manager, you see the Dashboard view, shown in Figure 1-2. The Dashboard shows a list of tasks you can perform, summarizes the installed roles, and shows the servers that are available to manage. The Welcome section can be hidden after you're familiar with Server Manager. This tool is used to access most of the configuration and monitoring tools for administering Windows servers, and you learn more about it throughout this book.

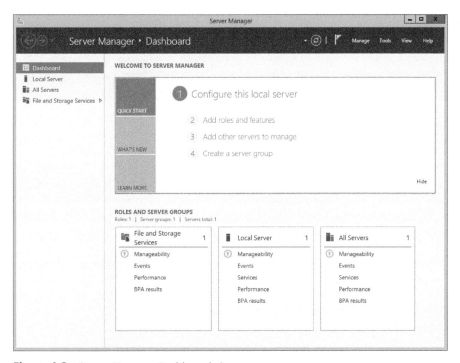

Figure 1-2   Server Manager Dashboard view

The forward and backward arrows at the upper left are used to navigate through recently opened windows. Moving to the right, your current location is displayed, followed by the refresh button and the notifications icon you click to view recent messages from Server Manager. Next is the Manage menu, used to perform major tasks, such as adding and removing roles and features and creating server groups. The Tools menu gives you quick access to administrative tools, such as Computer Management, Event Viewer, and Task Scheduler. Management consoles for server roles or features you install are added to this menu. You can use the View menu to choose a magnification option for fonts in Server Manager, and the Help menu is self-explanatory.

The left pane of Server Manager displays the major views: Dashboard (described previously), Local Server, and All Servers. You use the Local Server view to manage just the server where you're running Server Manager and the All Servers view to manage aspects of all servers. To add servers you want to manage, right-click All Servers and click Add Servers or use the Manage menu. Under the All Servers item in the left pane is a node for each installed server role. In Figure 1-2, you see File and Storage Services, which is a preinstalled role. Clicking a server role puts Server Manager into role management mode so that you can manage each role in the Server Manager interface. When you're managing a role, the options for it are displayed.

Activity 1-1: Reviewing System Properties

Time Required: 10 minutes
Objective: View system properties in Windows Server 2012 R2.

Required Tools and Equipment: 410Server1 with Windows Server 2012 R2 Standard or Datacenter Edition installed according to instructions in "Before You Begin"
Description: In this activity, you learn to find basic information about a Windows Server 2012 R2 installation, such as the server edition, processors, amount of RAM, and so forth.

1. Start 410Server1 and log on as **Administrator** with the password **Password01**. Server Manager starts automatically.

2. In the left pane of Server Manager, click **Local Server**. You see the Properties window for 410Server1, shown in Figure 1-3.

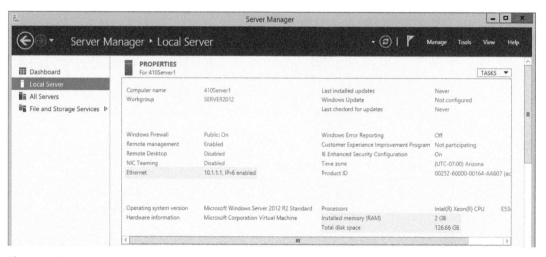

Figure 1-3 The Local Server Properties window

3. Review the fields highlighted in Figure 1-3: Ethernet, Installed memory (RAM), and Total disk space.

4. Write down the values listed in Step 3 for your server on the following lines:

   _____

   _____

   _____

5. Scroll down to explore other information available in Server Manager, such as a list of recent events, a summary of services, and a list of installed roles and features at the bottom.

6. Stay logged on if you're continuing to the next activity; otherwise, shut down the server by right-clicking **Start**, pointing to **Shut down or sign out**, and clicking **Shut down**. You can also press **Windows+C**, and click **Settings, Power**, and **Shut down**.

Activity 1-2: Exploring Server Manager

Time Required: 10 minutes
Objective: Review the features of Server Manager.

Required Tools and Equipment: 410Server1
Description: You have just installed Windows Server 2012 R2 and plan to install some roles and features soon. You open Server Manager to explore what's available in Windows Server 2012 R2.

1. Start 410Server1 and log on as **Administrator**, if necessary. If Server Manager isn't running, click the **Server Manager** icon on the taskbar.

2. Click **Dashboard** in the left pane, if necessary. (Notice the icon next to Dashboard; you'll need it to navigate back to this view later.) The Dashboard is divided into two sections: Welcome to Server Manager and Roles and Server Groups. The Welcome section lists common tasks you can access easily, including adding roles and features, adding other servers to manage, and creating server groups.

3. Scroll down, if necessary, to see the Roles and Server Groups section. This section contains a box for each installed role, a box for the local server, and a box for each server group (see Figure 1-4). Each box contains information about manageability, which tells you whether Server Manager can contact the role or server to perform management tasks. You can double-click other items in these boxes to get details about events, services, performance, and Best Practices Analyzer (BPA) results. In the File and Storage Services box, click **Events**. Any events related to this role are then displayed in the resulting dialog box. Click **Cancel**.

Figure 1-4   The Roles and Server Groups section

4. Scroll up to see the Welcome to Server Manager section, if necessary. In the right pane, click **Add roles and features** to start the Add Roles and Features Wizard; you use this wizard often in this book's activities. Read the information in the Before you begin window.

5. On the following lines, write three tasks that are recommended before installing new roles and features. When you're finished, click **Cancel**.

_____

_____

_____

6. Click **Local Server** in the left pane. The right pane is then divided into several sections, with the Properties section at the top. Scroll down to the Events section, which shows the most recent warning or error events that have occurred in your system. Clicking an event displays a description of it (see Figure 1-5).

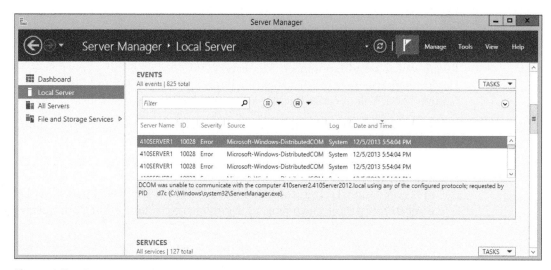

Figure 1-5   The Events section

7. Scroll down to the Services section, which displays a list of services installed on the server along with their status. You can start and stop services by right-clicking them and then selecting an action in the menu.

8. Scroll down to the Best Practices Analyzer section. The Best Practices Analyzer (BPA) is used to make sure a server role is installed in compliance with best practices to ensure effectiveness, trustworthiness, and reliability. Run a BPA scan by clicking the **Tasks** drop-down arrow and then clicking **Start BPA Scan** (see Figure 1-6). After a while, your results are displayed as shown in the figure.

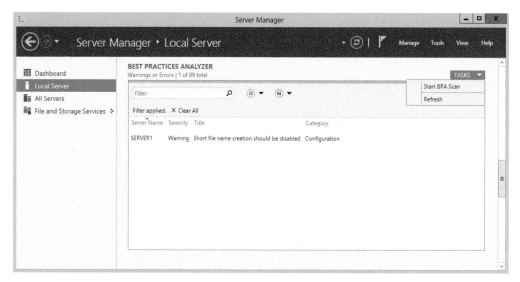

Figure 1-6   The Best Practices Analyzer

9. Scroll down to the Performance section. You can view and configure performance alerts for CPU and memory use. Performance monitoring is covered in more detail in *MCSA/MCSE Guide to Administering Windows Server 2012/R2, Exam 70-411* (Cengage Learning, 2015).

10. Scroll down to the Roles and Features section to see a list of roles and features installed on the local server. They're listed in the approximate order in which they were installed.

11. In the left pane, click **All Servers**. The right pane has the same sections as Local Server except the top section, which is Servers instead of Properties. In the Servers section, you can select one or more servers and see information about them in the other sections of this window.

12. In the left pane, click **File and Storage Services**. This server role is installed by default. The window changes to show you specific tools for working with this role. Click **Volumes** to see a summary of the server's volumes (see Figure 1-7). Click **Disks** to see information about the physical disks installed. Click **Storage Pools**. This new feature in Windows Server 2012/R2 is explained later in this chapter in "Storage Spaces" and in more detail in Chapter 4.

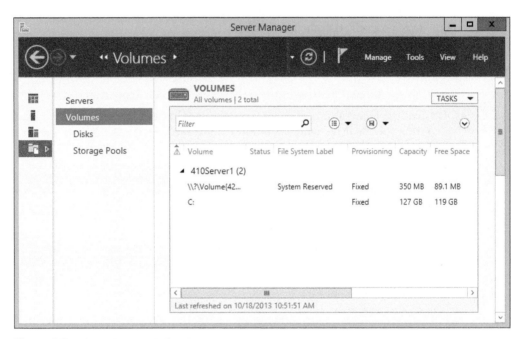

Figure 1-7   The Volumes window in Server Manager

13. Click the **Dashboard** icon in Server Manager to return to the Dashboard view.

14. Stay logged on if you're continuing to the next activity; otherwise, shut down the server.

NTFS

One of a server's main jobs is to store a variety of file types and make them available to network users. To do this effectively, a server OS needs a robust and efficient file system. **New Technology File System (NTFS)** was introduced in Windows NT in the early 1990s. Although it has been updated throughout the years, NTFS has remained a reliable, flexible, and scalable file system. Its predecessor was FAT/FAT32, which had severe limitations for a server OS. It lacked features such as native support for long filenames, file and folder permissions, support for large files and volumes, reliability, compression, and encryption. NTFS supports all these features and more.

Perhaps the most important feature of NTFS is the capability to set user and group permissions on both folders and files. With this feature, administrators can specify which users can access a file and what users can do with a file if they're granted access, which increase a server environment's security. FAT/FAT32 has no user access controls. NTFS and other supported file systems are covered in Chapter 5.

In Windows Server 2012/R2 and Windows 8.1, a new file system called Resilient File System has been introduced. It's discussed in "New Features in Windows Server 2012/R2."

The exFAT file system is similar to FAT/FAT32 except you can create volumes larger than 32 GB; with FAT32, you're limited to a maximum volume size of 32 GB.

Activity 1-3: Examining NTFS Permissions and Attributes

Time Required: 10 minutes
Objective: View NTFS file permissions and attributes.

Required Tools and Equipment: 410Server1
Description: You haven't worked with file permissions and attributes before, and you want to familiarize yourself with the features of NTFS.

1. Log on to 410Server1 as **Administrator,** if necessary.

2. Click the **File Explorer** icon on the taskbar, and then click **This PC** in the left pane, if necessary.

3. Right-click the **(C:)** drive in the right pane and click **Properties.**

4. Click the **General** tab, if necessary. You see that the file system is NTFS, which is the only option for the drive where Windows is installed. FAT/FAT32 lacks the security and features required by Windows.

5. Click the **Security** tab (see Figure 1-8).

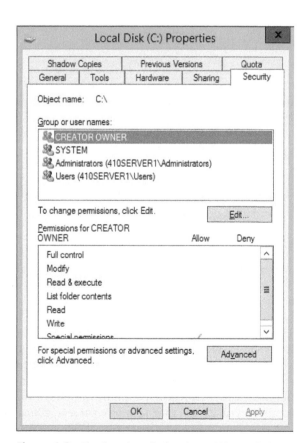

Figure 1-8   The Security tab showing NTFS permissions

6. Click each item in the Group or user names section, and view the permission settings for each in the bottom pane.

7. Next, click the **Quota** tab. Quotas, a feature available only on NTFS-formatted disks, are discussed more in Chapter 5. You should see that disk quotas are disabled, the default setting.

8. Now click the **Shadow Copies** tab. This feature enables you to restore previous versions of a file. Shadow copies are discussed more in Chapter 5 and, like quotas, aren't available on FAT/FAT32 disks.

9. Last, click the **General** tab again. Note the two check boxes at the bottom for enabling file indexing and compression, which are features of NTFS.

10. Click **Cancel** to close the Properties dialog box.

11. Double-click the **Documents** folder. Right-click in the right pane, point to **New**, and click **Text Document**.

12. Right-click **New Text Document** and click **Properties**. Notice the two check boxes at the bottom labeled Read-only and Hidden. They are common file attributes in both the FAT/FAT32 and NTFS/ReFS file systems. Click **Advanced**.

13. In the Advanced Attributes dialog box, notice four more check boxes for attributes. Only the archiving attribute is available with FAT/FAT32 volumes. The other three, for file indexing, file compression, and encryption, are available only with NTFS volumes.

14. Close all open windows. Stay logged on if you're continuing to the next activity; otherwise, shut down the server. As you can see, NTFS has numerous advantages over the older FAT file systems. You explore many of these features in Chapter 5.

Active Directory

Active Directory is the foundation of a Windows network environment. This directory service enables administrators to create and manage users and groups, set network-wide user and computer policies, manage security, and organize network resources. With Active Directory, you transform a limited, nonscalable workgroup network into a Windows domain with nearly unlimited scalability. (The differences between workgroup and domain models are explained in "Windows Networking Concepts" later in this chapter.) You learn more about using and configuring Active Directory in subsequent chapters. To summarize, the following are Active Directory's main purposes and features:

- Provides a single point of administration of network resources, such as users, groups, shared printers, shared files, servers, and workstations
- Provides centralized authentication and authorization of users to network resources
- Along with DNS, provides domain naming services and management for a Windows domain
- Enables administrators to assign system policies, deploy software to client computers, and assign permissions and rights to users of network resources

You delve into all these functions and more in later chapters. In Chapter 6, you install Active Directory and learn about its basic functions. Subsequent chapters go into more detail.

Microsoft Management Console

A server OS requires a multitude of tools that administrators must use to manage, support, and troubleshoot a server system. One challenge of having so many tools is the numerous user interfaces an administrator has to learn. Microsoft has lessened this challenge by including a common framework for running most administrative tools called the Microsoft Management Console (MMC). The MMC alone isn't very useful; it's just a user interface shell, as you can see in Figure 1-9. What makes it useful is the bevy of snap-ins you can install. Each snap-in is designed to perform a specific administrative task, such as the Disk Management snap-in shown in Figure 1-10.

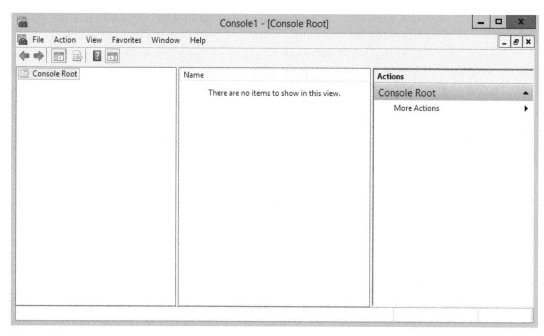

Figure 1-9   The Microsoft Management Console

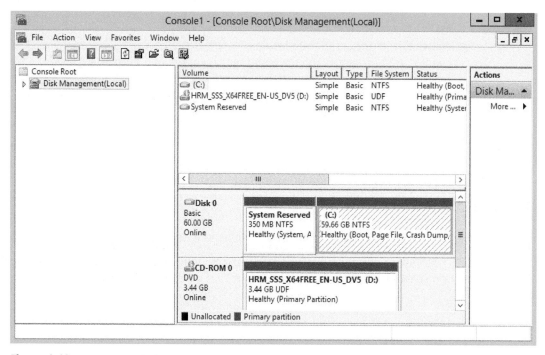

Figure 1-10   An MMC with the Disk Management snap-in

A number of MMCs are available in Server Manager's Tools menu, depending on the roles and features installed on the server. For example, after you install Active Directory, several new MMCs for managing it are created and added to the Tools menu. Not all administrative functions can be accessed from these prebuilt MMCs, however; you might have to create a customized MMC to access some functions or keep an MMC handy on your desktop with the administrative snap-ins you use most often. An important feature of an MMC is the capability to connect to servers remotely. Using this feature, you can install management tools on a Windows 8.1 workstation, for example, and manage a Windows Server 2012/R2 computer without having to log on at the server console.

Activity 1-4: Using a Prebuilt MMC

Time Required: 15 minutes

Objective: Explore the Tools menu in Server Manager and become familiar with prebuilt MMCs.

Required Tools and Equipment: 410Server1

Description: You're a junior administrator for a Windows server and have been told to familiarize yourself with the management tools on your server and check the status of the Windows Firewall service.

1. Log on to 410Server1 as **Administrator** and start Server Manager, if necessary.

2. In Server Manager, click **Tools, Computer Management** from the menu. You might notice that some tools in the Computer Management MMC, such as Task Scheduler and Event Viewer, are also available as separate MMCs in the Tools menu.

3. To explore a tool in Computer Management, click the tool name in the left pane. Some tools have an arrow next to them to indicate additional components. Each tool is called a snap-in.

4. Click the arrow next to **Services and Applications** to expand it, and then click the **Services** snap-in. This snap-in is also available as a stand-alone tool in the Tools menu.

5. Find and double-click **Windows Firewall**. Review the properties for this service, which are typical for most services. Click **Cancel** to close the Windows Firewall Properties window.

6. Explore several snap-ins in the left pane of Computer Management. Write the name of the snap-in that enables you to monitor application and hardware performance in real time:

_____

7. Close all open windows. Stay logged on if you're continuing to the next activity; otherwise, shut down the server.

Activity 1-5: Creating a Custom MMC

Time Required: 10 minutes

Objective: Create a custom MMC by selecting snap-ins.

Required Tools and Equipment: 410Server1

Description: You're a junior administrator for a Windows server, and three of your most common tasks are monitoring installed devices, managing and monitoring the server's disks, and checking on scheduled tasks. You have decided that putting tools for these tasks in their own MMC on your desktop would make you more efficient.

1. Log on to 410Server1 as **Administrator**, if necessary.

2. Right-click **Start** and click **Run**. Type **mmc** in the Open text box, and then click **OK**.

3. Click **File, Add/Remove Snap-in** from the MMC menu.

4. In the Available snap-ins list box, click **Device Manager**, and then click **Add**.

5. Note your choices in the next dialog box. You can decide whether to use the selected snap-in on the local computer or another computer. If you select the "Another computer" option, you can manage this computer remotely with your MMC. Leave the **Local computer** option selected, and then click **Finish**.

6. Repeat Steps 4 and 5, substituting the **Disk Management** and **Task Scheduler** snap-ins for Device Manager. Click **Finish** after adding Disk Management and **OK** after adding Task Scheduler. Then click **OK** to close the Add or Remove Snap-ins dialog box.

7. To name your MMC, click **File, Save As** from the menu.

8. In the Save As dialog box, click the **Desktop** icon, type **DevDiskTask** for the filename, and then click **Save**. You now have a customized MMC on your desktop.

9. Close all open windows. Stay logged on if you're continuing to the next activity; otherwise, shut down the server.

Disk Management

To manage the disks and volumes on a Windows Server 2012/R2 computer, you might use the Disk Management snap-in or the File and Storage Services role, which is integrated into Server Manager. With these tools, you can monitor the status of disks and volumes, initialize new disks, create and format new volumes, and troubleshoot disk problems. Both tools enable you to configure redundant disk configurations, such as RAID 1 and RAID 5 volumes. File and Storage Services also lets you create storage pools, a new feature in Windows Server 2012/R2. These tools are covered in more detail in Chapter 4, and the following activity walks you through using Disk Management.

Activity 1-6: Introducing the Disk Management Snap-in

Time Required: 15 minutes
Objective: Explore the features of the Disk Management snap-in.

Required Tools and Equipment: 410Server1
Description: You have just arrived at a customer site that's having problems with disk storage on its Windows Server 2012 R2 system. You don't know the configuration of the installed disks, so you need to view the disk configuration.

If your server is configured according to instructions in the "Before You Begin" section of the Introduction, you should have two physical disks. Disk 0 has the Windows OS installed, and Disk 1 is empty and offline.

1. Log on to 410Server1 as **Administrator**, if necessary.

2. Open the MMC you created in Activity 1-5, or in Server Manager, click **Tools, Computer Management**.

3. Click the **Disk Management** snap-in in the left pane. If you see a message about initializing a disk, click **OK**. There are two panes in Disk Management: The upper pane shows a summary of configured volumes and basic information about each volume. The lower pane shows installed disks and how each disk is being used.

4. Right-click the **(C:)** volume in the upper pane and note some of the options you have.

5. In the lower pane, find Disk 1. If its status is online and initialized, skip to the next step; otherwise, right-click **Disk 1** and click **Online**. Right-click it again and click **Initialize Disk** to open the dialog box shown in Figure 1-11. Leave the default option **MBR** selected, and click **OK**.

6. Right-click the unallocated space of **Disk 1**, and notice the options for making the unallocated space into a new volume. In Windows XP and Windows Server 2003, the term "partition" was used instead of "volume." In Windows Server 2008 and later, the term "volume" is often used instead when preparing disks for use.

7. Click **New Simple Volume** to start the New Simple Volume Wizard. In the welcome window, click **Next**.

8. In the Specify Volume Size window, type **500** to make a small 500 MB volume, and then click **Next**.

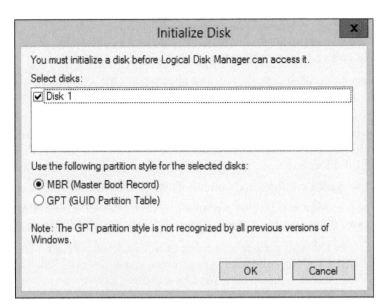

Figure 1-11   Initializing a disk in Disk Management

9. In the Assign Drive Letter or Path window, you have the option to assign a drive letter or mount the new volume into a folder on another volume. Click drive letter **S**, and then click **Next**. (If S isn't available, ask your instructor which drive letter to select.)

10. In the Format Partition window, click the **File system** list arrow, and note the available options. Click **FAT32** to select it as the file system. In the Volume label text box, type **Fat32Vol**, and then click **Next**.

11. Review the settings summary, and then click **Finish**. Watch the space where the new volume has been created. After a short pause, the volume should begin to format. When formatting is finished, the volume status should be Healthy (Primary Partition). If you see a message asking whether you want to format the disk, click **Cancel** because you just formatted it.

12. Close all open windows. If you're prompted to save changes to the MMC, click **No**. Stay logged on if you're continuing to the next activity; otherwise, shut down the server.

Activity 1-7: Comparing NTFS and FAT32 Volumes

Time Required: 15 minutes
Objective: Compare the features of FAT32 and NTFS volumes.

Required Tools and Equipment: 410Server1
Description: You can't remember which features are supported on NTFS and FAT32 volumes. Because the server you're working on has at least one volume in each file system, you decide to explore the properties of both file systems and compare them.

1. Log on to 410Server1 as **Administrator**, if necessary.

2. Open the Disk Management snap-in by using the method described in Activity 1-6.

3. In the upper pane, right-click the (**C:**) volume and click **Properties**.

4. Arrange the Properties dialog box so that you can see the list of disk drives in Disk Management. Right-click the **S** volume you created in Activity 1-6 and click **Properties**. Arrange the S volume's Properties dialog box next to the C volume's Properties dialog box.

5. Click the **General** tab, if necessary, in each volume's Properties dialog box. The first difference you should see is that the NTFS-formatted C volume has options to compress and index the drive, but the FAT32-formatted S volume does not.

6. The next three tabs, Tools, Hardware, and Sharing, are the same for both file system types. Click the **Security** tab for the C volume. Notice that the S volume doesn't have this tab.

7. Next, click the **Shadow Copies** tab for the C volume, where you can enable or disable shadow copies for a volume. Notice that the S volume doesn't have a Shadow Copies tab, and the S volume isn't listed in the Shadow Copies tab because the feature is supported only on NTFS and ReFS volumes.

8. Next, click the **Quota** tab for the C volume. This tab isn't available for the FAT32 volume.

9. Close all open windows. If you're prompted to save changes to the MMC, click **No**. Stay logged on if you're continuing to the next activity; otherwise, shut down the server.

As you can see, an NTFS volume has a number of advantages over a FAT/FAT32 volume. So what good is a FAT or FAT32 volume? One reason to use FAT or FAT32 on a Windows computer now is having a volume that will be used by another OS that might not support NTFS. In addition, removable drives, USB flash drives, and flash memory cards are often formatted with FAT32 or, for larger removable drives, exFAT.

A FAT/FAT32 formatted disk can be converted to NTFS without losing existing data by using the `convert` command-line utility.

File and Printer Sharing

Probably the most common reason for building a network and installing a server is to enable users to share files, printers, and other resources. Windows Server 2012/R2 has a full-featured system for file and printer sharing, offering advanced features such as shadow copies, disk quotas, and the Distributed File System (DFS). At its simplest, sharing files or a printer is just a few clicks away. More complex configurations that offer redundancy, version control, and user storage restrictions are also readily available. Windows Server 2012/R2 offers myriad tools and options for configuring file sharing; most are discussed in more detail in Chapter 5. The following activity shows you a method for basic file sharing.

Activity 1-8: Sharing a Folder in Windows Server 2012 R2

Time Required: 15 minutes
Objective: Create and share a folder.

Required Tools and Equipment: 410Server1
Description: You need to make a document available to several colleagues. You decide to create a folder and share it so that your colleagues can open or copy the document.

1. Log on to 410Server1 as **Administrator**, if necessary.

2. Press **Windows+X** and click **File Explorer** in the menu at the lower-left corner of the desktop. (You can also get to this menu in Windows Server 2012 R2 by right-clicking the Start button.)

3. Double-click the **(C:)** drive. Click the folder icon on the Quick Access toolbar at the upper left (see Figure 1-12). Type **DocShare** for the folder name.

4. Right-click the **DocShare** folder, point to **Share with**, and click **Specific people**.

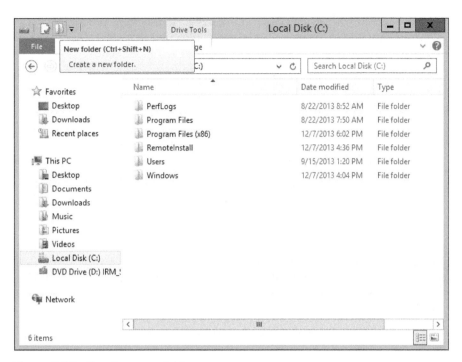

Figure 1-12   Creating a new folder

5. Type **Everyone** in the text box (see Figure 1-13) and click **Add**. Notice that the default permission level changes to Read, which allows all users with an account on the network to open or copy files in the DocShare folder.

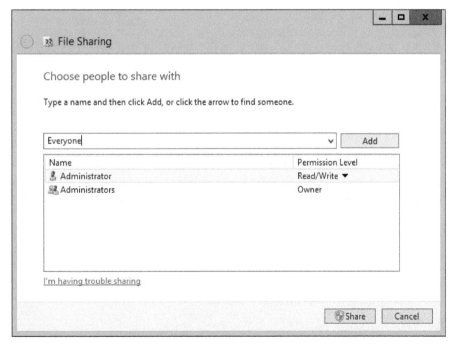

Figure 1-13   Sharing a folder

6. Click **Share.** If you see a message about network discovery and file sharing, click the response beginning with **No.** You see a message confirming that the folder is shared and the path to your new share is \\410Server1\DocShare. Click **Done.**

7. Close File Explorer and open Server Manager, if necessary. Click **File and Storage Services** in the left pane.

8. You should see that new tools have been added to the left pane: Shares and iSCSI. In Windows Server 2012 R2, you also see Work Folders. (If you don't see these new tools, press **F5**, click the **Refresh** button at the top of Server Manager, or close and restart Server Manager.) When you created a share, the File Server role service was installed automatically along with additional tools.

9. Click **Shares** to see a list of shares on your server (see Figure 1-14).

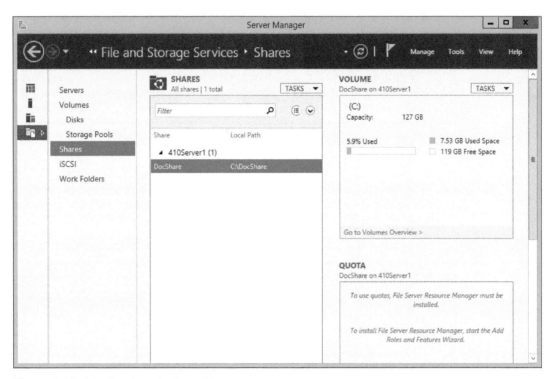

Figure 1-14   Viewing shares in Server Manager

10. Close all open windows. Stay logged on if you're continuing to the next activity; otherwise, shut down the server.

Windows Networking Concepts

Administering a Windows server requires extensive knowledge of networking components and protocols as well as a solid understanding of the network security models used in Windows. In a Windows network environment, computers can be configured to participate in one of two network security models: workgroup or domain.

The Workgroup Model   A **Windows workgroup** is a small collection of computers with users who typically have something in common, such as the need to share files or printers with each other. A workgroup is also called a peer-to-peer network sometimes because all participants are represented equally on the network, with no single computer having authority or control over another. Furthermore, logons, security, and resource sharing are decentralized, so each user has control over his or her computer's resources. This model is easy to configure, requires little expertise to manage, and works well for small groups of users (fewer than 10) who need to share files, printers, an Internet connection, or other resources. A Windows Server 2012/R2 server that participates in a workgroup is referred to as a **stand-alone server.**

The number of computers in a workgroup isn't limited to 10, but it's generally accepted that as more computers are added to a network, the domain model, although more expensive, is better from a management standpoint. For many situations and applications, the domain model is preferable even when the number of computers is far fewer than 10.

The Domain Model   A **Windows domain** is a group of computers that share common management and are subject to rules and policies defined by an administrator. The domain model is preferred for a computer network that has more than 10 computers or requires centralized security and resource management. Unlike the workgroup model, a domain requires at least one computer configured as a domain controller running a Windows Server OS. In the domain model, a computer running a Windows Server OS can occupy one of two primary roles: a domain controller or a member server.

A **domain controller** is a Windows server that has Active Directory installed and is responsible for allowing client computers access to domain resources. The core component of a Windows domain is Active Directory. A **member server** is a Windows server that's in the management scope of a Windows domain but doesn't have Active Directory installed.

Windows Networking Components

Every OS requires these hardware and software components to participate on a network: a network interface, a network protocol, and network client or network server software. Current OSs usually have both client and server software installed. In Windows, this collection of networking components working together is called a **network connection.**

Network Interface   A network interface is composed of two parts: the network interface card (NIC) hardware and the device driver software containing specifics of how to communicate with the NIC. In Windows Server 2012/R2, you configure the network interface in the Network Connections window (see Figure 1-15). To open it from Server Manager, click Local Server and then click the address next to the Ethernet label. Alternatively, right-click the network connection icon in the notification area, click Open Network and Sharing Center, and then click Change adapter settings.

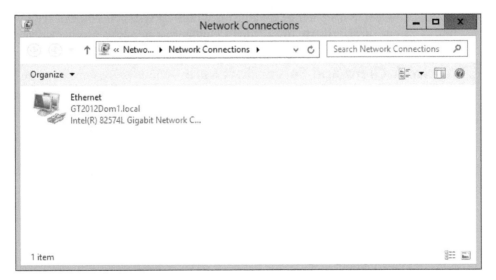

Figure 1-15   The Network Connections window

If you right-click a network connection and click Properties, a Properties dialog box similar to Figure 1-16 opens. The network interface used in this connection is specified in the Connect using text box. You can view details about the interface, including the device driver and configurable settings, by clicking the Configure button.

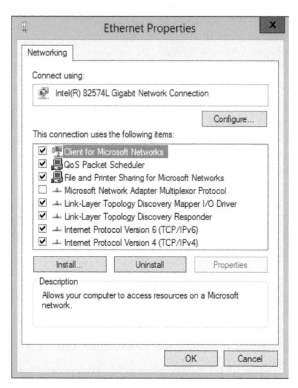

Figure 1-16   Properties of a network connection

Network Protocol   A **network protocol** specifies the rules and format of communication between network devices. Several years ago, network administrators usually had to understand and support two or more protocols on their networks. Today, most administrators need to work with only TCP/IP or, more specifically, TCP/IPv4. However, TCP/IPv4's successor, TCP/IPv6, is now being installed by default on Windows systems. You can see in Figure 1-16 that both versions of TCP/IP are installed. To configure a network protocol, select it and click the Properties button.

Network Client and Server Software   Windows systems have both network client and network server software installed. A **network client** is the part of the OS that sends requests to a server to access network resources. So if you want to access a file shared on a Windows computer, you need to have network client software that can make a request for a Windows file share. In Windows, this software is Client for Microsoft Networks. **Network server software** is the part of the OS that receives requests for shared network resources and makes these resources available to a network client. So if you want to share files that other Windows computers can access, you need to have network server software installed that can share files in a format Client for Microsoft Networks can read. In Windows, this server software is File and Printer Sharing for Microsoft Networks.

Windows networking is quite robust, with a number of client and server components and a variety of configuration options. Chapter 9 covers TCP/IP configuration, and throughout the book, you learn about many of the network services available in Windows Server 2012/R2.

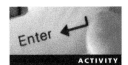

Activity 1-9: Exploring Windows Networking Components

Time Required: 15 minutes
Objective: Explore features of Windows networking components.

Required Tools and Equipment: 410Server1
Description: You're new to Windows Server 2012 R2 and need to know how to manage the network connections on your server.

1. Log on to 410Server1 as **Administrator,** if necessary.

2. Press **Windows+X,** click **Control Panel,** and click **View network status and tasks** (under the Network and Internet category) to open the Network and Sharing Center. (Alternatively, right-click the network connection icon in the notification area and click Open Network and Sharing Center.)

3. Active networks are listed at the top of the window. Depending on your network configuration, your network might have a name or be shown as "Unidentified network," as in Figure 1-17.

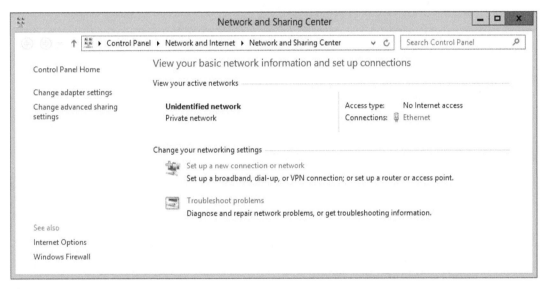

Figure 1-17   The Network and Sharing Center

4. Click the **Ethernet** link on the right to display information about your network connection and the number of bytes being sent and received (see Figure 1-18).

5. Click the **Details** button to view address information about TCP/IP and physical address information about your NIC, and then click **Close.**

6. Click the **Properties** button to see details on installed protocols, clients, and services. Each protocol and service has a check box for enabling or disabling it on the connection.

7. Click **Internet Protocol Version 4 (TCP/IPv4).** (Don't clear the check box, or you'll disable the protocol.) Then click **Properties** to open a dialog box where you can change your server's IP address settings. For now, leave the settings as they are. Click **Cancel,** and then click **Cancel** again.

8. Close all open windows. Stay logged on if you're continuing to the next activity; otherwise, shut down the server.

Figure 1-18   Viewing the status of a network connection

Windows Server 2012/R2 Roles

In Windows, a **server role** is a major function or service that a server performs. Probably the best known and most common server role is a file server (called the File and Storage Services role in Windows Server 2012/R2), which allows the server to share files on a network and manage storage devices. **Role services** add functions to the main role. For example, with the File and Storage Services role, you can install role services such as Distributed File System, Server for NFS, and File Server Resource Manager. Windows server roles and role services are installed in Server Manager.

You can also add **server features**, which provide functions that enhance or support an installed role or add a stand-alone function. For example, with the File and Storage Services role installed, you can add the Failover Clustering feature to provide fault tolerance for the file server. An example of a stand-alone feature is Internet Printing Client, which enables clients to use Internet Printing Protocol to connect to printers on the Internet. A server can be configured with a single role or several roles, depending on the organization's needs and the load a role puts on the server hardware. The following sections briefly describe some roles that can be installed in Windows Server 2012/R2. Several of these roles, particularly those covered in Exam 70-410, are explained in detail in later chapters. The coverage of roles in this chapter isn't exhaustive; it's meant to give you an overview of the roles you need to be most familiar with for the Windows Server 2012/R2 Microsoft Certified Solutions Associate (MCSA) certification. Figure 1-19 shows the list of available server roles in Windows Server 2012 R2.

The only new role in Windows Server 2012 R2 is the Windows Server Essentials Experience role.

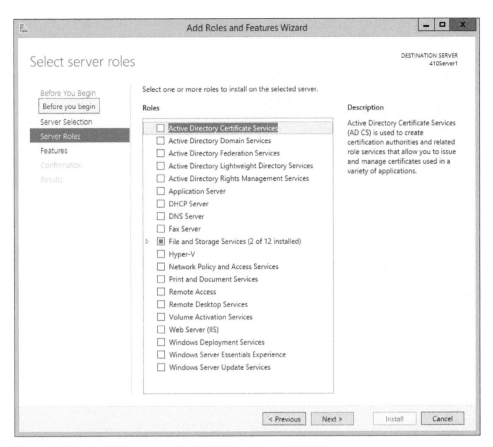

Figure 1-19   Available server roles in Windows Server 2012 R2

Active Directory Certificate Services

A driver's license provides information about the license holder, such as a photo, name, address, and so forth, and the state issuing the license. Similarly, a certificate, or digital certificate, is an electronic document containing information about the certificate holder and the entity that issued the certificate. This document is used to verify the identity of one or both parties who want to engage in a transaction.

The Active Directory Certificate Services (AD CS) role provides services for creating, issuing, and managing digital certificates that users and computers can use to verify their identities when engaging in secure transactions over a network. When this role is installed, a number of role services can also be deployed that have functions for managing certificates. The AD CS role is covered in *MCSA Guide to Configuring Advanced Windows Server 2012/R2 Services, Exam 70-412* (Cengage Learning, 2015) in detail.

Active Directory Domain Services

The Active Directory Domain Services (AD DS) role installs Active Directory and turns a Windows Server 2012/R2 computer into a domain controller. The main purpose of AD DS is to handle authentication and authorization for users and computers in a Windows domain environment. Active Directory stores information in a centralized database, giving administrators a tool for deploying user and computer policies, installing software, and applying patches and updates to client computers in the domain. As Active Directory is the cornerstone of the Windows Server network infrastructure, you learn about this role service in detail throughout this book and in *MCSA Guide to Administering Windows Server 2012/R2, Exam 70-411*, and *MCSA Guide to Configuring Advanced Windows Server 2012/R2 Services, Exam 70-412* (Cengage Learning, 2015).

Other Active Directory–Related Roles

Other server roles related to Active Directory can be installed. The following server roles are covered in *MCSA Guide to Configuring Advanced Windows Server 2012/R2 Services, Exam 70-412* (Cengage Learning, 2015):

- *Active Directory Federation Services (AD FS)*—This server role allows single sign-on access to Web-based resources, even when resources are located in a different network belonging to another organization.

- *Active Directory Lightweight Directory Services (AD LDS)*—This server role provides most of the functions of AD DS without the requirements of forests, domains, and domain controllers. The main purpose of AD LDS is to support directory-enabled applications with a flexibility that AD DS can't match.

- *Active Directory Rights Management Services (AD RMS)*—This role helps administrators control what users can do with documents and data after they have access. With AD RMS, an administrator can create usage policies that define how a document can be used; actions such as copying, saving, forwarding, and even printing documents can be restricted.

DHCP Server

The Dynamic Host Configuration Protocol (DHCP) Server role provides automatic IP address assignment and configuration for client computers. A DHCP server responds to requests from network computers for their IP address configurations, which include an IP address and a subnet mask. Optionally, a DHCP server can provide a default gateway address, DNS server addresses, WINS server addresses, and other options. This role is covered in Chapter 11 and in *MCSA Guide to Configuring Advanced Windows Server 2012/R2 Services, Exam 70-412* (Cengage Learning, 2015).

DNS Server

DNS is a critical component in the operation of the Internet and Windows domains. A DNS server resolves the names of Internet computers and computers that are members of a Windows domain to their assigned IP addresses. The DNS Server role can be tightly integrated with Active Directory, and your understanding of how to manage the DNS service in Windows Server 2012/ R2 is critical to proper Active Directory operation. When Active Directory is first installed in a Windows network, you're prompted to specify an existing DNS server or install DNS on the same server as Active Directory. Chapter 10 covers the DNS Server role in depth, and it's also covered in *MCSA Guide to Administering Windows Server 2012/R2, Exam 70-411*, and *MCSA Guide to Configuring Advanced Windows Server 2012/R2 Services, Exam 70-412* (Cengage Learning, 2015).

File and Storage Services

The File and Storage Services role, along with other role services that can be optionally installed, enables administrators to ensure highly available, reliable, shared storage to Windows and other client OSs. This server role has several related role services and features, given Microsoft's emphasis on the importance of data storage. "Storage Spaces," later in this chapter, describes some new capabilities of this role, and Chapters 4 and 5 cover this role and many of its related services in more detail.

Hyper-V

Hyper-V provides services for creating and managing virtual machines running on a Windows Server 2012/R2 computer. As mentioned, a virtual machine is a software environment that simulates the computer hardware an OS requires for installation. In essence, a virtual machine creates in software all the hardware you find on a computer, including BIOS, disk controllers, hard drives, CD/DVD drives, serial ports, USB ports, RAM, serial ports, network interfaces, video cards, and even processors. An OS can be installed on a virtual machine by using the same methods for installing one on a physical machine. The most common method is to insert a CD or DVD containing the OS you want to install. With a virtual machine, however, because the CD/DVD drive is virtual, you can simply point it to an image of the OS installation disk, thus making the physical media unnecessary. Hyper-V has been updated substantially in Windows Server 2012/R2, and some of these enhancements are discussed later in "New and Enhanced Features in Windows Server 2012/R2." Hyper-V is also covered in Chapter 12 and, to a lesser degree, in *MCSA Guide to Administering Windows Server 2012/R2, Exam 70-411*, and *MCSA Guide to Configuring Advanced Windows Server 2012/R2 Services, Exam 70-412* (Cengage Learning, 2015).

Network Policy and Access Services

This server role enables administrators to create and enforce network access policies that apply to client authentication and authorization and client health. Role services that can be installed include Network Policy Server (NPS), Health Registration Authority (HRA), and Host Credential Authorization Protocol (HCAP). The primary goal of these services is to give users secure access to network resources by using a variety of authentication and authorization protocols that are consistent with the company's network policies. With this role installed, network administrators can use Network Access Protection (NAP), an administrative tool for ensuring that all computers on the network are up to date with patches, antivirus software, and firewall settings. This role is covered in *MCSA/MCSE Guide to Administering Windows Server 2012/R2, Exam 70-411* (Cengage Learning, 2015).

Print and Document Services

The Print and Document Services role enables administrators to centralize and manage access to network printers. Available role services include Print Server, which is installed by default when you install the Print and Document Services role. The Internet Printing role service enables Web-based management of network printers and the capability to print to network printers by using HTTP. In addition, the Line Printer Daemon (LPD) role service provides print compatibility with Linux/UNIX clients. The Distributed Scan Server role service allows centralized management of network scanners. Chapter 5 covers this role in detail.

Remote Access

The Remote Access role allows configuring a server as a virtual private network (VPN) server and a router as well as a DirectAccess server. DirectAccess, like a VPN, enables users to connect to their work network securely wherever they have an Internet connection. DirectAccess is more user friendly than a typical VPN connection and makes managing remote computers an easier task for the IT administrator. The Remote Access role is covered in detail in *MCSA Guide to Administering Windows Server 2012/R2, Exam 70-411* (Cengage Learning, 2015).

Windows Deployment Services

Windows Deployment Services (WDS) makes installing multiple Windows systems across a network fast and simple. Administrators can not only install, but also remotely configure Windows 8.1 and Server 2012 systems. WDS provides all the tools needed to deploy Windows in an enterprise network on a large scale. You can find an in-depth discussion in *MCSA Guide to Administering Windows Server 2012/R2, Exam 70-411* (Cengage Learning, 2015).

New and Enhanced Features in Windows Server 2012/R2

Microsoft has added several new features and improved a host of existing features to make Windows Server 2012/R2 a secure, highly available, enterprise-class server OS. Microsoft's emphasis on the private cloud is clear, with several features focused on this burgeoning sector of IT. Some of the new and improved features, discussed briefly in the following sections, are covered in more detail in later chapters; others are covered in *MCSA Guide to Administering Windows*

Server 2012/R2, Exam 70-411, and *MCSA Guide to Configuring Advanced Windows Server 2012/R2 Services, Exam 70-412* (Cengage Learning, 2015).

- Server Core
- Minimal Server Interface
- Hyper-V 3.0
- PowerShell 3.0
- Storage Spaces
- Resilient File System (ReFS)
- IP Address Management (IPAM)
- Dynamic Access Control

Server Core

Server Core, introduced in Windows Server 2008, is more of an installation option than a feature. Microsoft recognized the need for a Windows Server OS with a smaller disk and memory footprint and a smaller attack surface that could be managed remotely instead of from the console. Server Core provides a minimal user interface environment and is intended to run specific server roles. It must be managed from a command line or remotely by using Server Manager, an MMC, PowerShell, or a Windows remote shell. Because of its smaller footprint, it makes an ideal virtual machine running in Hyper-V. Figure 1-20 shows the standard Server Core interface with a command prompt window running the text-based Server Configuration (`sconfig.exe`) program.

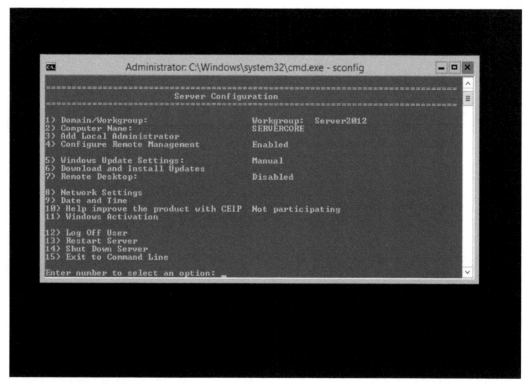

Figure 1-20   The Server Core interface

Not much to see, is there? Server Core has no taskbar or Start screen, just a command prompt window on a black background. Its use might not be obvious, but Server Core has quite a bit going on under the hood. Despite the austere user interface, Microsoft has made Server Core the recommended installation option, as you can see in the initial setup window in Figure 1-21.

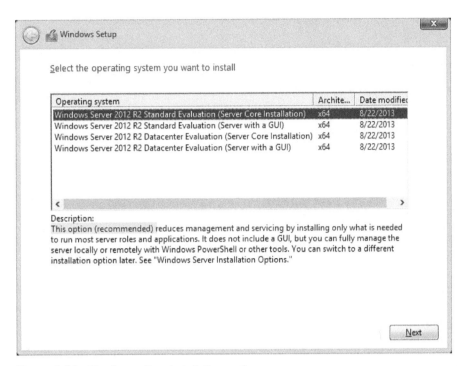

Figure 1-21   The Server Core installation option

Server Core's lightweight interface hides powerful server capabilities that aren't encumbered by a resource-intensive GUI. A fresh installation of Server Core uses a little more than 5 GB of disk space compared with more than 9 GB for a fresh installation of Windows Server 2012/R2 with a GUI. Although disk space is cheap, it's not free, and the disk space savings can add up if you're hosting dozens or hundreds of virtual machines running Windows Server 2012/R2. Maintenance of Server Core is also reduced considerably because fewer patches are needed. Fewer installed components and a reduced need for patches and updates result in a more secure and reliable system.

A major enhancement made to Server Core in Windows Server 2012/R2 is the ability to switch between Server Core mode and GUI mode. In the Windows Server 2008 version, after you installed it in Server Core mode or GUI mode, you couldn't switch to the other mode. With this improvement, administrators can install Windows Server 2012/R2 in GUI mode, configure the server with the familiar Server Manager and other GUI tools, and then switch to Server Core mode to benefit from the extra reliability and security.

Minimal Server Interface

The benefits of Server Core mode are substantial, but some people just can't live without being able to point and click. Microsoft recognized this fact and found a happy medium between Server Core mode and the full GUI: Minimal Server Interface (also called MinShell). Minimal Server Interface allows performing most local management tasks with a GUI tool but lacks many aspects of the full user interface. It includes the following GUI tools: Server Manager, some Control Panel applets, and the MMC. However, it doesn't include the taskbar, the desktop, Internet Explorer, File Explorer, or the Start screen. As in all interface modes, the command prompt and PowerShell are available. Figure 1-22 shows what you see when you boot into the Minimal Server Interface; like the full GUI, Server Manager starts automatically. To get to the

Minimal Server Interface from Server Core, enter the `Install-WindowsFeature Server-Gui-Mgmt-Infra` command at a PowerShell prompt.

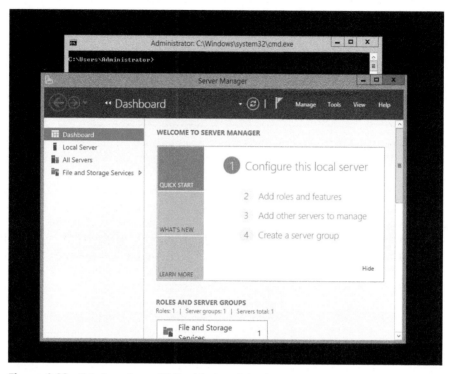

Figure 1-22   Windows Server 2012 with the Minimal Server Interface option

You can also get to Minimal Server Interface from the full GUI installation by using Remove Roles and Features in Server Manager and removing the Server Graphical Shell feature but keeping the Graphical Management Tools and Infrastructure feature.

The PowerShell command to install the Minimal Server Interface requires that the feature's binaries be available on the hard drive. If the command yields an error, add the following to the end of it: `-source wim:d:\sources\install.wim:4` (replacing `d:`, if necessary, with the letter of your CD/DVD drive with the Windows installation disc inserted).

Hyper-V 3.0

Hyper-V is the Windows Server virtualization environment introduced in Windows Server 2008. Although it's not new, the enhancements in Hyper-V version 3.0 make Windows Server among the leaders in virtualization software. Hyper-V 3.0 is a major component of Microsoft's private cloud initiative. Hyper-V and virtualization in general are a big part of Windows Server and warrant a full chapter (which is Chapter 12). The following list summarizes the new features in Hyper-V 3.0 compared with its predecessors:

- Multiple concurrent live migrations
- Hyper-V Replica
- Support for 32 virtual processors
- Virtual machines with up to 512 GB of RAM
- Clusters with up to 63 nodes

- Enhanced virtual networking
- Virtual disks up to 16 TB

All these enhancements mean Hyper-V 3.0 offers a lot of scalability and flexibility for building a virtualization environment.

PowerShell

PowerShell is a command-line interactive scripting environment that provides the commands for almost any management task in a Windows Server 2012/R2 environment. It can be used much like a command prompt, where you enter one command at a time and view the results, or as a powerful scripting engine that enables you to create and save a series of commands for performing complex tasks. To say PowerShell scripts are like a command-prompt batch file is like saying a two-seat propeller plane is similar to an F-35 fighter jet. Yes, they both fly, but the F-35 is much more powerful.

In a command-prompt environment, commands you type are called simply "commands"; PowerShell uses the term "cmdlets" (pronounced "command-lets"). Hundreds of cmdlets are available in PowerShell, ranging from performing simple tasks, such as displaying the date and time, to managing aspects of Active Directory. In addition, new cmdlets can be created and imported as modules for extending the capabilities of PowerShell. In addition, PowerShell cmdlets aren't limited to managing the local computer; remote management is a useful feature.

Getting the most out of PowerShell requires some effort because the number of available commands is staggering. Learning to use this powerful tool is no longer just an option, however; it's a requirement for enterprise server administrators. PowerShell 1.0 was introduced as a downloadable product in late 2006, and version 2.0 became an important part of Windows 7 and Windows Server 2008 R2. PowerShell 3.0 is an integrated component of Windows Server 2012 and Windows 8, and Windows Server 2012 R2 and Windows 8.1 are equipped with PowerShell 4.0.

The new features in PowerShell are too numerous to list, but the following note contains a link to the full list of enhancements in PowerShell 3.0 and 4.0. Here are some of the highlights:

- More than 50 new core cmdlets
- Job-scheduling cmdlets
- Language enhancements
- Remote module import
- Module auto-loading
- Enhanced command auto-completion
- Simplified command discovery
- Improved performance

For a complete list of PowerShell enhancements, see *http://technet. microsoft.com/en-us/library/hh857339.aspx*. For downloadable reference guides, see *www.microsoft.com/en-us/download/details.aspx?id=30002*.

For those familiar with PowerShell, the list of improvements means something; for everybody else, not so much. This book doesn't aim to make you a PowerShell guru, but with the new emphasis on Server Core and remote administration of servers, many of the tasks you learn to do in the GUI are also shown as PowerShell cmdlets and scripts.

Storage Spaces

Managing storage has become a full-time job for some administrators. The amount of data people need to store is always increasing, and the varying types of data they need to store are a challenge for server administrators. Windows Server 2012/R2 has a number of tools to meet today's increasing storage requirements and make managing storage, well, a little more manageable.

Storage Spaces is a new tool designed to make the most of local storage on small to medium business servers. It uses the power of virtual drives to give you a platform for creating volumes from storage pools that can be dynamically expanded and fault tolerant without the usual physical disk restrictions placed on volume creation. Volumes can be created from multiple drive types, including USB, SATA, and SAS. Drives can be internal or external, and RAID volumes need not be created from same-sized disks. By using virtual disks, Storage Spaces permits thin provisioning, which means the physical disk space isn't allocated for a volume until it's actually needed. For a glimpse of the Storage Spaces interface, take a look at Figure 1-23. Storage Spaces is covered in detail in Chapter 4.

Figure 1-23   The Storage Spaces interface

Resilient File System

Resilient File System (ReFS) is a new file system in Windows Server 2012/R2 that's intended for large data storage applications requiring a high degree of reliability. It's largely backward-compatible with NTFS but doesn't support some features, such as file-based compression, disk quotas, and Encrypting File System (EFS). In addition, the boot volume can't be an ReFS-formatted volume. ReFS does, however, have the following advantages over NTFS:

- Automatic on-the-fly file system repair (no need for the chkdsk utility)
- Support for huge volume sizes (2^{78} bytes or 274 billion terabytes)

ReFS is designed mainly for large file-sharing applications in which volumes are managed by Storage Spaces, giving you the most flexibility and reliability without the added expense of fault-tolerant hardware.

IP Address Management

IP Address Management (IPAM) takes some of the complexity out of managing an enterprise IP network. It has tools to monitor and manage servers running DHCP and DNS, including automatic discovery of domain controllers and DHCP and DNS servers. You can use IPAM to audit IP address use and track changes made to the IP address space. IPAM is an advanced topic covered in *MCSA Guide to Configuring Advanced Windows Server 2012/R2 Services, Exam 70-412* (Cengage Learning, 2015).

Dynamic Access Control

Dynamic Access Control (DAC) gives you fine-tuned control over shared resources without some of the limitations of traditional file permissions. However, instead of replacing traditional sharing and NTFS permissions, DAC works alongside these permissions, giving administrators more flexibility in assigning access to resources. Traditional permissions are based on user and group accounts, and in a large network with hundreds or thousands of users and resources, group-based permissions can be limiting and complex. DAC allows classifying data and assigning permissions by user attributes rather than group memberships. As a simple example, a folder can be classified as belonging to the Accounting Department, making access available only to users whose Department attribute equals Accounting, or classified as highly sensitive so that its contents are encrypted automatically, relieving an administrator from having to encrypt it manually. The possibilities with DAC are endless, and like IPAM, it's an advanced feature covered in *MCSA Guide to Configuring Advanced Windows Server 2012/R2 Services, Exam 70-412* (Cengage Learning, 2015).

Chapter Summary

- A server is largely defined by the software running on the computer hardware rather than the computer hardware on which the software is running. Although most client OSs now provide some server services, such as file and printer sharing, a true server OS is usually defined as providing these important network services: directory services, DNS, remote access, DHCP, and robust network application services. In addition, current server OSs include hardware support for multiple processors, disk fault tolerance, and clustering.

- Windows Server 2012/R2 is available in four main editions: Datacenter, Standard, Essentials, and Foundation. Datacenter and Standard edition are full-featured server OSs that differ only on the virtualization license. Essentials is aimed at small businesses and supports up to 25 users; Foundation is the entry-level server OS, supporting only 15 users.

- Windows Server 2012/R2 has several features for creating and supporting private cloud environments. Cloud computing abstracts the details of how computer services are delivered to users. Virtualization is a major component of cloud computing, and Windows Server 2012/R2 includes Hyper-V to create a virtual computing environment. Two major categories of cloud computing are public and private.

- The technologies that make up the core functions of Windows Server 2012/R2 include Server Manager, NTFS, Active Directory, the Microsoft Management Console, disk management, file and printer sharing, and Windows networking.

- Windows Server 2012/R2 includes more than a dozen primary server roles and many supporting role services and features. Administrators can configure a server as a narrowly focused device, providing just one or two specific services, or as a general, do-it-all system that's the center of a Windows network.

- Windows Server 2012/R2 builds on the success of Windows Server 2008 by adding a host of new services, including Minimal Server Interface, Storage Spaces, Resilient File System, IP Address Management, and Dynamic Access Control. In addition, enhancements have been made to Server Manager, Server Core, Hyper-V, and PowerShell.

Key Terms

Active Directory The Windows directory service that enables administrators to create and manage users and groups, set network-wide user and computer policies, manage security, and organize network resources.

client access licenses (CALs) A license required by law for each user who logs on to a Windows Server 2012/R2 Standard or Datacenter Edition server.

cloud computing A collection of technologies for abstracting the details of how applications, storage, network, and other computing resources are delivered to users.

Datacenter Edition A Windows Server 2012/R2 edition, intended primarily for organizations using virtualization on a large scale.

domain controller A Windows server that has Active Directory installed and is responsible for allowing client computers access to domain resources.

Essentials Edition A Windows Server 2012/R2 edition suitable for small businesses with 25 or fewer users. This edition doesn't support Hyper-V, and some services, such as Active Directory and DNS, are installed automatically during OS installation.

Foundation Edition A Windows Server 2012/R2 edition intended as an entry-level server edition. It's an OEM-only version that supports only 15 users and can only be purchased already installed on a server.

guest OS The operating system running in a virtual machine installed on a host computer. *See also* virtual machine (VM).

host computer The physical computer on which virtualization software is installed and virtual machines run.

hypervisor The virtualization software component that creates and monitors the virtual hardware environment, which allows multiple virtual machines to share physical hardware resources.

member server A Windows server that's in the management scope of a Windows domain but doesn't have Active Directory installed.

network client The part of the OS that sends requests to a server to access network resources.

network connection A collection of components consisting of a network interface, network protocols, and network client and server software that work together to connect a Windows computer to a network.

network protocol Software that specifies the rules and format of communication between devices on a network.

network server software The part of the OS that receives requests for shared network resources and makes these resources available to a network client.

New Technology File System (NTFS) A file system used on Windows OSs that supports compression, encryption, and fine-tuned permissions.

PowerShell A command-line interactive scripting environment that provides the commands needed for most management tasks in a Windows Server 2012/R2 environment.

private cloud A cloud computing service provided by a company's internal IT Department. *See* cloud computing.

public cloud A cloud computing service provided by a third party. *See* cloud computing.

role services Services that can be installed in Server Manager to add functions to the main role. *See also* server role.

root domain controller The first domain controller installed in an Active Directory forest. *See also* domain controller.

Server Core A Windows Server 2012/R2 installation option that doesn't have a traditional GUI.

server features Components you can install that provide functions to enhance or support an installed role or add a stand-alone feature.

server operating systems OSs designed to emphasize network access performance and run background processes rather than desktop applications.

server role A major function or service that a server performs.

stand-alone server A Windows server that isn't a domain controller or a member of a domain.

Standard Edition A Windows Server 2012/R2 edition suitable for most businesses that need a full-featured server and might need to use virtualization on a moderate scale.

virtual desktop infrastructure (VDI) A rapidly growing sector of private cloud computing whereby users access their desktops through a private cloud; the OS and applications run on servers in a corporate data center rather than on the local computer.

virtual machine (VM) The virtual environment that emulates a physical computer's hardware and BIOS.

virtualization   A technology that uses software to emulate multiple hardware environments, allowing multiple operating systems to run on the same physical server simultaneously.

virtualization software   The software for creating and managing virtual machines and creating the virtual environment in which a guest OS is installed.

Windows domain   A group of Windows computers that share common management and are subject to rules and policies that an administrator defines.

Windows workgroup   Also called a peer-to-peer network, it's a small collection of Windows computers whose users typically have something in common, such as the need to share files or printers with each other. No computer has authority or control over another. Logons, security, and resource sharing are decentralized.

Review Questions

1. Which of the following best defines a computer used as a server?

   a. Computer hardware that includes fast disk drives and a lot of memory

   b. A computer with OS software that has a Web browser and Client for Microsoft Networks

   c. A computer with OS software that includes directory services and domain name services

   d. A computer with Linux installed

2. Which of the following best describes a Windows client OS?

   a. Supports up to 64 processors

   b. Includes fault-tolerance features, such as RAID-5 and clustering

   c. Supports network connections based on the number of purchased licenses

   d. Supports a very limited number of logged-on network users

3. Which Windows Server 2012/R2 edition allows installing unlimited virtual instances?

4. Which of the following is true of Windows Server 2012/R2 Essentials Edition?

   a. It can't be installed as a virtual machine.

   b. It's configured as a root domain controller by default.

   c. Licensing is limited to 15 users.

   d. It supports up to four physical processors.

5. You have recently purchased a new computer that supports four processors and up to 512 GB of RAM. You want to be able to run six to eight virtual instances without incurring additional licensing costs. Which of the following Windows Server 2012/R2 editions should you install on your server?

   a. Essentials Edition

   b. Standard Edition

   c. Foundation Edition

   d. Datacenter Edition

6. Each core in a multicore processor counts toward the maximum number of processors that Windows Server 2012/R2 Foundation Edition supports. True or False?

7. You're starting a new business with five employees who need access to an application that runs on Windows Server 2012. You need to keep costs down, and you don't have a lot of computer expertise, so you want to keep things as simple as possible. Ideally, you'll buy a server with an OS already installed. Which edition of Windows Server 2012/R2 should you consider?

   a. Essentials

   b. Standard

   c. Foundation

   d. Datacenter

8. The IT Department sent out a memo stating that it will start delivering desktop computer interfaces through the IT data center via a Web browser interface. What technology is the IT Department using?

    a. Public cloud computing

    b. Server clustering

    c. Directory server

    d. Virtual desktop infrastructure

9. You need to support a large disk volume of 1 TB or more and use quotas to limit the amount of space users' files can occupy on the volume. Which file format should you use?

    a. exFAT

    b. FAT32

    c. NTFS

    d. ReFS

10. Which of the following disk formats supports Encrypting File System (EFS)?

    a. exFAT

    b. FAT32

    c. NTFS

    d. ReFS

11. What feature of the Windows Server 2012/R2 file system should you enable if you want users to be able to restore deleted or previous versions of a file in a shared folder?

    a. Distributed File System

    b. Disk quotas

    c. Shadow copies

    d. Bitlocker

12. You're a consultant for a small business with four computer users. The company's main reason for networking is to share the Internet connection, two printers, and several documents. Keeping costs down is a major consideration, and users should be able to manage their own shared resources. Which networking model best meets the needs of this business?

13. Which networking component includes a device driver?

    a. Network server software

    b. Network client software

    c. Network protocol

    d. Network interface

14. If you want to share files with other Windows computers, you should have _____ installed and enabled on your computer.

    a. Client for Microsoft Networks

    b. File and Printer Sharing for Microsoft Networks

    c. Active Directory

    d. Domain Name System

15. If you want to make a computer a domain controller, which of the following should you install?

    a. Client for Microsoft Networks

    b. File and Printer Sharing for Microsoft Networks

    c. Active Directory

    d. Domain Name System

16. Which of the following server roles resolves names of Internet computers?

    a. Active Directory Domain Services

    b. DNS Server

    c. DHCP Server

    d. Remote Access

    e. Hyper-V

17. Which of the following is the common framework in which most Windows Server 2012/R2 administrative tools run?

    a. Windows Management Center

    b. Microsoft Management Console

    c. Server Configuration Manager

    d. Windows Configuration Manager

18. You have been asked to advise a business on how best to set up its Windows network. Eight workstations are running Windows 8.1. The business recently acquired a new contract that requires running a network application on a server. A secure and reliable environment is critical to run this application, and security management should be centralized. There are enough funds in the budget for new hardware and software, if necessary. Which Windows networking model should you advise this business to use?

    a. A Windows domain using Active Directory

    b. A Windows workgroup using Active Directory

    c. A peer-to-peer network using File and Printer Sharing

    d. A peer-to-peer network using Active Directory

19. Which of the following is a feature (not a server role) that can be installed in Windows Server 2012/R2?

    a. Active Directory Domain Services

    b. Failover clustering

    c. File and Storage Services

    d. Hyper-V

20. Which of the following roles should you install if you want to create and manage virtual machines?

    a. Network Policy and Access Services

    b. Server Manager

    c. Hyper-V

    d. DHCP Server

21. Your manager has asked you to audit 150 Windows 8.1 client computers to make sure they're up to date with patches, antivirus software, and firewall settings. You realize that checking all these computers manually will take an inordinate amount of time. Which server role can you install in Windows Server 2012/R2 to make this job much easier?

    a. Active Directory Rights Management Services

    b. Network Policy and Access Services

    c. Print and Document Services

    d. AD Federation Services

22. Your boss has told you that he wants several employees to have a way to access the company network securely through an Internet connection. Further, the computers they use to access the network from should be manageable by the IT Department. What should you configure on your Windows Server 2012/R2 server?

    a. DirectAccess

    b. Windows Deployment Services

    c. Dynamic Access Control

    d. Storage Spaces

23. Server Core mode enables you to run certain GUI tools, such as Server Manager and some Control Panel applets, but doesn't include the taskbar or Start screen. True or False?

24. If you want to provide users with secure network transactions that verify the identity of sender and receiver with a digital certificate, which role should you consider installing?

    a. Active Directory Federation Services

    b. Active Directory Certificate Services

    c. Active Directory Rights Management Services

    d. Active Directory Lightweight Directory Services

25. You have just installed a human resources application that's directory service enabled on a Windows Server 2012/R2 server. You're running primarily Linux in your organization and don't have a Windows domain, but you want to take advantage of the benefits a directory service offers. Which Windows Server 2012/R2 role should you install?

    a. Active Directory Federation Services

    b. Active Directory Certificate Services

    c. Active Directory Rights Management Services

    d. Active Directory Lightweight Directory Services

Case Projects

Case Project 1-1: Selecting a Windows Server 2012/R2 Edition

You're installing a new network for CSM Tech Publishing, a new publisher of technical books and training materials. There will be 10 client computers running Windows 8.1, and CSM Tech Publishing plans to run a Web-based order processing/inventory program that for now is used only by in-house employees while they're on site. CSM Tech Publishing wants to be able to manage client computer and user policies and allow employees to share documents. Growth is expected, but the budget is tight, so the company needs to purchase only what's necessary to get running and leave high-end server features for future consideration. Management prefers to get the server with the OS already installed and wants to keep management tasks as simple as possible. Which Windows Server 2012/R2 edition do you recommend? Explain your answer.

Case Project 1-2: Choosing Server Roles

You have purchased a server for your client, CSM Tech Publishing. Review Case Project 1-1 for its computing requirements. Windows Server 2012 R2 is installed, and you're now installing and configuring services that your client will need. Based on the needs described in Case Project 1-1, which server roles should you install at a minimum, and which networking model should you use? Explain your answer.

Case Project 1-3: Performing Additional Server Configuration Tasks

CSM Tech Publishing has been operating for six months, and business is good. You do a spot check on server resources and find that RAM use is at 50%, which is fine, but the data volume is approaching 90% full. There are two volumes on this server: one for OS and program files and one for data storage. You inspect the data volume and find that some users are storing large amounts of data on the server. You check with the owner and determine that each user should require only about 4 GB of storage on the server for necessary documents. Because some users are clearly exceeding this limit, you're asked to come up with a solution. What file system option can you use, and which file system format must be used with this option?

Case Project 1-4: Explaining Cloud Computing

The owner of CSM Tech Publishing is always thinking about how he can use technology to improve the operation of his business. He read an article about cloud computing and has asked you to explain what cloud computing is and whether he needs it now or in the future for more efficient operations. Write a memo explaining what cloud computing is and whether you recommend using any form of it now or in the future.

chapter 2

Installing Windows Server 2012/R2

After reading this chapter and completing the exercises, you will be able to:

- Plan a Windows Server 2012/R2 installation
- Work with Windows Server Core
- Use the new Features on Demand

Once an arduous and sometimes intimidating task, installing a Windows server has become an easy, straightforward process. The installation process in Windows Server 2012/R2 is similar to the Windows 8.1 process and requires little user interaction from start to finish.

The real work of a Windows Server 2012/R2 installation takes place before you actually begin—in the planning phase. This chapter covers the actual installation process, but more important, it describes the planning that should go into installing a server in a production environment. Answers to questions about how the server will be used, whether the installation is an upgrade or a new installation, and what roles the server will play in the network factor into how you decide to install the operating system. After installing the server, you need to undertake a number of postinstallation tasks right away, many of which depend on decisions you made in the planning phase. This book doesn't cover in detail the tools for deploying Windows Server 2012/R2 in large numbers; instead, it focuses on the planning process for both small and large installations and the postinstallation tasks.

Other installation options in Windows Server 2012/R2 also affect installation-planning decisions, depending on whether you want a server with a full GUI, a minimal GUI, or the Server Core option. This chapter explores these options plus server upgrades, Features on Demand, and server role migration so that you can make wise choices when you deploy Windows Server 2012/R2 on your network.

Planning a Windows Server 2012/R2 Installation

Table 2-1 summarizes what you need for the hands-on activities in this chapter.

Table 2-1   Activity requirements

Activity	Requirements	Notes
Activity 2-1: Installing Windows Server 2012 R2	410Server2, Windows Server 2012 R2 installation medium	
Activity 2-2: Setting the Time, Date, and Time Zone	410Server2	
Activity 2-3: Setting a Static IP Address	410Server2	
Activity 2-4: Testing Network Connectivity	410Server1, 410Server2	
Activity 2-5: Changing the Computer Name and Workgroup	410Server2	
Activity 2-6: Configuring Windows Update	410Server2	Internet connection required
Activity 2-7: Installing Server Core	410ServerCore	
Activity 2-8: Restoring a Command Prompt Window in Server Core	410ServerCore	
Activity 2-9: Setting the Time, Date, and Time Zone in Server Core	410ServerCore	
Activity 2-10: Setting an IP Address in Server Core	410ServerCore	
Activity 2-11: Configuring the Server Core Firewall for Ping Packets	410Server2, 410ServerCore	
Activity 2-12: Setting Computer and Workgroup Names in Server Core	410ServerCore	
Activity 2-13: Configuring Windows Update in Server Core	410ServerCore	

The actual process of installing Windows Server 2012/R2 is simple enough that you might be inclined to get out the DVD and forge ahead without much forethought. However, this temptation could be a time-consuming and costly mistake if you don't have a well-thought-out plan for using the technologies in Windows Server 2012/R2. Aside from selecting an edition, choosing an upgrade or a new install, and deciding whether to use a domain controller, among other decisions, your installation options have expanded. You can do a GUI installation, a Minimal Server Interface installation, or just a Server Core installation. In addition, you can install your server on physical hardware or as a virtual machine.

Admittedly, a single server installation for a small business with 25 users doesn't pose a major challenge requiring weeks of careful consideration and planning. You can make a few decisions and get on with it. However, situations such as installing 400 servers or bringing a branch office online, which requires integrating its server with the existing network, involve more planning. This section doesn't attempt to cover every possible server installation you might encounter. Instead, it gives you the knowledge you need to understand some potential issues and arms you with questions you need to answer before proceeding.

This book doesn't cover Windows Deployment Services (WDS), a tool for deploying Windows OSs via a network installation, because it's not a topic of the 70-410 certification exam. WDS is covered in *MCSA Guide to Administering Windows Server 2012/R2, Exam 70-411* (Cengage Learning, 2015).

The network environment in which you're deploying a server and the roles a server will play on the network are the key considerations in planning Windows Server 2012/R2 installations. In the following sections, you examine these common installation situations and learn some of the issues and options involved:

- Installing the first server in a new Windows network

- Expanding a network by adding a second server or installing a server in a branch office

- Upgrading from earlier Windows versions

Installing the First Server in a New Network

Installing Windows Server 2012/R2 in a new network that doesn't already have Windows servers operating is usually the most straightforward installation situation. The following descriptions assume you're installing the first server in a small network with fewer than 100 users.

One issue to consider for any server installation is hardware features. The following list describes a few of these features:

The terms "CPU" and "processor" are often used interchangeably. A physical processor is a chip that installs in a socket on a motherboard. However, today's physical processors might have multiple processor cores, and each core can perform the same work as a single-core physical processor.

- *CPU architecture*—The major CPU manufacturers typically have a workstation line and a server line of processors. The server line includes Intel Xeon and AMD Opteron. Depending on the expected server workload, you must also consider how many physical processors and how many CPU cores each processor should have. Server virtualization, which has special CPU requirements, is also a factor. To sum up, here are some of the CPU architecture options:

  o Workstation or server line of processors: Typically, the workstation line supports only one or at most two physical CPUs; the server line supports up to 64.

  o Total number of physical processors: You can buy a system with one processor now and add more later if the motherboard supports multiple physical processors. Be aware, however, that you must use identical processors in multiprocessor systems, and finding an identical match three or four years later can be difficult. Also, keep in mind the Windows Server 2012/R2 edition you plan to install because the maximum number of processors supported varies.

o Number of cores in each processor: With multicore CPUs the norm today, buying a system that supports them makes sense. Multicore CPUs usually don't achieve the same performance as multiple physical processors, but they have become an inexpensive way to boost performance.

Recall from Chapter 1 that Microsoft considers a physical processor, regardless of the number of cores, as a single processor when considering how many processors a particular edition supports.

o 32-bit versus 64-bit processors: This option is no longer an issue for Windows Server products starting with Windows Server 2008 R2 because Microsoft no longer makes a 32-bit version of its server OS. In addition, unless you're using a very old processor, it's a moot point because any server or workstation processor manufactured after 2004 supports 64-bit processing.

o Virtualization extensions: With a 64-bit processor, chances are good that it supports virtualization extensions, but you need to be certain if you want to run Hyper-V. On Intel processors, look for the Intel Virtualization Technology (Intel-VT) label, and on AMD processors, look for AMD-V. These extensions are a prerequisite to installing the Hyper-V role.

- *Disk subsystem*—Before the arrival of serial ATA (SATA) drives, the only real choice of hard drives for servers was SCSI. Both specifications make performance improvements constantly. Between these two standards is serial attached SCSI (SAS). Current knowledge indicates that for entry-level or departmental servers, SATA is a good choice because it's inexpensive and offers excellent performance. For enterprise servers or servers accessed 24/7, SAS and the newest SCSI systems have a performance and reliability advantage. SCSI disks are generally designed for continuous use; SATA drives tend to be designed more for consumer use than around-the-clock use. Doing research on current technology and your network's needs before deciding is best.

- *Hot-add/hot-replace features*—Say you've noticed that memory use has increased to dangerously high levels after installing a new database application on your server. You need to add memory to the server before it crashes; in the past, this process meant shutting down the server first. Not so with Windows Server 2012/R2 Standard and Datacenter editions because both support **hot-add** memory, meaning the server doesn't have to shut down for this procedure. Unfortunately, the server hardware must also support this feature, and you find it only in high-end, enterprise-class servers. Some servers even support adding or replacing a processor without a system shutdown. The capability to hot-add disk drives is more common and can be found in almost all server classes. If you need more disk space or need to replace a failed disk in a RAID configuration, you can simply install the new drive without shutting down the server. All editions support disk **hot-replace** or hot-add if the hardware supports it.

This list covers just a few of the server hardware features you should consider before installing a new server. The best advice is to forge a good relationship with a knowledgeable vendor you can consult with when you need to make a purchase. This way, you can focus on managing your server, and your vendor can focus on keeping up with the latest hardware options.

To make sure your hardware selections are compatible with Windows Server 2012/R2, check the Windows Server Catalog at *www.windowsservercatalog.com*.

When installing the first server in a new network, you must make some decisions shortly after finishing the installation. Some are fairly straightforward, but others take some thought and consultation. Here's a list of some decisions you need to make:

- What should you name the server? This decision is more important than it sounds. Every computer needs a name so that it can be identified on the network. A server name must be unique on the network and should include some description, such as its location or primary function. Server names should also be simple and easy to remember because users often access servers by name.

Even if you expect the server to be the only server on the network, you shouldn't use just "Server" as the name. Situations often change and require adding a server, so at least give it a number, such as Server1. Subsequent server names can be a bit more descriptive, such as Mail1, Accounting1, or Building19DC.

- Which network protocols and addresses should you use? By default, Windows installs both TCP/IPv4 and TCP/IPv6 in Windows Server 2012/R2. You can't uninstall them, but you can disable them in a network connection's Properties dialog box. TCP/IPv4 is still the predominant local area network (LAN) protocol, but it won't be long before IPv6 takes hold in networks. Previous Windows versions had the option of installing other protocols and services, such as IPX/SPX (NWLink) and client/server components for NetWare. Windows Server 2012/R2 has no additional protocol or client options, so if they're important, you need to find a third-party solution or use Windows Server 2003 or earlier.

Although you might be tempted to disable IPv6 on your network connections, don't do it in Windows Server 2012/R2. Some features, such as DirectAccess, depend on IPv6.

- How should I assign an IP address to the server? By default, Windows Server 2012/R2 uses automatic IP addressing, but a server should have a static IP address. Some server roles (such as DHCP) actually require assigning a static address. If you haven't devised your addressing scheme, now is the time to do that. Generally, server administrators assign one of the first or last addresses in an address range, such as 192.168.1.1 or 192.168.1.254. Whatever you decide, be consistent so that when more servers are added, you can assign IP addresses easily.

- Setting the correct time zone isn't really a decision but a task you must complete because having the wrong time zone can cause all manner of problems, particularly in a domain environment. Certain functions in a domain network, such as user authentication, depend on client and server computers having their clocks well synchronized.

- Should I use the workgroup or domain model? As discussed in Chapter 1, the Windows domain model has a number of advantages in usability, manageability, and security. If you've invested in a Windows Server OS, it makes sense to get the most out of it by using the domain model and installing Active Directory. With a small network of only a few users, however, the workgroup model is a viable option, particularly if the main administrator isn't familiar with Active Directory. With either model, you need a workgroup or domain name, unless you're using the workgroup model and keep the default name "Workgroup." If you're using the domain model, the domain name you use should be registered with the Internet Corporation for Assigned Names and Numbers (ICANN; *www.icann.org*). If the Internet name isn't already registered, make sure the name you have in mind is still available.

For testing purposes and for domains that don't need a public Internet presence, you can use top-level names, such as `.local`, `.example`, and `.test` (`mycompany.local`, `mycompany.example`, or `mycompany.test`). For a production network that requires an Internet presence, however, you should use only valid top-level domain names and registered second-level domain names.

- What server roles should you install? This decision is one of the most important because it determines how the server will be used and what network services will be available to users. Chapter 1 summarized the available roles and many features you can install. For a first-server installation, however, there are some clear choices. With the domain model, you must install the Active Directory Domain Services (AD DS) role. AD DS requires DNS, so the DNS Server role is installed automatically. Other basic roles to consider on a first server include DHCP (for IP address configuration) and File and Print Services, which includes tools for sharing and managing file storage and printer resources. Many other roles and features can be installed to meet your network and business needs; several are discussed in later chapters.

Now that you have a plan, it's time to move on to the actual installation of Windows Server 2012 R2.

Performing a Clean Installation

A **clean installation** is one in which the OS is installed on a new disk partition and isn't an upgrade from any previous version of Windows. For the first server installation on a new network, you usually use a DVD. Like any other OS installation, make sure the BIOS is set to boot from the CD/DVD drive first if you have an OS already installed. After installation begins, a message is displayed to let you know that Windows is loading files. Next, you see the window shown in Figure 2-1, where you choose the language, time, and keyboard configuration. After clicking Next, a window is displayed with the options Install now or Repair your computer.

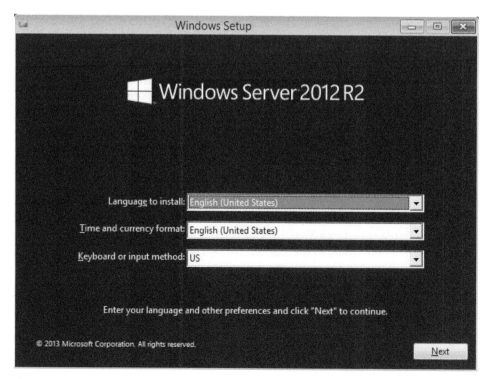

Figure 2-1   The initial installation window for Windows Server 2012 R2

After you click Install now, you're prompted to enter the product code (unless you're using the evaluation edition). The next window asks which edition you want to install and whether you want a server with a GUI or a Server Core installation (see Figure 2-2). This section covers a full GUI installation, and you perform a Server Core installation later in Activity 2-7. In subsequent windows, you accept the license terms and select an upgrade or a custom installation. The upgrade option is available only if a supported version of Windows is already installed. A custom installation, described in this section, performs a clean install of Windows.

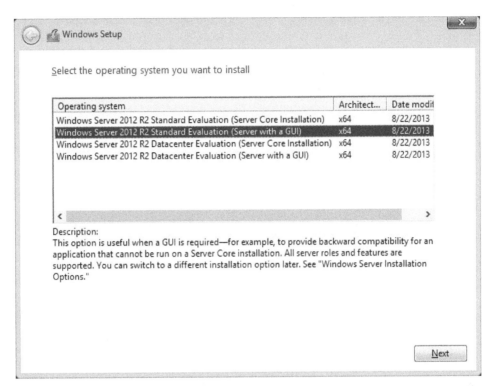

Figure 2-2   Choosing the edition and installation type

After selecting the custom option, choose from a list of disks and partitions to specify where you want to install Windows (see Figure 2-3). You can use the Load driver link to install a driver for a disk controller if your disk isn't shown. If you click the New link, you're prompted to create a new volume from the selected disk. If you just select a disk and click Next, Windows creates two volumes: one of about 350 MB for system boot files (which isn't assigned a drive letter) and the other for the C drive, where the Windows and other default folders are located. The entire disk is used and is formatted with NTFS.

Windows begins the installation (see Figure 2-4), and then your computer typically restarts twice. After the installation is finished, you're prompted to set the password for the built-in Administrator account (see Figure 2-5). The password you choose must meet complexity requirements, which means it must contain a minimum of six characters that include three of the following types: uppercase letters, lowercase letters, numerals, and special symbols, such as @, /, and #. You can use the icon at the lower-left corner to select ease of access options for hearing-, sight-, or mobility-impaired users. After you change the password, click Finish. When prompted, log on to open Server Manager.

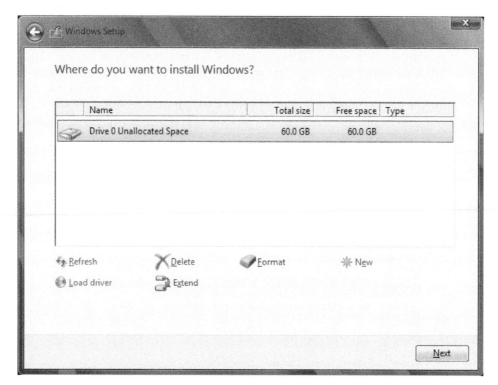

Figure 2-3   Specifying where to install Windows

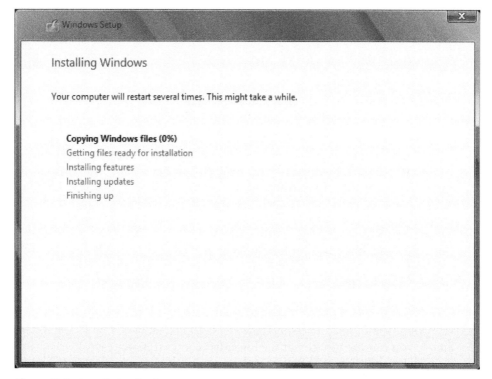

Figure 2-4   Installation begins

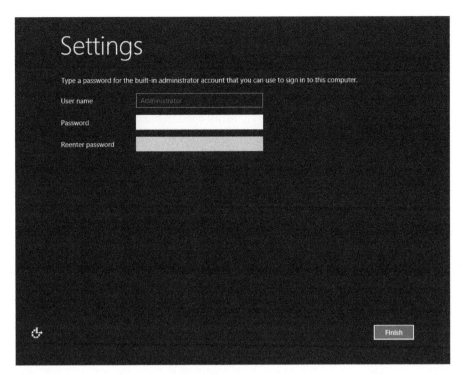

Figure 2-5   Setting the Administrator password

What If You Installed the Wrong Edition?   What happens if you install Standard Edition and your situation calls for Datacenter Edition, or you're using an evaluation edition and want to upgrade to the licensed edition without reinstalling? Fortunately, Microsoft devised a simple solution: using the dism.exe command. If you need to change the server edition from Standard to Datacenter, type the following at a command prompt:

```
dism /online /set-edition:ServerDatacenter /productkey:
  datacenter product key /accepteula
```

You can also use the dism command to upgrade an evaluation edition of Windows Server 2012/R2 to Standard or Datacenter licensed editions if you have the correct product key. To see what editions you can upgrade to, use the following command:

```
dism /online /get-targeteditions
```

For information on using the dism.exe command, type dism /? at a command prompt. For help on a specific dism option, type dism /option /?. For example, for help on the /online option, type dism /online /?.

Activity 2-1: Installing Windows Server 2012 R2

Time Required: 30 minutes to more than an hour
Objective: Install Windows Server 2012 R2.

Required Tools and Equipment: 410Server2 prepared according to instructions in "Before You Begin" and the Windows Server 2012 R2 installation medium

Description: You're ready to install Windows Server 2012 R2 on your network. You have verified the hardware configuration and have the installation DVD in hand. The server has a single hard drive and all space is unallocated, so there's no need to change the BIOS boot order.

1. Power on 410Server2 and insert the Windows Server 2012 R2 installation DVD.

2. You see a progress bar as files are loaded from the DVD. In the first installation window (shown previously in Figure 2-1), verify the language, time, and keyboard choices for your environment. Make changes if necessary, and click **Next**.

3. In the next window, click **Install now**.

4. If the next window asks for your product key, enter it now, and then click **Next**. The next window might differ slightly from Figure 2-2, but you should click **Windows Server 2012 R2 Standard (Server with a GUI)**, and then click **Next**.

5. Click the option to accept the license agreement, and then click **Next**. In the next window, click **Custom: Install Windows only (advanced)**.

6. In the Where do you want to install Windows? window, you can manipulate drive partitions and load drivers for a disk controller, if needed. If you simply click Next with an unallocated disk selected, Windows uses the entire disk and formats it as NTFS. If necessary, click to select **Drive 0 Unallocated Space**, and then click **Next**. Now you can just sit back and let Windows do the rest. Your computer restarts at least twice.

 In the Where do you want to install Windows? window, you can press Shift+F10 to open a command prompt window in the MINWINPC environment. From this command prompt, you can use a host of utilities, including `diskpart` for performing advanced disk configuration tasks.

7. In the Settings dialog box, set the Administrator password by typing **Password01** twice, and then clicking **Finish**. You see a message that Windows is finalizing your settings.

8. When prompted, press **Ctrl+Alt+Delete** to sign in. Type **Password01** and press **Enter**. After a short time, you see the desktop, Server Manager opens, and you're ready to go.

9. Stay logged on if you're continuing to the next activity; otherwise, log off or shut down the server.

What If Your Disk Isn't Found?

What If Your Disk Isn't Found?   If Windows setup doesn't recognize your disk controller during installation, you won't see the disk where you want to install Windows listed in the Where do you want to install Windows? window. In this case, click the Load driver link. You're prompted to insert a medium containing the disk controller driver. If you don't have the driver handy, check the disk controller's Web site. After the driver is loaded, the disk or disks connected to the controller should be displayed, and you can continue the installation.

Postinstallation Tasks

Now that Windows Server 2012 R2 is installed, it's time to attend to some postinstallation tasks. Some were discussed earlier, such as naming the server and configuring protocols and addresses. Here's a summary of the tasks you should perform immediately on the first server in a network:

- Activate Windows Server 2012 R2.
- Set the correct date, time, and time zone.
- Assign a static IP address.
- Assign a computer name.
- Configure automatic updates.
- Download and install available updates.

All these tasks can be accessed from Server Manager when you click Local Server in the left pane. Windows Server 2012/R2 requires activation within 10 days after installation. If you haven't activated Windows Server after 10 days, the desktop background turns black and your server restarts every hour. If you entered a product key during installation or are using an evaluation version, Windows Server 2012/R2 activates automatically if you're connected to the Internet. If you're using a volume license copy, you need to activate Windows manually in the Local Server Properties window or use the slmgr.vbs command-line program. In the following activities, you perform some of these postinstallation tasks.

Activity 2-2: Setting the Time, Date, and Time Zone

Time Required: 10 minutes
Objective: Perform the postinstallation task of setting the time, date, and time zone.

Required Tools and Equipment: 410Server2 with Windows Server 2012 R2 installed as specified in Activity 2-1
Description: You have finished the Windows installation and notice that the time zone is incorrect. You know that for all server functions to work correctly, the time, date, and time zone must be right on all clients and servers. In this activity, you use the Local Server Properties window in Server Manager to change the time zone.

1. Log on to 410Server2 as **Administrator**, if necessary. When Server Manager starts, click **Local Server** in the left pane to open the Properties window.
2. Click the **Time zone** link to open the Date and Time dialog box.
3. Click **Change date and time** and make changes, if necessary. Click **OK**.
4. Click **Change time zone**, and select your time zone in the drop-down list, if necessary. If your region observes daylight saving time, make sure the **Automatically adjust clock for Daylight Saving Time** check box is selected, and then click **OK**.
5. Click the **Additional Clocks** tab, where you can tell Windows to display the time in other time zones when you hover the mouse pointer over the taskbar clock.
6. Click the **Internet Time** tab, where you can select the option to synchronize with a time server on the Internet. By default, Windows Server 2012 R2 is set to synchronize with *time.windows.com*, and synchronization occurs weekly. Click **Change settings** to use a different time server or disable Internet time synchronization. You can choose from a list of time servers or enter the name of another server. You can also tell Windows to synchronize now by clicking **Update now**. If time synchronization isn't working, your company firewall might be blocking it.
7. Click **OK** twice to close the Internet Time Settings and Date and Time dialog boxes. Stay logged on if you're continuing to the next activity; otherwise, log off or shut down the server.

Activity 2-3: Setting a Static IP Address

Time Required: 15 minutes
Objective: Perform the postinstallation task of setting a static IP address.
Required Tools and Equipment: 410Server2
Description: After finishing the Windows Server 2012 R2 installation, you notice in the Local Server Properties window that the server's IP address is assigned by DHCP. Your server will be performing some server roles that require static addressing. You have already decided that all your servers will occupy addresses starting with 1 in the last octet. Server1 is already using 10.10.1.1, so you use 10.10.1.2.

This activity and many others in this book use 10.10.1.x/16 for IP addressing. If you will be using different addresses, make the necessary changes.

1. Log on to 410Server2 as **Administrator,** if necessary. Start Server Manager, if necessary, and open the Local Server Properties window.

2. Find Ethernet in the Properties dialog box and click **IPv4 address assigned by DHCP, IPv6 enabled.** The Network Connections window opens.

3. Right-click **Ethernet** and click **Properties** to open the Ethernet Properties dialog box (see Figure 2-6).

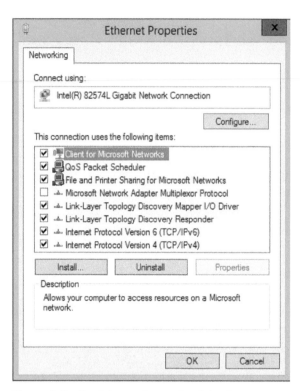

Figure 2-6   The Ethernet Properties dialog box

4. Notice that both TCP/IPv4 and TCP/IPv6 are installed and enabled, but you're going to configure only TCP/IPv4. Click **Internet Protocol Version 4 (TCP/IPv4),** being careful not to clear the check box next to it. Click the **Properties** button.

5. In the Internet Protocol Version 4 (TCP/IPv4) Properties dialog box, click the **Use the following IP address** option button, shown in Figure 2-7.

6. Fill in the following information:

 If you're using a different IP addressing scheme, see your instructor for these values.

IP address: **10.10.1.2**

Subnet mask: **255.255.0.0**

Default gateway: **10.10.1.250** (or an address supplied by your instructor)

Preferred DNS server: Your instructor should give you this address.

Alternate DNS server: Leave blank or enter a value specified by your instructor.

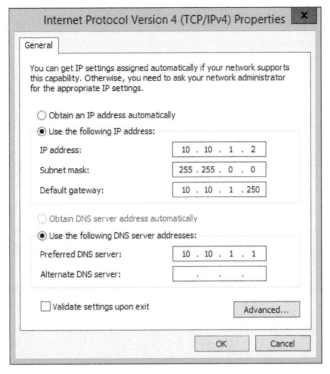

Figure 2-7   Configuring IP address settings

7. Click **OK** and then **Close**.

8. To verify your settings, right-click **Ethernet** and click **Status**. Then click the **Details** button to open the Network Connection Details dialog box.

9. Verify all the information, and then click **Close** twice. Close the Network Connections window.

10. For the server to register its DNS name, it needs a primary DNS suffix. To set it, click **Local Server** in Server Manager, if necessary, and then click the name of the server next to "Computer name" to open the System Properties dialog box.

11. Click **Change**, and then click **More**. In the DNS Suffix and NetBIOS Computer Name dialog box, type **410Server2012.local** in the "Primary DNS suffix of this computer" text box. Click **OK** twice.

12. The Computer Name/Domain Changes message box states that you must restart the computer to apply the changes. Click **OK**. Click **Close** to close the System Properties dialog box.

13. Click **Restart Now**. When the computer restarts, log on if you're continuing to the next activity.

After configuring networking on a server, most people test the configuration by using **ping**, a network testing and troubleshooting tool that sends a series of **Echo Request** packets to a destination IP address to see whether there's a reply. If the Echo Request reaches the destination computer, an **Echo Reply** packet is sent back to the sender.

Activity 2-4: Testing Network Connectivity

Time Required: 10 minutes
Objective: Test network connectivity after configuring a static IP address.
Required Tools and Equipment: 410Server1 and 410Server2
Description: You have just finished setting a static IP address on your server and want to be sure all the information is correct and working.

For `ping` to work, the network connection must be identified as a Private network. In Server Manager, find the Windows Firewall setting. If it's set to Public: On, follow the directions in the "Before You Begin" section to set the network type to Private.

1. Start 410Server1. Start 410Server2 and log on as **Administrator,** if necessary.

2. Open a command prompt window on 410Server2 by right-clicking **Start** and clicking **Command Prompt.**

3. At the command prompt, type **ping 10.10.1.1** (the address of 410Server1) and press **Enter.** If you get successful replies, the network connection between 410Server1 and 410Server2 is working.

4. If the `ping` command returns a "Request timed out" or "Destination host unreachable" message, verify your IP settings with your instructor.

It's not uncommon to get one "Request timed out" or "Destination host unreachable" message followed by three successful Reply messages, but if all four messages indicate an unsuccessful ping, recheck your address settings and the address settings of the computer you're trying to ping.

5. Ping the default gateway by typing **ping 10.10.1.250** (or the address you entered in Step 6 of Activity 2-3) and pressing **Enter.** Verify that you received a successful reply.

6. Ping the DNS server, using the address you entered in Step 6 of Activity 2-3. Verify that you received a successful reply.

7. Close the command prompt window.

8. Stay logged on if you're continuing to the next activity; otherwise, log off or shut down the server.

Activity 2-5: Changing the Computer Name and Workgroup

Time Required: 10 minutes
Objective: Change your computer name.

Required Tools and Equipment: 410Server2
Description: After installing Windows, you examine the Local Server Properties window and notice that the assigned computer name seems random and the workgroup name is the generic "Workgroup." You want to personalize these settings according to your network plan.

1. Log on to 410Server2 as **Administrator** and start Server Manager, if necessary. Open the Local Server Properties window.

2. Next to Computer name, click the name of the computer to open the System Properties dialog box.

3. Click the **Computer Name** tab, if necessary, and then click the **Change** button. In the Computer name text box, type **410Server2**.

4. In the Workgroup text box, type **Server2012** or another name assigned by your instructor, and then click **OK**. After a moment or two, you should see the message "Welcome to the Server2012 workgroup." Click **OK**. When prompted to restart your computer, click **OK**. Click **Close**, and then click **Restart Now**.

5. When Windows restarts, log on as **Administrator**.

6. Verify your changes in the Local Server Properties window. You can also right-click **Start** and click **System** to open the System dialog box, which displays the computer name, workgroup or domain, and other system information.

7. Close all open windows. Stay logged on if you're continuing to the next activity; otherwise, log off or shut down the server.

Installing Updates   One of the most important administrative tasks is installing updates. Almost immediately after an OS is released, bugs and security vulnerabilities are found and fixed. These fixes, normally released as **patches,** can be installed through Windows Update. Windows Update also downloads and installs new drivers and service packs. A **service pack** is generally a collection of all bug fixes and security updates made since the OS release. Service packs can also add features and performance enhancements or change the functioning of existing features, so you must understand the effects of a service pack on your server before installing it. Testing a service pack extensively on a test server is highly recommended before deploying it on production machines.

By default, Windows Update is set to "Not configured," and the options "Last installed updates" and "Last checked for updates" are set to Never, as shown in Figure 2-8. To configure Windows Update easily, click Not configured in the Local Server Properties window. The next activity walks you through the process of configuring Windows Update.

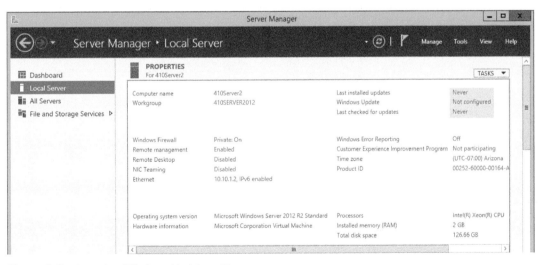

Figure 2-8   Accessing Windows Update settings

Activity 2-6: Configuring Windows Update

Time Required: 10 to 30 minutes, depending on number and size of updates
Objective: Configure automatic updates and download initial updates.

Required Tools and Equipment: 410Server2 and an Internet connection
Description: After installing Windows, you notice in the Local Server Properties window that automatic updates haven't been configured. You want to be sure your server is up to date on bug fixes and security updates.

You don't install updates in this activity because of the amount of time installation takes and because you might install an update (such as a service pack) that unexpectedly changes how Windows Server 2012/R2 works. In a production environment, however, you should install updates.

Before accessing the Internet with any computer, you should install antivirus software.

1. Log on to 410Server2 as **Administrator,** if necessary. In Server Manager, click **Local Server,** if necessary.

2. Click **Not configured** next to Windows Update to open the Windows Update dialog box (see Figure 2-9).

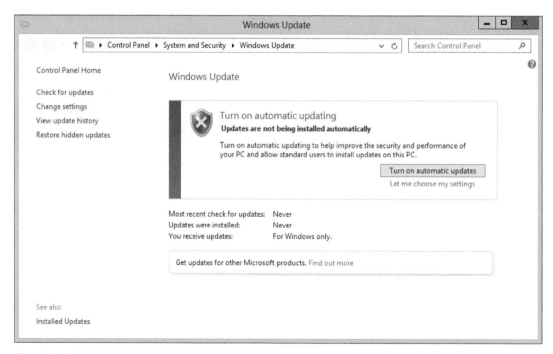

Figure 2-9   Windows Update configuration

3. Click the **Let me choose my settings** link. If you click "Turn on automatic updates," automatic updates is enabled with the default settings, which you might not want on a server. The default settings download and install updates automatically and might include a server restart.

4. The Change settings dialog box, shown in Figure 2-10, has sections called Important updates and Recommended updates. No options are selected by default. Under Important updates, click **Download updates but let me choose whether to install them.** This setting is the best choice for an administrator who wants to decide whether to install an update. Critical updates are downloaded as soon as they're available on the Internet, and a notification icon is displayed on the taskbar when they're ready to install. Any update requiring a server restart can be installed when a restart is convenient.

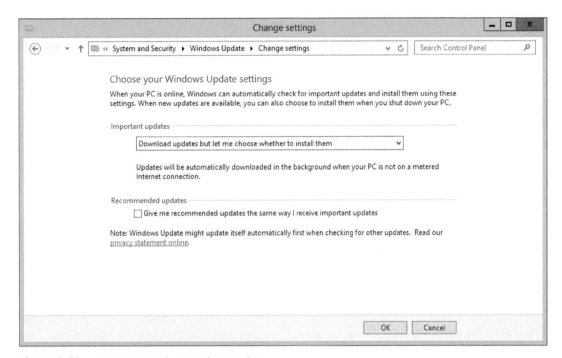

Figure 2-10   Changing Windows Update settings

5. Under Recommended updates, click the **Give me recommended updates the same way I receive important updates** check box. This option includes new drivers or updates to applications in downloaded updates. Click **OK.** Windows checks for updates immediately and downloads any updates it finds but doesn't install them.

6. After Windows finishes checking for updates, you see a window listing the number of updates found (see Figure 2-11). Click the message stating the number of updates found.

7. Windows lists the updates along with their size. Click an update to see its description in the right pane (see Figure 2-12). In this window, you can select or deselect the updates you want to install. For now, click **Cancel** because you don't want to install updates.

8. Close the Windows Update dialog box. Stay logged on if you're continuing to the next activity; otherwise, log off or shut down the server.

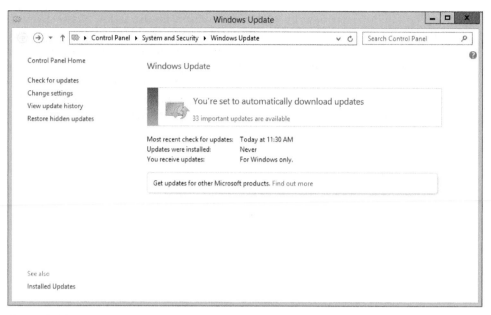

Figure 2-11 Downloaded updates ready to be installed

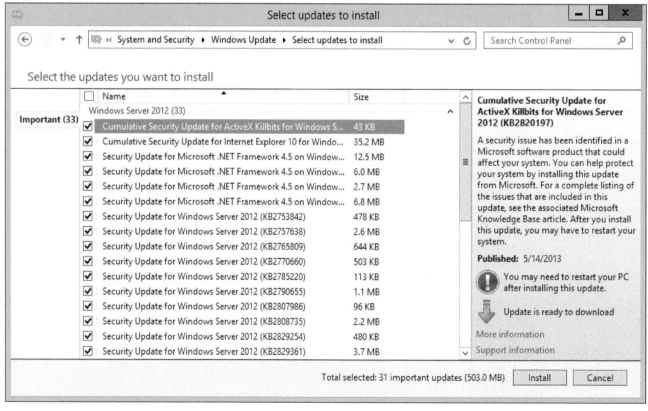

Figure 2-12 Selecting updates to install

Viewing Installed Updates   To view a list of installed updates in the Local Server Properties window, click the Windows Update link, and then click View update history. You can see the status of an update (whether the update was successful), the importance of the update, and the date it was installed (see Figure 2-13). After your computer is configured and up to date, you can start installing server roles and additional features. If this server is the first and only one (at least for now), you'll probably install several roles on it. As discussed, most networks in a domain environment usually run these services at a minimum: Active Directory Domain Services (AD DS), DNS, DHCP, and File and Storage Services. Other roles and features you install depend on how the network is used and what applications are running.

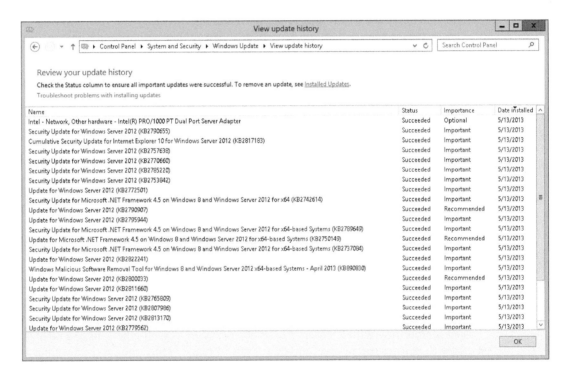

Figure 2-13   Update history

Expanding Your Network

Many businesses that start with a single server on the network eventually find a reason to install a second or third server and more. If your network requires two or more servers, you're almost certainly running in a domain environment, which is the perspective from which this topic is discussed.

When you're adding a server to an existing network, you must answer many of the same planning questions that you did for the first server. You need to decide on an IP address, a server name, and what roles the new server will play on the network. However, you probably don't need to choose a domain name because this new server will likely be part of the existing domain or a stand-alone server. What you must decide is whether the new server will be one of the following:

- A domain controller (DC) in the existing domain
- A read only domain controller (RODC) in the existing domain
- A member server in the existing domain
- A stand-alone server

If you're installing the second server in the network, there are some good arguments for making it a domain controller. The second server can share the load of managing directory services and handling user logons and provide fault tolerance for Active Directory should the first server go offline. A **read only domain controller** (**RODC**) provides much of a regular domain controller's functions, but changes can't be made on an RODC. Changes to the domain must be made on a regular (writeable) DC and then replicated to RODCs in the network. RODCs don't store password information, so they're more secure than writeable DCs. An RODC is better suited to handling domain services for branch offices than serving as a second DC. The RODC role is explored in *MCSA Guide to Administering Windows Server 2012/R2, Exam 70-411* (Cengage Learning, 2015).

A member server belongs to the domain and falls under domain management but doesn't run Active Directory or participate in managing directory services. Making a server a member server rather than a domain controller is best when you already have at least two DCs at a location or when you plan to run resource-intense applications on it that shouldn't share server resources with other services.

A stand-alone server, as the name implies, doesn't fall under the domain's management umbrella; instead, it's configured as part of a workgroup. Configuring a stand-alone server makes sense when, for example, the server will be acting as a public Web server, providing services (such as DNS or DHCP) for a group of non-Windows clients, or serving as a departmental server when you want local management.

Some reasons you need to add servers to a network include the following:

- Company growth
- Excessive load on existing servers
- Need to isolate an application
- Need for fault tolerance
- Addition of branch offices

A company that's growing, particularly in the number of users, should plan ahead for the inevitable network slowdowns caused by increased activity. A server that has been humming along smoothly with 25 users might not perform as well when this number doubles. Ideally, if growth is foreseen, new resources are put in place before the server becomes taxed. Even without additional users on a network, existing users' use tends to increase over time as users and administrators find more functions for the server to handle. This gradual increase in network and server use can sneak up on you. A server that was running fine six months ago can gradually bog down, sapping user productivity as it takes longer to log on to the network or access shared files. Monitoring a server's performance regularly before this problem becomes a crisis is a good idea. Server monitoring is discussed in *MCSA Guide to Administering Windows Server 2012/R2, Exam 70-411* (Cengage Learning, 2015).

Sometimes a network application works best when no other major services are competing for a server's CPU and memory resources. Even if your existing server isn't overused, introducing such an application into your network might prompt you to install it on its own server. Isolating applications in this way has the added benefit of not disturbing other network services when you perform maintenance on the server. The converse is also true: When you perform maintenance on other servers, you don't disturb the isolated application.

Access to network resources is so critical in business environments that loss of access to a server's services can reduce productivity and increase costs. Even in a smoothly running network where no server has an excessive load, adding a server for fault tolerance might still be wise. Load balancing or fault tolerance are built into several Windows server roles, such as AD DS, DNS, and file sharing with Distributed File System (DFS). If you need a complete hot replacement for an existing server, you can use failover clustering, in which a group of servers is connected by both cabling and software, so if one server fails, another takes over to provide those services.

When a business opens a branch office connected to the main office through a wide area network (WAN), installing a server at the branch office might be prudent. This setup can reduce WAN traffic created by authentication and authorization on a domain controller, DNS lookups, DHCP address assignment, access to shared files, and more. IT administrators are often concerned about security when installing a branch office server because a separate secure room to house the server might not be available. The server might be placed in somebody's office or a common area, which leaves it vulnerable to theft or even attacks by employees. Having physical access to a server makes compromising the server's security much easier. To address this problem, administrators can use RODCs. As mentioned, RODCs have many of the benefits of a standard DC, but administrators can filter what information is replicated to the RODC, including passwords. Therefore, an administrator can configure the RODC to keep only local users' passwords, which limits what damage could be done if someone were able to compromise the server. In addition, you can create a local administrator for an RODC so that maintenance activities can be carried out without giving the local administrator domain-wide administrative capabilities. Another option for a branch office server is using the Server Core installation mode to diminish the overall security risk.

Upgrading to Windows Server 2012/R2

When you upgrade to Windows Server 2012/R2, you can use two main methods: an in-place upgrade and server role migration. With an **in-place upgrade,** you boot to the existing OS and run `setup.exe` from the Windows Server 2012/R2 installation medium. With **server role migration,** you perform a clean install of Windows Server 2012/R2 and migrate the server roles the old OS version performed. Here's an overview of in-place upgrade considerations, followed by available upgrade paths in Table 2-2:

- The only previous Windows versions supported for upgrade are Windows Server 2008 and Windows Server 2008 R2.

- If you're running Server Core, you can upgrade only to Windows Server 2012/R2 Server Core, but you can install the GUI afterward.

- All Windows Server 2012/R2 versions are 64-bit, and cross-platform upgrades aren't supported, so you can upgrade only the Windows Server 2008 64-bit version to Windows Server 2012/R2. A Windows Server 2008 32-bit version requires a clean install.

- You can't upgrade to a different language.

Table 2-2   Windows Server 2012/R2 upgrade paths

Current edition	Server 2012/R2 upgrade path
Windows Server 2012 Datacenter	Windows Server 2012 R2 Datacenter
Windows Server 2012 Standard	Windows Server 2012 R2 Standard or Datacenter
Windows Server 2008 Standard or Enterprise	Windows Server 2012/R2 Standard or Datacenter
Windows Server 2008 Datacenter	Windows Server 2012/R2 Datacenter
Windows Server 2008 R2 Standard or Enterprise	Windows Server 2012/R2 Standard or Datacenter
Windows Server 2008 R2 Datacenter	Windows Server 2012/R2 Datacenter
Windows Web Server 2008 or Windows Web Server 2008 R2	Windows Server 2012/R2 Standard

© 2015 Cengage Learning®

If you're considering an in-place upgrade, Microsoft recommends removing any third-party software the manufacturer doesn't specifically support for a Windows Server 2012/R2 upgrade before the upgrade. In addition, make sure your system meets the minimum CPU, RAM, and disk requirements for Windows Server 2012/R2.

An upgrade is similar to a clean installation with a few exceptions. First, you must boot the existing OS and log on. Then you can start the `setup.exe` program from the installation medium. Next, you're asked whether Windows should go online to get the latest updates for installation. This option is recommended. You aren't prompted for the language, time, currency format, or keyboard layout; they must match the settings for the Windows Server 2012/R2 edition being installed. In addition, in an upgrade you aren't prompted for the location to install Windows. It's installed on the same disk partition as the OS you booted to.

Before an upgrade begins, Windows runs a compatibility check and produces a compatibility report. Any application, hardware, or driver issues discovered during the check are noted, and you can't continue the installation until you address issues known to prevent a successful upgrade.

Migrating from an Earlier Version   As you can see, in-place upgrades are somewhat limiting, and you could run into software incompatibility problems. In addition, upgrading isn't always possible if the specified upgrade path isn't available. For these reasons, Microsoft recommends a clean installation followed by server role migration, when possible. Windows Server 2012/R2 has a number of tools to help with this process, which avoids most of the upgrade path restrictions. For example, migration allows you to do the following:

- Migrate from a 32-bit Windows server installation to Windows Server 2012/R2.

- Migrate from Windows Server 2003 SP2 and later.

- Migrate from a Windows Server 2008 R2 Server Core installation to a GUI installation and vice versa.

Migrating Windows server roles and features isn't an all-or-nothing proposition. You can migrate roles and features from a server running an earlier version to a Windows Server 2012/R2 server, move a role or feature from one Windows Server 2012/R2 server to another, or move a role or feature from a virtual machine to a physical machine or vice versa. However, language migration isn't supported; both server versions must be running the same language package.

A migration is a multistep process. In the following steps, the *destination* computer is the new Windows Server 2012/R2 server you're migrating to, and the *source* computer is the computer you're migrating from:

1. To install the Windows Migration Tools feature on the destination Windows Server 2012/R2 server, use the Add Roles and Features Wizard in Server Manager or the PowerShell command `Install-WindowsFeature Migration`.

2. To create a distribution folder containing the tools the source server needs, use the `smigdeploy.exe` command. The specifics of using this command vary depending on the OS version and the source computer's architecture. For example, if the source computer is running a 32-bit version of Windows Server 2008, you use the following command to create a distribution folder in the `C:\distr` folder:

```
smigdeploy.exe /package /architecture x86 /os WS08 /path C:\distr
```

   You could also specify a network share in place of `C:\distr`.
3. Use any copying tool to copy the distribution folder created in Step 2 to the source computer.

4. To register Windows Server Migration Tools on the source computer, at an elevated command prompt change the directory to the distribution folder you copied in Step 3 and enter the `smigdeploy.exe` command.

An elevated command prompt is a command prompt run in Administrator mode. You can access one by right-clicking Start and clicking Command Prompt (Admin).

5. After the command finishes running, a PowerShell window opens, and you can begin using Windows Server Migration Tools cmdlets to migrate roles and features.

 The details of migrating roles and features are beyond the scope of this book, as each role and feature has different procedures to follow. For more information on using Windows Server Migration Tools, refer to *http://technet.microsoft.com/en-us/library/jj134202#BKMK_supported.*

Server Core: Windows That Doesn't Do Windows

As you learned in Chapter 1, the Server Core installation option provides a Minimal Server Interface environment designed for running Windows Server without the overheard of a GUI. Server Core's reduced codebase minimizes OS vulnerabilities and lessens maintenance and management tasks. In addition, the overall disk and memory footprint is smaller, thereby requiring fewer hardware resources than a full installation. The price you pay for these reductions and simplifications is a less user-friendly management interface.

Server Core is now the default and preferred operating mode for Windows Server 2012/R2. GUI management is intended to be performed from another Windows Server 2012/R2 server with a GUI or from a Windows 8.1 computer using remote server administration tools (RSAT). As you see in Chapter 3, Microsoft has improved and unified its remote administration tools with the goal that you rarely, if ever, need to visit a server's console to manage it. However, if you find that you simply must have a GUI, the advantage of Server Core mode in Windows Server 2012/R2 (unlike Windows Server 2008) is that you can change your mind and install the GUI if you decide the lonely command prompt in Server Core isn't your cup of tea.

Even if you prefer a server with the full GUI in most circumstances, Server Core is a good candidate for deployment in the following situations:

- As a secondary DC to provide redundancy for Active Directory running on a full installation
- As a branch office server when remote administration is likely and the reduced attack surface and maintenance are substantial benefits
- As an RODC for a department or branch office providing many of a standard DC's benefits but with reduced security risks
- As a virtual machine when reduced resource requirements are an important benefit
- As a specialized single-role server providing services such as DNS, DHCP, Web Services, or File and Storage Services
- As a departmental server, for many of the same reasons as a branch office server

Although Server Core supports most Windows server roles, there are a few it doesn't support. If you need to run any of these server roles, you must install the GUI version:

- Active Directory Federation Services
- Application Server
- Fax Server
- Network Policy and Access Services
- Remote Desktop Services: Gateway, Session Host, and Web Access
- Volume Activation Services
- Windows Deployment Services

Server Core's benefits are well and good, but you might be wondering how you carry out server management tasks without a desktop or Server Manager. That brings you to the next topic: performing initial configuration tasks on Server Core.

Server Core Installation and Postinstallation Tasks

A Server Core installation is nearly identical to a full installation, so there's no need to explain all the steps again. The only real difference is that you choose the Server Core Installation option when prompted to select the OS you want to install. From there, the process is the same, including changing the administrator password and logging on the first time. The first difference you'll probably notice is after you log on, when you see no desktop or Server Manager interface, just a command prompt.

Activity 2-7: Installing Server Core

Time Required: 30 minutes or longer, depending on the server's speed
Objective: Install Server Core.

Required Tools and Equipment: 410ServerCore configured according to the instructions in "Before You Begin"
Description: This activity doesn't give you step-by-step instructions because the steps are identical to installing Windows Server 2012 R2 with a GUI, except you choose the Server Core Installation option. You have verified the hardware configuration and have the installation DVD in hand. The server has a single hard drive and all space is unallocated, so there's no need to change the BIOS boot order.

1. Follow Steps 1 to 6 in Activity 2-1, but in Step 4, click the **Windows Server 2012 R2 Standard (Server Core Installation)** option.

2. If prompted, press **Ctrl+Alt+Delete** to sign in, and then click **Administrator**. When you're prompted to change the password, click **OK**.

3. Type **Password01** in the New password and Confirm password text boxes, click the arrow, and then click **OK**.

4. After you're logged on, you see a command prompt instead of the Server Manager interface. Type **sconfig** and press **Enter** to display the Server Configuration menu (see Figure 2-14).

```
==============================================================================
                          Server Configuration
==============================================================================
1) Domain/Workgroup:                         Workgroup:  WORKGROUP
2) Computer Name:                            WIN-HF1QO02APH3
3) Add Local Administrator
4) Configure Remote Management               Enabled

5) Windows Update Settings:                  Manual
6) Download and Install Updates
7) Remote Desktop:                           Disabled

8) Network Settings
9) Date and Time
10) Help improve the product with CEIP       Not participating
11) Windows Activation

12) Log Off User
13) Restart Server
14) Shut Down Server
15) Exit to Command Line

Enter number to select an option: ^F
```

Figure 2-14   The Server Configuration menu

5. In subsequent activities, you use the Server Configuration menu to perform initial installation tasks. For now, type **15** and press **Enter** to exit to the command prompt.

6. To shut down the 410ServerCore server, you can use option 14 in the Server Configuration menu. To shut down the computer immediately, however, type **shutdown /s /t 0** and press **Enter**.

In the shutdown command used in Step 6, the /s parameter specifies shutting down the server. You can use /r instead to specify a server restart. The /t parameter specifies the time to wait in seconds before the server should shut down. A 0 for the time period means to shut down immediately.

The immediate postinstallation tasks for Server Core are the same as in a full installation. The big difference is how you perform these tasks. The Server Configuration (sconfig) command you used in Activity 2-7 is the ideal way to do these essential first tasks in a Server Core installation. However, the menu the sconfig command opens is limited in the tasks it can perform. This chapter covers some initial configuration tasks you can perform with sconfig, netdom, and PowerShell; Chapter 3 covers more complex configuration tasks, such as installing roles and features.

Activity 2-8: Restoring a Command Prompt Window in Server Core

Time Required: 5 minutes
Objective: Open the command prompt window after it has been closed.

Required Tools and Equipment: 410ServerCore
Description: Out of habit, you typed "exit" at the command prompt or closed the command prompt window in Server Core. You need to restore the command prompt to finish some administration tasks.

1. Start 410ServerCore if necessary, and log on as **Administrator**.

2. If the command prompt window is open, close it by typing **exit** and pressing **Enter** or by clicking the **X** at the upper right. You now have a blank desktop.

3. Press **Ctrl+Alt+Delete** to open the window shown in Figure 2-15. Click **Task Manager**.

Figure 2-15   The Ctrl+Alt+Delete menu

4. In Windows Task Manager, click **More details** at the bottom.

5. Click **File**, **Run new task** from the menu. In the Create new task dialog box, type **cmd** and click **OK**.

6. Close Task Manager, but leave the command prompt window open for the next activity.

If you ever close the command prompt window in a Server Core installation, simply follow the preceding steps to restore it. You can also log off the server and log back on.

Activity 2-9: Setting the Time, Date, and Time Zone in Server Core

Time Required: 5 minutes
Objective: Perform the postinstallation task of setting the time, date, and time zone in a Server Core installation.

Required Tools and Equipment: 410ServerCore
Description: You have finished the Server Core installation and recall that setting the correct time, date, and time zone are essential for the server to operate.

1. Log on to 410ServerCore as **Administrator**, if necessary.

2. Open a command prompt window, if necessary, and type **sconfig** and press **Enter** to open the Server Configuration menu.

3. Type **9** and press **Enter** to start the Data and Time applet. Change the date, time, and time zone as needed, and then click **OK**.

4. Type **15** and press **Enter** to exit to the command line, but leave the command prompt window open for the next activity.

Any computer that becomes a member of a domain synchronizes its clock to a domain controller, so setting the time and date is unnecessary in these circumstances. You must still set the correct time zone, however.

Configuring Network, Firewall, and Name Settings in Server Core

Some of the first tasks you should perform on a new Server Core server are setting the IP address, naming the server, and activating the server. You can use different methods for each task. To configure IP address settings, for example, you can use sconfig, netsh, or PowerShell. Using sconfig, you simply select option 8 and follow the prompts. (Activity 2-10 walks you through using sconfig.) The netsh command and PowerShell cmdlets are described in detail in Chapter 6.

Activity 2-10: Setting an IP Address in Server Core

Time Required: 10 minutes
Objective: Set an IP address in Server Core.

Required Tools and Equipment: 410ServerCore
Description: By default, DHCP is used to assign IP addresses in all Windows OSs. For a server, however, you want to change to a static IP address assignment.

This activity and many others in this book use 10.10.X.X/16 for IP addressing. Please see your instructor for the actual addresses you should use.

1. Log on to 410ServerCore as **Administrator**, if necessary.

2. At the command prompt, type **ipconfig /all | more** and press **Enter**. You'll see that the IP address is set via DHCP (or if you don't have a DHCP server on the network, you see an APIPA address in the range 169.254.X.X). If necessary, press the **spacebar** to see the rest of the output from the ipconfig command.

3. Type **sconfig** and press **Enter** to open the Server Configuration menu. The input and output for the next three commands are shown in Figure 2-16. To configure network settings, type 8 and press **Enter**. You see a list of available network adapters and their current settings. Assuming you have only one network adapter, type the number shown in the Index# column and press **Enter**. Details about your network adapter settings are displayed. To set the network adapter address, type 1 and press **Enter**.

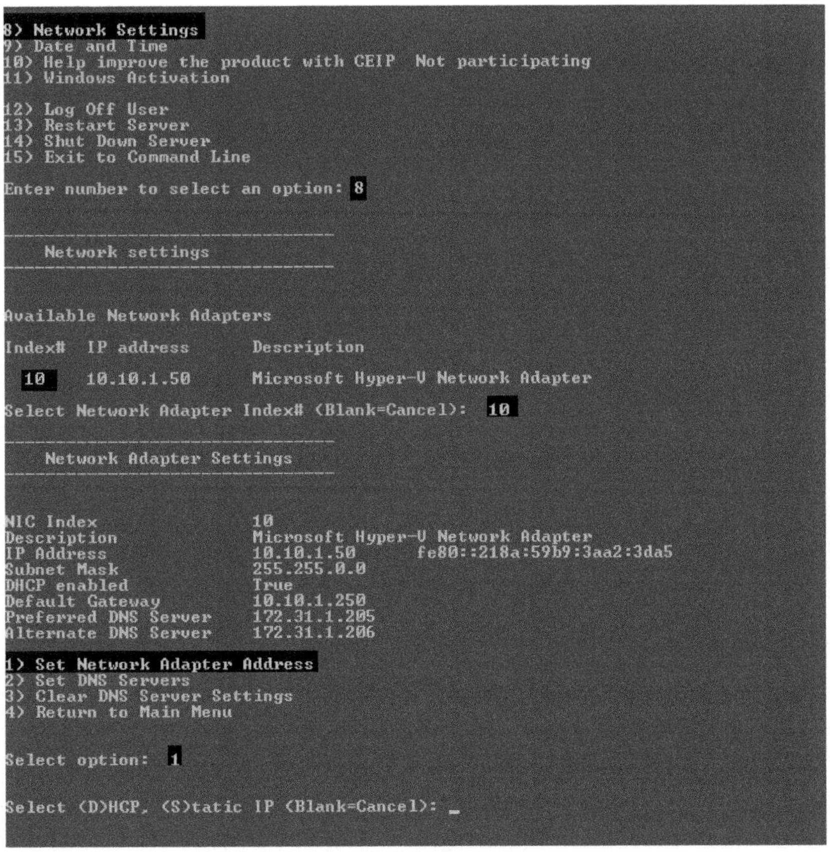

```
8) Network Settings
9) Date and Time
10) Help improve the product with CEIP  Not participating
11) Windows Activation

12) Log Off User
13) Restart Server
14) Shut Down Server
15) Exit to Command Line

Enter number to select an option: 8

_____
     Network settings
_____

Available Network Adapters

Index#  IP address       Description

  10    10.10.1.50       Microsoft Hyper-V Network Adapter

Select Network Adapter Index# (Blank=Cancel):  10

_____
     Network Adapter Settings
_____

NIC Index           10
Description         Microsoft Hyper-V Network Adapter
IP Address          10.10.1.50      fe80::218a:59b9:3aa2:3da5
Subnet Mask         255.255.0.0
DHCP enabled        True
Default Gateway     10.10.1.250
Preferred DNS Server  172.31.1.205
Alternate DNS Server  172.31.1.206

1) Set Network Adapter Address
2) Set DNS Servers
3) Clear DNS Server Settings
4) Return to Main Menu

Select option: 1

Select (D)HCP, (S)tatic IP (Blank=Cancel): _
```

Figure 2-16   Configuring network settings with sconfig

4. Type **s** and press **Enter** to specify a static IP address. To set this address, type **10.10.1.5** and press **Enter**. Type **255.255.0.0** and press **Enter** for the subnet mask. Type **10.10.1.250** (or an address specified by your instructor) for the default gateway and press **Enter**.

5. To set the DNS server address, type 2 and press **Enter**. Type the address specified by your instructor and press **Enter**. Click **OK** when prompted, and then press **Enter** to leave the alternate DNS server blank.

6. Type 4 and press **Enter** to return to the main menu. Type 15 and press **Enter** to exit to the command prompt. Leave the command prompt window open for the next activity.

Configuring the Firewall   If you try to ping a computer running a fresh installation of Windows Server, you might not get a reply. However, if you ping from a Windows Server 2012/R2 computer to the default gateway or another computer on the network, you probably get a response because the Windows Server 2012/R2 firewall blocks incoming ping (Echo Request) packets but allows ping reply (Echo Reply) packets. In the next activity, you configure the firewall to allow Echo Request packets so that your server can respond to ping packets.

The following activity uses the netsh command to configure the firewall. You can also set the firewall with PowerShell commands. For example, to configure the server to allow incoming ping packets, use the following command at a PowerShell prompt:

```
Set-NetFirewallRule -DisplayName "File and Printer Sharing (Echo Request
    - ICMPv4-In)" -enabled True
```

Chapter 3 explains how to manage many aspects of Server Core (including the firewall) remotely by using MMC plug-ins. However, the command line is the only way to manage most Server Core features locally.

Activity 2-11: Configuring the Server Core Firewall for Ping Packets

Time Required: 10 minutes
Objective: Configure the Windows Server 2012 R2 firewall to allow Echo Request packets.

Required Tools and Equipment: 410Server2 and 410ServerCore
Description: You have configured networking for your Windows Server 2012 R2 Server Core network, and now you want to test the configuration by pinging another server in your network. In this activity, you must have both 410Server2 and 410ServerCore computers running and connected to the network.

1. Log on to 410ServerCore as **Administrator** and open a command prompt window, if necessary.

2. To view basic IP address settings, type **ipconfig** and press **Enter**.

3. Ping 410Server2 by typing **ping 10.10.1.2** and pressing **Enter**. If it's successful, you should receive output that starts with "Reply from *ip_address*" (substituting the address you typed after the ping command for *ip_address*.). If it's not successful, ask your instructor for assistance. This step should be successful because 410Server2 has already been set up to allow ping packets.

4. When Step 3 is successful, log on to 410Server2 as **Administrator** and open a command prompt window. Type **ping 10.10.1.5** and press **Enter** to ping 410ServerCore. You should see the message "Request timed out."

5. Go back to the command prompt on 410ServerCore. To change the settings so that Echo Request packets are permitted through the firewall, type **netsh firewall set icmpsetting 8** and press **Enter**. You see a message that the command was successful but netsh firewall is deprecated. The replacement command is netsh advfirewall firewall add rule name="ICMP Allow incoming V4 echo request" protocol=icmpv4:8,any dir=in action=allow. It's long, but if the simpler command becomes unsupported, you can use the more complex netsh advfirewall command.

6. On 410Server2, type **ping 10.10.1.5** and press **Enter**. Your ping should be successful.

If you want to disable Echo Request packets again, simply type netsh firewall set icmpsetting 8 disable and press Enter.

7. On 410ServerCore, leave the command prompt window open for the next activity. You can shut down 410Server2, if you want.

Setting the Computer Name and Workgroup/Domain Membership The next postinstallation steps for configuring Server Core are setting the computer name and workgroup or domain name. The `sconfig` command can handle these tasks, as can `netdom.exe` and PowerShell commands. `Netdom.exe` is a useful command for working with computer names. You can rename a computer, set the primary DNS suffix, or join a domain by using `netdom.exe` at an elevated command prompt. The following command renames a computer. *Currentname* is the current name of the server, and *newname* is the name you want to change it to:

```
netdom renamecomputer currentname /newname:newname
```

The following command sets the primary DNS suffix. *Currentname.domainname* is the fully qualified domain name, and *domainname* is the primary DNS suffix:

```
netdom computername currentname /makeprimary:currentname.domainname
```

The following command joins a computer (specified by *computername*) to a domain (specified by *domainname*):

```
netdom join computername /domain:domainname
```

You can get more information about these commands by typing `netdom help`.

To use PowerShell to add a computer to a workgroup or domain, use these commands:

```
Add-Computer -WorkGroupName WorkGroup -Restart
```

```
Add-Computer -DomainName Domain -Restart
```

In Chapter 8, you use the command line to join a computer to a domain.

Activity 2-12: Setting Computer and Workgroup Names in Server Core

Time Required: 20 minutes
Objective: Set computer and workgroup names in Server Core.

Required Tools and Equipment: 410ServerCore
Description: You realize after installing Windows Server 2012/R2 Server Core that you need to provide a computer name and join a workgroup. You need to access this server by name, and the randomized name that Windows sets by default is too difficult to remember.

1. Log on to 410ServerCore as **Administrator** and open a command prompt window, if necessary.

2. To see the computer's current name, type **hostname** and press **Enter**. Make a note of this name because you need it for the next step.

3. Type **netdom renamecomputer** *currentname* **/newname:410ServerCore** (replacing *currentname* with the hostname you noted in Step 2) and press **Enter**. You see a message stating that certain services reply on a fixed machine name. Press **y** and then **Enter** to proceed. You see a message that the computer needs to be restarted to complete the operation.

You can also use the `sconfig` command or the PowerShell cmdlet `Rename-Computer` to rename your computer. Microsoft emphasizes using the command line and PowerShell in Windows Server 2012/R2, so this book often shows you how to perform tasks with PowerShell and other command-line utilities, even if you can use the GUI to do them.

4. When you see a message that the server needs to be restarted to complete the operation, restart it by typing **shutdown /r /t 0** and pressing **Enter**. After the server restarts, log on as **Administrator**.

5. To get the Server Core computer to register its name with the DNS server, you need to set the primary DNS suffix. The primary DNS suffix is the name of the zone created in DNS, which is 410Server2012.local (or another name specified by your instructor). At a command prompt, type **netdom computername 410ServerCore /add:410ServerCore.410Server2012.local** and press Enter to add the DNS suffix. Next, type **netdom computername 410ServerCore /makeprimary: 410ServerCore.410Server2012.local** and press Enter to make the DNS suffix the primary DNS suffix, which is used to register DNS names.

6. To complete the changes, restart the computer by typing **shutdown /r /t 0** and pressing **Enter**.

7. After your computer has restarted, log on to 410ServerCore as **Administrator**. To join a workgroup, start a PowerShell prompt by typing **powershell** and pressing **Enter**. Type **Add-Computer -WorkGroupName Server2012 -Restart** and press **Enter**.

8. After the server restarts, log on as **Administrator** and open a command prompt window. At the command prompt, type **ipconfig /all** and press **Enter** to see changes to the computer name, DNS suffix, and IP settings.

9. Leave the command prompt window open for the next activity.

Configuring Windows Update

Another postinstallation task is configuring Windows Update. The sconfig command is an easy way to configure basic settings for Windows Update on a Server Core computer. If you want to configure updates beyond using the default settings, you can edit the Registry. The Registry Editor is one of the few graphical utilities available in Server Core. For details on editing the Registry for Windows Update, consulting a good book on the subject is best. The best method for configuring updates in Server Core and to all computers in the domain is to use Group Policy in Active Directory. Group Policy is discussed in Chapter 11. The following activity uses sconfig to enable Windows Update with the default automatic settings.

Activity 2-13: Configuring Windows Update in Server Core

Time Required: 5 minutes
Objective: Configure Windows updates to keep your Server Core system up to date with patches and bug fixes.

Required Tools and Equipment: 410ServerCore
Description: You're working on a Windows Server Core system that you're unfamiliar with, so you want to verify that automatic updates are enabled and, if not, enable them.

1. Log on to 410ServerCore as **Administrator** and open a command prompt window, if necessary.

2. Type **sconfig** and press **Enter**. Notice that next to option 5, Windows Update Settings has been set to Manual. Type 5 and press **Enter**.

3. Type **a** and press **Enter** to enable automatic updates. You see a message stating "Windows Update set to Automatic. System will check for and install updates every day at 3:00 AM." Click **OK**.

4. You can also use option 6 to download and install updates immediately. Because you don't want updates installed automatically on this server, type **5** and press **Enter**. Type **m** and press **Enter** to set Windows Update back to Manual. Click **OK** in the message box stating that Windows Update is set to manual.

5. Type **15** and press **Enter** to exit the Server Configuration menu.

When Not to Use Server Core

As you might have noticed, a Server Core installation does have its drawbacks. You need to learn quite a few commands or keep them in a handy reference file. Server Core definitely has its place, especially after you master using remote administration tools, but it's not for all people or all situations. You might not want to use Server Core in situations such as the following:

- When it's the first server in a network
- When you need to install server roles and features that Server Core doesn't support
- When the server administrator isn't well versed in using command-line programs or remote administration tools
- When you absolutely, positively can't live without the Windows GUI running on your server

Because of Server Core's lower resource demands and smaller attack surface, however, it's likely to be a staple in many Windows networks, particularly large networks that use virtualization or have branch offices—that is, after administrators get used to not having a GUI.

Using Features on Demand

When you install Windows Server 2012/R2, all the files you need to install server roles and features are copied to the `C:\Windows\WinSxS` folder, so you don't need any installation medium to install new roles and features. However, these files use a lot of disk space. Although disk space is fairly cheap and abundant, it's neither free nor infinite. Besides, one reason for using Server Core is its small footprint. When you're talking about a server hosting several virtual machines, the disk space used for server roles and features can have an impact, and it can be used for better purposes.

To address this problem, Windows Server 2012/R2 has added **Features on Demand**, which enables you to remove these files and free up the disk space they normally consume. If the files are needed later, such as for adding a server role, Windows can be directed to a network share, installation medium, or Windows Update to get them. Another advantage of removing features you don't need is that Windows Update runs faster because it doesn't have to update files that have been removed.

Keep in mind that you can't remove these files from a feature that you want to remain installed; it's used only to remove features you aren't currently using. Say you have Windows Server 2012/R2 installed with a GUI, along with Active Directory and DHCP. You have configured the server the way you need it and now find that you can manage it remotely and no longer need the GUI components. To convert the server to a Server Core installation, use this command in PowerShell:

```
Uninstall-WindowsFeature Server-Gui-Shell, Server-Gui-Mgmt-Infra
  -Restart
```

This command removes the GUI features of Windows Server 2012/R2 and restarts the server, but it leaves the installation files in the `C:\Windows\WinSxS` folder. To uninstall the feature and remove these files, you add the `-Remove` option to the command:

```
Uninstall-WindowsFeature Server-Gui-Shell, Server-Gui-Mgmt-Infra
  -Restart -Remove
```

You can use this command on any role, role service, or feature you want. To see a list of available roles and features, use the following command, which yields the output shown in Figure 2-17:

```
Get-WindowsFeature
```

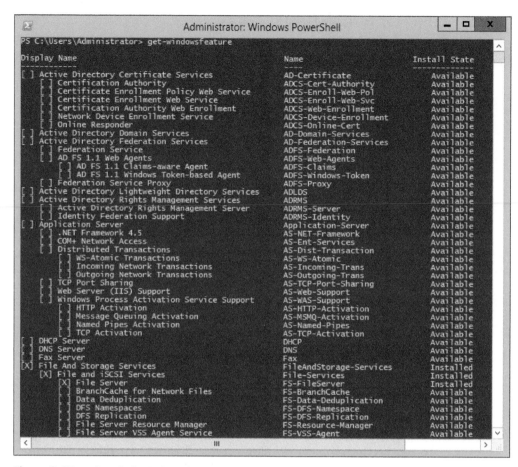

Figure 2-17 A list of all Windows features and their status

If you want to narrow the display down to only those features that are installed, use the following command to yield the output in Figure 2-18.

```
Get-WindowsFeature | where InstallState -eq Installed
```

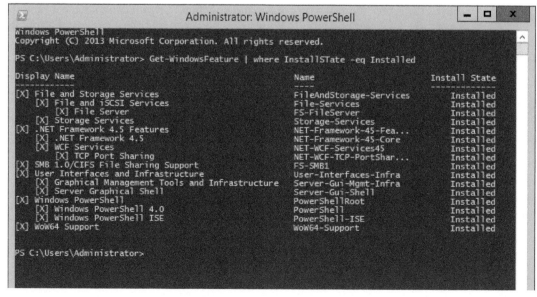

Figure 2-18 Viewing only installed features

You can replace the string `Installed` with `Removed` or `Available`, depending on the list you want to see. The `Removed` option displays features that no longer have installation files in the `C:\Windows\WinSxS` folder. The `Available` option shows features that are in the folder but not currently installed. For example, to remove all available features (leaving the installed features as they are) and restart the server, use the following command:

```
Get-WindowsFeature | where InstallState -eq Available|
    Uninstall-WindowsFeature -Remove
```

This command removes all files from the `C:\Windows\WinSxS` folder for features that aren't currently installed, and you need to specify another source if you want to install any removed features. It also creates a list of all features that have an install state of `Available` and pipes this list to the `Uninstall-WindowsFeature` cmdlet, which uninstalls the features (if necessary) and then removes the files. You can verify the results by using this command:

```
Get-WindowsFeature | where InstallState -eq Removed
```

Using this command also reduces the `C:\Windows\WinSxS` folder by about 2 GB, which, of course, is the objective.

If you have removed installation files and need to install a role or feature later, you can do so by specifying another location where Windows can find the installation files. The most common way to do this is to create a feature file store (also called a "side-by-side store"). A **feature file store** is a network share containing the files required to install roles, role services, and features on Windows Server 2012/R2 servers. To create a feature file store, create a network share and assign Read permissions for the Everyone group (or a group containing the computer accounts that will access the store). Then copy the `Sources\SxS` folder from the Windows Server 2012/R2 installation medium to the shared folder. You can then install a role or feature from the feature file store by using the following command.

```
Install-WindowsFeature FeatureName -Source \\Server\Share
```

In this command, you replace `FeatureName` with the name of the role or feature you want to install and `\\Server\Share` with the UNC path of the share you created for the feature file store.

Now that you're familiar with planning a Windows Server 2012/R2 installation, performing initial configuration tasks, and considering upgrade factors, it's time to get deeper into Windows Server 2012/R2 configuration. Chapter 3 covers many of the more detailed Windows Server 2012/R2 configuration tasks, along with options for managing servers remotely.

Chapter Summary

- The process of installing Windows Server 2012/R2 is fairly straightforward. Most of the work takes place in the planning phase. Some issues to consider include the server's CPU architecture, the total number of processors or cores the server requires, the number and types of disks, and advanced hardware features.

- Installing from a DVD is common for a single-server installation. Only a few choices must be made, such as whether to do a full or Server Core installation and deciding which disk or disk partition should be used for installing Windows Server 2012/R2.

- Postinstallation configuration tasks include giving the server a name, configuring network protocols, setting time zone information, selecting a network model (workgroup or domain), and installing and configuring Windows Updates. After completing these tasks, you can install server roles.

- When adding new servers to an existing network, you must decide whether the new server will be a new domain controller in the existing domain, a read only domain controller, a member server, or a stand-alone server. Reasons for adding new servers include company growth, excessive server load, application isolation, fault tolerance, and adding a branch office server.

- You can do an in-place upgrade to Windows Server 2012/R2 only if the existing OS is Windows Server 2008 or Windows Server 2008 R2. A clean install followed by server role migration is recommended.

- Windows Server Core is the default and recommended installation option. The traditional Windows GUI isn't available in Server Core. Initial configuration tasks, such as changing the server name and setting IP address information, must be done from the command line or through remote administration tools. However, you can convert from a Server Core installation to a GUI installation or vice versa.

- Features on Demand is a new feature in Windows Server 2012/R2 that enables you to remove Windows feature installation files from the local disk. Removing these unused files makes it possible to save disk space and allow Windows Update to run faster.

Key Terms

clean installation   A Windows OS installation in which the OS is installed on a new disk partition; it's not an upgrade from any previous version of Windows.

Echo Reply   An ICMP message that's the response when a computer receives an Echo Request, generated by the ping program.

Echo Request   An ICMP message generated by the ping program used to test network connectivity and IP configuration. If a computer receives an Echo Request, it responds with an Echo Reply.

feature file store   A network share containing the files required to install roles, role services, and features on Windows Server 2012/R2 servers. *See also* Features on Demand.

Features on Demand   A new feature in Windows Server 2012/R2 that enables you to remove the files used to install roles and features and free up the disk space these files normally consume.

hot-add   A high-end feature that allows adding hardware (usually memory, processors, or disk drives) to a system while it's running.

hot-replace   A high-end feature that allows replacing faulty hardware (usually memory, processors, or disk drives) in a system while it's running.

in-place upgrade   An upgrade that replaces the existing OS with the new OS but maintains all the roles and features installed on the existing OS.

patches   Software updates normally intended to fix security vulnerabilities and software bugs.

ping   A utility used to test network connectivity and IP address configuration.

read only domain controller (RODC)   A domain controller that stores a read-only copy of the Active Directory database but no password information. Changes to the domain must be made on a writeable DC and then replicated to an RODC.

server role migration   An upgrade in which you perform a clean install of Windows Server 2012/R2 and migrate existing server roles to the new OS.

service pack   A collection of bug fixes, security updates, and new features that can be installed on an OS to bring it up to date.

Review Questions

1. Which of the following is *not* a valid Windows Server 2012/R2 installation option?

   a.   A clean installation of Windows Server 2012/R2 (Server with a GUI)

   b.   An upgrade from Windows Server 2008 Server Core to Server with a GUI

   c.   An upgrade from Windows Server 2008 Enterprise to Windows Server 2012/R2 Datacenter

   d.   A clean installation of Windows Server 2012/R2 (Server Core)

2. What is required to install the Hyper-V server role? (Choose all that apply.)

    a. A 64-bit processor

    b. A 32-bit version of Windows Server 2012/R2

    c. AMD-V or Intel-VT extensions

    d. At least 384 MB RAM

3. Which of the following is true when purchasing a motherboard with multiple CPU sockets?

    a. Windows Server 2012/R2 doesn't support multiple CPU sockets.

    b. You must run a 32-bit version of Windows Server 2012/R2.

    c. All installed CPUs must be identical.

    d. Virtualization is not supported on multiple CPUs.

4. You're trying to decide which disk technology to use on your new server. The server will be in heavy use around the clock every day, so high performance is a necessity. Which technology is the best choice?

    a. IDE

    b. ATA-166

    c. SATA

    d. SAS

5. You can use a 32-bit processor to install the Hyper-V role as long as it supports virtualization extensions. True or False?

6. Which networking protocol is installed by default in Windows Server 2012/R2? (Choose all that apply.)

    a. TCP/IPv4

    b. IPX/SPX

    c. NetBEUI

    d. TCP/IPv6

7. Which of the following is *not* a typical Windows Server 2012/R2 postinstallation task?

    a. Installing the Server Core role

    b. Setting the correct time zone

    c. Setting IP configuration parameters

    d. Changing the server name

8. Which of the following is a task you must do *during* Windows Server 2012/R2 installation?

    a. Name the server.

    b. Choose the disk where it will be installed.

    c. Set the Administrator password.

    d. Set the workgroup or domain.

9. What command allows Echo Request packets through the firewall?

    a. `icmp set icmp-echo enabled`

    b. `Set-NetFirewallRule "Echo Request" -Enabled True`

    c. `netsh firewall set icmpsetting 8`

    d. `ipconfig -allow "ping requests"`

10. Which graphical utility runs in Server Core?

    a. File Explorer

    b. Date and Time control panel

    c. Computer Management

    d. Server Manager

11. You installed Windows Server 2012/R2 recently, and it has been running well for the past several days. You read about a critical security patch that has been available for about a week. You view the currently installed updates in the Programs and Features control panel and don't see any installed updates. You need to install this update immediately and make sure the server is kept up to date without your intervention in the future. What should you do?

12. Which of the following is a reason for installing a new server? (Choose all that apply.)

    a. Excessive load on existing servers

    b. Fault tolerance

    c. Adding a new network protocol

    d. To isolate a new application

13. You approach one of your servers running Server Core and see a completely blank desktop except for the mouse pointer. You need to do some management tasks on the server. What should you do?

    a. Right-click the mouse and click Open a command prompt.

    b. Press Start+X and click Run.

    c. Press Ctrl+Alt+Delete and click Start Task Manager.

    d. Right-click the desktop, point to New, and click Task.

14. You have just finished installing Windows Server 2012/R2. You have assigned the server a name and finished configuring IP addresses. You have tested your configuration by using `ping` to verify network connectivity with your default gateway and another server on the network, and everything worked fine. However, the next day, a colleague tells you that when he tried to ping the server, his request timed out. You try to ping your colleague's computer and receive a reply just fine. Why can't your colleague ping your server successfully?

    a. Your server's default gateway is incorrect.

    b. Windows Firewall is blocking the packets.

    c. Your colleague's IP address configuration is incorrect.

    d. You don't have DNS installed.

15. Which command do you use to restart Server Core?

    a. `shutdown /r /t 0`

    b. `restart /t 0`

    c. `net stop /r /t 0`

    d. `net computer /reset /t 0`

16. Which of the following is the default setting for Windows Update after you first turn on automatic updates?

    a. Download and install updates automatically.

    b. Download but do not install updates.

    c. Inform when updates are available but do not download updates.

    d. Download updates but let me choose whether to install them.

17. Which of the following is true about upgrading to Windows Server 2012/R2?

    a. A Windows Server 2008 32-bit edition requires a clean install.

    b. You can upgrade from a Chinese version to an English version.

    c. A Server Core install always requires a clean installation.

    d. You can upgrade from Windows Server 2003 R2.

18. In which of the following circumstances is server migration required when you want to upgrade to Windows Server 2012/R2 Server Core? (Choose all that apply.)

    a. When you're running Windows Server 2003

    b. When you're running a 32-bit version of Windows Server 2008

    c. When you're running a GUI installation of Windows Server 2008

    d. When you're running Windows Server 2008 Enterprise

19. Which command should you use in Windows Server 2012 Server Core to perform menu-based configuration tasks?

    a. `netsh.exe`

    b. `smigdeploy.exe`

    c. `sconfig`

    d. `command.com`

20. Why would you use Features on Demand?

    a. To free up system RAM

    b. To reduce disk space use

    c. To use the GUI interface

    d. To uninstall Server Core

21. If you want to see a list of available rolls and features, which command should you use?

    a. `sconfig`

    b. `Show-WindowsRoles`

    c. `dism.exe`

    d. `Get-WindowsFeature`

Case Projects

CASE PROJECTS

Case Project 2-1: Adding a Server to Your Network

Your client, CSM Tech Publishing, has been running Windows Server 2012 R2 Essentials Edition, which you installed about a year ago, and is using the AD DS, DNS, IIS, and File Services roles. The number of computer clients has grown from 25 to 50 in the past six months, and additional growth is expected. CSM Tech just purchased an expensive project management system to help manage project scheduling. This application has hefty memory (4 GB or more) and CPU requirements (recommended 3.0 GHz quad-core processor). All desktop computers will have the project management client application installed. The owner doesn't want to install the client application on mobile users' laptops, so a remote solution is needed for these laptops. The owner also mentions that he's familiar with this application and will need to log on to the server periodically to do maintenance and monitoring.

The owner tells you that in the future, CSM Tech Publishing might need system fault tolerance to ensure that there's little or no downtime because this critical application will eventually be accessed at all times of the day and night. For now, he's just concerned about getting the system up and running. You check the existing server's capacity and determine that the new application's memory and disk requirements will likely exceed the existing server's 4 GB capabilities. The owner explains that there's enough budget for a new server, so you should plan for growth. As an aside, he mentions that because all his employees log on at about the same time, the time it takes to log on has been increasing. You need to come up with specifications for a new server. Describe some hardware features you plan to recommend for this new server, in particular the CPU architecture, number of CPUs, amount of RAM, and disk system. Explain your answers.

Case Project 2-2: Choosing the Right Edition

You have your new server for the CSM Tech Publishing upgrade project and are ready to install Windows Server 2012 R2. Case Project 2-1 describes the current environment and requirements of CSM Tech. Which edition of Windows Server 2012 R2 will you install? Include information on whether it should be a full GUI or Server Core installation. Explain your answer.

Case Project 2-3: Selecting Server Postinstallation Tasks

You have finished installing Windows Server 2012 R2 on the new server for CSM Tech. Next, you need to decide what to name the server and how it will participate in the existing domain: as a domain controller, a member server, or a stand-alone server. The server will be named CSM-Server1-DC and located near the existing server in the equipment closet. List the postinstallation tasks you must perform on this server, including details on the server name and its role in the domain (if any). Don't include installing specific server roles just yet.

Case Project 2-4: Choosing Server Roles on the Second Server

You have finished postinstallation tasks for the new server, and now you need to decide which server roles to install on it. Reread Case Project 2-1 carefully because it contains most of the information you need to make an informed decision. List which server roles you plan to install and explain why.

Local and Remote Server Management

After reading this chapter and completing the exercises, you will be able to:

- Work with server roles and features
- Configure server modes
- Manage servers remotely
- Configure services
- Configure NIC teaming
- Work with downlevel servers

After you have installed a server and performed initial configuration tasks, next comes the task of configuring the server. This chapter covers how to add and remove server roles and features on both local and remote servers. You also learn how to add servers to Server Manager, configure firewall rules to allow remote management, move from a full GUI installation to a Server Core installation, and apply the Minimal Server Interface mode.

You might need to start or stop a Windows service or install and configure a new service; you learn how to perform these tasks using both the GUI and the command line. NIC teaming is a new feature in Windows Server 2012, and you learn how to configure a NIC team to give your servers optimal network performance and reliability. Finally, the steps for managing older (downlevel) servers in Server Manager are explained.

Working with Server Roles and Features

Table 3-1 describes what you need for the hands-on activities in this chapter.

Table 3-1   Activity requirements

Activity	Requirements	Notes
Activity 3-1: Installing Server Roles with Server Manager	410Server1	
Activity 3-2: Removing a Server Role with Server Manager	410Server1	
Activity 3-3: Installing and Uninstalling a Server Role with PowerShell in Server Core	410ServerCore	Can also be done on a server with a GUI
Activity 3-4: Converting a Server with a GUI to Server Core	410Server2	
Activity 3-5: Converting Server Core to Minimal Server Interface	410Server2	
Activity 3-6: Adding Servers to Server Manager	410Server1 and 410ServerCore	
Activity 3-7: Creating a Server Group	410Server1	
Activity 3-8: Configuring Windows Firewall for Remote MMC Management	410Server1 and 410ServerCore	
Activity 3-9: Working with Windows Services	410Server1	
Activity 3-10: Configuring NIC Teaming	410Server1	

© 2015 Cengage Learning®

Windows Server without roles and features installed is like an iPhone without apps installed. The basic installation does have some limited functions, such as basic file and printer sharing, but not much beyond that. You need to add server roles and features to take advantage of the power Windows Server 2012/R2 offers. This section covers how you work with server roles and features in both a GUI installation and a Server Core installation and how to update roles and features installed in offline images.

In Chapter 1, you learned the difference between server roles and features and explored the Add Roles and Features Wizard in Server Manager. In this chapter, you look more closely at the process of adding and removing roles and features.

Managing Server Roles in the GUI

In Server Manager, you can start the Add Roles and Features Wizard in the Welcome window or by clicking Manage, Add Roles and Features from the menu (see Figure 3-1). In either case, the Add Roles and Features Wizard opens to the Before You Begin window, shown in Figure 3-2. You can bypass this window in the future by selecting the option to skip it. If you're new to Windows Server, however, reading the information in this window is a good idea so that you can make sure you have performed these crucial tasks before installing server roles and features:

- The administrator has a strong password.
- Static IP addresses have been configured. Some server roles, such as DHCP and Active Directory, don't work correctly with dynamically assigned addresses. Although not all roles require static IP addresses, using them on servers is a recommended practice.
- Security updates are current.

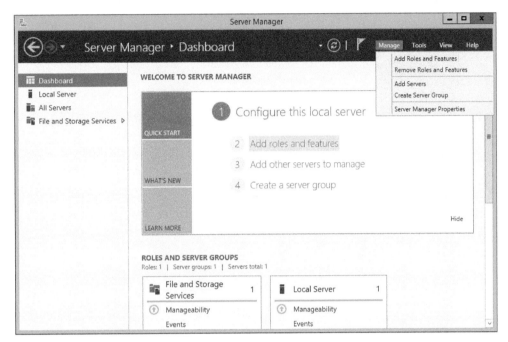

Figure 3-1   Starting the Add Roles and Features Wizard

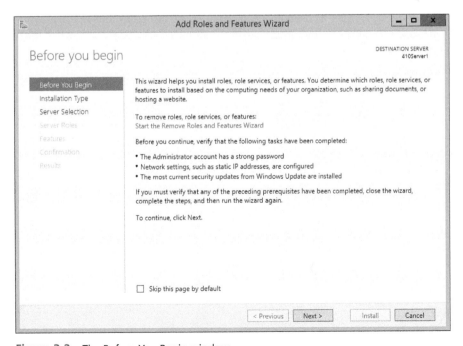

Figure 3-2   The Before You Begin window

The next window, Installation Type (see Figure 3-3), has two options:

- *Role-based or feature-based installation*—Use this default option to install a role or feature on a single physical or virtual server or an offline virtual hard disk (VHD). In most cases, you choose this option.
- *Remote Desktop Services installation*—Use this option to distribute components of the Remote Desktop Services role across different servers for use in a virtual desktop infrastructure.

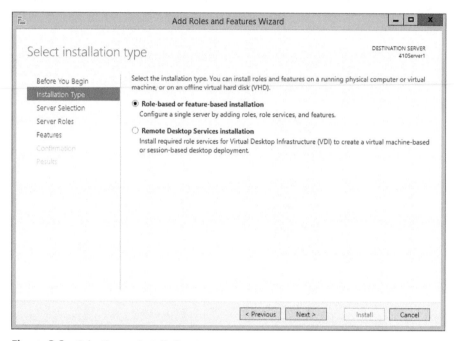

Figure 3-3   Selecting an installation type

In the next window, Server Selection (see Figure 3-4), you choose a server from the server pool for installing roles and features. You learn how to add servers to this list later in the chapter in "Managing Servers Remotely." You can also install roles and features on a virtual hard disk (VHD). If you choose this option, you're prompted to choose a server on which to mount the VHD and specify the path to the VHD file.

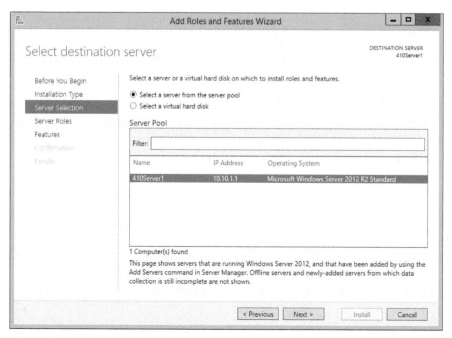

Figure 3-4   Selecting a destination server

The next window, Server Roles, lists all the server roles you can install (see Figure 3-5). Underneath each server role, you might see one or more role services. Next to each role or role service is a box. If it's selected, this role or role service, along with any subordinate role services, is installed. If the box is shaded, one or more role services or subordinate role services are installed. Figure 3-5 shows "File and Storage Services (2 of 12 installed)," which means 2 of the 12 role services (and subordinate role services) under File and Storage Services are installed. When you click the box next to a server role, Windows prompts you to include additional features and management tools, if necessary.

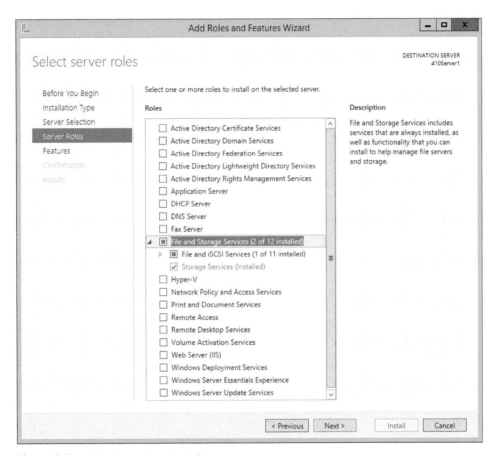

Figure 3-5   Selecting roles to install on a server

The next window, Features, lists the available features and works like the Server Roles window. If you selected a server role with multiple associated role services, the next step is selecting which role services you want. For example, the Remote Access server role has three role services associated with it (see Figure 3-6). If a role service requires installing other roles and role services, you're prompted to confirm their installation, too.

In the Confirmation window, shown in Figure 3-7, you can review your selections. Selecting the check box at the top ensures that the server restarts automatically, if needed, during installation. At the bottom of this window are links to two options:

- *Export configuration settings*—Select this option if you want to generate an XML script for installing the selected roles and features on another server with the PowerShell command `Install-WindowsFeature -ConfigurationFilePath XMLscript.xml`.

- *Specify an alternate source path*—Select this option to specify a path to an image file containing the installation files for roles and features if the files aren't available locally.

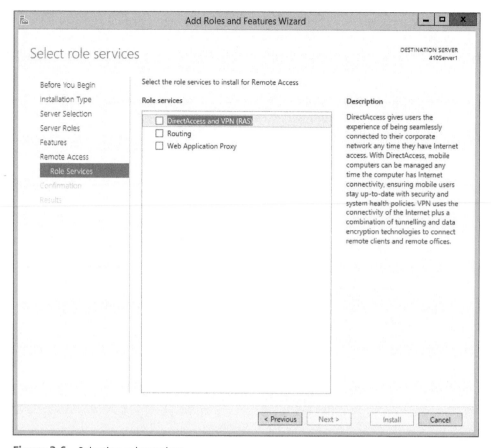

Figure 3-6 Selecting role services

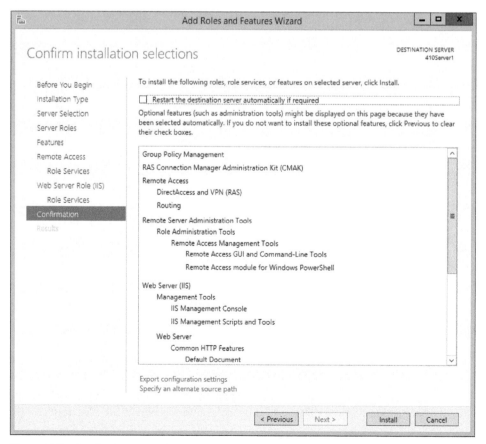

Figure 3-7 Confirming your selections

Clicking the Install button starts installing the server roles or features you've selected, and the Results window shows the progress of the installation.

The procedure for removing roles and features is similar. In Server Manager, click Manage, Remove Roles and Features from the menu to start the Remove Roles and Features Wizard. The main difference from the installation wizard is that you clear the box for the role or feature you want to remove. Roles and features that aren't installed are grayed out and can't be selected.

Managing Server Roles with PowerShell

You can use PowerShell to add and remove server roles from a Server Core or GUI server if you don't want to use Server Manager. To start PowerShell, type `powershell` at an elevated command prompt or right-click the PowerShell icon and click Run as Administrator. The following PowerShell commands are used to work with server roles and features:

- `Get-WindowsFeature`—Displays a list of available roles and features. You can also use `Get-WindowsFeature | where Installed` to display a list of installed roles and features or `Get-WindowsFeature | where InstallState -eq Available` to display roles and features that are available to be installed.

- `Install-WindowsFeature` *RoleOrFeatureName*—Installs the server role or feature specified by *RoleOrFeatureName*. To specify multiple roles and features, separate the names with a space. Variations on this command include `Install-WindowsFeature` *RoleOrFeatureName* `-IncludeAllSubFeatures -IncludeManagementTools`, which installs the specified role or feature and includes necessary subfeatures and management tools, and `Uninstall-WindowsFeature` *RoleOrFeatureName* `-IncludeManagementTools`, which uninstalls the specified role or feature along with management tools. Separate the names of multiple roles and features with a space.

PowerShell commands aren't case sensitive. They're shown with selective capitalization to make them more readable, but you can use all lowercase (or uppercase) letters when typing commands at a PowerShell prompt.

You can also install and uninstall roles and features to and from an offline VHD file by including the option `-VHD pathname` (replacing `pathname` with the path to the VHD file).

Using PowerShell on Remote Servers   All the PowerShell commands discussed in the previous section can be used to install or remove server roles and features on remote servers. You can perform the same commands on remote servers by including the parameter `string`, which specifies the name or IP address of the computer:

`-ComputerName` *string*

For example, if you're on Server1 and want to install the Windows Server Backup feature on a server named Server2, use this command:

```
Install-WindowsFeature Windows-Server-Backup -ComputerName Server2
  -IncludeAllSubFeature -IncludeManagementTools
```

For this command to work, Server2 must be in the same domain as the server where you entered the command. If the remote server isn't in the same domain, it must be added to the TrustedHosts setting, which is explained later in "Managing Servers Remotely."

Desired State Configuration   PowerShell 4.0 has a new feature, Desired State Configuration (DSC), that gives you a new way to manage and maintain servers with simple declarative statements. DSC's declarative syntax makes it possible for you to just tell the server how it should be configured without using the actual commands for performing configuration steps. DSC uses "pull" technology, so instead of DSC configurations having to be sent to remote servers, servers can pull their configurations from a central server by using standard Web protocols. This technology eliminates the need to open additional firewall ports.

You create a DSC script in PowerShell's **Integrated Scripting Environment (ISE)**, a Power-Shell development environment that you can open from the Tools menu in Server Manager. The basic steps for using DSC are as follows:

1. Create the script in the PowerShell ISE.

2. Run the script to create configuration files called management object files (MOF) files.

3. Enter the `Start-DscConfiguration` cmdlet at a PowerShell prompt.

Here's an example of using DSC to check whether DNS and DHCP are installed on ServerA and ServerB, and if not, install these services:

```
Configuration DNSDHCP

{
Node ServerA, ServerB
{
   WindowsFeature DNSserver
   {
     Ensure="Present"
     Name="DNS"
   }
   WindowsFeature DHCPserver
   {
     Ensure="Present"
     Name="DHCP"
   }
 }
}
```

The details of using DSC are beyond the scope of this book, but for a quick primer and examples, take a look at *http://technet.microsoft.com/en-us/library/dn249918.aspx*.

Working with Offline Images

You can install and uninstall features to and from an offline VHD file by using Server Manager or PowerShell cmdlets, as you have seen. Being able to work with VHD files offline can come in handy when you're maintaining a Hyper-V virtualization host. You might keep VMs in an offline state until you're ready to deploy them. If you need to add or remove roles and features from a VM, you can do so without having to start it. The ability to deploy roles and features on VHD files without having to start the virtual machine the VHD is associated with can save time and resources. The procedure for adding roles and features to an offline VHD file with PowerShell is identical to that for a live system (described previously), but you include the `-VHD` option in the command.

You might also need to manage features on an installation image that you deploy with Windows Deployment Server (WDS). For working with install images (`.wim` files), you use the Deployment Image Servicing and Management (`dism.exe`) command. This command and WDS roles are beyond the scope of this book. They're covered in *MCSA Guide to Administering Windows Server 2012/R2, Exam 70-411* (Cengage Learning, 2015), but here's the general procedure for deploying a feature on an offline image (`.wim`) file:

1. Mount the image by entering this command:

```
dism /mount-wim /wimfile:pathtowimfile /index:1 /mountdir:
  pathtomountedimage
```

2. Install the feature by entering this command:

```
dism /image:pathtomountedimage /enable-feature /featurename:
  roleorfeaturename
```

3. To commit the changes and dismount the image, enter this command:

```
dism /unmount-wim /mountdir:pathtomountedimage /commit
```

In Step 2, you can replace `/enable-feature` with `/disable-feature` to uninstall a role or feature or `/get-features` to list currently installed roles and features.

Activity 3-1: Installing Server Roles with Server Manager

Time Required: 15 minutes
Objective: Install a server role with Server Manager.

Required Tools and Equipment: 410Server1
Description: You've done the initial configuration on your server, so now it's time to install some roles and features. You know your server will be a print and document server, so you decide to install the Print and Document Services role.

1. Start 410Server1 and log on as **Administrator**.

2. In Server Manager, click **Manage, Add Roles and Features** from the menu to start the Add Roles and Features Wizard.

3. In the Before You Begin window, read the information to make sure you have the prerequisite tasks completed, and then click **Next**.

4. In the Installation Type window, accept the default option **Role-based or feature-based installation**, and then click **Next**.

5. In the Server Selection window, the only option is 410Server1 because you haven't added any other servers to be managed from this server. If you were installing the feature on an offline VHD file, you would click the "Select a virtual hard disk" option button. Accept the default setting **Select a server from the server pool**, and then click **Next**.

6. In the Server Roles window, click the box next to **Print and Document Services**. In the dialog box asking you to confirm the additional features needed for this role (see Figure 3-8), click the **Add Features** button.

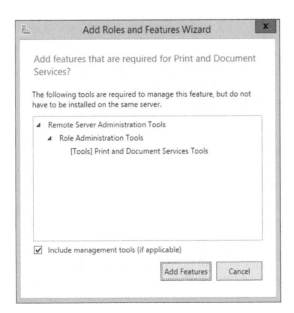

Figure 3-8 Adding features for a role service

7. Click **Next.** In the Features window, scroll through the list of features to review what's available, and then click **Next.**

8. Read the description of the Print and Document Services role in the next window, and then click **Next.**

9. In the Role Services window, you can choose other role services that work with this role, such as Internet Printing and LPD Service. Accept the default option **Print Server** and click **Next.**

10. In the Confirmation window, click **Install.** The Results window shows the progress of the installation. You can close this window without interrupting the installation; if you do, you can restore it to view your progress by clicking Notifications. Wait until the installation is finished, and then click **Close.**

11. A new icon named Print Services is added to Server Manager in the left pane. As shown in Figure 3-9, Print Services is also added in the Roles and Server Groups section.

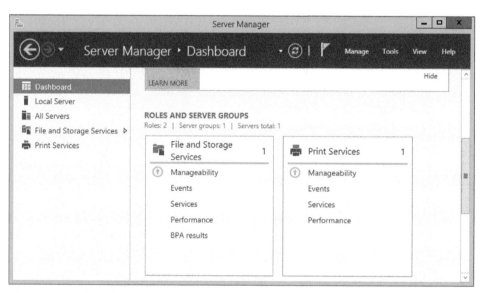

Figure 3-9   Adding Print Services to Server Manager

12. If you're continuing to the next activity, stay logged on; otherwise, log off or shut down the server.

Activity 3-2: Removing a Server Role with Server Manager

Time Required: 10 minutes
Objective: Remove a server role with Server Manager.

Required Tools and Equipment: 410Server1
Description: You no longer need the Print and Document Services role on your server, so you remove the role with Server Manager.

1. Log on to 410Server1 as **Administrator,** if necessary. When Server Manager starts, click **Manage, Remove Roles and Features** from the menu.

2. In the Before You Begin window, read the information, and then click **Next.** In the Server Selection window, click **Next.**

3. In the Server Roles window, click the box next to **Print and Document Services.**

4. In the Remove Roles and Features Wizard dialog box, click **Remove Features,** and then click **Next.** In the Features window, click **Next.**

5. In the Confirmation window, click **Remove**.

6. In the Results window, wait until the process is finished, and then click **Close**. Notice that Print Services has been removed from Server Manager.

7. If you're continuing to the next activity, stay logged on; otherwise, log off or shut down the server.

Activity 3-3: Installing and Uninstalling a Server Role with PowerShell in Server Core

Time Required: 10 minutes
Objective: Install and uninstall a server role with PowerShell.

Required Tools and Equipment: 410ServerCore (or a server with a GUI)
Description: For practice using PowerShell cmdlets, you install Print and Document Services with PowerShell and then uninstall it.

1. Start 410ServerCore and log on as **Administrator**.

2. At a command prompt, type **powershell** and press **Enter** to start PowerShell. The command prompt changes to PS C:\Users\Administrator>.

3. To see what roles and features are available to install, type **Get-WindowsFeature** and press **Enter**. You see a list of server roles, role services, and features (see Figure 3-10). Installed roles, role services, and features are preceded with an X. The left column shows the display name of the server role, role service, or feature, and the right column is the name you use in PowerShell commands.

Figure 3-10 Output of Get-WindowsFeature

4. Scroll up to Print and Document Services. Notice that the name in the right column is `Print-Services`.

5. Type **`Install-WindowsFeature Print-Services -IncludeManagementTools`** and press **Enter**.

6. Your progress is shown at the top of the PowerShell window. When the installation is finished, type **`Get-WindowsFeature | where Installed`** and press **Enter** to see a list of installed roles and features.

7. To uninstall Print and Document Services, type **`Uninstall-WindowsFeature Print-Services -IncludeManagementTools`** and press **Enter**.

8. When the role has been removed, you see a message stating that the server must be restarted. Type **`Get-WindowsFeature | where Installed`** and press **Enter**. You no longer see Print and Document Services in the list of installed features.

9. Shut down 410ServerCore by typing **`shutdown -s -t 0`** and pressing **Enter**.

Configuring Server Modes

As discussed in Chapter 1, you have two main options for installing Windows Server 2012/R2: Server with a GUI or Server Core. The good news is that after making this decision, you can always change your mind. If you like the Server Core interface but also want to use Server Manager, you can have the best of both worlds with Minimal Server Interface. Switching between interface modes is as easy as installing and uninstalling server roles and features. In Windows Server 2008, after you installed the Server with a GUI mode (called a full installation in Windows Server 2008), you couldn't switch to a Server Core installation without reinstalling Windows. The reverse was also true, and there was no middle ground between these two options. The following sections explain three ways to change server interface modes:

- Converting Server with a GUI to Server Core
- Converting Server Core to Minimal Server Interface
- Converting Server Core or Minimal Server Interface to Server with a GUI

Converting Server with a GUI to Server Core

You might wonder why you would want to convert a server with the full GUI to a Server Core installation. Perhaps you want to take advantage of Server Core's smaller footprint but you like a GUI's convenience for performing initial configuration tasks, such as setting IP addresses, joining a domain, setting up Windows Update, and installing server roles. The solution is to install the Server with a GUI option, and then perform all initial configuration tasks, including basic configuration of any roles and features. When you're finished with these tasks, convert to Server Core, which involves removing two features: Graphical Management Tools and Infrastructure and Server Graphical Shell.

Activity 3-4: Converting Server with a GUI to Server Core

Time Required: 10 minutes
Objective: Convert a server with a full GUI to Server Core.

Required Tools and Equipment: 410Server2
Description: You have installed a Windows Server 2012 R2 server with a GUI and performed the initial configuration tasks, and now you want to convert to the Server Core interface.

1. Start 410Server2 and log on as **Administrator**.

2. In Server Manager, start the Remove Roles and Features Wizard. Proceed through the wizard until you get to the Features window. Scroll through the roles, and click the arrow to expand **User Interfaces and Infrastructure**. You see a list of three features, two of which are currently installed (see Figure 3-11).

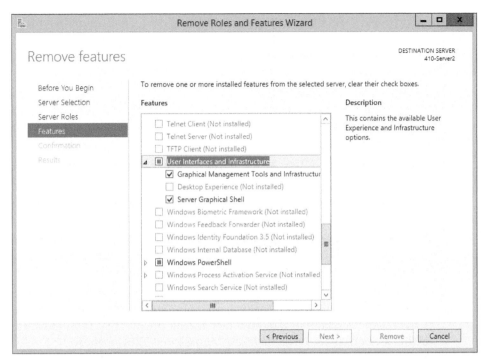

Figure 3-11   Viewing features for the User Interfaces and Infrastructure role

3. Click to clear the **Graphical Management Tools and Infrastructure** and **Server Graphical Shell** check boxes. In the dialog box that opens, click **Remove Features**. Click **Next**.

4. In the Confirmation window, click **Remove**. When the Results window confirms that the removal is finished, you see a message stating that a restart is required. Click **Close**.

5. If you're continuing to the next activity, restart 410Server2; otherwise, shut down 410Server2.

To perform this same task in PowerShell, enter the following command at a PowerShell command prompt opened as Administrator:

```
Uninstall-WindowsFeature Server-GUI-Mgmt-Infra, Server-GUI-Shell
  -Restart
```

With the PowerShell cmdlet, you can also remove installation files for the features you remove by adding the `-Remove` option. Removing these files saves space on the hard disk, but you have to specify another source for the installation files if you want to reinstall the features later.

Converting Server Core to Minimal Server Interface

Minimal Server Interface, a new feature in Windows Server 2012, takes up less disk space than Server with a GUI but more than Server Core. It's intended as a transition mode between the full GUI and Server Core. You can use this mode to perform tasks you're not well versed in doing from the command line. As mentioned in Chapter 1, this option includes the following GUI tools: Server Manager, the MMC, and some Control Panel applets. Applications that depend on File Explorer, Internet Explorer, or other Web client components might not work correctly running in Minimal Server Interface.

Activity 3-5: Converting Server Core to Minimal Server Interface

Time Required: 20 minutes
Objective: Convert Server Core to Minimal Server Interface.

Required Tools and Equipment: 410Server2

Description: Your server is currently running in Server Core mode, but you find that you need Server Manager and some MMCs to perform tasks that are more convenient to configure with a GUI.

1. Log on to 410Server2 as **Administrator**, if necessary. At the command prompt, start PowerShell.

2. At the PowerShell prompt, type **Install-WindowsFeature Server-GUI-Mgmt-Infra** and press **Enter**.

3. When the command finishes running, restart the server by typing **Restart-Computer** and pressing **Enter**. (Note: If you had added the `-Restart` option to the command you entered in Step 2, the server would have restarted automatically.)

4. After the features are installed and the server restarts, log on as **Administrator**. You see a command prompt first, and then Server Manager starts. Notice there's no Start button or taskbar, and pressing the Windows key doesn't open the Start window. However, you have the full array of tools available in the Manage and Tools menus.

5. What happens if you close Server Manager? Try it. Close Server Manager, and then restart it by typing **servermanager** and pressing **Enter**.

6. What if you close both Server Manager and the command prompt? Try it. Close Server Manager and the command prompt window. To restore the command prompt, press **Ctrl+Alt+Del** and click **Task Manager**. Click **More details**.

7. Click **File, Run new task**. Type **cmd** in the Open text box and click **OK**.

8. At the command prompt, type **servermanager** and press **Enter** to start Server Manager. Close Task Manager.

9. Log off or shut down 410Server2.

If you're installing Minimal Server Interface on a server that was originally installed in Server Core mode, you need to specify another source for the installation files (such as the `install.wim` file on the installation DVD).

Another helpful feature of using PowerShell cmdlets to install or uninstall roles and features is the `-WhatIf` option. You can add this option at the end of an `Install-WindowsFeature` or `Uninstall-WindowsFeature` command to see the results without actually performing the task. This way, you can see what features or role services might also be involved and whether you need to specify another source for the installation files.

Converting to Server with a GUI

If you just can't live without the full GUI, you can install the features `Server-GUI-Mgmt-Infra` and `Server-GUI-Shell`. If you're starting from a Server Core installation, you need to install both features, which can be done at the same time. If you're starting from Minimal Server Interface, you need to install only `Server-GUI-Shell`.

If you have Minimal Server Interface installed, you can use Server Manager or PowerShell; a Server Core installation requires using PowerShell. Use the following PowerShell command to switch from Minimal Server Interface to Server with a GUI:

```
Install-WindowsFeature Server-GUI-Shell -Restart
```

Use the following command to switch from Server Core to Server with a GUI:

```
Install-WindowsFeature Server-GUI-Mgmt-Infra, Server-GUI-Shell -Restart
```

Switching between any interface modes requires a server restart, so be sure to plan these changes ahead of time on production servers. The servers might be unavailable to users for several minutes while the changes are taking place and the server is restarting.

Managing Servers Remotely

The server management and configuration tools you have used so far perform tasks on the local server. Most networks have more than one server, and although you can perform a task by logging on to the console at each server or using Remote Desktop, there are more convenient ways to manage a multiserver environment remotely, covered in the following sections. By managing servers remotely, you can take advantage of the benefits of Server Core yet still be able to use a GUI on a remote machine. In addition, remote management reduces the need for a physical keyboard and monitor for each server. Most remote management tasks are handled by using Server Manager, MMCs, or the PowerShell command line.

Adding Servers to Server Manager

A new feature in Windows Server 2012 is the ability to manage all your servers from a single Server Manager interface. In Server Manager, you can manage all roles and features installed on any server and view the status of all servers, including events and performance data. To do this, you must add servers to Server Manager. To start the process, click Manage, Add Servers from the Server Manager menu. If the server where you're running Server Manager is a member of a domain and the server you want to add is also a domain member, you can add it by using any of these methods:

- *Searching Active Directory*—This method is probably the easiest. You can type the first few characters of the server name in the Name text box (see Figure 3-12) and click Find Now, or just click Find Now to see all computers in the domain. Then select one or more servers to manage. (Note that you can't manage computers running a client OS.)

- *Searching DNS*—Type the server name or IP address in the Search text box on the DNS tab, and select the servers you want to add.

- *Importing a text file*—Browse for and select a text file containing a list of server names or IP addresses, one per line, and all the servers listed in the file are added.

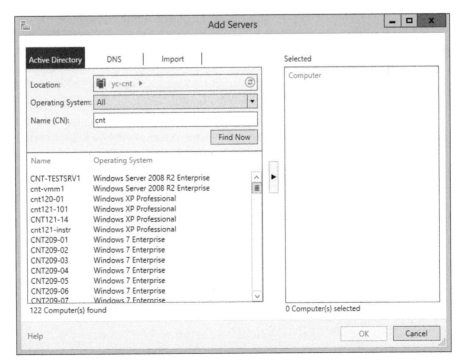

Figure 3-12   Adding a server to Server Manager

In Windows Server 2012 R2, you can manage servers running Windows Server 2003 and later. However, you can't manage a more recent version of Windows Server than the version on which Server Manager is running. For example, you can't manage a Windows Server 2012 R2 server from a Windows Server 2012 server, but you can manage a Windows Server 2012 server from a Windows Server 2012 R2 server.

If the server where you're running Server Manager is a member of a workgroup rather than a domain, or the server you want to manage is a workgroup member, first you need to add the remote server to the TrustedHosts list on the computer running Server Manager. To do this, use the following PowerShell cmdlet while logged on as Administrator:

```
Set-Item wsman:\localhost\Client\TrustedHosts RemoteServerName
  -Concatenate -Force
```

RemoteServerName is the name or IP address of the remote server you want to manage. The -Concatenate option adds the entry to the list instead of overwriting the existing list. After adding the remote server to the TrustedHosts list, you can add the server to Server Manager by using the previously described methods of searching DNS or importing a text file.

If you try to add a workgroup server that's not in the TrustedHosts list to Server Manager, Server Manager reports this error: "WinRM Negotiate authentication error."

Activity 3-6: Adding Servers to Server Manager

Time Required: 15 minutes
Objective: Add a Server Core computer to Server Manager.

Required Tools and Equipment: 410Server1 and 410ServerCore
Description: You have one server running the full GUI and one running Server Core. You want to manage the server running Server Core with Server Manager, so you add it to Server Manager on the server running the full GUI.

If you don't have the primary DNS suffix set on your servers and a running DNS server, you should substitute the IP address for the hostname in Steps 2 and 4.

1. Start 410Server1 and 410ServerCore, if necessary. Log on to 410Server1 as **Administrator**, and open a PowerShell command prompt.

2. If the servers you plan to manage aren't domain members, you must add them to the Trusted-Hosts list. In PowerShell, type **Set-Item wsman:\localhost\Client\TrustedHosts 410ServerCore.410Server2012.local -Concatenate -Force** and press **Enter**. (Substitute the correct domain name for 410ServerCore, if necessary.) Repeat this command, but substitute **410Server2** for 410ServerCore. Close the PowerShell window.

3. In Server Manager, click **Manage, Add Servers** from the menu to start the Add Servers Wizard.

4. Click the **DNS** tab. In the Search text box, type **410ServerCore** and press **Enter**. If you see a Server Manager message stating that no DNS entry was found, click **Yes**.

5. Click **OK**. In Server Manager, click **Dashboard** in the left pane, if necessary. Scroll down to the Roles and Server Groups section. Notice that the File and Storage Services box displays the number 2, indicating that two servers are running the File and Storage Services role. The All Servers box also displays a 2.

6. In the left pane of Server Manager, click **All Servers**. You should see both 410Server1 and 410ServerCore in the list of servers (see Figure 3-13).

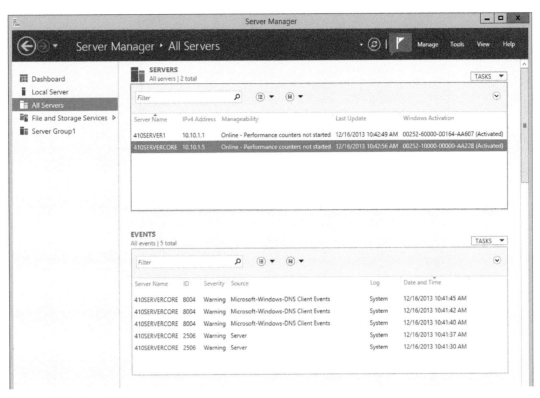

Figure 3-13   The All Servers window

7. Click **410ServerCore**. You see the Events box change to show recent events generated on the 410ServerCore server. Scroll down to view the Services box, which shows the status of services running on 410ServerCore.

8. Scroll back up to the list of servers and right-click **410ServerCore**. You see a number of management options you can perform on the server, including Add Roles and Features, Restart Server, Computer Management, and so forth. Click **Windows PowerShell**. At the PowerShell prompt, type **hostname** and press **Enter**. You see that the current host is 410ServerCore.

9. Type **Get-WindowsFeature** and press **Enter** to see a list of features on the 410ServerCore computer. You can add and remove features on a remote computer by using PowerShell or the GUI. Close the PowerShell window.

10. In Server Manager, right-click **410ServerCore** and click **Add Roles and Features** to start the Add Roles and Features Wizard. Click **Next** twice. In the Server Selection window, you see the 410ServerCore computer in the list of available servers. Click **Cancel**.

11. Right-click **410ServerCore** and click **Computer Management**. The message shown in Figure 3-14 indicates an error occurred in trying to manage a remote server. Before you can use MMCs to manage a remote server, you need to configure Windows Firewall on the remote server.

12. If you're continuing to the next activity, leave both servers running and stay logged on to 410Server1; otherwise, log off or shut down the servers.

Using Server Manager Groups

If you have only a few servers to manage, you can add them as described previously and access them by clicking All Servers in Server Manager. If you have dozens or even hundreds of servers to manage, however, you might want to organize them in groups, such as by department, location, or function. For example, you can group all servers related to the Operations Department, all servers in the Phoenix office, or all DNS servers. By organizing servers in this manner, you can

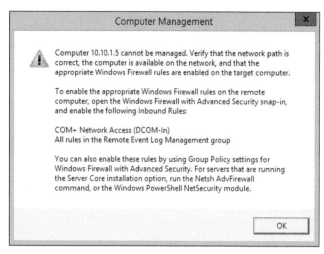

Figure 3-14   A Computer Management error message

see a group's status at a glance. Servers can be a member of more than one group, so you can place a domain controller in the Phoenix office in both the Domain Controllers group and the Phoenix group, for example.

To create a server group in Server Manager, click Manage, Create Server Group from the menu. Give the group a name, and then add servers to the group (see Figure 3-15). You can add servers from the existing list of servers managed by Server Manager, or you can add other servers to manage by using the methods described earlier. After you create a server group, the group name is added to the left pane of Server Manager and can be used just like the All Servers node.

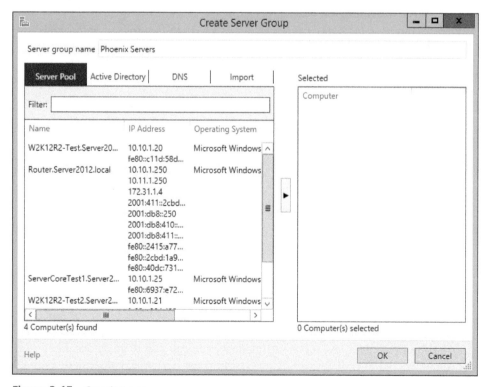

Figure 3-15   Creating a server group

Activity 3-7: Creating a Server Group

Time Required: 15 minutes

Objective: Create a server group and add a server to it.

Required Tools and Equipment: 410Server1

Description: In this activity, you create a server group and add 410Server1 and 410Server2 to it. Server groups are helpful when you're managing many servers and want to organize them by function, location, or another characteristic.

1. Start 410Server1, if necessary, and log on as **Administrator**.

2. In Server Manager, click **Manage, Create Server Group** from the menu to open the dialog box shown previously in Figure 3-15.

3. In the Server group name text box, type **Server Group1**. (In a production environment, you would make the group name more descriptive.)

4. In the list of servers, click **410Server1,** and then click the right-pointing arrow to move the server over to the Selected list box.

5. You can add a server to Server Manager and a group at the same time. Click the **DNS** tab. In the Search text box, type **410Server2.410Server2012.local** and press **Enter.** If you see a message stating that no DNS entry was found, click **Yes.** Click the arrow to move 410Server2 over to the Selected list box.

6. Click **OK.** In Server Manager, click **Server Group1** in the left pane. You see the two servers 410Server1 and 410Server2 listed. If 410Server2 isn't running, you see "Target computer not accessible" in the Manageability column (see Figure 3-16).

Figure 3-16   Viewing a server group

7. In the left pane of Server Manager, click **All Servers.** You see all three servers displayed in the list of servers.

8. If you're continuing to the next activity, leave both servers running and stay logged on to 410Server1; otherwise, log off or shut down the server.

Enabling and Disabling Remote Management

By default, Windows Server 2012/R2 remote management is enabled via **Windows Remote Management (WinRM).** WinRM provides a command-line interface for performing a variety of management tasks. Running in the background, it allows commands or applications that require Windows Management Instrumentation (WMI) or PowerShell to access the server remotely. To change the remote management setting, click the setting next to the label "Remote management" in the Local Server Properties window (see Figure 3-17).

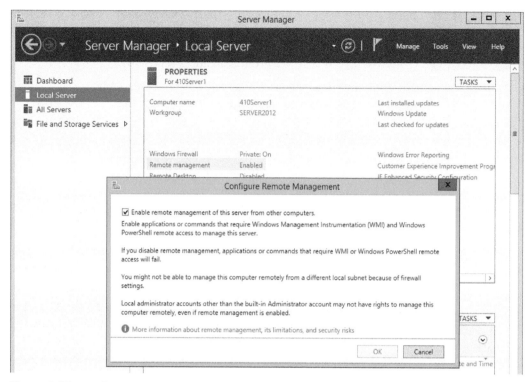

Figure 3-17   Configuring remote management

You can select or clear the check box in Figure 3-17 to enable or disable WinRM remote management. You can also enable or disable WinRM with the following commands:

- `Configure-SMRemoting.exe -Get` to display the current status of WinRM (enabled or disabled)
- `Configure-SMRemoting.exe -Enable` to enable WinRM
- `Configure-SMRemoting.exe -Disable` to disable WinRM

Configure Windows Firewall for Remote Management

Adding a server to Server Manager and enabling WinRM gives you only a few remote management capabilities. You can view the status of a remote server, run PowerShell, add and remove server roles, restart a server, and perform some additional tasks. However, to use an MMC to manage a remote server, you need to make some firewall rule changes on the remote server. To further complicate matters, different MMCs require different firewall rule changes. If you right-click a remote server in Server Manager and click Computer Management, for example, you get the error shown previously in Figure 3-14, which states that you must enable some firewall rules on the remote server.

Configuring Firewall Rules with the GUI   If the remote server you want to manage is running the full GUI, you can use the Windows Firewall with Advanced Security MMC to configure firewall rules. You need to log on to the remote server and open the Windows Firewall with Advanced Security MMC (explained in Activity 3-8). In the Inbound Rules section, enable the following rules (see Figure 3-18):

- COM+ Network Access (DCOM-In)
- Remote Event Log Management (NP-In)
- Remote Event Log Management (RPC)
- Remote Event Log Management (RPC-EPMAP)

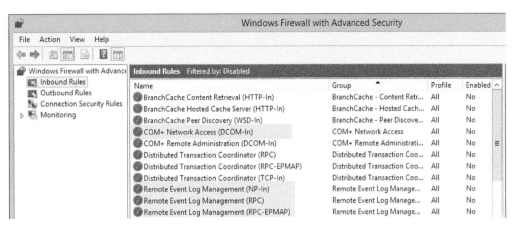

Figure 3-18 Windows Firewall rules for remote management

Enabling the preceding rules makes it possible to run most MMCs and snap-ins for managing a remote server.

Configuring Firewall Rules with the Command Line

You can configure the firewall with the `netsh` command or the `Set-NetFirewallRule` cmdlet in PowerShell. To enable the four rules highlighted in Figure 3-18 with `netsh`, use the following commands:

```
netsh advfirewall firewall set rule group="COM+ Network Access"
 new enable=yes
netsh advfirewall firewall set rule group="Remote Event Log Management"
 new enable=yes
```

Using the `group` keyword in these commands sets all three Remote Event Log Management rules at the same time.

The `netsh` command can be used to configure the firewall remotely, but *first* the Windows Firewall Remote Management group rules must be enabled on the remote computer, and they're disabled by default. To specify a remote computer in the `netsh` command, use the `-r RemoteComputer` parameter (replacing *RemoteComputer* with the name or IP address of the computer you're configuring).

To use PowerShell to configure the firewall, open a PowerShell command prompt window and enter the following commands:

```
Set-NetFirewallRule -DisplayGroup "COM+ Network Access" -enabled True
Set-NetFirewallRule -DisplayGroup "Remote Event Log Management"
 -enabled True
```

You can issue these commands while logged on to the remote computer or by opening a PowerShell command prompt remotely, as shown in Activity 3-6.

Special Considerations for Server Core

Server Core doesn't have the COM+ Network Access firewall group, and firewall rules for several MMC snap-ins might need to be enabled separately. You might want to enable the necessary firewall rules on the Server Core computer first so that you can manage the firewall remotely with the Windows Firewall with Advanced Security snap-in. To do so, open a PowerShell command prompt window on the Server Core computer and enter the following command:

```
Set-NetFirewallRule -DisplayGroup "Windows Firewall Remote Management"
 -enabled True
```

After you have enabled the firewall rule, you can create a Windows Firewall with Advanced Security MMC snap-in to manage the Server Core computer's firewall. Here are some other firewall rule groups you might want to enable on the Server Core computer for remote management with MMCs:

- *File and Printer Sharing*—Enables use of the Shared Folders snap-in and most of the other snap-ins in Computer Management, with the exception of Event Viewer and Device Manager.

- *Remote Event Log Management*—Allows using the Event Viewer snap-in.

- *Remote Volume Management*—Enables you to use the Disk Management snap-in to manage disks remotely. This firewall rule group must be enabled on both the Server Core computer and the computer where you're running Disk Management.

- *Remote Service Management*—Allows using the Services snap-in.

- *Performance Logs and Alerts*—Enables use of the Performance Monitor snap-in.

- *Remote Scheduled Tasks Management*—Allows using the Task Scheduler snap-in.

 You can't access Device Manager remotely on Windows Server 2012/R2 systems.

 ## Activity 3-8: Configuring Windows Firewall for Remote MMC Management

Time Required: 15 minutes
Objective: Configure Windows Firewall by using PowerShell remotely.

Required Tools and Equipment: 410Server1 and 410ServerCore
Description: You have added a server to Server Manager, and now you want to be able to manage the server remotely by using MMCs. In this activity, you use PowerShell commands remotely to configure the firewall.

1. Start 410Server1 and 410ServerCore and log on to both as **Administrator**, if necessary.

2. In Server Manager, click **All Servers** in the left pane. Right-click **410ServerCore** and click **Windows PowerShell**.

3. In PowerShell, type **Set-NetFirewallRule -DisplayGroup "Windows Firewall Remote Management" -enabled True** and press **Enter**.

4. Open an MMC by right-clicking **Start** and clicking **Run**. Type **mmc** and press **Enter**.

5. In the MMC console, click **File, Add/Remove Snap-in** from the menu. In Add or Remove Snap-ins dialog box, click **Windows Firewall with Advanced Security**, and then click **Add**.

6. In the Select Computer dialog box, click **Another computer** and type **410ServerCore** in the text box. Click **Finish** and then **OK**.

7. In the new MMC, click to expand **Windows Firewall with Advanced Security**, and then click **Inbound Rules**. Rules with a white checkmark on a green background are enabled. Those with a white checkmark on a gray background are disabled. Scroll through the rules to see which ones are enabled. Toward the bottom are the Windows Firewall Remote Management rules you just enabled.

8. In the MMC, click **File, Add/Remove Snap-in** from the menu. In Add or Remove Snap-ins dialog box, click **Services**, and then click **Add**.

9. In the Services dialog box, click **Another computer** and type **410ServerCore** in the text box. Click **Finish** and then **OK**.

10. Click the **Services** snap-in you just added. After a while, you see an error message stating that Windows can't open the Service Control Manager database. Click **OK**. You need to enable the Remote Services Management firewall rule group.

11. Click **Inbound Rules** under the Windows Firewall snap-in.

12. Find the three rules in the Remote Service Management group. Right-click each rule and click **Enable Rule**.

13. Click **Services** again to see that you can now view services on the 410ServerCore computer. Save the MMC console to your desktop with the name **FW-ServerCore**. Close the console.

14. In Server Manager, right-click **410ServerCore** and click **Computer Management**. You see an Event Viewer message stating that the computer can't be connected. Click **OK**.

15. The Computer Management MMC opens, but it's on the taskbar. Click the MMC on the taskbar to open it. You see that several snap-ins are available, but click **Event Viewer** to see that it's not available. Close Computer Management.

16. In PowerShell, type **Set-NetFirewallRule -DisplayGroup "Remote Event Log Management" -enabled True** and press **Enter**.

17. In Server Manager, right-click **410ServerCore** and click **Computer Management**. Click **Event Viewer**. You can now manage the event log on 410ServerCore.

18. Close Computer Management and PowerShell, and shut down 410ServerCore. If you're continuing to the next activity, leave both servers running and stay logged on to 410Server1; otherwise, log off or shut both servers down.

Configuring Services

A **service** is a task or process that runs in the background, behind the scenes. Just because you don't see a user interface for a service doesn't mean it doesn't need to be configured, however. Configuring services isn't a task you need to do often, but should the need come up, you must know how it's done. In Server Manager, you can access services via the Local Server node. After clicking Local Server, scroll down until you see the Services window shown in Figure 3-19. If you have added servers to Server Manager, you can click a server and see the Services window for that particular server.

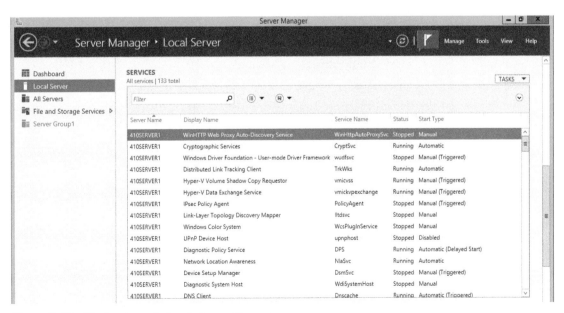

Figure 3-19   The Services window in Server Manager

You can use this window to view the status of a service. You can also right-click a service and perform the following actions:

- Start services
- Stop services
- Restart services
- Pause services
- Resume services
- Copy (used to copy text so that you can paste information about a service in a text file)

A Services MMC is also available from the Tools menu in Server Manager, and the Services snap-in is a standard part of the Computer Management MMC. If you need to perform configuration tasks beyond what's available in the Services window, you must use the Services snap-in. In addition to the actions listed previously, you can use the Services snap-in to perform the following operations:

- *Set the service startup type*—The settings are Manual, Automatic, Automatic (Delayed Start), and Disabled (see Figure 3-20). Manual requires an administrator to start the service. With the Automatic setting, the service starts at system boot. With the Automatic (Delayed Start) setting, the service starts a couple of minutes after all automatic services have started. If the startup type is Disabled, the service doesn't start. Services that are already installed in Windows usually don't require a change to the startup type; however, on occasion, you might want to disable a service you know isn't used to save system resources. Also, if you install an application that installs its own service, you might need to set the startup type according to the application's installation instructions. The Automatic (Delayed Start) setting is used when a service requires other services to be running before it starts.

Figure 3-20   Setting the service startup type

- *Set the service logon account*—A service must log on to a system to interact with it. You can specify an account (see Figure 3-21) or use the Local System account. As with the startup type, you usually need to configure the logon account only when installing a new service. The service installation instructions usually include guidelines.

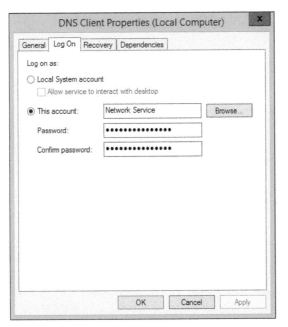

Figure 3-21 Setting the service logon account

- *Set service recovery options*—You can specify how a service should respond if it fails or is unable to start (see Figure 3-22). You can set the following options for the first, second, and subsequent failures: Take No Action, Restart the Service, Run a Program, and Restart the Computer.

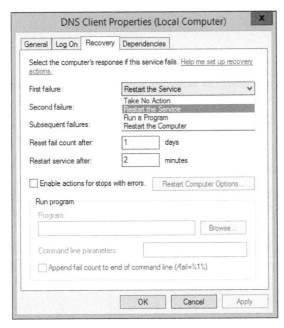

Figure 3-22 Setting service recovery options

- *View service dependencies*—Some services depend on other services to run, which is called **service dependencies**. The Dependencies tab shows other services the current service depends on, if any, and what system components depend on the current service (see Figure 3-23).

Figure 3-23 Viewing service dependencies

Configuring Services with PowerShell

As with most server functions, there are PowerShell cmdlets for configuring Windows services:

- `Get-Service`—Displays a list of services. To narrow the list, add the -DisplayName argument. For example, if you want to see a list of all services related to Hyper-V, use Get-Service -DisplayName Hy*.
- `Start-Service`—Starts a specified service. For multiple services, separate the names with a comma.
- `Stop-Service`—Stops a specified service. Separate multiple service names with a comma.
- `Restart-Service`—Stops and then starts a specified service. For multiple services, separate the names with a comma.
- `Suspend-Service`—Pauses a specified running service. For multiple services, separate the names with a comma.
- `Resume-Service`—Resumes a suspended service. For multiple services, separate the names with a comma.
- `Set-Service`—Allows you to change the properties of a service, including its status, description, start mode, and display name. You can also start, stop, and suspend services.
- `New-Service`—Creates a new service.

You can get detailed help on each command by typing `get-help cmdname -detailed` at a PowerShell command prompt (replacing *cmdname* with one of the service commands in the preceding list).

Activity 3-9: Working with Windows Services

Time Required: 15 minutes
Objective: Check the status of services and configure services.

Required Tools and Equipment: 410Server1
Description: Use the Services MMC and PowerShell to view and modify services.

1. Start 410Server1, and log on as **Administrator**, if necessary.

2. Open Server Manager, and click **Tools, Services** from the menu.

3. Scroll down and double-click **Print Spooler**. In the Print Spooler Properties dialog box, click the **Startup type** list arrow to see the available options. Make sure **Automatic** is selected.

4. Click the **Stop** button to stop the Print Spooler service.

5. Click the **Log On** tab, where you configure how a service logs on to the system.

6. Click the **Recovery** tab. Explore the available options for what should happen if the service fails.

7. Click the **Dependencies** tab. You see a list of other components that must be functioning for Print Spooler to run. Click **OK**. Notice that in the Service MMC, the Status column is blank, indicating that the service isn't running.

8. Open a PowerShell command prompt by clicking the **PowerShell** icon on the taskbar. Type **Get-Service -DisplayName Pr*** and press **Enter**. You see a list of services with a display name beginning with Pr, including the Print Spooler service. Its name is simply Spooler.

The Pr* in the command uses the * wildcard character, which means "any combination of characters can follow Pr in the service name."

9. Type **Start-Service Spooler** and press **Enter**. Type **Get-Service Spooler** and press **Enter**. The Print Spooler service is running again. Close PowerShell. Click the **Refresh** icon in the Services MMC to see that Print Spooler's status is Running.

10. Close the Services MMC. Stay logged on if you're continuing to the next activity; otherwise, log off or shut down 410Server1.

Configuring NIC Teaming

NIC teaming allows multiple network interfaces to work in tandem to increase available bandwidth and provide load balancing and fault tolerance. Another term for this feature is **load balancing and failover (LBFO)**. You can create a NIC team with a single network interface, but most of a NIC team's usefulness comes from having more than one NIC in the team. Windows Server 2012 supports up to 32 NICs in a team.

How does NIC teaming provide load balancing? **Load balancing** distributes traffic across two or more interfaces, thus increasing the overall network throughput a server is able to maintain. For example, two client stations are each transferring a 100 MB file to a share on a Windows Server 2012/R2 server. A server with a single NIC operating at 100 Mbps (megabits per second) could transfer both files in about 20 seconds (10 seconds for each file). A server with a two-NIC team load balances the data from the two clients, with each NIC able to handle one file in about 10 seconds, cutting the total transfer time in half.

Take a look at an example of how to use NIC teaming for fault tolerance, or failover. **Failover** in this context is a server's capability to recover from network hardware failure by having redundant hardware that can take over immediately for a device failure. Suppose you have a server that must be highly available. A server with a single NIC connected to a switch becomes unavailable if the switch or NIC fails. However, with a NIC team configured to provide failover, you can connect one NIC to one switch and the other NIC to another switch. If one NIC or switch fails, the other NIC takes over, maintaining server availability.

You can configure NIC teaming with Server Manager or PowerShell. In Server Manager, click Local Server. In the left column of the Properties dialog box is an entry for NIC Teaming, which is disabled by default. Click the Disabled link to open the NIC Teaming dialog box, shown in Figure 3-24.

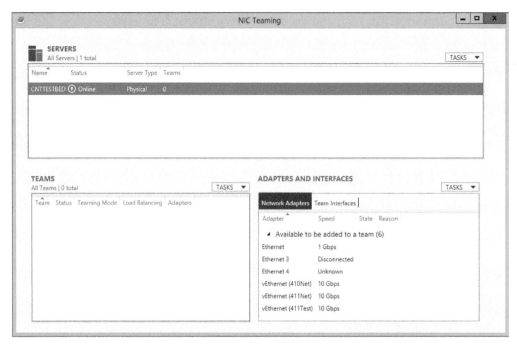

Figure 3-24   Configuring NIC teams

Figure 3-24 shows three panes, which have the following functions:

- *Servers*—This pane shows the available servers for which you can manage NIC teaming. You add servers to this list much like adding servers to Server Manager, by clicking the Tasks list arrow and clicking Add Servers. The Servers pane also shows whether a server is physical or virtual and the number of NIC teams defined.

- *Teams*—This pane lists NIC teams, their mode, their status, and which network adapters are part of a team. You can create or delete a NIC team by clicking Tasks.

- *Adapters and Interfaces*—This pane shows you the network adapters available to be added to a NIC team. You can add a NIC to an existing team or add one to a new team.

You can also use the following PowerShell cmdlets to list, create, remove, rename, and set properties of a team:

- `Get-NetLbfoTeam`—Shows a list of NIC teams on the server.

- `New-NetLbfoTeam`—Creates a NIC team and adds network adapters to it; you can optionally set the team's properties.

- `Remove-NetLbfoTeam`—Deletes a team.

- `Rename-NetLbfoTeam`—Renames a team.

- `Set-NetLbfoTeam`—Sets the properties of an existing team.

   To get help on using these PowerShell cmdlets, type `get-help` followed by the command name.

NIC Teaming Modes

A NIC team's mode of operation defines how it works. There are two main modes you can configure (see Figure 3-25): teaming modes and load-balancing modes.

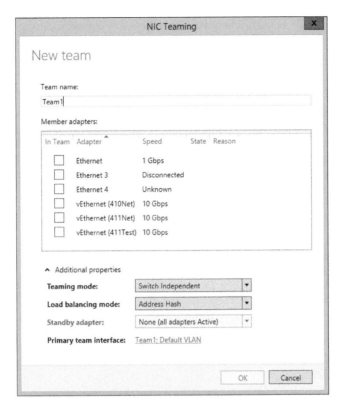

Figure 3-25   Configuring NIC teaming modes

There are three teaming modes:

- *Switch Independent*—The default mode is used to connect the NICs in a team to separate switches for fault tolerance. The switches aren't aware that a connected NIC is part of a team; the server provides all the teaming functions. You can also connect the NICs to the same switch. Switch Independent mode enables you to configure fault tolerance in one of two ways: Active or Standby. Active makes all NICs active, meaning you get the benefit of the bandwidth from all NICs in the team. If a NIC fails, the others continue to run. Standby lets you choose an adapter that remains in standby mode until there's a failure, when the NIC in standby mode becomes active. The default setting is Active.

- *Static Teaming*—This mode, also called switch dependent mode, is used primarily for load balancing. All NICs are connected to one switch, and the switch participates in the NIC teaming process. You must use a switch that supports IEEE 802.3ad, a standard that defines link aggregation. The switch must be configured manually to identify the ports switch team members are connected to. The switch load-balances network traffic between the NICs.

- *LACP*—Link Aggregation Control Protocol (LACP), defined in IEEE 802.1ax, allows a switch to automatically identify ports a team member is connected to and create a team dynamically. You must use a switch that supports LACP and enable the protocol before it can be used.

The load-balancing mode determines how the server load-balances outgoing data packets across NICs in the team:

- *Address Hash*—This mode uses an algorithm based on the outgoing packet's properties to create a hash value. The hash value is then used to assign the packet for delivery, using one of the NICs in the team. This mode is usually used when the team is connected to a physical switch rather than a Hyper-V switch. It's the default load-balancing mode in Windows Server 2012.

- *Hyper-V Port*—This mode is used when team members are connected to a Hyper-V switch. Each virtual NIC is associated with only one team member at system startup. It works well if a number of virtual machines are running to distribute the load evenly among NICs in the team.

- *Dynamic*—This mode is new in Windows Server 2012 R2 and is the default mode. In this mode, traffic is distributed evenly among all team members, including virtual NICs. With the other two modes, a NIC in the team could be overwhelmed during heavy traffic flow involving a single NIC, even if the other NICs have unused capacity. Dynamic mode balances heavy traffic flow over multiple NICs, thereby ensuring even distribution of traffic among all team members.

Activity 3-10: Configuring NIC Teams

Time Required: 7 minutes
Objective: Configure NIC teams.

Required Tools and Equipment: 410Server1
Description: Explore configuration options for NIC teams.

1. Start 410Server1 and log on as **Administrator**, if necessary.

2. In Server Manager, click **Local Server**. Click the **Disabled** link next to NIC Teaming to open the NIC Teaming dialog box.

3. In the Teams pane, click the **Tasks** list arrow, and then click **New Team**.

4. Type **NICTeam1** in the Team name text box. Click the **Ethernet** check box to add this adapter to the new team.

5. Click **Additional properties** at the bottom, and review the options. (*Note:* If you're running 410Server1 as a virtual machine, you might not be able to change the settings. In addition, if the NIC isn't connected to a real switch or a virtual switch with an external connection, you get an error if you create the team.)

6. Click **Cancel**, and then close the NIC Teaming dialog box.

7. Log off or shut down the server.

Working with Older Server Operating Systems

In most networks, you inevitably need to support multiple versions of the Windows Server OS. When you upgrade a network, you can rarely upgrade all servers to the newest OS version at the same time. This section discusses how to manage downlevel servers in Windows Server 2012 R2 by using Server Manager. A **downlevel server** is simply a server running an earlier version of the Windows Server OS. You can manage Windows Server 2012, Windows Server 2008 R2, and Windows Server 2008 servers remotely after installing the following updates:

- .NET Framework 4.5, which is the only update needed for Windows Server 2012.

- Windows Management Framework 4.0 for Windows Server 2008 R2 or 3.0 for Windows Server 2008.

- Performance update from Knowledge Base Article 2682011 (required only in Windows Server 2008/R2) to allow Server Manager to collect performance data. To find a Knowledge Base article, use the URL *http://support.microsoft.com/kb/articlenumber*. For example, to find the performance update article, go to *http://support.microsoft.com/kb/2682011*.

You can download updates from the Microsoft Download Center. Before installing these updates, it's a good idea to check Windows Update to make sure the server is already up to date.

A few other tasks you should do before you can get the most out of remote management of an older server:

- Make sure the WinRM service is running. On the remote server at an elevated command prompt, enter the `winrm qc` command and follow the prompts.
- Enable Windows PowerShell remote management. On the remote server at a PowerShell prompt, type `Enable-PSRemoting -Force`.

Now you can add the server to Server Manager by using the process described in Activity 3-6. On a Windows Server 2012 server, you can perform all remote management functions, including adding or removing roles and features. On Windows Server 2008/R2 servers, you can run Computer Management snap-ins and PowerShell cmdlets remotely, gather performance information, and restart the server, but you can't add or remove roles and features.

 You can add Windows Server 2003 servers to Server Manager, but the functionality is limited to Windows Server 2003 reporting online/offline status.

Chapter Summary

- You need to add roles and features to take advantage of Windows Server 2012's power. You can add and remove roles and features with Server Manager or PowerShell. You can also use PowerShell to query whether a role or feature is installed or available to be installed. You can use PowerShell to act on remote servers by using the `-ComputerName` argument.

- You can add and remove features to and from offline VHD and `.wim` file images with the `dism` command.

- You can switch between these server modes easily: Server with a GUI, Minimal Server Interface, and Server Core. Use Server Manager or PowerShell to add or remove the necessary features.

- You can add servers to Server Manager and perform most management tasks on remote servers. You can add servers by using Active Directory, DNS, and an import file. Remote computers that aren't domain members must be added to the TrustedHosts file on the managing computer.

- To organize the servers you're managing, create groups in Server Manager. Servers can belong to more than one group.

- WinRM has a command-line interface for performing a variety of tasks. This feature must be enabled to use PowerShell cmdlets remotely. The `Configure-SMRemoting` command enables and disables WinRM.

- You need to configure firewall rules to allow remote management with an MMC. You can use the Windows Firewall with Advanced Security MMC, the `netsh` command, or PowerShell cmdlets to set firewall rules.

- You configure services with the Services MMC or PowerShell. In the Services MMC, you can start, stop, and disable services. You can also configure the startup type, service logon account, recovery options, and service dependencies.

- NIC teaming allows multiple network interfaces to work in tandem to increase available bandwidth and provide load balancing and fault tolerance. You can configure the teaming mode and the load-balancing mode.

- Older operating systems need to be updated if you want to manage them in Server Manager. You need to update the .NET Framework and the Windows Management framework. You also need to make sure the WinRM service is running and PowerShell remote management is enabled.

Key Terms

downlevel server   A server running an earlier version of the Windows Server OS; usually in the context of managing that server remotely.

failover   A server's capability to recover from network hardware failure by having redundant hardware that can take over immediately for failed hardware.

Integrated Scripting Environment (ISE)   A PowerShell development environment that helps in creating PowerShell scripts.

load balancing   Distributing traffic between two or more interfaces, thus increasing the overall network throughput a server is capable of maintaining.

load balancing and failover (LBFO)   Another term for NIC teaming. *See* NIC teaming.

Minimal Server Interface   A new feature in Windows Server 2012 that takes up less disk space than the Server with a GUI option but more than the Server Core option. Includes Server Manager, MMCs, and some Control Panel applets.

NIC teaming   A feature that allows multiple network interfaces to work in tandem to increase available bandwidth and provide load balancing and fault tolerance.

service   A task or process that runs in the background.

service dependencies   A service that requires another service or Windows component to function correctly.

Windows Remote Management (WinRM)   A Windows 2012 feature that provides a command-line interface for performing a variety of remote management tasks.

Review Questions

1. Which of the following is a task you should perform before installing roles and features? (Choose all that apply.)

   a. Set a strong Administrator password.

   b. Read the Windows Server 2012 user manual.

   c. Configure static IP addresses.

   d. Make sure security updates are current.

2. Which of the following is true about installing roles and features in Windows Server 2012/R2?

   a. You can't install a server role by using the command line.

   b. All server role installations require a server restart.

   c. You can install more than one role at a time.

   d. Server roles can be installed only on online drives.

3. Which command shows a list of installed roles and features?

   a. `Installed-WindowsFeature -Show`

   b. `Get-WindowsFeature | where Installed`

   c. `List-InstalledFeature`

   d. `Show-Features .if. Installed`

4. You want to install a feature to an offline VHD file. What do you do first?

   a. Commit the changes.

   b. Install the feature by using `dism`.

   c. Mount the image.

   d. Import the `.wim` file.

5. You can convert a Server Core installation to a Minimal Server Interface installation but not vice versa. True or False?

6. Which of the following is true about the three server modes?

    a. Server Core uses the most resources.

    b. Server with a GUI doesn't have PowerShell.

    c. Minimal Server Interface can't run MMCs.

    d. Minimal Server Interface doesn't have File Explorer.

7. Which option can you add to the `Install-WindowsFeature` command that shows you what the results would be but doesn't actually perform the installation task?

    a. `-WhatIf`

    b. `-TestOnly`

    c. `-ShowResults`

    d. `-NoInstall`

8. Which features must be installed to convert a server from Server Core to the full GUI? (Choose all that apply.)

    a. `Server-GUI-Shell`

    b. `Server-MMC-Enable`

    c. `Server-Full-Interface`

    d. `Server-GUI-Mgmt-Infra`

9. Which of the following is a method for adding a server to Server Manager? (Choose all that apply.)

    a. Query NetBIOS.

    b. Search Active Directory.

    c. Import a file.

    d. Search DNS.

10. You add a server to Server Manager but see the error message "WinRM Negotiation authentication error." What should you do?

    a. Add the server with different credentials.

    b. Add the server to the TrustedHosts list.

    c. Install .NET Framework 4.5.

    d. Enter the `Configure-SMRemoting` command.

11. You're managing 75 servers from a single Server Manager console and find you're wasting a lot of time scrolling through the list of servers to find the one you want to manage. You have 5 locations with about 15 servers in each location. What can you do to make managing these servers in Server Manager easier?

12. What must be running to allow you to manage a server remotely with PowerShell?

    a. Windows Firewall

    b. LBFO

    c. Telnet

    d. WinRM

13. You right-click a Server Core server in Server Manager and click Computer Management. You see an error indicating that the server can't be managed. What should you do to solve the problem?

    a. Run `configure-SMRemoting.exe -Enable` on the local computer.

    b. Configure Windows Firewall on the remote computer.

    c. Install the Minimal Server Interface on the remote computer.

    d. Disable WinRM on the local computer.

14. You want to be able to manage a Server Core computer's firewall by using the Windows Firewall with Advanced Security snap-in. What should you do?

    a. On the local computer, disable the Windows Firewall Remote Management rule group.

    b. On the remote computer, enter the command `Configure-SMRemoting -ConfigureFirewallRules`.

    c. On the remote computer, use the PowerShell command `Set-NetFirewallRule -DisplayGroup "Windows Firewall Remote Management" -enabled True`.

    d. On the local computer, enable the COM+ Network Access firewall rule.

15. You need to stop a service so that you can do some troubleshooting. Before you stop it, you need to see whether any other services will be affected by this action. What should you do?

    a. Look at the Dependencies tab.

    b. View the service startup type.

    c. Right-click the service and click Show Requirements.

    d. Set the service recovery options.

16. Which cmdlet shows a list of services related to Hyper-V?

    a. `List-Services Hyper-V -all`

    b. `Show-Service -ServiceType Hyper*`

    c. `Get-Help Service Hyper-V`

    d. `Get-Service -DisplayName Hy*`

17. Which of the following is true about NIC teaming?

    a. You need a minimum of two NICs to create a NIC team.

    b. In failover mode, one NIC is always in standby mode.

    c. Static teaming is used mainly for load balancing.

    d. LACP is the default teaming mode.

18. Which load-balancing mode should you choose if you need to balance heavy traffic flow over multiple NICs?

    a. Address Hash

    b. Dynamic

    c. LACP

    d. Hyper-V Port

19. Which of the following must be installed if you want to remotely manage a Windows Server 2012 server from a Windows Server 2012 R2 server?

    a. Performance updates

    b. .NET Framework 4.5

    c. Windows Management Framework 4.0

    d. A full GUI

20. You want the switch to automatically identify the links between NICs on a NIC team and the switch so that teams can be created dynamically. What option should you set on the NIC team, and what feature should you look for on the switch?

    a. LACP, 802.3ad

    b. Static Teaming, LACP

    c. Switch Independent, Address Hashing

    d. LACP, 802.1ax

3

Case Projects

CASE PROJECTS

Case Project 3-1: Outfitting a Branch Office with Server Core

You have been supporting CSM Tech Publishing's Windows Server 2012 R2 server network for over a year. The office has two Windows Server 2012 R2 servers running Active Directory and a number of other roles. Management has informed you that a small sales office is opening in the same building three floors up. The sales manager wants to install a sales application on a server located in the sales office. This server will have limited physical security because there's no special room dedicated for it, which means it will be accessible to non-IT personnel and visitors. You're considering installing Windows Server 2012 R2 Server Core on the new server because accessing its console regularly probably won't be necessary, and this server will be managed from one of the other CSM Tech Publishing servers. What are the benefits and drawbacks of using Server Core for this branch office? What are some things you should do to set up this server management environment?

Case Project 3-2: Handling a NIC Failure

Last week, one of the servers at CSM Tech Publishing had a network failure that hindered operations for two days. You diagnosed the problem as a failed NIC and replaced it to solve the problem. The owner of CSM Tech Publishing wants to know whether you can do something to prevent downtime in a similar failure in the future. What can you suggest, and how does your suggestion help solve the problem?

Case Project 3-3: Dealing with Server Core Angst

The owner of CSM Tech Publishing was at the sales office last week and out of curiosity wanted to log on to the server there. The owner is somewhat tech savvy and has even worked a little with Active Directory in Windows Server 2003. He was shocked when he logged on and didn't see a familiar user interface—only a command prompt. He asked you about this and accepted your explanation of Server Core and why you chose this installation option. However, he was wondering what would happen if you stopped providing support or were unavailable for an extended period, and your replacement wasn't familiar with Server Core. Write a memo explaining how this situation could be handled easily.

chapter 4

Configuring Server Storage

After reading this chapter and completing the exercises, you will be able to:

- Describe server storage
- Configure local disks
- Work with virtual disks
- Use Storage Spaces

All screenshots, unless otherwise noted, are used with permission from Microsoft Corporation.

Configuring a server's storage is usually one of the first tasks you need to perform on a new server after finishing its initial configuration. In the past, server storage was simply a disk controller and one or two hard drives. Now advanced storage solutions are available to provide fault tolerance and high performance. This chapter covers the basics of server storage, and then explains configuring local disks. With virtualization becoming such an important part of network environments, it's no surprise that Windows Server 2012/R2 supports creating and mounting virtual disks. This chapter describes the basic steps to work with virtual disks. A major enhancement to configuring storage in Windows Server 2012 is Storage Spaces, a new storage model for Windows Server, and you see how to create and configure storage pools, virtual disks, and volumes with Storage Spaces.

An Overview of Server Storage

Table 4-1 describes what you need for the hands-on activities in this chapter.

Table 4-1   Activity requirements

Activity	Requirements	Notes
Activity 4-1: Configuring a New Disk	410Server1	A new disk is installed and can be a virtual or physical disk. Server 1 then has three disks installed.
Activity 4-2: Working with Volumes in Disk Management	410Server1	
Activity 4-3: Working with Virtual Disks	410Server1	
Activity 4-4: Creating a Storage Space	410Server1	
Activity 4-5: Cleaning Up Storage Spaces	410Server1	

© 2015 Cengage Learning®

One of the main reasons networks and servers were invented was to have a centralized repository for shared files. The need for faster, bigger, and more reliable storage is growing as fast as the technology can keep up. Everything is stored on digital media now—documents, e-mail, music, photographs, videos—and this trend is continuing. In addition, people want instant anywhere access to whatever it is they're storing. Just about every large Internet company has its own version of cloud storage, from DropBox to iCloud to Skydrive, and dozens more. Dozens of cloud storage services are competing to store your files, and although these services are convenient and seemingly work by magic, they all start with a server and some hard drives. The following sections cover some basics of server storage: what it is, why you need it, and the common methods for accessing storage.

What Is Storage?

Generally speaking, storage is any digital medium data can be written to and retrieved from. Technically, this definition includes random access memory (RAM), but the term "server storage" generally means long-term storage, maintaining data without a power source. Long-term storage includes the following types of media:

- USB memory sticks (flash drives)
- Secure Digital (SD) cards and Compact Flash (CF) cards
- CDs and DVDs
- Magnetic tape
- Solid state drives
- Hard disk drives

This discussion centers on server storage, which is based on hard disk drives (HDDs), although solid state drives are gaining popularity for applications requiring higher speed, smaller size, and lower power requirements. A **solid state drive (SSD)** uses flash memory and the same type of high-speed interfaces (usually SATA or the newer SATA Express) as traditional hard disks. An SSD has no moving parts, requires less power, and is faster and more resistant to shock than an HDD, but the cost is much higher per gigabyte than an HDD. SSDs also don't have the capacity of HDDs, so discussions of server storage are mainly about traditional HDD storage. Nonetheless, most of the discussion of HDD storage applies to SSDs, too, and as technology progresses and prices drop, you'll see SSDs replace HDDs in certain applications.

Reasons for Storage

Every computer needs some amount of storage, but servers generally require more than client computers because one of the server's main purposes is to store and serve files when they're requested. The following list isn't exhaustive, but it covers most uses:

- *Operating system files*—The OS itself requires a good bit of storage. The files that make up the OS include boot files, the kernel, device drivers, user interface files, and all the files for roles and features you can install. Together, they add up to around 9 GB on a server with the GUI installed and about 5 GB in Server Core.

- *Page file*—A **page file** is used as virtual memory and to store dump data after a system crash. Its size varies depending on how much RAM is installed, memory use patterns, and other factors. In the past, the page file was set to 1.5 times the amount of installed memory, but this formula is no longer valid. By default, the system manages the page file, which can change size depending on needs but is typically close to the amount of installed RAM, up to 4 GB.

- *Log files*—The log files you see in Event Viewer and other log files change size dynamically depending on how the system is used. You can use Event Viewer to configure the maximum size of many log files. Be aware that even if you aren't adding any files to the disk where Windows is installed, log files can slowly eat up disk space unless you keep an eye on them.

- *Virtual machines*—If the server is a virtualization server running Hyper-V, you need plenty of space to store files for virtual hard disks. Virtualization is one of largest uses of disk space in servers now.

- *Database storage*—If a server is running one or more databases, disk storage requirements vary depending on the size of databases. Because databases can grow dynamically, it's a good idea to store them on a drive separate from the Windows drive, preferably on a volume that can have its capacity expanded if needed.

- *User documents*—If a server is being used to store user files or user profiles, this purpose might be the largest use of disk space. Using disk quotas on servers that store user files is a good idea so that a single user can't monopolize disk space by storing his or her entire collection of movies, for example, on a network server.

When deciding how much disk space you need for a server, you should take all the preceding uses into account. Remember that certain storage uses benefit from being on separate disks from the disk where Windows is stored. This advice is particularly true of the page file and virtual machines, but ideally, the Windows directory should be on a separate drive from most other storage uses.

Storage Access Methods

The discussion on storage access methods revolves around where storage is located in relation to the server. There are four broad categories of storage access methods:

- Local storage
- Direct-attached storage (DAS)
- Network-attached storage (NAS)
- Storage area network (SAN)

Local Storage   Local storage has been around as long as computers have, but the interfaces to storage media have improved as speed and capacity requirements have grown. Local storage is the focus of this chapter, and disk interface technologies are discussed later in "Configuring Local Disks."

Local storage can be defined as storage media with a direct, exclusive connection to the computer's system board through a disk controller. Local storage is almost always inside the computer's case, attached to a disk controller via internal cables and powered by the computer's internal power supply. The term "local storage" usually refers to HDDs or SSDs instead of CDs/DVDs or other types of media. Local storage provides rapid and exclusive access to storage media through ever-faster bus technologies. The downside of local storage is that only the system where it's installed has direct access to the storage medium. Data on disks can be shared through network file sharing, but the system with the installed storage must fulfill requests for shared data.

Direct-Attached Storage   Direct-attached storage (DAS) is similar to local storage, in that it's connected directly to the server using it. In fact, local storage is a type of DAS because DAS includes hard drives mounted inside the server case. However, DAS can also refer to one or more HDDs in an enclosure with its own power supply. In this case, the DAS device is connected to a server through an external bus interface, such as eSATA, SCSI, USB, FireWire, and Fibre Channel.

A DAS device with its own enclosure and power supply can usually be configured as a disk array, such as a RAID configuration (discussed later in "Configuring Local Disks"). Although most DAS devices provide exclusive use to a single computer, some have multiple interfaces so that more than one computer can access the storage medium simultaneously. Most of the later discussion in "Configuring Local Disks" also applies to DAS devices because the computer usually sees an externally attached DAS device as local storage.

The term "DAS" was created to distinguish it from storage connected to a network, such as NAS and SAN.

Network-Attached Storage   Network-attached storage (NAS), sometimes referred to as a **storage appliance**, has an enclosure, power supply, slots for multiple HDDs, a network interface, and a built-in OS tailored for managing shared storage. An NAS is designed to make access to shared files easy to set up and easy for users to access. Because an NAS is typically dedicated to file sharing, it can be faster than a traditional server in performing this task because a server is often sharing its computing and networking resources among several duties. An NAS shares files through standard network protocols, such as Server Message Block (SMB), Network File System (NFS), and File Transfer Protocol (FTP). Some NAS devices can also be used as DAS devices because they often have USB, eSATA, or other interfaces that can be attached directly to a computer.

Storage Area Network   The most complex type of storage is a **storage area network** (**SAN**), which uses high-speed networking technologies to give servers fast access to large amounts of shared disk storage. The storage a SAN manages appears to the server OS as though it's physically attached to the server. However, it's connected to a high-speed network technology and can be shared by multiple servers. The most common network technologies used in SANs are Fibre Channel and iSCSI. These technologies are designed to connect large arrays of hard drive storage that servers can access and share. Client computers access shared data by contacting servers via the usual method, and the servers retrieve the requested data from the SAN devices and pass it along to the client computer. Figure 4-1 shows a SAN using Fibre Channel, in which disk arrays are connected to a Fibre Channel switch, and servers are connected to the Fibre Channel network as well as a traditional network. In this arrangement, all servers have access to the storage medium, which can be shared and allocated as needed.

SANs use the concept of **logical unit number (LUN)** to identify a unit of storage. A LUN is a logical reference point to a unit of storage that could refer to an entire array of disks, a single disk, or just part of a disk. To the server using the SAN, the LUN is easier to work with because the server doesn't have to know how the storage is provided; it needs to know only how much it has available.

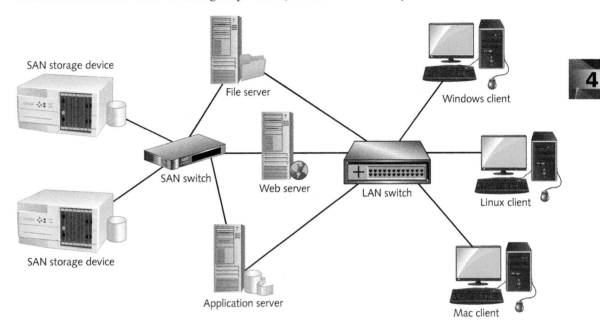

Figure 4-1   A storage area network
© 2015 Cengage Learning®

SANs are often used by server clusters so that all cluster members have access to shared storage for the purposes of load balancing and fault tolerance. Server clusters and the use of iSCSI with SANs are covered in *MCSE Guide to Designing and Implementing a Server Infrastructure, Exam 70-413* (Cengage Learning, 2015).

Configuring Local Disks

Configuration of local disks can be divided into two broad categories: physical disk properties and logical properties. Physical disk properties, which must be considered first before purchasing disk drives for a server, involve disk capacity, physical speed, and the interface for attaching a disk to the system. Logical disk properties include its format and the partitions or volumes created on it. Before you get too far into these properties, however, make sure you're clear on disk-storage terminology:

- *Disk drive*—A **disk drive** is a physical component with a disk interface connector (such as SATA or SCSI) and a power connector. A mechanical disk drive (usually called an HDD) has one or more circular magnetic platters storing the data's actual bits and one or more read/write heads—one for each side of the magnetic platters. The platters spin at high speed, and the read/write heads move from the inside of the platter to the outside to read data on the disk. An SSD has a disk interface and power connector but has flash memory chips instead of magnetic platters, and there are no read/write heads or other moving parts. Data is accessed in a similar fashion as RAM.

- *Volume*—Before an OS can use a disk drive, a volume must be created on the drive. A **volume** is a logical unit of storage that can be formatted with a file system. A disk drive can contain one or more volumes of different sizes. Disk drive space that hasn't been assigned to a volume is said to be unallocated. Volumes can also span two or more disks in an arrangement called RAID. Volumes, including RAID volumes, are discussed in more detail later in "Volumes and Disk Types."

- *Partition*—This older term means the same thing as "volume" but is used with basic disks. The term **partition** is still used at times, but in Windows, it has largely been replaced by "volume."

- *Formatting*—Before an OS can use a volume, the volume must be formatted. **Formatting** prepares a disk with a file system used to organize and store files. There are different format standards, and the format you choose for a disk depends on how the disk will be used. This topic is discussed in more detail later in "Disk Formats."

Disk Capacity and Speed

The disk capacity you need depends entirely on how the disk will be used. Will it be a system disk for storing the Windows OS and related files, a file-sharing disk, a disk storing a database, or maybe one that stores virtual machines? Perhaps you plan to have a combination of uses, but in general, distinct types of data should be kept on separate disks so that you can optimize some of the disk's logical properties for the type of data it will store.

Keep in mind that you might not be basing disk capacity decisions on a single disk because you could be configuring an array of disks in a RAID. HDD capacities are now measured in hundreds of gigabytes, with one and two terabyte (TB, 1000 gigabytes) disks being common. Disk capacity is fairly inexpensive, and having more than you need is better than having less. Here are some considerations for deciding how much disk capacity to buy and how many disks to use in a server:

- The Windows installation (the volume that stores the \Windows folder) should be on a separate disk from the data to be stored on the server. An SSD is a good candidate for the Windows installation.

- The page file should be on its own disk, if possible. An SSD is also a good candidate for the page file. If a separate disk is impractical, at least try to put the page file on its own volume.

- Take fault tolerance into account by using a RAID, which combines multiple disks to make a single volume so that data stored on the volume is maintained even if a disk fails. However, overall storage capacity is diminished.

The speed of HDDs is affected by a number of factors. The disk interface technology is an important performance factor that's discussed next. Other factors include rotation speed and the amount of cache memory installed. The rotation speed of disk platters in HDDs ranges from a low of about 5400 revolutions per minute (rpm) to 15,000 rpm, with speeds of 7200 and 10,000 rpm in between. A server should be outfitted with an HDD that rotates at a minimum of 7200 rpm, but for high-performance applications, look for 10,000 or 15,000 rpm drives.

The amount of cache in an HDD allows the drive to buffer read and write data locally, which speeds overall disk access. Cache sizes of 32 and 64 MB are common for server-class drives, but some very fast drives might have as little as 16 MB. What you're most interested in for disk performance is how fast data can be read from and written to the disk—the data rate. When researching disks for performance factors, look for the sustained data rate the manufacturer claims, which tells you how fast the drive can transfer data for an extended period.

Disk Interface Technologies

The disk interface connects a disk to a computer system, usually with some type of cable. The cable acts as a bus that carries data and commands between the disk and computer. The faster the bus, the faster the system can read from and write to the disk. The most common types of disk interfaces for locally attached disks are SATA, SAS, and SCSI. Each technology has advantages and disadvantages, discussed in the following sections.

You might also find a few parallel ATA (PATA) or Integrated Drive Electronics (IDE) drives on the low end and Fibre Channel drives on the high end, but for locally attached drives for servers, the most common by far are SATA, SAS, and SCSI. IDE drives are nearly obsolete, and Fibre Channel drives are most likely to be used in SANs.

Serial ATA Drives   Serial ATA (SATA) drives have mostly replaced parallel ATA (PATA) drives and have several advantages over this older technology, including faster transfer times and smaller cable size. Whereas the PATA interface is limited to about 167 megabytes per second (MB/s), SATA drives boast transfer times up to 6 gigabits per second (Gb/s; 600 MB/s). SATA drives are inexpensive, fast, and fairly reliable. They're a good fit for both client computers and lower-end servers. The SATA standard has evolved from SATA 1.0, supporting transfer speeds of 1.5 Gb/s (150 MB/s), to the current SATA 3.2, supporting speeds up to 16 Gb/s (or 1.6 gigabytes per second, GB/s). However, most readily available devices support SATA 2.0 (3 Gb/s) or SATA 3.0 (6 Gb/s). Even with their high transfer rates, however, SATA drives take a back seat to SCSI and SAS drives in the enterprise server realm.

SCSI and SAS Drives   **Small computer system interface (SCSI)** drives have been a mainstay in enterprise-class servers for decades, and this drive technology has endured through more than a half-dozen upgrades. The most recent SCSI variation, developed in 2003, is Ultra-640, with up to 640 MB/s transfer rates. SCSI is a parallel technology, like PATA, and has probably reached its performance limits. SCSI, however, has always provided high reliability and enterprise-level command features, such as error recovery and reporting. Its successor is **serial attached SCSI (SAS)**, which maintains the high reliability and advanced commands of SCSI and improves performance, with transfer rates up to 6 Gb/s and higher speeds underway. SAS has the benefit of having bus compatibility with SATA, so SATA drives can be connected to SAS backplanes. A **backplane** is a connection system that uses a printed circuit board instead of traditional cables to carry signals.

The SAS standard offers higher-end features than SATA drives do. SAS drives usually have higher rotation speeds and use higher signaling voltages, which allow their use in server backplanes. Overall, SAS is considered the more enterprise-ready disk interface technology, but enterprise features come with a price—SAS drives are also more expensive than SATA drives. As with many other things, server disk technologies have a tradeoff between performance and reliability versus price.

Volumes and Disk Types

Before data can be stored on a disk drive, space on the drive must be allocated to a volume. On a Windows system, each volume is typically assigned a drive letter, such as C or D. A volume can use some or all of the space on an HDD, or a single volume can span multiple drives. Before you go further, there are two Microsoft-specific volume definitions you need to know:

- *Boot volume*—The **boot volume** is the volume where the \Windows folder is located. It's usually the C drive but doesn't have to be. The boot volume is also called the "boot partition."

- *System volume*—The **system volume** contains files the computer needs to find and load the Windows OS. In Windows 2008 and later, it's created automatically during installation if you're installing an OS for the first time on the system, and it's not assigned a drive letter, so you can't see it in File Explorer. You can, however, see it in Disk Management (see Figure 4-2). In earlier Windows versions, the system volume is usually the C drive. In Figure 4-2, it's labeled "Active," which tells the BIOS to try booting from that volume. The system volume is also called the "system partition."

In Windows, the types of volumes you can create on a disk depend on how the disk is categorized. Windows defines two disk categories, discussed next: basic and dynamic.

The Windows boot and system volumes can be created only on basic disks.

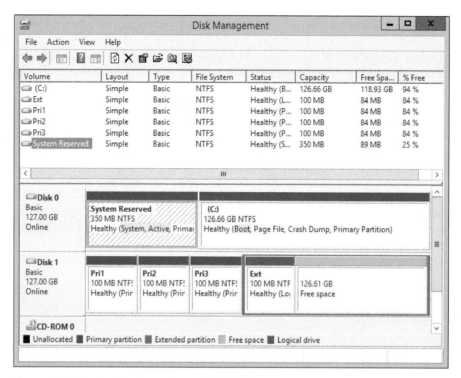

Figure 4-2   Boot and system volumes in Disk Management

Basic Disks   As the name implies, a **basic disk** can accommodate only basic volumes, called "simple volumes." A simple volume is a disk partition residing on only one disk; it can't span multiple disks or be used to create a RAID volume. The volumes on a basic disk are also called "partitions." The Disk Management snap-in uses both terms in its interface, but the term "partition" is more accurate and distinguishes it from a volume created on a dynamic disk. When Windows detects a new disk drive, it's initialized as a basic disk by default.

You can create a maximum of four partitions on a basic disk. The first three you create with Disk Management are primary partitions. A **primary partition** can be an active partition and can be the Windows system volume. It's usually assigned a drive letter but doesn't have to be, as with the Windows system partition. If you create a fourth partition, it's called an **extended partition**, which can be divided into one or more logical drives, each assigned a drive letter. A logical drive on an extended partition can hold the boot volume, but it can't hold the system volume because it can't be marked as active.

Dynamic Disks   If you need more than a simple volume, you must convert a basic disk to a **dynamic disk**. Volumes created on dynamic disks can span multiple disks and be configured for fault tolerance by using RAID. A dynamic disk can hold the Windows boot or system partition, but only if you convert the disk to dynamic after Windows is already installed on the volume. You can create up to 128 volumes on a dynamic disk.

To convert a basic disk to dynamic in Disk Management, simply right-click the disk and click Convert to Dynamic Disk. Existing volumes on the basic disk are converted to simple volumes on the dynamic disk, and all data on the disk is maintained. You can convert a dynamic disk to basic in the same manner, but you must first delete existing volumes on the dynamic disk, and existing data will be lost.

If you attempt to create a volume on a basic disk that isn't supported, Windows prompts you to convert it to dynamic before you can proceed.

4

Partitioning Methods   Windows offers two methods for partitioning disks. The most common method, **Master Boot Record (MBR)**, has been around since DOS. MBR partitions support volume sizes up to 2 TB. MBR-based disks are compatible with all Windows versions as well as most other OSs. When a disk is initialized in Disk Management, it's initialized as an MBR disk by default.

The second and newer method is **GUID Partitioning Table (GPT)**. GPT disks became an option starting with Windows Server 2008 and Vista. They support volume sizes up to 18 exabytes (EB, a million terabytes); however, Windows file systems currently support volume sizes only up to 256 TB. If you initialize a disk by using File and Storage Services in Server Manager, it's done with GPT. In Disk Management, you can convert an MBR disk to GPT and vice versa, but you must delete existing partitions first, which erases all data. In addition to larger volume sizes, GPT partitions offer improved reliability in the form of partition table replication (a backup copy of the partition table) and Cyclic Redundancy Check (CRC) protection of the partition table.

GPT partitions contain an area on the disk called the "protective MBR," which is maintained for backward-compatibility with disk utilities that work only with MBR disks.

Types of Volumes   A basic disk supports only simple volumes, but you can create several volume types on a dynamic disk, including RAID volumes. **Redundant array of independent disks (RAID)** is a disk configuration that uses space on multiple disks to form a single logical volume. Most RAID configurations offer fault tolerance, and some enhance performance. The following are the types of volumes you can create on a Windows Server 2012/R2 system. Some of these volume types are shown later in "Using Storage Spaces."

- *Simple volume*—A **simple volume**, as mentioned, resides on a single disk, basic or dynamic. On a basic disk, a simple volume can be extended (made larger) if unallocated space is available on the disk. A simple volume can also be shrunk on basic or dynamic disks. A simple volume on a dynamic disk can be extended on the same disk or to multiple disks as long as they have unallocated space. A simple volume can also be made into a mirrored volume by using two dynamic disks.

- *Spanned volume*—A **spanned volume** extends across two or more physical disks. For example, a simple volume that has been extended to a second disk is a spanned volume. When the first disk has filled up, subsequent disks are used to store data. Spanned volumes don't offer fault tolerance; if any disk fails, data on all disks is lost. There's also no performance advantage in using a spanned volume.

- *Striped volume*—A **striped volume** extends across two or more dynamic disks, but data is written to all disks in the volume equally. For example, if a 10 MB file is written to a striped volume with two disks, 5 MB is written to each disk. A striped volume can use from 2 to 32 disks. Striped volumes don't offer fault tolerance, but they do have a read and write performance advantage over spanned and simple volumes because multiple disks can be accessed simultaneously to read and write files. A striped volume is also referred to as a "RAID 0 volume." The Windows system and boot volumes can't be on a striped volume.

- *Mirrored volume*—A **mirrored volume** (or "RAID 1 volume") uses space from two dynamic disks and provides fault tolerance. Data written to one disk is duplicated, or mirrored, to the second disk. If one disk fails, the other disk has a good copy of the data, and the system can continue to operate until the failed disk is replaced. The space used on both disks in a mirrored volume is the same. Mirrored volumes might have a disk read performance advantage, but they don't have a disk write performance advantage.

- *RAID 5 volume*—A **RAID 5 volume** uses space from three or more dynamic disks and uses disk striping with parity to provide fault tolerance. When data is written, it's striped across all but one of the disks in the volume. Parity information derived from the data is written to the remaining disk. The system alternates which disk is used for parity information, so each disk has both data and parity information. Parity information is used to re-create lost data after a disk failure. A RAID 5 volume provides increased read performance, but write performance is decreased because of having to calculate and write parity information. The Windows system and boot volumes can't be on a RAID 5 volume.

Striped, mirrored, and RAID 5 volumes configured in Windows are referred to as "software RAID." You can also purchase a RAID disk controller that can create RAID disks by using the controller's firmware—called "hardware RAID." Hardware RAID is done at the disk level, whereas software RAID in Windows is done at the volume level. Hardware RAID typically results in better performance than software RAID. In addition, the restrictions on placing Windows system and boot volumes on RAID volumes applies to software RAID because the OS must be running before the RAID is recognized. In most cases, hardware RAID configurations don't have these restrictions.

Disk Formats

Before you can store data on a volume, it must be formatted with a file system. Formatting creates the directory structure needed to organize files and store information about each file. The information stored about each file depends on the file system used.

A **file system** defines the method and format an OS uses to store, locate, and retrieve files from electronic storage media. Windows supports three file systems for storing files on hard disks: FAT, NTFS, and ReFS (new in Windows Server 2012, as you learned in Chapter 1). NTFS is by far the most important and is dominant on Windows servers. However, FAT is still found occasionally on workstations and servers, and there are valid reasons to use this file system in certain circumstances. ReFS, the new kid in town, has limited features compared with NTFS.

Before going into detail on these disk formats, reviewing the components of a file system is helpful. Modern file systems have some or all of the following components:

- *Filenaming convention*—All files stored on a disk are identified by name, and the file system defines rules for how to name a file. These rules include length, special characters that can be used (such as $, #, %, &, and !), and case sensitivity (differentiating uppercase and lowercase letters).

- *Hierarchical organization*—Most file systems are organized as an inverted tree structure, with the root of the tree at the top and folders or directories underneath acting as branches. A folder can be empty or contain a list of files and additional folders. In most file systems, folders or directories don't contain the data that makes up the actual file; they contain information about the file along with a pointer to the file's location on the disk. Information for each file is usually called a "directory entry."

- *Data storage method*—Space on hard disks is divided into one or more partitions, with each partition containing its own file system. A partition is typically divided into 512-byte sectors. The file system groups one or more sectors into blocks or clusters, which are used as the basic unit of storage for file data. These blocks are indexed so that the file data they contain can be retrieved easily. A single file can occupy from one to many thousands of blocks. File systems vary in the methods used for indexing and managing these blocks, which affect the efficiency and reliability of data storage and retrieval.

- *Metadata*—Metadata is information about a file beyond its name and the data it contains. This information is generally stored by the directory or folder with the file's name or in a data structure the directory entry points to. Metadata can include timestamps indicating when a file was created, last changed, and last accessed; descriptive information about the file that can be used in searches; file attributes; and access control lists.

- *Attributes*—Attributes are usually on/off settings, such as Read Only, Hidden, Compressed, and so forth. File systems differ in the attributes that can be applied to files and folders.

- *Access control lists (ACLs)*—ACLs determine who can access a file or folder and what can be done with the file (read, write, delete, and so on).

File systems vary in whether and how each component is used. Generally, more advanced file systems have flexible filenaming rules, an efficient method of managing data storage, a considerable amount of metadata, advanced attributes, and ACLs. In Chapter 1, you reviewed some basic differences between FAT and NTFS. Next, you examine these file systems more closely.

For more information on other file systems and a comparison of features, see *http://en.wikipedia.org/wiki/Comparison_of_file_systems*. Wikipedia articles can be created and changed by anybody, but this article is accurate as of this writing and unique for this type of extensive file system comparison.

The FAT File System

The File Allocation Table (FAT) file system consists of two variations: FAT16 and FAT32. "File Allocation Table" vaguely describes the structure used to manage data storage. FAT16, usually referred to simply as "FAT," has been around since the mid-1980s, which is one of its biggest strengths—it's well known and well supported by most OSs. FAT32 arrived on the scene with the release of Windows 95 OSR2 in 1996.

A third variation, FAT12, is the original version of FAT developed in the late 1970s. It was limited to use on floppy disks.

The main difference between FAT16 and FAT32 is the size of the disk partition that can be formatted. FAT16 is limited to 2 GB partitions in most implementations (although Windows NT permits partitions up to 4 GB). FAT32 allows partitions up to 2 TB; however, in Windows 2000 and later, Microsoft limits them to 32 GB because the file system becomes noticeably slower and inefficient with larger partition sizes. This 32 GB limitation applies only to creating partitions. Windows can read FAT32 partitions of any size. FAT16 supports a maximum file size of 2 GB, and FAT32 supports files up to 4 GB.

The number in FAT versions refers to the number of bits available to address disk clusters. FAT16 can address up to 2^{16} disk clusters, and FAT32 can address up to 2^{32} disk clusters. The number of disk clusters a file system can address is directly proportional to the largest size partition it supports.

Already, you can see that FAT has severe limitations in current computing environments. The file size limitation alone prevents storing a standard DVD image file on a FAT file system. The limitations are even more apparent when you consider reliability and security requirements of current OSs. FAT doesn't support file and folder permissions for users and groups, so any user logging on to a computer with a FAT disk has full control over every file on that disk. In addition, FAT lacks support for encryption, file compression, disk quotas, and reliability features, such as transaction recovery and journaling, all of which NTFS supports.

You might think FAT isn't good for much, especially compared with the more robust NTFS, but FAT/FAT32 still has its place. It's the only file system option when using older Windows OSs, such as Windows 9x. In addition, FAT is simple and has little overhead, so it's still the file system of choice on removable media, such as flash drives. For hard drives, however, particularly on Windows servers, NTFS is usually the way to go, although some applications benefit from ReFS.

 Chapter 1 mentioned another variation of FAT, exFAT, which has the same features as FAT32 but can be used to format volumes larger than 32 GB, up to a theoretical 64 zettabytes (ZB, a billion terabytes) and file sizes up to 16 EB. When you format a volume larger than 32 GB in Disk Management, exFAT is offered as a format option.

The NTFS and ReFS File Systems

NTFS is a full-featured file system that Microsoft introduced with Windows NT in 1993. Since that time, its features have been expanded to help administrators gain control of ever-expanding storage requirements. NTFS has supported file and folder permissions almost since its inception, which was a considerable advantage over FAT. Many compelling features have been added, particularly starting with Windows 2000:

- *Disk quotas*—Enable administrators to limit the amount of disk space that users' files can occupy on a disk volume. Starting with Windows Server 2008, quotas can also be specified for folders.

- *Volume mount points*—Make it possible to associate the root of a disk volume with a folder on an NTFS volume, thereby forgoing the need for a drive letter to access the volume.

- *Shadow copies*—Enable users to keep historical versions of files so that they can revert a file to an older version or restore an accidentally deleted file.

- *File compression*—Allows users to store documents in a compressed format without needing to run a compression/decompression program to store and retrieve the documents.

- *Encrypting File System (EFS)*—Makes encrypted files inaccessible to everyone except the user who encrypted the file, including users who have been granted permission to the file. EFS protects files even if the disk is removed from the system.

NTFS permissions, disk quotas, and shadow copies are covered in Chapter 5. File compression and EFS are covered in *MCSA Guide to Administering Windows Server 2012, Exam 70-411* (Cengage Learning, 2015).

The Resilient File System   The main use of ReFS is in large file-sharing applications where volumes are managed by Storage Spaces. Although ReFS is mostly backward-compatible with NTFS, it doesn't support file compression, disk quotas, and EFS. Also, Windows can't be booted from an ReFS volume. ReFS can repair minor problems with the file system automatically and supports volume sizes up to 1 yottabyte (YB, a trillion terabytes).

ReFS works with Storage Spaces (discussed later in "Using Storage Spaces") to repair disk failure caused by corruption, whether from software or hardware problems. Unlike other fault-tolerant disk options, such as RAID 1 and RAID 5, that can only recover from failures, ReFS can also correct some types of data corruption automatically. This capability, when used with Storage Spaces, allows building highly reliable and scalable disk systems without using RAID disk controllers and the sometimes wasteful disk allocation schemes RAID configurations require.

Because of the features ReFS doesn't support, this file system isn't intended as a replacement for NTFS. ReFS is best for supporting volumes for high-availability applications that use very large files but don't require user-specific features, such as disk quotas and EFS.

Preparing a New Disk for Use

Now that you know most of the options for local disk storage in Windows Server 2012/R2, you can work through adding a disk to a working system. Depending on the system, you might be able to add a new HDD to a server while it's powered on, a process called "hot-add" or "hot-swap." Windows Server supports hot-adding a hard disk as long as the server hardware supports it. Don't attempt to add a disk to a running server unless you know the hardware supports it.

After the HDD has been physically attached to the server and the server is running, you need to use the Disk Management snap-in or File and Storage Services to make the disk accessible. By default, new disks must be initialized and brought online from their initial offline state, as explained in the following activity. After the disk is online and initialized, you can create a volume and format it. In Disk Management, you can convert the disk to dynamic or a GPT disk. Activity 4-1 walks you through configuring a new disk for use in a server.

Activity 4-1: Configuring a New Disk

Time Required: 10 minutes
Objective: Configure a new disk for use in a server.

Required Tools and Equipment: 410Server1
Description: You have just installed a new disk in your server, and you need to prepare it for use. First you bring the disk online and initialize it, and then you create a simple volume and format it. You need to install a new disk in the server before starting this activity. If you're using a virtual machine, you can install a new virtual disk with the default values for your virtualization software or one that's at least 40 GB.

Much of what's covered in this activity was done in Activity 1-5 with the Disk Management snap-in. This activity uses File and Storage Services.

The size of your disks might not match the size shown in screenshots.

1. Start 410Server1, and log on as **Administrator**.

2. In Server Manager, click **File and Storage Services**, and then click **Disks**.

3. Find the new disk you installed; you should be able to recognize it because its status will be Offline. Right-click the disk and click **Bring Online**. In the Bring Disk Online message box, click **Yes**.

4. Right-click the disk again and click **Initialize**. Click **Yes** in the Initialize Disk message box. A progress window is displayed. In the Partition column, the disk is labeled GPT because File and Storage Services creates GPT disks instead of MBR disks by default (see Figure 4-3). If you need to make it an MBR disk, use Disk Management.

5. To create a new volume, right-click the disk and click **New Volume** to start the New Volume Wizard. Read the information in the Before You Begin window, and then click **Next**. (*Note:* File and Storage Services initializes a disk only as a basic disk. If you want a dynamic disk, use Disk Management.)

6. In the Server and Disk window, make sure **410Server1** and the new disk are selected (see Figure 4-4), and then click **Next**.

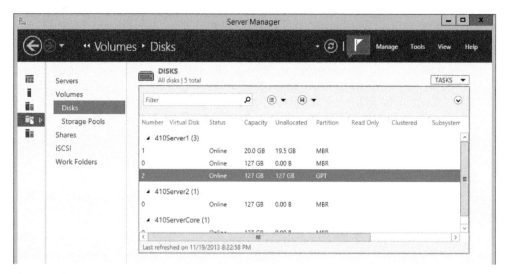

Figure 4-3   Initializing a disk in File and Storage Services

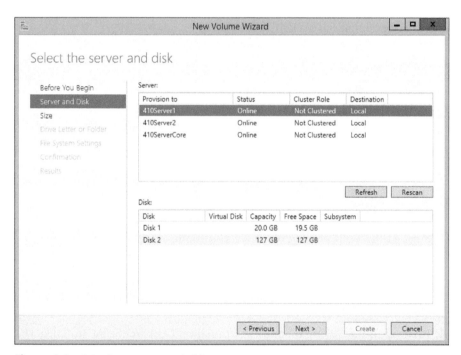

Figure 4-4   Selecting a server and disk

7. In the Size window, type **20** in the Volume size text box, and then click **Next**.

8. In the Drive Letter or Folder window, click **H** in the Drive letter list box. Notice that you can also mount the volume in an empty folder or not assign a drive letter or folder at all. Click **Next**.

9. In the File System Settings window, click the **File system** list arrow to see the options for formatting the volume. File and Storage Services lists only NTFS and ReFS as options. In Disk Management, you also have FAT32 as an option (or exFAT for volumes larger than 32 GB).

10. Type **NTFSvol** in the Volume label text box, and then click **Next**.

11. In the Confirmation window (see Figure 4-5), verify your choices, and then click **Create**. The Results window shows you the progress. Click **Close** when the process is finished.

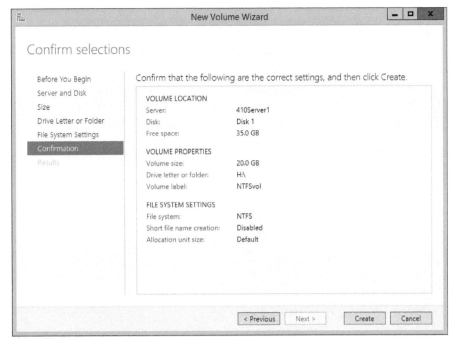

Figure 4-5   Confirming your selections

12. In Server Manager, click **Volumes** in the left pane to see the new volume.

13. If you're continuing to the next activity, stay logged on; otherwise, log off or shut down the server.

Activity 4-2: Working with Volumes in Disk Management

Time Required: 10 minutes
Objective: Work with basic and dynamic volumes.

Required Tools and Equipment: 410Server1, with three disks installed
Description: In this activity, you examine the options for working with basic and dynamic disks and FAT32 and NTFS volumes.

The size of your disks might not match the size shown in screenshots.

1. Start 410Server1, and log on as **Administrator**, if necessary.

2. Double-click the **DevDiskTask** MMC on your desktop that you saved in Chapter 1. If you don't have that MMC, open Server Manager, click **Tools, Computer Management** from the menu, and then click **Disk Management**. Notice that Disk 0 has two volumes: System Reserved and (C:). These volumes contain the system and boot partitions for Windows, so make sure you don't make any changes to Disk 0.

3. Disk 1 and the new disk you installed, Disk 2, are basic disks. Disk 1 contains the FAT32 volume you created in Chapter 1. Disk 2 contains the NTFSvol volume you just created. Right-click **FAT32VOL** to see the options you have for that volume (see Figure 4-6). The options for extending and shrinking the volume are grayed out because these actions require an NTFS or ReFS volume. Click **Delete Volume**, and click **Yes** when prompted to delete it.

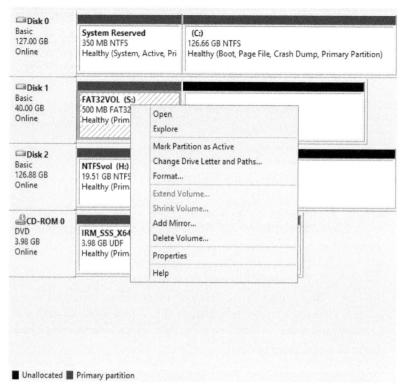

Figure 4-6   Options for FAT32 volumes

4. Right-click **NTFSvol** and notice the options for working with this volume (see Figure 4-7). Because it's a basic disk, if you choose an option not supported by a basic disk, you're prompted to convert the disk to dynamic.

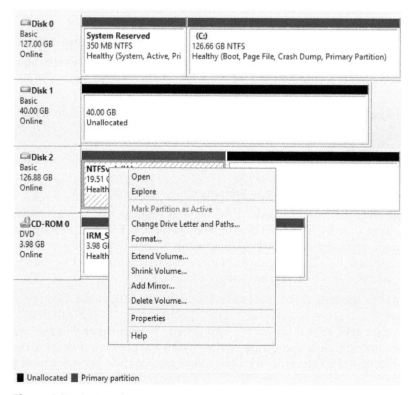

Figure 4-7   Options for NTFS volumes

5. Right-click **NTFSvol** again, if necessary, and click **Extend Volume**. In the Extend Volume Wizard welcome window, click **Next**.

6. In the Select Disks window, you can add disks to extend to, if you want. If you do so, you're prompted to convert the disk to dynamic because basic disks don't support extending to other disks (disk spanning). In the "Select the amount of space in MB" text box, type **10000**, which makes the volume 30 GB total. Click **Next**.

7. In the Completing the Extend Volume Wizard window, click **Finish**. The disk is extended to about 30 GB.

8. In Disk Management, right-click **NTFSvol** and click **Shrink Volume** to open the Shrink H: dialog box. In the "Enter the amount of space to shrink in MB" text box, type **10000** and click **Shrink**. The volume is back to 20 GB.

9. Right-click **NTFSvol** again and click **Add Mirror**. In the Add Mirror dialog box, click **Disk 1**, and then click **Add Mirror**. A Disk Management message states that the disks will be converted to dynamic disks if you continue. Click **No**. Mirrored volumes aren't supported on basic disks.

10. Right-click **Disk 2**. Notice the options you have for working with the disk (see Figure 4-8). The option for creating a RAID 5 volume is grayed out because you need at least three disks with available space for this configuration. The option to convert to MBR is grayed out because you need to delete existing volumes first. Click **Convert to Dynamic Disk**.

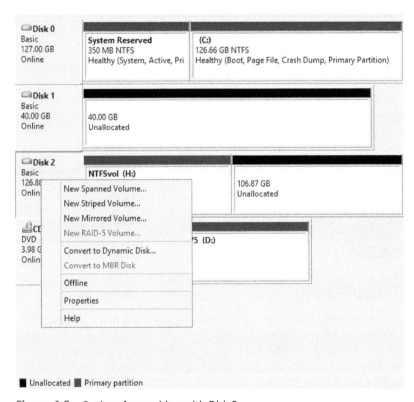

Figure 4-8 Options for working with Disk 2

11. In the Convert to Dynamic Disk dialog box, you have the option to convert more than one disk to dynamic. Leave the **Disk 2** check box selected and click **OK**. Click **Convert**, and then click **Yes**. The color of the volume label changes from blue to green to indicate it's now a simple volume rather than a primary partition.

12. Right-click **NTFSvol** and click **Add Mirror**. Click **Disk 1** and then **Add Mirror**. Click **Yes** to confirm that Disk 1 will be converted to a dynamic disk.

13. The volume label changes color to red, indicating a mirrored volume (see Figure 4-9). A status message states that resyncing (copying information from the primary disk to the mirrored disk) is taking place and shows the percentage. Disk 1 now has a volume named NTFSvol assigned the letter H. Close the MMC, and click **Yes** to save the changes.

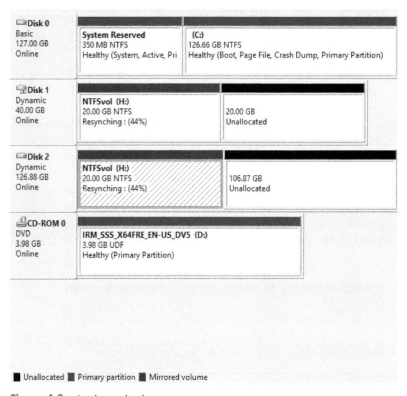

Figure 4-9   A mirrored volume

14. If you're continuing to the next activity, stay logged on; otherwise, log off or shut down the server.

 Disk 1 is an MBR disk, and Disk 2 is a GPT disk. You can use disks of different types in RAID configurations.

Working with Virtual Disks

In Windows Server 2012/R2, you can mount virtual hard disks (VHD files) and use them as though they were regular volumes. A **VHD file** is the format that virtual machines running in Hyper-V use for virtual disks. The Disk Management snap-in has options to create and mount virtual disks, but you can also mount a VHD simply by double-clicking it in File Explorer (or right-clicking it and clicking Mount).

You might want to use virtual disks instead of physical volumes to store data. Virtual disks have the advantage of being very portable. Because a virtual disk is just a file on an existing physical volume, you can copy it to any location quickly and easily for the purposes of backing up data on the virtual disk or allowing it to be used by another computer. The following activity guides you through creating and mounting a virtual disk.

 Virtual disks can have a .vhd or .vhdx extension. Windows Server 2012/R2 can mount either file type. The VHDX format, introduced in Windows Server 2012 Hyper-V, has more capacity (up to 64 TB), protection from corruption, and performance improvements over the VHD format.

Activity 4-3: Working with Virtual Disks

Time Required: 10 minutes
Objective: Create and mount a virtual disk.

4

Required Tools and Equipment: 410Server1
Description: Create and mount a virtual disk and view it in Disk Management and File Explorer.

1. Start 410Server1, and log on as **Administrator**, if necessary.
2. Open Disk Management. Click **Action, Create VHD** from the menu.
3. In the Create and Attach Virtual Hard Disk dialog box (see Figure 4-10), click **Browse**.
4. Click **NTFSvol (H:)** and type **Virtual1** in the File name text box. Click **Save**.
5. In the Virtual hard disk size text box, type **5000** to create a 5 GB virtual disk.
6. The virtual hard disk format is VHD by default. Because you're creating a small volume, you can accept this default setting. Click the **Dynamically expanding** option button so that the disk's file size is very small at first and then expands as you add data to it, up to the 5 GB you specified. Click **OK**.

Figure 4-10   Configuring a virtual hard disk

7. When you create a VHD file in Disk Management, it's mounted automatically. The disk should be listed as Disk 3, and its status is Not Initialized. Right-click **Disk 3** and notice the Detach VHD option in the menu. Click **Initialize Disk**.
8. In the Initialize Disk dialog box, click **OK**. Your new virtual disk is initialized and ready to have a volume created on it.
9. Right-click the unallocated space of Disk 3 and click **New Simple Volume**. Follow the New Simple Volume Wizard, using the following settings:

   Volume size: Use the maximum size.

   Drive letter: Assign drive letter **V:**.

   Format: Use the defaults, but make the volume label **Virtual1**.

10. When the volume has finished formatting, you can access it. The icon color of Disk 2 changes to light blue, indicating a virtual disk. Right-click the volume and click **Explore**. If you see a message box stating that you need to format the disk before you can use it, click **Cancel**.

11. File Explorer treats the virtual disk and volumes in it like any other disk and volume. In File Explorer, click the **H** drive. You should see a file named `Virtual1` with a disk icon next to it indicating a virtual disk.

12. Right-click **Virtual1 (V:)** in the left pane of File Explorer and click **Eject**. The disk is no longer shown in File Explorer or Disk Management.

13. Open File Explorer again and click the **H** drive. Notice that the virtual disk's file size is only about 41 MB. That size expands if you add data to the file. Right-click `Virtual1` and click **Mount**, or just double-click the file. The volume is mounted again. Dismount the virtual disk again, and then close all open windows.

14. If you're continuing to the next activity, stay logged on; otherwise, log off or shut down the server.

Using Storage Spaces

Storage Spaces, a new feature in Windows Server 2012, provides flexible provisioning of virtual storage. It uses the flexibility available with virtual disks to create volumes from storage pools. A **storage pool** is a collection of physical disks from which virtual disks and volumes are created and assigned dynamically. Volumes created from storage pools can be simple volumes, striped volumes, or fault-tolerant RAID volumes.

Unlike traditional physical disks and volumes created in Disk Management, Storage Spaces can allocate storage by using thin provisioning. **Thin provisioning** uses dynamically expanding disks so that you can provision a large volume, even if you have the physical storage for a volume only half the size. Later, you can add physical disks, and Storage Spaces expands into the additional storage as needed. If the disk pool becomes full, Windows takes it offline to alert you that you need to add physical storage to the pool.

Storage Spaces uses the concept of **just a bunch of disks (JBOD)**, in which two or more disks are abstracted to appear as a single disk to the OS but aren't arranged in a specific RAID configuration. JBOD gives you more flexibility because you can simply add a physical disk to a storage pool, and existing volumes can grow into the new space as needed. You can even add external disks to a pool via an external bus architecture, such as SAS or eSATA. If you use an external disk system, it should be a certified JBOD system, preferably using a SAS disk controller. You can find JBOD systems that are certified specifically for Storage Spaces.

 Using slower external bus architectures, such as USB, adversely affects your storage solution's overall performance and isn't recommended.

Storage Spaces brings storage flexibility to a Windows server for a fraction of the cost of a traditional SAN, which before Storage Spaces was the best way to achieve similar storage features and performance. Storage Spaces offers the following features that are usually found only in traditional SAN-based storage arrays:

- *Disk pooling*—A collection of physical disks viewed as a single storage space from which volumes can be provisioned for the server's use.

- *Data deduplication*—A new feature in Windows Server 2012 that finds data existing on a volume multiple times and reduces it to a single instance, thereby reducing space used on the volume. Data deduplication is a role service that can be installed and then enabled on volumes separately.

- *Flexible storage layouts*—Storage Spaces has three storage options, called **storage layouts:**

  o Simple space: A simple volume with no fault tolerance, or **resilience,** as Storage Spaces calls storage that can recover from disk failure. A simple space uses disk striping (RAID 0) if two or more physical disks are available, which provides better performance than a volume on a single disk or a spanned volume. Figure 4-11 shows a simple space using disk striping across two disks. It also shows two files, F1 and F2. F1 is spread across both disks in two parts (F1-a and F1-b). F2 is spread across both disks in four parts (F2-a, F2-b, F2-c, and F2-d).

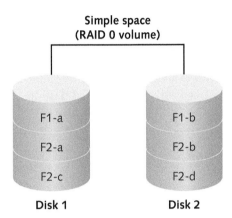

Figure 4-11   A simple space layout, using two disks

© 2015 Cengage Learning®

  o Mirror space: A two-way or three-way mirrored volume. A two-way mirror (RAID 1) requires at least two disks in the storage pool, and a three-way mirror requires three disks. This resilient storage layout maintains data if one disk (two-way mirror) fails or two disks (three-way mirror) fail. Mirror spaces are recommended for all storage applications that require resiliency. Figure 4-12 shows a mirror space with two disks, as in Figure 4-11. However, all parts of both files, F1 and F2, are on both Disk 1 and Disk 2, so if one disk fails, the other disk has a complete copy of all the data.

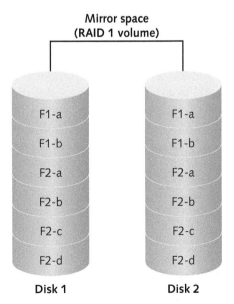

Figure 4-12   A mirror space layout, using two disks

© 2015 Cengage Learning®

    o Parity space: Similar to a RAID 5 volume, a parity space can be configured for single parity or dual parity. At least three disks are required for a single parity space, and four are required for a dual parity space. A dual parity space (new in Windows Server 2012 R2) can recover from simultaneous failure of two disks. Parity spaces are recommended for archival storage, not standard storage workloads, because calculating parity data decreases performance somewhat. Figure 4-13 shows a parity space with three disks. The same two files are represented in this figure, with the files striped across two disks and parity information written to the third disk. The parity information is spread across all three disks. If any disk fails, the parity information on the remaining disks is used to reconstruct missing data from the failed disk.

- *Storage tiering*—A new feature in Windows Server 2012 R2 that combines the speed of SSDs with the low cost and high capacity of HDDs. You can add SSDs to a storage pool with HDDs, and Windows keeps the most frequently accessed data on the faster SSD disks and moves less frequently accessed data to HDDs. This scheme improves performance substantially without the expense of moving all storage to costly SSDs.

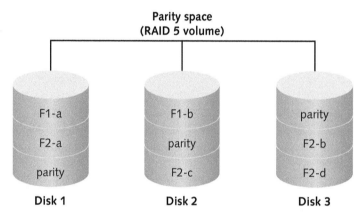

Figure 4-13   A parity space layout, using three disks
© 2015 Cengage Learning®

Creating Storage Spaces

Storage Spaces is configured with File and Storage Services in Server Manager or PowerShell cmdlets (more than 70 for working with Storage Spaces). There are three components of a storage space:

- *Storage pool*—Consists of one or more physical disks with unallocated space. Physical disks available for adding to a storage pool are listed as part of the **primordial pool**. If a disk already has a volume on it, it's still part of the primordial pool, but only the unallocated space is used for a storage pool. A disk added to a storage pool is no longer shown in Disk Management unless it contains a traditional volume. You need two or more physical disks in a pool if you want to create a resilient storage space. Figure 4-14 shows the primordial pool before any storage pools have been created. Available disks are shown in the Physical Disks pane.

A disk that has been converted to dynamic isn't listed in the primordial pool and can't be a member of a storage pool.

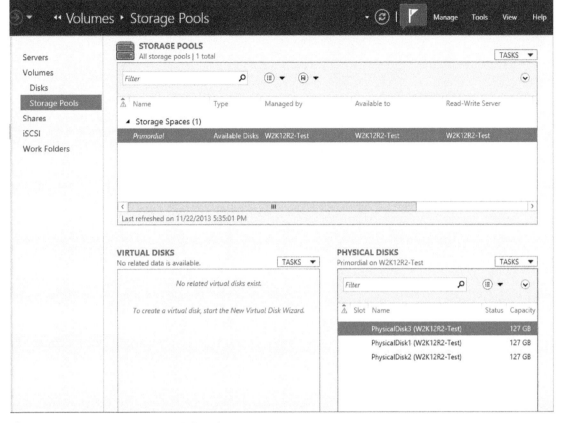

Figure 4-14 Viewing the primordial pool

- *Virtual disks*—You create virtual disks from storage pools and choose the storage layout: simple, mirror, or parity. If you choose a storage layout your pool can't support (for example, choosing a parity layout when you have only two disks in the pool), Storage Spaces prompts you to choose another one. Next, you select the provisioning type: thin provisioning (described previously) or **fixed provisioning,** which allocates all space for the virtual disk from the storage pool immediately. Then you specify the disk size. After a virtual disk is created, it's available in Disk Management like any other disk, and you can perform the usual operations on it. Storage Spaces creates the virtual disk as a GPT disk. Figure 4-15 shows a new storage pool with two member disks and a virtual disk that's been created.

You might hear the term "LUN" associated with virtual disks in Storage Spaces. As defined earlier, an LUN is a logical reference to a unit of storage that could be composed of part of a physical disk or an entire array of disks, which is exactly what a virtual disk is.

- *Volumes*—After you create a virtual disk, you create volumes. Every volume you create on the disk uses the virtual disk's storage layout and provisioning type. So if you create two volumes on a mirror space, both are mirrored volumes. You create a volume on a virtual disk in much the same way as on a traditional disk. You can use File and Storage Services or Disk Management. After a volume is formatted, it's ready to use like any other volume you create. The new volume is available in File Explorer, File and Storage Services, and Disk Management.

Figure 4-16 is a logical view of how these components work. You start with one or more disks that are part of the primordial pool. Next, you create storage pools from one or more of the disks in the primordial pool. In the figure, Pool1 is composed of two disks, and Pool2 is

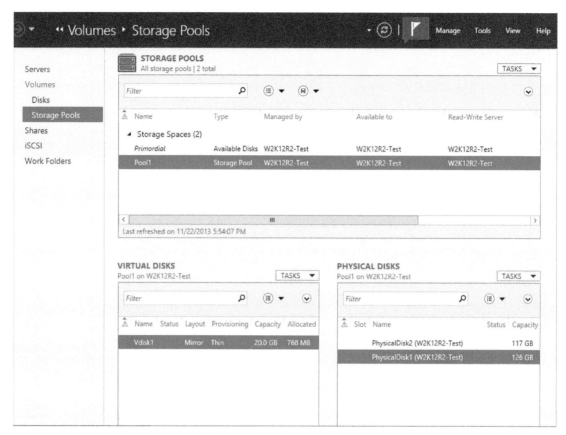

Figure 4-15 A new storage pool and virtual disk

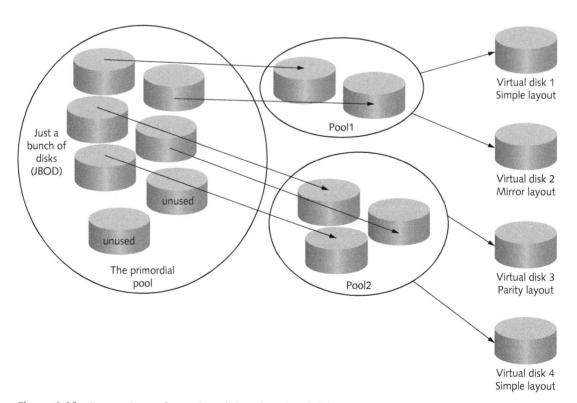

Figure 4-16 Storage Spaces from primordial pool to virtual disk

© 2015 Cengage Learning®

made up of three disks. After a disk is assigned to a pool, it's no longer part of the primordial pool. Two disks labeled "unused" remain part of the primordial pool after Pool1 and Pool2 are created. Two types of virtual disk layouts can be created from Pool1—simple and mirror—because you need at least two disks to create a mirror layout, and a simple layout can be created from any number of disks. You can create any of the three virtual disk layouts from Pool2 because a parity layout requires at least three disks. It's important to understand that you can create more than one virtual disk of any type supported from a pool until you run out of physical disk space in the pool. If you do, you can add disks from the primordial pool to make the pool larger.

From the virtual disks, you create volumes (not shown in Figure 4-16). The volumes you create match the virtual disk's layout, meaning any volume you create from a virtual disk with a mirror layout is a mirrored volume. You can create multiple volumes from a single virtual disk, as with regular physical disks.

Activity 4-4: Creating a Storage Space

Time Required: 20 minutes
Objective: Create a storage pool, virtual disk, and volume with Storage Spaces.

Required Tools and Equipment: 410Server1, with three disks installed
Description: First, you delete the mirror volume you created in Activity 4-3 because a dynamic disk can't be used in a storage pool. Then you create a storage pool, virtual disk, and volume with Storage Spaces. You also see how Disk Management displays physical disks that have been added to a storage pool.

1. Start 410Server1, and log on as **Administrator**, if necessary. Open Disk Management.

2. Right-click **NTFSvol** (the one created in Activity 4-3) and click **Delete Volume**. In the Delete mirrored volume message box, click **Yes**. If you see a Disk Management warning message about forcing a deletion of the volume, click **Yes**.

3. Close or minimize Disk Management.

4. In Server Manager, click **File and Storage Services**, and then click **Storage Pools**. Click the **Refresh** icon so that the disks are inventoried and displayed correctly. After the screen refreshes (which might take a minute or so), you see the primordial pool and three disks in the Physical Disks pane, similar to Figure 4-14, shown previously.

5. Right-click the **Primordial** pool and click **New Storage Pool**. In the Before You Begin window of the New Storage Pool Wizard, read the information and click **Next**.

6. In the Storage Pool Name window (see Figure 4-17), type **Pool1** in the Name text box, and then click **Next**.

7. In the Physical Disks window, click the **PhysicalDisk1** and **PhysicalDisk2** check boxes (see Figure 4-18). At the bottom of the window is the total capacity of the selected disks. Click **Next**.

8. In the Confirmation window, click **Create**. After the new pool is created, click **Close**. In the Storage Pools window, click **Pool1**. You see the members of the pool in the Physical Disks pane. You no longer see the primordial pool because you don't have more disks available to add to a pool.

9. Open or maximize Disk Management, and notice that Disk 1 and Disk 2 are no longer shown because they're part of a storage pool. Close or minimize Disk Management. If you're using the MMC you created earlier, click **Yes** to save the changes.

10. In Server Manager, right-click **Pool1** and click **New Virtual Disk**. Read the information in the Before You Begin window, and then click **Next**.

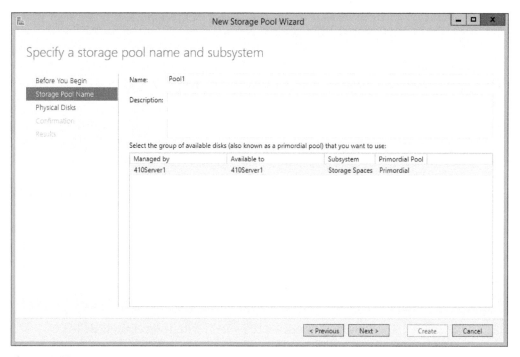

Figure 4-17   Naming a storage pool

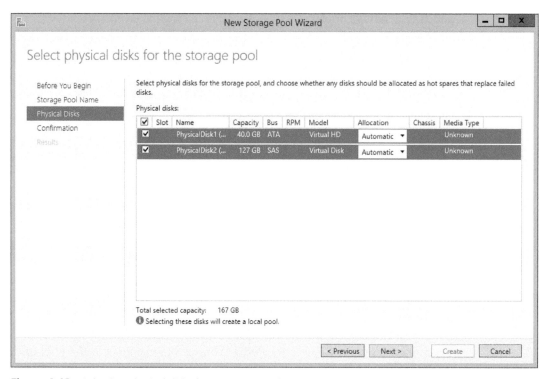

Figure 4-18   Selecting physical disks for a storage pool

11. The Storage Pool window lists only one pool, so click **Next**. In the Virtual Disk Name window, type **Vdisk1** in the Name text box. The check box for creating storage tiers is grayed out because an SSD isn't part of the pool. Click **Next**.

12. In the Storage Layout window, click **Parity** in the Layout list box, and then click **Next**. Read the error message (see Figure 4-19), which tells you that a parity layout isn't allowed because you have only two disks in the pool. Click **Mirror** in the Layout list box, and then click **Next**.

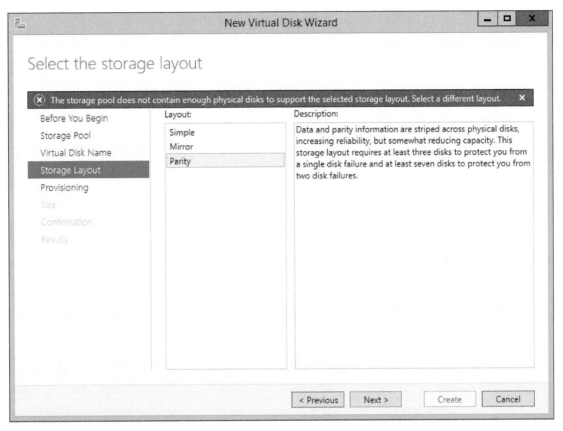

Figure 4-19   Selecting a storage layout

13. In the Provisioning window, click the **Thin** option button (see Figure 4-20), and then click **Next**.

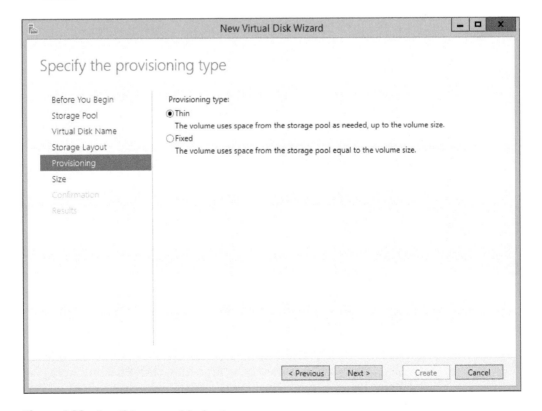

Figure 4-20   Specifying a provisioning type

14. In the Size window, type **10** to create a 10 GB virtual disk (changing the size units to GB, if necessary), and then click **Next**.

15. In the Confirmation window, verify your choices, and then click **Create**. Creating the virtual disk might take a few minutes. Click to clear the **Create a volume when this wizard closes** check box. Click **Close**. The new virtual disk is listed in the Virtual Disks pane (see Figure 4-21).

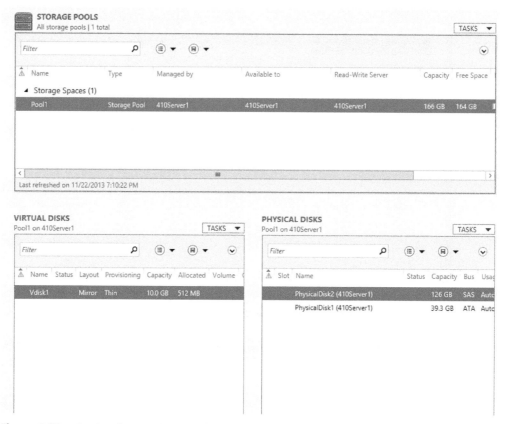

Figure 4-21   Viewing the new virtual disk

16. Open or maximize Disk Management to see that the new virtual disk is available. Close Disk Management. At this point, you don't need to create a new volume, but to do so, you follow the same procedure as in Activity 4-1 or 4-2, depending on whether you use File and Storage Services or Disk Management.

17. If you're continuing to the next activity, stay logged on; otherwise, log off or shut down the server.

Activity 4-5: Cleaning Up Storage Spaces

Time Required: 20 minutes
Objective: Delete the virtual disk and storage pool created in Activity 4-4.

Required Tools and Equipment: 410Server1
Description: You want to clean up the disk volumes from the preceding activities. You delete Vol1 and then the virtual disk you created in Activity 4-4.

1. Start 410Server1, and log on as **Administrator**, if necessary.

2. Open Server Manager, if necessary. If necessary, click **File and Storage Services**, and then click **Storage Pools**. In the Virtual Disks section, right-click **Vdisk1** and click **Delete Virtual Disk**. When prompted to continue, click **Yes**.

3. In the Storage Pools section, right-click **Pool1** and click **Delete Storage Pool**. When prompted to delete the pool, click **OK**. The disks are returned to the primordial pool.

4. If you're continuing to the next activity in the next chapter, stay logged on; otherwise, log off or shut down the server.

Using PowerShell to Manage Storage Spaces
As mentioned, many PowerShell cmdlets are available to work with Storage Spaces. Table 4-2 lists the most common ones. To get more information about these cmdlets, remember that you can type `Get-Help` at a PowerShell prompt followed by the command name.

Table 4-2   PowerShell cmdlets for working with Storage Spaces

PowerShell cmdlet	Function
New-StoragePool	Create a storage pool
New-VirtualDisk	Create a virtual disk from a storage pool
InitializeDisk	Initialize a new virtual disk
New-Partition	Create a volume
Format-Volume	Format a volume

© 2015 Cengage Learning®

Chapter Summary

- Storage is any digital media that data can be written to and later retrieved from. Long-term storage includes USB drives, SD cards, CDs/DVDs, magnetic tape, SSDs, and HDDs.

- All computers require at least some storage, but servers usually require more than client computers. Server storage is needed for OS files, page files, log files, virtual machines, database files, and user documents, among others.

- The main methods of storage access are local, DAS, NAS, and SAN. Local and DAS are similar, but DAS can also be a separate unit attached through an external interface. NAS is a stand-alone storage device with a network interface. A SAN is the most complex storage device, using high-speed networking technologies to provide shared storage.

- Configuration of local disks can be divided into two broad categories: physical disk properties and logical properties. Physical properties include disk capacity, rotation speed, and the disk interface technology. SATA and SAS are the most common disk interfaces on servers.

- Disk types include basic disks and dynamic disks. Partitioning types include MBR and GPT. Volume types are simple, spanned, striped, mirrored, and RAID 5. File systems include FAT, NTFS, and ReFS.

- Windows Server 2012/R2 can mount virtual disks and use them like regular volumes. Virtual disks are stored as files with a `.vhd` or `.vhdx` extension.

- Storage Spaces, a new feature in Windows Server 2012/R2, provides flexible provisioning of virtualized storage by using storage pools. A storage pool is a collection of physical disks from which virtual disks and volumes are created and assigned dynamically.

- Storage Spaces uses the concept of just a bunch of disks (JBOD), in which two or more disks are abstracted to appear as a single disk to the OS but aren't arranged in a specific RAID configuration.

- There are three components of a storage space: storage pools, virtual disks, and volumes.

Key Terms

backplane   A connection system that uses a printed circuit board instead of traditional cables to carry signals.

basic disk   A traditional Windows or DOS disk arrangement, in which the disk is partitioned into primary and extended partitions. A basic disk can't hold volumes spanning multiple disks or be part of a RAID.

boot volume   The volume where the \Windows folder is located; usually the C drive but doesn't have to be. Also referred to as the "boot partition."

direct-attached storage (DAS)   A storage medium directly connected to the server using it but differs from local storage in that it includes externally connected HDDs in an enclosure with a power supply.

disk drive   A physical component with a disk interface connector (such as SATA or SCSI) and a power connector.

dynamic disk   A disk arrangement that can hold up to 128 volumes, including spanned volumes, striped volumes, and RAID volumes.

extended partition   A division of disk space on a basic disk that must be divided into logical drives; can't be marked active and can't hold the Windows system volume.

file system   The method and format an OS uses to store, locate, and retrieve files from electronic storage media.

fixed provisioning   A method of creating virtual disks that allocates all space for the virtual disk from the storage pool immediately.

formatting   The process of preparing a disk with a file system used to organize and store files.

GUID Partitioning Table (GPT)   A disk-partitioning method that supports volume sizes up to 18 exabytes.

just a bunch of disks (JBOD)   A disk arrangement in which two or more disks are abstracted to appear as a single disk to the OS but aren't arranged in a specific RAID configuration.

local storage   Storage media with a direct and exclusive connection to the computer's system board through a disk controller.

logical unit number (LUN)   A logical reference point to a unit of storage that could refer to an entire array of disks, a single disk, or just part of a disk.

Master Boot Record (MBR)   A disk-partitioning method that supports volume sizes up to 2 TB.

mirrored volume   A volume that uses space from two dynamic disks and provides fault tolerance. Data written to one disk is duplicated, or mirrored, to the second disk. If one disk fails, the other disk has a good copy of the data, and the system can continue to operate until the failed disk is replaced. Also called a "RAID 1 volume."

network-attached storage (NAS)   A storage device that has an enclosure, a power supply, slots for multiple HDDs, a network interface, and a built-in OS tailored for managing shared files and folders.

page file   A system file in Windows used as virtual memory and to store dump data after a system crash.

partition   A logical unit of storage that can be formatted with a file system; similar to a volume but used with basic disks.

primary partition   A division of disk space on a basic disk used to create a volume. It can be assigned a drive letter, be marked active, and contain the Windows system volume.

primordial pool   A collection of physical disks available to be added to a storage pool.

RAID 5 volume   A volume that uses space from three or more dynamic disks and uses disk striping with parity to provide fault tolerance. When data is written, it's striped across all but one of the disks in the volume. Parity information derived from the data is written to the remaining disk and used to re-create lost data after a disk failure.

redundant array of independent disks (RAID)   A disk configuration that uses space on multiple disks to form a single logical volume. Most RAID configurations provide fault tolerance, and some enhance performance.

resilience   Another term for fault tolerance; indicates a disk arrangement's capability to maintain data if a disk fails.

Serial ATA (SATA)   A common disk interface technology that's inexpensive, fast, and fairly reliable with transfer speeds up to 6 Gb/s; used in both client computers and low-end servers and replaces the older parallel ATA (PATA) technology.

serial attached SCSI (SAS)   A newer serial form of SCSI with transfer rates up to 6 Gb/s and higher; the disk technology of choice for servers and high-end workstations. *See also* small computer system interface (SCSI).

simple volume   A volume that resides on a single disk, basic or dynamic.

small computer system interface (SCSI)   An older parallel bus disk technology still used on some servers but has reached its performance limits at 640 MB/s transfer rates.

solid state drive (SSD)   A type of storage medium that uses flash memory, has no moving parts, and requires less power than a traditional HDD. Also faster and more shock resistant than a traditional HDD but costs more per gigabyte and doesn't have as much capacity as an HDD.

spanned volume   A volume that extends across two or more physical disks, such as a simple volume that has been extended to a second disk.

storage appliance   *See* network-attached storage (NAS).

storage area network (SAN)   A storage device that uses high-speed networking technologies to give servers fast access to large amounts of shared disk storage. The storage a SAN manages appears to the server OS as though it's physically attached to the server.

storage layout   The method used to create a virtual disk with Storage Spaces; includes simple, mirror, and parity. *See also* Storage Spaces.

storage pool   A collection of physical disks from which virtual disks and volumes are created and assigned dynamically.

Storage Spaces   A new feature in Windows Server 2012/R2 that provides flexible provisioning of virtualized storage.

striped volume   A volume that extends across two or more dynamic disks, but data is written to all disks in the volume equally; provides no fault tolerance but does have a performance advantage over simple or spanned volumes.

system volume   A volume containing the files a computer needs to find and load the Windows OS. *See also* volume.

thin provisioning   A method for creating virtual disks, whereby the virtual disk expands dynamically and uses space from the storage pool as needed until it reaches the specified maximum size.

VHD file   The format virtual machines running in Hyper-V use for their virtual disks. VHD files can also be created and mounted with Disk Management and used like physical disks.

volume   A logical unit of storage that can be formatted with a file system.

Review Questions

1. Which of the following is an example of long-term storage? (Choose all that apply.)

   a. Magnetic tape

   b. CPU cache

   c. SSD

   d. RAM

2. Which of the following is true about an SSD?

   a. Uses magnetic platters

   b. Has no moving parts

   c. Uses a proprietary interface

   d. Uses EPROM

3. Which of the following is an example of what a server uses storage for? (Choose all that apply.)

   a. Page file

   b. Virtual machines

   c. Working memory

   d. Documents

4. Which of the following is true about a page file?

   a. It should be stored on a separate disk from the Windows folder.

   b. It's usually stored in fast random access memory.

   c. Windows stores frequently accessed drivers in it.

   d. The page file is usually smaller than 50 MB.

5. Local storage is rarely direct-attached storage. True or False?

6. You want shared network storage that's easy to set up and geared toward file sharing with several file-sharing protocols, but you don't want the device to be dedicated to file sharing. What should you consider buying?

   a. SAN

   b. DAS

   c. NAS

   d. LAS

7. What type of interface are you likely to find on a DAS device for connecting the device to the server that uses it?

   a. SATA

   b. IDE

   c. PATA

   d. eSATA

8. You have four servers that need access to shared storage because you're configuring them in a cluster. Which storage solution should you consider for this application?

   a. NAS

   b. SAN

   c. SCSI

   d. DAS

9. Which of the following is defined as a physical component with a disk interface connector?

   a. Format

   b. Partition

   c. Volume

   d. Disk drive

10. You have installed a new disk and created a volume on it. What should you do before you can store files on it?

    a. Format it.

    b. Partition it.

    c. Initialize it.

    d. Erase it.

11. You're planning to install a new database application that uses an enormous amount of disk space. You need this application to be highly available, so you need a disk system with the capability to auto-correct from disk errors and data corruption. Which of the following is the best option?

    a. MBR disk with `chkdsk`

    b. NTFS format with EFS

    c. ReFS format and Storage Spaces

    d. GPT disk with shadow copies

12. Which of the following is the correct sequence of steps for creating a volume with Storage Spaces?

    a. Disk pool, volume, virtual disk

    b. Primordial pool, virtual disk, volume

    c. Virtual disk, disk pool, volume

    d. Disk pool, virtual disk, volume

13. Which disk interface technology transfers data over a parallel bus?

    a. SATA

    b. USB

    c. SAS

    d. SCSI

14. What's created automatically when you install Windows Server 2012 R2 on a system with a disk drive that has never had an OS installed on it before?

    a. System volume

    b. Dynamic disk

    c. GPT

    d. Extended partition

15. What type of volumes or partitions can be created on a basic disk? (Choose all that apply.)

    a. Spanned volume

    b. Striped partition

    c. Extended partition

    d. Simple volume

16. Which of the following is true about GPT disks?

    a. They support a maximum volume size of 2 TB.

    b. GPT is the default when initializing a disk in Disk Management.

    c. They use CRC protection for the partition table.

    d. You can't convert a GPT disk to MBR.

17. You have a server with Windows Server 2012 R2 installed on Disk 0, a basic disk. You're using the server to store users' documents. You have two more disks that you can install in the server. What should you do if you want to provide fault tolerance for users' documents?

    a. Convert Disk 0 to dynamic. Create a striped volume using Disk 0, Disk 1, and Disk 2.

    b. Create a RAID 1 volume from Disk 1 and Disk 2.

    c. Convert the new disks to GPT. Create a spanned volume using Disk 1 and Disk 2.

    d. Create a RAID 5 volume from Disk 0, Disk 1, and Disk 2.

18. You need a disk system that provides the best performance for a new application that frequently reads and writes data to the disk. You aren't concerned about disk fault tolerance because the data will be backed up each day; performance is the main concern. What type of volume arrangement should you use?

    a. Spanned volume

    b. RAID 1 volume

    c. RAID 0 volume

    d. RAID 5 volume

19. You need to protect sensitive files from unauthorized users even if the disk is stolen. What feature should you use and on what file system?

    a. EFS, NTFS

    b. Disk compression, ReFS

    c. Quotas, NTFS

    d. Shadow copies, ReFS

20. You come across a file with a .vhd extension on your server's hard disk. What should you do to see this file's contents?

    a. Right-click the file and click Open.

    b. Open the file in Notepad.

    c. Burn the file to a DVD.

    d. Mount the file.

21. You see something named "primordial" in File and Storage Services. What can you do with it?

    a. Create a storage pool.

    b. Create a virtual disk.

    c. Format it.

    d. Create a new volume.

22. What type of storage layout does Storage Spaces support? (Choose all that apply.)

    a. Simple space

    b. Mirror space

    c. Parity space

    d. Striped space

23. Which of the following is a new feature in Windows Server 2012 R2 that combines the speed of SSDs with the low cost and capacity of HDDs?

    a. JBOD

    b. Thin provisioning

    c. Storage tiering

    d. Resilient spaces

24. Which feature in Storage Spaces finds data on a volume that exists multiple times and reduces it to a single instance?

    a. Disk quotas

    b. Storage tiering

    c. Fixed provisioning

    d. Data deduplication

25. Which of the following uses dynamically expanding storage?

    a. Thin provisioning

    b. Primordial pools

    c. Parity volumes

    d. Resilient File System

Case Projects

CASE PROJECTS

Case Project 4-1: Dealing with a Disk Crash

Last week, a disk containing CSM Tech Publishing's current project manuscripts crashed. Fortunately, there was a backup, but all files that had been added or changed that day were lost. A new disk had to be purchased for overnight delivery, and the data had to be restored. Several days of work time were lost. The owner of CSM Tech wants to know what can be done to prevent the loss of data and time if a disk crashes in the future. The server currently has two disks installed: one for the Windows boot and system volumes and one for manuscript files. The disk used for manuscript files is about one-third full. There's enough money in the budget to purchase up to two new drives if needed. What solution do you recommend, and why?

Case Project 4-2: Creating Flexible Storage

It's been six months since the disk crash at CSM Tech Publishing, and the owner is breathing a little easier because you installed a fault-tolerant solution to prevent loss of time and data if a disk crashes in the future. Business is good, and the current solution is starting to get low on disk space. In addition, he has some other needs that might require more disk space, and he wants to keep the data on separate volumes (what he understands as just drives). He wants a flexible solution in which drives and volumes aren't restricted in their configuration. He also wants to be able to add storage space to existing volumes easily without having to reconfigure existing drives. He has the budget to add a disk storage system that can contain up to 10 HDDs. Which Windows feature can accommodate these needs, and how does it work?

chapter 5

File and Printer Services

After reading this chapter and completing the exercises, you will be able to:

- Describe how Windows implements file and printer sharing
- Secure access to files with permissions
- Create file shares
- Describe Work Folders
- Configure and manage Windows printing

In the early days of computing, sharing files and printers was one of the main reasons to install a network and a primary task for servers. Sharing resources remains an essential function of servers, and developers of OSs dedicate a lot of effort to ensuring an efficient file- and printer-sharing environment with a wealth of features. This chapter discusses file- and printer-sharing protocols, file- and printer-sharing permissions, and ways to create and manage shared folders and printers.

An Overview of File and Printer Sharing

Table 5-1 describes what you need for the hands-on activities in this chapter.

Table 5-1   Activity requirements

Activity	Requirements	Notes
Activity 5-1 through Activity 5-13	410Server1	
Activity 5-14: Installing and Sharing a Printer	410Server1, network-attached printer	
Activity 5-15: Connecting to a Shared Printer	410Server1, 410Win8	

© 2015 Cengage Learning®

File- and printer-sharing functions in Windows Server 2012/R2 are in the File and Storage Services role and its many role services and related features. As you've seen, the File and Storage Services role is installed in Windows Server 2012/R2 by default, but the only role service installed is Storage Services, which can't be removed. If you create a shared folder on your computer, the File Server role service (under File and Storage Services) is installed automatically.

Windows clients access shared files and printers on a Windows server by using **Server Message Block (SMB)**, a client/server Application-layer protocol that provides network file sharing, network printing, and authentication. A common variation of SMB is Common Internet File System (CIFS), which is called a "dialect" of SMB. Windows Server 2012/R2 and Windows 8/8.1 introduced SMB 3.0, which has a number of new features you can read about at *http://support.microsoft.com/kb/2709568*.

Although SMB is the native file-sharing protocol for Windows clients and servers, Windows Server 2012/R2 also supports **Network File System (NFS)**, the native file-sharing protocol in UNIX and Linux OSs. Server for NFS is a role service found under File and Storage Services that you can install if you need to support clients using the NFS protocol.

Linux supports SMB in a variation of the protocol Linux calls Samba.

The capability to share printers on the network was one of the main reasons networks flourished during the 1980s and 1990s. Printers were expensive, and users were creating electronic documents with word processors, desktop publishers, and spreadsheets that needed to be printed. Networking computers together made it possible for everyone in the company to use a $3000 laser printer without having to carry documents on a floppy disk to the lone computer the printer was attached to. Basic printers now cost less, but color laser printers with a host of features are still too expensive to put on every employee's desk. In addition, by networking printers, administrators have a way to monitor and control use and know when a printer is low on toner or paper. Windows Server 2012/R2 offers advanced features for managing shared printers and making printing easy and convenient for users.

Windows shares printers by using the SMB protocol but also supports other printer-sharing protocols, such as Line Printer Remote/Line Printer Daemon (LPR/LPD), the native printer-sharing protocol on Linux/UNIX computers, and Internet Printing Protocol (IPP), which uses HTTP to send print jobs over the Internet. Windows Server 2012/R2 has print server features that enable you to manage any number of different printers that use different connectivity methods, whether directly attached or network attached. The details of sharing printers and configuring print servers are covered later in "Windows Printing."

Securing Access to Files with Permissions

Sharing files on a Windows server is a fairly straightforward process, but configuring permissions to secure shared files so that only authorized users can access them is a little more complex. There are two modes for accessing files on a networked computer: network (sometimes called remote) and interactive (sometimes called "local"). Similarly, there are two ways to secure files: share permissions and NTFS permissions. Share permissions are applied when a user attempts network access to shared files. NTFS permissions always apply, whether file access is attempted interactively or remotely, through a share. That last statement might sound confusing, so take a closer look at how permissions work.

As discussed in Chapter 1, **permissions** specify which users can access a file system object (a file or folder) and what users can do with the object if they're granted access. Each file system object has permissions associated with it, and each permission can be set to Allow or Deny. Permissions can be viewed as a gatekeeper to control who has access to folders and files. When you log on to a computer or domain, you're issued a ticket containing information such as your username and group memberships. If you attempt to access a file or folder, the gatekeeper examines your ticket and compares your username and group memberships to the file or folder's access list. If neither your username nor your groups are on the list, you're denied access. If you or your groups *are* on the list, you're issued an access ticket that combines all your allowed permissions. You can then access the resource as specified by your access ticket.

At least, that's how the process works when you're attempting interactive access to files. If you're attempting network access, there are two gatekeepers: one that checks your ticket against the share permissions access list and, if you're granted access by share permissions, another that checks your ticket against the NTFS permissions access list. The NTFS gatekeeper is required to examine your ticket only if you get past the share gatekeeper. If you're granted access by share permissions, you're issued an access ticket. Then if you're granted access by NTFS permissions, you're allowed to keep the access ticket that gives you the least permission between the two.

For example, Mike is granted Read access by share permissions and Read and Write access by NTFS permissions. Mike gets to keep only the Read access ticket because it's the lesser of the two permissions. Another example: Neither Mike nor any of his groups are on the share permissions access list. There's no need to even examine NTFS permissions because Mike is denied access at the share permissions gate. As a final example, Mike is granted Full Control access by share permissions and Modify access by NTFS permissions. Mike's access ticket gives him Modify permission because it allows less access than Full Control.

The general security rule for assigning permissions to resources is to give users the least access necessary for their job. This rule is often referred to as the "least privileges principle." Unfortunately, this axiom can be at odds with another general rule: Keep it simple. Sometimes determining the least amount of access a user requires can lead to complex permission schemes. The more complex a permission scheme is, the more likely it will need troubleshooting, and the more troubleshooting that's needed, the more likely an administrator will assign overly permissive permissions out of frustration.

 Because FAT volumes don't have permissions, everybody who logs on locally to a computer with a FAT volume has full access to all files on that volume. If a folder is shared on a FAT volume, network users' access is determined solely by share permissions. The ReFS file system supports the same permissions as NTFS and works the same way.

Security Principals

Three types of objects, called **security principals**, can be assigned permission to access the file system: users, groups, and computers. A file system object's security settings have three components that make up its **security descriptor:**

- *Discretionary access control list*—A list of security principals with permissions defining access to an object is called a **discretionary access control list (DACL)**. Each entry in the DACL is an **access control entry (ACE)**. A security principal or group not included in the DACL has no access to the object.

- *Object owner*—Usually the user account creating the object or a group or user who has been assigned ownership of the object is the **object owner**, which has special authority over the object. Most notably, even if the owner isn't in the object's DACL, the owner can still assign permissions to the object.

- *System access control list*—A **system access control list (SACL)** defines the settings for auditing access to an object.

How Permissions Are Assigned
Users can be assigned permission to an object in four different ways:

- The user creates the object. In this case, the user account is granted Full control permission to the object and all descendant objects and is assigned as owner of the object.

- The user's account is added to the object's DACL. This method is called **explicit permission**.

- A group the user belongs to is added to the object's DACL. This method is also considered explicit permission.

- Permission is inherited from the DACL of a parent object the user or group account has been added to. This is **inherited permission**.

When a user has been assigned permission to an object through a combination of methods, the user's **effective permissions** are a combination of the assigned permissions. For example, if Joe Tech1's account has been added to an object's DACL and assigned the Allow Read permission, and a group that Joe Tech1 belongs to has been added to the same object's DACL and assigned the Allow Write permission, Joe Tech1 has both Read and Write permissions to the object. A user's effective permissions determine the users effective access to an object.

Share Permissions

Share permissions apply to folders and files accessed across the network. Before a file can be accessed across the network, it must reside in a shared folder or a subfolder of a shared folder. Share permissions are configured on a shared folder and apply to all files and subfolders of the shared folder. These permissions can't be configured on files; NTFS permissions are used for that purpose. There are three share permissions levels (see Figure 5-1):

- *Read*—Users can view contents of files, copy files, run applications and script files, open folders and subfolders, and view file attributes.

- *Change*—All permissions granted by Read, plus create files and folders, change contents and attributes of files and folders, and delete files and folders.

- *Full Control*—All permissions granted by Change, plus change file and folder permissions as well as take ownership of files and folders. (File and folder permissions and ownership are available only on NTFS volumes.)

Windows assigns default permissions depending on how a folder is shared. (Several methods for sharing files are discussed later in "Windows File Sharing.") Generally, the default share permission is Read for the Everyone special identity. On FAT volumes, share permissions are the only way to secure files accessed through the network. NTFS permissions protect file accesses via the network and those done interactively.

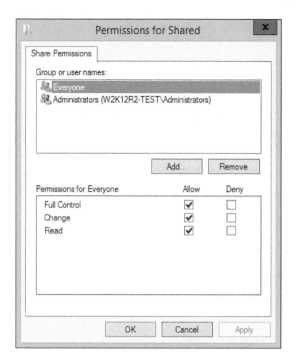

Figure 5-1   Share permission levels

Users, groups, and special identity groups are discussed in detail in Chapter 7.

NTFS Permissions

NTFS permissions give both network users and interactive users fine-grained access control over folders and files. Unlike share permissions, which can be configured only on a shared folder, NTFS permissions can be configured on folders and files. By default, when permissions are configured on a folder, subfolders and files in that folder inherit the permissions. However, inherited permissions can be changed when needed, making it possible to have different permission settings on files in a folder.

Permission inheritance defines how permissions are transmitted from a parent object to a child object. In a file system, parent objects can be a volume or folder, and child objects can be folders and files. For example, a folder can be the parent object, and any files and folders it contains, including other folders, are considered child objects. All objects in a volume are child objects of the volume. So if a user is assigned the Modify permission to a folder, all subfolders and files in the folder inherit the permission, and the user has Modify permission to these objects as well. Permission inheritance and how to change it are discussed later in "NTFS Permission Inheritance."

To view or edit permissions on an NTFS folder or file, you use the Security tab of the object's Properties dialog box. Unlike share permissions, which have only three permission levels, NTFS folders have six standard permissions, and NTFS files have five. Folders also have 14 special permissions, and files have 13. Special permissions aren't completely separate from standard permissions, however. Each standard permission is really a grouping of special permissions, as you see later.

NTFS standard permissions for folders and files are as follows (see Figure 5-2):

Figure 5-2   NTFS standard permissions

- *Read*—Users can view file contents, copy files, open folders and subfolders, and view file attributes and permissions. However, unlike the Read permission in share permissions, this permission doesn't allow users to run applications or scripts.

- *Read & execute*—Grants the same permissions as Read and includes the ability to run applications or scripts. When this permission is selected, List folder contents and Read are selected, too.

- *List folder contents*—This permission applies only to folders and grants the same permission as Read & execute. However, because it doesn't apply to files, Read & execute must also be set on the folder to allow users to open files in the folder.

- *Write*—Users can create and modify files and read file attributes and permissions. However, this permission doesn't allow users to read or delete files. In most cases, the Read or Read & execute permission should be given with the Write permission.

- *Modify*—Users can read, modify, delete, and create files. Users can't change permissions or take ownership. Selecting this permission automatically selects Read & execute, List folder contents, Read, and Write.

- *Full control*—Users can perform all actions given by the Modify permission with the addition of changing permissions and taking ownership. This permission is very powerful because it gives users complete control over who can access a file or folder as well as take ownership (discussed later in "File and Folder Ownership"). Full control should be assigned to non-administrator users only sparingly. In most cases, the Modify permission gives users enough capabilities to interact with the file system.

Standard permissions should work for most situations. Configuring special permissions should be reserved for, well, special circumstances. The temptation to configure special permissions to follow the least privileges principle can lead to breaking the "keep it simple" rule and result in administrators' and users' frustration. However, if you look at the NTFS permissions Windows sets by default on every volume, you see a few ACEs that use special permissions. So although you don't have to use them often, you need to understand them, particularly to figure out how initial volume permissions are set. Table 5-2 describes each special permission and lists which standard permissions include it.

Table 5-2   NTFS special permissions

Special permission	Description	Included in standard permission
Full control	Same as the standard Full control permission	Full control
Traverse folder/ execute file	For folders: Allows accessing files in folders or subfolders even if the user doesn't normally have access to the folder For files: Allows running program files	Full control, Modify, Read & execute, List folder contents
List folder/read data	For folders: Allows users to view subfolders and filenames in the folder For files: Allows users to view data in files	Full control, Modify, Read & execute, List folder contents, Read
Read attributes	Allows users to view file or folder attributes	Full control, Modify, Read & execute, List folder contents, Read
Read extended attributes	Allows users to view file or folder extended attributes	Full control, Modify, Read & execute, List folder contents, Read
Create files/write data	Allows users to create new files and modify the contents of existing files	Full control, Modify, Write
Create folders/ append data	Allows users to create new folders and add data to the end of existing files but not change existing data in a file	Full control, Modify, Write
Write attributes	Allows users to change file and folder attributes	Full control, Modify, Write
Write extended attributes	Allows users to change file and folder extended attributes	Full control, Modify, Write
Delete subfolders and files	Allows users to delete subfolders and files in the folder	Full control
Delete	Allows users to delete the folder or file	Full control, Modify
Read permissions	Allows users to read NTFS permissions of a folder or file	Full control, Modify, Read & execute, List folder contents, Read, Write
Take ownership	Allows users to take ownership of a folder or file, which gives the user implicit permission to change permissions on that file or folder	Full control

© 2015 Cengage Learning®

File and Folder Ownership   As mentioned, every file system object (files and folders) has an owner. An object owner is granted certain implicit permissions, regardless of how permissions are set in the object's DACL: viewing and changing permissions for the object and transferring ownership to another user. So it's possible that users can be file owners but not be able to open the files they own. However, because owners can change permissions on files they own, they can grant themselves the permissions they want.

A user can become the owner of a file system object in three ways:

- *Create the file or folder*—The user who creates a file or folder is automatically the owner.

- *Take ownership of a file or folder*—User accounts with Full control permission or the Take ownership special permission for a file or folder can take ownership of the file or folder. Members of the Administrators group can take ownership of all files.

- *Assigned ownership*—An Administrator account can assign another user as the owner of a file or folder.

NTFS Permission Inheritance

On an NTFS or ReFS volume, permissions are first set at the root of a volume, and all folders and files in the volume inherit these settings unless configured otherwise.

Windows changes the default inheritance settings on many folders created during installation so that they don't inherit all permissions from the root of the volume.

You can change how permission inheritance works by going to advanced settings in the Security tab of a file or folder's Shared Properties dialog box. When you select an ACE and click Edit, you see seven options for how permissions on a folder apply to other objects in the folder, as shown in Figure 5-3.

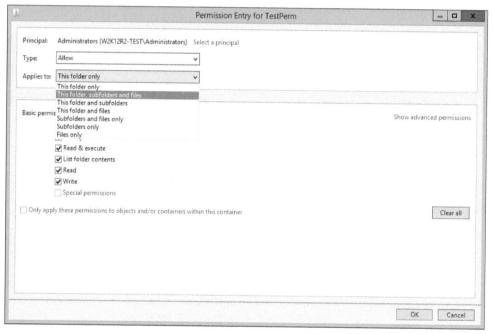

Figure 5-3   Configuring permission inheritance

All standard permissions have the Applies to option set to "This folder, subfolders and files," but there might be reasons to change this default setting. For example, you might want users to be able to create and delete files in a folder but not delete the folder itself. To do this, you could set the standard Read & execute and Write permissions on the folder, and then set the Delete special permission to apply to subfolders and files only.

Subfolders and files are configured to inherit permissions by default; however, permission inheritance can be disabled. If you need to remove permissions from a file or folder, you must disable inheritance first. You can add new ACEs or add permissions to an existing ACE with inheritance enabled, but you can't remove inherited permissions. To disable permission inheritance, open the Advanced Security Settings dialog box for an object (see Figure 5-4) and click the Disable inheritance button. When you disable inheritance, you're prompted to convert the existing inherited permissions into explicit permissions or remove all inherited permissions. In most cases, converting the permissions is best so that you have a starting point from which to make changes. The "Replace all child object permission entries with inheritable permission entries from this object" option forces the current folder's child objects to inherit applicable permissions. If a child object has inheritance disabled, this option reenables it.

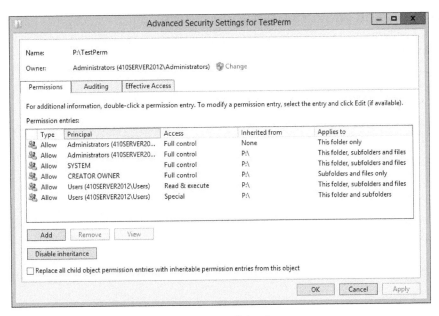

Figure 5-4   The Advanced Security Settings dialog box

Effective Access   With all the variables involved in permissions, determining what access a user account has to a file or folder isn't always easy, but Windows has a tool called **effective access** to help sort out object access. As shown previously in Figure 5-4, the Advanced Security Settings dialog box has an Effective Access tab where you can select a user or group to see its access to a file or folder after taking into account sharing permission, NTFS permissions, and group memberships (see Figure 5-5). You can also see which permissions a user or group has, and for permissions that aren't granted, the "Access limited by" column specifies whether the limiting factor is share or NTFS permissions.

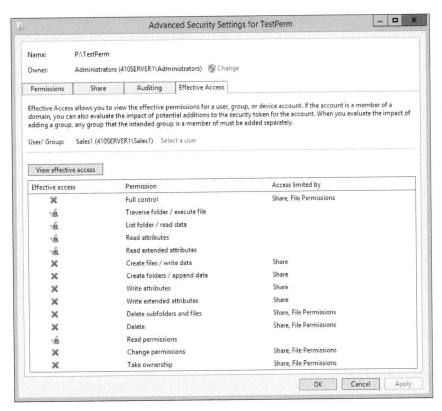

Figure 5-5   The Effective Access tab

Copying and Moving Files and Folders When you copy or move files and folders within or between volumes, you need to know how the permissions assigned to those files and folders are handled. Here's a list of rules:

- A file or folder copied within the same NTFS volume or to a different NTFS volume inherits permissions from the destination folder. If the destination is the root of the volume, it inherits permissions from the root of the volume.

- A file or folder moved within the same NTFS volume retains its original permissions.

- A file or folder moved to a different NTFS volume inherits the destination folder's permissions.

- A file or folder moved from a FAT or FAT32 volume to an NTFS volume inherits the destination folder's permissions.

- A file or folder moved or copied from an NTFS volume to a FAT or FAT32 volume loses all permission settings because FAT/FAT32 volumes don't support permissions.

 ReFS volumes behave the same way as NTFS volumes when copying and moving file system objects.

Activity 5-1: Examining Default Settings for Volume Permissions

Time Required: 10 minutes
Objective: Examine default permission settings on a volume.

Required Tools and Equipment: 410Server1

Description: You want a solid understanding of which permissions are inherited by files and folders created on a new volume.

1. Log on to 410Server1 as **Administrator,** if necessary.

2. Open Disk Management and create a new simple volume on Disk 1 that's **5 GB,** formatted as **NTFS,** and named **Vol1.** Assign drive letter **P** to the volume. Leave all other settings at their defaults, and wait for the volume to finish formatting.

3. Right-click **Vol1** and click **Properties.** Click the **Security** tab in the Properties dialog box.

4. Click each ACE in the volume's DACL to see the assigned permissions. You might need to scroll the Permissions for Everyone list box to see the Special permissions entry. Notice that several security principals are assigned special permissions.

5. Click the **Advanced** button. Notice that the Administrators group and SYSTEM and CREATOR OWNER special identities are granted Full control. Double-click the **CREATOR OWNER** entry. This special identity is given Full control but only over subfolders and files. This entry ensures that any user who creates a file or folder is granted Full control permission for that object. A user must have at least the Write standard permission to create files and folders. Click **Cancel.**

6. Double-click the **Users** entry with Create files/write data in the Access column. This entry and the Users entry above it allow users to create folders and files, but files can be created only in subfolders. This permission prevents users from creating files in the root of the volume. Click **Cancel.**

7. Double-click the **Everyone** entry. This set of permissions allows the Everyone special identity to read and execute files and view a list of files and folders in the root of the volume. The Applies to setting "This folder only" prevents child objects from inheriting these permissions. Click **Cancel** three times.

8. Create a folder in the root of the Vol1 volume named **TestPerm.**

9. Open the TestPerm folder's Properties dialog box, and click the **Security** tab. Click any ACE in the Group or user names list box. Permissions for the entries are grayed out, meaning you can't change them because they are inherited. Click **Cancel**.

10. Create a text file in the TestPerm folder named **Permfile1**.

11. Open the `Permfile1` file's Properties dialog box, and click the **Security** tab. Notice that the file inherits the TestPerm folder's permissions except the CREATOR OWNER special identity, which is assigned only to folders, not files. Close all open windows.

12. If you're continuing to the next activity, stay logged on; otherwise, log off or shut down 410Server1.

Activity 5-2: Creating a Regular User for Permission Experiments

Time Required: 5 minutes
Objective: Create a regular user.

Required Tools and Equipment: 410Server1
Description: You want to experiment with permissions, and you need a regular user to do so. You create one with the Local Users and Groups tool in Computer Management.

1. Log on to 410Server1 as **Administrator,** if necessary.

2. Open Computer Management, and click to expand **Local Users and Groups** in the left pane. Right-click **Users** and click **New User**.

3. In the User name text box, type **testuser,** and in the Password and Confirm password text boxes, type **Password01.**

4. Click to clear the **User must change password at next logon** check box and click to select the **Password never expires** check box. Click **Create** and then **Close.**

5. By default, new users are added to the Users group. Click **Groups** in the left pane of Computer Management. In the right pane, double-click **Users** to see that testuser is a member of this group. Click **Cancel,** and then close Computer Management.

6. If you're continuing to the next activity, stay logged on; otherwise, log off or shut down 410Server1.

Activity 5-3: Experimenting with NTFS Permissions

Time Required: 20 minutes
Objective: Experiment with NTFS permissions.

Required Tools and Equipment: 410Server1
Description: You're somewhat confused about NTFS permissions, so you create some files to use in a variety of permission experiments.

1. Log on to 410Server1 as **Administrator,** if necessary.

2. Open File Explorer, and navigate to the **TestPerm** folder you created on the Vol1 volume.

3. First, you want to be able to view file extensions in File Explorer so that you can create batch files easily. Click **View** on the toolbar, and then click **File name extensions.** You can now see the `.txt` extension on the `Permfile1` file you created previously.

4. Create a text file called **TestBatch.bat** in the TestPerm folder. When asked whether you want to change the file extension, click **Yes.**

5. Right-click **TestBatch.bat** and click **Edit**. Type **@ Echo This is a test batch file** and press **Enter**. On the next line, type **@ Pause**. Save the file, and then exit Notepad. To test your batch file, double-click it. A command prompt window opens, and you see "This is a test batch file. Press any key to continue . . ." Press the **spacebar** or **Enter** to close the command prompt window.

6. Open the Properties dialog box for **TestBatch.bat**, click the **Security** tab, and then click **Advanced**. Click the **Disable inheritance** button. In the message box that opens, click **Convert inherited permissions into explicit permissions on this object**. Notice that the three permissions entries now indicate "None" in the Inherited from column (refer back to Figure 5-4). Click **OK**.

7. Click **Edit**. Click **Users** in the Group or user names list box. In the Permissions for Users list box, click to clear the **Read & execute** check box in the Allow column and leave the **Read** check box selected. Click **OK** twice.

8. Log off and log on as **testuser** with **Password01**. In File Explorer, browse to the **TestPerm** folder on the Vol1 volume. Double-click the **TestBatch.bat** file. Read the error message, and then click **OK**.

9. Right-click the **TestBatch.bat** file and click **Edit**. Notice that you can still open this file because you have Read permission, but you can't run the batch file because you no longer have Read & execute permission. Exit Notepad.

10. In File Explorer, right-click the right pane and point to **New**. Strangely, the right-click New menu and the Quick Access toolbar menu offer only Folder as an option. However, you can create a file in Notepad and save it in this folder.

11. Right-click **Start**, click **Run**, type **notepad** in the Open text box, and press **Enter**. Type your name in the file and click **File, Save As** from the menu. In the Save As dialog box, click **This PC**, scroll down, and double-click the **Vol1** volume and the **TestPerm** folder. In the File name text box, type **Permfile2.txt**, and click **Save**. Exit Notepad.

12. Open the Properties dialog box for **Permfile2.txt**, and click the **Security** tab. Click **testuser**. This user has been assigned Full control of the file because of the CREATOR OWNER Full control permission on the parent folder. Click **Advanced**. You see testuser next to Owner. Notice that you can change the owner if you click the Change link.

13. Disable permission inheritance and convert the existing permissions. (Refer back to Step 6, if necessary.) Click **OK** until you get back to the Security tab of the **Permfile2** file's Properties dialog box.

14. Click **Edit**. Click **testuser**, and then click **Remove**. Click the **Users** entry, and then click **Remove**. Only SYSTEM and Administrators are left in the DACL. Click **OK** twice.

15. Double-click **Permfile2.txt**. You get an "Access is denied" message because you no longer have permission to open this file. Click **OK** and exit Notepad. Although you no longer have access to this file, you're still the file owner and, therefore, can assign yourself permissions.

16. Open the Properties dialog box for **Permfile2.txt**, click the **Security** tab, and then click **Edit**. Click **Add**. Type **testuser**, click **Check Names**, and then click **OK**. Click **Full control** in the Allow column in the Permissions for testuser list box. Click **OK** twice. Verify that you can open, change, and save **Permfile2.txt**.

17. Close all open windows, and log off 410Server1.

Creating Windows File Shares

The File Server role service is required to share folders. You can install this role service via Server Manager, or you can simply share a folder to have the role service installed automatically. Folders in Windows Server 2012/R2 can be shared only by members of the Administrators or Server Operators groups.

Sharing files on the network, as you saw in Chapter 1, isn't difficult in a Windows environment. Nonetheless, you should be familiar with some techniques and options before forging ahead with setting up a file-sharing server. You can use the following methods to configure folder sharing in Windows Server 2012/R2:

- *Simple file sharing*—To use simple file sharing, right-click a folder in File Explorer and click Share with or click Share in the Sharing tab of a folder's Properties dialog box. The File Sharing dialog box (see Figure 5-6) simplifies sharing for novices by using easy-to-understand terms for permissions and by setting NTFS permissions to accommodate the selected share permissions. If you share a file by using this method, the share permissions are always set to Full control for the Administrators group and Everyone. If you choose the Read permission for a specific user, the NTFS permissions are set to Read & execute, List folder contents, and Read for the specified user or group. If you choose Read/Write, the NTFS permissions are set to Full control for the specified user.

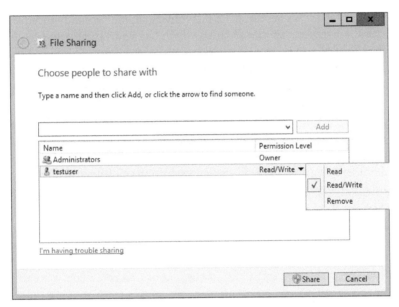

Figure 5-6   Simple file sharing

- *Advanced Sharing dialog box*—To open this dialog box, click Advanced Sharing in the Sharing tab of a folder's Properties dialog box. There are several options in this dialog box (see Figure 5-7):

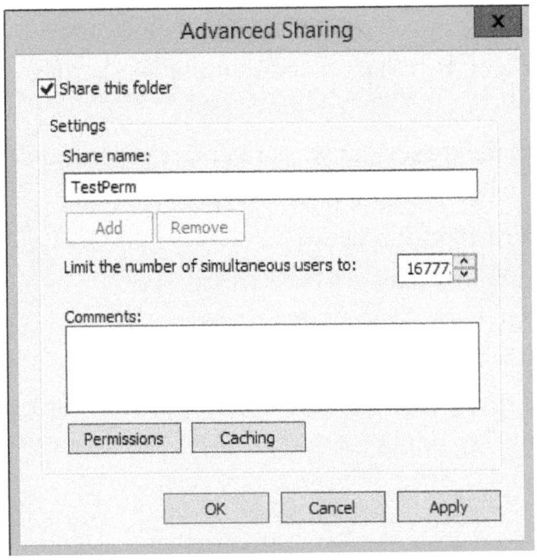

Figure 5-7   The Advanced Sharing dialog box

o Share this folder: Sharing can be enabled or disabled for the folder by clicking this check box.

o Share name: The share name is the name users see in the Network folder of File Explorer when browsing the server. To put it another way, the share name is the name you use to access the folder with the UNC path (*server**share name*). You can add or remove share names. A single folder can have multiple share names, each with different permissions, a different number of simultaneous users, and different caching settings.

o Limit the number of simultaneous users to: In Windows Server 2012/R2, the default limit is 16,777,216, which is, practically speaking, unlimited. In Windows 8.1, the maximum number of users who can access a share is 15.

o Comments: You can enter a description of the share's contents and settings in this text box.

o Permissions: Click this button to open the Permissions dialog box shown previously in Figure 5-1. In Windows Server 2012/R2, folders shared with advanced sharing are configured with the Everyone special identity, which has Read permission by default.

o Caching: This option controls how offline files are configured. Offline files enable users to disconnect from the network and still have the shared files they were working with available on their computers. When a user reconnects to the network, the offline and network copies of the file are synchronized.

- *Shared Folders*—You use this component of the Computer Management MMC to monitor, change, and create shares on the local computer or a remote computer. To create a new share, right-click the Shares node under Shared Folders and click New Share. The Create A Shared Folder Wizard walks you through selecting the folder to share or creating a new folder to share, naming the share, configuring offline files, and setting permissions.

- *File and Storage Services*—In Server Manager, click File and Storage Services, and then click Shares. Click Tasks and then New Share to start the New Share Wizard. This method, which is new in Windows Server 2012/R2, is the preferred method for creating and managing shares. Creating shares with File and Storage Services is discussed in more detail in the next section.

- *Share and Storage Management*—This snap-in can be installed as a feature in Windows Server 2012/R2. It was available in Windows Server 2008 but is being phased out in favor of tools in the File and Storage Services role.

Activity 5-4: Sharing a Folder with Simple File Sharing

Time Required: 10 minutes

Objective: Create a test folder and then share it with simple file sharing.

Required Tools and Equipment: 410Server1

Description: You understand that there are several ways to create shared folders. You decide to try simple file sharing to see how it sets permissions automatically.

1. Log on to 410Server1 as **Administrator**, if necessary.

2. Open File Explorer, and create a folder named **TestShare1** on Vol1.

3. Open TestShare1's Properties dialog box, and click the **Security** tab. Make a note of the permissions assigned on this folder, and then close the Properties dialog box.

4. Right-click **TestShare1**, point to **Share with**, and click **Specific people** to open the File Sharing dialog box. Notice that the Administrator user and Administrators group already have access.

5. Click the list arrow next to the Add button, and click **testuser** in the list. (You can also create a new user by clicking the "Create a new user" option.) Click the **Add** button. By default, the user has Read permission. Click the list arrow next to Read and click **Read/Write**.

6. Click **Share**. You see a message indicating the folder is shared. You can e-mail links to the shared folder or copy the links to the Clipboard. You can also click the "Show me all the network shares on this computer" link to open the network browse window for your server. Click **Done**.

7. Open **TestShare1**'s Properties dialog box. Click the **Sharing** tab, and then click **Advanced Sharing**.

8. Click **Permissions**. Notice that the Everyone group and Administrators group are assigned Full Control to the share, which is the default setting with simple file sharing. Permissions can be restricted by using NTFS permissions. Click **Cancel** twice.

9. In the TestShare1 folder's Properties dialog box, click the **Security** tab. Scroll through the ACEs in the DACL. Notice that testuser and Administrator ACEs were added to the DACL with Full control NTFS permissions. In addition, the CREATOR OWNER ACE has been removed. However, all other ACEs were maintained. In the real world, this may or may not be what you intended. Simple file sharing is just that—simple—but you might want to exert more control over file sharing.

10. Close all open windows. If you're continuing to the next activity, stay logged on; otherwise, log off or shut down 410Server1.

Activity 5-5: Sharing a Folder with Advanced Sharing

Time Required: 15 minutes
Objective: Create a new folder and share it with advanced sharing.

Required Tools and Equipment: 410Server1
Description: You're concerned that simple file sharing doesn't always have the results you want, so you decide to experiment with advanced sharing. You create a new folder, share it, and assign permissions. The permissions allow all members of the Users group to read files in the share, give all members of the Administrators group full control, and allow testuser to create new files (with full control over them) and read files created by other users.

1. Log on to 410Server1 as **Administrator**, if necessary.

2. Open File Explorer, and create a folder named **TestShare2** on Vol1. Open TestShare2's Properties dialog box, and click the **Security** tab. Examine the new folder's default permissions. The Users group has Read & execute, List folder contents, and Read permissions. The Administrators group has Full control permission, and the CREATOR OWNER special identity has special permissions that give any user who creates or owns a file full control over the file.

3. Click the **Sharing** tab, and then click **Advanced Sharing**. Click to select the **Share this folder** check box. Leave the share name as is, and then click **Permissions**. By default, the share permission is Allow Read for Everyone.

4. Because you don't want Everyone to have Read permission, click **Remove**. Click **Add**, type **Users**, click **Check Names**, and then click **OK**. Next, click **Add**, type **Administrators**, click **Check Names**, and then click **OK** to add the Administrators group to the DACL.

5. Click **Users** and click the **Full Control** check box in the Allow column. Click **Administrators** and click the **Full Control** check box in the Allow column. Even though the Users group permission is set to Full Control, NTFS permissions will restrict them to Read and Read & execute. You set additional permissions for testuser with NTFS permissions. Click **OK** twice.

6. Click the **Security** tab. Notice the permissions haven't changed as they did when you used simple file sharing. Click **Edit**, and then click **Add**. Type **testuser** and click **Check Names**. Click **OK**.

7. Click **testuser**. Notice the permissions for testuser are set to Read & execute, List folder contents, and Read. Click **Write** in the Allow column, which gives testuser the ability to create and make changes to files. Click **OK** and then **Close**.

8. Double-click TestShare2 to open it. Create a text file named `Testfile1.txt`. Open the file, type some characters in it, save it, and then exit Notepad.

9. Open the Properties dialog box for `Testfile1.txt`, and click the **Security** tab. `Testfile1.txt` has inherited permissions from the TestShare2 folder. Click **Advanced**, and notice that the file owner is the Administrators group. Click **Cancel** twice.

10. Log off and log back on to 410Server1 as **testuser**. To simulate access to the share from the network, right-click **Start**, click **Run**, type \\410Server1\TestShare2, and press **Enter**. Double-click `Testfile1` to open the file in Notepad. Close Notepad, and then try to delete `TestFile1`. When asked whether you're sure you want to delete the file, click **Yes**. You see a File Access Denied message box informing you that you need permission to perform the action. Click **Cancel**. You have read permission to `Testfile1`, but you don't have permission to delete the file.

11. Create a new text document named `Testfile2`. Open the Properties dialog box for `Testfile2`, and click the **Security** tab. Click **Advanced**, and notice that the owner of the file is testuser. As owner, you have full control over the file. Click **Cancel** twice and delete `Testfile2`. You are successful.

12. Close all open windows, and log off 410Server1.

Activity 5-6: Restricting Access to Subfolders of Shares

Time Required: 20 minutes
Objective: Restrict access to a subfolder of a share.

Required Tools and Equipment: 410Server1
Description: The Sales Department wants a subfolder of the Marketing share to store sensitive documents that should be available only to users in the Sales Department because some Marketing and Advertising users tend to leak information before it should be discussed outside the company. You could create a new share, but the Sales Department users prefer a subfolder of the existing share. To do this activity, you need to create a couple of groups and some users to put in the groups.

1. Log on to 410Server1 as **Administrator**.

2. Open Computer Management. Create two users named **Marketing1** and **Sales1**, following Steps 2 through 4 in Activity 5-2.

3. In the left pane, right-click **Groups** and click **New Group**. In the Group name text box, type **Marketing-G**.

4. Next, users in the Marketing and Sales departments should be added to the Marketing-G group. To do this, click **Add**. In the Select Users dialog box, type **Marketing1**, click **Check Names**, and then click **OK**. Click **Add**. In the Select Users dialog box, type **Sales1**, click **Check Names**, and then click **OK**. Click **Create** and then **Close**.

5. Create a group named **Sales-G** and add the **Sales1** user to the group. Close Computer Management.

6. Open File Explorer. On Vol1, create a folder named **MktgDocs**. In the MktgDocs folder, create a subfolder named **SalesOnly**.

7. Open the Properties dialog box for MktgDocs and click **Sharing**. Click **Advanced Sharing**, and then click **Share this folder**. Click **Permissions**, and then remove **Everyone** from the DACL.

8. Add the **Users** group to the DACL and give the group **Full Control** to the share. You limit access to files and subfolders by using NTFS permissions. Click **OK** until you're back to the MktgDocs Properties dialog box.

9. Click the **Security** tab. Currently, the Users group has Read permission to the folder and the Administrators group has Full Control. Click **Advanced**. Click **Disable Inheritance**, and then click the **Convert** option. Click **OK**.

10. Click **Edit**, click **Users**, and click **Remove**.

11. Add both the **Marketing-G** and **Sales-G** groups to the DACL. Click **Marketing-G** and click the **Write** check box in the Allow column so that Marketing-G has Read & execute, List folder contents, Read, and Write permissions to the folder. Repeat for **Sales-G**. Click **OK** and then **Close**.

12. In File Explorer, open the **MktgDocs** folder, and then open the Properties dialog box for the **SalesOnly** folder. Click the **Security** tab. The SalesOnly folder has inherited permissions from the MktgDocs folder.

13. Disable inheritance on the SalesOnly folder, being sure to convert existing permissions. In the Security tab, click **Edit**. Click **Marketing-G**, and then click **Remove**. Click **OK** twice.

14. Log off 410Server1 and log back on as **Sales1**. Open the MktgDocs share by right-clicking **Start**, clicking **Run**, typing \\410Server1\MktgDocs, and pressing **Enter**. Create a text file in MktgDocs named `Mktg1`.

15. Open the **SalesOnly** folder and create a text file named `SalesDoc`. You have verified that you can create files while logged on as a member of the Sales-G group. Open the Properties dialog box for `SalesDoc` and click the **Security** tab. Note that Sales-G and Sales1 are in the DACL. Click **Sales-G** and notice Sales-G has Read & execute, Read, and Write permissions. Click **Sales1**, and notice that Sales1 has Full control because it's the file owner.

16. Log off 410Server1 and log back on as **Marketing1**. Open the MktgDocs share by right-clicking **Start**, clicking **Run**, typing \\410Server1\MktgDocs, and pressing **Enter**. Create a text file in MktgDocs named `Mktg2`. You have verified that members of the Marketing-G group can create files in the MktgDocs share.

17. Try to delete the `Mktg1` file that Sales1 created. You can't because you have only Write permission to the file, which doesn't allow you to delete files.

18. Double-click the **SalesOnly** folder. You see a network error message because the Marketing1 user doesn't have access to the SalesOnly folder. Click **Close**.

19. Log off 410Server1.

In this activity, you restricted access to a folder by including in the DACL groups that are allowed access and excluding the Marketing-G group. The Marketing-G group was granted access to the MktgDocs share, but because the Marketing-G group wasn't in the SalesOnly folder's DACL, members of this group were effectively blocked from accessing this subfolder. Using a Deny permission might have worked, too, but it wasn't necessary in this example. The Deny permission should be used cautiously and only for exceptions. For example, if all members of a group except a few should have access to a resource, users can be added to a group and the group can be added to the DACL with a Deny permission, as you see in Activity 5-7.

Using Deny in an ACE

In Activity 5-6, you restricted access to a folder by including in the DACL groups that are allowed access and excluding the Marketing-G group. The Marketing-G group was granted access to the MktgDocs share, but because the Marketing-G group wasn't in the SalesOnly folder's DACL, members of this group were effectively blocked from accessing this subfolder. Using a Deny permission might have worked, too, but it wasn't necessary in this example. The Deny permission should be used cautiously and only for exceptions.

As stated, if a security principal isn't represented in an object's DACL, it doesn't have access to the object. For this reason, you don't need to add Deny ACEs to every object to prevent users from accessing objects. However, the Deny permission does have its place, usually when an exception is needed. For example, Bill is a member of the Accounting group, which has been given access to the Accounting share so that group members have access to accounting-related files. Bill is a new employee, so until he's fully trained, you don't want him to be able to make changes to files in the share. You can add Bill's user account to the Accounting share's DACL and assign the Deny Delete and Deny Create files/write data permissions to his account. Using Deny in this way enables you to assign broad permissions to groups yet make exceptions for certain group members. Another common use of the Deny permission is to override a permission inherited from a parent object.

As a rule, a Deny permission overrides an Allow permission. For example, a group Joe Tech1 belongs to has been added to an object's DACL and assigned the Allow Full control permission, and Joe Tech1's account has been added to the same object's DACL and assigned the Deny Write permission. In this case, Joe Tech1 could perform all actions on the object that Full control allows, except actions requiring the Write permission. There's an exception to this rule: If the Deny permission is inherited from a parent object, and the Allow permission is explicitly added to the object's DACL, the Allow permission takes precedence if there's a conflict. Activity 5-7 walks you through using Deny in an ACE.

Activity 5-7: Restricting Access with Deny Permissions

Time Required: 15 minutes
Objective: Deny access to a folder.

Required Tools and Equipment: 410Server1
Description: A new employee has just been hired in the Sales Department. Company policy states that all employees must be with the company for a 120-day probationary period before being allowed access to confidential material. This new employee should have access to all non-confidential material and, therefore, be a member of the Sales-G group. Your solution is to create a group called DenySales-G and add new users to this group. You then add this group to the DACL of any confidential folders and assign the Deny Full Control permission. After the user is past the probationary period, you can remove this user account from the DenySales-G group. By using a group instead of the user account to deny access, you don't need to hunt down all the confidential folders and remove the user account from their DACLs.

1. Log on to 410Server1 as **Administrator**.

2. Create a new user named **Sales2** and add Sales2 to the **Sales-G** group. Create a new group named **DenySales-G** and add Sales2 to the group.

3. Open File Explorer. In the Vol1 volume, double-click the **MktgDocs** folder to open it. Open the Properties dialog box for the **SalesOnly** subfolder, and click the **Security** tab. Click the **Edit** button, click **Add**, and type **DenySales-G**. Click **Check Names**, and then click **OK**.

4. Click **DenySales-G** in the DACL for SalesOnly and click **Full control** in the Deny column. Click **OK**. In the Windows Security message box, click **Yes**, and then click **OK**.

5. Log off and log back on as **Sales2**.

6. Open the **MktgDocs** share on 410Server1. Create a text file named **NewSales1** in the MktgDocs share to verify that you have access to the share.

7. Try to open the **SalesOnly** folder. You see a network error message. If necessary, click **Continue**, enter your password, click **Yes**, and then click **Close**. Sales2 is a member of Sales-G and DenySales-G, and both are in the SalesOnly DACL. However, the Deny permission takes precedence over the Allow permission. Log off 410Server1.

Creating Shares with File and Storage Services

You can create shares and set a number of sharing options with the New Share Wizard in the File and Storage Services role. To start the wizard, click File and Storage Services in the left pane of Server Manager, and then click Shares. In the Tasks list box, click New Share. The first window in the New Share Wizard is for setting the share profile (see Figure 5-8), which has five options:

- *SMB Share - Quick*—Creates a standard Windows share with default settings and permissions that you can customize by using the wizard or later in the shared folder's properties.

- *SMB Share - Advanced*—Allows you to create a Windows share with advanced options for setting the folder owner, the ability to classify data, and quotas. This option requires the File Server Resource Manager role service.

- *SMB Share - Applications*—Creates a Windows share that's suitable for Hyper-V, databases, and other applications.

- *NFS Share - Quick*—Creates an NFS share for Linux/UNIX clients with standard options.

- *NFS Share - Advanced*—Offers advanced options for creating a Linux/UNIX-style share.

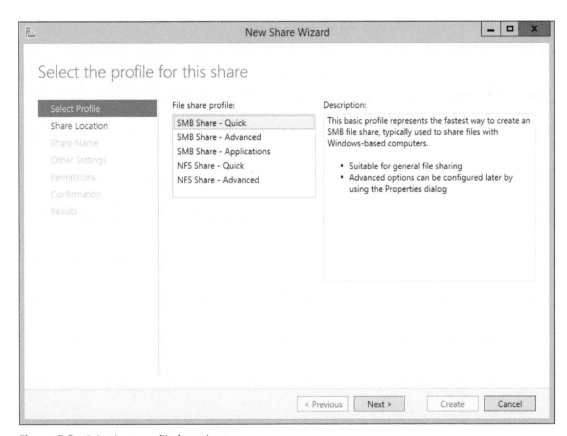

Figure 5-8   Selecting a profile for a share

The next windows described are based on the SMB Share - Quick profile. After selecting the profile, you choose a server and volume for the share's location (see Figure 5-9). By default, the share is created in the \Shares directory, but you can set a custom path. Next, you specify a share name and, if you like, add a description. The local and remote path are displayed, as shown in Figure 5-10.

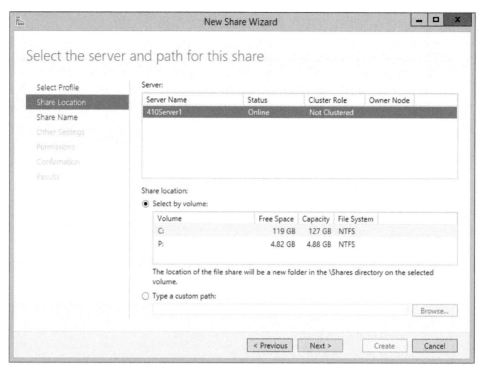

Figure 5-9   Specifying a share location

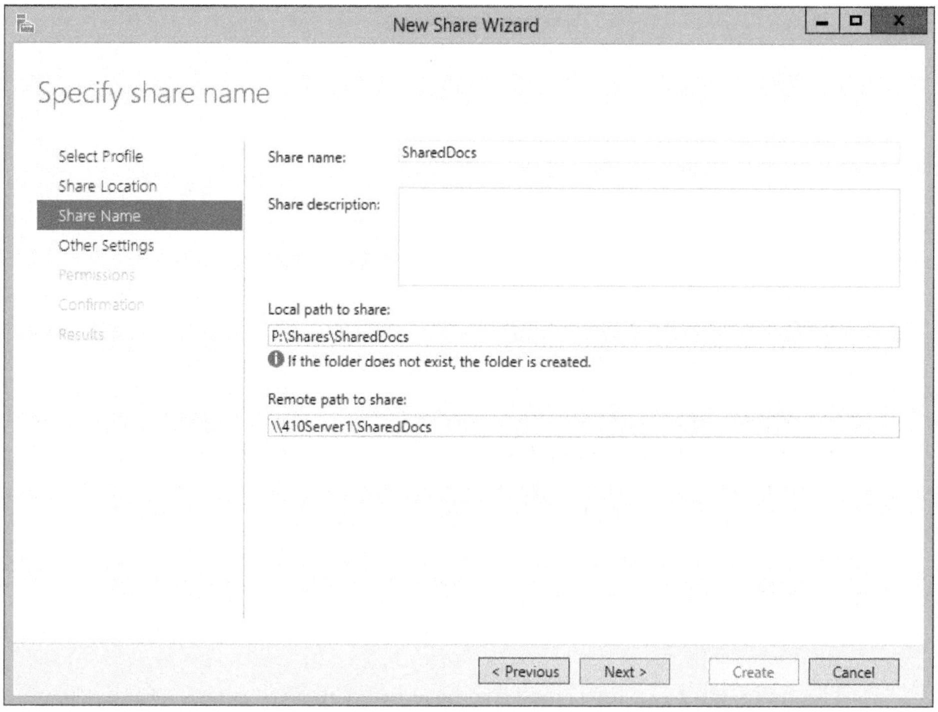

Figure 5-10   Specifying the share name

In the next window, you can set the following additional options for an SMB share (see Figure 5-11):

- *Enable access-based enumeration*—If enabled, **access-based enumeration** (**ABE**) shows only the files and folders to which a user has at least Read permission. If the user doesn't have at least Read permission, the files and folders in the share are hidden from the user. If ABE isn't enabled, users can still see files and folders they don't have access to but can't open them. ABE is disabled by default.

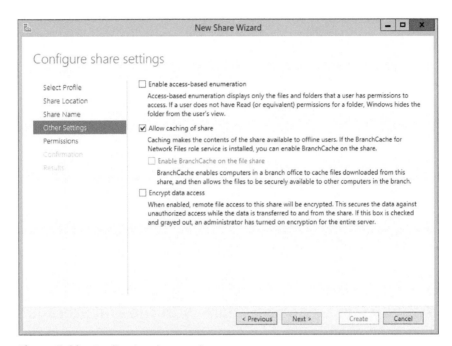

Figure 5-11   Configuring share settings

- *Allow caching of share*—Enables or disables offline files. **Offline files,** also known as "client-side caching," is a feature of shared folders that allows users to access the contents of shared folders when not connected to the network. If a file is opened in a share with caching enabled, it's downloaded to the client's local storage so that it can be accessed later, even if the client isn't connected to the network. Later, when the client reconnects, the file is synchronized with the copy on the share. A new feature of Windows Server 2012/R2 and Windows 8/8.1 clients is the capability to always use the locally cached version of files even when connected to the network. This feature can be enabled in Group Policy with the "Configure slow-link mode" policy setting. If caching is enabled and the BranchCache for Network Files role service is installed, the BranchCache feature can also be enabled on the share. BranchCache is discussed more in *MCSA Guide to Configuring Advanced Windows Server 2012 Services, Exam 70-412* (Cengage Learning, 2015).

- *Encrypt data access*—When this feature is enabled, retrieving files from the share is encrypted to prevent someone from using a network sniffer to view the contents of files as they're transferred across the network.

You set permissions for the share in the next window (see Figure 5-12). By default, new share permissions are set to Read Only for Everyone, and NTFS permissions are inherited from the parent folder. If you click the Customize permissions button, you can edit permissions in the Advanced Security Settings dialog box. Because it's a shared folder, a new tab is added for managing share permissions.

In the last window, you confirm your choices and create the share. When the new share is created, it's added to the list of shares in File and Storage Services. You can make changes to any settings configured in the New Share Wizard by right-clicking the share and clicking Properties.

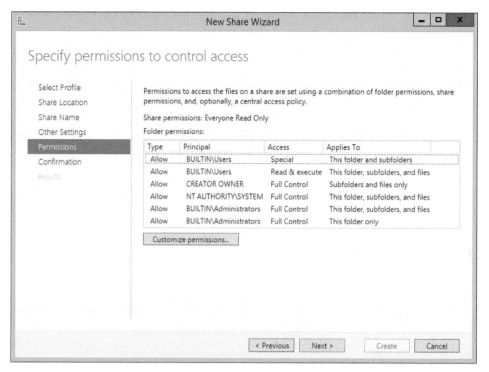

Figure 5-12   Setting permissions for the share

Activity 5-8: Creating a Share with File and Storage Services

Time Required: 5 minutes

Objective: Create a share with File and Storage Services.

Required Tools and Equipment: 410Server1

Description: You want to practice creating shares by using simple and advanced file sharing. In this activity, you use File and Storage Services to create a share.

1. Log on to 410Server1 as **Administrator,** if necessary.

2. In Server Manager, click **File and Storage Services,** and then click **Shares.**

3. Click the **Tasks** list box and click **New Share** to start the New Share Wizard. In the Select Profile window, click **SMB Share - Quick,** and then click **Next.**

4. In the Share Location window, click the **P:** volume in the Select by volume section, and then click **Next.**

5. In the Share Name window, type **NewShare1** in the Share name text box. By default, the local path to the share is set to P:\Shares\NewShare1. You can change the local path, but for now, leave it as is. Click **Next.**

6. In the Other Settings window, read the descriptions for the three options described previously. Leave the default settings and click **Next.**

7. In the Permissions window, review the default permissions. Note that the share permissions are Everyone Read Only, which means that only Read access to the share is allowed for all users. The Folder permissions lists the NTFS permissions. By default, Administrators have Full Control, and Users can read and create files when accessing the folder locally. Click the **Customize permissions** button to open the Advanced Security Settings for NewShare1 dialog box, where you can change the NTFS permissions and share permissions, if necessary. Click **Cancel,** and then click **Next.**

8. In the Confirmation window, review your choices, and then click **Create**. After the share is created successfully, click **Close**. You see the new share in the list of shares.

9. If you're continuing to the next activity, stay logged on; otherwise, log off or shut down 410Server1.

Creating and Managing Shares at the Command Line

Shared folders can be created and managed at the command line with the `net share` command or PowerShell cmdlets. Take a look at the `net share` command first:

- `net share MyDocs=D:\Documents`—Creates a share named MyDocs, using the D:\Documents folder
- `net share MyDocs`—Lists information about the MyDocs share
- `net share MyDocs /delete`—Deletes the MyDocs share
- `net share`—Lists shares on the computer

For more information and examples on using `net share`, type `net share /?` at a command prompt.

Managing and Creating Shares with PowerShell   Several dozen PowerShell cmdlets are available for working with file shares; Table 5-3 lists a few. For details on using a cmdlet, type `Get-Help cmdlet -Detailed` at a PowerShell prompt. To see a list of all cmdlets related to Windows shares, type `Get-Command -Module SmbShare` at a PowerShell prompt.

Table 5-3   PowerShell cmdlets for working with file shares

PowerShell cmdlet	Description
New-SmbShare	Creates a share
Get-SmbShare	Lists shares on the computer
Remove-SmbShare	Deletes a share
Set-SmbShare	Changes a share's properties
Get-SmbShareAccess	Displays permissions for a share
Grant-SmbShareAccess	Adds a permission to a share

© 2015 Cengage Learning®

Take a look at a few examples:

- `New-SmbShare MyDocs D:\Documents`—Creates a share named MyDocs, using the D:\Documents folder
- `Get-SmbShare MyDocs | Format-List -Property *`—Lists detailed information about the MyDocs share
- `Remove-SmbShare MyDocs`—Deletes the MyDocs share
- `Get-SmbShare`—Lists shares on the computer

Default and Administrative Shares

Every Windows OS since Windows NT (excluding Windows 9x and Windows Me) includes **administrative shares,** which are hidden shares available only to members of the Administrators group. On computers that aren't domain controllers, these shares are as follows:

- *Admin$*—This share provides network access to the Windows folder on the boot volume (usually C:\Windows).
- *Drive$*—The *drive* represents the drive letter of a disk volume (for example, C$). The root of each disk volume (except removable disks, such as DVDs and floppy disks) is shared and accessible by using the drive letter followed by a dollar sign.

- *IPC$*—IPC means interprocess communications. This share is less an administrative share than a system share. It's used for temporary connections between clients and servers to provide communication between network programs.

Domain controllers have all the previous hidden administrative shares as well as the following default shares, which aren't hidden but are considered administrative shares:

- *NETLOGON*—Used for storing default user profiles as well as user logon scripts for pre-Windows 2000 clients.
- *SYSVOL*—Used by Active Directory for replication between DCs. Also contains group policy files that are downloaded and applied to Windows 2000 and later clients.

Windows creates administrative shares automatically, and permissions on these shares can't be changed. An administrator can disable sharing on the Admin$ share or a volume administrative share, but the share is re-created the next time the system starts or when the Server service is restarted. The IPC$ share can't be disabled.

 You can prevent Windows from creating administrative shares automatically by creating the Registry subkey HKEY_LOCAL_MACHINE\SYSTEM\CurrentControlSet\Services\LanmanServer\Parameters\AutoShareServer, setting the value to 0, and restarting the server.

The dollar sign at the end of a hidden share name prevents the share from being displayed in a network browse list. To access a hidden share, you must use the UNC path. For example, entering \\410Server1\C$ opens the root of the C drive on 410Server1. You can create your own hidden shares by simply placing a $ at the end of the share name. Sometimes administrators use hidden shares to prevent users from attempting to access shares for which they don't have permission.

Managing Shares with the Shared Folders Snap-in

You use the Shared Folders snap-in to create, delete, and monitor shares; view open files; and monitor and manage user connections or sessions. To open this snap-in, add it to an MMC or open the Computer Management MMC. The Shared Folders snap-in has the following subnodes:

- *Shares*—In the Shares node (shown in Figure 5-13), you can view all shares, their path on the local file system, and how many clients are currently connected to each share. You can also open the folder on the local file system, stop sharing a folder, and create new shares.

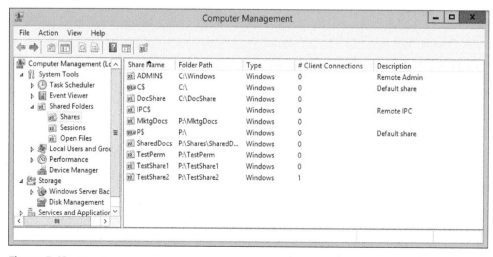

Figure 5-13   The Shares node

- *Sessions*—The Sessions node lists users who currently have a network connection to the server, which client computer they're connected from, how many files they have open, and how long they have been connected (see Figure 5-14). Administrators can select a user and close the session.

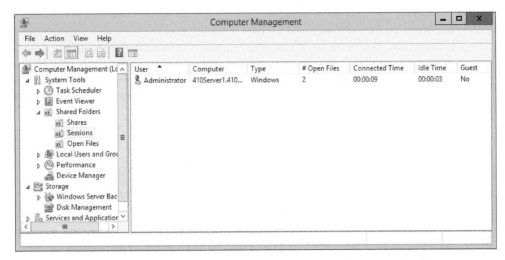

Figure 5-14   The Sessions node

- *Open Files*—The Open Files node lists files that network users have open and which user has opened the file (see Figure 5-15).

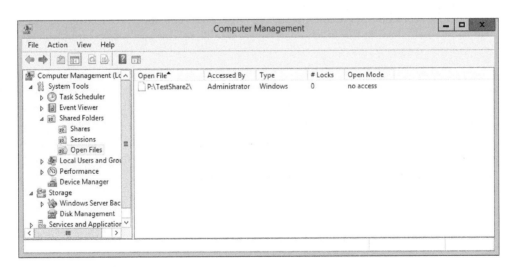

Figure 5-15   The Open Files node

The Shared Folders snap-in is useful for monitoring how much a server's shares are being used and by whom. You can also use this tool to see whether any files are being accessed over the network before shutting down the server or otherwise interrupting server access. You can also check the Idle Time column in the Sessions node to see whether a user is actively using shares on the server (a short idle time) or simply has a share open but hasn't accessed any files for a while (a longer idle time).

You can view and change a share's properties by double-clicking it in the Shares node. You can't change the share's name or the folder location, but you can change the user limit, offline settings, share permissions, and NTFS permissions. In addition, you can publish a share in Active Directory or change the publish options of a published share.

Activity 5-9: Creating a Hidden Share and Monitoring Share Access

Time Required: 10 minutes
Objective: Create a hidden share and monitor access to shared folders.

Required Tools and Equipment: 410Server1
Description: You want to be able to keep users from seeing certain shares on the network when they click Network in File Explorer or when they type the server's UNC path. You haven't worked with hidden shares yet, so you want to experiment with them. You create a new folder on Vol1 and then share it with the Shared Folders snap-in. You append a $ to the share name so that it's hidden, verify that the share is hidden, and then open it by using the full UNC path. Then you use the Shared Folders snap-in to monitor access to the share.

1. Log on to 410Server1 as **Administrator,** if necessary.

2. Open File Explorer and create a new folder on Vol1 named **HideMe.**

3. Open Computer Management and click to expand **Shared Folders.** Right-click **Shares** and click **New Share** to start the Create A Shared Folder Wizard. Click **Next.**

4. In the Folder Path window, type **P:\HideMe** in the Folder path text box, and then click **Next.**

5. In the Name, Description, and Settings window, type **HideMe$** in the Share name text box, and then click **Next.**

6. In the Shared Folder Permissions window, click **Administrators have full access; other users have read-only access,** and then click **Finish.**

7. In the Sharing was Successful window, click **Finish.**

8. Right-click **Start,** click **Run,** type **\\410Server1,** and press **Enter.** A File Explorer window opens listing the shares on 410Server1. The share you just created isn't listed. Close the File Explorer window.

9. Right-click **Start,** click **Run,** type **\\410Server1\HideMe$,** and press **Enter.** A window opens showing the share's contents. A hidden share is hidden only in network browse lists, but if you specify the share in a UNC path, it's available to all who have permission.

10. Minimize the File Explorer window, and open the Computer Management window. Click **Shares,** if necessary, and you see the HideMe$ share listed. The # Client Connections column displays the number 1 because you currently have the share open.

11. Click **Sessions,** and you see that the Administrator account has one open file. Click **Open Files,** and you see the P:\HideMe\ folder listed as an open file. (Folders are considered files in Windows.) Close Computer Management and File Explorer.

12. Log off or shut down 410Server1 because you log on as a different user in the next activity.

Accessing File Shares from Client Computers

The file-sharing discussion so far has focused on how to create and manage shared resources. However, for shared resources to be useful, users must know how to access them. You have already seen some access methods in this chapter's activities. The following methods of accessing shared folders are among the most common:

- *UNC path*—The UNC path, which you've seen in examples and activities, uses the syntax *\\server\share*[*\subfolder*][*\file*]. The parameters in brackets are optional. In fact, the *share* parameter is optional if all you want to do is list shared resources on a server. Using *\\server* by itself in a File Explorer window lists all shared folders and printers (except hidden shares) on that server. The disadvantage of this method is that the user must know the server name and share name, and in a network with dozens or hundreds of servers and shares, that might be asking a lot.

- *Active Directory search*—The Active Directory search allows you to search by keyword or simply list all shared folders in the directory. With this method, users don't need to know the hosting server's name. However, shares aren't published to Active Directory automatically, so this method might not find all shared folders on the network.

- *Mapping a drive*—Administrators often set up a logon script or configure a group policy in which a drive letter is mapped to a network folder where users can store documents. Users can also map a drive letter to shared folders that they access often. Users tend to be more comfortable using drive letters to access files in a Windows environment because all their local resources (hard drives, DVD drives, flash drives) are accessed in this manner. Drive letters can be mapped only to the root of the share, as in *server\share*, not to a subfolder of the share, as in *server\share\folder1*.

- *Browsing the network*—You can open the Network node in File Explorer and see a list of all computers found on the network (see Figure 5-16). You can then browse each computer to find the share you want. This method has the advantage of not requiring you to know the server's name. However, starting with Windows Vista, you must enable the Network Discovery feature for your computer to see other computers and for your computer to be seen by other computers. You can enable this feature in the Network and Sharing Center by clicking "Change advanced sharing settings." Browsing a network for shares might be convenient in a small network, but in a large network, you could be browsing for quite a while to find the right computer.

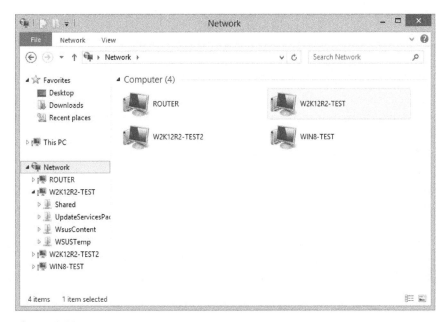

Figure 5-16   Browsing the network in Windows 8.1

Activity 5-10: Mapping a Drive

Time Required: 10 minutes
Objective: Map a drive letter to a shared folder.

Required Tools and Equipment: 410Server1
Description: A user in the Sales Department accesses the Marketing share often but forgets how to use the UNC path. You decide to show this user several ways to map a drive letter to the share.

1. Start 410Server1, if necessary, and log on as **Sales1**.

2. Right-click **Start**, click **Run**, type **\\410Server1**, and press **Enter**.

3. Right-click the **MktgDocs** share and click **Map network drive** to open the Map Network Drive dialog box (see Figure 5-17).

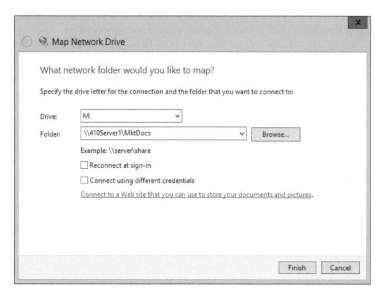

Figure 5-17   The Map Network Drive dialog box

4. Click the **Drive** list arrow, and click **M:**. By default, the "Reconnect at sign-in" check box is selected, which is what you usually want in this situation. This option means the M drive always connects to this share when the user logs on. For this activity, click to clear the **Reconnect at sign-in** check box. You can also use a different username to access this share, if necessary.

5. Click **Finish**. A File Explorer window opens, showing the contents of the MktgDocs share. Close this window.

6. In the File Explorer window that's still open, click **This PC**. Notice that the M drive is listed under Network locations, below the "Devices and drives" section. Right-click the **M** drive and click **Disconnect** to remove the drive mapping.

7. On the File Explorer menu bar, click **Computer**, and then click **Map network drive** on the ribbon. Click **Map network drive** in the list of options. Click the **M:** drive in the Drive list box. In the Folder text box, type **\\410Server1\MktgDocs**, and then click **Finish**.

8. Disconnect the M drive again.

9. Open a command prompt window. Type **net use m: \\410Server1\MktgDocs** and press **Enter**. In File Explorer, verify that the drive has been mapped. The net use command is good to use in batch files for mapping drives.

10. At the command prompt, type **net use** and press **Enter** to see a list of mapped drives. Type **net use m: /delete** and press **Enter** to disconnect the M drive again.

11. Close all open windows, and log off 410Server1.

Working with Disk Quotas

With the number and types of files used requiring more disk space on corporate servers, **disk quotas** are a welcome tool to help administrators get a handle on server storage because they set a limit on how much disk space a user's files can occupy on a volume. Disk quotas are set on an NTFS volume and, by default, apply to all users except administrators. Quotas are configured in the Quota tab of an NTFS volume's Properties dialog box (see Figure 5-18).

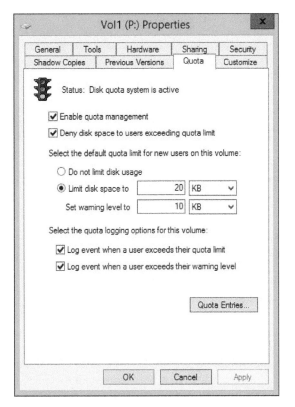

Figure 5-18   The Quota tab

The options for setting quotas are as follows:

- *Enable quota management*—When this check box is selected, quotas are enabled on the volume. (Quotas are disabled by default.) After they're enabled, the quota system begins tracking each user's disk use and creates quota entries with details on usage. To see quota entries, click the Quota Entries button.

- *Deny disk space to users exceeding quota limit*—This option prevents users from saving files to the volume when their limit is exceeded. When this check box isn't selected, administrators can still view disk quota entries and use the logging options to monitor how much space each user is using.

- *Do not limit disk usage*—When this option is selected, no disk use limits are set, but the quota system tracks usage for each user.

- *Limit disk space to*—When this option is selected, administrators can specify the maximum amount of space users can occupy and set a warning level that must be less than or equal to the limit. Disk space can be specified in kilobytes (KB), megabytes (MB), gigabytes (GB), terabytes (TB), petabytes (PB), or exabytes (EB).

- *Log event when a user exceeds their quota limit*—Selecting this option creates an entry in the event log when users exceed their quota limits. These events are written only after the NTFS driver scans the disk for quota entries that exceed the limit or warning level. Scanning occurs at one-hour intervals by default.

- *Log event when a user exceeds their warning level*—Selecting this option creates an entry in the event log when users exceed their warning levels.

- *Quota Entries*—Clicking this button opens the Quota Entries window (see Figure 5-19), where you can view users' disk use information. In addition, the limits specified in the Quota tab can be overridden by editing or creating an entry for a user.

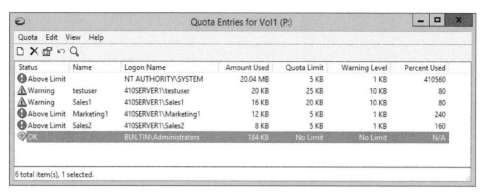

Status	Name	Logon Name	Amount Used	Quota Limit	Warning Level	Percent Used
Above Limit		NT AUTHORITY\SYSTEM	20.04 MB	5 KB	1 KB	410560
Warning	testuser	410SERVER1\testuser	20 KB	25 KB	10 KB	80
Warning	Sales1	410SERVER1\Sales1	16 KB	20 KB	10 KB	80
Above Limit	Marketing1	410SERVER1\Marketing1	12 KB	5 KB	1 KB	240
Above Limit	Sales2	410SERVER1\Sales2	8 KB	5 KB	1 KB	160
OK		BUILTIN\Administrators	184 KB	No Limit	No Limit	N/A

Figure 5-19 Disk quota entries

By default, administrators aren't subject to quota limits. For example, in Figure 5-19, the local Administrators group's entry specifies no limit. If you want to impose quotas on specific administrators, you can create a new quota entry for each of these administrators and set limits. You can create quota entries for regular users, too, if you want to specify a different limit or warning level from those in the volume's Quota tab. Note that quota entries can be created only for user accounts, not groups.

Be aware of how user disk use is calculated. Windows determines each user's disk usage based on the owner of each file on the volume. If ownership of a file changes, disk space use for the previous file owner decreases and increases for the new file owner. By default, the creator of a file is the file's owner, including files created when a user copies a file.

Although the volume disk quotas feature can be a useful tool for server administrators, it has limitations. Quotas can be enabled only on a per-volume basis, and all file types are treated the same way. Windows Server 2008 introduced File Server Resource Manager (FSRM), which allows enabling quotas on shares separately. In addition, you can create file filters with FSRM to restrict particular file types. FSRM is discussed in *MCSA Guide to Administering Windows Server 2012/R2, Exam 70-411* (Cengage Learning, 2015).

Activity 5-11: Working with Quotas

Time Required: 15 minutes
Objective: Enable and configure disk quotas on a new volume.

Required Tools and Equipment: 410Server1
Description: You need to see how quotas work. To start fresh, first you format the Vol1 volume, and then you enable quotas on Vol1 and create some folders and files.

1. Start 410Server1, if necessary, and log on as **Administrator**.

2. Open File Explorer, and click **This PC**. Right-click the **Vol1** volume and click **Format**. In the Format dialog box, accept the default choices and click **Start**. Click **OK** in the warning message box, and click **OK** in the Format Complete message box. Click **Close**.

3. Right-click the **Vol1** volume and click **Properties**. Click the **Quota** tab, and then click the **Enable quota management** and **Deny disk space to users exceeding quota limit** check boxes.

4. Click the **Limit disk space to** option button, and type **20**. In the Set warning level to text box, type **10**. The default unit is KB. These numbers are set very low just for demonstration purposes. Typically, quota limits and warning levels are set much higher.

5. Click both check boxes starting with **Log event when a user exceeds . . .**, and then click the **Quota Entries** button. You see only a single entry, the default Administrators group. Close the Quota Entries window, and then click **OK** to close the Properties dialog box. Click **OK** in the Disk Quota message box to enable the quota system.

6. On Vol1, create a folder called **TestQ**. Share the folder by using simple file sharing and assign Everyone Read/Write permissions.

7. Log off and log back on as **Sales1**. Open File Explorer, navigate to **C:\Windows**, and copy the **write** file, which should be the last file listed in the folder. It's an application file that's about 11 KB.

8. To simulate accessing the share across the network, right-click **Start**, click **Run**, type **\\410Server1\TestQ**, and press **Enter**.

9. Try pasting the **write** file into the TestQ share. You should be successful. Log off and log back on as **Administrator**.

10. Open File Explorer. Right-click **Vol1** and click **Properties**. Click the **Quota** tab, and then click the **Quota Entries** button. You should see an entry for the Sales1 account with Warning in the Status column because Sales1 has exceeded the warning level.

11. Log off and log back on as Sales1. Copy the **winhlp32** file from the C:\Windows folder. It's also about 11 KB.

12. Open the **TestQ** share, following the procedure in Step 8. Try to paste the **winhlp32** file into the TestQ share. In the error message stating that there's not enough space on the TestQ share, click **Cancel**. Your limit on the volume is 20 KB, and you have exceeded it by trying to copy two 11 KB files.

13. Close any open windows, and log off 410Server1.

Working with Shadow Copies

Like quotas, **shadow copies** are enabled on an entire volume. When this feature is enabled, users can access previous versions of files in shared folders and restore files that have been deleted or corrupted. This capability enables users to compare newer versions of files with older versions to see what has changed. An advantage of shadow copies is that administrators aren't burdened with having to restore files because users can access previous versions or deleted files themselves, as you see in Activity 5-13.

You configure shadow copies in the Shadow Copies tab of a volume's Properties dialog box (see Figure 5-20). Shadow copies are disabled by default.

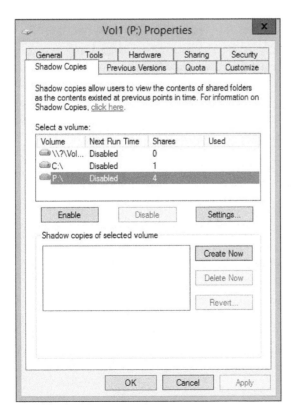

Figure 5-20 The Shadow Copies tab

When you enable shadow copies on a volume, Windows warns you that the default settings aren't suitable for heavily used servers and recommends configuring the settings manually. The most important setting is the location of shadow copies. By default, Windows allocates space on the same volume where shadow copies are enabled. On servers with a lot of shared files that are accessed and changed frequently, this default setting might not be ideal because of the additional load shadow copies place on the disk system. Volumes used heavily for sharing files should be configured to use a different volume for storing shadow copies—one that doesn't have shadow copies enabled. If you want to change the default volume, you should do so in the Settings dialog box (see Figure 5-21) before enabling shadow copies. Otherwise, you have to disable shadow copies, change the storage volume, and reenable shadow copies.

Figure 5-21 Settings for shadow copies

 Be aware that disabling shadow copies deletes all previous versions of documents maintained by shadow copies.

The Settings dialog box for shadow copies offers the following options:

- *Located on this volume*—Choose the volume for storing previous versions of files the Shadow Copies service creates. By default, the volume on which shadow copies are enabled is used. The volume must be an NTFS volume.

- *Details*—Click this button to view statistics on how much space shadow copies are using and how much free space is still available on the volume.

- *Maximum size*—By default, the Use limit option is set to 10% of the total volume size, but a minimum of 300 MB is required. You can also select the No limit option, but it's recommended only if you use a separate volume for storing shadow copies.

- *Schedule*—By default, shadow copies are created when they're first enabled on a volume and then two times a day at 7:00 a.m. and 12:00 p.m. Monday through Friday. You can change the schedule to suit your environment. To create shadow copies manually, click the Create Now button in the Shadow Copies tab of the volume's Properties dialog box (shown previously in Figure 5-20).

When the disk space that shadow copies use reaches the specified limit or available space on the volume can no longer accommodate a new shadow copy, older copies are deleted. Remember that shadow copies of files aren't created as each file is changed. Shadow copies are created for the entire volume at once on the prescribed schedule (or manually). So on a volume with many shared files that change often, considerable disk space might be required each time the Shadow Copies service runs. Regardless of the disk space available for shadow copies, a maximum of 64 previous versions are kept. When the 65th shadow copy is created, the oldest one is deleted. If necessary, shadow copies can be deleted to free up disk space. In the Shadow Copies tab, select the volume at the top, and shadow copies for the selected volume are listed at the bottom by the date and time they were created. Select the instance you want to delete, and then click the Delete Now button.

The total amount of disk space you need for shadow copies depends entirely on how files on the volume are used and your users' expectations of how many previous versions are available. If you have a lot of files that change frequently and users want the maximum number (64) of previous versions kept, obviously the amount of disk space required goes up. On volumes where shared files change less often or users require only a couple of previous versions, the disk space requirements are lower. If heavy use is expected, the best course of action is to dedicate a separate disk on which the free space far exceeds the size of the volume where shadow copies are enabled.

At times, you might need to revert all shared files in a volume to a previous shadow copy instance. The Revert button in the Shadow Copies tab does just that. Select the shadow copy instance you want, and click Revert to restore all shared folders on the volume to an earlier time. Keep in mind that if you use this feature, any files created since the selected shadow copy instance are deleted.

Shadow copies use the **Volume Shadow Copy Service (VSS)**, introduced in Windows Server 2003. VSS also facilitates backups by using Windows Server Backup and System Restore. VSS allows copying files that are open, essentially taking a snapshot of the data, which allows making backups of files and applications without taking them offline.

Activity 5-12: Configuring Shadow Copies

Time Required: 15 minutes
Objective: Enable shadow copies on a volume.

Required Tools and Equipment: 410Server1
Description: You have several shares on a volume that store documents employees use. These documents change frequently and have sometimes been deleted or corrupted accidentally. You have spent quite a bit of time restoring files from backup at users' requests, so you decide to enable shadow copies on the volume.

1. Log on to 410Server1 as **Administrator**.

2. Open File Explorer, open the Properties dialog box for Vol1, and click the **Shadow Copies** tab.

3. In the Select a volume list box, click **P:** if it's not already selected. Each volume on the computer has an entry so that you can configure shadow copies for all volumes in one place. Each volume entry tells you the next scheduled run time for shadow copies, the number of shares on the volume, and how much space shadow copies are currently using.

4. Click the **Settings** button. If necessary, you can change where shadow copies for this volume are stored. The Use limit option is set to 10% of volume size or 300 MB, whichever is higher. Click the **Schedule** button. The schedule currently contains two entries: one for 7:00 a.m. and one for 12:00 p.m. Monday through Friday. You can delete and add entries to the default schedule to create your own schedule. Click **Cancel**, and then click **OK**.

5. To enable shadow copies and create the first shadow copy, click to select the **P:** volume, and then click the **Enable** button. Read the resulting message and click **Yes**. Click the new entry in the "Shadow copies of selected volume" list box, and note that the Delete Now and Revert buttons are enabled.

6. Click the **Revert** button, and read the Volume Revert message. Click **Check here if you want to revert this volume**, and then click **Revert Now**. The shadow copy entry is deleted because this instance was used to revert the volume.

7. Click **Create Now**. A new shadow copy entry is created. Click **OK**.

8. Create a new text document named **Doc1.txt** in the TestQ folder on Vol1.

9. Open Vol1's Properties dialog box again, and click the **Shadow Copies** tab. If necessary, click the **P:** volume. Click the entry in the "Shadow copies of selected volume" list box, and then click **Revert**. Click **Check here if you want to revert this volume**, and then click **Revert Now**. Click **OK**.

10. In File Explorer, open the **TestQ** folder again. Notice that the text document you created is gone. Create another text document named **Doc2.txt**. Open it in Notepad, type your name and save the file, and exit Notepad.

11. Open the volume's Properties dialog box again, and click the **Shadow Copies** tab. If necessary, click the **P:** volume. Click **Create Now** so that you have a shadow copy for the next activity, and then click **OK**.

12. Close any open windows, and log off 410Server1.

Activity 5-13: Using Shadow Copies

Time Required: 5 minutes
Objective: Use shadow copies to revert to a previous version.

Required Tools and Equipment: 410Server1
Description: You want to test your shadow copies configuration. You access the TestQ share on 410Server1, make changes to the text document you created, and revert to the saved version.

In this activity, you restore a previous version when accessing a file from a share because that's the most common reason for using shadow copies. This feature also works when accessing files locally.

1. Log on to 410Server1 as **Sales1**.

2. Open the **TestQ** share by using the \\410Server1\TestQ UNC path.

3. In File Explorer, open **Doc2.txt**; you should see your name in this document. Add your address or any other text. Save the file, and then exit Notepad.

4. Right-click **Doc2.txt** and click **Restore previous versions**. The file's Properties dialog box opens to the Previous Versions tab. Only one previous version is listed, and you have options to open it to view its contents, copy it so that you don't overwrite the current version, or restore it and overwrite the current version.

5. Click **Restore** and then click **Restore** again in the prompt asking whether you are sure. You see a message stating that the file was restored successfully. Click **OK**, and then click **OK** again.

6. Open **Doc2.txt** and verify that it contains only your name. Exit Notepad.

7. Close any open windows, and log off 410Server1.

Work Folders

Windows Server 2012 R2 introduced a new remote file-sharing feature called Work Folders. **Work Folders** is a role service of the File and Storage Services role that allows users to synchronize documents between company file servers and mobile devices. It's not enabled by default and can be used only with Windows 8.1 and Windows RT 8.1 clients.

Work Folders functions much like offline files (client-side caching), but it works with mobile devices, such as phones and tablets, as well as Windows desktops and laptops. Offline files works only with Windows client OSs, such as Windows 8.1 and Windows 7. Work Folders uses HTTPS rather than the SMB protocol used with offline files, so it doesn't require additional network configuration, such as setting up a virtual private network (VPN) or configuring a firewall. Work Folders supports the following features:

- Files can be accessed while offline with automatic synchronization to company file servers the next time a network connection is established.

- Files can be encrypted on the server and while being copied between devices.

- Security policies can be used to force data encryption and to enforce password and device screen lock requirements.

- High-availability methods, such as failover clustering, are supported.

Before deciding to use Work Folders, you must be aware of some limitations. Work Folders isn't a collaboration service; for example, users can't share their Work Folders with other users and can sync only with their own Work Folders. After Work Folders is enabled, users can find the Work Folders folder in their user profiles. For example, if the user account is jsmith, the Work Folder is C:\Users\jsmith\Work Folder. Only this folder can be synced with company servers, so there's no public Work Folder or a Work Folder that can be accessed by a group of users. For these types of collaboration features, SkyDrive Pro is available. This cloud-based file-sharing service is available with Office 365 or SharePoint Server 2013.

Installing Work Folders

Work Folders has the following requirements:

- A Windows Server 2012 R2 server that acts as the Work Folders host server. It must be a member of a domain.

- An NTFS volume for file storage.

- A server certificate for each Work Folders host server. The certificate is used for validating the server and for data encryption. A certificate issued by a public certification authority is recommended.

- Client devices must run Windows 8.1 or 8.1 RT. Clients for Windows 7, iPad/iPhone, and Android are planned.

- Client devices must have at least 6 GB free space plus enough space for the stored files if the default Work Folders location is used (the Windows boot volume). The location for Work Folders can be changed to a different volume, and then only enough space for the stored files is required. The volume must be NTFS formatted.

To install Work Folders, use the Add Roles and Features function in Server Manager. The Work Folders role service is under File and Storage Services, File and iSCSI Services. You're prompted to install the IIS Hostable Web Core feature, too, which is required for Work Folders. You can also install Work Folders with the following PowerShell command:

```
Add-WindowsFeature FS-SyncShareService
```

Configuring Work Folders

After Work Folders has been installed, a few steps are required before client devices can start using this feature. The steps vary depending on whether users need to access Work Folders from the Internet:

1. Install an SSL certificate on the Work Folders host.

2. Create groups for users who will access Work Folders. If you already have suitable groups created, this step isn't necessary.

3. Create a sync share. At least one sync share must be created so that users can synchronize their Work Folders with the server. Multiple sync shares can be created on different volumes or even different servers if you want to distribute the load. To create a sync share in Server Manager, click File and Storage Services and then click Work Folders. Click Tasks and then New Sync Share to start the New Sync Share Wizard, which guides you through Steps 4 through 8.

4. Select a server and path for the new sync share (see Figure 5-22). Only servers that have Work Folders installed are available to select. You also specify the path to the new share or select an existing share. In Figure 5-22, the local path C:\SyncShare is specified.

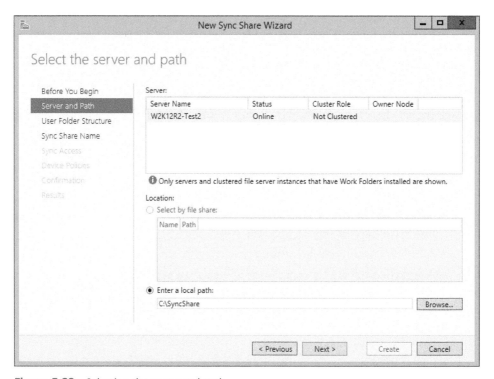

Figure 5-22   Selecting the server and path

5. Specify a user folder structure (see Figure 5-23). Select the User alias option if you want to maintain compatibility with other file-sharing options, such as folder redirection and home folders. The folder name is the same as the user's logon account. The User alias@domain option can be used in a multidomain environment to eliminate conflicts with identical user accounts in separate domains. You can also set a specific subfolder to sync instead of users' entire Work Folders.

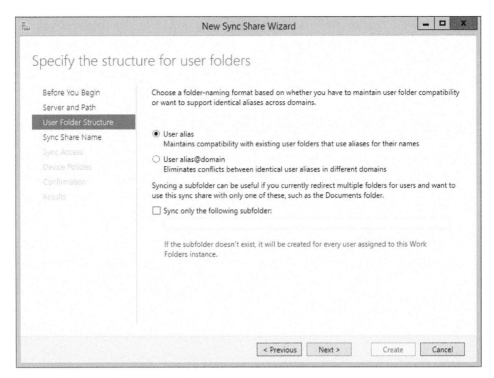

Figure 5-23   Specifying a user folder structure

6. Specify a sync share name (see Figure 5-24), which is the same name as the folder by default. You can also give the sync share a description.

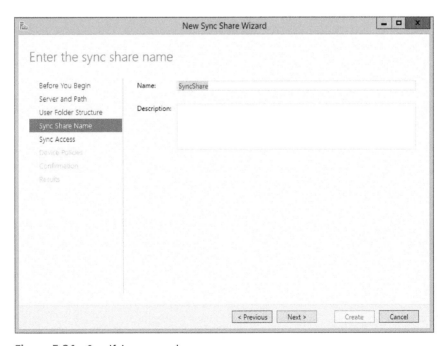

Figure 5-24   Specifying a sync share name

7. Grant access to the sync share (see Figure 5-25). For example, if you're setting up Work Folders for a department, such as Marketing, you can specify the Marketing group. By default, administrators don't have access to files on the sync share. If you want administrators to have access, clear the "Disable inherited permissions and grant users exclusive access to their files" check box.

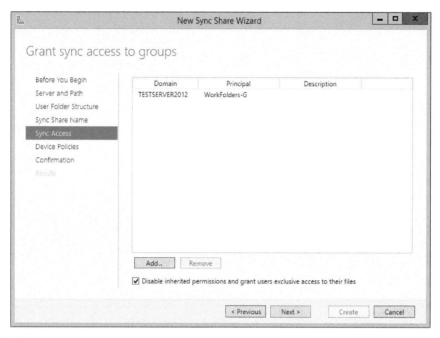

Figure 5-25   Granting sync access to groups

8. Define device policies (see Figure 5-26). You can specify that Work Folders are encrypted and a lock screen and password policies are enforced. The screen lock requirement is 15 or fewer minutes of inactivity, and the password policy requires a password of at least six characters. If a client device doesn't meet the policy, Work Folders can't be configured on the device.

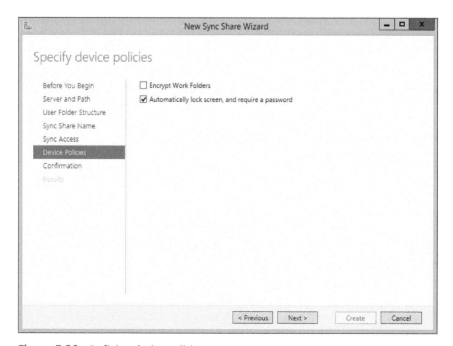

Figure 5-26   Defining device policies

9. To configure Windows 8.1, go to Control Panel, System Security, Work Folders. The server hosting Work Folders must be a member of a domain but the client need not be, which enables users to access Work Folders from their mobile Windows devices and home computers.

10. Enter your work e-mail address (see Figure 5-27) or server URL. The e-mail address is used only as an identifier so that your particular Work Folder can be identified and can be used only if Work Folders discovery is configured. Alternatively, you can enter a Work Folders URL, which has the format `https://server.domain`. After you enter an e-mail address or URL, you're prompted for domain credentials, unless the device is joined to the domain.

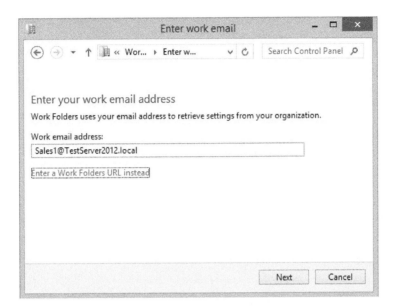

Figure 5-27   Entering an e-mail address or URL

11. Accept or change the local path to the Work Folders location (see Figure 5-28).

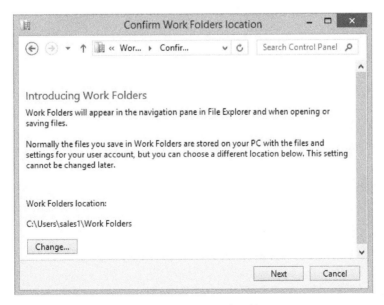

Figure 5-28   Setting the local path to Work Folders

12. Accept the security policies the Work Folders server requires. If you accept the security policies, you can click Set up Work Folders. Work Folders begins syncing with the device and continues to synchronize files as changes occur. After the synchronization is finished, the Work Folders Control Panel applet shows the Manage Work Folders window (see Figure 5-29). You can use this window to stop using Work Folders, manage your credentials, and synchronize files immediately.

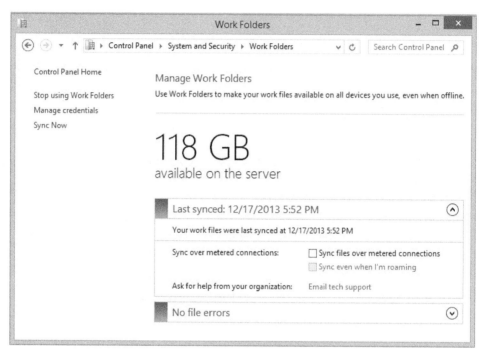

Figure 5-29   The Manage Work Folders window

Windows Printing

To understand how to work with and share printers in a Windows environment, first you need to understand the terminology for defining the components of a shared printer:

- *Print device*—The physical printer containing paper and ink or toner to which print jobs are sent. There are two basic types of print devices:

    o Local print device: A printer connected to an I/O port on a computer, usually with a USB cable.

    o Network print device: A printer attached directly to the network through a NIC.

- *Printer*—The icon in the Printers folder that represents print devices. Windows programs print to a printer, which uses a printer driver to format the print job and send it to the print device or print server. A printer can be a local printer, which prints directly to a local or network print device, or a network printer, which prints to a print server.

- *Print server*—A Windows computer that's sharing a printer. It accepts print jobs from computers on the network and sends jobs to the printer to be printed on the print device.

- *Print queue*—A storage location for print jobs awaiting printing. In Windows Server 2012/R2, the print queue is set up as a directory (by default, C:\Windows\System32\Spool\Printers) where files that make up each print job are stored until they're sent to the print device or print server.

The following sections focus on print servers—specifically, configuring and managing print servers in Windows Server 2012/R2.

Print Servers

A print server configured in Windows Server 2012/R2 can perform a host of printing functions that aren't possible when users' computers print directly to a print device:

- *Access control*—Using permissions, administrators can control who can print to a printer and who can manage print jobs and printers.

- *Printer pooling*—With **printer pooling,** a single printer represents two or more print devices. Users can print to a single printer, and the print server sends the job to the print device that's least busy.

- *Printer priority*—With **printer priority,** two or more printers can represent a single print device. Printers can be assigned different priorities so that jobs sent to the higher priority printer are sent to the print device first.

- *Print job management*—Administrators can pause, cancel, restart, reorder, and change preferences on print jobs waiting in the print queue.

- *Availability control*—Administrators can configure print servers so that print jobs are accepted only during certain hours of the day.

Printer Pooling   Printer pooling is used when a printer is heavily used and users are losing productivity waiting for their print jobs. You could just add another printer and another print device to the print server, but then users would have to know which printer is most available when they choose where to send a print job. With printer pooling, a single printer is defined on the print server, but the printer (the icon in the Printers folder in Windows) is connected to two or more print devices on separate ports. When a user prints a document, the document is sent to the printer, which then determines which print device is least busy and should get the job. Print devices in the pool must use the same print driver, and for convenience, they should be located close to one another. Users don't know which print device a job is sent to, so having all print devices in the same room means users don't have to wait around looking for their print jobs.

Printer Priority   Printer priority is in some ways the opposite of printer pooling. It solves the problem of small or important print jobs getting stuck in the print queue behind large or less important jobs. Two or more printers can be configured to send jobs to the same print device, and each printer can have a different priority set. The higher the number, the higher the priority. Print jobs sent to the highest priority printer are printed first. For example, you could set up two printers that print to a color laser print device. One printer is available only to managers, and the other is available to staff. Jobs sent to the managers' printer, with the priority setting 10, print before jobs sent to the staff printer, with the priority setting 1. Print jobs with higher priority get placed in the print queue before jobs with lower priority, but if the lower priority job is already printing, the job is not interrupted.

Configuring a Print Server   To configure a Windows Server 2012/R2 system as a print server, you just need to share a printer. After a printer is installed, right-click it, click Printer properties, and click the Sharing tab. The Sharing tab in a printer's Properties dialog box (see Figure 5-30) has the following options:

- *Share this printer*—When this check box is selected, the print server is shared. By default, the Everyone special identity is assigned Print permissions to shared printers.

- *Share name*—By default, it's the name of the printer in the Printers folder. You can enter a shorter share name or one that's easier to remember.

- *Render print jobs on client computers*—When this check box is selected (the default setting), client computers process the print job and send it to the print server in a format that's ready to go directly to the print device. If this option isn't selected, more processing occurs on the print server.

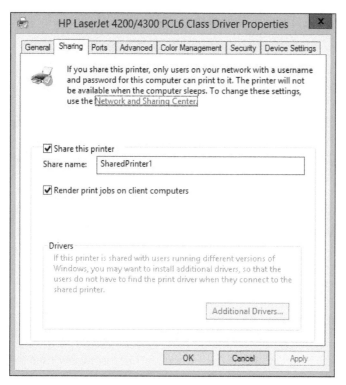

Figure 5-30   The Sharing tab in a printer's Properties dialog box

- *List in the directory*—This option is available only on servers that are domain members. When this check box is selected, the print server is displayed in Active Directory and can be found by Active Directory searches. By default, this option isn't selected.

- *Additional Drivers*—When a client connects to a shared printer, the printer driver is downloaded to the client from the server automatically when possible. You can click this button to install different printer drivers on the server to support different Windows versions or platforms.

The Advanced tab in a printer's Properties dialog box has more options for controlling the print server (see Figure 5-31):

- *Always available/Available from*—Select the Available from option to set the hours the print server accepts print jobs. Jobs that users submit outside the available hours wait in the local print queue until the print server is available.

- *Priority*—Printer priority was explained previously in "Printer Priority." Choose a number between 1 and 99 (with higher numbers having higher priority). The default priority is 1.

- *Driver*—This field specifies the print driver in use. To change the driver, click the New Driver button.

- *Spooling options*—Print jobs that are spooled are written as files to the print queue before being sent to the print device. You can specify whether jobs should start printing as soon as a page is received or an entire job should be written to the queue before printing starts. The default setting is "Start printing immediately." You can turn off spooling by selecting the "Print directly to the printer" option, but this option isn't recommended, as some applications have to wait until printing is finished before they can be resumed.

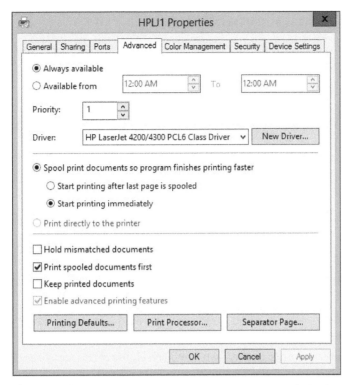

Figure 5-31   The Advanced tab in a printer's Properties dialog box

- *Hold mismatched documents*—If a print job at the head of the queue requires a different paper type than what's loaded in the print device, the print server normally stops all printing until the problem is solved. Setting this option (which is disabled by default) holds these print jobs and lets other jobs in the queue print. After the correct paper is loaded, the held document can print.

- *Print spooled documents first*—When this option is set, jobs already in the queue can start printing even if a job with higher priority starts spooling. This setting, which is enabled by default, minimizes printer idle time.

- *Keep printed documents*—Normally, print job files are deleted from the print queue after they have printed. This option, disabled by default, keeps files in the queue so that they can be reprinted if necessary. Setting this option might be a good choice with print jobs that are difficult to reproduce.

- *Enable advanced printing features*—This option, which is selected by default, enables you to use advanced printing options, such as page order and multiple pages per sheet (if supported by the driver). Turning the option off can solve some compatibility issues.

- *Printing Defaults*—You can select default settings for paper handling (one-sided, two-sided), paper sources, paper size, paper type, orientation (landscape or portrait), color or black and white, and so forth.

- *Print Processor*—Click this button to set the default print processor and data type. The existing defaults are normally okay, unless your network has older non-Windows clients.

- *Separator Page*—Click this button and then click Browse to select a separator page that's printed before each print job. Three separator pages are available in C:\Windows\System32: Pcl.sep for PCL printers, Sysprint.sep for PostScript printers, and Sysprtj.sep for PostScript printers with Japanese fonts.

Activity 5-14: Installing and Sharing a Printer

Time Required: 15 minutes
Objective: Install and share a printer.

Required Tools and Equipment: 410Server1 and a network-attached printer
Description: Most employees in the company have been printing directly to a network-attached printer. You have learned that a print server can offer some benefits, so you decide to install the printer and share it on your Windows Server 2012 R2 server.

This activity requires a network-attached printer and its IP address. Your instructor will provide this address.

1. Log on to 410Server1 as **Administrator,** if necessary.

2. Right-click **Start** and click **Control Panel.** Click **Hardware,** and then click **Devices and Printers.**

3. Click **Add a printer** to start the Add Printer Wizard. Windows searches for available printers. Click **The printer that I want isn't listed.**

4. In the Find a printer by other options window (see Figure 5-32), click the **Add a local printer or network printer with manual settings** option button, and then click **Next.**

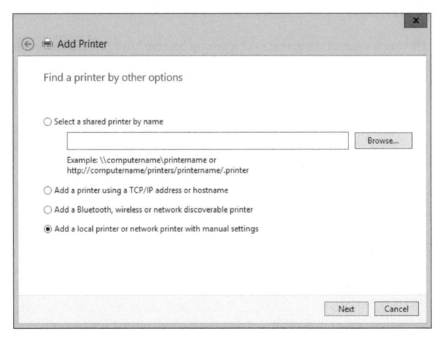

Figure 5-32   Adding a local or network printer

5. In the Choose a printer port window (see Figure 5-33), click the **Create a new port** option button. In the Type of port list box, click **Standard TCP/IP Port,** and then click **Next.**

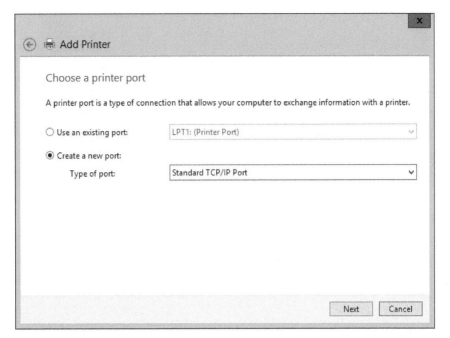

Figure 5-33   Specifying a printer port

6. In the Type a printer hostname or IP address window, type the network-attached printer's IP address (supplied by your instructor) in the Hostname or IP address text box. The port name is filled in automatically, but you can change it, if you like. By default, Windows attempts to query the printer to determine the driver to use. Click **Next**.

7. If Windows was able to determine the printer information, the printer name is filled in, which you can change, if you want. If Windows couldn't determine the printer information, select the printer manufacturer and model, and then click **Next**.

8. In the Printer Sharing window (see Figure 5-34), click the **Share this printer so that others on your network can find and use it** option button, and type **SharedPrinter1** in the Share name text box. (Normally, you give a printer a more descriptive name.) Click **Next**.

 If you don't share the printer in the Add Printer Wizard, you can share it later in the Sharing tab of the printer's Properties dialog box.

9. Click **Print a test page**, unless told otherwise by your instructor. If you printed a test page, click **Close**, and then click **Finish**.

10. In the Devices and Printers window, right-click the printer you installed and click **Printer properties**.

11. Click the **Ports** tab. You can add a port or change a port's configuration, such as changing the IP address of a TCP/IP port. If you have two or more identical printers, you can click the Enable printer pooling option and select additional ports for this printer.

12. Click the **Security** tab. Printers don't have share permissions; they have permissions only in the Security tab, and they work similarly to NTFS permissions. Click the ACEs in the Group or user names list box, and review the permissions for each one. Notice that the Everyone group has the Print permission by default. Click **Cancel**, and close any open windows.

13. Stay logged on if you're continuing to the next activity; otherwise, log off or shut down 410Server1.

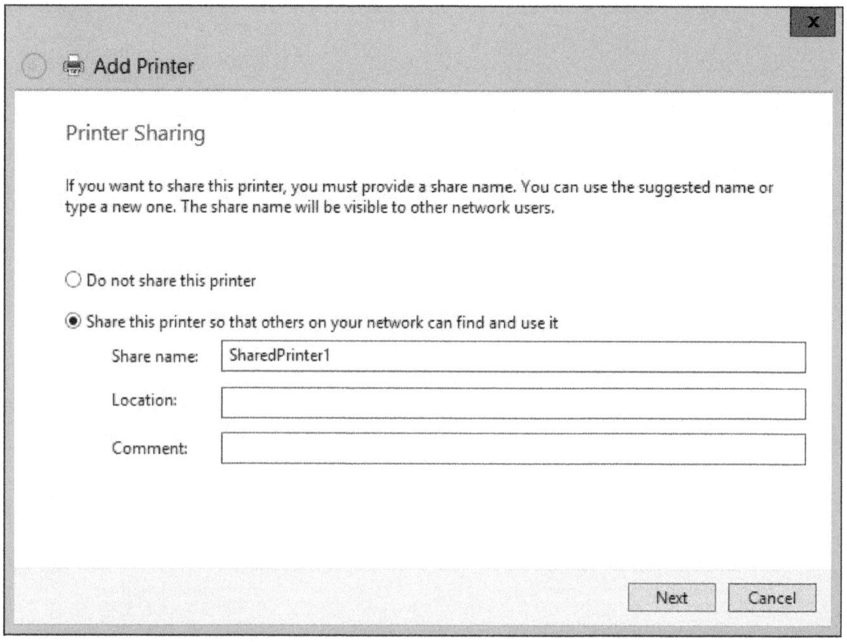

Figure 5-34 Setting share information for a printer

Printer Permissions   Access to printers is controlled much like access to folders and files. However, there's no need to be concerned with permission inheritance on printers. Printers have three standard permissions (see Figure 5-35) and six special permissions:

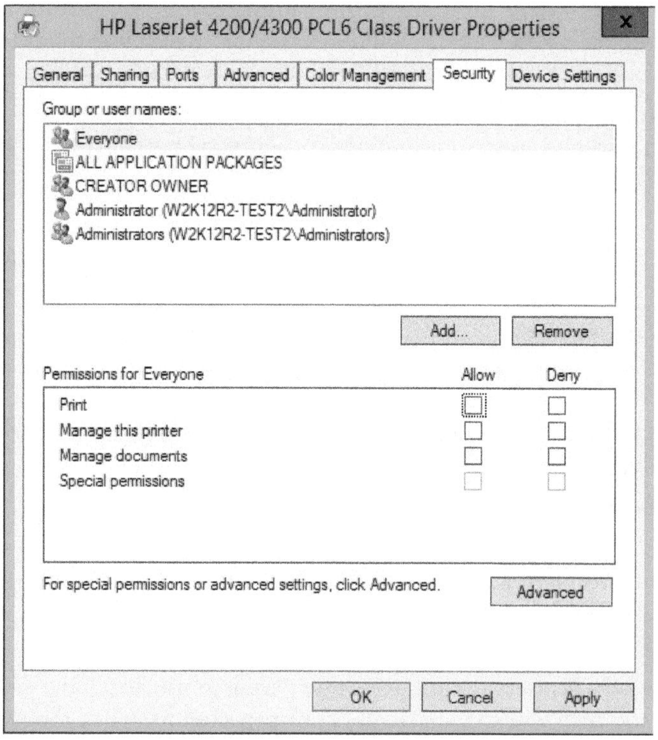

Figure 5-35 Printer permissions

- *Print*—Allows users to connect to a printer and send print jobs to it. By default, the Everyone special identity is assigned the Print permission.

- *Manage this printer*—Includes everything in the Print permission plus administering all aspects of the printer: pausing and restarting the printer, sharing the printer, changing permissions, and changing printer properties. By default, the Administrators group is assigned this permission along with the Print and Manage documents permissions. On domain controllers, the Server Operators and Print Operators groups are also assigned these permissions by default.

- *Manage documents*—Allows users to manage all jobs in the print queue. By default, the Administrators group and the CREATOR OWNER special identity are assigned this permission. Server Operators and Print Operators are assigned this permission by default on domain controllers. Because CREATOR OWNER is assigned this permission, users can manage their own print jobs (pause, cancel, restart, and change properties).

Special permissions include the three standard permissions as well as Read permissions, Change permissions, and Take ownership.

ACTIVITY

Activity 5-15: Connecting to a Shared Printer

Time Required: 10 minutes
Objective: Connect to a shared printer from a client workstation.

Required Tools and Equipment: 410Win8 and 410Server1
Description: After installing the printer and configuring sharing, you need to set up client workstations to connect to the shared printer.

1. Start 410Server1, if necessary. Start 410Win8, and log on as **Win8User**.

2. Log on to 410Server1, if necessary. Create a new user on 410Server1 named **Win8User** with the password **Password01**. Make sure the password is set to never expire. You need to create this user on 410Server1 so that you can access the shared printer from the 410Win8 client.

3. On 410Win8, right-click **Start**, click **Run**, type **\\410Server1** in the Open text box, and then press **Enter**. If necessary, enter the password for the Administrator account. Right-click **SharedPrinter1** and click **Connect**. Windows displays a message that it's connecting to the printer.

4. Right-click **Start**, click **Control Panel**, click **Hardware and Sound**, and click **Devices and Printers**. You see the printer you connected to. Right-click the printer, click **Printer properties**, and then click **Print Test Page**. Each test page can be identified by the computer name that printed it displayed on the test page. You see a message indicating a test page has been sent to the printer. Click **Close** and then click **Cancel** to close the printer's Properties dialog box.

5. On 410Server1, click **Devices and Printers** in Control Panel, and click the printer you installed. Click **See what's printing** on the menu bar. The print queue shows any jobs waiting to be printed. (At this point, there aren't any.) Figure 5-36 shows a print queue with two jobs.

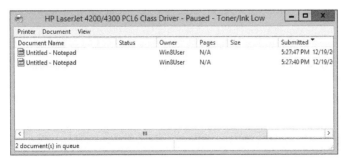

Figure 5-36 A print queue with jobs waiting to print

6. Click **Printer, Pause Printing** from the menu to prevent jobs in the queue from printing.

7. On 410Win8, print a test page to the printer.

8. On 410Server1, you see the print job in the print queue window. Right-click the print job and review the actions you can take. Leave the print queue window open.

9. On 410Server1, open File Explorer and navigate to the **C:\Windows\System32\spool\ PRINTERS** folder, which stores the jobs you see in the print queue. Two files representing the print job are listed. Close File Explorer.

10. On 410Win8, open the print queue for the printer. You see the job the same way you see it on the server. Right-click the print job and click **Cancel**. Click **Yes** to confirm. (If the print job is still displayed, click **View, Refresh** from the menu.) Recall that you can manage your own print jobs because of the CREATOR OWNER's Manage documents permission.

11. On 410Server1 in the print queue window, click **Printer, Properties** from the menu. Click the **Security** tab, click **CREATOR OWNER** in the list of ACEs, and then click **Remove**. Click **OK**.

12. On 410Win8, print another test page to the printer. In the print queue window, right-click the print job and click **Cancel**. Click **Yes** to confirm. You get an "Access denied" message in the status bar of the print queue window.

13. On 410Server1, right-click the print job and click **Cancel**. Click **Yes** to confirm. Click **Printer, Pause Printing** from the menu to unpause the printer.

14. Shut down 410Win8, and log off or shut down 410Server1.

Managing Print Documents

As you saw in the previous activity, you have several options for managing documents in the queue waiting to print. To access the print queue, right-click a printer and click "See what's printing." You can manage each document in the queue by right-clicking the document and using the shortcut menu or by selecting the document and clicking Document on the menu. You can take the following actions on a document:

- *Pause*—Pauses printing the document. You might need to pause a print job, for example, if you need to change the type of paper in the print device or want another job in the queue to print first.

- *Resume*—Resumes printing a paused document.

- *Restart*—Restarts a print job from the beginning. You might need to use this option if, for example, the document started printing on the wrong paper, and you changed the paper type and want to start the entire job over.

- *Cancel*—Cancels a print job and removes it from the queue.

- *Properties*—Opens the properties for a document in the queue. You can change the priority of the document, set a time restriction, and view or change print layout, paper, and quality options.

You can manage print documents with PowerShell commands, too. To get help on using any of the following PowerShell commands, type `Get-Help` *command* at a PowerShell prompt:

- `Get-PrintJob`—Lists current print jobs for a specified printer

- `Suspend-PrintJob`—Pauses a print job

- `Resume-PrintJob`—Resumes a paused print job

- `Restart-PrintJob`—Restarts a print job

- `Remove-PrintJob`—Cancels a print job

Solving Print Queue Problems One of the most common printing problems is getting jobs stuck in the print queue. When this happens, no other jobs can print. Sometimes canceling or restarting the job solves the problem, but if this fails, the next step is restarting the Print Spooler service. To do this, cancel the job that's trying to print and do one of the following things:

- Open the Services control panel, find the Print Spooler service, and restart it.
- Enter `net stop "print spooler"` at a command prompt, and then enter `net start "print spooler"`.
- Enter `Stop-Service Spooler` at a PowerShell prompt, and then enter `Start-Service Spooler`.

In most cases, stopping and restarting the Print Spooler service deletes the job that was stuck in the queue and starts the next job. If this method doesn't solve the problem, you might need to restart the server.

Remote Desktop Printing

When a client is connected to the network via a Remote Desktop Protocol (RDP) session, the applications and resources it uses are running on the RDP host computer. However, if the user wants to print a document, he or she probably wants to print to a local printer connected to the client computer. RDP uses the Easy Print printer driver to allow local printing during a RDP session. This driver redirects print jobs through the RDP session to the selected local printer. It's installed by default if Remote Desktop Services is installed on a computer, so no configuration or setup is required. When a client is connected to another computer via RDP and wants to print a document, the list of available printers includes printers connected to the RDP host and printers connected to the client computer. Those connected to the client computer show the printer name followed by "redirected" in parentheses (see Figure 5-37).

Figure 5-37 A printer redirected with Easy Print

Print Management with the Print and Document Services Role

You can create printer shares and manage the print server and print queue without installing the Print and Document Services role. However, this role includes many advanced options for managing a print server and additional ways to share printers. When you install the Print and Document Services role, you must also install the Print Server role service. It provides the Print

Management snap-in, which can be used to manage multiple printers and print servers. You can also migrate printers to and from other Windows print servers.

You have the option to install three other role services, too: Distributed Scan Server, LPD Service, and Internet Printing. Distributed Scan Server provides central administration for sharing and managing network scanners. To install this role service, the server must be a domain member and must be running the full GUI. Line Printer Daemon (LPD) Service allows UNIX/Linux computers using the Line Printer Remote (LPR) service to print to Windows shared printers. Internet Printing creates a Web site that allows managing print jobs through a Web browser and enables clients with Internet Printing Protocol (IPP) installed to connect to printers and send print jobs to shared printers via the Internet.

After the Print and Document Services role is installed, the Print Management console (see Figure 5-38) is available from the Tools menu in Server Manager. You use Print Management to view status information and manage all printers and print servers on the network. By default, local print servers are available in the console, and other print servers can be added to the console. Some tasks you can perform with Print Management include the following:

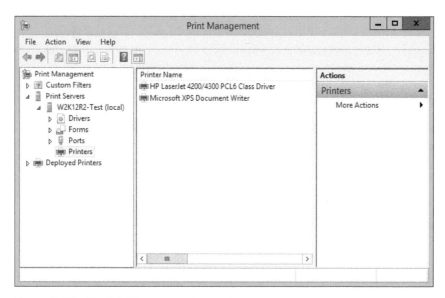

Figure 5-38   The Print Management console

- *Install a new printer*—Add new printers to any server on the network, not just the local server.
- *Share a printer*—Share an installed printer or change a shared printer's properties and permissions.
- *Migrate printers*—Export printers from one server and import them to another. This feature makes it easy to consolidate print servers or move printers from a server that's been taken out of service.
- *Deploy printers with Group Policy*—In domain environments, printer connections can be set up for users or computers by using Group Policy, which makes it unnecessary to set up printers on separate client workstations manually.
- *List or remove printers from Active Directory*—Publish printers in Active Directory or remove published printers.
- *Display printers based on a filter*—On a network with dozens or hundreds of printers, you can configure filters to display printers that meet certain criteria. Filters enable you to view in a single window, for example, all printers that have jobs waiting or all printers that are out of paper or toner. You can also set up notifications so that an e-mail is sent when criteria are met.

Branch Office Direct Printing Branch Office Direct Printing is a new feature in Windows Server 2012 and Windows 8 that makes it possible to print directly to a print device instead of the print server print queue. This feature can save bandwidth when branch office users print to a local print device, but the print server is located remotely in the central office.

With Branch Office Direct Printing enabled on a printer, the client computer receives printer information from the remote print server but prints the job directly to the print device without print data having to travel via a WAN link. Even if the WAN link is down and the print server is unavailable, users can print to the local print device. The print device must be network attached, the print server must be running at least Windows Server 2012, and the client must be running at least Windows 8. Branch Office Direct Printing can't be used with printer pooling or printer priorities.

To enable Branch Office Direct Printing, you use the Print Management console, which is installed with the Print and Document Services role, or PowerShell cmdlets. To enable Branch Office Direct Printing in the Print Management console, click Printer Servers in the left pane, and then click Printers. Right-click the printer where you want to enable the feature and click Enable Branch Office Direct Printing.

The PowerShell command to enable Branch Office Direct Printing is as follows:

```
Set-Printer -name PrinterName -ComputerName PrintServerName
  -RenderingMode BranchOffice
```

The `ComputerName` parameter is unnecessary if you're running the PowerShell command on the print server.

Chapter Summary

- File- and printer-sharing functions are in the File and Storage Services role, which includes the File Server role service. The SMB protocol is used to access Windows file shares, but Windows also supports NFS.

- There are two types of permissions to restrict access to files and folders: share and NTFS. Share permissions restrict network access to files and folders, and NTFS permissions restrict both interactive/local and network access.

- Three types of objects can be assigned permission to access the file system: users, groups, and computers. These object types are referred to as security principals.

- Permissions are assigned in four ways: The user creates an object, the user account is added to the DACL, a group the user belongs to is added to the DACL, and permission is inherited. Effective permissions are the combination of assigned permissions.

- There are three share permissions: Read, Change, and Full Control. There are six standard NTFS permissions: Read, Read & execute, List folder contents, Write, Modify, and Full control. On an NTFS or ReFS volume, permissions are set at the root of a volume first, and all folders and files in that volume inherit these settings unless configured otherwise.

- The File Server role service is required to share folders. You can install this role service in Server Manager, or you can simply share a folder to have it installed automatically. You can use the following methods to configure folder sharing in Windows Server 2012/R2: simple file sharing, advanced sharing, Shared Folders, File and Storage Services, and Share and Storage Management.

- You should use Deny permissions only when you need to create an exception to an Allow permission. Deny permissions take precedence over Allow permissions.

- Every recent Windows OS includes administrative shares, which are hidden shares available only to members of the Administrators group. They include Admin$, *Drive*$, and IPC$, and on domain controllers, the NETLOGON and SYSVOL shares are added.

- There are several ways for client computers to access shared folders: using the UNC path, doing an Active Directory search, mapping a drive, and browsing the network.

- Disk quotas are used to restrict how much space a user's files can occupy on a server. They are set on an NTFS volume and, by default, apply to all users except administrators.

- Shadow copies are enabled on an entire volume and allows users to access previous versions of files in shared folders and restore files that have been deleted or corrupted. You configure shadow copies in the Shadow Copies tab of a volume's Properties dialog box.

- Work Folders is a role service that's a component of the File and Storage Services role. It allows users to synchronize documents between company file servers and mobile devices. This role service isn't enabled by default and can be used only with Windows 8.1 and Windows RT 8.1 clients.

- Windows Server 2012/R2 offers advanced features for managing shared printers and making printing easy and convenient for users. A print server configured in Windows Server 2012/R2 can perform many printing functions that aren't possible when users' computers print directly to a print device, including access control, printer pooling, printer prioritization, and availability control.

- The Print and Document Services role includes the Print Management snap-in, which can be used to manage multiple printers and print servers. You have the option to install three other role services: Distributed Scan Server, LPD Service, and Internet Printing. With the Print and Document Services role installed, you can also enable Branch Office Direct Printing.

Key Terms

access-based enumeration (ABE)   A feature of a file share that shows only file and folders to which a user has at least Read permission.

access control entry (ACE)   An entry in a discretionary access control list (DACL); includes a security principal object and the object's assigned permissions. *See also* discretionary access control list (DACL).

administrative shares   Hidden shares created by Windows that are available only to members of the Administrators group; they include the root of each volume, the \Windows folder, and IPC$. Hidden shares' names end with a dollar sign.

Branch Office Direct Printing   A feature available with the Print and Document Services role that allows clients to print directly to a network-attached printer without the job having to go through the print server.

discretionary access control list (DACL)   A list of security principals; each has permissions that define access to an object. *See also* security principal.

disk quotas   An option on NTFS volumes that enables administrators to limit how much disk space a user can occupy with his or her files.

effective access   The access a security principal has to a file system object when taking sharing permissions, NTFS permissions, and group memberships into account. *See also* security principal.

effective permissions   The combination of permissions assigned to an account from explicit and inherited permissions; determines an account's effective access to an object. *See also* effective access.

explicit permission   A permission assigned by adding a user's account to an object's DACL.

inherited permission   A permission that comes from an object's parent instead of being assigned explicitly. *See also* explicit permission.

Network File System (NFS)   The native file-sharing protocol in UNIX and Linux OSs; also supported by Windows Server 2012.

NTFS permissions   Permissions set on folders or files on an NTFS-formatted volume; they protect both network and interactive/local file access.

object owner   Usually the user account that created the object or a group or user who has been assigned ownership of the object. An object owner has special authority over that object.

offline files   A feature of shared folders that allows users to access the contents of shared folders when not connected to the network; also called "client-side caching."

permission inheritance   A method for defining how permissions are transmitted from a parent object to a child object.

permissions   A property of the file system that specifies which users can access a file system object (a file or folder) and what users can do with the object if they're granted access.

printer pooling   A printer configuration in which a single printer represents two or more print devices. Users can print to a single printer, and the print server sends the job to the print device that's least busy.

printer priority   A printer configuration in which two or more printers can represent a single print device. Printers can be assigned different priorities so that jobs sent to the higher priority printer are sent to the print device first.

security descriptor   A file system object's security settings, composed of the DACL, owner, and SACL. *See also* discretionary access control list (DACL) *and* system access control list (SACL).

security principal   An object that can be assigned permission to access the file system; includes user, group, and computer accounts.

Server Message Block (SMB)   A client/server Application-layer protocol that provides network file sharing, network printing, and authentication.

shadow copies   A feature of the Windows file system that allows users to access previous versions of files in shared folders and restore files that have been deleted or corrupted.

share permissions   Permissions applied to shared folders that protect files accessed across the network; the only method for protecting files on FAT volumes.

system access control list (SACL)   A file system component that defines the settings for auditing access to an object.

Volume Shadow Copy Service (VSS)   A Windows service that enables shadow copies and allows copying files that are open, essentially taking a snapshot of the data, which allows making backups of files and applications without taking them offline. *See also* shadow copies.

Work Folders   A role service that's a component of the File and Storage Services role; allows users to synchronize documents between company file servers and mobile devices.

Review Questions

1. Which of the following is a file-sharing protocol supported by Windows Server 2012/R2 File and Storage Services role? (Choose all that apply.)

   a. SMB

   b. FTP

   c. TFTP

   d. NFS

2. Which of the following is *not* a standard NTFS permission?

   a. Read & execute

   b. Change

   c. Write

   d. List folder contents

3. In which of the following ways can a user become a file's owner? (Choose all that apply.)

   a. Take ownership of the file.

   b. Create the file.

   c. Belong to the File Owner special identity.

   d. Be assigned as the owner by an administrator.

4. Which SMB share option should you enable if you don't want users to see files they don't have at least Read permission to?

   a. Offline files

   b. Hidden shares

   c. Branch Cache

   d. Access-based enumeration

5. Which administrative share does Active Directory use for replication?

   a. NETLOGON

   b. SYSVOL

   c. Admin$

   d. IPC$

6. Which feature of Windows file sharing should you configure if you want users to be able to access their files securely from mobile devices without having to set up a VPN or configure the firewall?

   a. Client-side caching

   b. Offline files

   c. Access-based enumeration

   d. Work Folders

7. An expensive color laserjet printer is shared by a group of managers and some other employees. The managers complain that they often have to wait for their print jobs until other employees' large jobs have finished. Usually, the managers' print jobs are small and needed immediately, but other employees rarely need their print jobs in a hurry. What can you do to help solve this problem without buying additional equipment?

   a. Create two printers and assign them different priorities and permissions.

   b. Create another printer and configure a printer pool.

   c. Buy another printer and configure permissions so that only managers can access it.

   d. Make the printer available only during the hours managers are working.

8. Which of the following is *not* true about disk quotas?

   a. Users can be prevented from saving files on a volume.

   b. An event can be generated when a user exceeds the quota limit.

   c. Quotas can be overridden for groups.

   d. Quotas can be set without denying disk space to users.

9. You have been getting quite a few calls with requests to restore files from a backup because the file was accidentally deleted from a share or because the user needed a previous version of a file that was overwritten. Restoring the files has become a burden, and sometimes you need to repeat the process several times until you find the version the user needs. What can you do to give users a way to access the files they need and reduce your administrative burden?

    a. Adjust permissions on the shares so that users can't delete files except their own. Tell users to back up their own files to local backup media.

    b. Enable shadow copies for each share.

    c. Enable shadow copies on the volumes where the shares are hosted.

    d. Give each user a backup program and an external hard drive.

10. Which of the following is true about share and NTFS permissions?

    a. NTFS permissions are applied only to local file access.

    b. Share permissions take precedence over NTFS permissions.

    c. Share permissions are applied to network and local file access.

    d. NTFS permissions are applied to network access.

11. A user needs to create files and make changes to file contents. Aside from the Read permission, what other permission should the user be granted without allowing more access than is necessary?

    a. Write

    b. Full control

    c. Modify

    d. Create

12. The Tsmith user account has been granted the Read share permission. Tsmith is a member of the Sales group, which has been granted the Change share permission. In the shared folder's Security tab, Sales has been granted Full control, and the Users group has been granted Read permission. Which of the following can Tsmith do in the share when accessing it from the network? (Choose all that apply.)

    a. Change permissions on all files.

    b. Delete all files.

    c. Take ownership of all files.

    d. Create files.

13. You're the administrator of a file server. Tom, who is on vacation, had created a file that Mary needs access to, but neither her account nor the Administrator account has permission to access the file. What is the best way to allow Mary to access the file?

14. Which of the following can be used to create shares? (Choose all that apply.)

    a. Advanced sharing

    b. Disk Management

    c. Simple file sharing

    d. File and Storage Services

15. You need to prevent members of a group from accessing a subfolder of a folder the group *does* have access to. What's the best way to do this? (Choose two answers. Each correct answer represents part of the solution.)

    a. Disable permission inheritance on the subfolder, and convert existing permissions.

    b. Add each member of the group to the subfolder's DACL, and assign a Deny permission to each member.

    c. Create a new group, and add members of the existing group to this new group. Add the new group to the subfolder's DACL with a Deny permission.

    d. Remove the group from the subfolder's DACL.

16. You need to create a share containing confidential information that only a select group of people should know about. You don't want this share to appear in users' network browse lists. What can you do that involves the least administrative effort and disruption?

    a. Disable network discovery on all computers.

    b. Disable network discovery on the computers of users who you don't want to see the share.

    c. Put a $ character at the end of the share name.

    d. Put a @ character at the beginning of the share name.

17. What command can you put in a batch file to allow users to access the Public share on the ServPub1 server, using the drive letter P?

    a. `net share P: \\ServPub1\Public`

    b. `net use P: \\ServPub1\Public`

    c. `share \\ServPub1\Public P:`

    d. `share P: \\ServPub1\Public`

18. A folder can be shared only with a single name and single set of share permissions. True or False?

19. You're seeing heavy use on one of your shared printers, and users often have to wait in line to get their print jobs. What printing feature can you use to best alleviate the problem?

    a. Printer prioritization

    b. Change availability hours

    c. Change spooling options

    d. Printer pooling

20. You have installed a shared printer with the default permissions and want users to be able to manage their own documents in the print queue. What do you need to do?

    a. Do nothing.

    b. Assign the Everyone special identity the Manage documents permission.

    c. Assign the Everyone special identity the Manage printers permission.

    d. Add Domain Users to the Printer Operators group.

Case Projects

CASE PROJECTS

Case Project 5-1: Creating a Shared Folder Structure

CSM Tech Publishing has asked you to develop a file-sharing system for the company's departments, which include Management, Marketing, Sales, Development, and Editorial. The following are some requirements for the file-sharing solution:

- Management must be able to access all files in all the shares, unless stated otherwise, and must be able to create, delete, and change files.

- The Management Department must have a share that only it can access, and each member of the department must be able to create, delete, and change files in the share.

- Marketing and Sales should have one common folder that both departments' users have access to. Members of both departments should be able to create new files, have full control over files they create, and view and change files created by other group members. They should not be able to delete files created by other members.

- Sales should have its own share that only Sales and Management have access to. The Sales users must have full control over all files in the share.

- Development and Editorial have their own shares that only these departments and Management have access to. The users from these two departments must have full control over all files in their department shares.

- There should be a public share in which users in the Management Department can create, change, and delete documents, and all other users have the ability only to read the documents.

- There should be a share available to management that no other users can see in a browse list. It contains confidential documents that only selected users in the Management Department have access to.

- Users must be able to restore files they accidentally delete or restore an earlier version of a file without having to use a backup program.

- Sales users must be able to access the files in the Sales share when they're traveling whether they have an Internet connection or not. When Sales users are back in the office, any changed files should synchronize with their mobile devices automatically. All Sales users have a Windows 8.1 laptop or tablet computer running Windows RT 8.1.

- All users except Management users should be limited to 10 GB of space on the volume housing shares. Management users should be limited to 50 GB.

Given these requirements, perform the following tasks and answer the following questions:

- Design the folder structure and include information about the permissions (sharing and NTFS) you plan to assign to each share and group of users. Name each share appropriately.

- What tool will you use to create the shares? Why?

- What protocols and technologies (including file system) will be used to set up these shared folders? Explain the reason for using each protocol or technology.

chapter 6

Introducing Active Directory

After reading this chapter and completing the exercises, you will be able to:

- Describe the role of a directory service
- Install Active Directory
- Describe objects found in Active Directory
- Work with forests, trees, and domains
- Configure group policies

Windows Server 2012/R2 Active Directory is the core component in a Windows domain environment. The Active Directory Domain Services role provides a single point of user, desktop, and server administration. To understand Active Directory and its role in a network, you need to know what a directory service is and how it's used to manage resources and access to resources on a network. Before administrators can use Active Directory to manage users, desktops, and servers in a network, they need a good understanding of Active Directory's structure and underlying components and objects, which are covered in this chapter. You also learn how to install Active Directory and work with forests, trees, and domains. Finally, you learn the basics of using the Group Policy tool to set consistent security, user, and desktop standards throughout your organization.

The Role of a Directory Service

Table 6-1 summarizes what you need for the hands-on activities in this chapter.

Table 6-1   Activity requirements

Activity	Requirements	Notes
Activity 6-1: Installing Active Directory Domain Services	410Server1	
Activity 6-2: Exploring Active Directory Container Objects	410Server1	
Activity 6-3: Viewing Default Leaf Objects	410Server1	
Activity 6-4: Creating Objects in Active Directory	410Server1	
Activity 6-5: Using dsadd to Create Objects	410Server1	
Activity 6-6: Locating Objects with Active Directory Users and Computers	410Server1	
Activity 6-7: Locating Objects with File Explorer	410Server1	
Activity 6-8: Publishing a Shared Folder in Active Directory	410Server1	
Activity 6-9: Viewing the Operations Master Roles	410Server1	
Activity 6-10: Configuring a Global Catalog Server	410Server1	
Activity 6-11: Exploring Default GPOs	410Server1	
Activity 6-12: Working with Group Policies	410Server1	

© 2015 Cengage Learning®

A network **directory service**, as the name suggests, stores information about a computer network and offers features for retrieving and managing that information. Essentially, it's a database composed of records or objects describing users and available network resources, such as servers, printers, and applications. Like a database for managing a company's inventory, a directory service includes functions to search for, add, modify, and delete information. Unlike an inventory database, a directory service can also manage how its stored resources can be used and by whom. For example, a directory service can be used to specify who has the right to log on to a computer or restrict what software can be installed on a computer.

A directory service is often thought of as an administrator's tool, but users can use it, too. Users might need the directory service to locate network resources, such as printers or shared folders, by performing a search. They can even use the directory service as a phone book of sorts to look up information about other users, such as phone numbers, office locations, and e-mail addresses.

Whether an organization consists of a single facility or has multiple locations, a directory service provides a centralized management tool for users and resources in all locations. This capability does add a certain amount of complexity, so making sure the directory service is structured and designed correctly before using it is critical.

Windows Active Directory

Active Directory is a directory service based on standards for defining, storing, and accessing directory service objects. X.500, a suite of protocols the International Telecommunication Union (ITU) developed, is the basis for its hierarchical structure and for how Active Directory objects are named and stored. **Lightweight Directory Access Protocol (LDAP)**, created by the Internet Engineering Task Force (IETF), is based on the X.500 Directory Access Protocol (DAP). DAP required the seldom used, high-overhead Open Systems Interconnection (OSI) protocol stack for accessing directory objects. LDAP became a streamlined version of DAP, using the more efficient and widely used TCP/IP—hence the term "lightweight" in the protocol's name.

So why is knowledge of LDAP important? You run across references to LDAP periodically when reading material about Active Directory, and as an administrator, you'll be using tools such as ADSI Edit that incorporate LDAP definitions and objects or running programs that use LDAP to integrate with Active Directory. In addition, integrating other OSs, such as Linux, into an Active Directory network requires using LDAP. In fact, you use a tool that incorporates LDAP terminology in this chapter when you run the dsadd command. LDAP and its syntax are covered in more detail when you work with command-line tools in Chapter 7. For now, you focus on Active Directory and its structure and features.

Windows Active Directory became part of the Windows family of server OSs starting with Windows 2000 Server. Before Windows 2000, Windows NT Server had a directory service that was little more than a user manager; it included centralized logon and grouped users and computers into logical security boundaries called domains. The Windows NT domain system was a flat database of users and computers with no way to organize users or resources by department, function, or location. This single, unstructured list made managing large numbers of users cumbersome.

Active Directory's hierarchical database enables administrators to organize users and network resources to reflect the organization of the environment in which it's used. For example, if a company identifies its users and resources mostly by department or location, Active Directory can be configured to mirror this structure. You can structure Active Directory and organize the objects representing users and resources in a way that makes the most sense. Active Directory offers the following features, among others, that make it a highly flexible directory service:

- *Hierarchical organization*—This structure makes management of network resources and administration of security policies easier.

- *Centralized but distributed database*—All network data is centrally located, but it can be distributed among many servers for fast, easy access to information from any location. Automatic replication of information also provides load balancing and fault tolerance. **Active Directory replication** is the transfer of information between all domain controllers to make sure they have consistent and up-to-date information.

- *Scalability*—Advanced indexing technology provides high-performance data access, whether Active Directory consists of a few dozen or a few million objects.

- *Security*—Fine-grained access controls enable administrators to control access to each directory object and its properties. Active Directory also supports secure authentication protocols to maximize compatibility with Internet applications and other systems.

- *Flexibility*—Active Directory is installed with some predefined objects, such as user accounts and groups, but their properties can be modified, and new objects can be added for a customized solution.

- *Policy-based administration*—Administrators can define policies to ensure a secure and consistent environment for users yet maintain the flexibility to apply different rules for departments, locations, or user classes as needed.

Overview of the Active Directory Structure

As with most things, the best way to understand how Active Directory works is to install it and start using it, but knowing the terms used to describe its structure is helpful. There are two aspects of Active Directory's structure:

- Physical structure
- Logical structure

Active Directory's Physical Structure   The physical structure consists of sites and servers configured as domain controllers. An Active Directory **site** is nothing more than a physical location in which domain controllers communicate and replicate information regularly. Specifically, Microsoft defines a site as one or more IP subnets connected by high-speed LAN technology. A small business with no branch offices or other locations, for example, consists of a single site. However, a business with a branch office in another part of the city connected to the main office through a slow WAN link usually has two sites. Typically, each physical location with a domain controller operating in a common domain connected by a WAN constitutes a site. The main reasons for defining multiple sites are to control the frequency of Active Directory replication and to assign policies based on physical location.

Another component of the physical structure is a server configured as a domain controller, which is a computer running Windows Server 2012/R2 with the Active Directory Domain Services role installed. Although an Active Directory domain can consist of many domain controllers, each domain controller can service only one domain. Each domain controller contains a full replica of the objects that make up the domain and is responsible for the following functions:

- Storing a copy of the domain data and replicating changes to that data to all other domain controllers throughout the domain

- Providing data search and retrieval functions for users attempting to locate objects in the directory

- Providing authentication and authorization services for users who log on to the domain and attempt to access network resources

Active Directory's Logical Structure   The logical structure of Active Directory makes it possible to pattern the directory service's look and feel after the organization in which it runs. There are four organizing components of Active Directory:

- Organizational units
- Domains
- Trees
- Forests

These four components can be thought of as containers and are listed from most specific to broadest in terms of what they contain. To use a geographical analogy, an organizational unit represents a neighborhood, a domain is the city, a tree is the state, and a forest is the country.

An **organizational unit** (OU) is an Active Directory container used to organize a network's users and resources into logical administrative units. An OU contains Active Directory objects, such as user accounts, groups, computer accounts, printers, shared folders, applications, servers, and domain controllers. The OU structure often mimics a company's internal administrative structure, although this structure isn't required. For example, a corporation might create an OU for each department, but an educational institution might create separate OUs for students, faculty, and administration or for campus sites. You can use a combination of structures, too, because OUs can be nested as many levels as necessary. Besides being an organizational tool, OUs can represent policy boundaries, in which different sets of policies can be applied to objects in different OUs. Figure 6-1 shows OUs and the types of objects in them.

A **domain** is Active Directory's core structural unit. It contains OUs and represents administrative, security, and policy boundaries (see Figure 6-2). A small to medium company usually has one domain with a single IT administrative group. However, a large company or a company with several locations might benefit from having multiple domains to separate IT administration or accommodate widely differing network policies. For example, a company with major branches in the United States and the United Kingdom might want to divide administrative responsibilities into domains based on location, such as US.csmtech.local and UK.csmtech.local domains, each with a separate administrative group and set of policies. This arrangement addresses possible language and cultural barriers and takes advantage of the benefit of proximity.

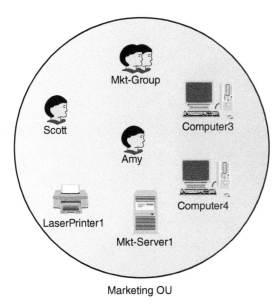
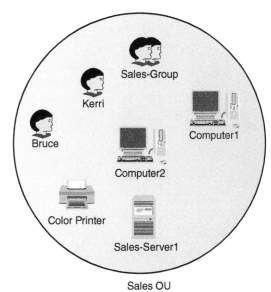

Figure 6-1 Active Directory organizational units
© Cengage Learning®

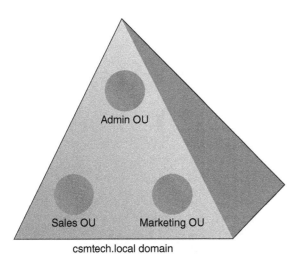

csmtech.local domain

Figure 6-2 An Active Directory domain and OUs
© 2015 Cengage Learning®

An Active Directory **tree** is less a container than a grouping of domains that share a common naming structure. A tree consists of a parent domain and possibly one or more **child domains** (also called "subdomains") that have the same second-level and top-level domain names as the parent domain. For example, US.csmtech.local and UK.csmtech.local are both child domains of the parent domain csmtech.local, and all three domains are part of the same tree. Furthermore, child domains can have child domains, as in phoenix.US.csmtech.local. Figure 6-3 depicts domains in an Active Directory tree.

An Active Directory **forest** is a collection of one or more trees. A forest can consist of a single tree with a single domain, or it can contain several trees, each with a hierarchy of parent and child domains. Each tree in a forest has a different naming structure, so although one tree might have csmtech.local as the parent, another tree in the forest might have csmpub.local as its parent domain. A forest's main purpose is to provide a common Active Directory environment, in which all domains in all trees can communicate with one another and share information yet allow

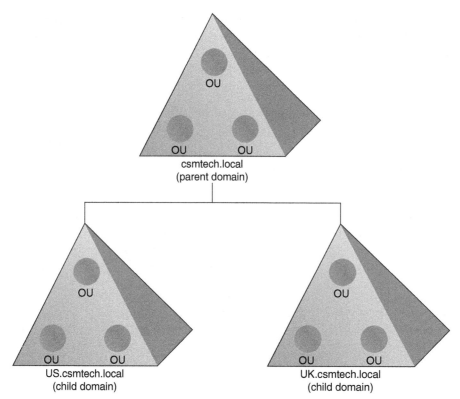

Figure 6-3   An Active Directory tree

© 2015 Cengage Learning®

independent operation and administration of each domain. Figure 6-4 shows an Active Directory forest and the trees and domains it contains. Every forest has a forest root domain, which is the first domain created in a new forest. This domain is discussed later in "The Role of Forests."

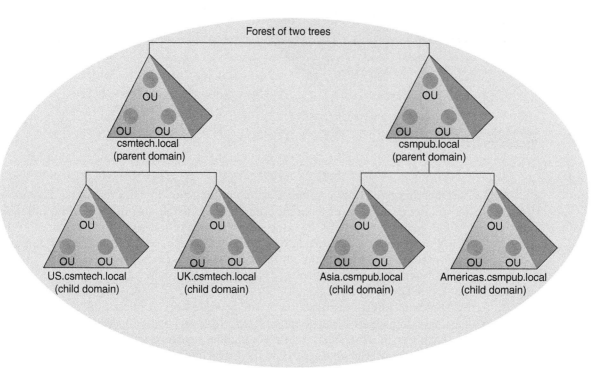

Figure 6-4   An Active Directory forest

© 2015 Cengage Learning®

This section has given you an overview of Active Directory components. You learn more about Active Directory account objects in Chapter 7. To understand its features and structure, you install and work with Active Directory in the next section.

Installing Active Directory

The Windows Active Directory service is commonly referred to as Active Directory Domain Services (AD DS). You must install this role for Active Directory to be part of your network. As with installing any server role, installing AD DS is fairly straightforward, with the real work in the planning and postinstallation tasks.

To begin installing AD DS in Windows Server 2012/R2 with a GUI, you use Server Manager. After selecting the Active Directory Domain Services role to install, you add the necessary features, which include a variety of administration tools and PowerShell modules. The installation program states that you must install the DNS Server role if DNS isn't already installed on the network and informs you that a few other services needed for Active Directory replication must be installed. In the confirmation window, you have the option to export the Active Directory deployment configuration settings, which creates an XML file with the installation settings you selected. This file can be used to automate Active Directory installations on other servers. After the installation is finished, you must configure Active Directory. To get started, click the notifications flag in Server Manager and click "Promote this server to a domain controller," which starts the Active Directory Domain Services Configuration Wizard.

 In previous versions of Windows Server, you needed to run the `Dcpromo.exe` program to promote a server to a DC. `Dcpromo.exe` has been deprecated in Windows Server 2012/R2.

In the Deployment Configuration window, you select from these options: Add a domain controller to an existing domain, Add a new domain to an existing forest, and Add a new forest (see Figure 6-5). For the first DC in the network, you should choose the option to add a new forest. Next, you're prompted for the **fully qualified domain name** (**FQDN**) for the new forest root domain. An FQDN is a domain name that includes all parts of the name, including the top-level domain.

 The first domain in a new forest is also the name of the forest. The wizard checks to be sure the forest name doesn't already exist.

The next window is Domain Controller Options, where you choose the forest and domain functional levels (see Figure 6-6). Microsoft has expanded Active Directory's functionality with each server OS since Windows 2000. For the most advanced features and security, you should choose the most current functional level, which is Windows Server 2012 R2. For the most backward-compatibility with older DCs on the network, you should choose Windows 2008 for the forest functional level. You can't choose a forest functional level earlier than Windows Server 2008. If you choose the Windows Server 2012 R2 forest functional level, you can't run DCs that run an OS version earlier than Windows Server 2012 R2. You can, however, still run older servers as member servers.

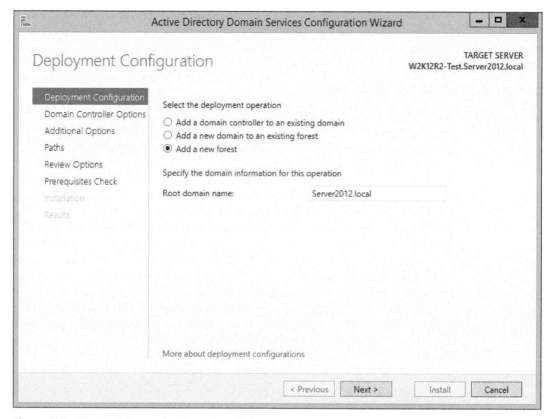

Figure 6-5 The Deployment Configuration window

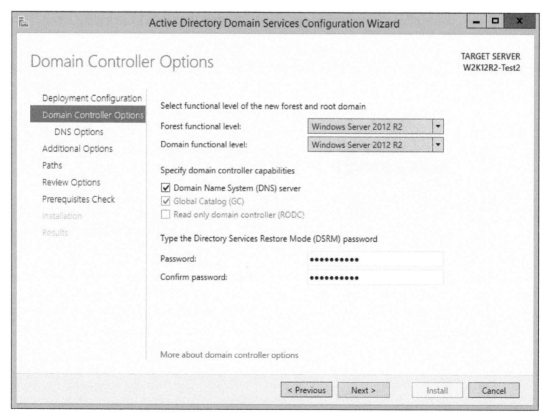

Figure 6-6 Choosing the forest and domain functional levels

You then have three options to specify capabilities for the DC:

- *Domain Name System (DNS) server*—For the first DC in a new domain, DNS should be installed unless you will be using an existing DNS server for the domain.
- *Global Catalog (GC)*—For the first DC in a forest, this check box is selected and disabled because the first DC in a new forest must also be a global catalog server.
- *Read only domain controller (RODC)*—This check box isn't selected by default. This option is disabled for the first DC in the domain because it can't be an RODC.

Next, you enter a password for **Directory Services Restore Mode (DSRM)**. This boot mode is used to perform restore operations on Active Directory if it becomes corrupted or parts of it are deleted accidentally.

The next window, DNS Options, prompts you to create DNS delegation, which allows Windows to create the necessary records on the DNS server for the new domain. You must enter valid credentials for the DNS server. In the Additional Options window, you specify a NetBIOS domain name, which is used for backward-compatibility with systems that don't use DNS. A default name is entered, but you can change it, if needed.

In the Paths window, you specify the location of the Active Directory database, log files, and SYSVOL folder (see Figure 6-7). The **SYSVOL folder** is a shared folder containing file-based information that's replicated to other domain controllers. Storing the database and log files on separate disks, if possible, is best for optimal performance. Next, you review your selections in the Review Options window. You can also view and export a PowerShell script with your settings if you want to duplicate them for another Active Directory configuration.

Windows then does a prerequisites check before starting the Active Directory installation and configuration (see Figure 6-8). This check notifies you of anything that could prevent successful installation and configuration of Active Directory. When the installation is finished, the server restarts. Server Manager then includes some new MMCs in the Tools menu for configuring and managing Active Directory.

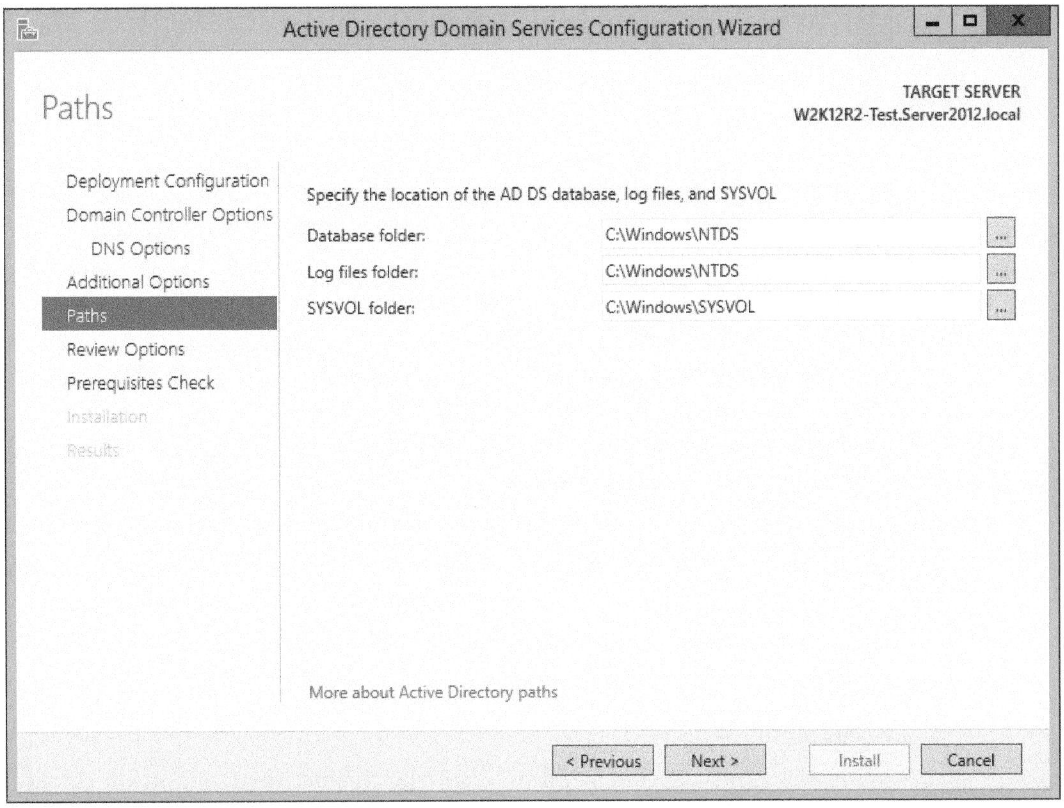

Figure 6-7 Specifying Active Directory paths

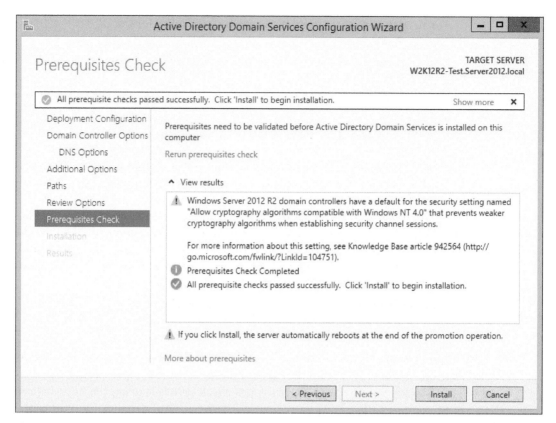

Figure 6-8   The Prerequisites Check window

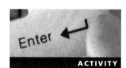

Activity 6-1: Installing Active Directory Domain Services

Time Required: 15 minutes
Objective: Install AD DS as a new domain controller in a new forest.

Required Tools and Equipment: 410Server1
Description: You're ready to start working with Active Directory. This server will be the first DC in a new forest. In addition, you install the DNS Server role as part of the installation because DNS is required for Active Directory to function.

1. Start 410Server1 and log on as **Administrator,** if necessary.

2. Click **Manage, Add Roles and Features.** The Before You Begin window warns you to be sure the Administrator account has a strong password, your network settings are configured, and the latest security updates are installed. Click **Next.**

3. In the Installation Type window, click **Role-based or feature-based installation,** and then click **Next.**

4. In the Server Selection window, make sure **410Server1** is selected, and then click **Next.**

5. In the Server Roles window, click the box next to **Active Directory Domain Services.** When you're prompted to add required features, click **Add Features,** and then click **Next.**

6. In the Features window, click **Next.** Read the information in the AD DS window, which explains that having two domain controllers is optimal, DNS must be installed on the network, and DFS Namespaces, DFS Replication, and File Replication services will also be installed. Click **Next.**

7. In the Confirmation window, click the **Restart the destination server automatically if required** check box. Click **Yes** to confirm automatic restart, and then click **Install.**

8. The Results window shows the progress of the installation. When the installation is finished, click **Close**.

9. Click the notifications flag, and then click **Promote this server to a domain controller**. The Active Directory Services Configuration Wizard starts.

10. In the Deployment Configuration window, click the **Add a new forest** option button, type **410Server2012.local** in the Root domain name text box, and then click **Next**.

11. In the Domain Controller Options window, verify that the forest and domain functional levels are set to **Windows Server 2012 R2**. Under Specify domain controller capabilities, click to select the **Domain Name System (DNS) server** check box, if necessary. The Global Catalog (GC) check box is always selected by default for the first DC in a forest. Notice that the Read only domain controller (RODC) option isn't available because the first DC in a new forest can't be an RODC.

12. In the Directory Services Restore Mode (DSRM) password section, type **Password01** in the Password and Confirm password text boxes. You can use a password different from the Administrator password, if you like, but for this activity, use the same password so that it's easier to remember. Click **Next**.

13. In the DNS Options window, make sure the **Create DNS delegation** check box is selected, and click **Change** to specify credentials for creating the delegation. Type **administrator** and **Password01** for the credentials, click **OK**, and then click **Next**.

14. In the Additional Options window, leave the default NETBIOS domain name and click **Next**.

15. In the Paths window, you can choose locations for the database folder, log files, and SYSVOL folder. Specifying different disks for the database and log files is ideal, but leave the defaults for now. Click **Next**.

16. Review your choices in the Review Options window, and go back and make changes if necessary. You can export your options to a Windows PowerShell script by clicking the View script button and saving the resulting text file with a `.ps1` extension; you can then run this file at a PowerShell prompt. Click **Next**.

17. In the Prerequisites Check window, Windows verifies that all conditions for installing Active Directory successfully have been met. If all prerequisites have been met, a green circle with a check is displayed. If they haven't been met, Windows displays a list of problems you must correct before installing Active Directory. Click **Install**. After the installation is finished, your computer restarts automatically.

18. After the server restarts, log on as **Administrator**. (*Note*: You're now logging on to the 410Server2012.local domain.) In Server Manager, click **Local Server** and verify the domain information shown under Computer name.

19. Click **Tools**. Note the new MMCs that have been added: Active Directory Administrative Center, Active Directory Domains and Trusts, Active Directory Module for Windows PowerShell, Active Directory Sites and Services, Active Directory Users and Computers, ADSI Edit, and DNS.

20. If you're continuing to the next activity, stay logged on; otherwise, log off or shut down 410Server1.

Installing Additional Domain Controllers in a Domain

Microsoft recommends at least two domain controllers in every domain for fault tolerance and load balancing. Even the smallest domain should have two DCs because a domain controller can disrupt user access to network resources if no backup DC is available. In larger networks, a single DC can become so overwhelmed serving requests for network logons, resource access validation, and the myriad other tasks a DC performs that network performance degrades. Having multiple DCs helps spread the load.

The procedure for installing additional domain controllers in an existing domain is not unlike installing the first domain controller. The biggest difference is that you select the "Add a domain controller to an existing domain" option instead of the "Add a new forest" option. When a new DC is added to an existing domain, you need to know the answers to the following questions:

- *Should you install DNS?* Installing DNS is recommended if you're installing the second DC in a domain because one reason you want to install another DC is for fault tolerance. You need at least two DNS servers as well as two DCs to achieve fault tolerance. If the DC is the only one at a remote site, DNS should also be installed. For DCs beyond the second, DNS installation is optional, and you must weigh the benefit of having an additional DNS server versus the additional load it places on the server.

- *Should the DC be a global catalog (GC) server?* The first DC is always configured as a GC server, but when you're installing additional DCs in a domain, this setting is optional. In most cases, it makes sense to make all your DCs global catalog servers as well, particularly in a single-domain forest. The global catalog and its importance in a network are discussed later in "Working with Forests, Trees, and Domains."

- *Should this be a read only domain controller (RODC)?* An RODC is most often used in branch office situations, where ensuring the server's physical security is more difficult. An RODC doesn't store account credentials, so if an RODC is compromised, no passwords can be retrieved. If the DC isn't at a branch office, there's no substantial advantage in making it an RODC.

- *In which site should the DC be located?* If you have more than one site defined for your network, you can choose where you want the DC to be located.

Because there's already a DC for the domain, you have the option to use a feature called "Install from media," discussed later in "Installing a DC with Install from Media."

Installing a New Domain in an Existing Forest

Another reason to install a new DC is to add a domain to an existing forest. There are two variations to the procedure:

- *Add a child domain*—In this variation, you're adding a domain that shares at least the top-level and second-level domain name structure as an existing domain in the forest. For example, if your current domain is named csmtech.local and you add a branch office in Europe, your new domain is named europe.csmtech.local. The new domain has a separate domain administrator, but the forest administrator has the authority to manage most aspects of both the child and parent domains. Figure 6-9 shows the window in the Active Directory installation where you choose to install a child domain. Notice that Child Domain is selected in the Select domain type list box. The other choice is Tree Domain, discussed next. The parent domain is the name of the existing domain you're creating a child domain for. In the figure, the existing domain is csmtech.local. The new domain name is the name of the new child domain, which in this example is europe. The new domain has the FQDN europe.csmtech.local. You must have the right credentials (a user who's a member of Domain Admins) for the csmtech.local domain to perform the operation. The new DC must be able to contact a DC from the parent domain, so DNS must be configured correctly. All the other steps are the same as installing a DC in a new forest.

- *Add a new tree*—In this variation, you're adding a new domain with a separate naming structure from any existing domains in the forest. So in a forest named csmtech.local, you can add a new domain (and, therefore, a new tree in the forest) named csmpub.local. Operationally, a new tree is the same as a child domain. Figure 6-10 shows the window in the Active Directory installation where you choose to install a new tree, with Tree Domain selected as the domain type. You need to enter the name of the forest, which is always the name of the first domain installed when the forest was created (the forest root domain); in this example, it's csmtech.local. As when adding a child domain, you need credentials to add the domain to the forest, but in this case, you need a user who's a member of Enterprise Admins and Schema Admins. The administrator account for the forest root domain is a member of both groups.

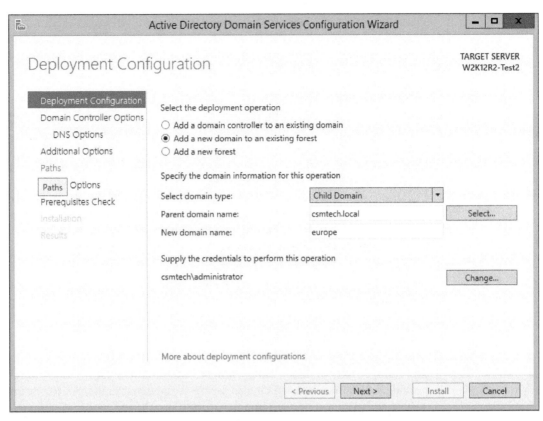

Figure 6-9   Adding a new child domain in an existing forest

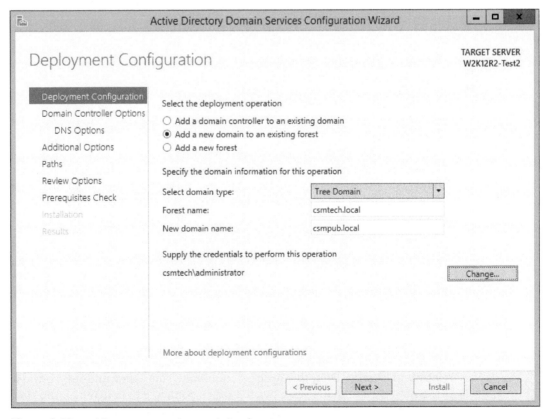

Figure 6-10   Adding a new tree in an existing forest

Working with multidomain forests and multiforest networks is an advanced topic. Some information you need to know is discussed later in "Working with Forests, Trees, and Domains." This topic is covered in more detail in *MCSA Guide to Configuring Advanced Windows Server 2012 Services, Exam 70-412* (Cengage Learning, 2015).

Installing Active Directory in Server Core

The preferred method of installing Active Directory in a Windows Server 2012/R2 Server Core installation is to use the PowerShell cmdlets designed for this purpose. However, for server administrators familiar with using `dcpromo.exe` along with an answer file, this option is still available. Just be aware that `dcpromo.exe` is a deprecated command starting with Windows Server 2012; eventually, it won't be available.

Installing Active Directory with PowerShell is a two-step process, just as it is when using Server Manager. First, you install the Active Directory Domain Services role, and then you promote the server to a DC by configuring Active Directory. Use the following command to install the Active Directory Domain Services role, like any other server role:

```
Add-WindowsFeature AD-Domain-Services
```

If you're using PowerShell in a GUI installation, you should probably include the `-IncludeManagementTools` parameter in this command. In a Server Core installation, however, you can't use the management tools. The preceding command prepares the server for promotion to a DC, but you must enter another command to start the promotion process. Which command you use depends on the type of installation you want:

- `Install-ADDSForest`—This command creates a new DC in a new forest. You must provide a domain name, which also serves as the forest name. So, for example, to create the 410Server2012.local domain in a new forest, use the following command:

```
Install-ADDSForest -DomainName "410Server2012.local"
```

- `Install-ADDSDomainController`—This command adds a DC to an existing domain. You specify the name of the existing domain as shown:

```
Install-ADDSDomainController -DomainName "410Server2012.local"
```

- `Install-ADDSDomain`—This command adds a new domain to an existing forest. You need to specify the new domain name, the parent domain, and the type of domain (`TreeDomain` or `ChildDomain`). The default is `ChildDomain`. To add a domain named europe to the existing forest named csmtech.local, use the following command:

```
Install-ADDSDomain -NewDomainName "europe" -ParentDomainName
    "csmtech.local" -DomainType ChildDomain
```

For the preceding commands, you need to specify credentials for an account with the necessary permissions to perform the installation. For each command, you can get detailed help in PowerShell with the `Get-Help` command, including examples of how to use the command. For instance, to get detailed help on using `Install-ADDSDomain`, including examples, use the following command:

```
Get-Help Install-ADDSDomain -detailed
```

If you want to see what a PowerShell cmdlet does without actually performing the operation, use the `-WhatIf` parameter. PowerShell displays the steps needed to perform the command, showing you the default settings and prompting you for other information the command requires.

Installing a DC with Install from Media

When you install a new DC in an existing domain, it must be updated with all existing data in the Active Directory database. Depending on the database's size and the new DC's location in relation to existing DCs, this process could take some time and use considerable bandwidth. If the new DC is the first in a branch office connected via a WAN, the time and bandwidth use might be a concern. Using the **Install from media (IFM)** option during Active Directory configuration can substantially reduce the replication traffic needed to update the new DC. This utility copies the contents of an existing DC's Active Directory database (and optionally the SYSVOL folder) to disk. These contents are then used to populate the new DC's Active Directory database, thereby reducing the replication needed to bring the new DC's database up to date.

The procedure for using IFM is as follows:

1.   Select a suitable DC from which you'll create the IFM data. If you're creating IFM data for a standard DC (a writeable DC, not an RODC), you must use a standard DC to create this data. If you're creating IFM data for an RODC, you can use an RODC or a standard DC.

2.   On the selected DC, run the `ntdsutil` command-line program at an elevated command prompt. `Ntdsutil` is an interactive program, where you enter commands as shown in Figure 6-11 and explained in the following list:

     o `ntdsutil`—Starts the command-line program.

     o `activate instance ntds`—Sets the program focus on the Active Directory database.

     o `ifm`—Sets the program to IFM mode.

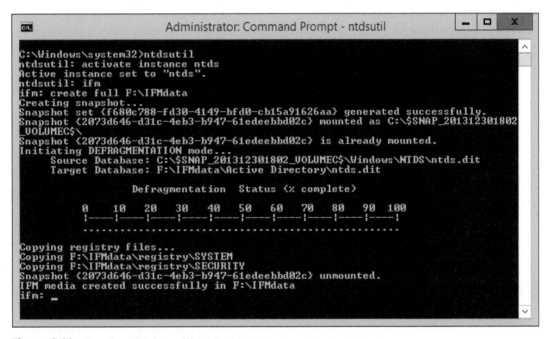

Figure 6-11   Creating IFM data with `ntdsutil`

The next command creates the IFM data and has the following four variations. The *path* parameter specifies where to store IFM data and can be a local drive, a network share, or removable media. A network share is ideal so that the new DC has access to IFM data without having to copy data or transfer removable media. In addition, you can use the network share for multiple DC installations easily.

o `create full` *path*—Creates IFM data for a writeable DC.

o `create RODC` *path*—Creates IFM data for an RODC.

o `create Sysvol Full` *path*—Creates IFM data for a writeable DC and includes the SYSVOL folder.

o `create Sysvol RODC` *path*—Creates IFM data for an RODC and includes the SYSVOL folder.

3. Install the new DC and select the IFM option. If you're using Server Manager, click the Install from media check box in the Additional Options window (see Figure 6-12) of the Active Directory Domain Services Configuration Wizard, and specify the path to the media. If you're using PowerShell, use the `-InstallationMediaPath` parameter and specify the path to the storage location.

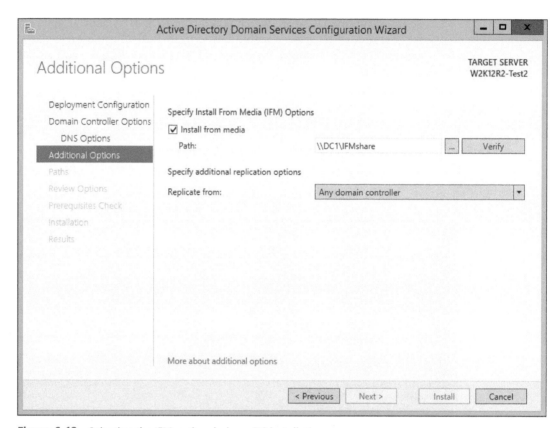

Figure 6-12   Selecting the IFM option during a DC installation

What's Inside Active Directory?

After Active Directory is installed, you can explore it by using the Active Directory Administrative Center (ADAC) or Active Directory Users and Computers MMC; several PowerShell cmdlets are also available for working with Active Directory. The ADAC, shown in Figure 6-13, is a central console for performing many Active Directory tasks, including creating and managing user, group, and computer accounts; managing OUs; and connecting to other domain controllers in the same or a different domain. You can also change the domain's functional level and enable the Active Directory Recycle Bin.

ADAC is built on PowerShell, so each command you use in ADAC issues a PowerShell command to perform the task. You can take advantage of this new feature in Windows Server 2012 by using the Windows PowerShell History pane in ADAC (see Figure 6-14). This pane shows a list of commands generated by creating a new user named Test User3. These commands can be copied and edited to make a PowerShell script so that you can handle tasks such as creating users and adding users to groups by running a PowerShell script instead of using the GUI or typing PowerShell commands. You use ADAC in Chapter 7.

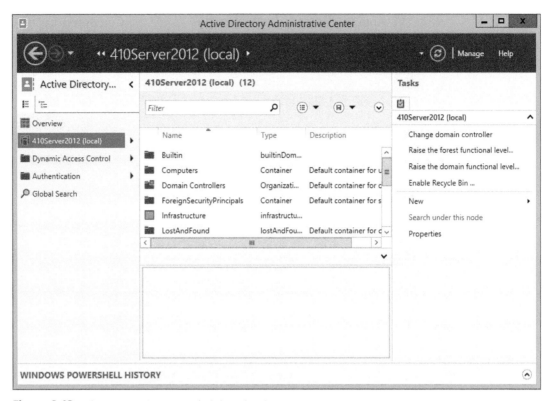

Figure 6-13   The Active Directory Administrative Center

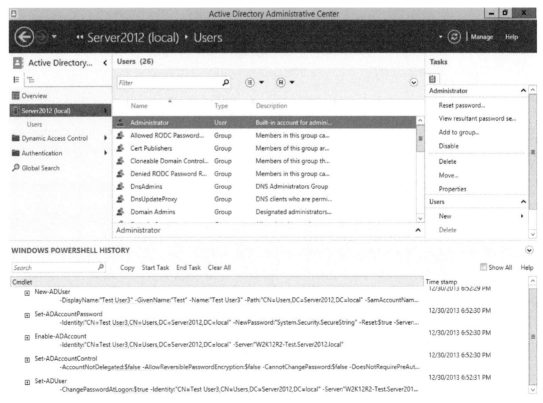

Figure 6-14   Viewing the PowerShell history

As shown in Figure 6-15, Active Directory Users and Computers has two panes. In the left pane, the top node shows the server and domain being managed. The Saved Queries folder contains a list of Active Directory queries you can save to repeat Active Directory searches easily. The third node represents the domain and contains all the objects that make up the domain. In Figure 6-15, the domain being managed is 410Server2012.local. In this figure, the Users container is open, and objects in this container are displayed in the right pane.

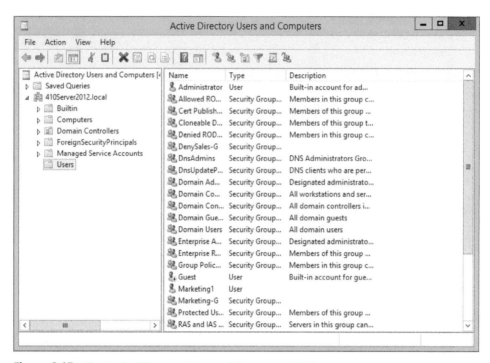

Figure 6-15 The Active Directory Users and Computers MMC

Before you continue working with Active Directory, knowing something about the information you find in the database is helpful. Active Directory's contents and the functions it performs in your network are defined by the schema, objects, and Group Policy Objects (GPOs, discussed later in "Introducing Group Policies").

The Active Directory Schema

All information in the Active Directory database is organized as objects. An **object** is a grouping of information that describes a network resource, such as a shared printer; an organizing structure, such as a domain or OU; or an account, such as a user or group. The **schema** defines the type, organization, and structure of data stored in the Active Directory database and is shared by all domains in an Active Directory forest. The information the schema defines is divided into two categories: schema classes and schema attributes. **Schema classes** define the types of objects that can be stored in Active Directory, such as user or computer accounts. **Schema attributes** define what type of information is stored in each object, such as first name, last name, and password for a user account object. The information stored in each attribute, such as "Mary" in the first name attribute, is called the **attribute value.**

Figure 6-16 shows the relationship between schema classes, attributes, and Active Directory objects. As you can see, some schema attributes, such as the description attribute used for both objects, can be shared by more than one Active Directory object. When Active Directory is first installed, a default schema describes all available default objects, but you can extend this schema to add attributes to existing object classes or create new object classes.

This discussion of Active Directory refers to several different object classes in Active Directory. Figure 6-17 shows object classes and their associated icons in Active Directory Users and Computers. Active Directory objects can be organized into two basic groups, discussed in

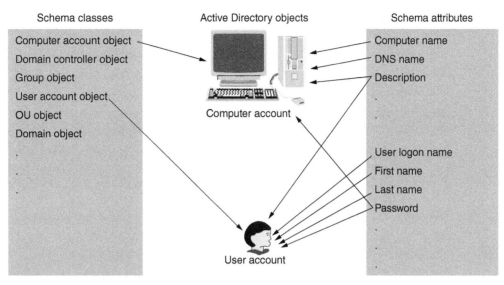

Figure 6-16 Schema classes, schema attributes, and Active Directory objects
© *Cengage Learning*®

Figure 6-17 Icons used to represent Active Directory objects
© *Cengage Learning*®

the next sections: container objects and leaf objects. Similar icons are used in ADAC but are black and white.

Active Directory Container Objects

A container object, as the name implies, contains other objects. Container objects are used to organize and manage users and resources in a network. They can also act as administrative and security boundaries or a way to group objects for applying policies. Three container objects, explained in the following sections, are found in Active Directory: OU, folder, and domain.

Organizational Units   An OU is the primary container object for organizing and managing resources in a domain. Administrators can use OUs to organize objects into logical administrative groups, which makes it possible to apply policies to the OU that affect all objects in it. For example, you could apply a policy that prohibits access to Control Panel for all users in an OU. In addition, you can delegate administrative authority for an OU to a user, thereby allowing the user to manage objects in the OU without giving the user wider authority. Object types typically found in an OU include user accounts, group accounts, computer accounts, shared folders, shared printers, published applications, and other OUs. By nesting OUs, administrators can build a hierarchical Active Directory structure that mimics the corporate structure for easier object management.

In Active Directory Users and Computers, an OU is represented by a folder with a book inside, as shown previously in Figure 6-17. When Active Directory is installed, a single OU called Domain Controllers is created and contains a computer object representing the domain controller. When a new DC is installed in the domain, a new computer object representing it is placed in the Domain Controllers OU by default. A GPO is linked to the Domain Controllers OU and used to set security and administrative policies that apply to all DCs in the domain.

Folder Objects   When Active Directory is installed, five folder objects are created:

- *Builtin*—Houses default groups created by Windows and is mainly used to assign permissions to users who have administrative responsibilities in the domain.

- *Computers*—The default location for computer accounts created when a new computer or server becomes a domain member.

- *ForeignSecurityPrincipals*—Initially empty but later contains user accounts from other domains added as members of the local domain's groups.

- *Managed Service Accounts*—Added to the schema in Windows Server 2008 R2; created specifically for services to access domain resources. In this account, the password is managed by the system, alleviating the administrator of this task. This folder is empty initially.

- *Users*—Stores two default users (Administrator and Guest) and several default groups.

These folder objects are represented in Active Directory Users and Computers with the folder icon shown previously in Figure 6-17. You can't create new folder objects, nor can you apply group policies to folder objects. You can delegate administrative control on all folders but the Builtin folder. All objects in a folder are subject to group policies defined at the domain level. You can move objects from the default folders (except the Builtin folder) into OUs you have created. For example, because all computer accounts are created in the Computers folder by default, they're subject to the same policies defined at the domain level. If you want to apply different policies to different computers in your domain, you create one or more OUs, move the computer accounts to the new OUs, and apply group policies to these OUs.

Domain Objects   The domain is the core logical structure container in Active Directory. Domains contain OU and folder container objects but can also contain leaf objects, such as users, groups, and so forth. A domain typically reflects the organization of the company in which Active Directory is being used, but in large or geographically dispersed organizations, you can create multiple domains, each representing a business unit or location. The main reasons for using multiple domains are to allow separate administration, define security boundaries, and define policy boundaries. Each domain object has a default GPO linked to it that can affect all objects in the domain. The domain object in Active Directory Users and Computers is represented by an icon with three tower computers (refer back to Figure 6-17).

Activity 6-2: Exploring Active Directory Container Objects

Time Required: 10 minutes
Objective: Explore Active Directory container objects.

Required Tools and Equipment: 410Server1
Description: After installing Active Directory, you want to view its structure by exploring the default container objects in Active Directory Users and Computers.

1. Log on to 410Server1 as **Administrator**.

2. In Server Manager, open Active Directory Users and Computers by clicking **Tools**, **Active Directory Users and Computers** from the menu.

3. Click the domain object (**410Server2012.local**) in the left pane.

4. Right-click the domain object and click **Properties**. Click the **General** tab, if necessary, and verify that both the domain and forest functional levels are Windows Server 2012 R2.

5. Enter a description for the domain, such as Windows Server 2012 R2 Domain for 410 Exam, and then click **OK**.

6. Click to expand the domain node, if necessary. Click the **Builtin** folder in the left pane to view its contents in the right pane: a list of group accounts created when Active Directory was installed.

7. Click the **Computers** folder in the left pane. This folder is empty.

8. Click the **Domain Controllers** OU. A computer object representing your domain controller is displayed in the right pane. The DC Type column displays GC, meaning the domain controller is a global catalog server.

9. Click the **Users** folder in the left pane. The right pane displays groups and two user accounts created by default when Active Directory is installed. It also contains the user accounts you created before you promoted the server to a DC. These converted accounts in the Users folder—DenySales-G, Marketing1, Marketing-G, Sales1, Sales2, Sales-G, testuser, and Win8User—aren't needed, so you can delete them now. To do so, right-click the user account and click **Delete**, and then click **Yes** to confirm.

10. Leave Active Directory Users and Computers open for the next activity.

Active Directory Leaf Objects

A leaf object doesn't contain other objects and usually represents a security account, network resource, or GPO. Security account objects include users, groups, and computers. Network resource objects include servers, domain controllers, file shares, printers, and so forth. GPOs aren't viewed as objects in the same way as other Active Directory objects. In Windows Server 2012/R2, GPOs are managed by the Group Policy Management MMC, discussed later. The following paragraphs explain some common leaf objects in Active Directory.

User Accounts A user account object contains information about a network user. Typically, when a user account is created, the administrator enters at least the user's name, logon name, and password. However, the user account object contains much more information, such as group memberships, account restrictions (allowed logon hours and account expiration date, for example), profile path, and dial-in permissions. In addition, administrators can fill in descriptive fields, such as office location, job title, and department. The main purpose of a user account is to allow a user to log on to a Windows computer or an Active Directory domain to access computer and domain resources. By supplying a user logon name and password, a user is authenticated on the computer or network. **Authentication** confirms a user's identity, and the account is then assigned permissions and rights that authorize the user to access resources and perform certain tasks on the computer or domain.

Windows Server 2012/R2 defines three user account types: local user accounts, domain user accounts, and built-in user accounts. A **local user account**, defined on a local computer, is authorized to access resources only on that computer. Local user accounts are mainly used on stand-alone computers or in a workgroup network with computers that aren't part of an Active Directory domain. A **domain user account**, created in Active Directory, provides a single logon for users to access all resources in the domain they're authorized for. Windows creates two **built-in user accounts** automatically: Administrator and Guest. They can be local user accounts or domain user accounts, depending on the computer where they're created. On a workgroup or stand-alone Windows computer, these two accounts are created when Windows is installed, and they're local accounts that have access to resources only on the local computer. When Active Directory is installed on a Windows Server 2012/R2 computer, these two accounts are converted from local user accounts to domain user accounts. User accounts are discussed in more detail in Chapter 7.

Groups A group object represents a collection of users with common permissions or rights requirements on a computer or domain. **Permissions** define which resources users can access and what level of access they have. For example, a user might have permission to open and read a certain document but not to change it. A **right** specifies what types of actions a user can perform on a computer or network. For example, a user might have the right to log on to and log off a computer but not shut down the computer. Groups are used to assign members permissions and rights. This method is more efficient than assigning permissions and rights to each user account separately because you have to perform the assignment task only once, and it applies to all accounts that are members of the group. For example, if all users in the Accounting Department need access to a shared folder, you can create a group containing all users in this department as members and assign permission to access the shared folder to the group as a whole. In addition, if a user leaves the department, you can remove his or her account as a group member, and the user loses all rights and permissions assigned to this group. Groups are explained in more detail in Chapter 7.

Computer Accounts   A computer account object represents a computer that's a domain controller or domain member and is used to identify, authenticate, and manage computers in the domain. Computer accounts are created automatically when Active Directory is installed on a server or when a server or workstation becomes a domain member. Administrators can also create computer accounts manually if they don't want to allow automatic account creation. By default, domain controller computer accounts are placed in the Domain Controllers OU, and domain member computer accounts are placed in the Computers folder.

The computer account object's name must match the name of the computer that the account represents. Like user accounts, computer accounts have a logon name and password, but a computer account password is managed by Active Directory instead of an administrator. A computer must have a computer account in Active Directory for users to log on to it with their domain user accounts. You learn about managing computer accounts in Chapter 7.

Other Leaf Objects   The following list describes other leaf objects that are commonly created in Active Directory:

- *Contact*—A person who is associated with the company but is not a network user. You can think of a contact object as simply being an entry in an address book, used purely for informational purposes.

- *Printer*—Represents a shared printer in the domain. Printers shared on Windows 2000 or later computers that are domain members can be added to Active Directory automatically. If a printer is shared on a non-domain member or a pre-Windows 2000 computer, you must create the printer object manually and specify the path to the shared printer.

- *Shared folder*—Represents a shared folder on a computer in the network. Shared folder objects can be added to Active Directory manually or by using the publish option when creating a shared folder with the Shared Folders MMC snap-in.

Both printer and shared folder objects enable users to access shared printers and folders on any computer in the domain without knowing exactly which computer the resource was created on. Users can simply do a search in Active Directory to find the type of resource they want. In a large network, shared printers and folders could be located on any one of dozens or hundreds of servers. Publishing these resources in Active Directory makes access to them easier.

There are other leaf objects, but the previous sections cover the most common objects you find in Active Directory.

Activity 6-3: Viewing Default Leaf Objects

Time Required: 15 minutes
Objective: View the properties of a variety of leaf objects.

Required Tools and Equipment: 410Server1
Description: You want to learn more about Active Directory objects, so you view the properties of several default leaf objects.

1. If necessary, log on to 410Server1 as **Administrator**, and open Active Directory Users and Computers.

2. Click to expand the domain node so that folders and OUs are displayed under it, and then click the **Builtin** folder.

3. In the right pane, right-click the **Administrators** group and click **Properties** (or double-click the **Administrators** group).

4. Click the **General** tab, if necessary. Notice that the option buttons under Group scope and Group type are disabled because you can't change this information for built-in groups. (You learn more about group scope and group type in Chapter 7.)

5. Click the **Members** tab. You should see one user and two groups listed as members (see Figure 6-18). The Name column displays the name of the user or group member, and the Active Directory Domain Services Folder column displays the domain and folder or OU where the member is located. Groups can be nested, as shown here; the Domain Admins and Enterprise Admins groups are members of the Administrators group.

6. Click the **Member Of** tab. Because built-in groups can't be members of any other group, the Add and Remove buttons are disabled.

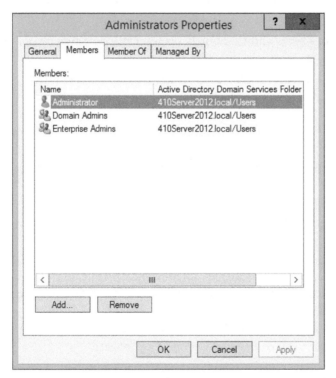

Figure 6-18   Viewing properties of the Administrators group

7. Click the **Managed By** tab. An administrator can specify another user or group that has the right to manage this group. Click **Cancel**.

8. In the left pane of Active Directory Users and Computers, click the **Domain Controllers** OU. Double-click the **410Server1** computer object in the right pane to open its Properties dialog box.

9. If necessary, click the **General** tab. Notice that only the Description text box can be changed for this object.

10. Click the **Operating System** tab, which displays the name, version, and service pack (if any) installed on the computer this computer object represents.

11. Click the **Member Of** tab. Because this computer object represents a domain controller, it's a member of the Domain Controllers group. (If this computer object represents a domain member, it's a member of the Domain Computers group.) Click **Cancel**.

12. In the left pane of Active Directory Users and Computers, click the **Users** folder. Double-click the **Administrator** user to open its Properties dialog box.

13. If necessary, click the **General** tab. The information here is optional for user accounts but can be used as part of an employee directory. Type your first name and last name in the corresponding text boxes.

14. Click the **Account** tab. Here you can specify the user logon name, logon restrictions, and account options.

15. Click the **Member Of** tab. Note the groups the Administrator account belongs to, and then click **Cancel**.

16. Find the Guest user, and notice the down arrow on its icon. Double-click the **Guest** user to open its Properties dialog box.

17. Click the **Account** tab. In the Account options list box, scroll down to view the available account options. The down arrow on the Guest user icon means the Guest user is disabled by default because it's created with a blank password, which can pose a security risk. Click **Cancel**.

18. Leave Active Directory Users and Computers open for the next activity.

Activity 6-4: Creating Objects in Active Directory

Time Required: 15 minutes
Objective: Create an OU and add some objects to it.

Required Tools and Equipment: 410Server1
Description: You want to learn more about Active Directory objects, so you create an OU and add a user object and a group object.

1. If necessary, log on to 410Server1 as **Administrator**, and open Active Directory Users and Computers.

2. Click to expand the domain node so that folders and OUs are displayed under it. Right-click the domain node, point to **New**, and click **Organizational Unit**. In the Name text box, type **TestOU1**. Click to clear the **Protect container from accidental deletion** check box, and then click **OK**.

3. Make sure **TestOU1** is selected in the left pane, and then right-click in the right pane, point to **New**, and click **User** to start the New Object - User Wizard.

4. In the First name text box, type **Test**, and in the Last name text box, type **User1**. Notice that the "Full name" text box is filled in automatically.

5. In the User logon name text box, type **testuser1**. The User logon name (pre-Windows 2000) text box is filled in automatically. (A user logon name longer than 20 characters is truncated to 20 characters in this text box.)

6. Click **Next**. In the Password text box, type **mypassword**, and type it again in the Confirm password text box. Click to clear the **User must change password at next logon** check box. Click **Next**, and then click **Finish**.

7. You see an error message; read it carefully. By default, Windows Server 2012/R2 requires a complex password, meaning one of a minimum length with at least three characters of the following types: uppercase letters, lowercase letters, numbers, and special symbols (such as #, ?, and so forth). Click **OK**.

8. In the New Object - User window, click **Back**. In the Password text box, type **Password01**, making sure the P is capitalized and the last two characters are the numbers 0 and 1. Retype the password in the Confirm password text box. Click **Next**, and then click **Finish**.

9. Right-click in the right pane of Active Directory Users and Computers, point to **New**, and click **Group**.

10. Type **TestGroup1** in the Group name text box (see Figure 6-19). Verify that the Group scope setting is **Global** and the Group type setting is **Security**, and then click **OK**.

Group scope and group type are explained in Chapter 7.

Figure 6-19   Creating a group

11. Double-click **Test User1** to open its Properties dialog box, and click the **Member Of** tab. This user account is already a member of the Domain Users group; all new users are members of this group by default.

12. Click the **Add** button to open the Select Groups dialog box. In the "Enter the object names to select" text box, type **TestGroup1**, as shown in Figure 6-20, and then click the **Check Names** button. Active Directory verifies that the group name you entered exists and underlines it if it does. If the group doesn't exist, a Name Not Found message box is displayed, where you can correct the group name. Click **OK**, and then click **OK** again.

13. Double-click **TestGroup1** to open its Properties dialog box. Click the **Members** tab to verify that Test User1 has been added as a member. Users can be added to groups in the Member Of tab of the user account's Properties dialog box or the Members tab of the group's Properties dialog box. Click **Cancel**.

14. Close Active Directory Users and Computers, but stay logged on if you're continuing to the next activity.

As you can tell, Active Directory Users and Computers is a fairly straightforward, easy-to-use tool for managing Active Directory objects, but not every administrator wants to use a graphical utility to create and modify Active Directory objects. Sometimes using command-line tools is easier or even necessary. Although this topic is explored more thoroughly in Chapter 7, the following activity introduces you to the `dsadd` command-line tool for creating objects in Active Directory.

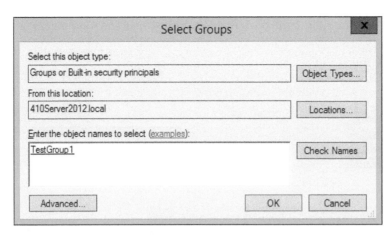

Figure 6-20   The Select Groups dialog box

Activity 6-5: Using `dsadd` to Create Objects

Time Required: 10 minutes
Objective: Create a user with the `dsadd` command-line tool.

Required Tools and Equipment: 410Server1
Description: You want to get more practice creating Active Directory objects, so you decide to create a test user with the `dsadd` command-line tool and add this user to the group you created earlier.

1. Log on to 410Server1 as **Administrator**, if necessary, and open a command prompt window by right-clicking **Start** and clicking **Command Prompt**.

2. At the command prompt, type **dsadd user "cn=Test User2, ou=TestOU1, dc=410Server2012, dc=local" -upn testuser2@410Server2012 -Samid testuser2 -fn Test -ln User2 -pwd Password01 -memberof "cn=TestGroup1, ou=TestOU1, dc=410Server2012, dc=local"** and press **Enter**. This complex command creates a user named Test User2 with the logon name testuser2 and the password Password01, places the user in TestOU1, and makes the user a member of TestGroup1. If you get a response other than "dsadd succeeded: cn=Test User2, ou=TestOU1,dc=410Server2012,dc=local," check the command for typos and try again.

3. Close the command prompt window. Open Active Directory Users and Computers, and click **TestOU1** in the left pane.

4. Verify that Test User2 is there. Double-click **TestGroup1** to open its Properties dialog box, and then click the **Members** tab to verify that this new user is a member. Click **OK**.

5. Leave Active Directory Users and Computers open for the next activity.

These steps might seem like a lot of work to create a single user, but as you learn in Chapter 7, you can create several users at once quickly and easily with command-line tools and a text file. Microsoft has placed an increased emphasis on command-line tools, especially with Server Core and the new PowerShell suite of tools.

Recovering Objects with the Active Directory Recycle Bin

Working with Active Directory objects is usually straightforward, but what happens if you delete an object by mistake? There's no undo feature, as in word processors, image editors, and other tools you use to create, modify, and delete things. Before Windows Server 2008 R2, the procedure for recovering deleted objects in Active Directory was laborious and required cumbersome command-line syntax. Even worse, the domain controller the object was deleted from had to be taken offline. In Windows Server 2008 R2, Microsoft introduced the Active Directory Recycle Bin, and it has been improved on in Windows Server 2012/R2. Before you see this feature in action, you should be aware of the following:

- Active Directory Recycle Bin is disabled by default; it can be enabled in Active Directory Administrative Center (ADAC).

- After it's enabled, the Recycle Bin can't be disabled without reinstalling all domain controllers in the forest.

- To use the Recycle Bin, all DCs in the forest must be running Windows Server 2008 R2 or later, and the forest functional level must be at least Windows Server 2008 R2.

To enable the Recycle Bin, open ADAC, click the domain node in the left pane, and in the Tasks pane, click Enable Recycle Bin. Click OK in the warning message stating that the Recycle Bin can't be disabled after you enable it. You see a message stating that the Recycle Bin is being enabled and won't function reliably until all DCs are updated with the change. You need to refresh ADAC to see the new container added under the domain node named Deleted Objects. To undelete an object, double-click the Deleted Objects container. All objects that have been deleted since the Recycle Bin was enabled are listed. To restore an object, right-click it and choose one of these options from the menu: Restore (which restores the object to its original container, if it's still available) or Restore To (which restores the object to a container you select).

Locating Active Directory Objects

In a large Active Directory environment with hundreds or thousands of users, groups, computers, and other domain objects, locating objects can be difficult for administrators and users alike. Luckily, Active Directory Users and Computers has a search function for administrators, and File Explorer incorporates an Active Directory search function for users.

You search for Active Directory objects by first selecting the type of object you're searching for. For example, you can search for users, contacts, groups, computers, printers, shared folders, and so forth. In a multidomain environment, you can search in a single domain or in the entire directory (all domains). You can also limit your search to a folder or an OU in a domain. The Find dialog box shown in Figure 6-21 is identical whether you're searching for objects with Active Directory Users and Computers or File Explorer. However, not all objects are available to all users, depending on the object's security settings and its container.

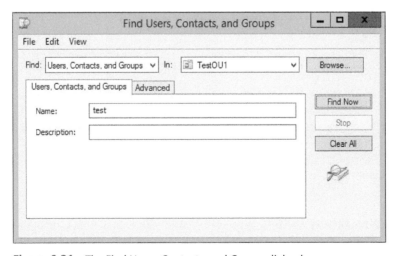

Figure 6-21 The Find Users, Contacts, and Groups dialog box

Activity 6-6: Locating Objects with Active Directory Users and Computers

Time Required: 5 minutes
Objective: Search for user and group objects with Active Directory Users and Computers.

Required Tools and Equipment: 410Server1

Description: Before Active Directory grows too large, you need to experiment with the search feature in Active Directory Users and Computers so that you're comfortable finding objects.

1. If necessary, log on to 410Server1 as **Administrator**, and open Active Directory Users and Computers.

2. Right-click the domain node in the left pane and click **Find**.

3. Click the **Find** list arrow and verify that **Users, Contacts, and Groups** is selected. In the In text box, make sure the domain is selected. You could click Find Now, but if you do, all users, contacts, and groups in the entire domain are displayed. You want to narrow down the choices first.

4. In the Name text box, type **test**. By specifying this name, all users, groups and contacts starting with "test" are displayed. Click the **Find Now** button. You should see results similar to Figure 6-22.

Figure 6-22   Results from an Active Directory find operation

5. In the Search results section, you can double-click any entry to access its properties. Close the Find Users, Contacts, and Groups dialog box and Active Directory Users and Computers.

Activity 6-7: Locating Objects with File Explorer

Time Required: 10 minutes

Objective: Search for user and group objects with File Explorer.

Required Tools and Equipment: 410Server1

Description: Part of your job as network administrator is assisting users in using Active Directory, so you want to familiarize yourself with the Active Directory search tool in File Explorer.

 These instructions work in both Windows Server 2012 R2 and Windows 8.1.

6

1. Log on to 410Server1 as **Administrator,** if necessary.

2. Open File Explorer, and click **Network** in the left pane.

3. Click **Network, Search Active Directory** from the menu to open the Find Users, Contacts, and Groups dialog box. It's the same as the one in Figure 6-22, shown previously. By default, Entire Directory is set as the search scope.

4. In the Find drop-down list, click **Computers**. In the Role drop-down list, click **All Active Directory Domain Controllers** to specify that you want to search only for computers that are domain controllers.

5. Click the **Find Now** button. You should see 410Server1 in the search results.

6. Close all open windows.

Activity 6-8: Publishing a Shared Folder in Active Directory

Time Required: 25 minutes

Objective: Publish a shared folder in Active Directory and then find the folder.

Required Tools and Equipment: 410Server1

Description: You have heard that users can access shared folders by locating them in Active Directory. You decide to create a shared folder and then publish it in Active Directory. Then you use the find feature in File Explorer to locate the shared folder in Active Directory.

1. Log on to 410Server1 as **Administrator,** if necessary.

2. Open File Explorer. Create a folder in the root of Vol1 named **PubShare**.

3. Share this folder with simple file sharing, giving the Everyone group Read permission and leaving the Administrator and Administrators accounts with the default permissions. Close File Explorer.

4. Open Computer Management. Click to expand the **Shared Folders** node, and then click the **Shares** folder.

5. In the right pane, double-click **PubShare** to open its Properties dialog box. Click the **Publish** tab (see Figure 6-23), and then click the **Publish this share in Active Directory** check box.

6. In the Description text box, type **A share to test publishing in Active Directory**.

7. Click the **Edit** button. In the Edit Keywords dialog box, type **testing**, and then click **Add**. Click **OK** twice.

8. Close Computer Management. Open File Explorer, and click **Network**.

9. Click **Network, Search Active Directory** from the menu.

Figure 6-23   The Publish tab of a shared folder's Properties dialog box

10. In the Find drop-down list, click **Shared Folders**. In the Keywords text box, type **test**, and then click **Find Now**.

11. In the Search results section, right-click **PubShare** and click **Explore**. A File Explorer window opens, showing the contents of the PubShare shared folder (currently empty).

12. Close all open windows. Open Active Directory Users and Computers.

13. When you publish a shared folder or printer, the published share appears as a child object of the server where the share is located. To view child objects of servers, click **View, Users, Contacts, Groups, and Computers as containers** from the menu.

14. Click to expand the **Domain Controllers** OU, and then click the server icon. You see the share you published in the right pane (see Figure 6-24).

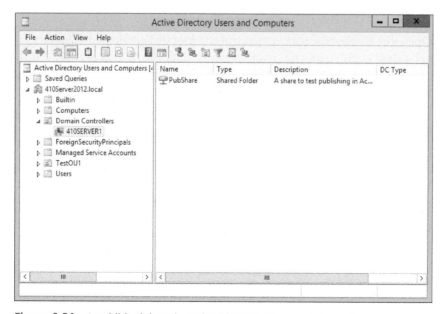

Figure 6-24   A published share in Active Directory Users and Computers

15. Click **View, Users, Contacts, Groups, and Computers as containers** from the menu again to disable this feature, and then close Active Directory Users and Computers.

Now that you've gotten your feet wet using Active Directory, it's time to delve into some details of how Active Directory is structured and how it functions. The next section discusses working with forests, trees, and domains and describes how information from one DC is transferred (replicated) to another DC.

Working with Forests, Trees, and Domains

In the day-to-day administration of an Active Directory domain, most administrators focus on OUs and their child objects. In a small organization, a solid understanding of OUs and leaf objects might be all that's needed to manage a Windows domain successfully. However, in large organizations, building an Active Directory structure composed of several domains, multiple trees, and even a few forests might be necessary.

When the first DC is installed in a network, the structure you see in Active Directory Users and Computers—a domain object and some folder and OU containers—isn't all that's created. In addition, a new tree and the root of a new forest are created, along with elements that define a new site. As a business grows or converts an existing network structure to Active Directory, there might be reasons to add domains to the tree, create new trees or forests, and add sites to the Active Directory structure. This section starts by describing some helpful terms for understanding how Active Directory operates and is organized. Next, you learn the forest's role in Active Directory and how to use multiple forests in an Active Directory structure. Then you examine trust relationships and domains, particularly situations involving multiple domains and multiple trees.

Active Directory Terminology

A number of terms are used to describe Active Directory's structure and operations. In the following sections, you examine terms associated with replication, directory partitions, operations masters, and trust relationships.

Active Directory Replication
Replication is the process of maintaining a consistent database of information when the database is distributed among several locations. Active Directory contains several databases called partitions that are replicated between domain controllers by using intrasite replication or intersite replication. **Intrasite replication** takes place between domain controllers in the same site; **intersite replication** occurs between two or more sites. The replication process differs in these two types, but the goal is the same—to maintain a consistent set of domain directory partitions.

Active Directory uses **multimaster replication** for replicating Active Directory objects, such as user and computer accounts, which means changes to these objects can occur on any DC and are propagated (replicated) to all other domain controllers. A process called the **Knowledge Consistency Checker (KCC)** runs on every DC to determine the replication topology, which defines the domain controller path through which Active Directory changes flow. This path is configured as a ring (or multiple rings, if there are enough domain controllers), with each DC in the path constituting a hop. The KCC is designed to ensure there are no more than three hops between any two domain controllers, which can result in multiple rings, as shown in Figure 6-25.

Intrasite replication occurs 15 seconds after a change is made on a domain controller, with a 3-second delay between each replication partner. A **replication partner** is a pair of domain controllers configured to replicate with one another. The KCC also configures the topology for intersite replication, but it's different from intrasite replication's topology. Site replication and configuration is discussed more in *MCSA Guide to Configuring Advanced Windows Server 2012 Services, Exam 70-412* (Cengage Learning, 2015).

6

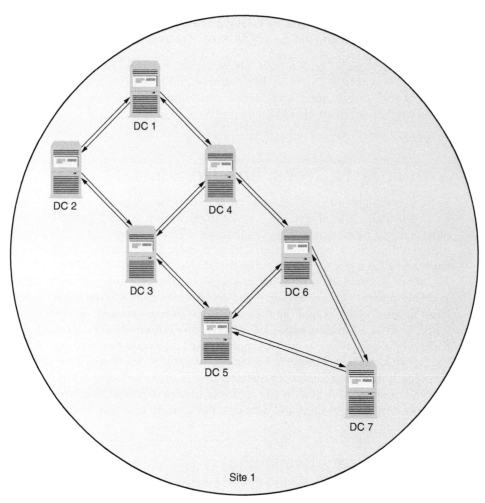

Figure 6-25   Replication topology
© Cengage Learning®

Directory Partitions   An Active Directory database has many sections stored in the same file on a DC's hard drive. These sections must be managed by different processes and replicated to other domain controllers in an Active Directory network. Each section of an Active Directory database is referred to as a **directory partition**. There are five directory partition types in the Active Directory database:

- *Domain directory partition*—Contains all objects in a domain, including users, groups, computers, OUs, and so forth. There's one **domain directory partition** for each domain in the forest. Changes made to objects in domain directory partitions are replicated to each DC in the domain. Some object attributes are also replicated to global catalog servers (described later in "The Importance of the Global Catalog Server") in all domains. Changes to the domain directory partition can occur on any DC in the domain except read-only domain controllers.

- *Schema directory partition*—Contains information needed to define Active Directory objects and object attributes for all domains in the forest. The **schema directory partition** is replicated to all domain controllers in the forest. One domain controller in the forest is designated as the schema master domain controller (discussed in the next section) and holds the only writeable copy of the schema.

- *Global catalog partition*—The **global catalog partition** holds the global catalog, which is a partial replica of all objects in the forest. It stores the most commonly accessed object attributes to facilitate object searches and user logons across domains. The global catalog is built automatically by domain replication of object attributes flagged for inclusion. Administrators can't make changes to this partition.

- *Application directory partition*—Used by applications and services to hold information that benefits from automatic Active Directory replication and security. DNS is the most common service to use an **application directory partition** for the DNS database. The information in this partition can be configured to replicate to specific domain controllers rather than all domain controllers, thereby controlling replication traffic. There can be more than one application directory partition.

- *Configuration partition*—By default, the **configuration partition** holds configuration information that can affect the entire forest, such as details on how domain controllers should replicate with one another. Applications can also store configuration information in this partition. This partition is replicated to all domain controllers in the forest, and changes can be made to information stored in this partition on all domain controllers.

Operations Master Roles

Operations Master Roles   A number of operations in a forest require having a single domain controller, called the **operations master**, with sole responsibility for the function. In most cases, the first DC in the forest takes on the role of operations master for these functions. However, you can transfer the responsibility to other domain controllers when necessary. There are five operations master roles, referred to as **Flexible Single Master Operation (FSMO) roles**, in an Active Directory forest:

- *Schema master*—As mentioned, the schema partition can be changed on only one DC, the schema master. This DC is responsible for replicating the schema directory partition to all other domain controllers in the forest when changes occur.

- *Infrastructure master*—This DC is responsible for ensuring that changes made to object names in one domain are updated in references to these objects in other domains. For example, if a user account in Domain A is a member of a group in Domain B and the user account name is changed, the infrastructure master in Domain A is responsible for replicating the change to Domain B. By default, the first DC in each domain is the infrastructure master for that domain.

- *Domain naming master*—This DC manages adding, removing, and renaming domains in the forest. There's only one domain naming master per forest, and the DC with this role must be available when domains are added, deleted, or renamed.

- *RID master*—All objects in a domain are identified internally by a **security identifier (SID)**. An object's SID is composed of a domain identifier, which is the same for all objects in the domain, and a **relative identifier (RID)**, which is unique for each object. Because objects can be created on any DC, there must be a mechanism that keeps two domain controllers from issuing the same RID, thereby duplicating an SID. The RID master is responsible for issuing unique pools of RIDs to each DC, thereby guaranteeing unique SIDs throughout the domain. The RID master must be available when adding a DC to an existing domain. There's one RID master per domain.

- *PDC emulator master*—This role provides backward-compatibility with Windows NT servers configured as Windows NT backup domain controllers or member servers. In addition, the PDC emulator master manages password changes to help make sure user authentication occurs without lengthy delays. When a user account password is changed, the change is replicated to all domain controllers but can take several minutes. Meanwhile, the user whose password was changed might be authenticated by a DC that hasn't yet received the replication, so the authentication fails. To reduce this problem, password changes are replicated immediately to the PDC emulator master, and if authentication fails at one DC, the attempt is retried on the PDC emulator master.

Because domain controllers that manage FSMO role data are, by definition, single masters, special attention must be paid to them. When removing domain controllers from a forest, make sure these roles aren't removed from the network accidentally. Domain administrators should keep track of which server holds each role and move the role to another DC if that machine is to be taken offline.

Activity 6-9: Viewing the Operations Master Roles

Time Required: 15 minutes

Objective: Discover where operations master roles are configured.

Required Tools and Equipment: 410Server1

Description: You're a consultant called in to document the Active Directory configuration for a company, in particular the operations master roles. You use Active Directory Users and Computers, Active Directory Domains and Trusts, and Active Directory Schema to view these roles.

1. Log on to 410Server1 as **Administrator**, if necessary, and open Active Directory Users and Computers.

2. In the left pane, right-click the top node **Active Directory Users and Computers [410Server1.410Server2012.local]**, point to **All Tasks**, and click **Operations Masters**.

3. The RID tab shows which DC performs the RID master role (see Figure 6-26). Click the **Change** button. The error message tells you that the DC you're connected to is the operations master, and you must first connect to the DC where you want to transfer the operations master role. You aren't going to transfer the role, however, so click **OK**.

Figure 6-26   Viewing the RID master role

4. Click the **PDC** tab to view the DC that's the PDC emulator master, and then click the **Infrastructure** tab to view the DC that's the infrastructure master. Only one DC per domain performs the three operations master roles you just saw. Click **Close**.

5. Right-click **Active Directory Users and Computers [410Server1.410Server2012.local]** and click **Change Domain Controller**. If your domain had more than one DC, you could connect to any of them here, and then change the operations master role to another DC. Click **Cancel**, and close Active Directory Users and Computers.

6. In Server Manager, click **Tools, Active Directory Domains and Trusts** from the menu.

7. Right-click **Active Directory Domains and Trusts [410Server1.410Server2012.local]** and click **Operations Master**. Here's where you can find which DC is the domain naming master.

Note that only one DC in the entire forest performs this function. Click **Close**, and close Active Directory Domains and Trusts.

8. To view the schema master, you must use a different process because this role isn't shown in any standard MMCs. Right-click **Start**, click **Run**, type **regsvr32 schmmgmt.dll** in the Open text box, and click **OK**. In the message box stating "DllRegisterServer in schmmgmt. dll succeeded," click **OK**.

 The command in Step 8 is needed to register, or activate, certain commands that aren't normally available in Windows—in this case, the Active Directory Schema snap-in.

9. Right-click **Start**, click **Run**, type **MMC** in the Open text box, and click **OK**.

10. Click **File**, **Add/Remove Snap-in** from the MMC menu.

11. In the Available snap-ins list box, click **Active Directory Schema**. Click **Add**, and then click **OK**.

12. Click **Active Directory Schema**, and then right-click **Active Directory Schema** and click **Operations Master**. As with the domain naming master, only one DC in the entire forest performs the schema master role. Click **Close**, and close the MMC. When prompted to save your console settings, click **No**. Close all open windows, but stay logged on to 410Server1.

Using PowerShell to View FSMO Roles   You can use PowerShell commands to view the FSMO roles. To view the holder of the three domain-wide roles, use the following PowerShell command:

```
Get-ADDomain
```

This command produces several lines of output (Figure 6-27). The highlighted lines show the three domain-wide FSMO roles.

To view the folder of the two forest-wide roles, use the following PowerShell command. Figure 6-28 shows its output.

```
Get-ADForest
```

```
Windows PowerShell
Copyright (C) 2013 Microsoft Corporation. All rights reserved.

PS C:\Users\Administrator> get-addomain

AllowedDNSSuffixes               : {}
ChildDomains                     : {}
ComputersContainer               : CN=Computers,DC=410Server2012,DC=local
DeletedObjectsContainer          : CN=Deleted Objects,DC=410Server2012,DC=local
DistinguishedName                : DC=410Server2012,DC=local
DNSRoot                          : 410Server2012.local
DomainControllersContainer       : OU=Domain Controllers,DC=410Server2012,DC=local
DomainMode                       : Windows2012R2Domain
DomainSID                        : S-1-5-21-175752861-1735658318-850774572
ForeignSecurityPrincipalsContainer : CN=ForeignSecurityPrincipals,DC=410Server2012,DC=local
Forest                           : 410Server2012.local
InfrastructureMaster             : 410Server1.410Server2012.local
LastLogonReplicationInterval     :
LinkedGroupPolicyObjects         : {CN={31B2F340-016D-11D2-945F-00C04FB984F9},CN=Policies
                                   DC=local}
LostAndFoundContainer            : CN=LostAndFound,DC=410Server2012,DC=local
ManagedBy                        :
Name                             : 410Server2012
NetBIOSName                      : 410SERVER2012
ObjectClass                      : domainDNS
ObjectGUID                       : 3a0f97af-7dab-4cfa-ac83-079588740fc6
ParentDomain                     :
PDCEmulator                      : 410Server1.410Server2012.local
QuotasContainer                  : CN=NTDS Quotas,DC=410Server2012,DC=local
ReadOnlyReplicaDirectoryServers  : {}
ReplicaDirectoryServers          : {410Server1.410Server2012.local}
RIDMaster                        : 410Server1.410Server2012.local
SubordinateReferences            : {DC=ForestDnsZones,DC=410Server2012,DC=local,
                                   DC=DomainDnsZones,DC=410Server2012,DC=local,
                                   CN=Configuration,DC=410Server2012,DC=local}
SystemsContainer                 : CN=System,DC=410Server2012,DC=local
UsersContainer                   : CN=Users,DC=410Server2012,DC=local
```

Figure 6-27   Output of `Get-ADDomain`

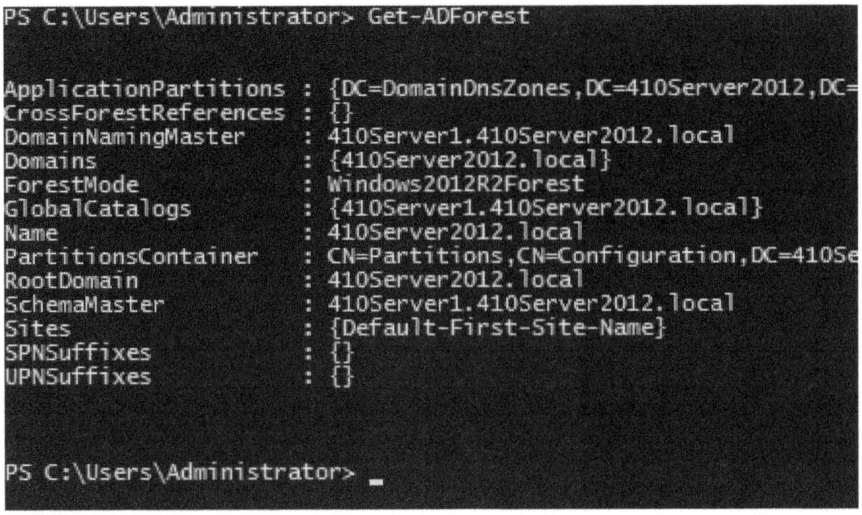

```
PS C:\Users\Administrator> Get-ADForest

ApplicationPartitions : {DC=DomainDnsZones,DC=410Server2012,DC=
CrossForestReferences : {}
DomainNamingMaster    : 410Server1.410Server2012.local
Domains               : {410Server2012.local}
ForestMode            : Windows2012R2Forest
GlobalCatalogs        : {410Server1.410Server2012.local}
Name                  : 410Server2012.local
PartitionsContainer   : CN=Partitions,CN=Configuration,DC=410Se
RootDomain            : 410Server2012.local
SchemaMaster          : 410Server1.410Server2012.local
Sites                 : {Default-First-Site-Name}
SPNSuffixes           : {}
UPNSuffixes           : {}


PS C:\Users\Administrator> _
```

Figure 6-28   Output of `Get-ADForest`

Trust Relationships   In Active Directory, a **trust relationship** defines whether and how security principals from one domain can access network resources in another domain. Trust relationships are established automatically between all domains in a forest. Therefore, when a user authenticates to one domain, the other domains in the forest accept, or trust, the authentication.

Don't confuse trusts with permissions. Permissions are still required to access resources, even if a trust relationship exists. When there's no trust relationship between domains, however, no access across domains is possible. Because all domains in a forest have trust relationships with one another automatically, trusts must be configured only when your Active Directory environment includes two or more forests or when you want to integrate with other OSs. Trusts are discussed in more detail in *MCSA Guide to Configuring Advanced Windows Server 2012 Services, Exam 70-412* (Cengage Learning, 2015).

The Role of Forests

The Active Directory forest is the broadest logical component of the Active Directory structure. Forests contain domains that can be organized into one or more trees. All domains in a forest share some common characteristics:

- *A single schema*—The schema defines Active Directory objects and their attributes and can be changed by an administrator or an application to best suit the organization's needs. All domains in a forest share the same schema, so a change to the schema affects objects in all domains. This shared schema is one reason that large organizations or conglomerates with diverse business units might want to operate as separate forests. With this structure, domains in different forests can still share information through trust relationships, but changes to the schema—perhaps from installing an Active Directory–integrated application, such as Microsoft Exchange—don't affect the schema of domains in a different forest.

- *Forest-wide administrative accounts*—Each forest has two groups defined with unique rights to perform operations that can affect the entire forest: Schema Admins and Enterprise Admins. Members of Schema Admins are the only users who can make changes to the schema. Members of Enterprise Admins can add or remove domains from the forest and have administrative access to every domain in the forest. By default, only the Administrator account for the first domain created in the forest (the forest root domain) is a member of these two groups.

- *Operations masters*—As discussed, certain forest-wide operations can be performed only by a DC designated as the operations master. Both the schema master and the domain naming master are forest-wide operations masters, meaning only one DC in the forest can perform these roles.

- *Global catalog*—There's only one global catalog per forest, but unlike operations masters, multiple domain controllers can be designated as global catalog servers. Because the global catalog contains information about all objects in the forest, it's used to speed searching for objects across domains in the forest and to allow users to log on to any domain in the forest.

- *Trusts between domains*—These trusts allow users to log on to their home domains (where their accounts are created) and access resources in domains throughout the forest without having to authenticate to each domain.

- *Replication between domains*—The forest structure facilitates replicating important information between all domain controllers throughout the forest. Forest-wide replication includes information stored in the global catalog, schema directory, and configuration partitions.

6

The Importance of the Global Catalog Server The first DC installed in a forest is always designated as a global catalog server, but you can use Active Directory Sites and Services to configure additional domain controllers as global catalog servers for redundancy. The following are some vital functions the global catalog server performs:

- *Facilitates domain and forest-wide searches*—As discussed, the global catalog is contacted to speed searches for resources across domains.

- *Facilitates logon across domains*—Users can log on to computers in any domain by using their **user principal name (UPN)**. A UPN follows the format *username@domain*. Because the global catalog contains information about all objects in all domains, a global catalog server is contacted to resolve the UPN. Without a global catalog server, users could log on only to computers that were members of the same domain as their user accounts.

- *Holds universal group membership information*—When a user logs on to the network, all the user's group memberships must be resolved to determine rights and permissions. Global catalog servers are the only domain controllers that hold universal group membership information, so they must be contacted when a user logs on. A universal group (discussed in Chapter 7) is the only type of group that can contain accounts from other domains, which is why this information must be stored in the global catalog.

Because of the critical functions a global catalog server performs, having at least one DC configured as a global catalog server in each location (such as a company's branch offices) is a good idea to speed logons and directory searches for users in all locations.

Activity 6-10: Configuring a Global Catalog Server

Time Required: 5 minutes
Objective: Use Active Directory Sites and Services to see how to configure a global catalog server.

Required Tools and Equipment: 410Server1
Description: You have installed a DC at a branch office but chose not to make it a global catalog server during installation. You have heard about the importance of having a global catalog server at all locations. A junior administrator is currently at the branch office, and you want to be able to instruct her on how to configure the DC as a global catalog server.

1. Log on to 410Server1 as **Administrator**, if necessary.

2. In Server Manager, click **Tools, Active Directory Sites and Services** from the menu.

3. Click to expand the **Sites** node, if necessary. Click to expand **Default-First-Site-Name,** **Servers,** and then **410Server1.** Your screen should look similar to Figure 6-29.

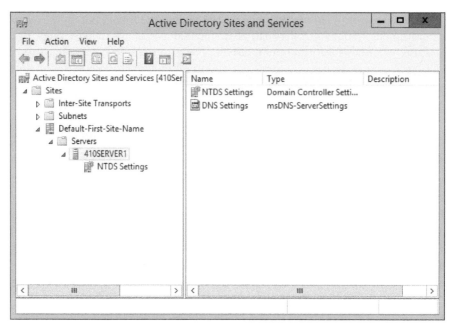

Figure 6-29   Active Directory Sites and Services

4. Right-click **NTDS Settings** under 410Server1 and click **Properties.** Click the **General** tab, if necessary. When the Global Catalog check box is selected, the DC is a global catalog server. Because it's the only global catalog server in the forest, clearing the check box generates a warning message stating that users can't log on if there's no global catalog server. Click **Cancel.**

5. Right-click **410Server1** and click **Properties.** Click the **General** tab, if necessary. Note that Global Catalog is specified in the DC Type text box. Click **Cancel,** and close Active Directory Sites and Services. If you're continuing to the next activity, stay logged on.

Forest Root Domain   As discussed, when the first domain is created in a Windows network, the forest root is also created. In fact, the first domain *is* the forest root and is referred to as the **forest root domain.** It has a number of important responsibilities and serves as an anchor for other trees and domains added to the forest. Certain functions that affect all domains in the forest are conducted only through the forest root domain, and if this domain becomes inoperable, the entire Active Directory structure ceases functioning. Figure 6-30 shows the forest root domain with multiple domains and trees. (Figure 6-4 showed the same structure, but for simplicity, it didn't show one of the domains as the forest root.)

What makes the forest root domain so important? It provides functions that facilitate and manage communication between all domains in the forest as well as between forests, if necessary. Some functions the forest root domain usually handles include the following:

- DNS server
- Global catalog server
- Forest-wide administrative accounts
- Operations masters

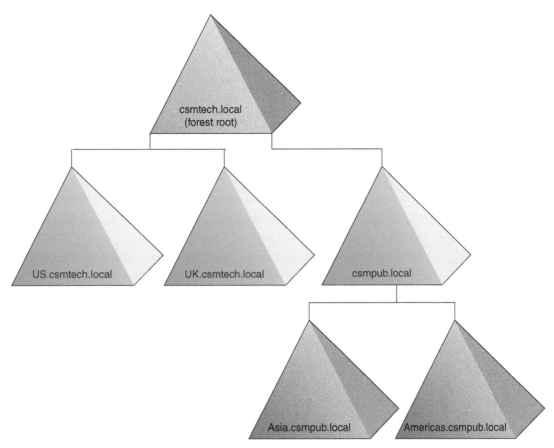

Figure 6-30   The forest root domain
© 2015 Cengage Learning®

The DNS server and global catalog server functions can be installed on other servers in other domains for fault tolerance. However, the forest-wide operations masters and forest-wide administrative accounts can reside only on a DC in the forest root domain. For these reasons, the forest root domain is a critical component of the Active Directory structure.

Understanding Domains and Trees

As discussed, an Active Directory tree is a group of domains sharing a common naming structure. A tree can consist of a single domain or a parent domain and one or more child domains, which can have child domains of their own. An Active Directory tree is said to have a contiguous namespace because all domains in the tree share at least the last two domain name components: the second-level domain name and the top-level domain name.

Organizations operating under a single name internally and to the public are probably best served by an Active Directory forest with only one tree. However, when two companies merge or a large company splits into separate business units that would benefit from having their own identities, a multiple tree structure makes sense. As you've learned, there's no major functional difference between domains in the same tree or domains in different trees, as long as they're part of the same forest. The only operational difference is the necessity of maintaining multiple DNS zones (discussed in Chapter 10).

Designing the Domain Structure   A domain is the primary identifying and administrative unit in Active Directory. A unique name is associated with each domain and used to access network resources. A domain administrator account has full control over objects in the domain, and certain security policies apply to all accounts in a domain.

Additionally, most replication traffic occurs between domain controllers in a domain. Any of these factors can influence your decision to use a single-domain or multidomain design. Most small and medium businesses choose a single domain for reasons that include the following:

- *Simplicity*—The more complex something is, the easier it is for things to go wrong. Unless your organization needs multiple identities, separate administration, or differing account policies, keeping the structure simple with a single domain is the best choice.

- *Lower costs*—Every domain must have at least one DC and preferably two or more for fault tolerance. Each DC requires additional hardware and software resources, which increases costs.

- *Easier management*—Many management tasks are easier in a single-domain environment:

  o Having a single set of administrators and policies prevents conflicts caused by differing viewpoints on operational procedures and policies.

  o Object management is easier when personnel reorganizations or transfers occur. Moving user and computer accounts between different OUs is easier than moving them between different domains.

  o Managing access to resources is simplified when you don't need to consider security principals from other domains.

  o Placement of domain controllers and global catalog servers is simplified when your organization has multiple locations because you don't need to consider cross-domain replication.

- *Easier access to resources*—A single domain provides the easiest environment for users to find and access network resources. In a multidomain environment, mobile users who visit branch offices with different domains must authenticate to their home domain. If their home domain isn't available for some reason, they can't log on to the network.

Although a single-domain structure is usually easier and less expensive than a multidomain structure, it's not always better. Using more than one domain makes sense or is even a necessity in the following circumstances:

- *Need for differing account policies*—Account policies that govern password and account lockout policies apply to all users in a domain. If you need to have differing policies for different business units, using separate domains is the best way to meet this requirement. A feature introduced in Windows Server 2008 called "fine-grained password policies" can be used to apply different password policies for users or groups in a domain, but this feature can be difficult to manage when many users are involved.

- *Need for different name identities*—Each domain has its own name that can represent a separate company or business unit. If each business unit must maintain its own identity, child domains can be created in which part of the name is shared, or multiple trees with completely different namespaces can be created.

- *Replication control*—Replication in a large domain maintaining several thousand objects can generate substantial traffic. When multiple corporate locations are connected through a WAN, the amount of replication traffic could be unacceptable. Replication traffic can be reduced by creating separate domains for key locations because only global catalog replication is required between domains.

- *Need for internal versus external domains*—Companies that run public Web servers often create a domain used only for publicly accessible resources and another domain for internal resources. In fact, Microsoft recommends that all companies have separate domain names for their public presence and their internal network.

- *Need for tight security*—With separate domains, stricter resource control and administrative permissions are easier. If a business unit prefers to have its own administrative staff, separate domains must be created.

Introducing Group Policies

A **Group Policy Object (GPO)** is a list of settings administrators use to configure user and computer operating environments remotely. Group policies can specify security settings, deploy software, and configure a user's desktop, among many other computer and network settings. They can be configured to affect an entire domain, a site, and, most commonly, users or computers in an OU. The **GPO scope** defines which objects a GPO affects.

Despite the name, GPOs don't apply to group objects. You can link GPOs to sites, domains, and OUs, and GPOs linked to these containers affect only user or computer accounts in the containers. When Active Directory is installed, two GPOs are created and linked to two containers:

- *Default Domain Policy*—This GPO is linked to the domain object and specifies default settings that affect all users and computers in the domain. The settings in this policy are related mainly to account policies, such as password and logon requirements, and some network security policies.

- *Default Domain Controllers Policy*—This GPO is linked to the Domain Controllers OU and specifies default policy settings for all domain controllers in the domain (provided the computer objects representing domain controllers aren't moved from the Domain Controllers OU). The settings in this policy pertain mainly to user rights assignments, which specify the types of actions users can perform on a DC.

These default policies don't define any user-specific policies; instead, they're designed to provide default security settings for all computers, including domain controllers, in the domain. You can view, create, and manage GPOs by using the Group Policy Management console (GPMC), shown in Figure 6-31. Each GPO has two main nodes in GPMC (shown in the right pane of Figure 6-31):

- *Computer Configuration*—Used to set policies that apply to computers within the GPO's scope. These policies are applied to a computer when the computer starts.

- *User Configuration*—Used to set policies that apply to all users within the GPO's scope. User policies are applied when a user logs on to any computer in the domain.

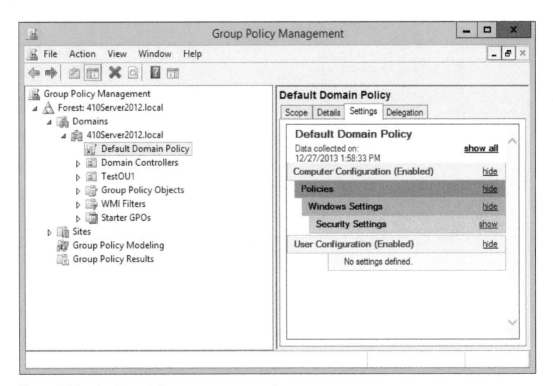

Figure 6-31   The Group Policy Management console

Each node contains a Policies folder and a Preferences folder. Settings configured in the Policies folder are applied to users or computers and can't be overridden by users. Settings in the Preferences folder are applied to users or computers but are just that: preferences. Therefore, users can change settings configured in the Preferences folder.

The Policies folder under both the Computer Configuration and User Configuration nodes contains three folders: Software Settings, Windows Settings, and Administrative Templates. They can store different information, depending on whether they're under Computer Configuration or User Configuration.

 In GPMC, you see only folders containing configured settings. By default, there are no configured settings in the User Configuration node in the Default Domain Policy, which is why you don't see a Policies folder under User Configuration in Figure 6-31. Likewise, you don't see the Preferences folder in this figure because no preferences have been configured.

To change a GPO's settings, you use the Group Policy Management Editor (GPME, shown in Figure 6-32), which you open by right-clicking a GPO and clicking Edit.

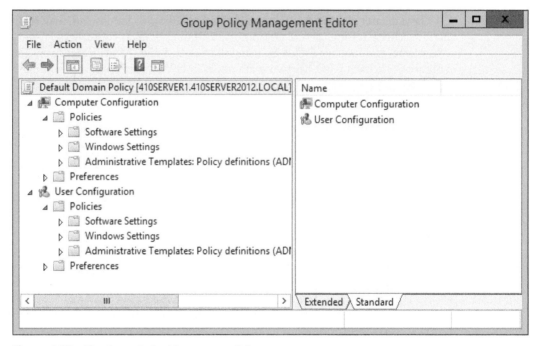

Figure 6-32   The Group Policy Management Editor

The Computer Configuration Node

In the Computer Configuration node, the three folders under the Policies folder contain the following information:

- *Software Settings*—This folder contains an item (**extension**) called Software installation, which enables administrators to install and manage applications remotely. Application installation packages can be configured so that the next time a computer in the GPO's scope starts, the application is installed automatically. This feature is called "assigning" the application to the computer.

- *Windows Settings*—This folder contains the Name Resolution Policy node, Scripts extension, Security Settings node, and Policy-based QoS node. The Name Resolution Policy stores configuration settings for DNS security and DirectAccess. Administrators can use the Scripts extension to create scripts that run at computer startup or shutdown. The Security Settings node contains the lion's share of policies that affect computer security, including account policies, user rights, wireless network policies, Registry and file system permissions, and network communication policies, among others. The Policy-based QoS node can be used to prioritize and control outgoing network traffic from a computer.

- *Administrative Templates*—This folder contains Control Panel, Network, Printers, System, and Windows Components folders. The settings in these folders affect computer settings that apply to all logged-on users. For example, the Network folder contains settings for configuring Windows Firewall, and Windows Components contains settings for configuring Windows Update. You can control hundreds of computer settings with the Administrative Templates folder.

Remember that policies configured in the Computer Configuration node affect all computers in the container (and child containers) to which the GPO is linked. So a policy set in the Computer Configuration node of a GPO linked to the domain object affects all computers in the domain, including all computers in the Domain Controllers OU and the Computers folder.

The User Configuration Node

In the User Configuration node, the Policies folder contains the same three folders as in the Computer Configuration node. However, the policies defined here affect domain users within the GPO's scope, regardless of which computer the user logs on to. The following list describes other differences from folders under the Computer Configuration node:

- *Software Settings*—This folder also contains the Software installation extension. However, application packages configured here can be assigned or published. An **assigned application** is made available as an icon in the Start screen the next time a user affected by the policy logs on to a computer in the domain. The first time the user tries to run the application or open a document associated with it, the application is installed. A **published application** is made available via Group Policy for a user to install by using Programs and Features in Control Panel.

- *Windows Settings*—This folder contains four items: the Scripts extension, the Security Settings node, the Folder Redirection node, and the Policy-based QoS node. The Scripts extension enables administrators to create scripts that run at user logon and logoff. The Security Settings node contains policies for configuring certificates and controlling what software users can run. Administrators can use the Folder Redirection node to redirect users' profile folders to a network share. The Policy-based QoS node provides the same functions as in the Computer Configuration node, except that the policy is applied to a computer when a user affected by the policy logs on to the computer.

- *Administrative Templates*—This folder contains a host of settings that enable administrators to tightly control users' computer and network environments. For example, Control Panel can be completely hidden from a user, specific Control Panel items can be made available, or items on a user's desktop and Start screen can be hidden or disabled, just to name a few of the settings that can be configured here.

Group Policy is a powerful tool, but with this power comes complexity. This chapter serves as an introduction to group policies, and you learn more about working with their complexities in Chapter 8. For now, take the time to explore the default GPOs in Active Directory in the following activity.

Activity 6-11: Exploring Default GPOs

Time Required: 30 minutes

Objective: Explore the two default GPOs in Active Directory.

Required Tools and Equipment: 410Server1

Description: You want to begin using GPOs to manage users and computers in your network, so as a first step, you decide to familiarize yourself with the default GPOs linked to the domain and the Domain Controllers OU.

1. Log on to 410Server1 as **Administrator**, if necessary.

2. In Server Manager, click **Tools, Group Policy Management** from the menu.

3. In the left pane, click to expand the **Forest** and **Domains** nodes, if necessary. Click to expand **410Server2012.local** under the Domains node, if necessary.

4. Click **Default Domain Policy**. If a Group Policy Management console message is displayed, read the message, click the **Do not show this message again** check box, and then click **OK**.

5. In the right pane, click the **Scope** tab, if necessary (see Figure 6-33). The Links section shows you which container objects are linked to this GPO. In this case, your domain should be the only container linked. All objects in a container linked to the GPO are affected by that GPO.

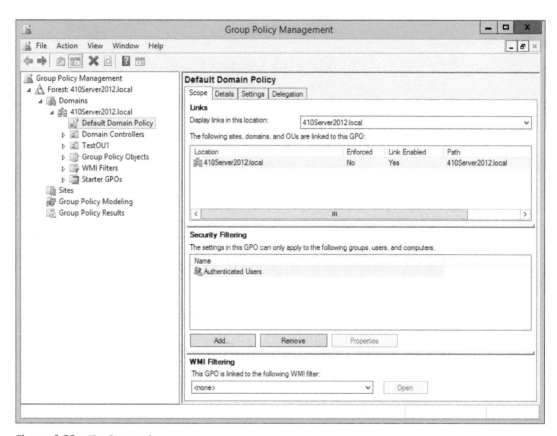

Figure 6-33   The Scope tab

6. Click the **Settings** tab. (The settings might take a few seconds to be displayed.) You can view GPO settings here, but you can't change them.

7. The two main nodes are highlighted: Computer Configuration and User Configuration. Click the **show all** link to expand the settings to see a window similar to Figure 6-34. Only nodes that have configured settings are shown.

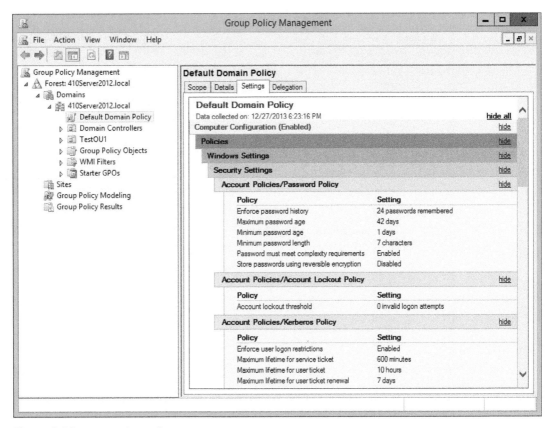

Figure 6-34   The Settings tab

8. Scroll through the settings for the Default Domain Policy, which pertain to user account settings, such as password policies, or security. Take some time to see how Windows initially configures security settings for the domain. You might want to make changes to the default security settings on your own domain. Notice that no settings are displayed under the User Configuration node because no settings have been configured.

9. Click to expand **Domain Controllers** in the left pane, and then click **Default Domain Controllers Policy**.

10. In the right pane, click the **Settings** tab, if necessary, and then click **show all**. Scroll through the settings for the Default Domain Controllers Policy. Most pertain to user rights assignments, such as which users are allowed to log on to the computer locally or change the system time. Again, take some time to see how Windows initially configures security settings for domain controllers.

11. Right-click **Default Domain Policy** in the left pane and click **Edit** to open the Group Policy Management Editor.

12. If necessary, click to expand **Computer Configuration** and **User Configuration**. Under Computer Configuration, click to expand the **Policies** folder. You see the three folders described earlier.

13. Click to expand **Windows Settings** and then **Security Settings**. Click to expand the **Account Policies** node, and explore the settings in this node and the nodes under it. Figure 6-35 shows the settings in the Password Policy node. By default, account policies are defined only in the Default Domain Policy, and all domain users are subject to these settings.

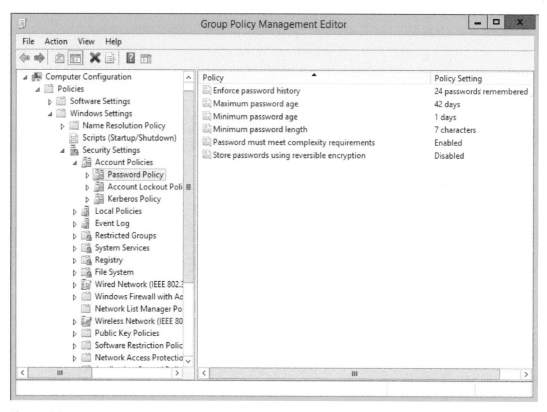

Figure 6-35   Password policies

14. Click to expand the **Local Policies** node, and explore the three nodes under it. Most settings in Local Policies are displayed as Not Defined. In fact, only three policies in the Local Policies node are defined. Can you find them?

15. Browse through some nodes in the Policies folder under User Configuration. No policies are configured in this node. Configuration of user policies is up to the server administrator.

16. Close the Group Policy Management Editor. In the Group Policy Management console, click to expand **Domain Controllers**, if necessary, and then right-click **Default Domain Controllers Policy** and click **Edit**.

17. Under the Computer Configuration node, click to expand the **Policies** folder, if necessary, and then click to expand **Windows Settings** and then **Security Settings**. Click to expand **Account Policies** and **Local Policies**, and explore the settings in these nodes. Notice that no account policies are defined, but a number of user rights assignments are. Default settings that apply to domain controllers focus on what types of actions users can perform on domain controllers. Most actions are limited to members of the Administrators, Backup Operators, and Server Operators groups.

18. Take some time to explore several GPOs to familiarize yourself with what's available. Leave the Group Policy Management console open for the next activity.

How Group Policies Are Applied

After reading about group policies and examining the two default policies, you might wonder how the Default Domain Policy can affect all computers in the domain when domain controllers have their own default policy. You might have noticed that the Default Domain Policy defines several account policies, such as password and account lockout settings, but no user rights assignment policies; the Default Domain Controllers Policy defines user rights assignment policies but no account policies. In addition, many policies are left undefined or not configured because GPOs, like Active Directory, work in a hierarchical structure.

GPOs can be applied in four places: local computer, site, domain, and OU. Policies are applied in this order, too. Policies that aren't defined or configured are not applied at all, and the last policy to be applied is the one that takes precedence. For example, a GPO linked to a domain affects all computers and users in the domain, but a GPO linked to an OU overrides the domain policies if there are conflicting settings. You learn more about using GPOs in Chapter 8.

You can remember the order in which GPOs are applied with the acronym LSDOU: local computer, site, domain, and OU.

6

Activity 6-12: Working with Group Policies

Time Required: 30 minutes
Objective: Create a GPO and see how policies you configure affect user objects in the OU to which the GPO is linked.

Required Tools and Equipment: 410Server1
Description: You want to see how some group policy settings affect users in your domain. You know that you want to restrict some users' access to Control Panel, so you decide to start with this policy. Because you want the policy to affect certain users, you configure it in the User Configuration node.

1. If necessary, log on to 410Server1 as **Administrator**, and open the Group Policy Management console.

2. Click to expand the **Forest** and **Domains** nodes and then the domain node, if necessary.

3. Right-click **TestOU1** (created earlier) and click **Create a GPO in this domain, and Link it here**. In the New GPO dialog box, type **GPO1** in the Name text box, and then click **OK**.

4. In the left pane, click to expand **TestOU1**, and then right-click **GPO1** and click **Edit** to open the Group Policy Management Editor.

5. Under User Configuration, click to expand **Policies** and then **Administrative Templates**. Click the **Control Panel** node. In the right pane, double-click the **Prohibit access to Control Panel and PC settings** policy to open the dialog box shown in Figure 6-36.

6. Read the description of the policy in the Help box, and then click the **Enabled** option button. Note that there are three possible settings: Enabled, Disabled, and Not Configured. If the policy is enabled, users affected by the policy are prohibited from accessing the Control Panel and PC settings. If the policy is disabled, users have access. If the policy is not configured, it has no effect on users' access to the Control Panel and PC settings. Click **OK**. Notice that the State column in the Group Policy Management Editor for the policy you changed then shows "Enabled."

7. Close the Group Policy Management Editor and Group Policy Management console.

8. Log off your server and log back on as **testuser1**. To do so, after you press **Ctrl+Alt+Delete**, click **Other user**. Type **testuser1** in the User name text box and **Password01** in the Password text box, and then press **Enter**.

9. You see a message stating that the sign-in method you're trying to use isn't allowed. This is because of a policy that prevents regular users from logging on locally to a server. Click **OK**, and then click the back arrow.

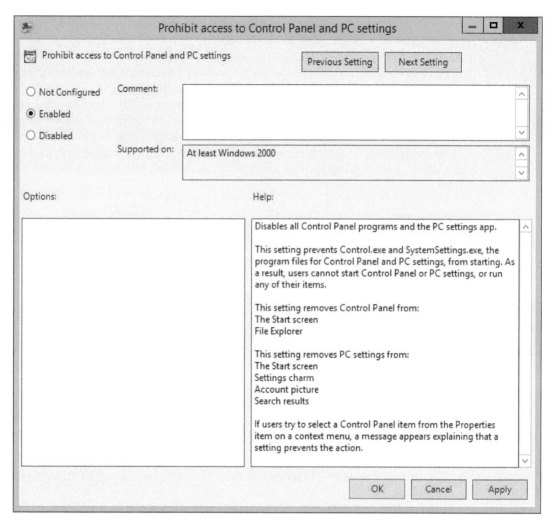

Figure 6-36 Configuring a policy setting

10. Log back on as **Administrator**. Open the Group Policy Management MMC, and click to expand the **Domain Controllers** OU. Right-click **Default Domain Controllers Policy** and click **Edit** to open the Group Policy Management Editor.

11. Under Computer Configuration, click to expand **Policies, Windows Settings,** and then **Security Settings**. Click to expand **Local Policies,** and then click **User Rights Assignment**. You should see a list of User Rights Assignment policies in the right pane (see Figure 6-37).

12. In the right pane, double-click the **Allow log on locally** policy. Click **Add User or Group**. In the Add User or Group dialog box, type **Domain Users,** and then click **OK** twice.

13. Log off and log back on as **testuser1**. If you still can't log on, you might need to wait a few minutes and try again. Group policies take some time to take effect.

14. After you're logged on, right-click **Start** and click **Control Panel**. In the Restrictions message box stating that the operation has been cancelled because of restrictions on the computer, click **OK**.

15. Right-click the desktop and click **Screen Resolution**. In the same Restrictions message box, click **OK**. Your policy has clearly taken effect. (If you see an Explorer.EXE message box stating "Unspecified error," click **OK**.)

16. Log off 410Server1. Shut down the server unless you're continuing to the activities in the next chapter.

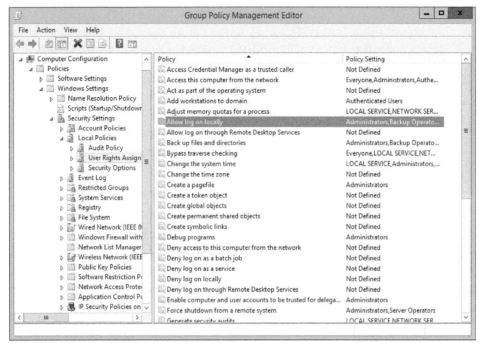

Figure 6-37   The User Rights Assignment node

In Activity 6-12, you might have noticed a delay between setting a policy and the policy taking effect. You can run the command-line program `gpupdate.exe`, which applies group policies immediately to the computer on which `gpupdate.exe` is running and to the currently logged-on user. This program is an invaluable tool for testing GPOs because it saves considerable time. As mentioned, computer policies are applied when a computer restarts, which can take some time, and user policies are applied when a user logs on. GPOs are also updated on domain controllers every 5 minutes and on workstations and servers every 90 minutes, even if the computers don't restart.

There's a lot more to group policies than the overview in this chapter. You learn more about managing and configuring GPOs in Chapter 8.

Chapter Summary

- A directory service is a database that stores network resource information and can be used to manage users, computers, and resources throughout the network. A directory service provides network single sign-on for users and centralizes management in geographically dispersed networks.

- Active Directory is based on the X.500 standard and LDAP. Active Directory is the Windows directory service and has been part of the Windows Server family since Windows 2000 Server. Active Directory is a hierarchical, distributed database that's scalable, secure, and flexible. Active Directory's physical structure is composed of sites and domain controllers, and the logical structure is composed of organizational units, domains, trees, and forests.

- You use Server Manager to install the Active Directory Domain Services role. After running the wizard in Server Manager, you must finish the Active Directory installation by promoting the server to a domain controller using the Active Directory Domain Services Configuration Wizard. After Active Directory is installed, a number of new MMCs are added to the Administrative Tools folder. The main tools for managing an Active Directory domain are Active Directory Administrative Center and Active Directory Users and Computers.

- Installing the first DC in a network creates a new forest and the domain is called the forest root domain. Adding additional domain controllers to a domain, or new domains in a forest are similar to creating a new forest. You can use Install from media (IFM) to install subsequent DCs in a domain, which reduces the amount of initial replication traffic required to bring a DC up to date.

- The data in Active Directory is organized as objects. Available objects and their structure are defined by the Active Directory schema, which is composed of schema classes and schema attributes. The data in a schema attribute is called an attribute value.

- There are two types of objects in Active Directory: container objects and leaf objects. Container objects contain other objects and include domains, folders, and OUs. OUs are the primary organizing container in Active Directory. Domains represent administrative, security, and policy boundaries. OUs are organizing and management containers mainly used to mimic a company's structure and apply group policies to collections of users or computers.

- Leaf objects generally represent security accounts, network resources, and GPOs. Security accounts include users, groups, and computers. There are three categories of user account objects: local user accounts, domain user accounts, and built-in user accounts. Groups are used to assign rights and permissions to collections of users. Computer account objects are used to identify computers that are domain members. Other leaf objects include contacts, printers, and shared folders.

- The AD Recycle Bin can be enabled in ADAC, but after it's enabled, it can't be disabled. This feature requires a forest functional level of at least Windows Server 2008 R2.

- Active Directory objects can be located easily with search functions in Active Directory Users and Computers and Windows Explorer. Users can use the Active Directory search function to find network resources (such as shared printers and folders), other users, and contacts, among many other items.

- Large organizations might require multiple domains, trees, and forests. Some terms for describing the Active Directory structure include directory partitions, operations master roles, Active Directory replication, and trust relationships.

- Directory partitions are sections of the Active Directory database that hold varied types of data and are managed by different processes. Directory partitions can be replicated from one domain controller to another. FSMO roles are functions carried out by a single domain controller per domain or forest and perform vital functions that affect Active Directory operations.

- The forest is the broadest logical Active Directory component. All domains in a forest share some common characteristics, such as a single schema, the global catalog, and trusts between domains. The global catalog facilitates several important functions, such as cross-domain logon and forest-wide searching. The forest root domain is the first domain created in a forest.

- A domain is the primary identifying and administrative unit of Active Directory. Each domain has a unique name, and there's an administrative account with full control over objects in the domain. Some organizations can benefit by using multiple domains when different security or account policies are required, among other reasons. A tree consists of one or more domains with a contiguous namespace. An Active Directory forest might require multiple trees when an organization is composed of companies with a noncontiguous namespace.

- GPOs are lists of settings that enable administrators to configure user and computer operating environments remotely. GPOs have two main nodes: Computer Configuration and User Configuration. Each node contains a Policies folder and a Preferences folder. Under the Policies folder are three additional folders called Software Settings, Windows Settings, and Administrative Templates.

- Policies defined in the Computer Configuration node affect all computers in the Active Directory container to which the GPO is linked. Policies defined in the User Configuration node affect all users in the Active Directory container to which the GPO is linked. Group objects aren't affected by GPOs. GPOs can be applied in these four places in order: local computer, site, domain, and OU. User policies are applied when a user logs on, and computer policies are applied when a computer restarts.

Key Terms

6

Active Directory replication   The transfer of information between all domain controllers to make sure they have consistent and up-to-date information.

application directory partition   A directory partition that applications and services use to store information that benefits from automatic Active Directory replication and security.

assigned application   An application package made available to users via Group Policy and places a shortcut to the application in the Start screen. The application is installed automatically if a user tries to run it or opens a document associated with it. If the assigned application applies to a computer account, the application is installed the next time Windows boots.

attribute value   Information stored in each attribute. *See also* schema attributes.

authentication   A process that confirms a user's identity, and the account is assigned permissions and rights that authorize the user to access resources and perform certain tasks on the computer or domain.

built-in user accounts   User accounts created by Windows automatically during installation.

child domains   Domains that share at least the top-level and second-level domain name structure as an existing domain in the forest; also called "subdomains."

configuration partition   A directory partition that stores configuration information that can affect the entire forest, such as details on how domain controllers should replicate with one another.

directory partition   A section of an Active Directory database stored on a domain controller's hard drive. These sections are managed by different processes and replicated to other domain controllers in an Active Directory network.

directory service   A database that stores information about a computer network and includes features for retrieving and managing that information.

Directory Services Restore Mode (DSRM)   A boot mode used to perform restore operations on Active Directory if it becomes corrupted or parts of it are deleted accidentally.

domain   The core structural unit of Active Directory; contains OUs and represents administrative, security, and policy boundaries.

domain directory partition   A directory partition that contains all objects in a domain, including users, groups, computers, OUs, and so forth.

domain user account   A user account created in Active Directory that provides a single logon for users to access all resources in the domain for which they have been authorized.

extension   An item in a GPO that allows an administrator to configure a policy setting.

Flexible Single Master Operation (FSMO) roles   Specialized domain controller tasks that handle operations that can affect the entire domain or forest. Only one domain controller can be assigned a particular FSMO.

forest   A collection of one or more Active Directory trees. A forest can consist of a single tree with a single domain, or it can contain several trees, each with a hierarchy of parent and child domains.

forest root domain   The first domain created in a new forest.

fully qualified domain name (FQDN)   A domain name that includes all parts of the name, including the top-level domain.

global catalog partition   A directory partition that stores the global catalog, which is a partial replica of all objects in the forest. It contains the most commonly accessed object attributes to facilitate object searches and user logons across domains.

GPO scope   The objects affected by a GPO linked to a site, domain, or OU.

Group Policy Object (GPO)   A list of settings that administrators use to configure user and computer operating environments remotely through Active Directory.

Install from media (IFM)   An option when installing a DC in an existing domain; much of the Active Directory database contents are copied to the new DC from media created from an existing DC.

intersite replication   Active Directory replication that occurs between two or more sites.

intrasite replication   Active Directory replication between domain controllers in the same site.

Knowledge Consistency Checker (KCC)   A process that runs on every domain controller to determine the replication topology.

Lightweight Directory Access Protocol (LDAP)   A protocol that runs over TCP/IP and is designed to facilitate access to directory services and directory objects. It's based on a suite of protocols called X.500, developed by the International Telecommunication Union.

local user account   A user account defined on a local computer that's authorized to access resources only on that computer. Local user accounts are mainly used on stand-alone computers or in a workgroup network with computers that aren't part of an Active Directory domain.

multimaster replication   The process for replicating Active Directory objects; changes to the database can occur on any domain controller and are propagated, or replicated, to all other domain controllers.

object   A grouping of information that describes a network resource, such as a shared printer, or an organizing structure, such as a domain or OU.

operations master   A domain controller with sole responsibility for certain domain or forest-wide functions.

organizational unit (OU)   An Active Directory container used to organize a network's users and resources into logical administrative units.

permissions   Settings that define which resources users can access and what level of access they have to resources.

published application   An application package made available via Group Policy for users to install by using Programs and Features in Control Panel. The application is installed automatically if a user tries to run it or opens a document associated with it.

relative identifier (RID)   The part of a SID that's unique for each Active Directory object. *See also* security identifier (SID).

replication partner   A domain controller configured to replicate with another domain controller.

right   A setting that specifies what types of actions a user can perform on a computer or network.

schema   Information that defines the type, organization, and structure of data stored in the Active Directory database.

schema attributes   A category of schema information that defines what type of information is stored in each object.

schema classes   A category of schema information that defines the types of objects that can be stored in Active Directory, such as user or computer accounts.

schema directory partition   A directory partition containing the information needed to define Active Directory objects and object attributes for all domains in the forest.

security identifier (SID)   A numeric value assigned to each object in a domain that uniquely identifies the object; composed of a domain identifier, which is the same for all objects in a domain, and an RID. *See also* relative identifier (RID).

site   A physical location in which domain controllers communicate and replicate information regularly.

SYSVOL folder   A shared folder that stores information from Active Directory that's replicated to other domain controllers.

tree   A grouping of domains that share a common naming structure.

trust relationship   An arrangement that defines whether and how security principals from one domain can access network resources in another domain.

user principal name (UPN)   A user logon name that follows the format *username@domain*. Users can use UPNs to log on to their own domain from a computer that's a member of a different domain.

6

Review Questions

1. Which of the following best describes a directory service?

   a. Similar to a list of information in a text file

   b. Similar to a database program but with the capability to manage objects

   c. A program for managing the user interface on a server

   d. A program for managing folders, files, and permissions on a distributed server

2. The protocol for accessing Active Directory objects and services is based on which of the following standards?

   a. DNS

   b. LDAP

   c. DHCP

   d. ICMP

3. Which of the following is a feature of Active Directory? (Choose all that apply.)

   a. Fine-grained access controls

   b. Can be distributed among many servers

   c. Can be installed on only one server per domain

   d. Has a fixed schema

4. Which of the following is a component of Active Directory's physical structure?

   a. Organizational units

   b. Domains

   c. Sites

   d. Folders

5. Which of the following is the responsibility of a domain controller? (Choose all that apply.)

   a. Storing a copy of the domain data

   b. Providing data search and retrieval functions

   c. Servicing multiple domains

   d. Providing authentication services

6. Which of the following is *not* associated with an Active Directory tree?

    a.   A group of domains

    b.   A container object that can be linked to a GPO

    c.   A common naming structure

    d.   Parent and child domains

7. Which of the following is *not* part of Active Directory's logical structure?

    a.   Tree

    b.   Forest

    c.   DC

    d.   OU

8. Which of the following is associated with an Active Directory forest? (Choose all that apply.)

    a.   Can contain trees with different naming structures

    b.   Allows independent domain administration

    c.   Contains domains with different schemas

    d.   Represents the broadest element in Active Directory

9. Which of the following is associated with installing the first domain controller in a forest?

    a.   RODC

    b.   Child domain

    c.   Global catalog

    d.   DHCP

10. When installing an additional DC in an existing domain, which of the following is an option for reducing replication traffic?

    a.   New site

    b.   Child domain

    c.   GC server

    d.   IFM

11. Which MMC is added after Active Directory installation? (Choose all that apply.)

    a.   Active Directory Domains and Trusts

    b.   Active Directory Groups and Sites

    c.   ADSI Edit

    d.   Active Directory Restoration Utility

12. Which of the following is the core logical structure container in Active Directory?

    a.   Forest

    b.   OU

    c.   Domain

    d.   Site

13. Which of the following defines the types of objects in Active Directory?

    a.   GPOs

    b.   Attribute values

    c.   Schema attributes

    d.   Schema classes

14. Which of the following defines the types of information stored in an Active Directory object?

    a. GPOs

    b. Attribute values

    c. Schema attributes

    d. Schema classes

15. Which of the following specifies what types of actions a user can perform on a computer or network?

    a. Attributes

    b. Rights

    c. Permissions

    d. Classes

16. Which of the following is considered a leaf object? (Choose all that apply.)

    a. Computer account

    b. Organizational unit

    c. Domain controller

    d. Shared folder

17. Which of the following is a default folder object?

    a. Computers

    b. Domain Controllers

    c. Groups

    d. Sites

18. Which type of account is *not* found in Active Directory?

    a. Domain user account

    b. Local user account

    c. Built-in user account

    d. Computer account

19. Which of the following is a directory partition? (Choose all that apply.)

    a. Domain directory partition

    b. Group policy partition

    c. Schema directory partition

    d. Configuration partition

20. Which is responsible for management of adding, removing, and renaming domains in a forest?

    a. Schema master

    b. Infrastructure master

    c. Domain naming master

    d. RID master

21. All domains in the same forest have which of the following in common? (Choose all that apply.)

    a. Domain name

    b. Schema

    c. Domain administrator

    d. Global catalog

22. You have an Active Directory forest of two trees and eight domains. You haven't changed any operations master domain controllers. On which domain controller is the schema master?

   a.   All domain controllers

   b.   The last domain controller installed

   c.   The first domain controller in the forest root domain

   d.   The first domain controller in each tree

23. To which of the following can a GPO be linked? (Choose all that apply.)

   a.   Trees

   b.   Domains

   c.   Folders

   d.   Sites

24. Which container has a default GPO linked to it?

   a.   Users

   b.   Printers

   c.   Computers

   d.   Domain

25. By default, when are policies set in the User Configuration node applied?

   a.   Every 5 minutes

   b.   Immediately

   c.   At user logon

   d.   At computer restart

Case Projects

Case Project 6-1: Configuring Active Directory

When CSM Tech Publishing started its Windows network almost a year ago, the network was small enough that you simply used the default Users and Computers containers for the user account and computer account objects you created. However, now that the company has grown to more than 50 users and computers, you decide that some structure is needed. You talk to the owner to understand how the business is organized and learn that there are four main departments: Executive, Marketing, Engineering, and Operations. Draw a diagram of the Active Directory structure based on this information, including the types of objects in each container. Include the objects you know about and where these objects should be located, and state whether you need to move any existing objects. Use triangles and circles to represent container objects in your diagram, as shown in Figures 6-1 through 6-4.

Case Project 6-2: Explaining GPOs

The owner of CSM Tech Publishing has told you he needs to lock down some desktops so that these users can't access certain Windows components, such as Control Panel. He also wants some standardization in the look of users' desktops, such as wallpaper and so forth. However, he's not sure how to make these changes without affecting all users and computers. Write a short explanation of how GPOs can be applied. Include information about how policies defined in one place can take precedence over policies defined elsewhere.

chapter 7

Managing OUs and Active Directory Accounts

After reading this chapter and completing the exercises, you will be able to:

- Work with organizational units
- Manage user accounts
- Manage group accounts
- Work with computer accounts
- Automate account management

A directory service should be thought of as a tool to help administrators manage network resources. Like any tool, the better designed it is, the more useful it will be. In its default configuration, Active Directory is a useful directory service, but its real power is apparent when thought has been put into its design and configuration. An efficient Active Directory design that reflects how a business is organized improves the ease and efficiency of managing a Windows network. Likewise, correct configuration of Active Directory is paramount to a smoothly running and secure network. You learn more about organizational units, how to use them in a hierarchical design, and how to manage access to them.

A major task for an Active Directory domain administrator is managing user, group, and computer accounts. Users are hired, leave the company, change departments, and change their names. Passwords are forgotten and must be reset. New resources become available, and users or, more likely, groups of users must be given access to them. New computers are installed on the network and must be added to the domain. All these tasks, particularly in large networks, keep administrators busy.

This chapter discusses GUI and command-line tools for creating and managing all aspects of Active Directory accounts. You also examine the use of several user account properties. Next, you learn about group account types and group scopes, including how to use groups to maintain secure access to resources. In addition, you learn the purpose of computer accounts and how to work with them. Finally, you explore some command-line tools that are useful for automating account management.

Working with Organizational Units

Table 7-1 describes what you need for the hands-on activities in this chapter.

Table 7-1 Activity requirements

Activity	Requirements	Notes
Activity 7-1: Creating a Single-Level OU Structure	410Server1	
Activity 7-2: Delegating Control of an OU	410Server1	
Activity 7-3: Viewing Object Permissions	410Server1	
Activity 7-4: Working with Permission Inheritance	410Server1	
Activity 7-5: Determining Effective Access	410Server1	
Activity 7-6: Creating User Accounts in Active Directory Users and Computers	410Server1	
Activity 7-7: Creating User Accounts in Active Directory Administrative Center	410Server1	
Activity 7-8: Creating a User Template	410Server1	
Activity 7-9: Editing Multiple Accounts	410Server1	
Activity 7-10: Creating Contacts and Distribution Groups	410Server1	
Activity 7-11: Creating Groups with Different Scopes	410Server1	
Activity 7-12: Working with Default Groups	410Server1	
Activity 7-13: Joining a Computer to the Domain	410Server1 and 410Win8	
Activity 7-14: Joining a Server Core Computer to the Domain with PowerShell	410Server1 and 410ServerCore	
Activity 7-15: Creating a Batch File for the `dsadd` Command	410Server1	
Activity 7-16: Using `dsquery` and `dsmod` with a Pipe	410Server1	
Activity 7-17: Using `csvde` to Create Users	410Server1	
Activity 7-18: Using `ldifde` to Create Users	410Server1	

As you learned in Chapter 6, organizational units (OUs) are the building blocks of the Active Directory structure in a domain. Thoughtful planning of the OU structure eases managing users and computers and applying group policies and makes Active Directory easier for users and technical staff to work with. Here are some benefits of using OUs:

- You can create a familiar hierarchical structure based on the organizational chart that enables users and administrators to locate network users and resources quickly.

- You can delegate administration of network resources to other IT staff without assigning more comprehensive administrative permissions.

- You can change the OU structure easily to accommodate corporate reorganizations.

- You can group users and computers for the purposes of assigning administrative and security policies with the Group Policy tool.

- You can hide Active Directory objects for confidentiality or security reasons by configuring access permissions on OUs.

 An OU can't be used to assign permissions to objects it contains. Groups, not OUs, are the main Active Directory object for permission assignments and are discussed in detail later in "Managing Group Accounts."

OUs are containers holding objects such as user and computer accounts, but they can also contain other OUs. This ability to nest OUs gives you the flexibility to create a hierarchy with as many levels as needed for your organization. Take a look at a fictitious company, csmtech.local, which has about 40 employees and this top-level organizational structure:

- Administration

- Marketing

- Research and Development (R&D)

- Operations

This organization will likely have a single-level OU structure, as shown on the left in Figure 7-1. Dividing R&D into the Engineering and Research departments and Marketing into Sales and Advertising creates the multilevel OU structure shown on the right in Figure 7-1.

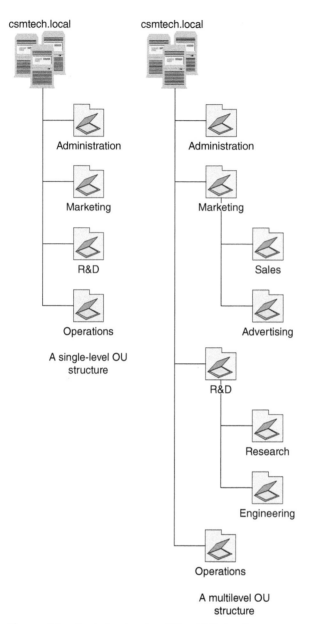

Figure 7-1 Single-level and multilevel OU structures
© 2015 Cengage Learning®

Now look at a larger organization with departments in different locations. If the company uses departments rather than locations for identification purposes, the OU structure could reflect that focus, as shown on the left in Figure 7-2. The top-level structure remains intact, but under each department is an OU for each location. Conversely, if the business is organized mainly by location, the OU structure looks like the one on the right in Figure 7-2. Notice that some OUs have the same name, which is allowed as long as they're in different parts of the Active Directory hierarchy. For example, the R&D OU is under both the Boston and Seattle OUs.

There are other approaches to OU hierarchy design. For example, a current trend is designing OUs based on grouping users and resources according to their security levels.

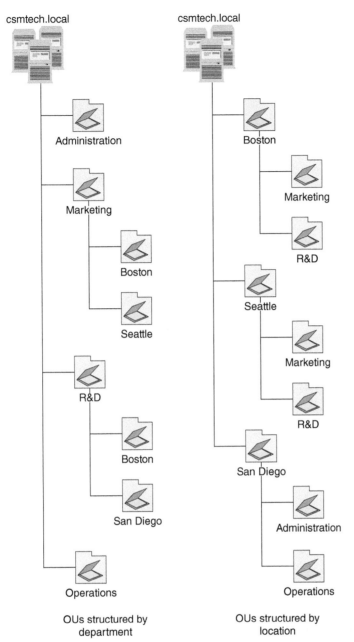

Figure 7-2   A multilocation domain organized by department and location
© 2015 Cengage Learning®

Activity 7-1: Creating a Single-Level OU Structure

Time Required: 10 minutes

Objective: Create OUs to reflect a company's departmental structure.

Required Tools and Equipment: 410Server1

Description: You have been asked to create the OU structure for a business with four main departments: Administration, Marketing, Research and Development, and Operations. You create a single-level OU structure based on these requirements, using Active Directory Administrative Center for this task.

1. Log on to 410Server1 as **Administrator,** if necessary.

2. Open Active Directory Administrative Center.

3. In the left pane, right-click the domain node, which should be 410Server2012 (local), point to **New,** and click **Organizational Unit.**

4. In the Name text box, type **Administration**. Leave the other settings at their defaults and click **OK**.

5. Repeat Steps 3 and 4 to create the **Marketing, Research and Development,** and **Operations** OUs. When finished, click the domain node in the left pane to display the folders and OUs in the middle pane, if necessary. Your OU structure should be similar to Figure 7-3.

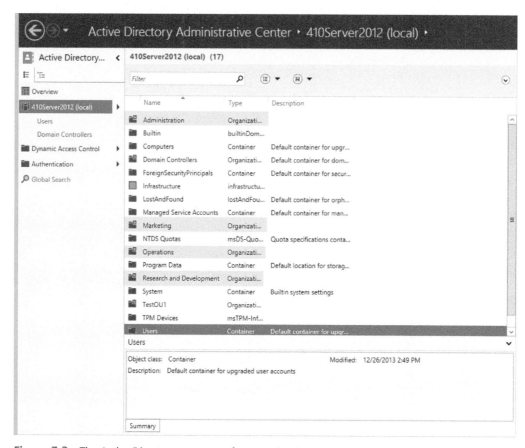

Figure 7-3   The Active Directory structure after creating OUs

6. Close Active Directory Administrative Center. If you're continuing to the next activity, stay logged on; otherwise, log off or shut down 410Server1.

OU Delegation of Control

As you've learned, one benefit of using OUs is that you can delegate administration of the OU and its contents to other users without giving them broader administrative capability. **Delegation of control,** in the context of Active Directory, means a person with higher security privileges assigns authority to a person of lesser security privileges to perform certain tasks. Delegation of control of an OU is not an all-or-nothing proposition. You can assign specific tasks the user can perform on objects in that OU and even delegate other tasks to different users or groups. The following are the most common tasks that can be delegated:

- Create, delete, and manage user accounts.
- Reset user passwords and force password change at next logon.
- Read all user information.
- Create, delete, and manage groups.
- Modify the membership of a group.
- Manage group policy links.
- Generate Resultant Set of Policy (Planning).
- Generate Resultant Set of Policy (Logging).

Three more predefined tasks can be delegated for the object class `inetOrgPerson`, which is a user and contact class defined in Active Directory for LDAP compatibility.

In addition to these tasks, you can define custom tasks, which allow fine-grained control over the management tasks a user can perform in an OU. When you create a custom task, you must fully understand the nature of objects, permissions, and permission inheritance. Even if you delegate control only by using predefined tasks, your understanding of how permissions and permission inheritance work is important. After all, the Delegation of Control Wizard does nothing more than assign permissions for Active Directory objects to selected users or groups.

Activity 7-2: Delegating Control of an OU

Time Required: 10 minutes
Objective: Create a user and delegate control of an OU to this user.

Required Tools and Equipment: 410Server1
Description: Your responsibilities as IT administrator have been keeping you busy, and you're trying to focus on plans for a sizable network expansion. Your plans have been slowed considerably because the Marketing Department is expanding, and you're fielding frequent requests to create users and groups and reset forgotten passwords. You have hired a new technician and think he's ready for additional responsibilities, so you decide to delegate control of user accounts to him. You need to create an account for him first. You use Active Directory Users and Computers for these tasks because there's no Delegation of Control Wizard in Active Directory Administrative Center.

1. If necessary, log on to 410Server1 as **Administrator**, and open Active Directory Users and Computers.

2. Expand **410Server2012.local**. Right-click the **Operations** OU you created in Activity 7-1, point to **New**, and click **User**.

3. Type **Joe** in the First name text box, **Tech1** in the Last name text box, and **jtech1** in the User logon name text box. Click **Next**.

4. Type **Password01** in the Password text box and again in the Confirm password text box. Click to clear the **User must change password at next logon** check box and click to select the **Password never expires** check box. Click **Next**, and then click **Finish**.

5. Right-click the **Marketing** OU and click **Delegate Control** to start the Delegation of Control Wizard. In the welcome window, click **Next**.

6. In the Users or Groups window, click **Add**. In the "Enter the object names to select" text box, type **jtech1**. Click **Check Names**, and then click **OK**. Click **Next**.

7. Click the **Create, delete, and manage user accounts** check box. Click **Next**, and then click **Finish**.

8. Leave Active Directory Users and Computers open for the next activity.

After you have delegated control to a user, there's no clear indication that this change has been made. By default, the OU's properties don't show that another user has been delegated control. To verify who has been delegated control of an OU, you must view the OU's permissions, as explained in the following section.

Active Directory Object Permissions

Active Directory object permissions work almost identically to file and folder permissions (discussed in Chapter 5). Recall that three types of security principals can be assigned permission to an object: users, groups, and computers. An Active Directory object's security settings are composed of the same three components, collectively referred to as the object's security descriptor:

- Discretionary access control list (DACL)
- Object owner
- System access control list (SACL)

DACL, object owner, and SACL were defined in Chapter 5 in the "Security Principals" section.

Like file system objects, every Active Directory object has a list of standard permissions and a list of special permissions that can be assigned to a security principal. For simplicity's sake, the term "users" is used when discussing permissions, but keep in mind that permissions can be assigned to any type of security principal: users, groups, and computers. Each permission can be set to Allow or Deny, and five standard permissions are available for most objects:

- *Read*—Users can view objects and their attributes and permissions.
- *Write*—Users can change an object's attributes.
- *Create all child objects*—Users can create new child objects in the parent object.
- *Delete all child objects*—Users can delete child objects in the parent object.
- *Full control*—Users can perform all actions granted by the previous four standard permissions, plus change permissions and take ownership of the object.

Different object types have other standard and special permissions. For example, a user object has the Reset password and Read logon information permissions; an OU object has the Create Account objects and Create Printer objects permissions.

Users can be assigned permissions by any of the four methods described in Chapter 5 in "How Permissions are Assigned"; however, there's one difference. Unlike an object's creator becoming its owner in file system permissions, the Domain Admins group is assigned ownership of new Active Directory objects by default.

Permission Inheritance in OUs

Permission inheritance in OUs also works much the same way as it does in the file system. For example, an OU containing other objects is the parent object, and any objects contained in the OU, including other OUs, are considered child objects. All objects in Active Directory are child objects of the domain. By default, permissions applied to the parent OU with the Delegation of Control Wizard are inherited by all child objects of the parent OU. So if a user has been given permissions to manage user accounts in an OU, these permissions apply to all existing and future user accounts in this OU, including user accounts created in child OUs. In the OU design structured by department in Figure 7-2, if a user is delegated control to create, delete, and manage user accounts in the R&D OU, this user could perform these actions on users in the R&D OU as well as the Boston and San Diego OUs.

Advanced Features Option in Active Directory Users and Computers

The default display settings in Active Directory Users and Computers hide some system folders and advanced features, but you can display them by enabling the Advanced Features option from the View menu. After selecting this option, five new folders are shown under the domain node:

- *LostAndFound*—Contains objects created at the same time their container is deleted, perhaps by another administrator on another domain controller.
- *Program Data*—Initially empty; is available to store application-specific objects.
- *System*—Used by Windows system services that are integrated with Active Directory.
- *NTDS Quotas*—NTDS stands for NT Directory Service. Stores quota information that limits the number of Active Directory objects a user, group, computer, or service can create.
- *TPM Devices*—Stores Trusted Platform Module (TPM) information about Windows 8 and later computer accounts. This folder is new in Windows Server 2012.

After Advanced Features is enabled, the Properties dialog box of domain, folder, and OU objects has three new tabs:

- *Object*—Used to view detailed information about a container object, such as the object class, created and modified dates, and sequence numbers for synchronizing replication. It also includes a check box you can select to protect an object from accidental deletion.

- *Security*—Used to view and modify an object's permissions.
- *Attribute Editor*—Used to view and edit an object's attributes, many of which aren't available in standard Properties dialog boxes.

For now, you're most interested in the Security tab of an OU's Properties dialog box (see Figure 7-4). The top section lists all accounts (user, group, and computer) that have an access control entry (ACE) in the DACL. The bottom section lists permission settings for each ACE. In Figure 7-4, Joe Tech1's ACE is selected, and the bottom section shows Allow Special permissions for his permission settings. To view details for this permission, you can click the Advanced button.

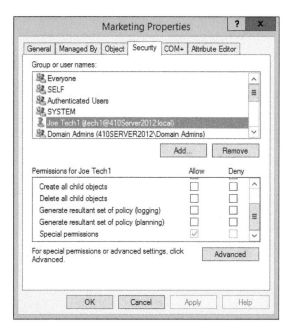

Figure 7-4   The Security tab of an OU's Properties dialog box

Activity 7-3: Viewing Object Permissions

Time Required: 10 minutes
Objective: Explore the Advanced Features option in Active Directory Users and Computers.

Required Tools and Equipment: 410Server1
Description: You have just delegated control of the Marketing OU to one of your technicians and are curious to see how the OU's DACL has changed. To view the settings, you need to enable the Advanced Features option in Active Directory Users and Computers.

1. If necessary, log on to 410Server1 as **Administrator,** and open Active Directory Users and Computers.

2. Right-click the **Marketing** OU and click **Properties.** Note the three tabs that are available now: General, Managed By, and COM+. (In the next step, you enable a feature that adds tabs.) Click **Cancel.**

3. Click **View, Advanced Features** from the menu, and verify that Advanced Features is selected with a check mark. The display changes to include the five new folders described previously.

4. Right-click the **Marketing** OU and click **Properties.** Click the **Object** tab, where you can find information that's useful in troubleshooting. In addition, when the "Protect object from accidental deletion" check box is selected, the object can't be deleted unless this check box is cleared.

5. Click the **Security** tab. Scroll through the list of group and user names so that you know what ACEs are in the DACL. Click each ACE to view its permission settings at the bottom.

6. Click the **Joe Tech1** ACE, and notice in the permissions list that the Allow Special permissions check box is selected. Click the **Advanced** button to open the Advanced Security Settings for Marketing dialog box (see Figure 7-5).

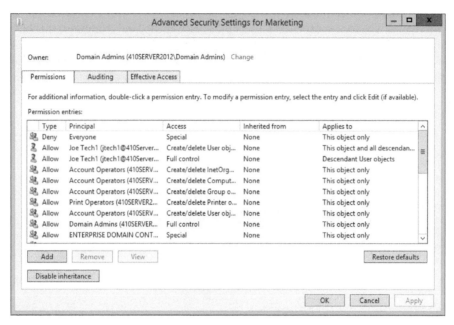

Figure 7-5   An OU's Advanced Security Settings dialog box

7. Double-click the first **Joe Tech1** entry to open the Permission Entry for Marketing dialog box (see Figure 7-6). Scroll down to see that the Create User objects and Delete User objects check boxes are selected, so Joe Tech1 has permission to create and delete users in the Marketing OU. The "This object and all descendant objects" option in the "Applies to" list means Joe Tech1 can create and delete users in any OUs under Marketing.

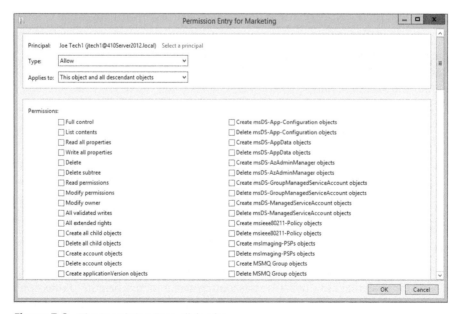

Figure 7-6   The Permission Entry dialog box

The term "descendant objects" means all objects underneath the object are also affected by the permission settings.

8. Click **Cancel**, and then double-click the second **Joe Tech1** entry. Notice that all check boxes in the permissions list are selected. In addition, the Descendant User objects option is selected in the "Applies to" list, which means Joe Tech1 has all permissions for all new and existing user objects in the Marketing OU.

9. Click **Cancel** three times, until only Active Directory Users and Computers is open. Leave this window open if you're continuing to the next activity; otherwise, log off or shut down 410Server1.

Effective Permissions   As discussed, effective permissions for an object are a combination of the allowed and denied permissions assigned to a security principal. These permissions can come from assignments made directly to a user account or to a group the user belongs to. Before examining the nuances of object permissions, take a look at some examples of how to determine a user's effective permissions for an object. Table 7-2 lists two groups with their group members, and Table 7-3 lists the ACEs for an OU.

Table 7-2   Group membership

Group	Members
Group1	Bill, Tom, Mary, Susan
Group2	Bill, Mary, Jane, Alex

© 2015 Cengage Learning®

Table 7-3   ACEs for an OU: Example 1

ACE	Permission	How assigned
Bill	Allow Read	Explicit
Tom	Allow Full control	Explicit
Group1	Allow Write	Inherited
Group2	Allow Create all child objects	Inherited

© 2015 Cengage Learning®

The effective permissions are as follows:
- Bill: Allow Read, Write, and Create all child objects
- Tom: Allow Full control
- Mary: Allow Write and Create all child objects
- Susan: Allow Write
- Jane and Alex: Allow Create all child objects

All the permissions assigned are Allow permissions, so you just add them together to arrive at the effective permissions for each user. Tom is granted Full control, which encompasses all other permissions. Take a look at another example with the same group memberships but using the ACEs in Table 7-4.

Table 7-4   ACEs for an OU: Example 2

ACE	Permission	How assigned
Bill	Deny Delete all child objects	Inherited
Mary	Deny Full control	Inherited
Group1	Allow Full control	Inherited
Group2	Allow Create all child objects	Inherited

© 2015 Cengage Learning®

The effective permissions are as follows:

- Bill: Allow Full control, except for deleting all child objects
- Tom: Allow Full control
- Mary: Deny Full control
- Susan: Allow Full control
- Jane and Alex: Allow Create all child objects

The Deny permission overrides the Allow permission, so although Bill, as a member of Group1, inherited Full control, the Deny Delete all child objects entry prevents him from deleting objects in the OU. Mary inherited Full control because of her membership in Group1, but the Deny Full control entry for her user account overrides the inherited permission. Look at the next example with the same group memberships but using the ACEs in Table 7-5.

Table 7-5   ACEs for an OU: Example 3

ACE	Permission	How assigned
Bill	Allow Full control	Explicit
Jane	Allow Create all child objects	Explicit
Group1	Deny Full control	Inherited
Group2	Deny Create all child objects	Inherited

© 2015 Cengage Learning®

The effective permissions are as follows:

- Bill: Allow Full control
- Jane: Allow Create all child objects
- Tom, Mary, Susan, Alex: Denied access

In this example, the Deny permissions are inherited, so any explicitly assigned Allow permissions take precedence. Remember that it's the exception to the rule that Deny permissions override Allow permissions. So although Bill and Jane are denied permission because of their group memberships, these permissions are inherited, and the Allow permissions for their user accounts are assigned explicitly.

Now take a closer look at permission inheritance. As stated, permissions for an object are inherited from its parent automatically. In Active Directory, the domain is the top-level object for permission inheritance. So the domain object doesn't inherit any permission settings because it has no parent container from which to inherit settings. OUs inherit some permissions from the domain object or, with nested OUs, from their parent OU. In addition, several permissions are added to an OU's DACL by default when it's created. You can see which permissions are inherited and which have been added to a DACL by viewing the Advanced Security Settings dialog box, shown previously in Figure 7-5. The Inherited from column shows "None" or the complete path to the object from which permission was inherited. The "Applies to" column shows whether the permission is set to be inherited by child objects. The following are some of the most common settings for permission inheritance:

- *This object only*—The permission setting isn't inherited by child (descendant) objects. This setting is the default when a new ACE is added to an object's DACL manually instead of with the Delegation of Control Wizard.

- *This object and all descendant objects*—The permission setting applies to the current object and is inherited by all child objects.

- *All descendant objects*—The permission setting doesn't apply to the selected object but is inherited by all child objects.

- *Descendant [object type] objects*—The permission is inherited only by specific child object types, such as user, computer, or group objects.

Permission inheritance is enabled by default on child objects but can be disabled. Inherited permissions can't be changed or removed without disabling permission inheritance first. However, you can add permissions to an object without disabling inheritance.

Use caution before changing permissions and permission inheritance. Incorrect settings can cause Active Directory access problems, so be sure you know what effect your changes will have on Active Directory before applying them. If your changes cause problems, you can click the Restore defaults button in the Advanced Security Settings dialog box, which resets permissions for the object to the default security settings defined in the Active Directory schema.

Activity 7-4: Working with Permission Inheritance

Time Required: 15 minutes

Objective: Create two OUs under an existing OU and view the effect of different permission inheritance settings.

Required Tools and Equipment: 410Server1

Description: You have been told that the Marketing Department is growing to the point that Sales and Advertising departments will be added under it to make management easier. You decide to create two OUs to reflect this organizational structure.

1. If necessary, log on to 410Server1 as **Administrator,** and open Active Directory Users and Computers.

2. Right-click the **Marketing** OU, point to **New,** and click **Organizational Unit.** In the Name text box, type **Sales,** and then click **OK.** Repeat this procedure, but type **Advertising** in the Name text box.

3. Click to expand the **Marketing** OU, if necessary. Right-click the **Sales** OU and click **Properties.** Click the **Security** tab.

4. Scroll down in the Group or user names list box, and click **Enterprise Admins.** Note that the check boxes in the Allow column of the Permissions section are disabled. Because Sales is a child OU of Marketing, its permissions have been inherited.

5. Click the **Remove** button. A Windows Security message box opens, explaining that you can't remove the Enterprise Admins entry because the permission was inherited

from the parent object. You must disable inheritance if you want to remove the entry. Click **OK.**

6. Click **Joe Tech1,** and click **Remove.** You see the same message as in Step 5. Click **OK,** and then click **Advanced.**

7. Click one of the **Joe Tech1** entries in the Permission entries list box. Place your mouse pointer over the **Inherited from** column to see the full path of the object from which the permission was inherited. In this case, the path is the Marketing OU in your domain.

8. Click the **Disable inheritance** button. The Block Inheritance message box shown in Figure 7-7 is displayed. Notice that disabling inheritance applies to all entries in the permissions list, not just the selected entry. (If you want to enable inheritance again, you can click the Enable inheritance button in the Advanced Security Settings dialog box.)

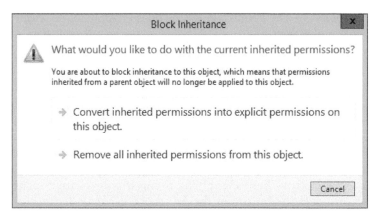

Figure 7-7   The Block Inheritance message

9. Click the line in the message starting with **Convert.** The Inherited from column for all entries changes to "None." Click **OK.** You see a warning message explaining that permissions are being added to the DACL. These "added" permissions are simply ones that have been changed from inherited to not inherited. When permissions are added to a DACL, Windows must apply these permissions to all child objects, if required by the permission's Applies to setting. Windows is informing you that if many child objects are present, the process can take more time and storage. Click **Yes.**

10. Click **Joe Tech1** in the Sales Properties dialog box, and then click **Remove.** Because you have disabled inheritance, you can now remove or edit any permissions that were previously inherited and couldn't be removed or changed. Click **OK.**

11. Right-click the **Advertising** OU and click **Properties.** Click the **Security** tab. Click **Joe Tech1,** and then click **Remove.** Note that disabling inheritance on the Sales OU doesn't affect the Advertising OU. Click **OK,** and then click **Cancel.** Joe Tech1 now has permission to access the Marketing and Advertising OUs but not the Sales OU.

12. Leave Active Directory Users and Computers open if you're continuing to the next activity; otherwise, log off or shut down 410Server1.

The Advanced Security Settings dialog box for Active Directory objects has the same Effective Access tab as in file system permissions, allowing you to view the effective permissions for a user or group (see Figure 7-8). You can only view permissions here; you can't change them.

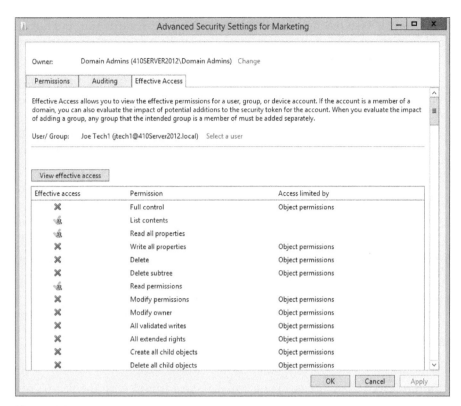

Figure 7-8 The Effective Access tab for viewing effective permissions

Activity 7-5: Determining Effective Access

Time Required: 15 minutes

Objective: Set up permissions and then verify the results by checking the Effective Access tab.

Required Tools and Equipment: 410Server1

Description: A junior administrator has some questions about how permissions work. You create an account for her to use and delegate control of a test OU to her so that she can work with some different permission situations and use the Effective Access tab to verify her results.

1. If necessary, log on to 410Server1 as **Administrator**, and open Active Directory Users and Computers.

2. Create an OU under the domain node named **TestOU2**. Create a user under the Operations OU with the logon name **jradmin**, full name **JrAdmin**, and password **Password01**. Make sure the user's password never expires.

3. Right-click **TestOU2** and click **Delegate Control**. In the welcome window, click **Next**.

4. Click **Add** to open the Select Users, Computers, or Groups dialog box. Type **jradmin**, click **OK**, and then click **Next**.

5. Click the **Create a custom task to delegate** option button, and then click **Next**.

6. Click the **This folder, existing objects in this folder, and creation of new objects in this folder** option button, if necessary, and then click **Next**.

7. Click the **Full Control** check box in the Permissions list box. Click **Next**, and then click **Finish**.

8. Right-click **TestOU2** and click **Properties**. Click the **Security** tab, and then click the **JrAdmin** ACE. Verify that the **Full control** check box in the Allow column is selected.

9. Click the **Advanced** button. Click the **Effective Access** tab, and then click **Select a user**.

10. Type **jradmin**, click **Check Names**, and then click **OK**. Click the **View effective access** button. The effective permissions for jradmin are less than Full control because the Everyone group has a Deny Delete permission for this OU. The Deny Delete permission is added to every new OU by default and can be removed by clearing the "Protect object from accidental deletion" check box in the Object tab of an object's properties. Click **OK** twice.

11. Log off and log on as **jradmin**. Start Server Manager. You see the User Account Control (UAC) message asking you to enter administrator credentials. Enter these credentials and click **Yes**.

12. Open Active Directory Users and Computers. Create an OU named **TestOU2-L2** under TestOU2 and an OU named **TestOU2-L3** under TestOU2-L2 so that the OU structure looks like Figure 7-9.

> ▲ 🗐 TestOU2
>   ▲ 🗐 TestOU2-L2
>   ▷ 🗐 TestOU2-L3

Figure 7-9   The Test OU structure

13. In the TestOU2 container, create a user named **jrtest1** with the password **Password01**; the other properties don't matter. Create a global security group called **jrgroup1** in TestOU2, and add jrtest1 as a member of this group. If you need help with this step, refer to Activity 6-4 in Chapter 6.

Group scope and group type are explained later in "Managing Group Accounts."

14. Click **View, Advanced Features** from the menu. Click to expand **TestOU2**, and then right-click **TestOU2-L2** and click **Properties**.

15. Click the **Security** tab, and then click the **Advanced** button. In the Advanced Security Settings for TestOU2-L2 dialog box, note that Domain Admins is the owner of this OU, even though jradmin created the OU. As mentioned, an object created in Active Directory is owned by the Domain Admins group, unlike an object created in the file system, which is owned by the account that created the object. Click **OK**.

16. In the TestOU-L2 Properties dialog box, click the **Add** button. Type **jrgroup1**, and then click **OK**. By default, the ACE for jrgroup1 has the Allow Read permission.

17. Click **jrgroup1** in the Group or user names list box, and then click the **Write** and **Create all child objects** check boxes in the Allow column. Click to clear the **Read** check box in the Allow column, and then click **Apply**.

18. Click the **Advanced** button, and then click the **Effective Access** tab. Click **Select a user**, type **jrtest1**, and then click **OK**. Click the **View effective access** button. In the list of permissions, notice that jrtest1 gets the Write and Create objects permissions because jrtest1 is a member of jrgroup1. As a member of the special group Authenticated Users (discussed later in "Special Identity Groups"), jrtest1 also gets the Read permission. Click **OK**.

19. Click the **Add** button. Type **jrtest1**, and then click **OK**. Click **jrtest1** in the Group or user names list box, and then click the **Write** check box in the Deny column. Click to clear the **Read** check box in the Allow column, and then click **Apply**.

20. View the effective permissions for jrtest1. Notice that jrtest1 no longer has the Write permission because you applied the Deny permission. Click **OK** twice.

21. Click to expand **TestOU2-L2**. Right-click the **TestOU2-L3** OU and click **Properties**. Click the **Security** tab.

22. Scroll through the Group or user names list box. There are no entries for jrtest1 and jrgroup1 because when you add an ACE to a DACL manually, the default inheritance setting is for the ACE to apply to "This object only." Again, this is different from the way permissions inheritance works with the file system. This setting can be changed, however. Click **Cancel**.

23. Open the Properties dialog box for TestOU-L2, click the **Security** tab, and then click the **Advanced** button. Double-click the **jrtest1** entry. In the "Applies to" list, change the setting to **This object and all descendant objects**, and then click **OK**. Double-click the **jrgroup1** entry. In the "Applies to" list, change the setting to **This object and all descendant objects**, and then click **OK**. Click **OK** twice to close all dialog boxes.

24. Open the Properties dialog box for TestOU-L3, and click the **Security** tab. Notice that there are entries for jrtest1 and jrgroup1 now. Click the **Advanced** button, and view the effective permissions for jrtest1. Notice that jrtest1's permissions are the same as for the TestOU1-L2 OU. Click **OK**.

25. Click **jrtest1** in the Group or user names list box, and then click the **Write** check box in the Allow column. The Write check box in the Deny column is disabled because the permission was inherited. Click **Apply**, and then click the **Advanced** button.

26. View the effective permissions for jrtest1. Jrtest1 has write permissions now because the explicit Allow Write permission you added overrides the inherited Deny Write permission. Click **OK** twice.

27. Log off 410Server1.

As you can see, permissions in Active Directory behave similarly to file system permissions, but there are some important differences, as you saw in the preceding activity. Active Directory permissions can become complex with the multitude of inheritance rules and options, so as with file system permissions, it's best to keep things as simple as possible without compromising security. Until you fully understand permissions in Active Directory, use the Delegation of Control Wizard to assign other users or groups the ability to perform specific functions in Active Directory containers.

Managing User Accounts

Working with user accounts is one of the most important Active Directory administrative tasks. User accounts are the main link between real people and network resources, so user account management requires not only technical expertise, but also people skills. When users can't log on or access a needed resource, they often turn to the administrator to solve the problem. Fortunately, an administrator's understanding of how user accounts work and how to best configure them can reduce the need to exercise people skills with frustrated users. User accounts have two main functions in Active Directory:

- *Provide a method for user authentication to the network*—The user logon name and password serve as a secure method for users to log on to the network to access resources. A user account can also contain account restrictions, such as when and where a user can log on or an account expiration date.

- *Provide detailed information about a user*—For use in a company directory, user accounts can contain departments, office locations, addresses, and telephone information. You can modify the Active Directory schema to contain just about any user information a company wants to keep.

As you learned in Chapter 6, Windows OSs have three categories of user accounts: local, domain, and built-in. Local user accounts are found in Windows client OSs, such as Windows 8.1 and Windows 7, as well as Windows Server OSs on systems that aren't configured as domain controllers. These accounts are stored in the **Security Accounts Manager (SAM) database** on local computers, and users can log on to and access resources only on the computer where the account resides. A network running Active Directory should limit the use of local user accounts on client computers, however, as they can't be used to access domain resources. Local user accounts are mainly used in a peer-to-peer network where Active Directory isn't running. Administrators can also log on to a computer with a local Administrator account for the purposes of joining the computer to a domain or troubleshooting access to the domain. Local user accounts are usually created in Control Panel's User Accounts applet or the Computer Management MMC's Local Users and Groups snap-in. Because these accounts don't participate in Active Directory, they can't be managed from Active Directory or be subject to group policies. The number of attributes in a local user account pales in comparison with those in Active Directory user accounts, as shown in Figure 7-10.

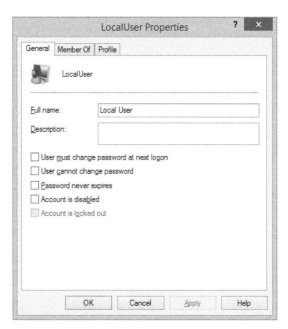

Figure 7-10   A domain user account (left) and local user account (right)

User accounts created in Active Directory are referred to as "domain user accounts." Generally, these accounts enable users to log on to any computer that's a domain member in the Active Directory forest. They also provide single sign-on access to domain resources in the forest and other trusted entities to which the account has permission. Domain user accounts can be managed by group policies and are subject to account policies linked to the domain.

Built-in user accounts include the Administrator and Guest accounts created during Windows installation. They can be local or domain user accounts, depending on whether they're stored in the computer's SAM database or in Active Directory. Built-in accounts have the same qualities as regular local or domain accounts, except they can't be deleted. When Active Directory is installed on a Windows Server 2012/R2 computer, the Administrator and Guest accounts, along with any other local accounts, are converted from local user to domain user accounts.

The Administrator and Guest accounts require special handling because of their unique role in being the two accounts on every Windows computer. The following guidelines apply to the built-in Administrator account:

- The local Administrator account has full access to all aspects of a computer, and the domain Administrator account has full access to all aspects of the domain.

- The domain Administrator account in the forest root domain has full access to all aspects of the forest. This administrator account is the only default member of the Enterprise Admins group, discussed later in "Managing Group Accounts."

- Because the Administrator account is created on every computer and domain, it should be renamed and given a very strong password to increase security. With these measures in place, a user attempting to gain unauthorized access has to guess not only the administrator's password, but also the logon name.

- The Administrator account should be used to log on to a computer or domain only when performing administrative operations is necessary. Network administrators should use a regular user account for logging on to perform nonadministrative tasks.

- The Administrator account can be renamed or disabled but can't be deleted.

The following guidelines apply to the built-in Guest account:

- After Windows installation, the Guest account is disabled by default and must be enabled by an administrator before it can be used to log on.

- The Guest account can have a blank password, so if you enable this account, be aware that anybody can log on with it without needing a password. The Guest account should be assigned a password before it's enabled.

- Like the Administrator account, the Guest account should be renamed if it's going to be used.

- The Guest account has limited access to a computer or domain, but it does have access to any resource for which the Everyone group has permission.

Creating and Modifying User Accounts

User accounts can be created with GUI tools, such as Active Directory Users and Computers (ADUC) and Active Directory Administrative Center (ADAC), and with command-line tools, such as dsadd and the PowerShell cmdlet New-ADUser. Using command-line tools to create and manage accounts is discussed later in "Automating Account Management." When you create a user account in an Active Directory domain, keep the following considerations in mind:

- A user account must have a unique logon name throughout the domain because it's used to log on to the domain. However, user accounts in different domains in the same forest can be the same.

- User account names aren't case sensitive. They can be from 1 to 20 characters and use letters, numbers, and special characters, with the exception of ", [,], :, ;, <, >, ?, *, +, @, |, ^, =, and ,.

- Devise a naming standard for user accounts, which makes creating users easier and can be convenient when using applications, such as e-mail, that include the username in the address. The downside of using a predictable naming standard is that attackers can guess usernames easily to gain unauthorized access to the network. Common naming standards include a user's first initial plus last name (for example, kwilliams for Kelly Williams) or a user's first name and last name separated by a special character (such as Kelly.Williams or Kelly_Williams). In large companies where names are likely to be duplicated, adding a number after the username is common.

- By default, a complex password is required, as described in Chapter 6. Passwords are case sensitive.

- By default, only a logon name is required to create a user account. If a user is created without a password and the password policy requires a non-blank password, the user is created but disabled. Descriptive information, such as first and last name, should be included to facilitate Active Directory searches.

You have created a few users already, but take a closer look at the process, particularly some of the fields in ADUC and ADAC. Figure 7-11 shows the New Object - User dialog box in ADUC.

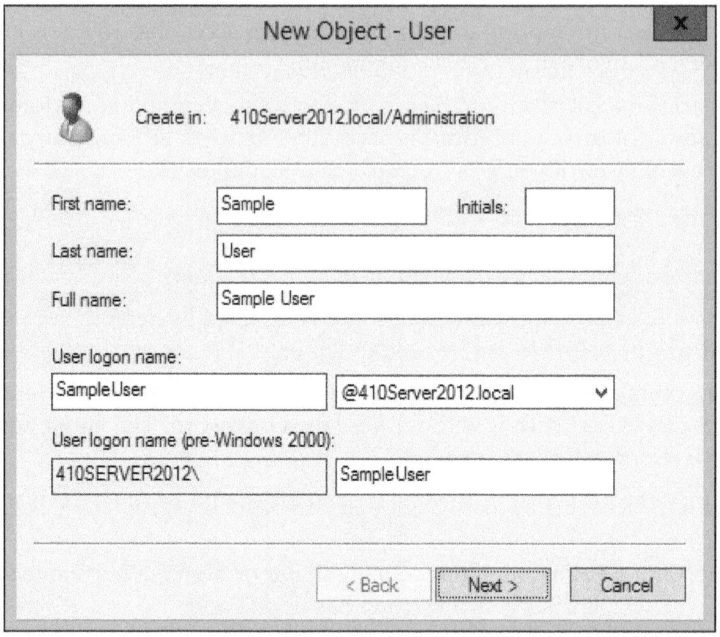

Figure 7-11   The New Object - User dialog box

As mentioned, the only field *required* for a valid user is a user logon name—or more specifically, only the User logon name (pre-Windows 2000) field shown in Figure 7-11. However, you can get away with skipping the other fields only when you're using command-line tools. When you use ADUC, you must enter a value for the following attributes:

- *Full name*—This field is normally a composite of the First name, Initials, and Last name fields, but you can enter a name that's different from what's in these three fields.

- *User logon name*—This field isn't actually required, but it's highly recommended. It's called the user principal name (UPN), and the UPN format is *logon name@domain*. The "@domain" part is the UPN suffix. You can fill in the logon name and select the domain in the drop-down list, which is set to the current domain controller's domain by default. By using the UPN, users can log on to their home domains from a computer that's a member of a different domain or from a remote application. In ADAC, this field is called User UPN logon. If you omit this field and fill in only the User logon name (pre-Windows 2000) field, the user account is still valid. Windows creates an implicit UPN, using the User logon name (pre-Windows 2000) field and the domain name. Microsoft recommends making the UPN the same as the user's e-mail address.

- *User logon name (pre-Windows 2000)*—This field is called the **downlevel user logon name** because of its backward-compatibility with older applications and Windows versions. Generally, it's the same as the User logon name field but need not be. It consists of the domain name (without the top-level domain), a backslash, and the user logon name. Users running applications that don't recognize the UPN format can use this format to log on: *domain\user*. Although the User logon name and User logon name (pre-Windows 2000) fields can be different, it's not recommended. This field is required when creating a user account. In ADAC, this field is called "User SamAccountName logon."

- *Password and Confirm password*—These fields (see Figure 7-12) are required when creating a user in ADUC because account policies in a Windows Server 2012/R2 domain don't allow blank passwords. The default password policy requires a minimum length of 7 characters and a maximum of 127, and the password must meet complexity requirements, meaning it must have at least three characters of the following types: uppercase letters, lowercase letters, numbers, and special characters. You can change this password policy by using Group Policy (discussed in Chapter 8). When creating users with ADAC, dsadd, or PowerShell, you have the option of leaving the password blank, but the account is disabled. You must set a suitable password before the account can be enabled.

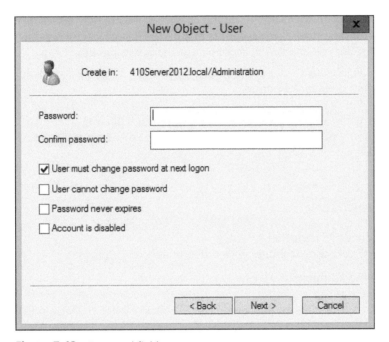

Figure 7-12   Password fields

The four check boxes in Figure 7-12 are as follows:

- *User must change password at next logon*—This option, enabled by default, requires users to create a new password the next time they log on. Typically, you use this option when users are assigned a generic password at account creation for logging on to the domain for the first time. After the first logon, the user is prompted to change the password so that it complies with the password policy. This option is also used when an existing user's password is reset.

- *User cannot change password*—This option is useful when multiple users log on with the same user account, a practice common with part-time employees or guests who need access to the network. However, this option can't be set if "User must change password at next logon" is already selected. If you attempt to set both options, Windows displays a message stating that only one can be set.

- *Password never expires*—This option overrides the password policy that sets a maximum password age to force users to change their passwords periodically. It applies only to password expiration, not to account expiration, and can't be set when "User must change password at next logon" is already selected. Later in "Understanding Account Properties," you see how to set an expiration date for a user account.

- *Account is disabled*—This option, which prevents using the user account, is sometimes set when user accounts are created before users need them, as when you've hired a new employee who hasn't started yet. You can also set this option on existing user accounts, as discussed in the following section.

Disabling User Accounts You disable a user account to prevent someone from logging on with it. There are a number of reasons you might want to do this:

- *A user has left the company*—You disable the account instead of deleting it so that all the user's files are still accessible and all group memberships are maintained. If the user's position will be replaced, you can rename the account to match the new employee, and the new employee will have the previous user's rights and permissions. Even if a user isn't being replaced, you might want to disable rather than delete the account for auditing purposes.

- *The account is not ready to use*—You might want to create new accounts in anticipation of new hires. You can create these accounts in a disabled state, and when the users are ready to use the system, you enable the accounts for their first logons.

- *A user goes on extended leave*—For security reasons, it's best to disable an account that will be inactive for an extended period.

Aside from using ADUC and ADAC to enable and disable accounts, you can use the PowerShell cmdlets `Enable-ADAccount` and `Disable-ADAccount` as well as the `dsmod user` command.

Activity 7-6: Creating User Accounts in Active Directory Users and Computers

Time Required: 15 minutes
Objective: Create user accounts with different account options.

Required Tools and Equipment: 410Server1
Description: You want to experiment with some user account options that can be set during account creation. In this activity, you use Active Directory Users and Computers.

1. Log on to 410Server1 as **Administrator**, and open Active Directory Users and Computers.

2. Click to expand the domain node, if necessary. Click **TestOU1**, and then click the **New User** toolbar icon. (*Hint:* Hover your mouse pointer over toolbar icons to see their descriptions.) Type **testuser3** in the User logon name text box. The User logon name (pre-Windows 2000) text box is filled in automatically. However, the Next button is still disabled, which means you haven't filled in all the required fields. Type **Test** in the First name text box and **User3** in the Last name text box. Now the Full name text box is filled in automatically, and the Next button is enabled. (Alternatively, you could just fill in the full name.) Click **Next**.

3. In the Password text box, type **p@$$word**. Type **p@$$word** again in the Confirm password text box.

4. Click to select the **User cannot change password** check box. Read the warning message, and then click **OK**. Click to clear the **User must change password at next logon** check box, and then click **User cannot change password**. Click **Next**, and then click **Finish**.

5. Read the error message that's displayed. What can you do to change the password you typed in Step 3 so that it meets complexity requirements? Click **OK**, and then click **Back**.

6. Type **p@$$word1** in the Password and Confirm password text boxes. Adding a number at the end meets complexity requirements, but you could also change one letter to uppercase, such as **p@$$Word**. Click **Next**, and then click **Finish**.

7. Log off, and then log on as **testuser3** with the password you just set.

8. Press **Ctrl+Alt+Delete**, and then click **Change a password**.

9. In the Old password text box, type **p@$$word1**. In the New password text box, type **p@$$word2**, and type it again in the Confirm password text box. Click the **arrow** icon. You see an "Access is denied" message because the account is prohibited from changing the password. Click **OK**, and then click the **left arrow** icon. Click **Sign out**.

10. Log on as **Administrator**, and open Active Directory Users and Computers.

11. Create a user in TestOU1 with the logon name **testuser4** and the first and last names **Test User4**. Enter a suitable password, and then click **Account is disabled**. Click **Next**, and then click **Finish**.

12. In Active Directory Users and Computers, notice that testuser4's icon has a down arrow to indicate that the account is disabled. If you open the Users folder, you'll see the Guest user has this icon, too, to indicate its disabled status. Close Active Directory Users and Computers, and stay logged on for the next activity.

Activity 7-7: Creating User Accounts in Active Directory Administrative Center

Time Required: 15 minutes
Objective: Create a user account in Active Directory Administrative Center.

Required Tools and Equipment: 410Server1
Description: You understand there are some differences in account creation when using ADAC, so you decide to create a test user with this tool. You also explore the Windows PowerShell History feature of ADAC that you first saw in Chapter 6.

1. Log on to 410Server1 as **Administrator**, if necessary, and open Active Directory Administrative Center.

2. Click the domain node. In the middle pane, right-click **TestOU1**, point to **New**, and click **User**.

3. In the Create User window, notice the two fields with asterisks next to them: Full name and User SamAccountName logon. In Active Directory Administrative Center, only these two fields are required to create a user. Type **Test User5** in the Full name box and **testuser5** in the User SamAccountName logon box (see Figure 7-13).

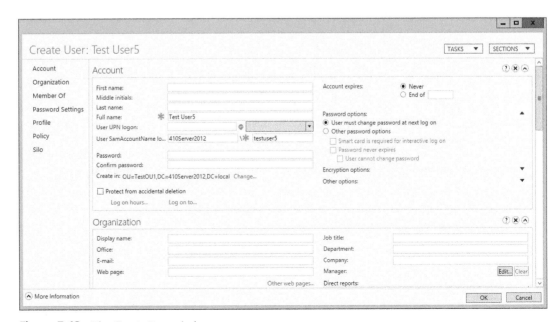

Figure 7-13   The Create User window

4. Click **OK**. In Active Directory Administrative Center, double-click **TestOU1** and notice that Test User5 is grayed out and has a down arrow icon to indicate the account is disabled. (If you don't see Test User5, refresh the view.) Right-click **Test User5** and click **Enable**. In the message stating that the password doesn't meet complexity requirements, click **OK**. You can't enable the account until a suitable password has been set.

5. Right-click **Test User5** and click **Reset password**. In the Reset Password dialog box, type **Password01** in the Password and Confirm password text boxes, and then click **OK**.

6. Right-click **Test User5** and click **Enable**. The account is enabled.

7. At the bottom of Active Directory Administrative Center, you see the Windows PowerShell History. Click the **up arrow** on the right to expand the Windows PowerShell History Viewer.

8. Scroll to the top of the history, if necessary, to see the `New-ADUser` command. Click to select **New-ADUser** and click **Copy** on the viewer's menu bar.

9. Open Notepad, and paste the Clipboard contents into Notepad. You see the full PowerShell command that was generated when you created Test User5. Close Notepad without saving the file.

10. Scroll through the PowerShell history to see other commands that were generated for setting the password and other account properties. It isn't obvious which command enables the account. Find the last **Set-ADObject** command in the history. The `userAccountControl=8389120` part of the command is what does the job. This parameter sets account properties that specify the account is a normal user and the password must be changed at next logon.

 You can learn more about the `userAccountControl` parameter at *https://support.microsoft.com/kb/305144*.

11. Although the PowerShell commands generated by Active Directory Administrative Center aren't always the most straightforward way to accomplish a task (the `Enable-ADAccount` cmdlet is more straightforward), they can help you learn how to use these commands for writing scripts. Close Active Directory Administrative Center.

12. If you're continuing to the next activity, stay logged on; otherwise, log off or shut down the computer.

Using User Templates   Creating users can be a repetitive task, especially when you're creating several users with similar group memberships, account options, and descriptive fields. Fortunately, you can reduce some of this repetition by using a **user template**, which is simply a user account that's copied to create users with common attributes. You can copy many user account attributes in this template to accounts you're creating, except for name, logon name, password, and some contact and descriptive fields (such as phone number and e-mail address) that are generally unique for each user. You use ADUC to copy an account, and then the same wizard for creating a user starts so that you can fill in the name, logon name, password, and other unique fields. Here are some tips for creating user templates:

- Create one template account for each department or OU, as users in the same department often have several common attributes.

- Disable the template account so that it doesn't pose a security risk.

- Add an underscore or other special character to the beginning of a template account's name so that it's easily recognizable as a template and is listed first in an alphabetical list of accounts.

- Fill in as many common attributes as you can so that after each account is created, less customizing is necessary.

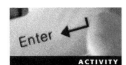

Activity 7-8: Creating a User Template

Time Required: 10 minutes

Objective: Create a user template for populating the Sales OU with users.

Required Tools and Equipment: 410Server1

Description: You need to create several users for the Sales Department and want to reduce the work by using a user template.

1. If necessary, log on to 410Server1 as **Administrator,** and open Active Directory Users and Computers.

2. Click to expand the **Marketing** OU and then click the **Sales** OU.

3. In the Sales OU, create a group named **Sales-G** with the default group scope and group type. You'll add the user template to this group so that all Sales OU users belong to this group by default.

4. In the Sales OU, create a user with the full name **_Sales Template,** the logon name **_SalesTemplate,** and the password **Password01.** Make sure the **Account is disabled** and **User must change password at next logon** check boxes are selected.

5. After you've created this user, right-click the **_Sales Template** user and click **Properties.**

6. In the General tab, type **Sales Template User Account** in the Description text box, **Building 1** in the Office text box, **555-5555** in the Telephone number text box, and **www. allaboutcomputernetworks.com** in the Web page text box.

7. Click the **Address** tab. Type **555 First St.** in the Street text box, **Metropolis** in the City text box, **AZ** in the State/province text box, and **12121** in the Zip/Postal Code text box. Click **United States** in the Country/region drop-down list.

8. Click the **Organization** tab. Type **Salesperson** in the Job Title text box, **Sales** in the Department text box, and **All About Computer Networks** in the Company text box.

9. Click the **Member Of** tab. Add the account to the **Sales-G** group. Click **OK** until the Properties dialog box is closed.

10. In the right pane of Active Directory Users and Computers, right-click the **_Sales Template** user and click **Copy.** Type **Sales** in the First name text box, **Person1** in the Last name text box, and **sales1** in the User logon name text box, and then click **Next.**

11. Type **Password01** in the Password and Confirm password text boxes. Notice that the Account is disabled check box is selected because you set this option for the _Sales Template account. Click to clear the **Account is disabled** check box, and then click **Next.** Click **Finish.**

12. Right-click **Sales Person1** and click **Properties.** Arrange the Properties dialog box so that you can see the _Sales Template user in Active Directory Users and Computers. Right-click **_Sales Template** and click **Properties.** Arrange the two Properties dialog boxes side by side so that you can compare them (see Figure 7-14). Make sure the General tab is visible in both.

13. Notice that no fields in the template's General tab were copied to the Sales Person1 user. Click the **Address** tab in both Properties dialog boxes, and notice that the Street field wasn't copied but the rest of the address was. Click the **Organization** tab, and notice that only the Job Title field wasn't copied.

14. Click the **Member Of** tab in both Properties dialog boxes, and notice that the group membership *was* copied.

15. Click **Cancel** to close both Properties dialog boxes, and leave Active Directory Users and Computers open if you're continuing to the next activity; otherwise, log off or shut down the computer.

User templates are useful for creating several users with a number of similar attributes. Unfortunately, some attributes aren't copied to the new user account, such as the Description, Office, Telephone number, Web page, and other fields. In addition, if one of the attributes that's

Figure 7-14   Comparing user properties

copied changes, quite a bit of manual configuration might be required. However, there's a way to work around these limitations, discussed in the following section.

You can use the Active Directory Schema snap-in to change whether an attribute is copied when the user account is copied. Load the snap-in into an MMC, double-click the attribute, and click the "Attribute is copied when duplicating a user" check box.

Modifying Multiple Users   As you learned in Activity 7-8, user templates don't copy all the common attributes you might want to set for multiple users, such as department members who have the same telephone number or office location. In addition, you might need to add several users to a group after the users are created. Fortunately, Active Directory Users and Computers supports making changes to several accounts simultaneously. To select multiple accounts, hold down Ctrl and click each one separately. If the accounts are listed consecutively, click the first one, hold down Shift, and click the last account in the list, or drag over the accounts to select them. After making a selection, right-click it or click Action on the menu bar to perform the following actions on all selected accounts simultaneously:

- *Add to a group*—Adds the selected accounts to a group you specify
- *Disable Account*—Disables the selected accounts
- *Enable Account*—Enables the selected accounts
- *Move*—Moves the selected accounts to a new OU or folder
- *Send Mail*—Opens the configured e-mail application and places each user's e-mail address in the To field
- *Cut*—Cuts the selected accounts so that you can paste them into another OU or folder
- *Delete*—Deletes the selected accounts
- *Properties*—Opens the Properties for Multiple Items dialog box, where you can edit certain attributes of the selected accounts

Activity 7-9: Editing Multiple Accounts

Time Required: 10 minutes

Objective: Create users and change attributes on several accounts simultaneously.

Required Tools and Equipment: 410Server1

Description: You need to change some attributes on several users in your Sales OU, so you decide to use the Properties for Multiple Items dialog box to make this task easier.

1. If necessary, log on to 410Server1 as **Administrator,** and open Active Directory Users and Computers.

2. Click to expand the **Marketing** OU, if necessary, and then click the **Sales** OU.

3. Create two user accounts by using the _Sales Template account. The accounts should have the first and last names **Sales Person2** and **Sales Person3** and logon names **sales2** and **sales3.** Enter **Password01** for the password on both accounts. Make sure the **Account is disabled** check box is selected. Click to clear the **User must change password at next logon** check box so that these users *don't* have to change their passwords.

4. After you have created the two users, click **Sales Person1,** and then hold down **Shift** and click **Sales Person3.** Release **Shift,** and then click **Action, Properties** from the menu to open the Properties for Multiple Items dialog box (see Figure 7-15).

Figure 7-15   The Properties for Multiple Items dialog box

5. Click the **Description** check box, and then type **AACN Sales Person** in the text box. Click the **Web page** check box, and then type **www.allaboutcomputernetworks.com** in the text box.

6. Click the **Account** tab. Scroll down in the Account options list box, and click to select the **Account is disabled** check box on the far left (see Figure 7-16). Click **Apply.**

7. Click the **Address** and **Profile** tabs to review which attributes you can change. Click the **Organization** tab. Click the **Job Title** check box, type **Sales Associate** in the text box, and then click **OK.**

8. Open the Properties dialog box for each Sales Person user to verify that the changes were made for all. When you're finished with each one, click **OK.**

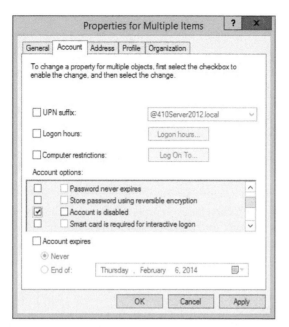

Figure 7-16   Setting account properties for multiple items

9. Leave Active Directory Users and Computers open if you're continuing to the next activity; otherwise, log off or shut down the computer.

Editing multiple items isn't limited to user accounts, although it's most useful with these objects. You can edit multiple computer and group accounts and even objects of differing types, but the only attribute you can edit for these object types is the Description field.

Understanding Account Properties

After an account is created, your work as an administrator is just beginning. User account properties aren't static and require modification from time to time. Users might need their password changed, their group memberships altered, their logon restrictions modified, and other account changes. First you learn how to perform common actions on accounts such as resetting passwords and moving accounts to different containers:

- *Reset a password*—If users forget their passwords or are prohibited from changing them, administrators can reset a password by right-clicking the user account and clicking Reset Password. In ADAC, the Overview window has a Reset Password check box so that you can quickly reset a password or unlock an account. To reset a user account password with PowerShell, enter the following command. You're prompted to enter and confirm the new password.

```
Set-ADAccount Password LogonName -Reset
```

- *Rename an account*—The object name shown in the Name column of ADUC and ADAC is referred to as the "common name" (CN). For example, the CN of the user you created in Activity 7-8 is Sales Person1. A user account's CN is taken from the Full name field when the user is created. You can change the CN by right-clicking the account and clicking Rename in ADUC or by changing the Full name field in ADAC. In PowerShell, enter the following command. You need to specify the object's distinguished name, the first part of which is the common name:

```
Rename-ADObject DistinguishedName -NewName "NewName"
```

An object's distinguished name (DN) is used in some commands to identify Active Directory objects. It uses LDAP syntax. For example, `CN=Jr Admin,OU=Operations,DC=410Server2012,DC=local` identifies a user named Jr Admin in the Operations OU in the 410Server2012.local domain. CN means common name, OU means organizational unit, and DC means domain component.

- *Move an account*—You can move a user account, or any Active Directory object, with any of the following methods:
  - o Right-click the user and click Move. (You can also click Action, Move from the menu.) You're then prompted to select the container to which you're moving the object.
  - o Right-click the user and click Cut. Then open a container object and paste the user into the container. This method works only in ADUC.
  - o In ADUC, drag the user from one container to another.
  - o Use the `Move-ADObject` cmdlet in PowerShell.

This book has covered only a small fraction of the many user account properties that can be configured. The following sections describe some other properties you might need to set on a user account. These sections are organized according to the tabs of an account's properties in ADUC. The same properties are available in ADAC but can be accessed in one place by scrolling down the Properties window.

The General Tab   The General tab of a user account's Properties dialog box contains descriptive information about the account, none of which affects a user account's logon, group memberships, rights, or permissions. However, some fields in the General tab do bear mentioning:

- *Display name*—The value in this field is taken from the Full name field during account creation and is usually the same as the CN. However, changing the display name doesn't change the CN, and changing the CN doesn't affect the display name. This field can be used in Active Directory searches.

- *E-mail*—You can use the value in this field to send an e-mail to the user associated with the account. If you right-click the user account and click Send Mail, the default mail application starts, and the value in this field is entered in the e-mail's To field.

- *Web page*—This field can contain a URL. If this field is configured, you can right-click the user account and click Open Home Page, and a Web browser opens the specified Web page.

The remainder of the fields in the General tab can be used to locate an object with an Active Directory search.

If you want to see more account properties in ADUC, click View, Add/Remove Columns. In ADAC, right-click any column name and click the property you want to display.

The Account Tab   The Account tab (see Figure 7-17) contains the information that most affects a user's logon to the domain. Aside from a password reset, this tab is the best place to check when a user is having difficulty with the logon process.

- *User logon name and User logon name (pre-Windows 2000)*—These fields were described previously in "Creating and Modifying User Accounts."

- *Logon Hours*—Clicking this button opens a dialog box (see Figure 7-18) where administrators can restrict days and hours that users can log on to the domain.

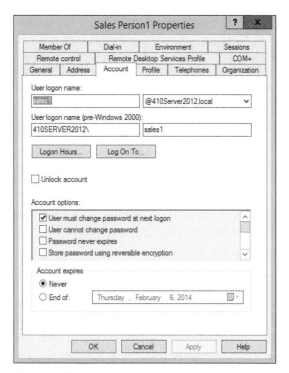

Figure 7-17   The Account tab

By default, all days and all hours are permitted. To exclude hours, click the Logon Denied option button and select the boxes for the hours you want to exclude; each box represents one hour. You can drag over the hour boxes to select several days or hours at a time. In Figure 7-18, logging on is denied to Sales Person1 every day from 12:00 a.m. to 3:00 a.m. The default behavior of this feature denies new attempts to log on during denied hours but doesn't affect a user who's already logged on. However, you can set a group policy to force a user to be disconnected when logon hours are denied.

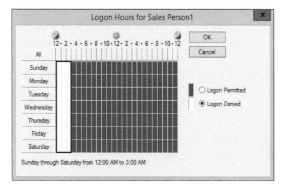

Figure 7-18   Setting logon hours

- *Log On To*—Click this button to specify by computer name which computers the user account can use to log on to the domain. By default, a user can use all computers in the domain. However, you might want to limit accounts that have access to sensitive information to logging on only at designated computers.
- *Unlock account*—If this check box is selected, the user has too many failed logon attempts. In this case, the account is locked out and the user can't log on. Clearing the check box unlocks the account.

- *Account options*—Five of these options were described previously. Most account options pertain to the user's password and Kerberos authentication properties, but a few warrant more explanation:

  o Store password using reversible encryption: Allows applications to access an account's stored password for authentication purposes. Enabling this option poses a considerable security risk and should be used only when no other authentication method is available.

  o Smart card is required for interactive logon: Requires a smart card for the user to log on to a domain member. When this option is enabled, the user's password is set to a random value and never expires.

  o Account is sensitive and cannot be delegated: Used to prevent a service from using an account's authentication credentials to access a network resource or another service. This option increases security and is most often set on administrator accounts.

- *Account expires*—An administrator uses this option to set a date after which the account can no longer log on. You might set an expiration on a temporary or guest account.

The Profile Tab   The Profile tab (see Figure 7-19) is used to specify the location of files that make up a user's profile, a logon script, and the location of a home folder:

- *Profile path*—Used to specify the path to a user's profile. By default, a user's profile is stored on the computer where the user is currently logged on. In Windows 8.1 or Server 2012/R2, the profile is in the C:\Users*logonname* directory by default, and this field is blank. It needs to be filled in only if you want to change the profile path. It's most often used when creating roaming profiles, a topic covered in the Microsoft exam Implementing a Desktop Infrastructure (Exam 70-415). When you're creating a user template, you can use the %username% variable instead of the actual logon name, and the variable is replaced automatically with the user logon name.

- *Logon script*—Used to specify a script that runs when the user logs on. The preferred method for specifying a logon script is with a group policy, so this field is rarely used with domain accounts, but it can be used with local accounts.

Figure 7-19   The Profile tab

- *Local path*—Used to specify the path to a user's home folder. In general, the home folder has been replaced by the Documents folder. Some older applications use this field as the default location for storing user documents, however. You can also use it to specify the location on a terminal server where user documents are stored during Terminal Services sessions. The home folder can be a local path or a drive letter that points to a network share.

- *Connect*—Used to map a drive letter to a network share that's the user's home folder.

The Member Of Tab   The Member Of tab lists groups the user belongs to and can be used to change group memberships. Every new user is added to the Domain Users group automatically. You can remove a user from Domain Users, but it's not recommended because membership in this group is one way to give users default rights and permissions. The Set Primary Group button in this tab is needed only when a user is logging on to a Mac OS, UNIX, or Linux client computer.

Using Contacts and Distribution Groups

User accounts are security principals, which means permissions and rights can be assigned to them so that users can access network resources and perform certain operations on their computers. You can create two other user-related accounts that aren't security principals: contacts and distribution groups. A **contact** is an Active Directory object that usually represents a person for informational purposes only, much like an address book entry. Like a user account, a contact is created in Active Directory Users and Computers, but a contact isn't a security principal and, therefore, can't be assigned permissions or rights. The most common use of a contact is for integration into Microsoft Exchange's address book. The Full name field is the only information required to create a contact, but a contact's Properties dialog box has General, Address, Telephones, Organization, and Member Of tabs for adding detailed information about the contact. You use the Member Of tab to add a contact to a group or a distribution group.

A **distribution group** is created the same way as a group. The only real difference is the group type, which is distribution rather than security (explained later in "Managing Group Accounts"). Like a contact, a distribution group is used mostly with Microsoft Exchange for sending e-mails but to several people at once. Both regular user accounts and contacts can be added as members of a distribution group.

You can't create contacts and distribution groups in ADAC.

Activity 7-10: Creating Contacts and Distribution Groups

Time Required: 5 minutes
Objective: Create a contact and a distribution group.

Required Tools and Equipment: 410Server1
Description: You need to have a marketing business partner's contact information readily available. Because your users are well versed in using Active Directory to find other directory information, you decide to create contact and distribution group objects in Active Directory for outside business contacts. For organizational purposes, you place outside contacts in separate OUs.

1. If necessary, log on to 410Server1 as **Administrator**, and open Active Directory Users and Computers.

2. If necessary, click to expand the **Marketing** OU, and then create an OU called **External** under it.

3. Click the **External** OU you just created. Right-click a blank spot in the right pane, point to **New**, and click **Contact**.

4. Type **Partner** in the First name text box and **One** in the Last name text box, and then click **OK**.

5. Right-click a blank spot in the right pane, point to **New**, and click **Group**.

6. In the Group name text box, type **MktEmail**. Under Group type, click the **Distribution** option button, and then click **OK**.

7. Right-click **Partner One** and click **Properties** to open its Properties dialog box. Click each tab to view the information you can enter for a contact.

8. Click the **Member Of** tab. Click **Add** to open the Select Groups dialog box. Type **MktEmail** in the "Enter the object names to select" text box, click **Check Names**, and then click **OK** twice.

9. Close Active Directory Users and Computers. If you're continuing to the next activity, stay logged on; otherwise, log off or shut down the computer.

Managing Group Accounts

Active Directory group objects are the main security principal administrators use to grant rights and permissions to users. Using groups to assign user rights and permissions is preferable to using separate user accounts, mainly because groups are easier to manage. Users with similar access requirements to resources can be made members of a group, and instead of creating ACEs for each user in a network resource's DACL, you can make a single entry for the group. Furthermore, if a user changes departments or positions in the company, you can remove the user from one group and place the user in another group that meets his or her new access requirements. With a single administrative action, you can completely alter a user's access to resources. If permissions are assigned to a single user account, the administrator must find each resource for which the user has an ACE, make the necessary changes, and then add the user account to the DACL for each resource the new department or position requires. When an administrator creates a group in Active Directory Users and Computers, aside from assigning a name, there are two other settings, discussed in the following sections: group type and group scope.

Group Types

There are two group types: security groups and distribution groups. As mentioned, a distribution group is used to group users together, mainly for sending e-mails to several people at once with an Active Directory–integrated e-mail application, such as Microsoft Exchange. Distribution groups aren't security principals and, therefore, can't be used to assign rights and permissions to their members. A distribution group can have the following objects as members: user accounts, contacts, other distribution groups, security groups, and computers.

Because you can mix user accounts and contacts, you can build useful distribution groups that include people outside your organization. You can also nest groups, which makes organizing users and contacts more flexible. However, because distribution groups aren't used for security and are useful only with certain applications, their use in Active Directory is more limited than security groups.

Security groups are the main Active Directory object administrators use to manage network resource access and grant rights to users. Most discussions about groups focus on security groups rather than distribution groups, and in general, when the term "group" is used without a qualifier, a security group should be assumed. Security groups can contain the same types of objects as distribution groups. However, if a security group has a contact as a member and the security group is granted permission to a resource, the permission doesn't extend to the contact because a contact isn't a security principal. Security groups can also be used as distribution groups by applications such as Microsoft Exchange, so re-creating security groups as distribution groups isn't necessary for e-mail purposes.

Converting Group Type You can convert the **group type** from security to distribution and vice versa. However, only a security group can be added to a resource's DACL. If a security group is an entry in the DACL for a shared folder, for example, and the security group is converted to a distribution group, the group remains in the DACL but has no effect on access to the resource for any of its members.

The need to convert group type isn't all that common, but when it's necessary, usually a distribution group is converted to a security group. This conversion might be necessary when, for example, a group of users is assigned to collaborate on a project. Distribution groups composed of team members might be created for the purpose of e-mail communication about the project, but later, it's determined that the project requires considerable network resources that team members need access to. The distribution group could be converted to a security group for the purpose of assigning rights and permissions, and the security group could still be used as an e-mail distribution group.

Group Scope

The **group scope** determines the reach of a group's application in a domain or a forest: which security principals in a forest can be group members and to which forest resources a group can be assigned rights or permissions. Three group scope options are possible in a Windows Server 2012/R2 forest: domain local, global, and universal. A fourth scope—local—applies only to groups created in the SAM database of a member computer or stand-alone computer. Local groups aren't part of Active Directory. For each group scope, Table 7-6 summarizes possible group members, which groups the scope can be a member of, and to which resources permissions or rights can be assigned.

Table 7-6   Group scope membership and resource assignment

Group scope	Possible members	Can be a member of	Permissions and rights assignments
Domain local	User accounts, computer accounts, global groups from any domain in the forest, and universal groups Other domain local groups from the same domain User accounts, computer accounts, global groups, and universal groups from trusted domains in another forest	Domain local groups in the same domain Local groups on domain member computers; domain local groups in the Builtin folder can be members only of other domain local groups	Resources on any DC or member computer in the domain; domain local groups in the Builtin folder can be added to DACLs only on DCs, not on member computers
Global	User accounts, computer accounts, and other global groups in the same domain	Global groups in the same domain and universal groups Domain local groups or local groups on member computers in any domain in the forest or trusted domains in another forest	Resources on any DC or member computer in any domain in the forest or trusted domains in another forest
Universal	User accounts, computer accounts, global groups from any domain in the forest, and other universal groups	Universal groups from any domain in the forest Domain local groups or local groups on member computers in any domain in the forest or trusted domains in another forest	Resources on any DC or member computer in any domain in the forest or trusted domains in another forest

Domain Local Groups   A **domain local group** is the main security principal recommended for assigning rights and permissions to domain resources. Although both global and universal groups can also be used for this purpose, Microsoft best practices recommend using these groups to aggregate users with similar access or rights requirements. Global and universal groups should then be added as members of domain local groups, which are added to a resource's DACL. The process can be summarized with the abbreviations AGDLP and AGGUDLP. In single-domain environments or when users from only one domain are assigned access to a resource, use AGDLP:

- Accounts are made members of
- Global groups, which are made members of

- Domain Local groups, which are assigned
- Permissions to resources

In multidomain environments where users from different domains are assigned access to a resource, use AGGUDLP:

- Accounts are made members of
- Global groups, which when necessary are nested in other
- Global groups, which are made members of
- Universal groups, which are then made members of
- Domain Local groups, which are assigned
- Permissions to resources

The repeating theme is that permissions should be assigned to as few different security principals as possible, namely domain local groups. Using this method to assign permissions keeps the list of ACEs short, making resource access management considerably easier. This rule isn't hard and fast, as there are circumstances in which other group scopes and individual user accounts should be assigned permissions. Whenever possible, however, these rules should be followed.

Some administrators create a domain local group for each level of access to each shared resource. For example, you have a shared folder called SalesDocs that requires two levels of access by different groups: Read access and Modify access. You could create two domain local groups named SalesDocs-Read-DL, with Read permission, and SalesDocs-Mod-DL, with Modify permission. By using this group-naming standard, you have identified the resource, access level, and group scope. Next, you need only add the global or universal groups containing users to the correct domain local group. Keep in mind that the "local" in domain local refers to where resources this group scope is assigned to can be located. You can't, for example, add a domain local group from Domain A to the DACL of a resource in Domain B.

Global Groups   As mentioned, a **global group** is used mainly to group users from the same domain with similar access or rights requirements. A global group's members can be user accounts, computer accounts, and other global groups from the same domain. However, a global group is considered global because it can be made a member of a domain local group in any domain in the forest or trusted domains in other forests. Global groups can also be assigned permissions to resources in any domain in the forest or trusted domains in other forests.

A common use of global groups is creating one for each department, location, or both. In a single-domain environment, global groups are added to domain local groups for assigning resource permissions. You might wonder why user accounts aren't simply added directly to a domain local group, bypassing global groups altogether. In a single-domain environment, you can do this, but this approach has some drawbacks:

- Domain local group memberships can become large and unwieldy, particularly for resources to which many users from several departments must have access. Examine Figure 7-20 and think about which group you would rather manage.
- If the company ever adds a domain, you need to redesign group memberships to grant permissions to cross-domain resources. This task is necessary because a domain local group can't be a member of a group or assigned permission to a resource in another domain.

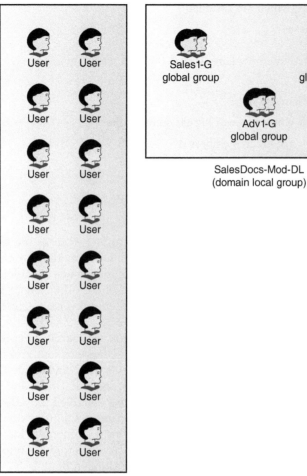

Figure 7-20   Global groups nested inside a domain local group is easier to manage
© *Cengage Learning®*

In multidomain environments where departments are represented in more than one domain, departmental global groups from each domain can be aggregated into a universal group, which is then made a member of a domain local group for resource access. For example, in Figure 7-21, both the US and UK csmtech.local domains have a global group called Sales. These global groups are added to the universal group Sales-U in the csmtech.local parent domain; Sales-U is then made a member of the domain local group assigned permissions to the shared folder. Keep in mind that the shared resource could be located in any of the three domains, as long as the domain local group is in the same domain as the shared resource. The universal group in this example can be added to a domain local group in any domain in the forest as well as trusted domains in other forests.

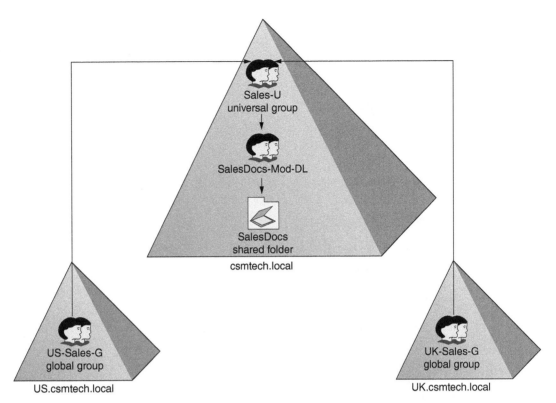

Figure 7-21 Using global and universal groups
© 2015 Cengage Learning®

Universal Groups A **universal group** is special in a couple of ways. First, a universal group's membership information is stored only on domain controllers configured as global catalog servers. Second, they are the only type of group with a truly universal nature:

- User accounts, computer accounts, global groups, and universal groups from any domain in the forest can be a member.
- They can be a member of other universal groups or domain local groups from any domain in the forest.
- They can be assigned permissions to resources in any domain in the forest.

Because universal groups' membership information is stored only on global catalog servers, you need to plan the placement of domain controllers configured as global catalog servers in multidomain networks carefully. When users log on, a global catalog server must be available to determine their memberships in any universal groups. For that reason, a remote office with many users should have at least one domain controller configured as a global catalog server to reduce WAN traffic during user logons.

An alternative to having a global catalog server at each site is to enable **universal group membership caching** on a remote office's domain controller. With caching enabled, a domain controller queries a global catalog server to determine universal group membership, and then keeps a local copy of this information to use for future logons.

Universal group membership changes require replication to all global catalog servers. If you're operating a WAN with global catalog servers in remote locations, extra bandwidth is required to replicate universal group membership changes. Plan your Active Directory group design carefully so that changes to universal groups don't happen often.

Local Groups A **local group** is created in the local SAM database on a member server or workstation or a stand-alone computer. Because groups and users created on a stand-alone computer can't interact with Active Directory, this discussion focuses on local groups created on computers that are members of an Active Directory domain.

Local groups can be found on any Windows computer that isn't a domain controller, and you manage them with the Local Users and Groups snap-in in the Computer Management MMC. Using local groups to manage resources on a member computer is generally discouraged because it decentralizes resource management. Assigning permissions and rights on member computers to domain local groups is better. However, when a Windows computer becomes a domain member, Windows changes the membership of two local groups automatically:

- *Administrators*—The Domain Admins global group is made a member of this local group, so any Domain Admins group member has administrative access to every member computer in the domain.

- *Users*—The Domain Users global group is made a member of this local group, giving Domain Users group members a set of default rights and permissions appropriate for a regular user on every member computer in the domain.

Local groups can have the following account types as members:

- Local user accounts created on the same computer

- Domain user accounts and computer accounts from any domain in the forest or trusted domains in another forest

- Domain local groups from the same domain (except domain local groups in the Builtin folder)

- Global or universal groups from any domain in the forest or trusted domains in another forest

Local groups can be assigned permissions only to resources on the local computer. The most common use of local groups, besides the Administrators and Users local groups, is in a workgroup environment on non-domain computers. However, when a member computer's user requires considerable autonomy for managing local computer resources, you can grant the user enough rights on the local computer for this autonomy.

Nesting Groups

Nesting groups is exactly what it sounds like: making one group a member of another group. There are few restrictions on group nesting, as long as you follow the group scope's membership rules. Group nesting is often used to group users who have similar roles but work in different departments. For example, you can create a global group for supervisors in each department and place users in each department with a supervisory role in this group. Next, create a Super-All global group and place the department supervisor groups in this group (see Figure 7-22). In this way, all department supervisors can easily be assigned the rights and permissions their role specifies. Furthermore, in a multidomain environment, a similar group configuration can be developed for each domain. The SuperAll global groups from each domain can then be added to a universal supervisors group for assigning permissions and rights throughout the forest. This example follows the AGGUDLP rule described earlier.

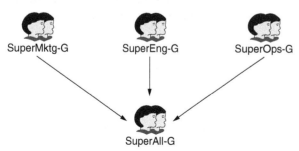

Figure 7-22   Nesting global groups
© *Cengage Learning®*

Although there are few restrictions on group nesting, the complexity of tracking and troubleshooting permissions increases as the number of levels of nested groups increases. Like OUs, groups can be nested an unlimited number of levels, but that doesn't mean you should. In most circumstances, one level of nesting groups of the same type is enough, as in Figure 7-22. An additional level, such as aggregating nested global groups into a universal group, should work for most designs. The last step is to put your group of groups, whether global or universal, into a domain local group for resource access.

Converting Group Scope

When you create a group, the default setting is a security group with global scope. However, just as you can convert group type from security to distribution and vice versa, you can convert the group scope, with some restrictions, as explained in the following list:

- Universal to domain local, provided the original universal group isn't a member of another universal group because you would have a domain local group as a member of a universal group, which isn't allowed.

- Universal to global, provided no universal group is a member of the universal group because universal groups can't be members of global groups.

- Global to universal, provided the global group isn't a member of another global group because global groups can't be members of universal groups.

- Domain local to universal, provided no domain local group is a member because domain local groups can't be members of universal groups.

Group scope conversions not mentioned in this list aren't allowed. Even though you can't do certain group scope conversions directly, however, you can do some conversions with two steps. For example, to convert from domain local to global, first convert the domain local group to universal and then convert the universal group to global.

Activity 7-11: Creating Groups with Different Scopes

Time Required: 20 minutes
Objective: Create groups with different scopes.

Required Tools and Equipment: 410Server1
Description: You want to experiment to see how nesting groups and converting group scope work.

1. If necessary, log on to 410Server1 as **Administrator**, and open Active Directory Users and Computers.

2. Click **TestOU1**, and create the following security groups with the indicated scope: **Group1-G** (global), **Group2-G** (global), **Group1-DL** (domain local), **Group2-DL** (domain local), **Group1-U** (universal), and **Group2-U** (universal).

3. In the right pane of Active Directory Users and Computers, click **Group1-G**, and open its Properties dialog box. In the Group scope section, notice that the Domain local option is disabled because converting from global to domain local isn't allowed.

4. Click the **Members** tab, and then click **Add**. Type **Group2-G**, click **Check Names**, and then click **OK**.

5. Click **Add**. Type **Group1-DL** and click **Check Names**. The Name Not Found message box is displayed because domain local groups can't be members of global groups. Click **Cancel**.

6. Click **Advanced**, and then click **Find Now**. Active Directory displays only valid objects that can be made a group member, so no domain local or universal groups are listed. Click **Cancel** twice, and then click **OK**.

7. Click **Group2-G** and open its Properties dialog box. In the Group scope section, click the **Universal** option button, and then click **OK**. You should get an error message stating that a global group can't have a universal group as a member. Because Group2-G is a member of Group1-G, attempting to convert it to universal violates that rule. Click **OK**, and then click **Cancel**.

8. Click **Group1-DL** and open its Properties dialog box. In the Group scope section, the Global option is disabled because you can't convert a domain local group to a global group.

9. Click the **Members** tab and add **Group1-G** as a member. Adding a global group as a member of a domain local group is in line with the AGDLP best practice. Click **OK** twice.

10. Click **Group1-U** and open its Properties dialog box. Add **Group2-U** as a member, and then click **OK** twice. Click **Group2-U** and open its Properties dialog box. In the Group scope section, click **Domain local**, and then click **OK**. You get an error message, which reinforces the rule that universal groups can be converted to domain local groups only if they're already a member of another universal group. Click **OK**, and then click **Cancel**.

11. Click **Group1-U** and open its Properties dialog box. Try to add **Group1-DL** as a member. Nesting domain local groups in universal groups isn't permitted. Add **Group1-G** as a member. Success! Global groups can be members of universal groups.

12. Leave Active Directory Users and Computers open for the next activity.

Default Groups in a Windows Domain

When an Active Directory domain is created, some default groups are created automatically to establish a framework for assigning users rights and permissions to perform common tasks and access default resources. Windows assigns default groups a variety of rights and permissions so that users can carry out certain tasks simply by being added to the appropriate group. For example, the default Backup Operators group is assigned the right to back up all files and directories on all computers in the Domain Controllers OU. To give users this capability, simply add them as members of the Backup Operators group.

There are three categories of default groups in a Windows domain: groups in the Builtin folder, groups in the Users folder, and special identity groups that don't appear in Active Directory management tools and can't be managed. A fourth category, the default local groups in the SAM database on member computers, corresponds roughly to groups in the Builtin folder.

Default Groups in the Builtin Folder   All default groups in the Builtin folder are domain local groups used for assigning rights and permissions in the local domain. Neither the group scope nor type can be converted. Each group in this folder has a brief description in ADUC or ADAC. Table 7-7 describes the most prominent of these groups in more detail.

Table 7-7   Default groups in the Builtin folder

Group	Description
Account Operators	Members can administer domain user, group, and computer accounts, except computers in the Domain Controllers OU and the Administrators, Domain Admins, Enterprise Admins, Schema Admins, and Read Only Domain Controllers groups. Members can log on locally and shut down domain controllers in the domain. There are no default members.
Administrators	Members have full control of all DCs in the domain and can perform almost all operations on DCs. Default members are Domain Admins, Enterprise Admins, and the Administrator user account.
Backup Operators	Members can back up and restore all files and directories on DCs in the domain with an Active Directory–aware backup program. Members' ability to access all files and folders doesn't extend beyond their use of backup software. Members can log on locally to and shut down DCs. There are no default members.
Event Log Readers	Members can read event logs on the local machine. This default group is helpful because you want a technician to be able to read event logs without having broader administrative capabilities. There are no default members.
Guests	This group has no default rights or permissions. The Domain Guests group and Guest user account are default members.
Hyper-V Administrators	Members have full access to all Hyper-V features. A virtualization specialist can be added to this group without giving the user broader administrative capabilities on the server. There are no default members.

(continues)

Group	Description
IIS_IUSRS	Internet Information Services uses this group to allow anonymous access to Web resources.
Network Configuration Operators	Members can change TCP/IP settings and release and renew DHCP-assigned addresses on DCs. There are no default members.
Print Operators	Members can manage all aspects of print jobs and printers connected to DCs. Members can log on locally to and shut down DCs in the domain. There are no default members.
Remote Desktop Users	Members can log on remotely to DCs with the Remote Desktop client. There are no default members.
Server Operators	Members can log on locally to DCs, manage some services, manage shared resources, back up and restore files, shut down DCs, format hard drives, and change the system time. There are no default members.
Users	Members can run applications and use local printers on member computers, among other common tasks. Members of this group can't, by default, log on locally to DCs. Domain Users and the special identity Authenticated Users and Interactive groups are members of the Users group by default. Because all user accounts created in a domain are automatically members of the Domain Users global group, all domain users become members of this group as well.

© 2015 Cengage Learning®

7

Default Groups in the Users Folder

The default groups in the Users folder are a combination of domain local, global, and, in the forest root domain, universal scope. User accounts are generally added to global and universal groups in this folder for assigning permissions and rights in the domain and forest. Table 7-8 describes several groups in the Users folder.

Table 7-8   Default groups in the Users folder

Group/scope	Description
Allowed RODC Password Replication Group/domain local	Members can have their passwords replicated to RODCs. There are no default members.
Denied RODC Password Replication Group/domain local	Members can't have their passwords replicated to RODCs, so this group is a security measure to ensure that passwords for sensitive accounts don't get stored on RODCs. Default members include Domain Admins, Enterprise Admins, and Schema Admins.
DnsAdmins/domain local	This group is created when DNS is installed in the domain. Members have administrative control over the DNS Server service. There are no default members.
Domain Admins/global	Members have full control over domain-wide functions. This group is a member of all domain local and local Administrators groups. The domain Administrator account is a member by default.
Domain Computers/global	All computers that are domain members (excluding DCs) are added to this group by default.
Domain Controllers/global	All DCs are members of this group by default.
Domain Users/global	All user accounts in the domain are added to this group automatically. This group is used to assign rights or permissions to all users in the domain, but it has no specific rights by default. This group is a member of the Users domain local group by default.
Enterprise Admins/universal	This universal group is found only on DCs in the forest root domain. Members have full control over forest-wide operations. This group is a member of the Administrators group on all DCs. The Administrator account for the forest root domain is a member by default.
Group Policy Creator Owners/global	Members can create and modify group policies throughout the domain.
Read Only Domain Controllers/global	RODCs are members by default.
Schema Admins/universal	This universal group is found only on DCs in the forest root domain. Members can modify the Active Directory schema. The Administrator account for the forest root domain is a member by default.

© 2015 Cengage Learning®

Special Identity Groups   Special identity groups, some of which are described in Table 7-9, don't appear as objects in ADUC or ADAC, but they can be assigned permissions by adding them to resources' DACLs. Membership in these groups is controlled dynamically by Windows, can't be viewed or changed manually, and depends on how an account accesses the OS. For example, membership in the Authenticated Users group is assigned to a user account automatically when the user logs on to a computer or domain. No group scope is associated with special identity groups, and users can be members of more than one special identity group at a time. For example, anyone who authenticates to a Windows computer is a member of the Authenticated Users group. In addition, users who log on remotely with Remote Desktop are members of both the Interactive group and the Remote Interactive Logon group. Special identity groups are also called "well-known groups." You can view all your group memberships, including current membership in special identity groups, by entering whoami /groups at a command prompt.

For more information on using the whoami command, enter whoami /? at a command prompt.

Table 7-9   Special identity groups

Group	Description
Anonymous Logon	Users and services that access domain resources without using an account name or a password. Typically used when a user accesses an FTP server that doesn't require user account logon.
Authenticated Users	Members include any user account (except Guest) logging on to a computer or domain with a valid username and password. Often used to specify all users in a forest.
Creator Owner	A user becomes a member automatically for a resource he or she created (such as a folder) or took ownership of. Often assigned Full control permission for subfolders and files only on the root of a drive so that a user who creates a file or folder on the drive has full control of the object automatically.
Dial-up	A user logged on through a dial-up connection is a member.
Everyone	Refers to all users who access the system. Similar to the Authenticated Users group but includes the Guest user.
Interactive	Members are users logged on to a computer locally or through Remote Desktop. Used to specify that only a user sitting at the computer's console is allowed to access a resource on that computer.
Local	Includes all users who have logged on locally.
Network	Members are users logged on to a computer through a network connection. Used to specify that only a user who's trying to access a resource through the network can do so.
Remote Interactive Logon	Members include users who log on to a computer remotely through Remote Desktop.
Owner Rights	Represents the current owner of a folder or file. Permissions set on this group can be used to override implicit permissions granted to the owner of a file, such as Change Permissions and Take Ownership.
Service	Any security principal logged on as a service is a member.
System	Refers to the Windows OS.
Self	Refers to the object whose permissions are being set. If this group is an ACE in the object's DACL, the object can access itself with the specified permissions.

© 2015 Cengage Learning®

Activity 7-12: Working with Default Groups

Time Required: 15 minutes
Objective: View properties of default groups.

Required Tools and Equipment: 410Server1
Description: You want to see the scope and membership of some default groups that Windows creates.

1. If necessary, log on to 410Server1 as **Administrator,** and open Active Directory Users and Computers.

2. Click the **Builtin** folder. Click the **Administrators** group, and open its Properties dialog box. The options in the Group scope and Group type sections are disabled because you can't

change the scope or type of groups in the Builtin folder. Notice that the selected scope is Builtin local. These groups are considered domain local, but there are some differences between Builtin local and other domain local groups, as you'll see.

3. Click the **Members** tab to see this group's members, and then click **Cancel**.

4. Next, view the membership of the **Guests** and **Users** groups. Notice that the Users group has two special identities as members: Authenticated Users and Interactive. Close both Properties dialog boxes.

5. Click the **Users** folder. Click **Domain Admins**, and open its Properties dialog box. Click the **General** tab, if necessary. Notice that you can't change this group's scope or type. Click the **Members** tab to view the group membership, and then click **Cancel**.

6. Next, view the membership of the **Domain Users** group. Notice that all the users you have created became members of this group automatically. Close this Properties dialog box.

7. View the membership of the **Domain Computers** group. There are currently no members, but after a computer is joined to the domain, the computer account is added to this group.

8. To see the groups your currently logged-on account is a member of, open a command prompt window. Type **whoami /groups** and press **Enter**. You see a long list of groups the local administrator is a member of, including several special identity groups, such as Everyone, Interactive, Authenticated Users, and Local. In the output, these groups are identified as well-known groups. Close the command prompt window.

9. Stay logged on if you're continuing to the next activity; otherwise, log off or shut down the computer.

Working with Computer Accounts

Computer accounts are created in Active Directory when a client computer becomes a member of the domain. Like a user account, a computer account is a security principal with an SID and a password and must authenticate to the domain. Unlike a user account, an administrator can't manage a computer account's password, which each computer changes automatically every 30 days.

Don't confuse logging on to a computer connected to a computer account in Active Directory with a user's ability to access domain resources. A user can log on to a workgroup computer with any Windows version installed and still access domain resources. For example, if users log on to a Windows 8.1 computer that isn't a domain member, they can access domain resources in the usual way by using the UNC path. However, they must log on to each domain resource they want to access in the format *domain\username*. Just the same, having users log on to computers that are domain members has these advantages:

- *Single sign-on*—Users who log on from domain member computers have access to any permitted resources throughout the forest without needing to authenticate again.

- *Active Directory search*—Users of domain member computers can search Active Directory for objects and resources throughout the forest.

- *Group policies*—Administrators can manage aspects of member computers by using group policies, including security settings and use restrictions.

- *Remote management*—Administrators can right-click a computer object and click Manage to run the Computer Management MMC for member computers.

Creating Computer Accounts

Computer accounts are created in Active Directory in two ways:

- A user changes the computer membership from Workgroup to Domain in the System Properties dialog box of a computer, thereby joining the domain and creating the computer account automatically.

- An administrator creates the account manually in Active Directory.

Usually, computer accounts are created when a computer joins the domain. When a computer account is created in this way, the account is placed in the Computers folder by default. This behavior applies to both client OS computers, such as Windows 8.1 computers, and server OS computers running a version of Windows Server.

By default, the Authenticated Users group is granted the "Add workstations to domain" right so that users need only a valid username and password to join their computers to the domain if the computer account doesn't already exist. This right permits users to join computers to the domain and create up to 10 computer accounts in the domain. If administrators don't want users to have this right, they can change it through group policies. Other groups that can add workstations to a domain are Domain Admins, Account Operators, and Enterprise Admins.

You can also create computer accounts manually before a computer joins a domain. When a computer attempts to join a domain, Active Directory attempts to find a computer account matching the computer name. If it finds the account, the user is prompted for domain credentials. The computer is joined to the domain if the user has correct credentials. When a computer account is created manually, the administrator chooses which users or groups can join a computer matching the account name to the domain. By default, the Domain Admins group has the right (see Figure 7-23). Using this method for creating computer accounts means more work for an administrator but more control over which computers can join the domain.

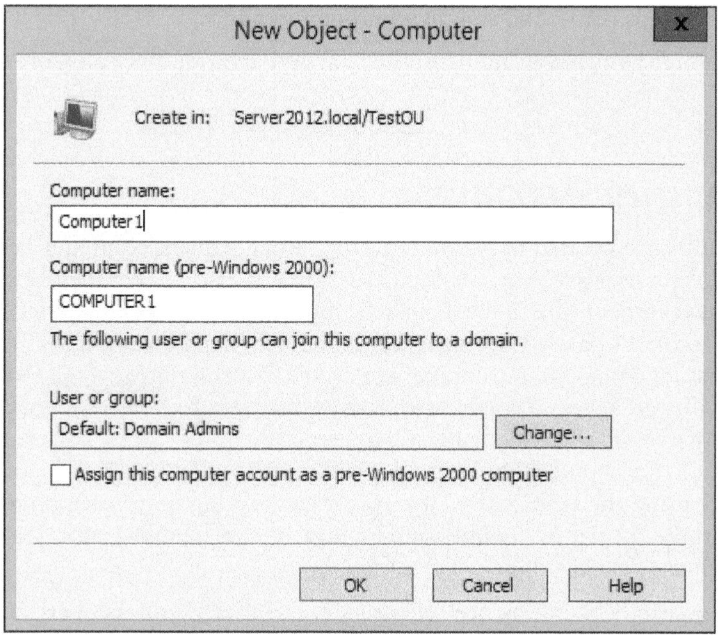

Figure 7-23   Creating a computer account

Changing the Default Computer Account Location   To gain the full benefit of computer accounts, move them to an OU you have created because the Computers folder can't have a group policy linked to it. Furthermore, because you usually require different policies for servers and user computers, you can move computer accounts for servers and user computers to separate OUs and link different group policies to these OUs.

You can change the default location for computer accounts created automatically when they join the domain by using the redircmp.exe command-line program. You might want to do this so that computers joined to the domain are immediately subject to group policies, and you don't have to remember to move them later. For example, to change the default location for computer accounts to the MemberComputers OU in the csmtech.local domain, type the following command on a domain controller:

```
redircmp ou=MemberComputers,dc=csmtech,dc=local
```

Joining a Domain   The process for joining a domain is straightforward: On the computer joining the domain, go to the Computer Name tab in the System Properties dialog box, click Change, click the Domain option button, and type the name of the domain you want the computer to join. You're prompted for credentials for a domain user account and then prompted to restart the computer to finish the operation. If the computer account doesn't already exist, it's created automatically if the domain user account has the "Add workstations to the domain" right. If the computer account does exist, the user account must have been granted the right to join the computer to the domain when the computer account was created.

As with most tasks you perform in the GUI, a command-line program is available to perform the same task. These commands are particularly useful when you're joining a Server Core computer to the domain. To join a domain, enter this command:

```
netdom join ComputerName /Domain:DomainName /UserD:UserName
   /PasswordD:Password
```

In this command, `ComputerName` is the name of the computer you want to join to the domain, and `DomainName` is the name of the domain. `UserName` is the logon name of a user account that has the right to join the computer to the domain. `Password` is the password for `UserName`. You can use * instead of specifying the password so that users are prompted for a password and the password is masked when they type it.

To join a domain by using PowerShell, enter this command:

```
Add-Computer -DomainName DomainName -Restart
```

In this command, `DomainName` is the name of the domain you want to join. You're prompted for credentials for a user account that has the necessary permissions, and then the computer restarts. You can use this cmdlet to join multiple computers to the domain at the same time. For more information and examples on using this cmdlet, type `Get-Help Add-Computer -detailed`.

Use the PowerShell cmdlet `Remove-Computer` to remove a computer from the domain.

Performing an Offline Domain Join   The capability to join a domain without contacting a domain controller became available in Windows Server 2008 R2 and Windows 7. With an **offline domain join**, the computer joining the domain doesn't have to be connected to the network when the join occurs. Later, when the computer does communicate with a DC in the domain where the offline join occurred, the computer is authenticated to the domain.

Offline domain joins are useful for large deployments of virtual machines or for mobile device deployments where network connectivity might not be available when the VM or device is deployed. It can also be useful as part of an unattended Windows installation and during setup of branch offices when there's no DC and WAN connectivity hasn't been established. In addition, offline domain joins can be done when regular domain joins can't be performed reliably, as with some WAN connections.

Offline domain joins can be done on a running computer or an offline virtual hard drive (VHD or VHDX) image.

To perform an offline domain join, you use the `djoin.exe` command. There are two phases to the process. In the first phase, you run the `djoin.exe` command to create the computer account in the domain and create a file with metadata that's used with the `djoin.exe` command on the computer you're joining. The syntax for this command in the first phase is as follows:

```
djoin /provision /domain DomainName /machine ComputerName
   /savefile filename.txt
```

In this command, the `/provision` option creates the computer account in Active Directory. *DomainName* is the name of the domain you're joining, and *ComputerName* is the computer account name of the computer joining the domain. *Filename.txt* is the name of the file where metadata is saved. You transfer this file to the computer joining the domain. The next phase is done on the computer joining the domain or an offline image. The following is the syntax for a running computer:

```
djoin /requestODJ /loadfile filename.txt /windowspath %systemroot%
  /localos
```

In this command, the `/requestODJ` option requests an offline domain join at the next system start. *Filename.txt* is the name of the file created in the first phase. The `/windowspath` option specifies the path to the Windows directory of an offline image. If the `/localos` option is used, the path to the local Windows directory is specified by using `%systemroot%` or `%windir%`. `Djoin.exe` has a number of other optional parameters. To learn more about using them, type `djoin /?` at an elevated command prompt.

The metadata file created with the `djoin.exe` command contains very sensitive information, such as the computer account password and the domain's security ID. Take precautions when transferring this file.

Activity 7-13: Joining a Computer to the Domain

Time Required: 20 minutes
Objective: Join a computer to a domain.

Required Tools and Equipment: 410Server1 and 410Win8
Description: In this activity, you join the 410Win8 computer to the domain and create the computer account automatically.

The 410Win8 computer must be configured according to the lab setup instructions in this book's Introduction. In particular, it must be in the same IP network as 410Server1 and have its DNS server configured to 410Server1's address (10.10.1.1).

1. Start 410Server1. Start and log on to 410Win8 as **Win8User** with the password **Password01**.

2. In 410Win8's Start screen, click **Desktop**. From the desktop, right-click **Start** and click **System**. In the System control panel, click **Change settings** next to Computer name. The System Properties dialog box opens. In the Computer Name tab, click **Change**.

3. Click the **Domain** option button, type **410Server2012.local**, and then click **OK**. You're prompted for credentials.

4. Type **testuser1** in the User name text box and **Password01** in the Password text box. Click **OK**. You see a message welcoming you to the domain. Click **OK**. In the message stating that you need to restart the computer to apply the changes, click **OK** and then click **Close**.

5. When prompted to restart your computer, click **Restart Now**. While 410Win8 is restarting, log on to 410Server1 as **Administrator**, and open Active Directory Users and Computers.

6. Click the **Computers** folder, and you see a computer object named 410WIN8. It was created automatically when you joined 410Win8 to the domain.

7. When 410Win8 restarts, log on to the domain as **testuser1** from 410Win8. Press **Ctrl+Alt+Delete**, and then you're prompted to enter the password for the local Win8User. Click the **back arrow** and click **Other user**. Now you can log on as testuser1.

8. Shut down 410Win8, but stay logged on to 410Server1.

Activity 7-14: Joining a Server Core Computer to the Domain with PowerShell

Time Required: 20 minutes
Objective: Join a Server Core computer to a domain.

Required Tools and Equipment: 410Server1 and 410ServerCore
Description: In this activity, you join the 410ServerCore computer to the domain after creating the computer account manually.

The 410ServerCore computer must be configured according to the lab setup instructions in this book's Introduction. In particular, it must be in the same IP network as 410Server1 and have its DNS server configured to 410Server1's address (10.10.1.1).

1. Start 410ServerCore. While it's starting, log on to 410Server1 as **Administrator** and open Active Directory Users and Computers, if necessary.

2. On 410Server1, create an OU named **MemberServers** under the domain node. Right-click **MemberServers**, point to **New**, and click **Computer**.

3. In the Computer name text box, type **410ServerCore**, and then click the **Change** button. In the Select User or Group dialog box, type **jradmin** and click **Check Names**. (You created this user account in Activity 7-5.) Click **OK** twice.

4. On 410ServerCore, log on as **Administrator** and start PowerShell by typing **powershell** at the command prompt and pressing **Enter**. Type **Set-DnsClientServerAddress -InterfaceAlias Ethernet -ServerAddresses 10.10.1.1** and press **Enter**. Type **Get-Help Add-Computer -detailed** and press **Enter** to see detailed help and examples of using this cmdlet.

5. Type **Add-Computer -DomainName 410Server2012.local -Restart** and press **Enter**.

6. When prompted for credentials, type **testuser1** in the User name text box and **Password01** in the Password text box. Click **OK**. You see a message stating that the computer failed to join the domain because access was denied. That's because when you created the computer account, you specified jradmin had the right to join the computer to the domain.

7. Repeat Step 5. When prompted for credentials, type **jradmin** in the User name text box and **Password01** in the Password text box. Click **OK**, and the computer restarts.

8. When 410ServerCore restarts, log on to the domain as **Administrator** to verify that you can. Press **Ctrl+Alt+Delete**, and then you're prompted to enter the password for the local administrator. Click the **back arrow** and click **Other user**. Enter the username in the format Administrator@410Server2012 (or 410Server2012\Administrator) because Windows assumes you're logging on to the local computer instead of the domain when you log on as Administrator. If you try to log on as any other domain user, you can just enter the logon name without the domain.

9. On 410ServerCore, type **systeminfo** at the command prompt and press **Enter**. Information about the computer is displayed, including the domain membership and which DC logged you on (see Figure 7-24). The systeminfo command works on computers with a GUI, too.

10. Shut down 410ServerCore. Stay logged on to 410Server1 if you're continuing to the next activity.

```
C:\Users\Administrator.410SERVER2012>systeminfo

Host Name:                      410SERVERCORE
OS Name:                        Microsoft Windows Server 2012 R2 Standard Evaluation
OS Version:                     6.3.9600 N/A Build 9600
OS Manufacturer:                Microsoft Corporation
OS Configuration:               Member Server
OS Build Type:                  Multiprocessor Free
Registered Owner:               Windows User
Registered Organization:
Product ID:                     00252-10000-00000-AA228
Original Install Date:          10/20/2013, 2:12:20 PM
System Boot Time:               1/9/2014, 4:33:29 PM
System Manufacturer:            Microsoft Corporation
System Model:                   Virtual Machine
System Type:                    x64-based PC
Processor(s):                   1 Processor(s) Installed.
                                [01]: Intel64 Family 6 Model 15 Stepping 7 GenuineInt
el ~2333 Mhz
BIOS Version:                   American Megatrends Inc. 090006 , 5/23/2012
Windows Directory:              C:\Windows
System Directory:               C:\Windows\system32
Boot Device:                    \Device\HarddiskVolume1
System Locale:                  en-us;English (United States)
Input Locale:                   en-us;English (United States)
Time Zone:                      (UTC-07:00) Arizona
Total Physical Memory:          512 MB
Available Physical Memory:      253 MB
Virtual Memory: Max Size:       768 MB
Virtual Memory: Available:      519 MB
Virtual Memory: In Use:         249 MB
Page File Location(s):          C:\pagefile.sys
Domain:                         410Server2012.local
Logon Server:                   \\410SERVER1
Hotfix(s):                      N/A
Network Card(s):                1 NIC(s) Installed.
                                [01]: Microsoft Hyper-V Network Adapter
                                      Connection Name: Ethernet
                                      DHCP Enabled:    No
                                      IP address(es)
                                      [01]: 10.10.1.5
                                      [02]: fe80::218a:59b9:3aa2:3da5
Hyper-V Requirements:           A hypervisor has been detected. Features required for
Hyper-V will not be displayed.

C:\Users\Administrator.410SERVER2012>
```

Figure 7-24   Output from the `systeminfo` command

Managing Computer Accounts

Computer account objects are, for the most part, a set-it-and-forget-it proposition. After creating them and possibly moving them to another OU, you might not need to do anything with these objects. However, sometimes administrators must attend to computer accounts—usually when something has gone wrong.

As mentioned, a computer account has an associated password and must log on to the domain. The computer changes this password automatically every 30 days by default. If the password becomes unsynchronized between the computer and the computer account in Active Directory, the computer can no longer access the domain. Sometimes the password can become unsynchronized if a computer has been turned off or is otherwise unable to contact a domain controller for an extended period and, therefore, can't change its password. In effect, the password expires, and the only solution is to reset the computer account by right-clicking the computer object in Active Directory Users and Computers and clicking Reset Account. After resetting, the computer must leave the domain (by joining a workgroup) and then join it again. You can also use the `netdom` command on member servers with an unsynchronized account. This command resets the password on the local server and the corresponding computer account, so the server doesn't have to leave and rejoin the domain.

If the computer does become unsynchronized with its account in Active Directory, users get a message stating that the trust relationship between the workstation and the domain failed.

Another reason for an administrator to access a computer account is to run the Computer Management MMC remotely on a member computer. As mentioned, clicking Manage in the right-click menu of a computer account opens Computer Management on that computer. The Computer Management MMC includes the Task Scheduler, Event Viewer, Shared Folders, Local Users and Groups, Reliability and Performance, Device Manager, Disk Management, and Services and Applications snap-ins—quite a bit of management capability available at a click.

Disabling Computer Accounts   Computer accounts can be deleted or disabled, just as user accounts can be. You might need to delete a computer account if it's no longer a permanent domain member or if resetting the account doesn't solve the problem of a computer not being able to log on to the domain. In these cases, you can delete the account and re-create it. The computer must also leave and rejoin the domain.

When a computer leaves the domain, its associated computer account is disabled automatically. If the same computer rejoins the domain, the account is enabled again. You might need to disable a computer account manually if the computer (a laptop, for example) won't be in contact with the domain for an extended period. When the computer needs access to the domain again, you can reenable the computer account. You enable, disable, and reset a computer account by right-clicking it and choosing the option from the shortcut menu in ADUC or ADAC.

You might wonder why you would want to place computer accounts into groups. A common reason for creating groups for computer accounts is to use group policy filtering to configure exceptions for a group of users or computers that would normally be affected by a policy. Group policy filtering is discussed in Chapter 8.

Automating Account Management

Account management has been discussed mostly from the standpoint of using ADUC and ADAC to work with accounts. When only a few accounts require action, using a GUI tool is convenient. When many accounts require action or certain tasks must be repeated many times, however, a command-line program is often the most efficient tool for the job. Administrators can take advantage of batch files to handle lengthy and cumbersome command-line syntax. A batch file is a text file with the .bat extension that's used to enter a command or series of commands normally typed at the command prompt. Batch files can take arguments to replace variables in the command. Bulk import/export programs also make account management faster and easier. These programs can read an input file (import) to create several Active Directory objects at once or produce an output file (export) from Active Directory objects. In the following sections, examples and activities walk you through using command-line tools and bulk import/export programs to manage accounts.

Command-Line Tools for Managing Active Directory Objects

The GUI interfaces of ADUC and ADAC are convenient for creating a few accounts or making changes to a few objects. Even with the help of a template, however, quite a bit of manual entry is still required to create a user. Many administrators prefer a command-line tool, often used with a batch file, to create or change accounts. The following commands are used at a command prompt or in a batch file for managing accounts:

- dsadd—Adds objects to Active Directory. Used mainly for adding account objects but can also be used to create OUs and contacts.
- dsget—Displays an object's properties onscreen by default, but the output can be redirected to a file.
- dsmod—Modifies existing Active Directory objects.
- dsmove—Moves objects in a domain to another folder or OU or renames the object.
- dsquery—Finds and displays objects in Active Directory that meet specified criteria. The output can be displayed onscreen or sent (piped) to other commands. For example, dsquery could find and display a list of all users in an OU, and this list could be piped to a dsmod command that adds the users to a group.
- dsrm—Removes, or deletes, objects from Active Directory.

You can type a command followed by /? to get help on syntax and use. For example, if you need to know more about the dsadd command, type dsadd /? at the command prompt.

You used `dsadd` in Chapter 6 to create a user. Now take a closer look at its syntax and see how you can use it in a batch file to make account creation easier. The syntax for using `dsadd` to create objects is as follows:

```
dsadd ObjectType ObjectDN [options]
```

- *ObjectType* is the type of object you want to create, such as a user or group.
- *ObjectDN* is the object's distinguished name (DN), which includes the full path in Active Directory where the object should be created. The path is specified by starting with the object name, followed by each parent container object up to the top-level domain name. Each component of the path is separated by a comma. A DN's components are as follows:

  o CN (common name): The name of the object as shown in Active Directory.
  o CN (common name): The CN component can be repeated if the object is in a folder, such as the Users or Computers folder, rather than an OU.
  o OU (organizational unit): Use this component if the object is in an OU. It's repeated for as many levels as necessary, starting with the lowest OU level.
  o DC (domain component): Each part of the domain name is specified separately until the top-level domain name is reached.

For example, to create a user account named BSmith in the Sales OU, which is in the Marketing parent OU in the csmtech.local domain, the command is as follows:

```
dsadd user CN=BSmith,OU=Sales,OU=Marketing,DC=csmtech,DC=local
```

To create a computer account named New Computer in the Computers folder in the same domain, the command is as follows:

```
dsadd computer "CN=New Computer,CN=Computers,DC=csmtech,DC=local"
```

The quotation marks around the distinguished name path are required if the path contains any spaces, including after commas. Following the DN, a command can include options specified with this syntax:

```
-OptionName OptionValues
```

For example, if you want to add BSmith and include the first name and last name attributes, the command uses the `-fn` and `-ln` options, as shown:

```
dsadd user CN=BSmith,OU=Sales,OU=Marketing,DC=csmtech,DC=local
 -fn Bill -ln Smith
```

The `dsadd` command's syntax is somewhat intimidating, and if you had to type this entire command over and over, you might start to wonder how useful it is. The command's usefulness is apparent, however, when you have to create several accounts with similar properties except a few that are unique for each user. You can construct the command once in a batch file with a placeholder for the unique information that varies each time the command is used. For example, you could type the following command in a text file saved as `uadd.bat`:

```
dsadd user "CN=%1,OU=Sales,OU=Marketing,DC=csmtech,DC=local"
 -fn %2 -ln %3 -pwd Password01 -memberof Sales-G -mustchpwd yes
```

 The distinguished name path in the preceding commands isn't case sensitive, so you can use "ou" and "dc" instead of "OU" and "DC." The capitalization just makes the commands easier to read.

This command creates a user in the specified container and domain, assigns the password Password01, places the user in the Sales-G group, and requires that the user change the password at next logon. The %1, %2, and %3 are variables replaced with username, first name, and last name. For example, to run the `uadd.bat` batch file to create a user named Susan Martin with the username SMartin, you enter the following:

```
uadd SMartin Susan Martin
```

For each user you need to create, you have to specify only the username, first name, and last name. If you have several users with similar properties to create, you could perform the task much faster than in Active Directory Users and Computers, even if you used a user template.

Activity 7-15: Creating a Batch File for the `dsadd` Command

Time Required: 15 minutes
Objective: Create a batch file for the `dsadd` command.

Required Tools and Equipment: 410Server1
Description: A new department, Advertising, has been added to your company, and 15 new employees will be hired immediately. You have already created the OU structure to accommodate this new department: the Advertising OU under the Marketing OU. All users will belong to a global group called Advert-G, which you need to create first.

1. If necessary, log on to 410Server1 as **Administrator**, and open a command prompt window.

2. To create a security group called **Advert-G** with global scope, type **dsadd group "CN=Advert-G,OU=Advertising,OU=Marketing,DC=410Server2012, DC=Local"** and press **Enter**. If you typed it correctly, you'll see a message starting with "dsadd succeeded." You don't need to specify the scope because global is the default.

3. Right-click **Start**, click **Run**, type **Notepad** in the Open text box, and press **Enter**.

4. In Notepad, type the following on one line: **dsadd user "CN=%1, OU=Advertising,OU=Marketing,DC=410Server2012,DC=local" -fn %2 -ln %3 -upn %1@410Server2012.local -pwd Password01 -memberof "CN=Advert-G, OU=Advertising, OU=Marketing, DC=410Server2012, DC=local" -mustchpwd yes**.

5. Save the file as **"C:\uadd.bat"**. Because Notepad adds the `.txt` extension automatically, enclose the filename in quotation marks to preserve the `.bat` extension. Exit Notepad.

6. At the command prompt, type **C:\uadd AdvUser1 Advertising User1** and press **Enter**.

7. The last line of the command output should start with "dsadd succeeded." If `dsadd` failed, check the syntax in the `uadd.bat` file. Make sure there's a space between the option name and the option value; for example, make sure there's a space between `-fn` and `%2`.

8. Refresh the view in Active Directory Users and Computers by clicking **Action, Refresh** from the menu or clicking the **Refresh** toolbar icon. The user you just created should appear in the Advertising OU and be a member of the Advert-G group.

9. Create two more users named **AdvUser2** and **AdvUser3** (with first names and last names in the format shown in Step 6) by using the batch file. Leave Active Directory Users and Computers and the command prompt window open if you're continuing to the next activity; otherwise, log off or shut down 410Server1.

Piping Output A benefit of some command-line programs is that you can use one command's output as input to another, which is called **piping**. You can use piping with the `dsquery` and `dsmod` commands, but it's not unique to directory service commands. It's also used extensively with PowerShell commands. One of the most common uses of piping is sending the output of any command producing more than one screen of information to the `more` command. You can try it by displaying the help information for a command:

```
dsmod user /? | more
```

The vertical bar, called a "pipe," specifies sending the output of `dsmod user /?` to the `more` command, which simply paginates information it receives so that you can view one page of output at a time. In the following activity, you use `dsquery` to find and display Active Directory information, and then use a pipe to `dsmod` to add users to a group.

Activity 7-16: Using `dsquery` and `dsmod` with a Pipe

Time Required: 10 minutes
Objective: Pipe output from `dsquery` to `dsmod` to add users to a group.

Required Tools and Equipment: 410Server1
Description: All users in the Marketing OU and all OUs under it need to be added to a new group called Marketing-G. You create the group and use `dsquery` and `dsmod` to assign group memberships.

1. If necessary, log on to 410Server1 as **Administrator**, open a command prompt window, and open Active Directory Users and Computers.

2. At the command prompt, type **dsadd group "CN=Marketing-G, OU=Marketing, DC=410Server2012, DC=local"** and press Enter.

3. Type **dsquery user "OU=Marketing,DC=410Server2012,DC=local"** and press **Enter**. The output should be a list of all users, shown in DN format, in the Marketing OU and all its child OUs. This data is what's piped to the `dsmod` command in the next step.

4. Type **dsquery user "OU=Marketing,DC=410Server2012,DC=local" | dsmod group "CN=Marketing-G,OU=Marketing,DC=410Server2012,DC=local" -addmbr** and press **Enter**.

5. If you get a message indicating that `dsmod` was successful, open Active Directory Users and Computers, if necessary. If you get an error, check the syntax and spelling, and make sure there are no spaces between DN components.

6. In Active Directory Users and Computers, click the **Marketing-G** group in the Marketing OU. (You might need to refresh the view before you can see this group.) Open its Properties dialog box, and then click the **Members** tab. You should see all the users the `dsquery` command displayed in Step 3. Close the Properties dialog box.

7. At some point, the passwords of some users you have created will expire. To set their passwords to never expire, type **dsquery user | dsmod user -pwdneverexpires yes** and press **Enter**.

8. Close the command prompt window and Active Directory Users and Computers. If you're continuing to the next activity, stay logged on; otherwise, log off or shut down 410Server1.

Another feature of many command-line programs is redirecting output to a file instead of displaying it onscreen. The syntax to redirect output is as follows:

```
command > outputfile
```

For example, you could use the `dsquery` command from the previous activity to send the results to a file named `MktgUsers.txt`:

```
dsquery user OU=Marketing,DC=410Server2012,DC=local > MktgUsers.txt
```

Commands such as `dsadd` work well when you have many objects to create, especially when used with a batch file. `Dsquery` is also useful for displaying a list of objects based on particular criteria or piping data to commands such as `dsmod` for further processing. What if you already have a database or spreadsheet of possibly hundreds of users to create, however? When you have a file with Active Directory objects to create, two command-line tools can import that information into Active Directory: `csvde` and `ldifde`.

Managing Accounts with PowerShell

There are numerous PowerShell cmdlets you can use to manage Active Directory accounts and just about every other aspect of Active Directory. Table 7–10 lists some commands that work with user, group, and computer accounts. As always, to see how to use any of these commands, type Get-Help *cmdlet* at a PowerShell prompt (replacing *cmdlet* with the name of the command). To see an entire list of Active Directory PowerShell commands, type the following at a PowerShell prompt:

```
Get-Command -module ActiveDirectory
```

Table 7-10   PowerShell cmdlets for account management

Cmdlet	Description
New-ADUser	Creates a user account
Remove-ADUser	Deletes a user account
Set-ADUser	Changes user account properties
Get-ADUser	Gets information about user accounts
New-ADGroup	Creates a group account
Remove-ADGroup	Deletes a group account
Set-ADGroup	Changes group account properties
Get-ADGroup	Gets information about group accounts
New-ADComputer	Creates a computer account
Remove-ADComputer	Deletes a computer account
Set-ADComputer	Changes computer account properties
Get-ADComputer	Gets information about computer accounts
Disable-ADAccount	Disables a user or computer account
Enable-ADAccount	Enables a user or computer account
Search-ADAccount	Searches for accounts that match specific properties
Unlock-ADAccount	Unlocks a locked user account
Set-ADAccountPassword	Resets a user account password

© 2015 Cengage Learning®

As with the commands described previously, you can use pipes with PowerShell commands. For example, to get a list of disabled user accounts, use this command:

```
Search-ADAccount -AccountDisabled
```

To enable all accounts that are disabled, you can use the following command:

```
Search-ADAccount -AccountDisabled | Set-ADUser -Enabled $true
```

When using PowerShell commands that might produce results you're not entirely sure of, you can add the -whatif parameter to the command. PowerShell shows the results of the command without actually performing it.

Some of the real power of PowerShell comes when using filters to list Active Directory objects that have particular properties. Say you want to get a list of all computer accounts that haven't logged on for one month. They might be considered inactive accounts. First, you need to construct a variable representing the current date minus 30 days. Then use the Get-ADComputer cmdlet to produce the list of computers meeting the criteria:

```
$InactiveDate=$(get-date).AddDays(-30)

Get-ADComputer -Properties * -Filter 'LastLogonDate -lt
  $InactiveDate'
```

Bulk Import and Export with `csvde` and `ldifde`

The `csvde` and `ldifde` commands can bulk import or export Active Directory data; the difference between them is mainly the format of files they use. `csvde` uses the comma-separated values (CSV) format common in database and spreadsheet programs. `ldifde` uses LDAP Directory Interchange Format (LDIF), which isn't as common but is useful when you're working with LDAP applications. Another difference is that `csvde` can only create objects in Active Directory, and `ldifde` can create or modify objects.

Neither command-line program has a simple method for importing a list of people directly from a database or spreadsheet, but with a little database or spreadsheet programming know-how, you can do it without too much trouble. The easiest way to get an idea of the file format these programs use is to use their export functions to create an output file. In `csvde`, the following command creates a file called `MktUsers.csv` that can be opened in Notepad, as shown in Figure 7-25:

```
csvde -m -f mktusers.csv -d "ou=marketing,dc=410Server2012,dc=local"
  -r (objectClass=user)
```

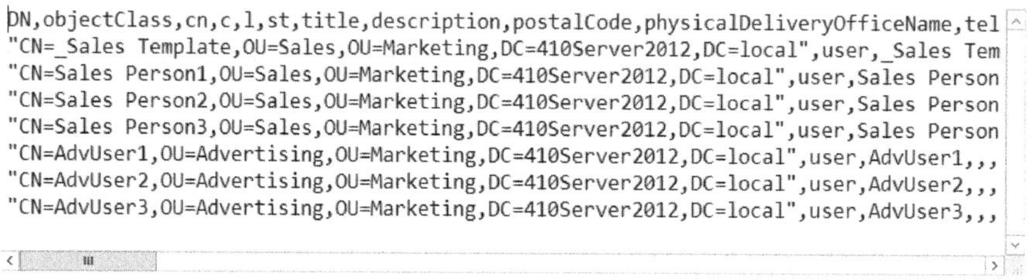

```
DN,objectClass,cn,c,l,st,title,description,postalCode,physicalDeliveryOfficeName,tel
"CN=_Sales Template,OU=Sales,OU=Marketing,DC=410Server2012,DC=local",user,_Sales Tem
"CN=Sales Person1,OU=Sales,OU=Marketing,DC=410Server2012,DC=local",user,Sales Person
"CN=Sales Person2,OU=Sales,OU=Marketing,DC=410Server2012,DC=local",user,Sales Person
"CN=Sales Person3,OU=Sales,OU=Marketing,DC=410Server2012,DC=local",user,Sales Person
"CN=AdvUser1,OU=Advertising,OU=Marketing,DC=410Server2012,DC=local",user,AdvUser1,,,
"CN=AdvUser2,OU=Advertising,OU=Marketing,DC=410Server2012,DC=local",user,AdvUser2,,,
"CN=AdvUser3,OU=Advertising,OU=Marketing,DC=410Server2012,DC=local",user,AdvUser3,,,
```

Figure 7-25 An export file created by `csvde`

To see the same output in `ldifde` format (see Figure 7-26), use the following command:

```
ldifde -f MktUsers -d "ou=Marketing,dc=410Server2012,dc=local"
  -r (objectClass=user)
```

As mentioned, `ldifde` is more powerful because of its capability to modify Active Directory objects. One method is exporting the objects you want to modify, making changes to the attributes you're modifying, and importing the file. Each object in the exported file has an associated action specified by the `changetype` line (the second line of output in Figure 7-26). To modify objects, change the action in this line to `modify`. The `ldifde` command is also useful for bulk moving of users from one domain to another.

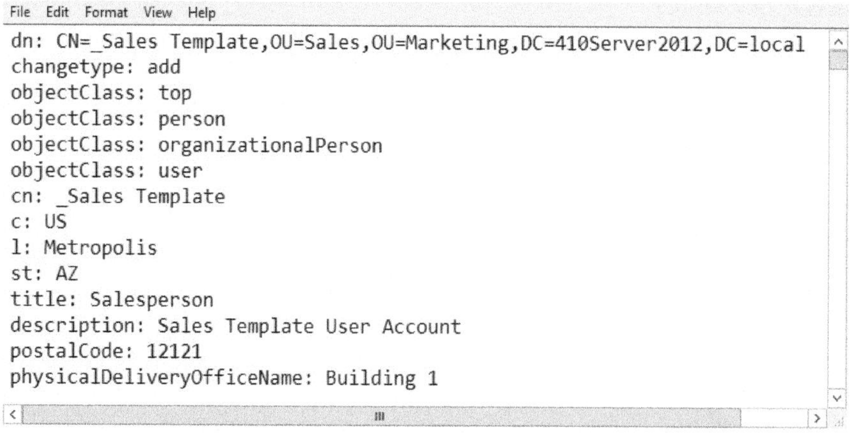

```
File  Edit  Format  View  Help
dn: CN=_Sales Template,OU=Sales,OU=Marketing,DC=410Server2012,DC=local
changetype: add
objectClass: top
objectClass: person
objectClass: organizationalPerson
objectClass: user
cn: _Sales Template
c: US
l: Metropolis
st: AZ
title: Salesperson
description: Sales Template User Account
postalCode: 12121
physicalDeliveryOfficeName: Building 1
```

Figure 7-26 An export file created by `ldifde`

Creating Users with `csvde` You can use a regular text file to import users (and other objects) into Active Directory with `csvde`, but the file must be formatted correctly. A CSV file must have a header record (the first line of a file) listing attributes of the object to be imported. For a user, it normally includes at minimum the distinguished name, the SAM account name, the UPN, and the object class attribute. Here's an example of a header record:

```
dn,SamAccountName,userPrincipalName,objectClass
```

To find a list of any object's attributes, open the Attribute Editor tab of its Properties dialog box. To see this tab, you must enable Advanced Features on Active Directory Users and Computer's View menu.

A data record for this CSV file looks like this:

```
"cn=New User,ou=TestOU,dc=csmtech,dc=local",NewUser,
    NewUser@410Server2012,user
```

You add a data record for each user you need to create. Creating this file manually is no time saver compared with using `dsadd` in a batch file or even using Active Directory Users and Computers. If you have a database of several hundred users you need to create, however, you could create this file from the database easily if you have a little experience in Access or other database programs. A major drawback of `csvde` is that you can't set passwords with it, so all accounts are disabled until you create a password for each account that meets complexity requirements. As a workaround, you can temporarily set the password policy for the domain to allow blank passwords.

Activity 7-17: Using `csvde` to Create Users

Time Required: 10 minutes
Objective: Create a text file to use with `csvde` to import users.

Required Tools and Equipment: 410Server1
Description: You have a large database of users, and you need to create user accounts for them. You have heard of the `csvde` command but haven't used it. You want to create a file to import test users before writing code to create the file with a database program.

1. If necessary, log on to 410Server1 as **Administrator**.

2. Start Notepad and type the following, pressing Enter after each line:

In the following example, take care to type the second and third lines on one line, and then type the fourth and fifth lines on one line.

```
dn,SamAccountName,userPrincipalName,objectClass
"cn=CSV User1,ou=TestOU1,dc=410Server2012,dc=local",CSVUser1,
CSVUser1@410Server2012.local,user
"cn=CSV User2,ou=TestOU1,dc=410Server2012,dc=local",CSVUser2,
CSVUser2@410Server2012.local,user
```

4. Click **File**, **Save As** from the menu. In the File name text box, type **"C:\csvusers.csv"**, and then click **Save**. Exit Notepad.

5. Open a command prompt window. Type **cd ** and press **Enter** to move to the root of the C drive where you saved the file. Type **csvde -i -f csvusers.csv** and press **Enter**. You should see a message stating that two entries were modified successfully and the command was successful.

6. Close the command prompt window, and open Active Directory Users and Computers. Click the **TestOU1** OU and verify that the users were created. You'll see that the accounts are disabled.

7. Leave Active Directory Users and Computers open if you're continuing to the next activity; otherwise, log off or shut down 410Server1.

Creating Users with `ldifde`   The LDIF format is considerably different from the CSV format, but the idea is the same. Instead of a header line followed by data records, each object consists of several lines, with each one specifying an action or attribute. Here's an example of a file for creating a user:

```
dn: cn=LDF User1,ou=TestOU1,dc=410Server2012,dc=local

changetype: add

ObjectClass: user

SamAccountName: LDFUser1

UserPrincipalName: LDFUser1@410Server2012.local
```

Aside from the format, the data is no different from what's in a CSV file, except the `changetype` entry, which can be `add`, `modify`, or `delete` (depending on what you're doing with objects). One common use of `ldifde` is exporting users from one domain and importing them to another domain.

Activity 7-18: Using `ldifde` to Create Users

Time Required: 10 minutes
Objective: Create a text file to use with `ldifde` to import users.

Required Tools and Equipment: 410Server1
Description: You have a large database of users, and you need to create user accounts for them. You have heard of the `ldifde` command but haven't used it. You want to create a file to import a test user before writing code to create the file with a database program.

1. If necessary, log on to your server as **Administrator**.

2. Start Notepad and type the following, pressing **Enter** after each line:

```
dn: cn=LDF User1,ou=TestOU1,dc=410Server2012,dc=local

changetype: add

ObjectClass: user

SamAccountName: LDFUser1

UserPrincipalName: LDFUser1@410Server2012.local
```

4. Click **File, Save As** from the menu. In the File name text box, type **"C:\ldfusers.ldf"**, and then click **Save**. Exit Notepad.

5. Open a command prompt window. Type **cd ** and press **Enter**. Type **ldifde -i -f ldfusers.ldf** and press **Enter**. You should see a message stating that the command was successful.

6. Close the command prompt window, and open Active Directory Users and Computers, if necessary. Click the **TestOU1** OU and verify that LDFUser1 was created. If necessary, refresh the view so that you can see this user.

7. Log off or shut down 410Server1.

Chapter Summary

- OUs, the building blocks of the Active Directory structure in a domain, can be designed to mirror a company's organizational chart. Delegation of control can be used to give certain users some management authority in an OU. You need to be familiar with OU permissions and permission inheritance to understand delegation of control.

- OU permissions and permission inheritance work much the same way as they do in the file system. You must enable the Advanced Features option in ADUC to view an object's Security tab and other folders and tabs.

- User accounts provide a way for users to authenticate to the network and contain user information that can be used in a company directory. There are three categories of users in Windows: local, domain, and built-in. The two built-in accounts are Administrator and Guest.

- Active Directory Users and Computers and Active Directory Administrative Center are GUI tools for creating and maintaining user accounts. User account names must be unique in a domain, aren't case sensitive, and must be 20 or fewer characters. A complex password is required by default. A naming standard should be devised before creating user accounts. At the very least, the user's full name, logon name, and password are required to create a user account in Active Directory Users and Computers.

- User templates facilitate creating users who have some attributes in common, such as group memberships. Administrators can use the multiple edit feature of Active Directory Users and Computers to edit certain fields for several users at once.

- This chapter covers the user account properties in the General, Account, Profile, and Member Of tabs. The Account tab contains information that controls many aspects of logging on to the domain, such as logon name, logon hours, logon locations, account lockout, and account expiration. The Profile tab contains information about where a user's profile data is stored and can specify a logon script.

- Groups are the main security principal used to grant rights and permissions. The two group types are security and distribution, but only security groups are used to assign permissions and rights. The group type can be converted from security to distribution and vice versa.

- There are three group scopes in Active Directory: domain local, global, and universal. (Local groups are found on domain member computers and stand-alone computers.) The recommended use of groups can be summarized with the acronyms AGDLP and AGGUDLP. Groups can be nested, as long as the rules for group membership are followed. Group scope can be converted, with some restrictions. There are default groups in the Builtin and Users folders, and there are special identity groups with dynamic membership that can't be managed.

- Computers that are domain members have computer accounts in Active Directory. Domain users logging on to member computers can use single sign-on forest-wide and perform Active Directory searches. Computers can be managed by using group policies and remote MMCs.

- Computer accounts are created automatically when a computer joins a domain or manually by an administrator. By default, computer accounts are created in the Computers folder, but to use group policies, they must be moved to an OU that has a group policy linked to it.

- You can automate account management by using command-line tools, such as `dsadd` and `dsmod`, or PowerShell cmdlets. There are also the bulk import/export command-line programs `csvde` and `ldifde`. Command-line tools can be simplified by using batch files and piping.

Key Terms

contact An Active Directory object that usually represents a person for informational purposes only, much like an address book entry.

delegation of control The process of a user with higher security privileges assigning authority to perform certain tasks to a user with lesser security privileges; usually used to give a user administrative permission for an OU.

distribution group A group type used when you want to group users together, mainly for sending e-mails to several people at once with an Active Directory–integrated e-mail application, such as Microsoft Exchange.

domain local group A group scope that's the main security principal recommended for assigning rights and permissions to domain resources.

downlevel user logon name The user logon name field defined in a user account object that's used for backward-compatibility with OSs and applications that don't recognize the UPN format.

global group A group scope used mainly to group users from the same domain who have similar access and rights requirements. A global group's members can be user accounts and other global groups from the same domain. *See also* group scope.

group scope A property of a group that determines the reach of a group's application in a domain or a forest—for example, which security principals in a forest can be group members and to which forest resources a group can be assigned rights or permissions.

group type A property of a group that defines it as a security group or a distribution group.

local group A group created in the local SAM database on a member server or workstation or a stand-alone computer.

offline domain join A feature that allows a running computer or offline virtual disk to join a domain without contacting a domain controller.

piping Sending the output of one command as input to another command.

Security Accounts Manager (SAM) database A database on domain member and workgroup computers that holds the users and groups defined on the local computer.

security groups A group type that's the main Active Directory object administrators use to manage network resource access and grant rights to users. *See also* group type.

special identity group A group whose membership is controlled dynamically by Windows and doesn't appear as an object in Active Directory Users and Computers or Active Directory Administrative Center; can be assigned permissions by adding it to resources' DACLs.

universal group A group scope that can contain users from any domain in the forest and be assigned permission to resources in any domain in the forest. *See also* group scope.

universal group membership caching A feature enabled on a domain controller that causes it to keep a local copy of universal group membership after querying a global catalog server.

user template A user account that's copied to create users with common attributes.

Review Questions

1. Which of the following is true about organizational units? (Choose all that apply.)

   a. OUs can be added to an object's DACL.

   b. OUs can be nested.

   c. A group policy can be linked to an OU.

   d. Only members of Domain Administrators can work with OUs.

2. You want to see the permissions set on an OU, so you open Active Directory Users and Computers, right-click the OU, and click Properties. After clicking all the available tabs, you can't seem to find where permissions are set in the Properties dialog box. What should you do?

   a. Log on as a member of Enterprise Admins and try again.

   b. In the Properties dialog box, click the Advanced button.

   c. Right-click the OU and click Security.

   d. In Active Directory Users and Computers, click View, Advanced Features.

3. You have hired a new junior administrator and created an account for her with the logon name JrAdmin. You want her to be able to reset user accounts and modify group memberships for users in the Operations department whose accounts are in the Operations OU. You want to do this with the least effort and without giving JrAdmin broader capabilities. What should you do?

   a. In Active Directory Administrative Center, right-click the Operations OU, click Properties, and click Managed By.

   b. In Active Directory Users and Computers, right-click the Operations OU and click Delegate Control.

   c. Open the Operations Security tab and add JrAdmin to the DACL.

   d. Add JrAdmin to the Password Managers domain local group.

4. Another administrator has been changing permissions on the Operations OU by adding some groups and users to the DACL. You're concerned that the JrAdmin account has been given more access to the OU than it should have. You need to see all permissions the JrAdmin account has to the Operations OU. What should you do?

   a. In Active Directory Users and Computers, right-click the JrAdmin account, click Properties, and view her group memberships.

   b. In Active Directory Administrative Center, run the Permissions Wizard and select JrAdmin as the target.

   c. In Active Directory Users and Computers, enable Advanced Features, open the Operations OU's Properties dialog box, and navigate to the Effective Access tab.

   d. In Active Directory Administrative Center, open JrAdmin's account properties and click the Manager Of tab.

5. An account named SrAdmin created an OU named QandA under the Operations OU. Which of the following is true by default?

   a. Domain Admins is the owner of the QandA OU.

   b. SrAdmin is the owner of the QandA OU and all objects created inside it.

   c. SrAdmin has all standard permissions except Full control for the QandA OU.

   d. The Everyone group has Read permission to the QandA OU.

6. Which of the following is a user account category? (Choose all that apply.)

   a. Local

   b. Global

   c. Domain

   d. Universal

7. Which of the following is a built-in user account? (Choose all that apply.)

   a. Administrator

   b. Operator

   c. Anonymous

   d. Guest

8. Sam*Snead is a valid user account name. True or False?

9. Which of the following is true about user accounts in a Windows Server 2012/R2 domain? (Choose all that apply.)

    a. The name can be from 1 to 20 characters.

    b. The name is case sensitive.

    c. The name can't be duplicated in the domain.

    d. Using default settings, PASSWORD123 is a valid password.

10. Which of the following account options can't be set together? (Choose all that apply.)

    a. User must change password at next logon.

    b. Store password using reversible encryption.

    c. Password never expires.

    d. Account is disabled.

11. Global groups can have domain local groups as members. True or False?

12. Jane has left the company. Her user account is a member of several groups and has permissions and rights to a number of forest-wide resources. Jane's replacement will arrive in a couple of weeks and needs access to the same resources. What's the best course of action?

    a. Find all groups Jane is a member of and make a note of them. Delete Jane's user account and create a new account for the new employee. Add the new account to all the groups Jane was a member of.

    b. Copy Jane's user account and give the copy another name.

    c. Disable Jane's account. When the new employee arrives, rename Jane's account, assign it a new password, and enable it again.

    d. Export Jane's account and then import it when the new employee arrives. Rename the account and assign it a new password.

13. Over the past several months, Tom, who has access to sensitive company information, has logged on to computers in other departments and left them without logging off. You have discussed the matter with him, but the problem continues to occur. You're concerned that someone could access these sensitive resources easily. What's the best way to solve this problem?

    a. Ensure that all computers Tom is logging on to have screen savers set to lock the computer after 15 minutes of inactivity.

    b. Specify which computers Tom can log on to in the domain by using the Log On To option in his account's properties.

    c. Move Tom's account and computer to another domain, thereby making it impossible for him to log on to computers that are members of different domains.

    d. Disable local logon for Tom's account on all computers except Tom's.

14. You have noticed inappropriate use of computers for gaming and Internet downloads by some employees who come in after hours and on weekends. These employees don't have valid work assignments during these times. You have been asked to devise a solution for these employees that doesn't affect other employees or these employees' computers during working hours. What's the best solution?

    a. Install personal firewall software on their computers in an attempt to block the gaming and Internet traffic.

    b. Request that the Maintenance Department change the locks on their office doors so that they can enter only during prescribed hours.

    c. Set the Logon Hours options for their user accounts.

    d. Before you leave each evening and before the weekend, disable these employees' accounts and reenable them the next working day.

15. The Users domain local group in the Builtin folder can be a member of the local Administrators group on a Windows client OS computer. True or False?

16. Which of the following is considered a security principal? (Choose all that apply.)

    a. Contacts

    b. Computer accounts

    c. User accounts

    d. Distribution groups

17. Which of the following is a valid group scope? (Choose all that apply.)

    a. Global

    b. Domain local

    c. Forest

    d. Domain global

18. What happens if a security group that's an ACE in a shared folder is converted to a distribution group?

    a. A security group can't be converted to a distribution group if it has already been assigned permissions.

    b. The group is removed from the DACL automatically.

    c. The group remains in the DACL, but the ACE has no effect on members' access to the resource.

    d. The group remains in the DACL, and permissions assigned to the group affect access to the resource as though it were still a security group.

19. Which of the following can be a member of a universal group? (Choose all that apply.)

    a. User accounts from the local domain only

    b. Global groups from any domain in the forest

    c. Other universal groups

    d. Domain local groups from the local domain only

20. Which direct group scope conversion is allowed?

    a. Domain local to universal, provided no domain local group is already a member

    b. Global to domain local, without restriction

    c. Domain local to global, provided no domain local group is already a member

    d. Universal to global, without restriction

21. Which of the following is true about the Users domain local group?

    a. It's in the Users folder.

    b. It can be converted to a global group.

    c. Domain Users is a member.

    d. Its members can log on locally to a domain controller.

22. A domain user logging on to the domain becomes a member of which special identity group?

    a. Creator Owner

    b. System

    c. Authenticated Users

    d. Anonymous Logon

23. Which of the following creates a file named `disabled.txt` containing a list of disabled Active Directory accounts?

    a. `net accounts /show disabled`

    b. `ldifde -accounts -property=enabled -value=false`

    c. `Query-Account -Disable=True | disabled.txt`

    d. `Search-ADAccount -AccountDisabled > disabled.txt`

24. A user is having trouble logging on to the domain from a computer that has been out of service for several months, and nobody else can seem to log on from the computer. What should you try first to solve the problem?

    a. Reinstall Windows on the workstation and create a new computer account in the domain.

    b. Rename the computer and create a new computer account with the new name.

    c. Reset the computer account, remove the computer from the domain, and rejoin it to the domain.

    d. Disable the computer account, remove the computer from the domain, and rejoin it to the domain.

25. Which commands can you use together to change attributes of several users at once?

    a. `dsget` and `dsadd`

    b. `dsget` and `dsmod`

    c. `dsquery` and `dsmod`

    d. `dsquery` and `dsget`

Case Projects

Case Project 7-1: Creating an OU Structure

In Case Project 6-1, you outlined the OU structure for CSM Tech Publishing. Now it's time to put it into practice. Because you're unlikely to have a domain controller to dedicate to these activities, your OU structure should simulate the csmtech.local domain container. CSM Tech Publishing has four main departments: Executive, Marketing, Engineering, and Operations. Create this OU structure on your domain controller after creating an OU named csmtech.local to simulate the domain container. When you're finished, your OU structure should look like Figure 7-27.

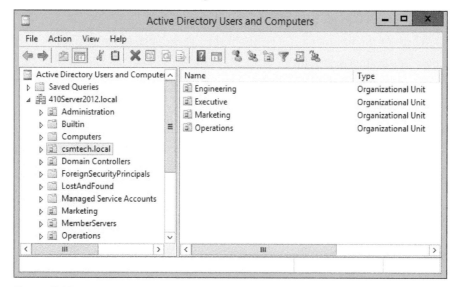

Figure 7-27   The CSM Tech Publishing OU structure

Case Project 7-2: Creating Groups for Your Domain

Create groups in the OUs under csmtech.local that are suitable for the domain structure. The group members are the users in each department the OU represents. Explain your group-naming standard, and specify the group scope you're using for these groups. Are any groups candidates for nesting?

Case Project 7-3: Creating User Templates for Each Department

You know you'll be creating several users for each department in csmtech.local. Users in each department will have some common attributes, specifically membership in their departmental groups and information in the Organization tab's Department and Company fields. Create a user template for each department. What are some best practices you should follow when creating this user template?

Case Project 7-4: Creating Users for Your Departments

Using the user template from Case Project 7-3, create two users in each department. For simplicity's sake, name each user *Department*User*X* with the full name *Department* User*X*. For example, in the Operations Department, the first user is OperationsUser1 with the full name Operations User1. Assign the password Password01 to each user. Create a third user in each department named Mgr*Department*, so for the Operations Department, the user is MgrOperations with the full name Manager Operations.

Case Project 7-5: Using Command-Line Account Management

Use dsadd to create a Managers group in the csmtech.local OU. Next, use dsquery and dsmod with a pipe to add the manager accounts you created in Case Project 7-4 to the Managers group. Write down the commands you used and turn them into your instructor, or take a screenshot of the commands and their output.

chapter 8

Configuring Group Policies

After reading this chapter and completing the exercises, you will be able to:

- Describe the architecture and processing of group policies

- Configure group policy settings, and manage and monitor group policies

- Work with security templates

- Configure Windows Firewall with Group Policy

Group Policy is a powerful tool for network administrators to manage domain controllers, member servers, member computers, and users. It allows administrators to manage most aspects of computer and user environments centrally through Active Directory. An administrator's solid understanding of how to get the most out of group policies can relieve some of the burden of user and computer management. Even more important, designing and applying group policies correctly result in a more secure network.

This chapter covers the architecture of group policies so that you understand what a GPO is and how and where GPOs can be applied to your Active Directory structure. In addition, you learn about the myriad security settings and user and computer environment settings that can be configured through group policies. You also examine how to apply standard security settings throughout your network and audit computers that aren't in compliance with designated standards. Finally, you take a look at how to configure Windows Firewall with Group Policy.

Group Policy Architecture

Table 8-1 describes what you need for the hands-on activities in this chapter.

Table 8-1 Activity requirements

Activity	Requirements	Notes
Activity 8-1: Working with Local GPOs	410Server1, 410Win8	
Activity 8-2: Browsing GPTs	410Server1	
Activity 8-3: Viewing the Properties of a GPC	410Server1	
Activity 8-4: Creating, Linking, and Unlinking GPOs	410Server1	
Activity 8-5: Configuring and Testing a GPO	410Server1, 410Win8	
Activity 8-6: Creating and Using Starter GPOs	410Server1	
Activity 8-7: Demonstrating GPO Inheritance Blocking	410Server1, 410Win8	
Activity 8-8: Demonstrating GPO Enforcement	410Server1, 410Win8	
Activity 8-9: Setting a Domain Policy	410Server1	
Activity 8-10: Using GPO Security Filtering	410Server1, 410Win8	
Activity 8-11: Disabling Default Auditing	410Server1, 410Win8	
Activity 8-12: Working with Audit Policies	410Server1	
Activity 8-13: Reviewing User Rights Assignment and Security Options Settings	410Server1	
Activity 8-14: Creating a Software Restriction Policy	410Server1, 410Win8	
Activity 8-15: Creating an Application Control Policy	410Server1, 410Win8	
Activity 8-16: Creating the ADMX Central Store	410Server1	
Activity 8-17: Creating a Security Template	410Server1, 410Win8	
Activity 8-18: Exploring the `secedit.exe` Command	410Server1, 410Win8	
Activity 8-19: Creating an Inbound Firewall Rule	410Server1, 410Win8	

© 2015 Cengage Learning®

The processes of centrally maintaining lists of computer and user settings, replicating these settings to all domain controllers, and applying these settings to users and computers are complex. The architecture of group policies is equally complex, at least when you're trying to envision the architecture as a whole. When broken down into their constituent parts, however, the architecture is easier to grasp. Group policy architecture and functioning involve the following components:

- *GPOs*—A GPO is an object containing policy settings that affect user and computer operating environments and security. GPOs can be local (stored on users' computers) or Active Directory objects linked to sites, domains, and OUs.

- *Replication*—Replication of Active Directory–based GPOs ensures that all domain controllers (DCs) have a current copy of each GPO. Changes to GPOs can be made on any DC and are replicated to all other DCs.

- *Scope and inheritance*—The scope of a group policy defines which users and computers are affected by its settings. The scope can be a single computer (in the case of a local GPO) or an OU, a domain, or a site. Like permissions, policy settings applied to users and computers are inherited from parent containers, and like permission inheritance, an administrator can override the default behavior of group policy inheritance.

- *Creating and linking*—GPOs are created in the Group Policy Management console and can then be linked to one or more Active Directory containers. Multiple GPOs can be linked to the same container.

Group Policy Objects

A GPO, the main component of group policies, contains policy settings for managing many aspects of domain controllers, member servers, member computers, and users. There are two main types of GPOs: local GPOs and domain GPOs.

Local GPOs   Local GPOs are stored on local computers and can be edited with the Group Policy Object Editor snap-in (see Figure 8-1). To use this tool, you add the Group Policy Editor snap-in to a custom MMC or enter `gpedit.msc` at the command line to open an already con-figured MMC called Local Group Policy Editor. You use one of these tools to edit local GPOs on workgroup computers manually. The policy settings on domain member computers can be affected by domain GPOs linked to the site, domain, or OU in Active Directory. Settings in local GPOs that are inherited from domain GPOs can't be changed on the local computer; only settings that are undefined or not configured by domain GPOs can be edited locally.

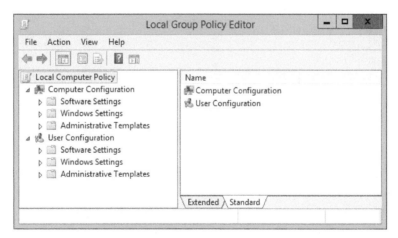

Figure 8-1   The Local Group Policy Editor

When you run `gpedit.msc`, you open a local GPO named Local Computer Policy containing Computer Configuration and User Configuration nodes. The policies defined in this GPO, when configured on non-domain member computers, apply by default to all users who log on to the computer. For example, a computer used in a public environment, such as a kiosk, might have policies that severely restrict what users can do on the computer.

Windows has a preconfigured MMC called Local Security Policy that enables you to edit policies in just the Security Settings node of the local GPO. You access this MMC via Administrative Tools in Control Panel or by entering `secpol.msc` at the command line.

In addition to the Local Computer Policy GPO, there are local GPOs, described in the following list, that allow different policy settings depending on who logs on to the computer. The policies in these GPOs aren't configured, so they have no effect on users until they're configured. In addition, these GPOs have only a User Configuration node, so policies are limited to user-related settings:

- *Local Administrators GPO*—Members of the local Administrators group are affected by settings in this GPO. The default membership includes the local Administrator account and the Domain Admins global group when the computer is a domain member.

- *Local Non-Administrators GPO*—All users who log on to the computer who aren't members of the local Administrators group are affected by settings in this GPO, including domain users when the computer is a domain member.

- *User-specific GPO*—A user-specific GPO is created for each account (except Guest) in the local Security Accounts Manager (SAM) database.

To access these GPOs, first add the Group Policy Object Editor snap-in to an MMC. Instead of accepting the default Local Computer Policy when asked to select a GPO, click Browse to open the dialog box shown in Figure 8-2, click the Users tab, and select one of the GPOs. Local GPOs are intended to be configured on non-domain computers because domain GPOs take precedence over local GPOs, and administration is centralized by using domain GPOs. Configuring the domain-based group policy "Turn off Local Group Policy objects processing" causes member computers to ignore local GPOs. Doing so is a good idea to ensure that all policies are controlled from the domain.

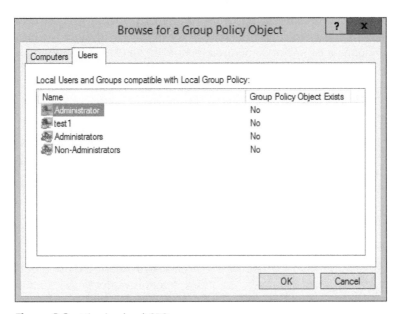

Figure 8-2   Viewing local GPOs

Three of the four local GPOs can contain settings that affect a particular user logging on to a Windows computer. The Local Computer Policy object is processed first for all users and is the only local GPO that affects the computer configuration. The local Administrators or local Non-Administrators GPO is processed next, if configured, and the user-specific GPO is processed last, if configured. Any conflicting settings are resolved in the same order. In other words, the last configured policy setting that's applied takes precedence.

Take a look at an example: User MSmith has an account on a computer that's not a domain member. The Local Computer Policy is configured to prohibit access to Control Panel, and the Control Panel policy isn't configured in the Non-Administrators GPO. MSmith has a user-specific GPO that enables access to Control Panel. When MSmith logs on, the Local Computer Policy is processed first, which disables access to Control Panel; next, the Non-Administrators policy is processed, which has no effect on the Control Panel policy because it's not configured. Finally, the user-specific MSmith GPO is processed, which allows Control Panel access, so MSmith has Control Panel access.

Local GPOs (except for the Local Computer Policy) were introduced in Windows Server 2008 and Vista, so they weren't available in Windows XP and earlier.

Activity 8-1: Working with Local GPOs

Time Required: 20 minutes
Objective: Configure local GPOs.

Required Tools and Equipment: 410Win8 and 410Server1
Description: You want to become familiar with the local GPOs in Windows, so you log on to 410Win8 with the *local* Administrator account, configure some local GPOs, and create a local user account. Then you see how local GPOs can affect different users.

1. Log on to 410Win8 with the *local* **Win8User** account. You need to enter the username as **410Win8\Win8User**; otherwise, Windows assumes you want to log on to the domain.

2. Click the **Desktop** tile. Right-click **Start** and click **Control Panel** to make sure you have access to it, and then close Control Panel. Right-click **Start**, click **Run**, type **gpedit.msc** in the Open text box, and press **Enter** to open the Local Group Policy Editor for the Local Computer Policy GPO.

3. Click to expand **User Configuration, Administrative Templates,** and then click the **Control Panel** node.

4. In the right pane, double-click **Prohibit access to Control Panel and PC settings**. In the Prohibit access to Control Panel and PC settings dialog box, click **Enabled,** and then click **OK.** Close the Local Group Policy Editor.

5. Right-click **Start** and click **Control Panel.** In the message box explaining that the action has been canceled because of restrictions in effect on the computer, click **OK.**

6. Right-click **Start,** click **Run,** type **mmc** in the Open text box, and press **Enter.** If necessary, in the User Account Control message box, click **Yes.**

7. In the MMC window, click **File, Add/Remove Snap-in** from the menu. In the Available snap-ins list box, click **Group Policy Object Editor,** and then click **Add.** The Group Policy Wizard starts.

8. In the Select Group Policy Object window, click **Browse.** In the Browse for a Group Policy Object dialog box, click the **Users** tab. Click **Administrators** in the Name list box, and then click **OK.** Click **Finish** and then **OK.**

9. Click to expand **Local Computer\Administrators Policy.** Click to expand **User Configuration** and **Administrative Templates,** and then click the **Control Panel** node. (*Hint:* You might want to click the Standard tab at the bottom so that you can see the policy setting descriptions better.)

10. In the right pane, double-click **Prohibit access to the Control Panel and PC settings.** In the dialog box for configuring the policy, click **Disabled,** and then click **OK.**

11. Right-click **Start** and click **Control Panel,** which opens. The Administrators local GPO overrode the Local Computer Policy (because you're logged on as Win8User, which is a member of the Administrators group). Close Control Panel.

12. Open Computer Management by right-clicking **Start** and clicking **Computer Management.** Click to expand the **Local Users and Groups** snap-in, and then click the **Users** folder. Right-click the middle pane and click **New User.**

8

13. In the New User dialog box, type **TestGPO** in the User name text box and **Password01** in the Password and Confirm password text boxes.

14. Click to clear the **User must change password at next logon** check box. Click **Create**, and then click **Close**. Close Computer Management.

15. Log off 410Win8 and log back on as **TestGPO** with **Password01**. You have to enter the username as **410Win8\TestGPO** so that Windows knows you're logging on to the local computer. While you're waiting for TestGPO to log on, start 410Server1, if necessary.

16. On 410Win8, click the **Desktop** tile, and then right-click **Start** and click **Control Panel**. You see the same message as in Step 5. Click **OK**. Because TestGPO isn't an administrator and doesn't have a user-specific GPO configured, the default Local Computer Policy takes effect.

17. Log off 410Win8, and log back on to the domain from your 410Win8 computer as **testuser1**.

18. Right-click **Start** and click **Control Panel**. You see the same message as in Steps 5 and 16, which demonstrates that the Local Computer Policy affects domain users as well as local users. The only local GPO that doesn't affect domain users is the user-specific GPO, which can be configured for users only in the local SAM database. Click **OK**.

19. Log off and log back on to 410Win8 as **Win8User**. (Remember to log on as 410Win8\ Win8User.) Open the Group Policy Object Editor for the Local Computer Policy (referring to Step 2 if you need help). Change the "Prohibit access to the Control Panel and PC settings" policy back to **Not Configured**, and then click **OK**. Close the Local Group Policy Editor.

20. Shut down 410Win8, but leave 410Server1 running if you're continuing to the next activity.

Domain GPOs   Domain GPOs are stored in Active Directory on domain controllers. They can be linked to a site, a domain, or an OU and affect users and computers whose accounts are stored in these containers. A domain GPO is represented by an Active Directory object, but it's composed of two separate parts: a Group Policy Template (GPT) and a Group Policy Container (GPC). The GPT and GPC have different functions and hold very different information, but they do have these things in common:

- *Naming structure*—Each GPO is assigned a globally unique identifier (GUID), a 128-bit value represented by 32 hexadecimal digits that Windows uses to ensure unique object IDs. The GPT and GPC associated with a GPO are stored in a folder with the same name as the GPO's GUID. This naming structure makes associating each GPO with its GPT and GPC easier.

- *Folder structure*—Each GPT and GPC has two subfolders: Machine and User. The Machine folder stores information related to a GPO's Computer Configuration node, and the User folder stores information about the User Configuration node.

One reason administrators must understand the structure of GPOs is so that they know where to look when problems happen, particularly with replication of GPOs (covered later in this chapter in "Group Policy Replication"). To that end, you examine GPT and GPC components more closely in the following sections.

Group Policy Templates   A Group Policy Template (GPT) isn't stored in Active Directory but in a folder in the SYSVOL share on a domain controller. It contains all the policy settings that make up a GPO as well as related files, such as scripts. Every GPO has a GPT associated with it. The local path to GPT folders on a domain controller is *%systemroot%*\SYSVOL\ sysvol*domain*\Policies; *%systemroot%* represents the drive letter and folder name where the Windows OS is stored, usually C:\Windows, and *domain* is the domain name. Each GPT is actually a series of folders and files, but the root folder has the name of the GPO's GUID. Figure 8-3 shows the Policies folder with three GPT folders.

The names of GPT folders look random, but two folders have the same name on every domain controller. The folder starting with 6AC1 is the GPT for the Default Domain Controllers Policy, and the folder starting with 31B2 is the GPT for the Default Domain Policy. The third folder is the GPT for GPO1 you created in Chapter 6.

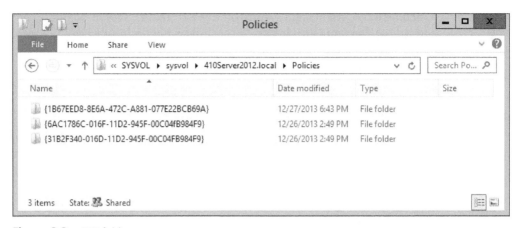

Figure 8-3 GPT folders

When a GPO is created, files and subfolders are created under the root folder. The number of files and subfolders in each GPT folder varies depending on which policies have been configured, but each one has at least these three items:

- GPT.INI—This file contains the version number used to determine when a GPO has been modified. Every time a GPO changes, the version number is updated. When GPO replication occurs, DCs use this version number to determine whether the local copy of the GPO is up to date.
- *Machine*—This folder contains subfolders that store policy settings related to the Computer Configuration node.
- *User*—This folder contains subfolders that store policy settings related to the User Configuration node.

A GPO with few policy settings defined or configured has only a few other subfolders and files under the root folder. For example, you have made only a few changes to the Default Domain Controllers Policy, which is in the folder starting with 6AC1. If you browse the Machine and User subfolders, you'll likely find only one additional file, GptTmpl.inf. This file contains settings configured in the Security Settings node under Computer Configuration.

Activity 8-2: Browsing GPTs

Time Required: 15 minutes
Objective: Browse subfolders and files in a GPT folder.

Required Tools and Equipment: 410Server1
Description: You want to get a better idea of how group policies are structured, so you explore the folders where the GPT component of GPOs is located.

1. Log on to 410Server1 as **Administrator**, if necessary.

2. Open File Explorer, and navigate to **C:\Windows\SYSVOL\sysvol\410Server2012.local\ Policies**, where you should see a list of folders similar to Figure 8-3, shown previously.

3. Double-click the folder starting with **6AC1**, which is the Default Domain Controllers Policy GPT. Double-click the **GPT.INI** file to open it in Notepad. Notice the version number, which changes each time the GPO is modified. Exit Notepad.

4. Click to expand the **MACHINE\Microsoft\Windows NT\SecEdit** folder, and double-click the **GptTmpl.inf** file to open it in Notepad. Knowing the details of what's in this or other GPT files isn't important; you just need to know that they exist and how to find them. You'll probably recognize some information, however. Find the line starting with

"SeInteractiveLogonRight," and you'll see Domain Users in this line. In Activity 6-12, you added the Domain Users group to the "Allow log on locally" right, which is the setting this line pertains to. Exit Notepad.

5. Browse to the third GPT folder (the one that doesn't start with 6AC1 or 31B2), which is associated with the GPO (GPO1) you created and linked to TestOU1 in Activity 6-12. Double-click the **GPT.INI** file and make a note of the version number; you'll compare it with the GPC version number in the next activity.

6. Double-click the **User** folder, which contains the `Registry.pol` file, used to store policy settings that affect the Registry of the computer the policy is applied to. Double-click **Registry.pol.** You see a message stating that Windows can't open the file. Click **Try an app on this PC** to display a list of apps. Click to select the **Use this app for all .pol files** check box, and then click **Notepad**.

7. The `Registry.pol` file opens in Notepad. Scroll to the right to see all the information in it. This file contains the key and value of Registry entries. In this case, the key is related to File Explorer, and the value is NoControlPanel, which is the policy you set in Activity 6-12. Exit Notepad.

8. Close all open windows, but stay logged on if you're continuing to the next activity.

Group Policy Containers   A **Group Policy Container (GPC)** is an Active Directory object stored in the System\Policies folder and can be viewed in Active Directory Users and Computers with the Advanced Features option enabled. A GPC stores GPO properties and status information but no actual policy settings. Like a GPT, the folder name of each GPC is the same as the GPO's GUID.

A GPC is composed of several attributes you can view in the Attribute Editor tab of its Properties dialog box, as shown in Figure 8-4. Although deciphering the purpose of each attribute isn't always easy, some information the GPC provides includes the following:

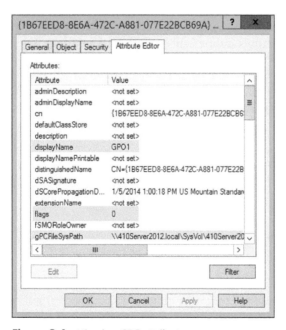

Figure 8-4   Viewing GPC attributes

- *Name of the GPO*—The displayName attribute tells you the name of the GPO the GPC is associated with.

- *File path to GPT*—The gPCFileSysPath attribute specifies the Universal Naming Convention (UNC) path to the related GPT folder.

- *Version*—The versionNumber attribute should have the same version number as the `GPT.INI` file in the GPT folder.

- *Status*—The flags attribute contains a value that indicates the GPO's status. In Figure 8-4, it has the value 0, which indicates that the GPO is enabled. The value 3 means the GPO is disabled.

A GPC might seem less interesting than a GPT, but it's just as important. This Active Directory object links the GPO to Active Directory, which is critical for GPO replication to all domain controllers.

Activity 8-3: Viewing the Properties of a GPC

Time Required: 20 minutes
Objective: View the properties of a GPC.

Required Tools and Equipment: 410Server1
Description: You want to get a better idea of how group policies are structured. Now that you have a handle on the purpose and location of GPTs, you want to explore the other component of GPOs, the GPC.

1. Log on to 410Server1 as **Administrator**, if necessary.

2. Open Active Directory Users and Computers. To verify that the Advanced Features option is enabled, click **View** on the menu bar, and click **Advanced Features** if it's not already selected with a check mark.

3. Click to expand the **System** folder and then click the **Policies** folder to see the list of GPC folders, shown in Figure 8-5.

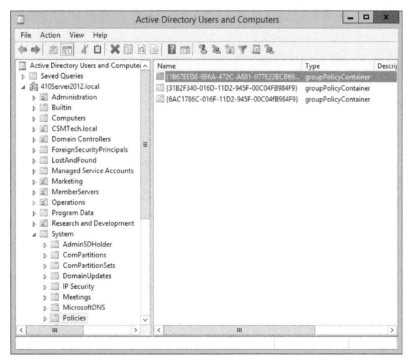

Figure 8-5   GPC folders in Active Directory

4. In the right pane, right-click the GPC folder associated with GPO1 (the one that *doesn't* start with 6AC1 or 31B2) and click **Properties**. In the Properties dialog box, click the **Attribute Editor** tab. Scroll down to view some attributes of the GPC; attributes are listed in alphabetical order. Although you can edit attributes here, it isn't recommended unless you're sure of the results.

5. Find the **versionNumber** attribute. It should have the same value you noted for the GPT.INI file in Activity 8-2.

6. Find the **flags** attribute. Its value should be 0, indicating that the GPO is enabled. Click **Cancel**.

7. Open the Group Policy Management console from the Tools menu in Server Manager. In the left pane, click to expand **TestOU1**. Click **GPO1**, and in the right pane, click the **Details** tab (see Figure 8-6).

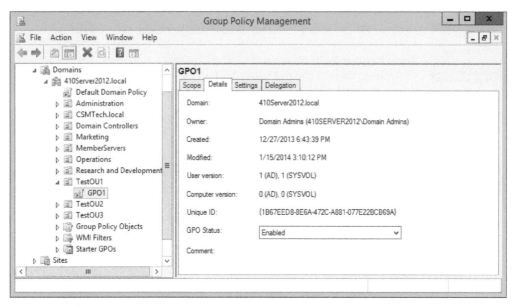

Figure 8-6   The Details tab for a GPO

8. Click the **GPO Status** list arrow, click **All settings disabled**, and then click **OK**.

9. In Active Directory Users and Computers, open the Properties dialog box of the GPC folder associated with GPO1. Click the **Attribute Editor** tab, and then view the value of the flags attribute. It's 3, indicating that the GPO is disabled.

10. Click the **flags** attribute and click the **Edit** button. Type 0, and then click **OK** twice.

11. In the Group Policy Management console, click the **Refresh** toolbar icon or click **Action**, **Refresh** from the menu. The GPO status changes to Enabled because you changed the flags attribute to 0.

12. Close all open windows, and stay logged on for the next activity.

Group Policy Replication

Because the two components of a GPO are stored in different places on a DC, different methods are required to replicate GPOs to all domain controllers. GPCs, which are Active Directory objects, are replicated during normal Active Directory replication. GPTs, located in the SYSVOL share, are replicated by using one of these methods:

- *File Replication Service (FRS)*—FRS is used if you have DCs in your domain that are running versions of Windows Server earlier than Windows Server 2008.

- *Distributed File System Replication (DFSR)*—DFSR is used when all DCs are running Windows Server 2008 or later.

Of these two replication methods, DFSR is the more efficient and reliable. It's efficient because it uses an algorithm called remote differential compression (RDC) in which only data blocks that have changed are compressed and transferred across the network. DFSR is more reliable because of improvements in handling unexpected service shutdown that could corrupt data and because it uses a multimaster replication scheme.

Because GPCs and GPTs use different replication methods, they can become out of sync. As mentioned, GPCs are replicated when Active Directory replication occurs. Between DCs in the same site, this interval is about 15 seconds after a change occurs. Between DCs in different sites, the interval is usually much longer—minutes or even hours. DFSR of the SYSVOL share (and, therefore, the GPT) occurs immediately after a change is made. Strange and unpredictable results could occur when a client computer attempts to apply a GPO when the GPC and GPT aren't synchronized. However, starting with Windows XP, the client computer checks the version number of both components before applying GPO settings.

As long as replication services are running correctly, the most likely problem with GPO replication is a delay in clients receiving changes in policy settings. This problem usually occurs when multiple sites are involved. Replication problems can be diagnosed with `gpotool.exe`, which verifies the version and status of GPOs on all DCs and reports any discrepancies. This tool is part of the Windows Resource Kit and can be downloaded from the Microsoft Download Center.

Creating and Linking GPOs

Chapter 6 introduced you to the Default Domain Policy and Default Domain Controllers Policy, but undoubtedly you'll need to create your own GPOs and link them to Active Directory containers. In fact, if changes are necessary for domain policies or domain controller policies, creating new GPOs and linking them to containers is recommended instead of editing the default GPOs.

As you have learned, the main tools for managing, creating, and editing GPOs are the Group Policy Management console (GPMC, also called the Group Policy Management MMC) and the Group Policy Management Editor (GPME), both of which you used in Chapter 6. The purpose of using these tools is to carry out changes to the security and/or working environment for users or computers. There are several ways to go about this task:

- Edit an existing GPO that's linked to an Active Directory container.
- Link an existing GPO to an Active Directory container.
- Create a new GPO for an Active Directory container.
- Create a new GPO in the Group Policy Objects folder, which isn't linked to an Active Directory object.
- Create a new GPO by using a Starter GPO.

If you edit an existing GPO that's already linked to an Active Directory container, keep in mind that changes in policy settings take effect as soon as clients download them. In other words, there's no Save option in the GPME; changes are saved immediately. By default, client computers download GPOs at restart, and user policies are downloaded at the next logon. Therefore, the best practice is usually creating GPOs in the Group Policy Objects folder, and then linking them to the target Active Directory container after all changes have been made and tested. When you're changing several policy settings at once or are unsure of the effect policy changes will have, you should test policies before enabling them by using the following method:

1. Set up at least one test computer per OS used in the organization.
2. Join test computers to the domain and place their accounts in a test OU.
3. Create one or more test user accounts in the test OU.
4. Create the new GPO in the Group Policy Objects folder and set the policies you want.
5. Link the GPO to the test OU.
6. Restart and log on to the test computers with the test user accounts to observe the policy effects.
7. Make changes to the GPO, if necessary, and repeat Step 6 until the policy has the desired effect.
8. Unlink the policy from the test OU, and link it to the target Active Directory container.

Editing an Existing GPO   To edit an existing GPO, right-click it in the GPMC and click Edit, which opens the GPO in the GPME. In the GPMC, all GPOs are stored in the Group Policy Objects folder, and you can also find GPOs linked to an Active Directory container displayed as shortcut objects in the container to which they're linked. Checking whether and where a GPO is linked is a good idea before editing. To do this, select the GPO in the left pane of the GPMC and view the Scope tab in the right pane (see Figure 8-7). All Active Directory objects the GPO is linked to are listed for the selected location. In this figure, the domain is selected as the location, and you can also select Entire forest or All sites in the Display links in this location list box.

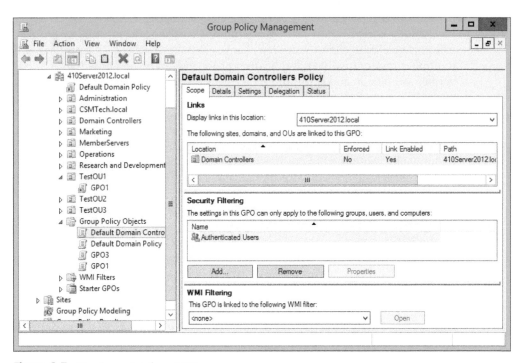

Figure 8-7   The Scope tab for a GPO

As mentioned, editing the two default GPOs is not advisable. One reason is that you can't test the GPO adequately because it's already linked to the domain or the Domain Controllers OU. Another reason is that you might want to revert to the default settings, and you could have difficulty remembering what was changed. The recommended method for making changes to domain policies is creating a new GPO and linking it to the domain. Remember: you can have multiple GPOs linked to the same container. The steps for making policy changes that affect the whole domain are as follows, assuming you already have the test computers, users, and OU set up as described previously:

1. Create the new GPO in the Group Policy Objects folder, and set the policies you want.

2. Link the GPO to the test OU, making sure to unlink any GPOs that are linked there from previous tests.

3. Test your policies by following Steps 6 to 8 in the previous list.

4. Make changes to the GPO, if necessary, and repeat testing until the policy has the effect you want.

5. Unlink the policy from the test OU, and link it to the domain.

You might wonder how this procedure tests domain-wide settings. Because a GPO can be linked to multiple containers, you could have linked the Default Domain Policy to the test OU as well. However, by default, policy settings are inherited by child objects, so settings in the Default Domain Policy affect objects in all Active Directory containers in the domain, including containers with another GPO linked. If you have two or more GPOs linked to the domain, as in Figure 8-8, GPOs are applied to objects in reverse of the specified link order. In this example, the NewGPO policy is applied, and then the Default Domain Policy is applied. If any settings conflict, the last setting applied takes precedence. GPO processing and inheritance are discussed later in the chapter in "Group Policy Scope."

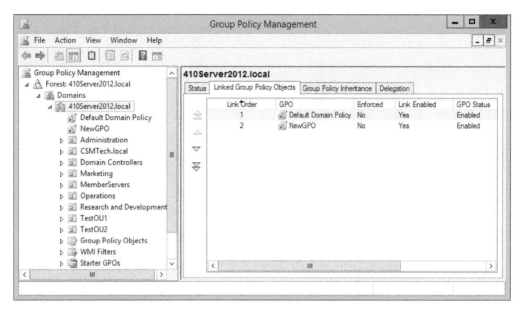

Figure 8-8   Multiple GPOs linked to a container

Creating a New GPO   There are two ways to create a new GPO in the GPMC. You can right-click the container you're linking the GPO to and select "Create a GPO in this domain, and Link it here," or you can right-click the Group Policy Objects folder and click New. The latter method is preferable for the reasons stated earlier. After creating a GPO, you can edit it and link it to an Active Directory container, if necessary. Because several GPOs can be linked to the same container, the best practice is to create GPOs that set policies narrowly focused on a category of settings, and then name the GPO accordingly. For example, if you need to config-ure policy settings related to the Network node under Computer Configuration, create a GPO named CompNetwork. If this policy will apply only to a certain container, you could include the container name in the GPO name—for example, TestOU-CompNetwork. Creating and nam-ing GPOs in this manner make it easier to identify the GPO that sets a particular policy and to troubleshoot GPO processing problems.

Activity 8-4: Creating, Linking, and Unlinking GPOs

Time Required: 15 minutes
Objective: Create, link, and unlink GPOs.

Required Tools and Equipment: 410Server1
Description: You want to be sure you know how to create and test GPOs, so you create a test OU and a GPO linked to it.

1. Log on to 410Server1 as **Administrator**, if necessary.

2. Open Active Directory Users and Computers, and create an OU named **TestOU3** under the domain node.

3. Open the Group Policy Management console. Right-click **TestOU3** and click **Create a GPO in this domain, and Link it here**. In the New GPO dialog box, type **GPO3** in the Name text box, and then click **OK**.

4. If necessary, click **TestOU3**. In the right pane, notice that GPO3 is listed as Enabled. Changes you make to the GPO take effect on any users or computers in TestOU3 that update their policies.

5. Right-click **GPO3** and click **Delete**. Click **OK**. This action deletes only the link to the GPO, not the GPO itself.

6. Click the **Group Policy Objects** folder to see all your GPOs, including the default GPOs.

7. Right-click **GPO3** and point to **GPO Status**. You can enable or disable a GPO or just disable the Computer Configuration or User Configuration settings.

8. Right-click the **TestOU3** OU and click **Link an Existing GPO**. In the Select GPO dialog box, click **GPO3**, and then click **OK**.

9. To link the same GPO to another container, right-click **TestOU1** and click **Link an Existing GPO**. In the Select GPO dialog box, click **GPO3**, and then click **OK**.

10. Click **TestOU1**. Notice that both GPO1 and GPO3 are linked to TestOU1. If both GPOs had the same policy setting configured but with different values, the value of the policy setting in GPO1 would take precedence because it would be applied last.

11. Click **GPO3** in the right pane and click the **up arrow** to the left of the Link Order column. GPO3 now has link order 1 and GPO1 has link order 2, so GPO3 takes precedence if any settings conflict.

12. Right-click **GPO3** and click **Delete**. Click **OK** in the message box asking you to confirm the deletion. Next, right-click **GPO1** and click **Delete**, and then click **OK**. No policies should be linked to TestOU1 now.

13. If you're continuing to the next activity, leave the Group Policy Management console and Active Directory Users and Computers open; otherwise, log off or shut down 410Server1.

Activity 8-5: Configuring and Testing a GPO

Time Required: 25 minutes
Objective: Configure and test a GPO.

Required Tools and Equipment: 410Server1 and 410Win8
Description: Now that you have a new GPO and an OU to test it on, you move the 410Win8 computer account to the new OU and test some computer settings in the GPO.

1. Start 410Win8. Log on to 410Server1 as **Administrator** and open Active Directory Users and Computers, if necessary.

2. Click the **Computers** folder, and drag the **410Win8** computer account to the **TestOU3** OU. If necessary, click **Yes** in the warning message about moving Active Directory objects.

3. Open the Group Policy Management console, if necessary. Click to expand the **TestOU3** OU. Right-click **GPO3** and click **Edit** to open it in the Group Policy Management Editor.

4. Click to expand **Computer Configuration, Policies, Windows Settings, Security Settings,** and **Local Policies,** and then click **User Rights Assignment**.

5. In the right pane, double-click **Allow log on locally** to open its Properties dialog box. Notice that the policy setting is currently not defined. Click the **Define these policy settings** check box, and then click **Add User or Group**. In the Add User or Group dialog box, click **Browse**. Type **Administrators** in the "Enter the object names to select" text box, and click **Check Names**. Click **OK** three times.

6. On 410Win8, log on to the domain as **Administrator**. Click the **Desktop** tile, right-click **Start**, click **Run**, type **secpol.msc** in the Open dialog box, and press **Enter**. The Local Security Policy MMC contains only the security settings for the local computer and is the section of the policy that was modified in Step 5.

7. Click to expand **Local Policies** and then click **User Rights Assignment.** Notice in Figure 8-9 that the icon next to the "Allow log on locally" policy looks like two towers and a scroll instead of the torn-paper icon next to the other policies. This icon indicates that the policy is defined by a domain GPO.

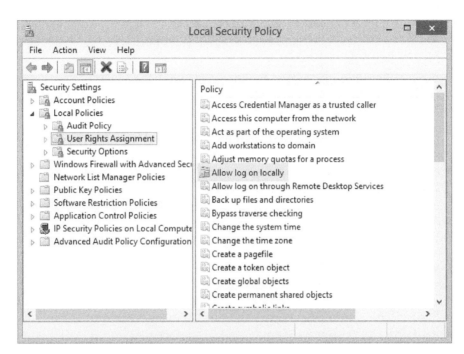

Figure 8-9 The Local Security Policy MMC with a policy set by a domain GPO

8. If the "Allow log on locally" policy doesn't have the domain GPO icon, the policy hasn't been updated yet on your 410Win8 computer. If so, do the following: Close the Local Security Policy MMC, open a command prompt window, type **gpupdate**, and press **Enter.** Gpupdate.exe immediately updates group policies on the local computer. When it's finished, open the Local Security Policy MMC and navigate back to User Rights Assignment.

In this chapter's activities, if gpupdate.exe doesn't seem to update policies on the local computer, try using gpupdate /force, which reapplies all policy settings, even those that haven't changed.

9. In the right pane, double-click **Allow log on locally.** In the list box of users and groups, click **Administrators.** Neither the Add User or Group nor the Remove button is active because no users, not even administrators, can override domain polices on the local computer. Click **Cancel.**

10. Log off 410Win8, and then try to log back on as **testuser1.** Because you have restricted local logon to Administrators only, you'll see the following message: "The sign-on method you're trying to use isn't allowed. For more info, contact your network administrator." The logon method referred to in the message is interactive logon or local logon. Click **OK.**

11. On 410Server1, change the **Allow log on locally** policy on GPO3 to undefined by clearing the **Define these policy settings** check box, and then click **OK** to close the Properties dialog box. Close Group Policy Management Editor.

12. On 410Win8, try again to log on as **testuser1**. You'll probably get the same message about not being able to log on because the policy hasn't been updated yet. Click **OK**. Restart the computer by clicking the button at the lower right of the logon window and clicking **Restart**. Recall that computer policies are updated every 90 minutes or when the computer restarts.

13. Log on to 410Win8 as **testuser1**. Only an administrator can run the Local Security Policy MMC, but there's a workaround with the `runas` command. On the desktop, right-click **Start** and click **Command Prompt (Admin)**. When prompted, type the username and password for Administrator, and click **Yes**.

14. At the command prompt, type **secpol.msc** and press **Enter**.

15. In the Local Security Policy console, click to expand **Local Policies** and **User Rights Assignment**. In the right pane, double-click **Allow log on locally** to view the list of users and groups assigned this permission. Notice that this right is now assigned from a local GPO rather than a domain GPO, so you can make changes if needed. Click **OK**.

16. Unlink **GPO3** from TestOU3.

17. Log off 410Win8. Stay logged on to 410Server1 if you're continuing to the next activity.

Using Starter GPOs   A **Starter GPO** is a GPO template, for lack of a better word, not to be confused with the GPTs discussed earlier. An administrator creates a Starter GPO to be used as a baseline for new GPOs, much like the user account templates discussed in Chapter 7.

When you create a GPO, the New GPO Wizard includes an option to use a Starter GPO. Starter GPOs are stored in the Starter GPOs folder in GPMC. As discussed, creating GPOs that focus on a narrow category of settings is a best practice. Starter GPOs can be used to specify a baseline for certain settings categories and then modified when the Starter GPO is used to create the new GPO.

To use a Starter GPO to create a new GPO, select one in the Source Starter GPO list box in the New GPO Wizard, or right-click a Starter GPO in the Starter GPOs folder and click New GPO From Starter GPO. To create a Starter GPO, right-click the Starter GPOs folder and click New. After creating a Starter GPO, you can edit it just like any GPO. However, Starter GPOs don't contain all the nodes of a regular GPO; only the Administrative Templates folder in both Computer Configuration and User Configuration is included.

Activity 8-6: Creating and Using Starter GPOs

Time Required: 20 minutes
Objective: Create Starter GPOs to be used to create new GPOs.

Required Tools and Equipment: 410Server1
Description: Now that you're more comfortable working with GPOs, you want to start building a library of Starter GPOs for creating new GPOs. You create two: one in the Computer Configuration node for configuring printers and one in the User Configuration node for configuring Start menu options.

1. Log on to 410Server1 as **Administrator**, if necessary.

2. Open the Group Policy Management console. Right-click the **Starter GPOs** folder and click **New**.

3. In the New Starter GPO dialog box, type **StartPrintersC** in the Name text box. ("Start" stands for Starter GPO, "Printers" refers to the Printers node, and "C" refers to the Computer Configuration node of the GPO.) In the Comment text box, type **Starter GPO for the Printers node of Computer Configuration**, and then click **OK**.

4. Right-click the **StartPrintersC** GPO you created and click **Edit**. In the Group Policy Starter GPO Editor, click to expand **Computer Configuration** and **Administrative Templates**, and then click the **Printers** node. In the right pane, double-click **Automatically publish new**

printers in **Active Directory**. In the Properties dialog box, click **Enabled**, and then click **Apply**. Read the explanation of this policy setting, and then click **OK**.

5. Double-click **Always render print jobs on the server**. In the Properties dialog box, click **Enabled**, and then click **Apply**. Read the explanation of this policy setting, and then click **OK**.

6. Close the Group Policy Starter GPO Editor. In the Group Policy Management console, right-click the **Group Policy Objects** folder and click **New**. In the New GPO dialog box, type **PrintConfigGPO** in the Name text box, click **StartPrintersC** in the Source Starter GPO list box, and then click **OK**.

7. Right-click **PrintConfigGPO** in the Group Policy Objects folder and click **Edit**. In the Group Policy Management Editor, expand **Computer Configuration**, and navigate to the **Printers** node under Administrative Templates to verify that your Starter GPO settings are there. Now you can link this new GPO to a container with computer accounts that have print servers installed, and the printer policies will be in effect on these servers. Close the Group Policy Management Editor.

8. To see the other method of using Starter GPOs to create new GPOs, click the **Starter GPOs** folder in the Group Policy Management console. Right-click **StartPrintersC** and click **New GPO From Starter GPO**. The New GPO Wizard starts. Click **Cancel**.

9. Create another Starter GPO named **StartU**, which is used as a baseline for Start screen options in a later activity.

10. Right-click the **StartU** GPO and click **Edit**. In the Group Policy Management Editor, click to expand **User Configuration** and **Administrative Templates**, and then click **Start Menu and Taskbar**.

11. Configure the following policies as shown:

    - Lock the taskbar: **Enabled**
    - Go to the desktop instead of Start when signing in or when all the apps on a screen or closed: **Enabled**
    - Remove Run menu from Start Menu: **Enabled**

12. Stay logged on if you're continuing to the next activity.

Starter GPOs can be useful for making sure your policies are consistent throughout the domain by defining a baseline for group policy setting categories. You can change the baseline settings as needed in the GPO created from the Starter GPO. However, after a new GPO is created from a Starter GPO, any changes to the Starter GPO aren't propagated to the new GPO.

Starter GPOs can also be shared with other administrators by placing them in cabinet files (CAB files). If you click the Starter GPOs folder in GPMC (see Figure 8-10), all Starter GPOs are listed in the right pane. You can use the Load Cabinet and Save as Cabinet buttons to load a Starter GPO from a CAB file or save a Starter GPO as a CAB file.

8

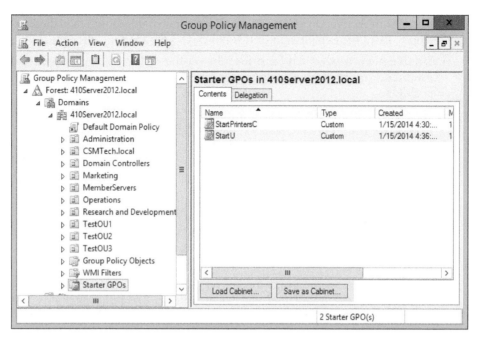

Figure 8-10   Saving Starter GPOs as CAB files

Group Policy Scope

The scope of a group policy defines which objects in Active Directory are affected by settings in the policy. As stated, GPOs can be linked to sites, domains, and OUs and are applied to objects (users or computers) in this order. When conflicts exist, the last policy setting applied takes precedence. When OUs are nested, the GPO applied to the OU nested the deepest takes precedence over all other GPOs. When a policy setting isn't configured, its status is Not defined or Not configured. When a GPO is applied to an object, only the configured settings have any effect on that object. If two GPOs are applied to an object, and a certain setting is configured on one GPO but not the other, the configured setting is applied. For example, Table 8-2 shows an Active Directory structure similar to what you have been using in this book's activities (shown later in Figure 8-11). In particular, notice that Marketing is a parent OU of the Advertising OU.

Table 8-2   GPO inheritance and precedence: Example 1

GPO	Linked to	Policy	Setting
Default Domain Policy	Domain	Lock the Taskbar	Disabled
StTaskMktGPO	Marketing OU	Lock the Taskbar	Enabled
StTaskAdvGPO	Advertising OU	Lock the Taskbar	Not configured

© 2015 Cengage Learning®

Referring to Table 8-2, the Lock the Taskbar policy, which is in the User Configuration node, is enabled for users in the Marketing OU and any of Marketing's child OUs. The policy is also enabled for users in the Advertising OU (a child of Marketing) because it's not configured in the GPO linked to the Advertising OU. The policy is disabled for all other users in the domain who aren't in the scope of the StTaskMktGPO because the Default Domain Policy disables the setting.

Every computer also has one or more local policies, but policies defined in GPOs in Active Directory take precedence over all local policies. So taken together, policies are applied in this order:

1. Local policies
2. Site-linked GPOs
3. Domain-linked GPOs
4. OU-linked GPOs

The last policy applied takes precedence over policies applied earlier, so OU-linked GPOs have the strongest precedence when conflicting policies exist.

Understanding Site-Linked GPOs   GPOs linked to a site object affect all users and computers physically located at the site. Because sites are based on IP address, GPO processing determines from where a user is logging on and from what computer based on that computer's IP address. So users who log on to computers at different sites might have different policies applied to their accounts. In addition, mobile computers can have different policies applied depending on the site where the computer connects to the network. Keep in mind that if a site contains computers and domain controllers from multiple domains, a site-linked GPO affects objects from multiple domains. For simplicity, when you have only one site and one domain, domain GPOs should be used rather than site-linked GPOs. As you might imagine, using site-linked GPOs can be confusing for users, particularly with a lot of user mobility between sites, so site-linked GPOs should be used with caution and only when there are valid reasons for different sites to have different policies.

Understanding Domain-Linked GPOs   GPOs set at the domain level should contain settings that you want to apply to all objects in the domain. The Default Domain Policy is configured and linked to the domain object by default and mostly defines user account policies. Account policies that affect domain logons can be defined only at the domain level. Typically, they're configured by using the Default Domain Policy but can use a different GPO, as long as it's linked to the domain object.

Active Directory folders, such as Computers and Users, are not OUs and, therefore, can't have a GPO linked to them. Only domain-linked GPOs and site-linked GPOs affect objects in these folders. If you need to manage objects in these folders with group policies, moving the objects to OUs is recommended instead of configuring domain or site GPOs to manage them.

It might be tempting to define most group policy settings at the domain level and define exceptions at the OU level, but in a large Active Directory structure, that strategy could become unwieldy. Best practices suggest setting account policies and a few critical security policies at the domain level and setting the remaining policies on GPOs linked to OUs.

NOTE   Domains and their child domains aren't subject to GPO inheritance. In other words, GPO settings applied to the csmtech.local domain are *not* inherited by objects in the US.csmtech.local domain.

Understanding OU-Linked GPOs   Most fine-tuning of group policies, particularly user policies, should be done at the OU level. Because OU-linked policies are applied last, they take precedence over site and domain policies (with the exception of account policies, which can be applied only at the domain level). Because the majority of policies are defined at the OU level, the correct OU design is paramount in your overall Active Directory design. Users and computers with similar policy requirements should be located in the same OU when possible.

Because OUs can be nested, so can the GPOs applied to them. When possible, your OU structure should be designed so that policies defined in GPOs linked to the top-level OU apply to all objects in that OU. GPOs applied to nested OUs should be used for exceptions to policies set at the higher level OU or when certain computers or users require more restrictive policies. For example, all full-time employees in the Engineering Department need complete access to Control Panel, but part-time employees should be restricted from using it. You can configure a policy allowing Control Panel access in a GPO linked to the Engineering OU. Then you create an OU under the Engineering OU that contains part-time employees' accounts and link a GPO to it that restricts use of Control Panel.

Changing Default GPO Inheritance Behavior

By default, GPO inheritance is enabled and settings linked to a parent object are applied to all child objects. Therefore, settings in a GPO linked to the domain object are inherited by all OUs and their child objects in the domain. Settings in a GPO linked to the site are inherited by all objects in that site. To see which policies affect a domain or OU and where the policies are inherited from, select a container in the left pane of the GPMC and click the Group Policy Inheritance tab in the right pane. There are several ways to affect GPO inheritance, discussed in the following sections:

- Blocking inheritance
- Enforcing inheritance
- GPO filtering

Blocking GPO Inheritance   Although the default inheritance behavior is suitable for most situations, as with NTFS permission inheritance, sometimes you need an exception to the default. One method is blocking GPO inheritance, which prevents GPOs linked to parent containers from affecting child containers. To block GPO inheritance, in the GPMC, right-click the child domain or OU and click Block Inheritance. You can block inheritance on a domain or an OU. On a domain object, this setting blocks GPO inheritance from a site, and on an OU, it blocks inheritance from parent OUs (if any), the domain, and the site. If inheritance blocking is enabled, the OU or domain object is displayed with a blue exclamation point. Inheritance blocking should be used sparingly; if you find that you need to block GPO inheritance frequently, it's an indication that your OU design is probably flawed and should be reexamined.

What happens if you have a nested OU and want to block GPO inheritance from its parent OU, but you still want domain- and site-linked GPOs to apply? This is where GPO enforcement comes in.

Enforcing GPO Inheritance   When GPO inheritance is enforced by setting the Enforced option, the GPO's settings are applied to all child objects, even if a GPO with conflicting settings is linked to a container at a deeper level. In other words, a GPO that's enforced has the strongest precedence of all GPOs in its scope. If multiple GPOs are enforced, the GPO that's highest in the Active Directory hierarchy has the strongest precedence. For example, if a GPO linked to an OU and a GPO linked to a domain are both set to be enforced, the GPO linked to the domain has stronger precedence. GPO enforcement overrides GPO inheritance blocking.

Take a look at some examples of how blocking and enforcing GPO inheritance affect the application of policies. Table 8-3 is similar to Table 8-2, except the Advertising OU has the Block Inheritance option set. Figure 8-11 shows the relevant part of the Active Directory structure in the GPMC.

Table 8-3   GPO inheritance and precedence: Example 2

GPO	Linked to	Policy	Setting
Default Domain Policy	Domain	Lock the Taskbar	Disabled
StTaskMktGPO	Marketing OU	Lock the Taskbar	Enabled
StTaskAdvGPO	Advertising OU (**Block Inheritance**)	Lock the Taskbar	Not configured

© 2015 Cengage Learning®

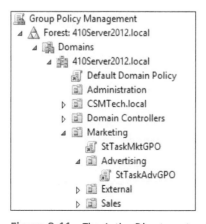

Figure 8-11   The Active Directory structure for GPO inheritance examples

In Table 8-3, users in the Advertising OU aren't affected by GPOs linked to the Marketing OU or the domain because inheritance is blocked. The Lock the Taskbar policy isn't configured on the Advertising OU, so settings in local GPOs apply. If the policy isn't set in local GPOs, the setting remains unchanged from its current state (whatever that might be). Table 8-4 uses the same example, but with the Enforced option set on the Default Domain Policy.

Table 8-4   GPO inheritance and precedence: Example 3

GPO	Linked to	Policy	Setting
Default Domain Policy **(Enforced)**	Domain	Lock the Taskbar	Disabled
StTaskMktGPO	Marketing OU	Lock the Taskbar	Enabled
StTaskAdvGPO	Advertising OU **(Block Inheritance)**	Lock the Taskbar	Not configured

© 2015 Cengage Learning®

With the configuration shown in Table 8-4, the Lock the Taskbar policy is disabled for all users in the domain because the Enforced option set on the Default Domain Policy takes precedence over all other settings, including the Block Inheritance option on the Advertising OU. The next example in Table 8-5 illustrates the effect of the Enforced option set on two GPOs.

Table 8-5   GPO inheritance and precedence: Example 4

GPO	Linked to	Policy	Setting
Default Domain Policy **(Enforced)**	Domain	Lock the Taskbar	Disabled
StTaskMktGPO **(Enforced)**	Marketing OU	Lock the Taskbar	Enabled
StTaskAdvGPO	Advertising OU	Lock the Taskbar	Not configured

© 2015 Cengage Learning®

When two GPOs have the Enforced option set, the GPO linked to the container highest in the Active Directory hierarchy takes precedence. Therefore, as in the previous example, the Lock the Taskbar policy is disabled for all users in the domain.

 Remember that the Block Inheritance option is set on an OU or domain, and the Enforced option is set on a GPO.

Activity 8-7: Demonstrating GPO Inheritance Blocking

Time Required: 20 minutes
Objective: Enable the Block Inheritance option on an OU.

Required Tools and Equipment: 410Server1 and 410Win8
Description: You want to set some policies for personnel in the Marketing Department. However, salespeople don't need to be subject to these policies, so you must block inheritance on the Sales OU.

1. Log on to 410Server1 as **Administrator**, if necessary.

2. Open the Group Policy Management console, and click the **Group Policy Objects** folder. Create a GPO in this folder named **StTaskMktGPO**, using the StartU Starter GPO you created earlier. (Refer to Activity 8-6, if you need a reminder of how to create a GPO from a Starter GPO.)

3. In the left pane, right-click **StTaskMktGPO** and click **Edit**. In the Group Policy Management Editor, click to expand **User Configuration**, and then navigate to the **Start Menu and**

Taskbar node. Verify that the three settings you configured in the starter GPO are configured. Notice that many of the settings you see are relevant only to Windows 7/Windows Server 2008 and earlier OSs.

4. Close the Group Policy Management Editor. In the Group Policy Management console, link the **StTaskMktGPO** GPO to the **Marketing** OU. (Refer to Activity 8-4 for a reminder of how to link GPOs to containers.)

5. Click to expand the **Marketing** OU, if necessary, and then click the **Sales** OU. In the right pane, click the **Group Policy Inheritance** tab. Notice that Sales is inheriting policies from both StTaskMktGPO and Default Domain Policy, and StTaskMktGPO has a higher precedence than Default Domain Policy. Leave the Group Policy Management console open.

6. Log on to the domain from 410Win8 as **sales1** with **Password01**. Notice that you logged on directly to the desktop instead of the Start screen as a result of a policy you configured.

7. Right-click the taskbar. The taskbar should be locked, and the Lock the taskbar option should be disabled. Right-click **Start** and click **Run**. You see an error message informing you the operation was canceled because of restrictions in effect on the computer. Click **OK** in the message box, and stay logged on to 410Win8.

8. On 410Server1, in the left pane of the Group Policy Management console, right-click the **Sales** OU under the Marketing OU and click **Block Inheritance**. Notice that the list of GPOs in the Group Policy Inheritance tab is empty.

9. On 410Win8, open a command prompt window. Type **gpupdate** and press **Enter**. After gpupdate.exe updates group policies, close the command prompt window. (You can also log off and log back on again to update user policies.)

10. Right-click the taskbar. The Lock the taskbar option is no longer disabled. Click to clear **Lock the taskbar**. Right-click **Start** and click **Run**. The Run option is now available. Click **Cancel**.

11. Leave the Group Policy Management console open, and stay logged on to 410Win8 for the next activity.

Activity 8-8: Demonstrating GPO Enforcement

Time Required: 15 minutes
Objective: Enable the Enforced option on a GPO.

Required Tools and Equipment: 410Server1 and 410Win8
Description: You have decided that the Start menu policies you configured in your Starter GPO should be applied to all users in the domain. You create a GPO based on the Starter GPO, link the new GPO to the domain object, and enforce that GPO. (Refer to Figure 8-11 for the relevant Active Directory structure.)

1. Log on to 410Server1 as **Administrator**, if necessary.

2. Open the Group Policy Management console, if necessary, and click the **Group Policy Objects** folder. Create a GPO in this folder named **StTaskDomainGPO**, using the StartU Starter GPO you created earlier.

3. Link **StTaskDomainGPO** to the domain object. In the left pane, click the domain object. In the right pane, click the **Linked Group Policy Objects** tab, if necessary. The GPO with link order 1 has the stronger precedence—in this case, the Default Domain Policy.

4. In the right pane, click **StTaskDomainGPO**. To change the link order, click the up arrow to the left of the Link Order column. Click the down arrow so that StTaskDomainGPO again has link order 2.

5. Right-click **StTaskDomainGPO** and click **Enforced**. Click **OK**. Notice the padlock icon next to StTaskDomainGPO indicating that GPO inheritance is enforced.

6. Click the **Sales** OU. In the right pane, click the **Group Policy Inheritance** tab, if necessary. Even though the Sales OU has the Block Inheritance option set, it's forced to inherit settings from StTaskDomainGPO.

7. On 410Win8, log on as **sales1**, if necessary, and open a command prompt window. Type **gpupdate** and press **Enter**. Close the command prompt window.

8. Verify that the settings from StTaskDomainGPO are now in effect: The taskbar should be locked, and the Run option from the Start menu no longer works. Log off 410Win8.

9. On 410Server1, right-click **StTaskMktGPO** under the Marketing OU and click **Delete**. Click **OK**. This action unlinks the GPO from the OU but doesn't delete the GPO. Repeat for StTaskDomainGPO linked to the domain object.

10. Right-click the **Sales** OU and click **Block Inheritance** to remove the Block Inheritance setting.

11. Close all open windows, and stay logged on to 410Server1 for the next activity.

Activity 8-8 has quite a bit going on with group policy processing, so examine the final settings to review. Table 8-6 lists the relevant GPOs, OUs, and policy settings from Activity 8-8. Both Default Domain Policy and StTaskDomainGPO are linked to the domain. StTaskDomainGPO is enforced so that the enabled policies apply to all users in the domain. The Sales OU blocks inheritance so that objects in this OU aren't affected by Default Domain Policy or StTaskMktGPO. However, objects in the Sales OU are affected by the enabled policies in StTaskDomainGPO because this GPO has the Enforced option set, which takes precedence over the Block Inheritance option.

Table 8-6   Blocking and enforcing GPO inheritance

GPO	Linked to	Policy	Setting
Default Domain Policy	Domain	Lock the Taskbar	Not configured
		Go to the desktop instead of Start	Not configured
		Remove Run menu from Start Menu	Not configured
StTaskDomainGPO (**Enforced**)	Domain	Lock the Taskbar	Enabled
		Go to the desktop instead of Start	Enabled
		Remove Run menu from Start Menu	Enabled
StTaskMktGPO	Marketing OU	Lock the Taskbar	Enabled
		Go to the desktop instead of Start	Enabled
		Remove Run menu from Start Menu	Enabled
None	Sales OU (**Block Inheritance**)		

© 2015 Cengage Learning®

Activity 8-9: Setting a Domain Policy

Time Required: 5 minutes
Objective: Enable logon directly to the desktop by setting a policy at the domain level.

Required Tools and Equipment: 410Server1
Description: You prefer going straight to the desktop when you log on to a Windows 8 or Windows 8.1 computer, so you decide to create a GPO, set a logon policy, and link it to the domain so that it affects all users.

1. Log on to 410Server1 as **Administrator**, if necessary.

2. Open the Group Policy Management console, if necessary. Right-click the domain object and click **Create a GPO in this domain, and Link it here**. Name the GPO **LogToDeskDomGPO**. Don't use a Starter GPO.

3. Edit the GPO you just created by configuring the "Go to the desktop instead of Start when signing in or when all the apps on a screen are closed" policy as **Enabled**.

4. The next time you log on to 410Win8, you go straight to the desktop instead of the Start screen. Close the Group Policy Management Editor, and leave the Group Policy Management console open for the next activity.

GPO Filtering   You have seen how to exclude all objects in an OU from inheriting GPO settings, but what if you want to exclude only some objects in the OU? This is where GPO filtering comes into play. There are two types of **GPO filtering**: security filtering and Windows Management Instrumentation (WMI) filtering.

Security filtering uses permissions to restrict objects from accessing a GPO. Like any object in an Active Directory, a GPO has a discretionary access control list (DACL) in which lists of security principals are granted permission to access the GPO. User and computer accounts must have the Read and Apply Group Policy permissions for a GPO to apply to them. By default, the Authenticated Users special identity is granted these permissions to every GPO; Authenticated Users applies to both logged-on users and computers. You can see a GPO's DACL in Active Directory Users and Computers in the System\Policies folder and in the Delegation tab in the GPMC, but for basic GPO filtering, you can use the simpler GPMC interface. To view the current security filtering settings, click a GPO in the Group Policy Objects folder in the GPMC and click the Scope tab on the right (see Figure 8-12).

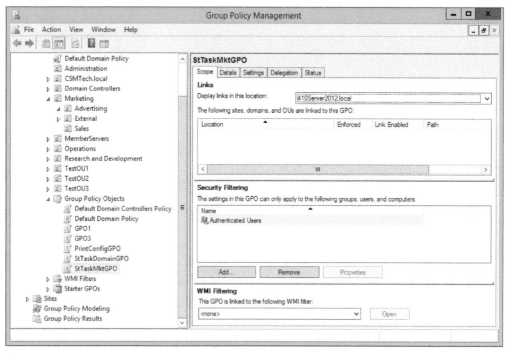

Figure 8-12   Viewing security filtering settings

You use the Security Filtering dialog box in the GPMC to add or remove security principals from the GPO access list. For example, if you want a GPO to apply to all users in a domain or OU except a few, follow these steps:

1. Create a security group in Active Directory Users and Computers.

2. Add all the users who should be subject to the GPO as members of the new group.

3. In the GPMC, click the GPO in the Group Policy Objects folder and click the Scope tab in the right pane.

4. Use the Security Filtering dialog box to add the new group to this GPO.

5. Use the Security Filtering dialog box to remove the Authenticated Users special identity from this GPO.

Remember that computer accounts are also affected by GPOs. So if the GPO you're filtering contains computer settings, you must add a group containing the computer accounts that should be subject to the GPO's policies.

Another way to use security filtering is to edit the GPO's DACL directly. This method is often easier when the GPO must be applied to many users or computers with just a few exceptions. In the GPMC, click the GPO in the Group Policy Objects folder, and click the Delegation tab in the right pane to see the complete list of ACEs for the GPO, as in Figure 8-13. You can add security principals to the DACL or click the Advanced button to open the Advanced Security Settings dialog box you have used with other Active Directory objects.

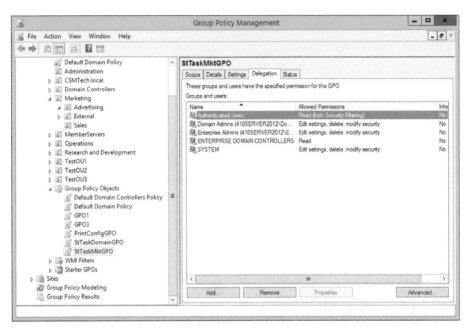

Figure 8-13   The Delegation tab for a GPO

By using the Advanced Security Settings dialog box, you can assign Deny permissions as well as Allow permissions. Assigning the Deny Read permission, for example, enables you to create exceptions to normal GPO processing. You can add a single user or computer account or a group to the DACL and prevent these security principals from being affected by the GPO.

For example, you have a GPO configuring some Internet Explorer settings in the Computer Configuration node that restricts access to advanced features. You have more than 500 computer accounts in different OUs, so you want to link the GPO to the domain so that it affects all computers in the domain. However, you have a dozen or so power users whose computers you want to exempt from these policies. You can create a group, add the power users' computers as members, add the group to the GPO's DACL, and then configure Deny Read permission.

WMI Filtering   The second type of filtering is **WMI filtering**. Windows Management Instrumentation (WMI) is a Windows technology for gathering management information about computers, such as the hardware platform, the OS version, available disk space, and so on. WMI filtering uses queries to select a group of computers based on certain attributes, and then applies or doesn't apply policies based on the query's results. You need to have a solid understanding of the complex WMI query language before you can create WMI filters. Here's an example of using one to select only computers running Windows 8 Enterprise:

```
Root\CimV2; Select * from Win32_OperatingSystem where
   Caption = "Microsoft Windows 8 Enterprise"
```

You can learn more about WMI and WMI filtering by searching on the Microsoft TechNet Web site at *http://technet.microsoft.com.*

Activity 8-10: Using GPO Security Filtering

Time Required: 25 minutes
Objective: Change the default security filtering on a GPO and examine the results.

Required Tools and Equipment: 410Server1 and 410Win8
Description: You're unsure how GPO security filtering works, so you decide to test some settings with a test OU and test GPO.

1. Log on to 410Server1 as **Administrator**, if necessary.

2. Open the Group Policy Management console, if necessary. Click to expand the **Group Policy Objects** folder, and then click **GPO1**. In the right pane, click the **Scope** tab, if necessary.

3. In the Security Filtering dialog box in the right pane, click the **Add** button. Type **testuser1**, click **Check Names**, and then click **OK**.

4. In the Name list box, click **Authenticated Users** and click the **Remove** button. Click **OK** to confirm that you want to remove the delegation privilege. The testuser1 account is now the only security principal with Read and Apply Group Policy permissions for GPO1.

5. Click the **Settings** tab, and then click the **show all** link. The "Prohibit access to Control Panel and PC settings" policy should be set to Enabled.

6. Link **GPO1** to the **TestOU1** OU.

7. On 410Win8, log on to the domain as **testuser1**.

8. From the desktop, right-click **Start** and click **Control Panel**. You see a message that the operation was canceled because of restrictions on the computer. Click **OK**. Because GPO1 is linked to TestOU1, the Control Panel is restricted for testuser1.

9. Log off and log on as **testuser2**, and open the Control Panel. You have access because testuser2 isn't in the WMI filter for GPO1. Close the Control Panel.

10. On 410Server1, change the security filtering for GPO1 to add **Authenticated Users** back and remove **testuser1**.

11. With GPO1 selected in the left pane of the Group Policy Management console, click the **Delegation** tab in the right pane, and then click the **Advanced** button.

12. In the GPO1 Security Settings dialog box, click **Add**. Type **testuser1**, click **Check Names**, and then click **OK**.

13. If necessary, click **Test User1** in the list box at the top, click the **Read** check box in the Deny column, and then click **OK**. Click **Yes** to confirm that you want to set a Deny permission. The current permissions on the GPO allow Authenticated Users members, except Test User1, to access the GPO.

14. On 410Win8, you should still be logged on as testuser2. Open a command prompt window, type **gpupdate**, and press **Enter** to update group policies.

15. After the policy update is finished, try to open the Control Panel to verify that it's no longer available to testuser2.

16. Log off 410Win8 and log on as **testuser1**. Verify that the Control Panel is available to testuser1. Log off 410Win8.

17. On 410Server1, remove **testuser1** from GPO1's DACL, and then unlink **GPO1** from **TestOU1**. Close the Group Policy Management console, but stay logged on if you're continuing to the next activity.

Group Policy Settings

As you have learned, GPOs have a Computer Configuration node, affecting all computer accounts in a GPO's scope, and a User Configuration node, affecting all user accounts in a GPO's scope. Most policies in these two nodes affect different aspects of the working environment, but a few policies are the same. If the same policy is configured in both nodes and the settings conflict (for example, one disables a policy and the other enables it), the setting in Computer Configuration takes precedence.

Both nodes have a Policies folder and a Preferences folder. Under the Policies folder are these three folders: Software Settings, Windows Settings, and Administrative Templates. Chapter 6 covered the types of policies in these folders briefly, but now you examine some of them more closely. *MCSA Guide to Configuring Advanced Windows Server 2012/R2 Services, Exam 70-412* (Cengage Learning, 2015) covers many additional policy settings and Group Policy preferences. The Software Settings and Windows Settings folders include items called "extensions" because they extend the functionality of Group Policy beyond what was available in Windows 2000. The Administrative Templates folder contains categorized folders or nodes with settings that affect users' or computers' working environments, mainly by changing Registry settings.

Policy settings can be managed or unmanaged. A **managed policy setting** is applied to a user or computer when the object is in the scope of the GPO containing the setting. When the object is no longer in the GPO's scope or the policy is set to Not configured, however, the setting on the user or computer reverts to its original state. You have seen this behavior in earlier activities, when the Prohibit access to the Control Panel policy affected the user only as long as the user was in the GPO's scope. An **unmanaged policy setting** is persistent, meaning it remains even after the computer or user object falls out of the GPO's scope until it is changed by another policy or manually. The policies already loaded in Active Directory are managed policies, but you can customize Group Policy by adding your own policies, which are unmanaged.

Policies in the Computer Configuration Node

The Computer Configuration node applies policies to computers regardless of who logs on to the computer. Most important, this node contains most of the security-related settings in the Account Policies, User Rights Assignment, Audit Policy, and Security Options nodes. Computer Configuration policies are uploaded to a computer when the OS starts and are updated every 90 minutes thereafter. Although many policies take effect when the GPO is updated, some might require a computer restart. The next sections cover some important policies in the Computer Configuration node of a GPO.

NOTE This book covers only some of the many policies in Group Policy. Many others are covered in *MCSA Guide to Administering Windows Server 2012/R2, Exam 70-411* (Cengage Learning, 2015) and *MCSA Guide to Configuring Advanced Windows Server 2012/R2 Services, Exam 70-412* (Cengage Learning, 2015).

Computer Configuration: Software Settings The Software Settings node contains the Software Installation extension, which can be configured to install software packages remotely on computers, regardless of who logs on to the computer. Applications are deployed with the Windows Installer service, which uses installation packages called "MSI files." An MSI file is a collection of files packaged into a single file with an `.msi` extension and contains the instructions Windows Installer needs to install the application correctly. Software installation through Group Policy is discussed more in *MCSA Guide to Administering Windows Server 2012/R2, Exam 70-411* (Cengage Learning, 2015).

Computer Configuration: Windows Settings The Windows Settings folder contains four subnodes:

- *Name Resolution Policy*—This policy, added in Windows Server 2008 R2, is used to deploy DNS security (DNSSEC) policies to clients. DNSSEC is covered in *MCSA Guide to Configuring Advanced Windows Server 2012/R2 Services, Exam 70-412* (Cengage Learning, 2015).

- *Scripts (Startup/Shutdown)*—You can create scripts in a variety of scripting languages, including VBScript, JScript, and batch files. Startup scripts run when the computer starts, and shutdown scripts run before the computer shuts down. Scripts must be placed in the Scripts folder under the GPO's GPT folder in the SYSVOL share.

- *Security Settings*—This node consists of a number of subnodes and is discussed in more detail in the following section.
- *Policy-based QoS*—Quality of service (QoS) policies, new in Server 2008, enable administrators to manage network bandwidth use on a per-computer or per-user basis and prioritize network packets based on the type of data the packet carries.

Security Settings

There are well over 100 policies under Security Settings. Some of the most important are under Account Policies and Local Policies because they contain baseline security options for your computers. The following list describes the types of policies found under Security Settings, and some are covered in more detail in the next sections:

- *Account Policies*—Contains settings that affect user authentication and logon. A GPO with settings configured in Account Policies must be linked to the domain for these policies to have any effect on domain logons. If a GPO linked to an OU has settings configured in Account Policies, they only affect the account policy settings on local computer accounts within the scope of the GPO, which only pertains to local user accounts. The Default Domain Policy is configured with default account policies settings, and many administrators keep all account policies in this GPO. This policy is discussed in detail in *MCSA Guide to Administering Windows Server 2012/R2, Exam 70-411* (Cengage Learning, 2015).
- *Local Policies*—Local Policies is so named because all settings in its subnodes pertain to security options applied to computers and what users can and can't do on the local computer to which they log on. Because these policies affect computers, they're defined in GPOs linked to OUs containing computer accounts, such as the Default Domain Controllers Policy. There are three subnodes under Local Policies: Audit Policy, User Rights Assignment, and Security Options.
- *Event Log*—Controls parameters of the main logs in Event Viewer on target computers. Policies include log file sizes and retention parameters.
- *Restricted Groups*—Controls group membership for both domain groups and local SAM groups. After the policy is applied, existing members of the target group are deleted and replaced with the membership specified in the policy.
- *System Services*—Manages the startup mode and security settings of services on target computers.
- *Registry*—Sets NTFS permissions on Registry keys on target computers.
- *File System*—Sets NTFS permissions and controls auditing and inheritance on files and folders on target computers.
- *Wired Network (IEEE 802.3) Policies*—Controls a variety of authentication parameters on computers with wired connections to the network.
- *Windows Firewall with Advanced Security*—Controls firewall settings on Windows Vista and Server 2008 and later computers. Configuring the Windows Firewall with Group Policy is discussed later in "Configuring Windows Firewall with Group Policy."
- *Network List Manager Policies*—Controls aspects of the networks identified by Windows, such as location type (for example, public, private, domain) and network name and whether users can change information.
- *Wireless Network (IEEE 802.11) Policies*—Controls how wireless clients can connect to wireless networks, including network type (ad hoc or infrastructure), service set identifier (SSID), authentication, and encryption protocols.
- *Public Key Policies*—Controls parameters associated with public key infrastructure, including EFS and certificate handling.
- *Software Restriction Policies*—Controls which software can run on a computer.
- *Network Access Protection*—Controls the NAP environment for target computers, including enforcement services, user interface, and servers used for health registration certificates.

- *Application Control Policies*—Contains the subnode AppLocker, which extends the function of Software Restriction Policies. This policy can be used only on computers running Windows 7/Windows 2008 R2 and later.

- *IP Security Policies on Active Directory*—Controls IPsec policies on target computers. IPsec is a network protocol that provides secure, encrypted communication between computers.

Local Policies: Audit Policy   An administrator can audit events occurring on a computer, including logon and logoff, file and folder access, Active Directory access, and system and process events (see Figure 8-14). Auditing can be enabled for successful events, failed events, or both. For example, you can audit a user's successful access to a file or attempted accesses that fail or both. Auditing file and folder access should be used sparingly and for only short periods because of the system overhead it creates when monitoring objects and writing events to the Security log when access occurs. By default, no audit policies are defined on either default GPO. However, in Windows Server 2012/R2, certain events, such as logons and directory service access, are audited by default and can be changed only by using the command-line tool `auditpol.exe`. Events created by auditing are listed in the Security log, which you can view with Event Viewer.

Figure 8-14   Auditing policies

Auditing Object Access   Auditing, particularly auditing access to file system objects, requires additional explanation. There are two steps for auditing objects:

1. Enable the "Audit object access" policy for success, failure, or both.
2. Enable auditing on target objects for success, failure, or both.

After object access auditing is enabled in Group Policy, you need to enable auditing on the target object, such as a file or folder. You do this by changing the system access control list (SACL) for the object in the Auditing tab of the Advanced Security Settings dialog box for the object (see Figure 8-15). By default, there are no entries in the Auditing tab. Figure 8-15 shows an entry in which testuser1 is being audited for successful write access to the P:\TestShare1 folder. As you can see in the figure, there are inheritance considerations with auditing, too. By default, when you audit a folder, the auditing extends to the subfolders and files, but like permissions inheritance, you can change this outcome.

A single object access, such as opening a file, can create several log entries. For this reason, auditing objects should be done for only brief periods or when an object is accessed infrequently. In highly secure environments, however, auditing access to sensitive data on an ongoing basis can be useful. Because auditing writes events to the Security log, it makes little sense to enable auditing unless logs are checked regularly.

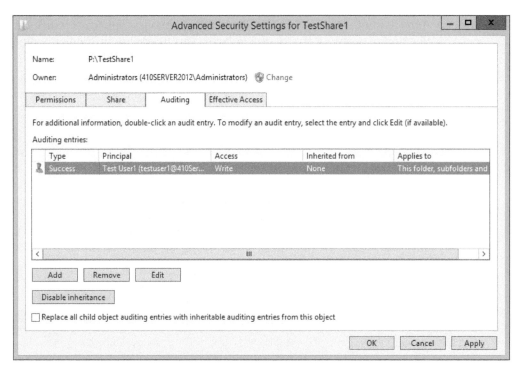

Figure 8-15   The Auditing tab for a folder

Changing Default Auditing   As mentioned, Windows Server 2012/R2 logs successful logon events and certain other events by default, even though auditing isn't enabled in Group Policy. If you check the Security log, you'll see quite a few events logged there, most pertaining to computer accounts logging on and off. Each category of audit events shown previously in Figure 8-14 has a number of subcategories, which give you more control over the types of events that are audited. Unfortunately, these subcategories can't be managed with the GPME; you must use the auditpol.exe command-line tool. As mentioned, some subcategories are enabled by default, such as logon and logoff events, and these subcategories take precedence over policies set in GPOs.

To clear all audit policy subcategories so that auditing is controlled only by Group Policy, type auditpol /clear at a command prompt. This command stops all auditing on the computer where you run it, unless auditing is enabled in the local policy or a GPO in the computer's scope.

For more information on auditpol.exe, see *http://support.microsoft. com/kb/921469/*.

Activity 8-11: Disabling Default Auditing

Time Required: 15 minutes
Objective: Disable default event auditing on a domain controller.

Required Tools and Equipment: 410Server1 and 410Win8
Description: Your event logs have become much too large because of Windows Server 2012's default logging. You want to turn off default logging by using the auditpol.exe command.

1. Log on to 410Server1 as **Administrator**, if necessary.

2. In Server Manager, click **Tools, Local Security Policy**.

3. Click to expand **Local Policies,** and then click **Audit Policy**. Verify that all audit policies are set to **No auditing,** which is the default setting. "Not defined" is the default setting in the Default Domain Policy and Default Domain Controllers Policy. Close the Local Security Policy MMC.

4. In Server Manager, click **Tools, Event Viewer**. Click to expand **Windows Logs** in the left pane, and then click the **Security** log. Scroll through the events in the right pane. You'll probably see quite a few events pertaining to logon, logoff, and directory service access. (If necessary, expand the middle pane so that you can see the Task Category column.)

5. Right-click the **Security** log in the left pane and click **Clear Log**. Click **Clear**. One event is created, which indicates the event log was cleared. This event is always logged.

6. On 410Win8, log off, if necessary, and then log on as **testuser1**.

7. On 410Server1, right-click the **Security** log and click **Refresh**. You should see several events created by the logon from 410Win8.

8. Open a command prompt window, type `auditpol /get /category:* | more`, and press **Enter**. Notice that the Logon event is set for Success and Failure, and the Logoff event is set for Success. Press the **spacebar** to page through the results. This command displays all the subcategories of audit policies and their current settings.

9. Type `auditpol /clear` and press **Enter**. When prompted, type **y** and press **Enter**. Type `auditpol /get /category:* | more` and press **Enter**. Press the **spacebar** to page through the resulting output. Notice that all audit policies have been set to "No Auditing." Close the command prompt window.

10. In Event Viewer, clear the **Security** log again. On 410Win8, log off and log on again as **testuser1**. Refresh the Security log again to verify that no new events were created (aside from the event of clearing the log). Close Event Viewer.

11. Log off 410Win8. Stay logged on to 410Server1 if you're continuing to the next activity.

Activity 8-12: Working with Audit Policies

Time Required: 15 minutes
Objective: Enable and test auditing of object access.

Required Tools and Equipment: 410Server1
Description: You have a share containing very sensitive files. These files aren't accessed often, and only a few users access them. Because of the files' sensitive nature, you want to know who is accessing them (include those who shouldn't be attempting access) and when. You enable auditing object access and auditing the sensitive files.

1. Log on to 410Server1 as **Administrator**, if necessary.

2. Open the Group Policy Management console, and click the **Group Policy Objects** folder. Create a GPO in this folder named **LocalGPO**.

3. Right-click **LocalGPO** and click **Edit**. In the Group Policy Management Editor, expand **Computer Configuration, Policies, Windows Settings, Security Settings,** and **Local Policies,** and then click **Audit Policy**. In the right pane, double-click **Audit object access**. In the Properties dialog box, click the **Define these policy settings** check box. Click **Success** and **Failure**, and then click **OK**. Close the Group Policy Management Editor.

4. In the Group Policy Management console, link **LocalGPO** to the **Domain Controllers** OU. Close the Group Policy Management console. Open a command prompt window, and then type **gpupdate** and press **Enter**. Then type `auditpol /get /category:* | more` and press **Enter**. Page through the output, noting that all subcategories under Object Access are set to Success and Failure. Close the command prompt window. If you want to limit auditing to just some subcategories, you need to enable auditing with `auditpol`.

5. Open File Explorer, and create a folder named **TestShare1** on Vol1.

6. Create a file in the TestShare1 folder called `Confidential.txt`. Right-click `Confidential.txt` and click **Properties**. Click the **Security** tab, and then click the **Advanced** button.

7. In the Advanced Security Settings for Confidential.txt dialog box, click the **Auditing** tab, and then click the **Add** button. In the Auditing Entry for Confidential.txt dialog box, click **Select a principal**, type **Domain Users**, click **Check Names**, and then click **OK**.

8. In the Type list box, click **All**, which means you want to audit both successful and failed attempts to access the object. Under Basic permissions, leave the default settings of **Read** and **Read & execute** selected. Click **OK** until you get back to the File Explorer window.

9. Open **Confidential.txt** in Notepad, and then exit Notepad. In Server Manager, click **Tools, Event Viewer**. Click to expand **Windows Logs** and click the **Security** log. You'll probably find several events listed. Unfortunately, when object access auditing is enabled in Group Policy, many types of access are audited, as indicated by the list of subcategories you saw under Object Access in Step 4. Close Event Viewer.

10. Open the Group Policy Management console. Right-click **LocalGPO** and click **Edit**. In the Group Policy Management Editor, navigate to the **Audit Policy** node. In the right pane, double-click **Audit object access**. In the Properties dialog box, click to clear the **Define these policy settings** check box, and then click **OK**. Close the Group Policy Management Editor.

11. In the Group Policy Management console, unlink **LocalGPO** from the **Domain Controllers** OU. Stay logged on for the next activity.

Local Policies: User Rights Assignment   User rights define the actions users can take on a computer, such as shutting down the system, logging on locally, and changing the system time. More than 40 user rights policies can be assigned (see Figure 8-16), and for each

Figure 8-16   Viewing User Rights Assignment policies

policy, you can add users or groups. The Default Domain Controllers Policy specifies User Rights Assignment policies that define the default actions users can take on domain controllers. It's a good idea to spend some time examining the policies you can define in this node so that you know what types of rights you can enable and disable for users.

Local Policies: Security Options   This subnode includes almost 100 settings; only a small percentage are shown in Figure 8-17. Available policies are organized into 15 categories, such as Accounts, Interactive logon, Network access, and User Account Control. Only a handful of the policies are defined in Default Domain Policy and Default Domain Controllers Policy. Most of these policies are configured with a simple Enable or Disable setting. For example, if "Interactive logon: Do not display last user name" is enabled, the account name of the last user to log on isn't displayed in the logon window.

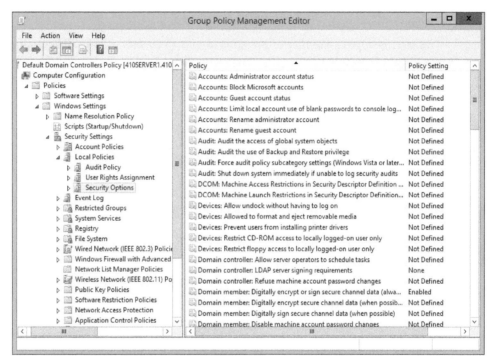

Figure 8-17   Viewing Security Options policies

One category of security policies you might want to configure right away is User Account Control. The **User Account Control policies** determine what happens on a computer when a user attempts to perform an action that requires elevation. When User Account Control is fully enabled, users logged on with administrator credentials run with regular user privileges. When users attempt to perform an action requiring administrative rights (such as installing applications and changing system settings), they're prompted to enter credentials. Being prompted for credentials in this situation is called **elevation**; the user is giving explicit consent to the system to perform the action. Regular user accounts can't be elevated, but user accounts in the Administrators group can. By default, the built-in Administrator account doesn't require elevation. With Group Policy, you can determine which types of action prompt for elevation and the behavior of the elevation prompt for regular users and administrators.

Some additional settings that are commonly configured in Security Options include the following, but you should be familiar with most of the settings in Security Options:

- *Accounts: Administrator account status*—Enable or disable the local Administrator account. In client OSs, the Administrator account is disabled by default.

- *Accounts: Guest account status*—Disabled by default, but you can enable it with this setting.

- *Accounts: Limit local account use of blank passwords to console logon only*—Enabled by default; this policy disallows network users from logging on to the computer if their password is blank.

- *Accounts: Rename administrator account*—Allows you to rename the administrator account; if set on a domain-based GPO, the Administrator account on all member computers affected by the GPO is renamed.

- *Accounts: Rename guest account*—Similar to the "Rename administrator account" setting.

- *Interactive logon: Do not display last user name*—Prevents the logon screen from showing the username of the last logged on user; disabled by default.

- *Interactive logon: Do not require CTRL+ALT+DEL*—If this setting is enabled, users don't have to press Ctrl+Alt+Del to log on to the local computer.

- *Interactive logon: Message text for users attempting to log on*—Allows the administrator to define a message that users see on the logon screen.

- *Interactive logon: Number of previous logons to cache*—Allows the computer to locally cache logon information so that users can log on to the computer if no domain controller is available. By default, 10 logons are cached. If it's set to 0, a DC must be available for a user to log on to the local computer.

- *Microsoft network server: Disconnect clients when logon hours expire*—Enabled by default, if user accounts have restricted logon hours, their sessions are disconnected from file shares if they're connected outside valid logon hours. If it's disabled, users can continue to work after logon hours expire if they're already logged on.

Activity 8-13: Reviewing User Rights Assignment and Security Options Settings

Time Required: 20 minutes
Objective: Review several User Rights Assignment and Security Options settings.

Required Tools and Equipment: 410Server1
Description: You have some experience using group policies to set User Rights Assignment and Security Options policies, but you haven't taken the time to see everything that's available in these nodes. You open the Group Policy Management Editor and explore these two nodes.

1. Log on to 410Server1 as **Administrator,** if necessary.

2. Open the Group Policy Management console, and navigate to **LocalGPO.** Open this GPO in the Group Policy Management Editor.

3. Click to expand **Computer Configuration, Policies, Windows Settings, Security Settings,** and **Local Policies,** and then click **User Rights Assignment.** Browse the list of policies, and double-click any that look interesting or that aren't self-explanatory. Click the **Explain** tab and read the detailed description. Suggested policies to view in detail include Add workstations to domain, Back up files and directories, Bypass traverse checking, Allow log on locally, Deny log on locally, Load and unload device drivers, Shut down the system, and Take ownership of files or other objects.

4. Browse the **Security Options** node in a similar manner. Suggested policies to view in detail include Accounts: Administrator account status, Accounts: Rename administrator account, Accounts: Limit local account use of blank passwords to console logon only, Audit: Force audit policy subcategory settings, Devices: Prevent users from installing printer drivers, Interactive logon: Do not display last user name, Interactive logon: Message text for users attempting to log on, Interactive logon: Prompt user to change password before expiration, Network access: Shares that can be accessed anonymously, Network security: Force logoff

when logon hours expire, Shutdown: Clear virtual memory pagefile, User Account Control: Behavior of the elevation prompt for standard users, and User Account Control: Run all administrators in Admin Approval Mode.

5. When you have time, you should explore these nodes more thoroughly to become more familiar with the settings. Stay logged on if you're continuing to the next activity.

Restricted Groups   The Restricted Groups policy allows an administrator to control the membership of both domain groups and local groups on member computers. By default, this node is empty; you configure it by adding groups you want to restrict. This policy is typically used on groups that require especially high security, perhaps because the group has been assigned powerful rights or permissions to sensitive data. You can control both the Members and Member Of properties of a group (see Figure 8-18). The Members property controls which accounts can be members of the group. Current members of the target group not on the list are removed (unless the Administrator account is among them), and those in the list that aren't already members of the target group are added.

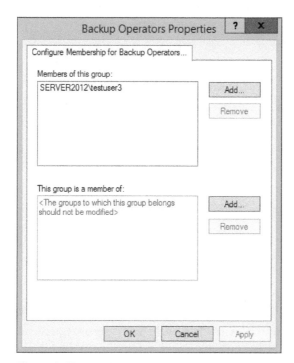

Figure 8-18   Configuring a restricted group

The Member Of property operates somewhat differently. It adds the target group to groups on the list that it isn't already a member of, but it doesn't remove the target group from existing memberships. For example, in Figure 8-18, the Backup Operators group is configured with testuser3 as a member. The GPO in which this policy is configured is linked to the domain. Because Backup Operators is a group in both the domain and on local computers, testuser3 is added to the group on all domain members and domain controllers in the domain. Furthermore, any existing members of Backup Operators are removed, and testuser3 is the sole member. Because there are no entries in the "This group is a member of" list, the groups Backup Operators is a member of are unchanged.

File System   The File System node enables an administrator to configure permissions and auditing on files and folders on any computers that fall in the scope of the GPO on which the policy is configured. Similar to Restricted Groups, there are no File System policies defined by default, so you need to add a folder or file and then configure the settings as you would configure permissions and auditing on any file or folder. When you're done, the file system settings are transmitted to the file system of target computers. If the file or folder doesn't exist on a computer within the GPO's scope, the policy has no effect. For example, say you configure a File System policy for a folder named scripts on the C drive, giving the Administrators group Full control and the Users group Read permissions. Any computer that falls in the scope of the GPO that has a folder named scripts on the C drive receives these permissions. Any existing permissions are replaced.

Software Restriction Policies   Software restriction policies are designed to prevent users from running certain applications or to allow users to run only certain applications. Aside from preventing users from using programs at work that don't contribute to their productivity, software restriction policies can add a layer of security to your network by preventing malware from running.

There's a Software Restriction Policies node under both the Computer Configuration and User Configuration nodes. By default, it's empty, but you can create a policy by right-clicking the folder and clicking New Software Restriction Policies. When a new policy is created, Software Restrictions Policies contains two folders and three policies (see Figure 8-19).

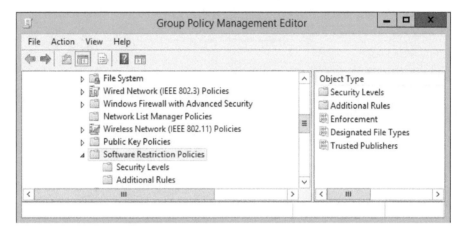

Figure 8-19   The Software Restriction Policies node

The Security Levels folder contains three rules explained in the following list, one of which you select as the default rule for the policy. You can then create exceptions to the default rule.

- *Disallowed*—No software can run, regardless of the user's security access.

- *Basic User*—All software can run with access rights of a normal user, regardless of the user's actual rights on the system. This rule prevents users with administrative access from running programs that could cause harm with that level of access.

- *Unrestricted*—This is the default setting on a new policy. All programs can run according to the user's actual access rights. This setting, with no additional rules defined, is the same as having no software restriction policy assigned.

A user must have the Read & execute permission to run a file, regardless of what a software restriction policy permits.

The Additional Rules folder is where you create exceptions to the default rule by identifying applications or application locations that are allowed or disallowed. There are four ways to identify applications designated as exceptions to the default rule:

- *Hash*—A digital fingerprint of the application file is created, based on the file's attributes, to identify it uniquely.

- *Certificate*—Some software publishers provide a digital certificate to identify an application uniquely.
- *Path*—The path on the local system or a UNC path to the application file.
- *Network zone*—An Internet zone that defines the Web sites from which applications can run.

For each additional rule you create, you can specify whether applications meeting the rule criteria should be disallowed, run as a basic user, or unrestricted. When you create a new software restriction policy, two path rules are created automatically to define unrestricted locations programs can run from: one specifying the default Program Files directory and one specifying the Windows directory. Three policies can be configured in the Software Restriction Policies folder:

- *Enforcement*—Specifies how restrictions should be enforced. You can exempt members of the Administrators group, and you can exempt library files, such as DLLs.
- *Designated File Types*—Specifies which file types are to be considered executable files. You can add your own file types or remove certain types from the list.
- *Trusted Publishers*—Specifies trusted publisher policy options, such as who can manage the list of trusted publishers (users or administrators) and certificate verification parameters.

You should edit software restriction policies only when the GPO is disabled or not linked to a container because a policy you haven't finished configuring might be applied to a user or computer, causing undesirable results.

Activity 8-14: Creating a Software Restriction Policy

Time Required: 20 minutes
Objective: Create a software restriction policy and test it.

Required Tools and Equipment: 410Server1 and 410Win8
Description: You want to begin locking down some computers in your company by restricting which programs users can run. You want to use settings in the Software Restriction Policies folder, so you decide to create a simple policy to test this feature. This policy is created in the Computer Configuration section of the GPO, but the process is the same in the User Configuration section.

1. Log on to 410Server1 as **Administrator**, if necessary.

2. Open the Group Policy Management console, and then open **GPO1** in the Group Policy Management Editor. Expand **Computer Configuration, Policies, Windows Settings, Security Settings**, and **Software Restriction Policies**. Right-click **Software Restriction Policies** and click **New Software Restriction Policies**.

3. Click the **Security Levels** folder in the left pane to see the three default rules in the right pane. The Unrestricted rule has a small check mark, indicating that it's currently selected as the default. Double-click **Disallowed** to open this rule's Properties dialog box, and click **Set as Default**. Click **Yes**, and then click **OK**.

4. Click the **Additional Rules** folder. As mentioned, two path rules were created automatically that refer to a Registry key specifying the Windows directory and the Program Files directory. They can be deleted or you can leave them as is (recommended). Double-click the path rule listed first to open the dialog box shown in Figure 8-20. This path rule refers to the SystemRoot folder, which is C:\Windows on most systems, and it's set to Unrestricted. Click **Cancel**. Look at the second path rule, which refers to the Program Files folder and is also unrestricted. Click **Cancel**.

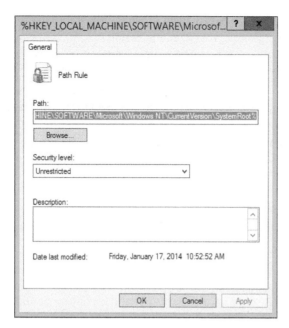

Figure 8-20   Viewing a path rule

5. Click **Software Restriction Policies** in the left pane. Double-click **Enforcement** in the right pane (see Figure 8-21). In the Properties dialog box, click the **All users except local administrators** option button. Read the other options and their descriptions, and then click **OK**.

Figure 8-21   The Enforcement Properties dialog box

6. Double-click **Designated File Types** in the right pane. In the Properties dialog box, scroll through the list of file types that are considered executable files, and then click **Cancel**. Close the Group Policy Management Editor.

7. In the Group Policy Management console, link **GPO1** to **TestOU3**. TestOU3 is where the 410Win8 computer account is located, so this policy applies only to applications on that computer.

8. Log on to the domain from 410Win8 as **Administrator**. Open a command prompt window, type **gpupdate**, and press **Enter**. Close the command prompt window.

9. Open Notepad and type the command **dir /s**. Save the file as **"c:\test.bat"** and exit Notepad. Remember to use quotes around the filename so that Notepad doesn't add the .txt extension. This simple batch file runs the dir command and lists files in subdirectories to test the software restriction policy you just created.

10. To be sure your batch file works, right-click **Start**, click **Run**, type **c:\test.bat** in the Open text box, and press **Enter**. You exempted local administrators from the policy, so the Administrator account can still run this program. You see a long listing of all files and folders on the C drive.

11. Log off 410Win8 and then log on again as **testuser1**.

12. Start Notepad to verify that you can run programs in the C:\Windows directory. Exit Notepad.

13. Right-click **Start**, click **Run**, type **c:\test.bat** in the Open text box, and press **Enter**. You see a message stating that your system administrator has blocked the program. Click **OK**.

14. Log off 410Win8. On 410Server1, unlink **GPO1** from **TestOU3**. In the Group Policy Objects folder, open **GPO1** in the Group Policy Management Editor. Navigate to the **Software Restriction Policies** node under Computer Configuration, and then right-click it and click **Delete Software Restriction Policies**. Click **Yes**.

15. Stay logged on if you're continuing to the next activity.

Application Control Policies   The Application Control Policies node contains a subnode named AppLocker. As mentioned, AppLocker extends the functionality in Software Restriction Policies and affects only Windows 7 and later computers. This node is found only under Computer Configuration, so its policies are applied to computer accounts, not user accounts. This doesn't mean the policy can't be configured to specify which users can run particular applications. It can but only if the specified users log on to a computer in the GPO's scope. When you click AppLocker in the GPME, the dialog box shown in Figure 8-22 opens. It has three sections: Getting Started, Configure Rule Enforcement, and Overview.

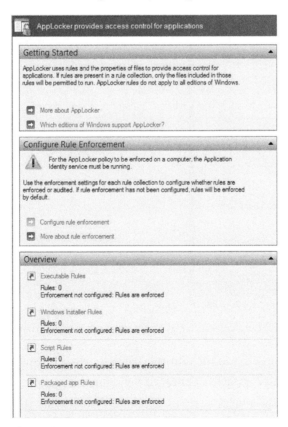

Figure 8-22   AppLocker configuration

AppLocker is fully supported only in Windows Server 2012/R2, Windows Server 2008 R2, Windows 8 and 8.1 Enterprise Edition, and Windows 7 Ultimate and Enterprise editions. Windows 7 Professional and Windows 8 Pro support only AppLocker auditing, not enforcement.

The Getting Started section simply provides information about AppLocker. In the Configure Rule Enforcement section, you can specify whether rules are enforced or just audited. By auditing rather than enforcing a rule, you can monitor which applications are being used without enforcing the rule. When a user runs an application that matches a rule, an event is generated in the AppLocker event log (whether the rule is enforced or audited). There are four categories of rules (described shortly), and each category has its own enforcement setting, as shown in Figure 8-23:

- *Not configured*—The default setting. An unconfigured enforcement rule defaults to "Enforce rules." If the rule category isn't configured, another GPO can override the setting.

- *Enforce rules*—If the setting is configured with "Enforce rules," the rule category is enforced. The setting can be overridden only by a GPO that has higher precedence.

- *Audit only*—If the setting is configured with "Audit only," the rule category is audited, as explained previously. The setting can be overridden only by a GPO that has higher precedence.

Figure 8-23 Rule enforcement settings

The Overview section contain links to the four rule categories where you build rules:

- *Executable Rules*—These rules apply to applications with an .exe or a .com file extension.

- *Windows Installer Rules*—These rules apply to Windows Installer files that have the .msi or .msp extension.

- *Script Rules*—These rules apply the following types of script files: batch files (`.bat` or `.cmd` extension), PowerShell scripts (`.ps1`), Visual Basic scripts (`.vbs`), and JavaScript (`.js`).
- *Packaged app Rules*—These rules apply to apps purchased through the Windows app store.

To see events generated by AppLocker, open Event Viewer, and click Applications and Services Logs, Microsoft, Windows, AppLocker.

Creating Rules   There are three ways to create AppLocker rules:

- Create default rules.
- Create a custom rule by using the Create Executable Rules Wizard.
- Let Windows generate rules automatically.

Before you start creating rules such as "Allow members of the Accounting Group to run Executable applications in the C:\AcctApps folder," you need to create some default rules. If you create a rule without defining the default rules, only users and applications specified by the created rule are allowed. So if you created the aforementioned rule, nobody besides members of the Accounting group would be able to run executable applications on the affected computers, and the Accounting group members would be able to run applications only in the C:\AcctApps folder. These results probably aren't what you want.

You create default rules by right-clicking the rule category under AppLocker and clicking Create Default Rules. The default rules for executable files are similar to those created by Software Restriction Policies (see Figure 8-24). Each rule category has its own default rules that are created the same way and have a similar intent: to allow everyone to run applications in the standard locations and to give administrators unrestricted access to applications.

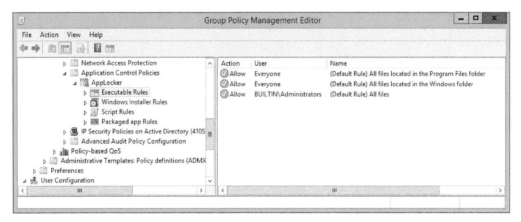

Figure 8-24   Default rules for executable files

Creating Custom Rules   You create custom rules by right-clicking the rule category and clicking Create New Rule to start the Create Executable Rules Wizard. First, you choose Allow or Deny to specify whether the rule allows or denies the type of application. Then you choose the group or users you want the rule to affect. Next, you select conditions for the rule:

- *Publisher*—Base the rule on a specific publisher of an application, such as Microsoft or Symantec.
- *Path*—Select the folder the application can be run from. All subfolders are affected by default.
- *File hash*—Create a rule for an unsigned application.

The next window depends on the condition you choose. If you choose Publisher, you're prompted to specify details (see Figure 8-25). You must first select a signed reference file, which can be the actual application you're creating the rule for or just a sample application from the application publisher. You can use the slider (shown in the figure) to change the rule from more specific to less specific. For example, with the slider all the way down, the actual application filename and version are specified. With the slider all the way up, any publisher is allowed. If you set the slider at Publisher, all applications from Microsoft are included in the rule. You can click the "Use custom values" check box to change aspects of the application's properties. If you're finished creating the rule, click Create or click Next if you want to specify exceptions. You can also specify a name for the rule or accept the default name, which is based on the rule's properties.

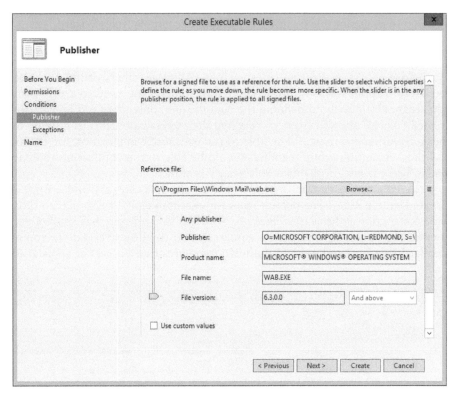

Figure 8-25   Specifying details for the Publisher condition

If you choose the Path condition, you're prompted to specify a folder or file the rule should affect. If you select a folder, all files in the folder are affected by the rule. After specifying the path, you can add exceptions to the rule and give it a name.

If you choose the File hash condition, you're prompted to select a file from which the hash is created. This option is used for unsigned applications, and the hash value is used to positively identify the file. This option prevents a user from renaming a disallowed application with the name of an allowed application.

Creating Automatically Generated Rules   Rules that are generated automatically are created by Windows after analyzing files in a folder you select. You create automatically generated rules by right-clicking the rule category and clicking Automatically Generate Rules. You select the users or groups to which the rule should apply, the folder to analyze, and a name for the set of rules to be generated. By default, the C:\Program Files folder is selected for analysis. Next, you select rule preferences (see Figure 8-26). You can create publisher rules (described previously in "Creating Custom Rules") for digitally signed files, and if the file isn't digitally signed, you can choose a file hash rule or a path rule. Optionally, you can create hash rules for all files in the folder, but this method isn't recommended because each time a file is revised (for example, with an application update), the hash rules must be updated.

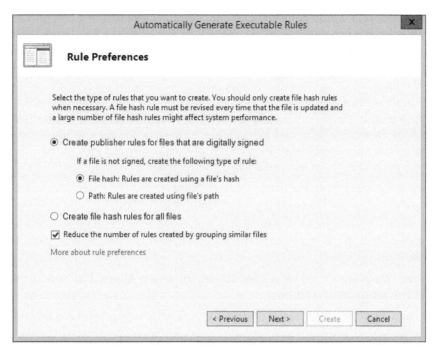

Figure 8-26   The Rule Preferences window

In the last window of the wizard, you can review the files that were analyzed and view the rules to be generated automatically. If you want, you can exclude one or more files on the list, and then a rule isn't created for that file.

 Computers affected by AppLocker policies must have the Application Identity service set to Automatic, which you can do with a Group Policy setting, as shown in Activity 8-15.

Activity 8-15: Creating an Application Control Policy

Time Required: 20 minutes
Objective: Create an application control policy.

Required Tools and Equipment: 410Server1 and 410Win8
Description: You want to see how the Application Control Policies settings work differently from software restriction policies, so you create a rule in the AppLocker node.

 If you aren't running Windows 8.1 Enterprise Edition, this lab won't work as written. You can configure the AppLocker policy, but it won't affect Windows 8.1 Pro Edition. Alternatively, you can link the GPO to the Domain Controllers OU and test the policy with 410Server1.

1. Log on to 410Server1 as **Administrator**, if necessary.

2. Open the Group Policy Management console, and then open **GPO1** in the Group Policy Management Editor. Expand **Computer Configuration, Policies, Windows Settings, Security Settings,** and **Application Control Policies.** Click **AppLocker** and in the right pane, read the Getting Started, Configure Rule Enforcement, and Overview sections to see what's available. If you have time, click **More about AppLocker** in the Getting Started section to read more about this policy online.

3. Click **Configure rule enforcement**. Notice that none of the Configured check boxes are selected; rules are enforced by default unless you click the Configured check box and then click "Audit only." You need to click the Configured check box to enforce rules only if you need to override settings on a conflicting GPO. For now, leave the default settings, and click **Cancel**.

4. Click to expand **AppLocker** so that you see the four rule categories under it. Click **Executable Rules**. In the right pane, right-click empty space and click **Create Default Rules**. Click each of the default rules and examine the properties so that you know how you can change the default rules if needed. Be careful not to make any changes to the rules; click **Cancel** to close the properties of each rule when you're finished examining it.

5. Delete the first rule in the list by right-clicking it, clicking **Delete**, and clicking **Yes**. The rule you deleted allows Everyone to run executable files in the C:\Program Files folder.

6. In the left pane, right-click **Executable Rules** and click **Create New Rule** to start the Create Executable Rules Wizard. Read the information in the Before You Begin window, and then click **Next**.

7. In the Permissions window, accept the default action **Allow**, and click the **Select** button next to the User or group text box.

8. In the Select User or Group dialog box, type **TestGroup1**, click **Check Names**, and click **OK**. TestGroup1 contains the users testuser1 and testuser2. By specifying that only this group is allowed, all other users are prohibited from accessing the applications defined in the rule. Click **Next**.

9. In the Conditions window, accept the default option **Publisher** and click **Next**. In the Publisher window, click **Browse** next to the Reference file text box. In the Open dialog box, double-click **Windows NT**, double-click **Accessories**, and click **wordpad.exe**. Click **Open**.

10. In the Publisher window, move the slider up and down to see how it changes which properties are included in the rule. Leave the slider all the way down at File version, and then click **Next**.

11. In the Exceptions window, click **Next**. In the Name window, type **WordPad** in the Name text box. In the description text box, type **Allow TestGroup1 wordpad.exe** and click **Create**.

12. The Application Identity service must be set to Automatic on computers affected by AppLocker. Under the Security Settings node, click **System Services** and double-click **Application Identity** in the right pane. Click **Define this policy setting** and then click **Automatic**. Click **OK**.

13. Close the Group Policy Management Editor, and in the Group Policy Management console, link **GPO1** to **TestOU3**.

14. Log on to 410Win8 as sales1. Open a command prompt window. Type **gpupdate /force** and press **Enter** to make sure the new policy is applied. Close the command prompt window.

15. Start Notepad to verify that you can run programs in the C:\Windows directory. Exit Notepad.

16. Right-click **Start**, click **Run**, type **wordpad** in the Open text box, and press **Enter**. You see a message stating that your system administrator has blocked the program. Because sales1 isn't included in the rule (only members of TestGroup1 are), this user account isn't permitted to run the application. Click **OK**.

17. Log off 410Win8. On 410Server1, unlink **GPO1** from **TestOU3**. In the Group Policy Objects folder, open **GPO1** in the Group Policy Management Editor. Navigate to the **Application Control Policies** node, and then right-click **AppLocker** and click **Clear Policy**. Click **Yes**, and then click **OK**.

18. Stay logged on if you're continuing to the next activity.

 A common use of AppLocker is controlling which version of applications users can run. For example, for compatibility or security reasons, you might want users to run only Internet Explorer 10 and later as their Web browser.

Computer Configuration: Administrative Templates

Both Computer Configuration and User Configuration have an Administrative Templates folder. In the Computer Configuration node, the settings in Administrative Templates affect the HKEY_LOCAL_MACHINE key of the computer's Registry. Hundreds of settings are defined in this node, and many more can be added through customization. The Administrative Templates folder uses policy definition files, called **administrative template files**, in XML format, which makes creating your own policies fairly easy if you need to control a setting not provided by default. These text files, referred to as "ADMX files" because of their `.admx` extension, specify Registry entries that should be controlled and the type of data the entries take. Many software vendors provide administrative template files for controlling their applications' settings through group policies. For example, Microsoft offers administrative template files for the Microsoft Office suite.

Windows versions before Vista and Server 2008 used `.adm` files. This format can still be used on the same system as ADMX files, but you can create and edit ADMX files only on Windows Vista or later computers. ADMX files can also have an `.adml` extension, which provides a language-specific user interface in the Group Policy Management Editor. On a Windows Server 2008 or Vista and later computer, you can find all ADMX and ADML files under %*systemroot%* PolicyDefinitions and open them in Notepad or another text editor. Administrative Templates settings and ADMX files are covered in more detail in *MCSA Guide to Administering Windows Server 2012/R2, Exam 70-411* (Cengage Learning, 2015).

The Administrative Templates folder in the Computer Configuration node, where many aspects of the computer working environment are controlled, contains the following folders and nodes, most with additional subnodes:

- *Control Panel*—This folder has three subfolders: Personalization, Regional and Language Options, and User Accounts. Personalization has settings that affect the look of Windows; in particular the lock screen and background. Settings in Regional and Language Options allow administrators to set and restrict the language in the Control Panel user interface. The policy in User Accounts configures a default user logon picture for all users on target computers.

- *Network*—A host of network settings can be controlled on target computers, including but not limited to Background Intelligent Transfer Service (BITS) parameters, DNS client settings, Microsoft Peer-to-Peer Networking Services, network connection settings, offline files configuration, and TCP/IP settings.

- *Printers*—Policies in this folder control how computers interact with network printers, including automatic printer publishing in Active Directory, automatic printer pruning, and Internet printing parameters.

- *Server*—Policies in this folder control options for backing up a computer.

- *Start Menu and Taskbar*—Policies in this folder allow you to specify a Start screen layout and pin apps to the Start screen.

- *System*—This folder contains more than 30 subnodes. Some computer functions that can be controlled in this node include disk quotas, group policies, system logon, power management, and user profiles.

- *Windows Components*—This folder contains more than 50 subnodes with policies for configuring the CD/DVD autoplay feature, Internet Explorer, and Windows Update, among others. Some settings in this folder have an identical counterpart in the User Configuration node. When a conflict exists, the setting in Computer Configuration takes precedence.

An additional node under Administrative Templates called All Settings displays all Administrative Template settings and can be sorted in alphabetical order. You can select View, Filter Options from the GPME menu to list policies by certain criteria or keywords, too.

Policies in the User Configuration Node

Policies set under the User Configuration node follow a user wherever he or she logs on. As mentioned, this node has both a Policies and Preferences folder and the same top-level folders under Policies as the Computer Configuration node: Software Settings, Windows Settings, and Administrative Templates. Many of the policy categories are the same, but there are important differences in the actual policies. Notably, because most security settings and account policies apply to computers rather than users, the User Configuration node has far fewer security settings. User Configuration policies tend to focus on the user working environment: Windows features the user can and can't access, the desktop look and feel, user profile settings, and so forth. The following sections describing policies available in the User Configuration node use an approach similar to the "Policies in the Computer Configuration Node" section.

User Configuration: Software Settings   The Software Installation extension under Software Settings performs the same function as in Computer Configuration—deploying software to remote destinations—but because it's defined in the User Configuration node of a GPO, it affects users in the scope of the GPO no matter where they log on. As mentioned, software installation using group policies is covered in depth in *MCSA Guide to Administering Windows Server 2012/R2, Exam 70-411* (Cengage Learning, 2015).

User Configuration: Windows Settings   Windows Settings contains four subnodes, three of which have the same name as in the Computer Configuration node:

- *Scripts (Logon/Logoff)*—Identical to the Scripts (Startup/Shutdown) policy, except scripts specified here are run only by users in the GPO's scope. If both a startup and logon script are to run, the startup script runs first. If both a shutdown and logoff script are to run, the logoff script runs first.

- *Security Settings*—This subnode contains two folders: Public Key Policies, which defines parameters for using certificate services, and Software Restriction Policies, which is the same as the Software Restriction Policies node in Computer Configuration except the policies are targeted at specific users, regardless of which computer they log on to.

- *Folder Redirection*—Controls which folders in a user's profile are redirected to a location outside the user's profile folder. Redirecting users' profile folders to a network share is recommended when roaming profiles are used to reduce logon and logoff delays and reduce the bandwidth needed to upload and download profile data.

- *Policy-based QoS*—The same function as in the Computer Configuration node but applied to users.

User Configuration: Administrative Templates   The settings in Administrative Templates under User Configuration affect the HKEY_CURRENT_USER section of the computer's Registry. Most of the previous information about Administrative Templates in the Computer Configuration node applies to the User Configuration node, too. Administrative Templates in User Configuration also contain the Control Panel, Network, Start Menu and Taskbar, System, and Windows Components subnodes as well as the following subnodes:

- *Desktop*—Controls the look of users' desktops, determines which icons are available, and can limit actions users can take on the desktop.

- *Shared Folders*—Controls whether a user can publish shared folders and DFS root folders.

Hundreds of settings are available in Administrative Templates—far too many to explain in detail in this book. The best way to become acquainted with the myriad settings that can be controlled through Group Policy is to read the Help box in the properties of policies you want to investigate further.

Group Policy Management and Monitoring

Creating, configuring, and testing group policies are essential parts of managing a Windows network. As you have seen, it's no small job to get policies tested and working in an optimal fashion. Windows includes tools for managing GPOs and monitoring group policies to help make designing and testing easier. The following sections cover these aspects of group policy management and monitoring:

- Managing GPO status and link status
- Creating and working with an ADMX central store

Managing GPO Status and Link Status   After a GPO is created, it can be in one of the following states:

- *Link status: unlinked*—The GPO is in the Group Policy Objects folder but hasn't been linked to any container objects.
- *Link status: enabled*—The GPO is listed under the container object, and the link is enabled. This status is set by right-clicking a container, clicking Link an Existing GPO, and choosing a GPO from the Group Policy Objects folder or by right-clicking a container and clicking "Create a GPO in this domain, and Link it here."
- *Link status: disabled*—The GPO is listed under the container object and the link is disabled. Link status can be toggled between enabled and disabled by right-clicking a GPO linked to a container and clicking Link Enabled.
- *GPO status: Enabled*—The GPO is fully functional. In the Group Policy Objects folder, right-click a GPO, point to GPO Status, and click Enabled.
- *GPO status: User Configuration Settings Disabled*—The User Configuration node isn't processed by computers running the group policy client. In the Group Policy Objects folder, right-click a GPO, point to GPO Status, and click User Configuration Settings Disabled.
- *GPO status: Computer Configuration Settings Disabled*—The Computer Configuration node isn't processed by computers running the group policy client. In the Group Policy Objects folder, right-click a GPO, point to GPO Status, and click Computer Configuration Settings Disabled.
- *GPO status: All Settings Disabled*—The GPO is disabled. In the Group Policy Objects folder, right-click a GPO, point to GPO Status, and click All Settings Disabled.

The ADMX Central Store   ADMX files, as discussed, contain the settings in the Administrative Templates folder. The **ADMX central store** is a centralized location for maintaining ADMX files so that when an ADMX file is modified from one domain controller, all DCs receive the updated file. You can also create custom ADMX files that are available to all administrators to use without having to copy the files from one location to another.

The default location of ADMX files is in the *%systemroot%*\PolicyDefinitions folder. Without a central store, any ADMX file you customize or create would have to be copied manually to all other systems where group policies are being configured and managed. In a large network with many people working with group policies, ADMX files would get out of sync rapidly without a central store.

To create a central store, simply create a folder named PolicyDefinitions in the *%systemroot%*\SYSVOL\sysvol*domainname*\Policies folder (the same folder where GPTs are stored). Under the PolicyDefinitions folder, create a language-specific folder that uses the two-character ISO standard for worldwide languages. Variations of some languages use an additional two characters to specify the country. For example, English is en-us for U.S. English or en-GB for Great Britain English. In a network with multiple domain controllers, the central store should be created on the DC that controls the PDC emulator role.

After creating folders for the central store, you just need to copy the ADMX files from their current location to the central store location. If you're managing ADMX files from a computer other than where you created the central store, the process is easy—simply copy the ADMX files to the SYSVOL share (*server*\SYSVOL*domainname*\Policies\PolicyDefinitions). Because the SYSVOL share is replicated, the files and folders in the PolicyDefinitions folder are, too.

Activity 8-16: Creating the ADMX Central Store

Time Required: 10 minutes
Objective: Create the ADMX central store.

Required Tools and Equipment: 410Server1
Description: You want administrators to be able to work on group policies and customize administrative templates from any Windows Server 2012 R2 or Windows 8.1 computer. To keep ADMX files from becoming unsynchronized, you need to create a central store.

1. Log on to 410Server1 as **Administrator**, if necessary.

2. Open File Explorer and navigate to **C:\Windows**. Click the **Windows** folder in the left pane. Right-click the **PolicyDefinitions** folder in the right pane and click **Copy**.

3. Navigate to **C:\Windows\SYSVOL\sysvol\410Server2012.local\Policies**. Right-click the **Policies** folder and click **Paste**. By pasting the entire PolicyDefinitions folder, there's no need to create the folder structure.

4. Double-click the new **PolicyDefinitions** folder to inspect the contents. There should be more than 170 ADMX files and a language-specific folder.

5. To see the contents of an ADMX file, you can open it with Notepad. To associate ADMX files with Notepad, double-click `Desktop.admx`. You see a message stating that Windows can't open this type of file. Click **Try an app on this PC**. When asked how you want to open the file, click the **Use this app for all .admx files** check box, and then click **Notepad**.

6. Browse through the `Desktop.admx` file to get an idea of how these files are structured, and then close all open windows. Stay logged on if you're continuing to the next activity.

ADMX files are complex. If you want to learn more about them to customize existing ADMX files or create your own administrative templates for use in Group Policy, search for "managing ADMX files" on the Microsoft Web site. You'll find a number of documents, including a step-by-step guide for managing ADMX files. The topic is also covered in more detail in *MCSA Guide to Administering Windows Server 2012/R2, Exam 70-411* (Cengage Learning, 2015).

Using Security Templates

Security templates are text files with an `.inf` extension that contain information to define policy settings in the Computer Configuration\Policies\Windows Settings\Security Settings node of a local or domain GPO. You can use them to create and deploy security settings to a local or domain GPO. Simply right-click the Security Settings node and click Import policy, and then select a security template file to apply. Security templates can also be used to verify the current security settings on a computer against the settings in a template. There are three tools for working with security templates, discussed in the following sections: the Security Templates snap-in, the Security Configuration and Analysis snap-in, and `secedit.exe`.

The Security Templates Snap-in

You use the Security Templates snap-in to create and edit security templates. You can create templates for computers with differing security requirements, such as servers with different roles installed or different physical locations. Servers in branch offices that don't have tight physical security, for example, might require stronger security settings than servers in a secure location. Computers used by employees who have access to sensitive information often require tighter security than computers used by employees with limited access on the network.

 **NOTE** Before Windows Server 2008, preconfigured security templates were designed for servers, domain controllers, and workstations with varying needs for security. These templates are no longer available. However, when Windows Server 2012/R2 is configured as a domain controller, the initial security settings are in *%systemroot%*\security\templates\DC security.inf.

Figure 8-27 shows the Security Templates snap-in with a new security template named LowSecurityWS. Notice that only a subset of the policies in a GPO are available in the template. When a user creates a new template, it's stored in the user's Documents folder in Security\Templates. After the template is created, it can be imported into a local or domain GPO or be used by the Security Configuration and Analysis snap-in. If you configure account policies in your template to import into a GPO, remember that settings in the Account Policy node are used only when linked to a domain or applied to a local GPO.

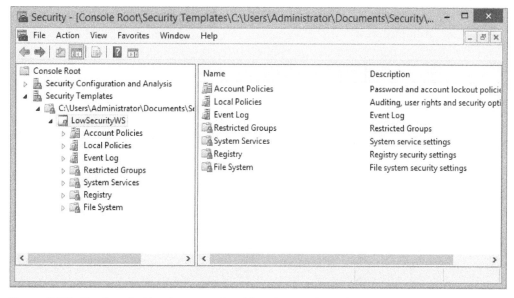

Figure 8-27   The Security Templates snap-in with an imported template

The Security Configuration and Analysis Snap-in

The Security Configuration and Analysis snap-in is useful for checking a computer's existing security settings against the known settings in security template files that have been imported into a security database. You can also use this snap-in to apply a security template to a computer. Windows doesn't supply a preconfigured MMC, so you have to add this snap-in to an MMC. If you'll be working with security templates quite a bit, you can create a custom MMC containing the Security Templates and Security Configuration and Analysis snap-ins.

When you analyze a template against the current security settings on a computer, a report is generated. For each policy setting, there are five possible results:

- An X in a red circle indicates that the template policy and current computer policy don't match.

- A check mark in a green circle indicates that the template policy and computer policy are the same.

- A question mark in a white circle indicates that the policy wasn't defined in the template or the user running the analysis didn't have permission to access the policy.

- An exclamation point in a white circle indicates that the policy doesn't exist on the computer.

- No indicator indicates that the policy wasn't defined in the template.

Activity 8-17: Creating a Security Template

Time Required: 15 minutes
Objective: Create a security template.

Required Tools and Equipment: 410Server1 and 410Win8
Description: You want to create a set of security baselines for your servers and computers. You start by exporting the current security settings on 410Win8 to a new security template and editing some settings that are suitable for computers that don't require a high level of security. Then you analyze the template settings against 410Win8's current security settings.

You create the security template on 410Win8 in this activity, but you could create all your templates on a server share, and then access them as needed from workstations to perform a security configuration analysis.

1. Start 410Server1 and 410Win8, if necessary. Log on to the domain from 410Win8 as **Administrator**.

2. Open the Local Security Policy MMC by right-clicking **Start**, clicking **Run**, typing **secpol. msc**, and pressing **Enter**. Right-click **Security Settings** and click **Export policy**. In the File name text box, type **LowSecurityWS**, and then click **Save**. Close the Local Security Policy MMC.

3. Start an MMC console. Add the **Security Templates** and **Security Configuration and Analysis** snap-ins to it, and save the console to your desktop with the name **Security**.

4. Click to expand **Security Templates**. Click to expand the folder under Security Templates, and then click **LowSecurityWS**. (If you want to create a new template from scratch, you right-click the folder and click New Template.)

5. Click to expand **LowSecurityWS** and **Local Policies**, and then click **User Rights Assignment**. In the right pane, double-click **Back up files and directories**. In the Properties dialog box, verify that the **Define these policy settings in the template** check box is selected. Click **Add User or Group**. In the User and Group names text box, type **Users**, and then click **OK** twice.

6. Double-click **Change the time zone**. Click **Users**, click the **Remove** button, and then click **OK**.

7. Double-click **Force shutdown from a remote system**. In the Properties dialog box, click **Add User or Group**. In the User and Group names text box, type **Users**, and then click **OK** twice.

8. In the left pane, click **Security Options**. In the right pane, double-click **Accounts: Limit local account use of blank passwords to console logon only**. Click **Disabled**, and then click **OK**.

9. Double-click **Interactive logon: Do not require CTRL+ALT+DEL**. Click to select the **Define this policy setting in the template** check box. Click **Enabled**, and then click **OK**.

10. In the left pane of the Security console, right-click **LowSecurityWS** and click **Save**.

11. Click the **Security Configuration and Analysis** snap-in, and then right-click it and click **Open Database**. In the File name text box, type **wslowsec**, and then click **Open**. In the Import Template dialog box, click **LowSecurityWS**, and then click **Open**. Read the message in the middle pane.

12. Right-click **Security Configuration and Analysis** and click **Analyze Computer Now**. In the Perform Analysis dialog box, click **OK**. The security analysis is performed.

13. Under Security Configuration and Analysis, expand **Local Policies**, and then click **User Rights Assignment**. You should see a window similar to Figure 8-28. Each policy has a Database Setting column and a Computer Setting column. (The red and green indicators you see on some policies were explained previously.)

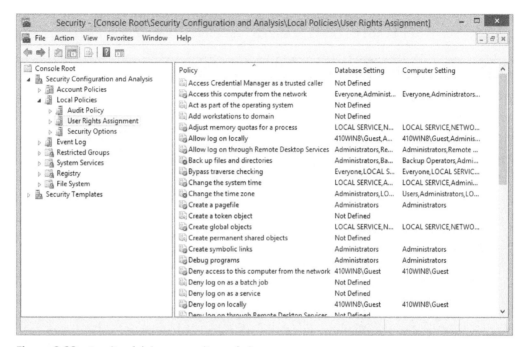

Figure 8-28   Results of doing a security analysis

14. Click the **Security Options** node to see the results of the analysis on that node.

15. Close all open windows, but stay logged on to 410Win8 and leave 410Server1 running for the next activity. When prompted to save the Security MMC, click **No**.

The `secedit.exe` Command-Line Program

`Secedit.exe` is a command-line program that performs many of the same functions as the Security Configuration and Analysis snap-in. Because it's run from the command line, however, you can use it in scripts and batch files to automate the process of working with security templates. `Secedit.exe` has options to import or export some of or all the settings between a security database and a template file. It can also compare settings between a security database and a computer's current settings or apply a security database to a computer.

Activity 8-18: Exploring the `secedit.exe` Command

Time Required: 10 minutes
Objective: Explore the syntax of the `secedit.exe` command.

Required Tools and Equipment: 410Server1 and 410Win8
Description: You want to start working with `secedit.exe` so that you can create batch files and scripts to work with security templates more easily. You start by using the command to display its options and syntax.

1. Start 410Server1 and 410Win8, if necessary. Log on to the domain from 410Win8 as **Administrator**, if necessary.

2. On 410Win8, open a command prompt window, type **secedit**, and press **Enter** to see a list of options to use with `secedit.exe`.

3. Type **secedit /configure | more** and press **Enter**. You see a description of the /configure option followed by the correct syntax for using it.

4. Repeat Step 3 five times, substituting **/analyze, /import, /export, /validate**, and **/ generaterollback** for /configure to see the syntax for these options.

5. Type **cd \users\administrator\documents\security\database** and press **Enter** to change to the directory where the wslowsec database from the previous activity was created. Type **dir** and press **Enter**. You should see the wslowsec.sdb file.

6. Type **secedit /analyze /db wslowsec.sdb /log seclog.txt** and press **Enter**.

7. Type **notepad seclog.txt** and press **Enter** to see a text file of the security analysis report. Exit Notepad.

8. Close the command prompt window. Stay logged on to 410Win8 and keep 410Server1 running for the next activity.

Configuring Windows Firewall with Group Policy

Windows Firewall is the last defense against outside intrusions into a computer. It's much too important to leave up to regular users to configure on their own. Fortunately, you can centrally manage all client and server firewall settings with Group Policy. If different computers require different settings, you simply place these computers in separate OUs with different GPOs linked, or you use one of the GPO-filtering methods described earlier.

Windows Firewall settings are in Computer Configuration, Policies, Windows Settings, Security Settings, Windows Firewall with Advanced Security. In this folder is the Windows Firewall with Advanced Security extension followed by the LDAP path of the GPC in Active Directory. When you click the extension, you see the window shown in Figure 8-29, which looks identical to the Windows Firewall with Advanced Security MMC. If you've used that console, configuring the firewall in Group Policy will seem familiar. Configuring Windows Firewall with Advanced Security is covered in detail in "Configuring Windows 8, Exam 70-687." This section covers some details of configuring it in Group Policy.

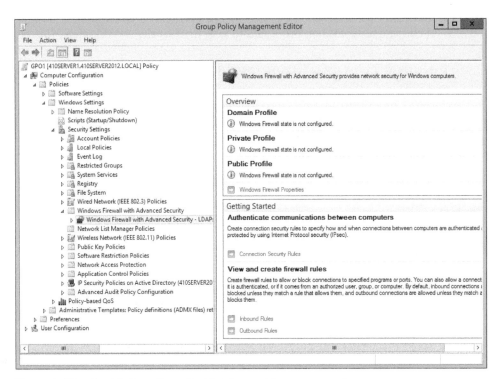

Figure 8-29   The Windows Firewall with Advanced Security extension

Configuring Rules for Multiple Profiles

The Overview section in Figure 8-29 has three headings: Domain Profile, Private Profile, and Public Profile. Each refers to a Network Location Awareness setting. The **Network Location Awareness** feature in Windows configures each network connection on your computer with one of the three settings: Domain, Private, and Public. The network location setting for each connection determines which firewall profile is applied to that connection. This feature provides flexibility so that, for example, if you're connected to your home or work network, you can have the Private or Domain profile set, which allows services such as file and printer sharing. If you're connected to a public network, such as at school or a library, you probably want the Public profile set, which restricts these services. If you have multiple connections at the same time, the correct profile is applied to each connection.

To configure a profile, click Windows Firewall Properties (shown at the bottom of the Overview section in Figure 8-29) to open the dialog box shown in Figure 8-30. You see tabs for configuring each profile as follows:

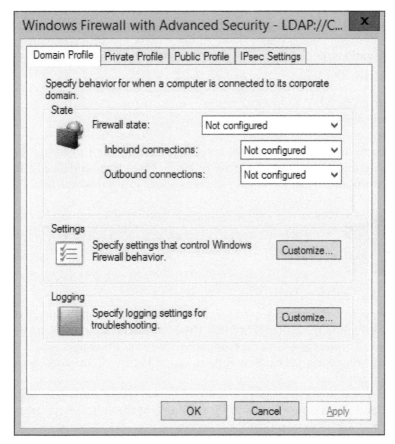

Figure 8-30 Configuring Windows Firewall properties

- *Firewall state*—You can choose from the following settings:

  o Not configured: The firewall profile is not configured. The computer's local settings or settings from another linked GPO are used.

  o On: The firewall has been enabled for the selected profile.

  o Off: The firewall has been disabled for the selected profile. This option isn't recommended.

- *Inbound connections*—Has an effect only if the firewall profile is on. An inbound connection refers to other computers trying to connect to the local computer or send it network packets. Inbound connections can be configured as follows:

   o Not configured: The computer's local settings or settings from another linked GPO are used.

   o Block (default): Blocks all inbound connections unless there's a firewall rule that allows it.

   o Block all connections: Blocks all inbound connections even if there's a firewall rule that allows it.

   o Allow: Allows all inbound connections unless there's a firewall rule that blocks it.

- *Outbound connections*—Has an effect only if the firewall profile is on. An outbound connection refers to the local computer initiating a connection with other computers.

   o Not configured: The computer's local settings or settings from another linked GPO are used.

   o Block: Blocks all outbound connections unless there's a firewall rule that allows it.

   o Allow (default): Allows all outbound connections unless there's a firewall rule that blocks it.

In most situations, you should configure these default settings for each of the three profiles:

- *Firewall state*—On
- *Inbound connections*—Block (default)
- *Outbound connections*—Allow (default)

You probably noticed a fourth tab, IPsec Settings. It's used to define the default settings when IPsec is used in a connection security rule. The IPsec settings defined here can be overridden by connection security rules, which you learn about in the next section.

 When you configure firewall settings in Group Policy, the settings apply only to computers in the scope of the linked GPO. All the normal inheritance and precedence rules described earlier apply.

Configuring Connection Security Rules

Connection security rules allow you to specify which connections should be authenticated and encrypted by using Internet Protocol Security (IPsec). By default, no rules are defined. To create a connection security rule, right-click the Connection Security Rules node under Windows Firewall with Advanced Security and click New Rule to start the New Connection Security Rule Wizard (see Figure 8-31).

There are several steps to creating a new connection security rule. The first step is specifying the rule type, and the last step is specifying the name of the rule. The steps in between depend on the rule type, which can be one of the following:

- *Isolation*—Connections rules are based on authentication type and connection profile. For example, you can prevent computers in the domain from connecting to computers outside the domain. When this rule type is selected, you must specify the following: authentication requirements, authentication method, and connection profile settings.

- *Authentication exemption*—Creates a rule that exempts certain computers from authentication. You use this rule for servers that provide key services in your network, such as domain controllers, DNS servers, and DHCP servers. These servers must be communicated with before authentication can occur, so they must be exempted from authentication. You also use this rule to exempt computers that can't use the type of authentication you have configured. When you select this rule type, you must configure the computers to exempt and the connection profile settings.

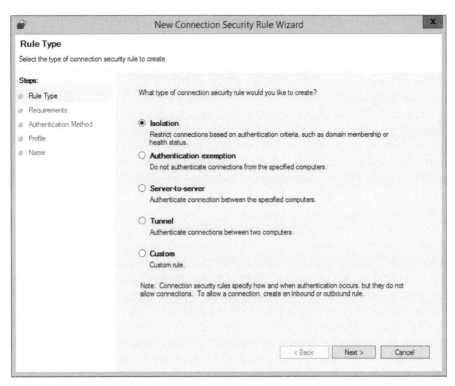

Figure 8-31   The New Connection Security Rule Wizard

- *Server-to-server*—Used to require authentication between two specific computers, between IP subnets, or between a specified computer and a group of computers in a subnet. When this rule type is specified, you must configure the following: endpoints (which computers or subnets are subject to the rule), authentication requirements, authentication method, and connection profile settings.

- *Tunnel*—Use tunnel mode instead of transport mode to secure communication. In transport mode, authentication and encryption occur at each computer. In tunnel mode, you specify an endpoint, such as a router or gateway, and authentication and encryption occur between the endpoints. When you specify tunnel mode, you must configure the following: tunnel type, authentication requirements, tunnel endpoints, authentication method, and connection profile settings.

- *Custom*—Create a custom rule if no other rule types meet your needs.

Configure Inbound and Outbound Rules

You configure inbound and outbound rules to allow or block specific applications from communicating on the network or to allow or block specific network ports. Ports are used to specify source and destination applications when two computers are communicating. For example, when you open a Web browser, the window is assigned a port number so that when a Web page is requested from a Web server, Windows knows the data should be sent to this window. The Web server is also assigned a port number—usually port 80, the standard port number for the HTTP protocol. When the computer running the Web browser sends a request to the Web server, the port number assigned to the Web browser window is the source port, and the Web server port number is the destination port. Likewise, when the Web browser sends data back to the computer running the Web browser, the Web server port number is the source port, and the port number assigned to the Web browser window is the destination port. You can also configure rules to allow an inbound or outbound connection if the computers are authenticated.

You can define inbound and outbound rules for each network connection profile, and the rules can be different depending on which profile is active for a connection. For example, you have a computer with two network interfaces. One interface is connected to the company network, which has the domain profile applied, and the other interface is connected to a wireless network that has the public profile applied. You can define an inbound rule for the domain profile that allows computers to connect to shared folders on your computer if the communication occurs on the network interface connected to the company network. By default, the public profile disallows this communication, so computers on the wireless network wouldn't be able to access the network shares.

Creating Inbound and Outbound Rules
Inbound rules control what kind of network connections the computer allows when another computer initiates the connection. Outbound rules control communication initiated by the local computer. In Group Policy, no rules are defined by default, but rules you create in Group Policy can override rules already defined on the computers the policy affects. On a local computer, there are predefined rules for each profile, depending on what services a computer is running.

To create an inbound rule or outbound rule, right-click the Inbound Rules or Outbound Rules node under the Windows Firewall with Advanced Security node and click New Rule to start the New Inbound Rule (or Outbound Rule) Wizard. You choose from the following rule types:

- *Program*—Creates a new rule that applies to all programs or a specific program. If you select "All programs," the rule applies to all programs that match other rules. If the rule should apply to a specific program, you enter the path to the executable program file.
- *Port*—Creates a rule that specifies a particular TCP or UDP port, a range of ports, or all ports.
- *Predefined*—Creates one or more rules for a built-in Windows service. The rules are listed for you to select which rules you want to create.
- *Custom*—Allows you to create a custom rule in which you can specify programs, ports, Windows services, and IP addresses to which the rule should apply.

After you specify the rule type and related parameters for the rule type, you specify an action that should be taken when a connection matches the specified rule:

- *Allow the connection.*
- *Allow the connection if it is secure*—The connection is allowed only if it has been authenticated by IPsec. When this option is selected, it's referred to as an "authenticated firewall exception." It's an exception because all other connections are blocked except those made by applications that meet authentication requirements. By clicking the Customize button, you can specify authentication requirements and whether the connection must be encrypted. You can also include or exclude specific users from the rule.
- *Block the connection.*

After you specify an action, you choose which profiles the rule should apply to: Domain, Private, or Public. Last, you name the rule. In most cases, the rules you define are inbound rules because the biggest security risks lie with outside computers attempting to make connections with computers inside your network. However, you might need to create outbound rules to prevent users from accidentally or purposely running applications that make unsafe or undesirable network connections to other computers.

Activity 8-19: Creating an Inbound Firewall Rule

Time Required: 15 minutes

Objective: Create an inbound firewall rule and examine its effect.

Required Tools and Equipment: 410Server1 and 410Win8

Description: You want to experiment with configuring Windows Firewall in Group Policy. By default, Windows Firewall blocks `ping` packets, so you create a rule that allows `ping` packets on the domain profile only. You apply the GPO to the OU holding your 410Win8 computer account.

1. Start 410Server1 and 410Win8, if necessary. On 410Server1, log on as **Administrator**, if necessary.

2. Open a command prompt window. Type **ping 410Win8** and press **Enter**. The `ping` messages should not be successful. You should see a "Request time out" message repeated four times. (If the `ping` messages are successful, log on to the domain from 410Win8 as **Administrator**, open Windows Firewall in Control Panel, and click **Restore defaults**. The default settings block incoming `ping` packets.)

3. On 410Server1, open the Group Policy Management console. Create a GPO in the Group Policy Objects folder named **TestFW**, and open **TestFW** in the Group Policy Management Editor.

4. In the Group Policy Management Editor, navigate to **Computer Configuration, Policies, Windows Settings,** and **Security Settings.** Click to expand **Windows Firewall with Advanced Security,** and then click the **Windows Firewall with Advanced Security** node under it. In the right pane, read the information in the Overview and Getting Started sections.

5. In the left pane, click to expand **Windows Firewall with Advanced Security.** Click to select **Inbound Rules,** and then right-click **Inbound Rules** and click **New Rule.** The New Inbound Rule Wizard starts, shown in Figure 8-32. Click each rule type to see how the steps in the left pane change. When you're finished, click the **Custom** option button, and then click **Next.**

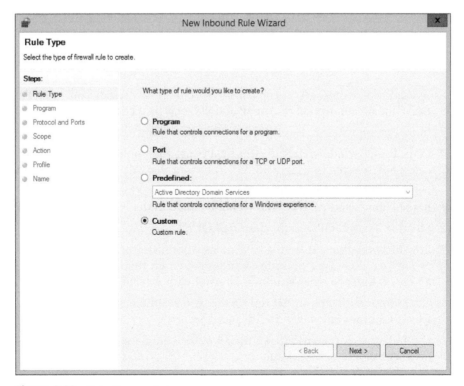

Figure 8-32 Selecting a rule type

6. In the Program window, click **Next** because you're not specifying a particular program.

7. In the Protocol and Ports window, click **ICMPv4** in the Protocol type list box, which is the protocol that `ping` messages use (see Figure 8-33). Then click the **Customize** button. Click the **Specific ICMP types** option button, and click to select **Echo Request**. Echo Request is the specific type of packets the `ping` program generates. Click **OK**, and then click **Next**.

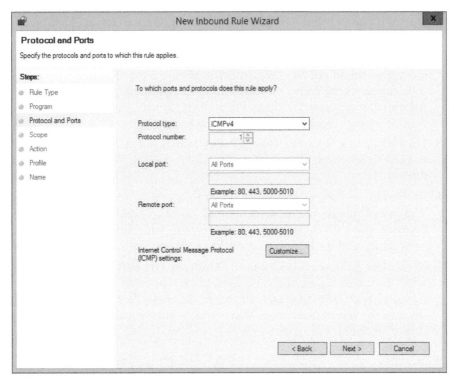

Figure 8-33   Specifying protocols and ports

8. In the Scope window, you can choose specific IP addresses you want the rule to apply to. Leave the default option of **Any IP address**, and then click **Next**.

9. In the Action window, leave the default option **Allow the connection**, and click **Next**.

10. In the Profile window, click to clear the **Private** and **Public** check boxes, but leave the **Domain** check box selected (see Figure 8-34). You want this rule to apply only to the Domain profile. Click **Next**.

11. In the Name window, type **Allow Ping-Domain** in the Name text box, and then click **Finish**.

12. Link the **TestFW** GPO to the **TestOU3** OU.

13. Log on to the domain from 410Win8 as **Administrator**, if necessary, and open a command prompt window. Type **gpupdate** and press **Enter**. Right-click **Start**, click **Run**, type **wf.msc**, and press **Enter** to open Windows Firewall with Advanced Security.

14. Click **Inbound Rules**. In the right pane, you see the new rule you created listed at the top. Close Windows Firewall with Advanced Security.

15. On 410Server1, type **ping 410Win8** at the command prompt and press **Enter**. The `ping` messages should be successful.

16. Close the command prompt window. Unlink **TestFW** from **TestOU3**. Log off or shut down 410Win8 and 410Server1.

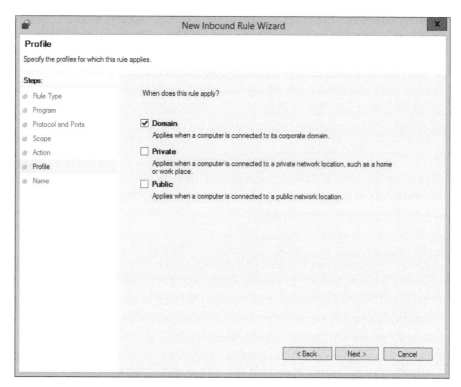

Figure 8-34 The Profile window

Export and Import Windows Firewall Settings

You can spend quite a bit of time getting your firewall rules just right. You might need to use the rules you have created in more than one domain, or you might need to use the rules on a non-domain member that can't be configured with Group Policy. Fortunately, you can export and import firewall settings with the Import Policy and Export Policy options.

To export a policy, in the GPME, right-click the Windows Firewall with Advanced Security node and click Export Policy. You're prompted to save the policy file with the extension `.wfw`. Enter a name and save the file.

To import a policy, right-click the Windows Firewall with Advanced Security node and click Import Policy. You're warned that your current settings will be overwritten. Select a previously exported policy file and click Open. That's all there is to it. You can also export and import policies in the Windows Firewall with Advanced Security console on any computer.

Chapter Summary

- Group policy architecture and function involves these components: GPOs, replication, scope and inheritance, and creating and linking GPOs. GPOs can be local or domain. Windows Vista and Server 2008 have three new local GPOs (stored on the local computer). A domain GPO consists of a Group Policy Template (GPT), stored in the SYSVOL share, and a Group Policy Container (GPC), stored in Active Directory.

- GPO replication is handled by Active Directory replication for GPCs and by FRS or DFSR for GPTs. DFSR is used only when all DCs are running Windows Server 2008 and later.

- You use the Group Policy Management console to create, link, and manage GPOs and the Group Policy Management Editor to edit GPOs. Changes to linked GPOs take effect as soon as the user logs on or the computer restarts or at the time of the next policy refresh, whichever comes first. GPO changes should be made when the GPO is not linked to a container object.

- Starter GPOs are like template files for GPOs. You can create a GPO by using a Starter GPO as a baseline. Starter GPOs contain only the Administrative Templates folder in the Computer Configuration and User Configuration nodes.

- GPOs can be linked to sites, domains, and OUs. Policies are applied in this order, and the last policy setting applied takes precedence when conflicts exist. Local policies are applied before domain policies, so when conflicts exist, domain policies take precedence over local policies.

- Default GPO inheritance can be changed by using inheritance blocking, enforcement, and GPO filtering.

- The Computer Configuration and User Configuration nodes contain three subnodes: Software Settings, Windows Settings, and Administrative Templates. If settings in these two nodes conflict, computer settings take precedence. Software Settings can be used to assign or publish software packages remotely to users and assign software packages remotely to computers.

- The Security Settings node in Computer Configuration contains the Account Policies subnode with settings that affect all domain users. The Account Policies subnode contains Password Policy, Account Lockout Policy, and Kerberos Policy subnodes.

- The Local Policies subnode in the Security Settings node contains Audit Policy, User Rights Assignment, and Security Options. To audit object access, you must enable the object access audit policy and then enable auditing on the target object.

- Administrative Templates can control hundreds of settings on computers and for users. Administrative Templates use ADMX files to define the policies that affect settings in the HKLM and HKCU sections of the Registry.

- Security templates are used to transfer security settings easily from one GPO or computer to another and can be used to analyze a computer's current settings against a security database created from one or more security templates.

- The ADMX central store can be created to ensure that ADMX files are synchronized among all computers where group policies are managed.

Key Terms

administrative template files   These XML format text files define policies in the Administrative Templates folder in a GPO. You can create custom ADMX files to create your own policies.

ADMX central store   A centralized location for maintaining ADMX files so that when an ADMX file is modified from one domain controller, all DCs receive the updated file.

domain GPOs   Group Policy Objects stored in Active Directory on domain controllers. They can be linked to a site, a domain, or an OU and affect users and computers whose accounts are stored in these containers.

elevation   A process that occurs when a user attempts to perform an action requiring administrative rights and is prompted to enter credentials.

GPO filtering   A method to alter the normal scope of a GPO and exclude certain objects from being affected by its settings. GPO filtering methods include security filtering, which uses GPO permissions, and WMI filtering, which uses Windows Management Instrumentation queries to select objects. *See also* WMI filtering.

Group Policy Container (GPC)   A GPO component that's an Active Directory object stored in the System\Policies folder. The GPC stores GPO properties and status information but no actual policy settings.

Group Policy Template (GPT)   A GPO component that's stored as a set of files in the SYSVOL share. It contains all the policy settings that make up a GPO as well as related files, such as scripts.

local GPOs   A Group Policy object that's stored on local computers and can be edited by the Group Policy Object Editor snap-in.

managed policy setting　A type of group policy setting whereby the setting on the user or computer account reverts to its original state when the object is no longer in the scope of the GPO containing the setting.

Network Location Awareness　A Windows feature for configuring each network connection on your computer with one of three settings, called profiles: Domain Profile, Private Profile, and Public Profile.

security templates　Text files with an `.inf` extension that contain information to define policy settings in the Computer Configuration, Policies, Windows Settings, Security Settings node of a local or domain GPO.

Starter GPO　A GPO template that can be used as a baseline for creating new GPOs, much like user account templates.

unmanaged policy setting　A type of group policy setting whereby the setting on the user or computer account is persistent, meaning it remains even after the computer or user object falls out of the GPO's scope.

User Account Control policies　Policies that determine what happens on a computer when a user attempts to perform an action that requires elevation. *See also* elevation.

WMI filtering　A GPO filtering method that uses Windows Management Instrumentation (WMI), a Windows technology for gathering management information about computers.

8

Review Questions

1. Which of the following is a local GPO on a Windows 8.1 computer? (Choose all that apply.)

   a. Local Administrators

   b. Local Default User

   c. Local Default Domain

   d. Local Non-Administrators

2. Where is a GPT stored?

   a. In a folder named the same as the GPO in the SYSVOL share

   b. In a folder named the same as the GUID of the GPO in Active Directory

   c. In a folder named the same as the GUID of the GPO in the SYSVOL share

   d. In a folder named the same as the GPO in Active Directory

3. A user-specific local GPO takes precedence over a site-linked GPO. True or False?

4. You're having replication problems with your GPOs and suspect that the version numbers have somehow gotten out of sync between the GPT and the GPC. What can you do to verify the version numbers on a GPO?

   a. Check the versionNumber attribute of the GPC and open the `GPT.INI` file.

   b. Check the versionNumber attribute of the GPT and open the `GPC.INI` file.

   c. Right-click the GPO in the Group Policy Management console, click Properties, and view the version in the General tab.

   d. Right-click the GPO in the Group Policy Management Editor, click Properties, and view the version in the General tab.

5. All your domain controllers are running Windows Server 2012 R2. You're noticing problems with GPT replication. What should you check?

   a. Verify that Active Directory replication is working correctly.

   b. Verify that FRS is operating correctly.

   c. Verify that DFSR is operating correctly.

   d. Check the GPOReplication flag for the GPT in the Attribute Editor.

6. Which of the following is an inbound and outbound rule type you can create with Windows Firewall with Advanced Security? (Choose all that apply.)

   a. Program

   b. Port

   c. Server

   d. Isolation

7. You have created a GPO that defines settings only in the Local Policies node. You want the settings to apply to all computers in the domain and take precedence over any other GPOs. Which of the following is the best approach?

   a. Link the new GPO to the domain, and unlink the Default Domain Policy. Right-click the domain object and click Enforced.

   b. Link the new GPO to each OU containing computer accounts, and make sure it has link order 1.

   c. Link the new GPO to the domain, and then right-click the new GPO and click Enforced.

   d. Link the new GPO to the domain, make sure it has the highest link order, and then right-click the domain object and click Block Inheritance.

8. Which of the following represents the correct order in which GPOs are applied to an object that falls within the GPO's scope?

   a. Site, domain, OU, local GPOs

   b. Local GPOs, domain, site, OU

   c. Domain, site, OU, local GPOs

   d. Local GPOs, site, domain, OU

9. Your network consists of three sites and two domains, with some computers from both domains at each site. Each site has certain security settings that should apply to all computers from both domains when they're located at the site. What's the best way to ensure that the correct security settings are applied to the computers at each site?

   a. Create three OUs in each domain, one for each site. In both domains, place the computer accounts in the OU corresponding to the site where the computer is located. Apply a GPO with the appropriate security settings to each OU in both domains.

   b. Create three GPOs, one for each site, with the appropriate security settings. Apply the GPOs to the corresponding site, and enforce the GPO.

   c. Create three GPOs, one for each site. Apply the GPOs to the domain object in both domains. Create three groups, one for each site, and place the computer accounts in the appropriate groups. Use GPO filtering to make sure the policy configured for each site affects only the corresponding group of computers.

   d. On each computer in each site, configure the local GPO in GPOE with the appropriate security settings. In the Group Policy Object Editor, right-click the Computer Configuration node and click Block Inheritance.

10. Objects in an OU with the Block Inheritance option set are affected by a domain-linked GPO with the Enforced option set. True or False?

11. You have created a GPO named RestrictU and linked it to the Operations OU (containing 30 users) with link order 3. RestrictU sets several policies in the User Configuration node. After a few days, you realize the Operations OU has three users who should be exempt from the restrictions in this GPO. You need to make sure these three users are exempt from

RestrictU's settings, but all other policy settings are still in effect for them. What's the best way to proceed?

a. Move the three users to a new OU. Create a GPO with settings appropriate for the three users, and link it to the new OU.

b. Create an OU under Operations, and move the three users to this new OU. Create a GPO, and link it to this new OU. Configure the new OU to block inheritance of the RestrictU GPO.

c. Create a global group and add the three users as members. Configure GPO security filtering so that the global group is denied access to the GPO.

d. Set the Enforced option on RestrictU with an Enforce filter that excludes the three user accounts.

12. You want to make changes to policy settings that affect File Explorer. The settings are in the Administrative Templates folder of the User Configuration node. You want the settings to affect all users in the domain. Which of the following is the best way to accomplish this?

a. Create a GPO, configure the policy, and link the GPO to the Domain object.

b. Create a GPO, configure the policy, and link the GPO to the Users OU.

c. Configure the policy in the Default Domain Controllers Policy GPO.

d. Configure the policy in the Default Domain Policy GPO and set a security filter for the Domain Users group.

13. In Active Directory, all your computer accounts are in the Computers folder, and all your user accounts are in the Users folder. You need to configure an AppController policy that affects users who log on to computers in the Engineering Department. Which of the following is the best way to accomplish this?

a. Place the Engineering Department user accounts in a group. Create a new GPO, configure the AppController policy, and link the GPO to the group you created.

b. Place the Engineering Department computer accounts in a group named Eng. Create a new GPO, configure the AppController policy, and link it to the domain object. Set a security filter for the Eng group.

c. Move the Engineering Department user accounts to a new OU named Eng. Configure the AppController policy on the Default Domain Policy GPO. Set Block Inheritance on the Users folder.

d. Move the Engineering Department computer accounts to a new OU named Eng. Create a new GPO, configure the AppController policy, and link the GPO to the Eng OU.

14. You have been working with ADMX files to modify existing Administrative Templates and create new templates. You work on different domain controllers, depending on your location. Despite a concerted effort, your ADMX files are getting out of sync. How can you solve this problem?

a. Remove group policy management tools from all but one domain controller so that policies can be managed from only one computer.

b. Create an ADMX store in the SYSVOL share, and copy the ADMX files to the ADMX store.

c. Create an ADMX store in Active Directory, and move all your ADMX files to Active Directory.

d. Share the %systemroot%\PolicyDefinitions folder on all your domain controllers, and set up Task Scheduler to copy ADMX files automatically from one system to all other systems.

15. What Group Policy feature should you use if you have a policy linked to an OU that contains computer accounts but want the policy to affect only computers running Windows 7? You don't know exactly which computer accounts represent the computers running Windows 7.

    a. Disabling inheritance

    b. Policy enforcement

    c. WMI filtering

    d. Security filtering

16. You're concerned that some domain controllers and workstations don't meet security requirements. What should you do to verify security settings on a computer against a list of known settings?

    a. Create a security template and run Group Policy Modeling.

    b. Create a security database from a template and run `secedit.exe`.

    c. Load the Security Templates snap-in and use the Group Policy Results feature.

    d. Export the Security Settings node on the computer and run Security Configuration and Analysis.

17. None of the computers in an OU seem to be getting computer policies from the GPO linked to the OU, but users in the OU are getting user policies from this GPO. Which of the following is a possible reason that computer policies in the GPO aren't affecting the computers? (Choose all that apply.)

    a. The GPO link is disabled.

    b. The Computer Configuration settings are disabled.

    c. The computer accounts have Deny Read permission.

    d. The OU has the Block Inheritance option set.

18. Which of the following sets the profile for each network connection on your computer?

    a. The Network Connection policy under the Software Settings node

    b. The Windows Firewall with Advanced Security policy

    c. The Properties dialog box of each network interface

    d. The Network Location Awareness feature

19. You want to configure an inbound firewall rule that allows a connection only if the computer trying to make the connection is authenticated. What option should you select?

    a. Allow the connection if it is secure

    b. Block unauthenticated connections

    c. Isolation mode

    d. Allow Domain connections

20. You want to configure an encrypted and authenticated connection between two gateway computers. What rule type should you configure in the New Connection Security Rule Wizard?

    a. Isolation

    b. Server-to-server

    c. Tunnel

    d. Authentication exemption

21. You want to create policies in a new GPO that affects only computers with Windows 7 installed. You don't want to reorganize your computer accounts to do this, and you want computers that are upgraded to Windows 8.1 to fall out of the GPO's scope automatically. What can you do?

    a. For each policy, use selective application to specify Windows 7 as the OS.

    b. Create a new OU, place all computer accounts representing computers with Windows 7 installed in this OU, and link the GPO to this OU.

    c. Create a group called W7Computers. Place all computer accounts representing computers with Windows 7 installed in this group, and use this group in a security filter on the GPO. Link the GPO to the domain.

    d. Configure a WMI filter on the GPO that specifies Windows 7 as the OS. Link the GPO to the domain.

22. When a policy setting in Computer Configuration and User Configuration in the same GPO conflict, the Computer Configuration policy setting takes precedence. True or False?

23. You're a consultant for a small company that uses eight Windows 8.1 computers in a work-group configuration. The owner asked you to set restrictive policies on users to prevent them from making Control Panel, desktop, and other changes. The owner wants to be exempt from these policies but shouldn't be a member of the local Administrators group. What should you do?

    a. Configure the Local Computer Policy object, and then configure a user-specific GPO for the owner.

    b. Configure the Local Computer Policy object, and use GPO filtering to exempt the owner from this policy.

    c. Install Windows Server 2012 R2 and configure Active Directory. Add the Vista computers to the domain, configure a GPO for the domain, and use filtering to exempt the owner.

    d. Configure the Local Computer Policy object, and then configure a logon script for the owner that changes the restrictive settings.

24. You want to have a library of GPOs that specify baseline settings for different policy categories, and you can use this library to create new GPOs with baseline settings already configured. What's the best way to accomplish this?

    a. Create a number of GPOs in the Group Policy Objects folder and export the settings.

    b. Create Starter GPOs for each policy category you want to configure.

    c. Configure the GPOs in the Group Policy Modeling folder.

    d. Create GPOs in offline mode and save them to the central store.

25. Which type of connection security rule should you configure if you want to prevent computers in your domain from connecting to computers outside the domain?

    a. Isolation

    b. Authentication exemption

    c. Server-to-server

    d. Tunnel

Case Projects

The following case projects work with GPOs for the csmtech.local OU structure. When possible, GPOs should be named CSM-OU*whereLinked*-C/U. For example, a GPO linked to the csmtech.local OU that configures computer settings should be named CSM-csmtech-C.

Case Project 8-1: Creating a Computer GPO for CSM Tech Publishing

Create a GPO that meets the following requirements:

- Set computer security policies that affect all computers as follows:
  - Deny guests the ability to log on to computers from the network.
  - Do not display the last username that logged on to a computer.
  - Do not allow a system to be shut down unless somebody is logged on.
  - When logon hours expire, users should be logged off the system.
- Set the following additional policies that affect all computer accounts:
  - Change the default group policy refresh interval to 45 minutes for computers, with the random time interval set to 15 minutes.
  - Configure user profiles to be deleted after 90 consecutive days of nonuse.
  - Configure Windows Update so that updates are downloaded and installed automatically every day at 3:00 a.m.

Case Project 8-2: Analyzing Security Settings

Create a security database with Security Configuration and Analysis, using a template file created by exporting settings from the GPO you created in Case Project 8-1. Use this security database to analyze the security settings of your 410Win8 computer. Print the log file and hand it in to your instructor.

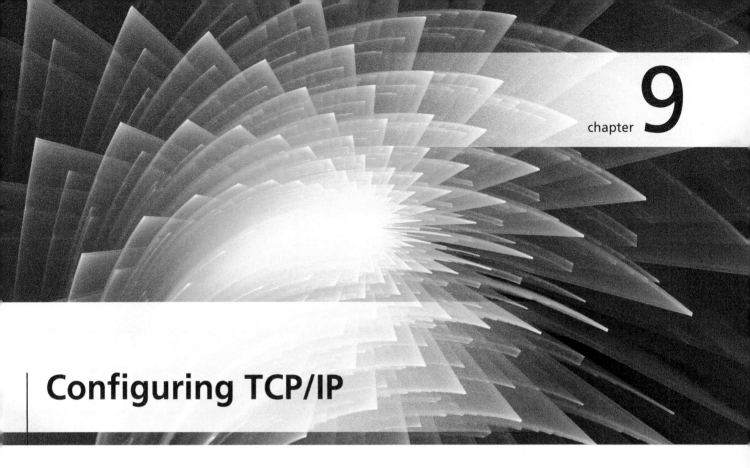

chapter 9

Configuring TCP/IP

After reading this chapter and completing the exercises, you will be able to:

- Describe the TCP/IP protocol and its components
- Define IPv4 addressing and calculate subnet masks
- Configure IPv4 addresses
- Describe IPv6 addresses
- Define IPv6 address types
- Autoconfigure IPv6 addresses
- Transition from IPv4 to IPv6

The TCP/IP protocol suite has been used to facilitate communication between computers for more than 40 years. From the smallest LAN to the worldwide Internet, computers use this enduring protocol because of its reliability, flexibility, and scalability. Although it has undergone changes throughout the years, the underlying protocol remains. In this chapter, you learn about some components of the TCP/IP protocol suite and how to subnet IPv4 addresses. Next, you learn how to configure IPv4 addresses on Windows computers with both GUI and command-line tools.

Although TCP/IP is scalable, developing a replacement for IPv4 has become necessary with the explosion of the Internet that started in the 1990s. This replacement, IPv6, provides a nearly unimaginable number of IP addresses with its 128-bit address space. You learn about the structure of IPv6 addresses, a variety of methods for configuring IPv6 addresses on host computers, and ways to transition from an IPv4 network to an IPv6 network.

An Overview of TCP/IP

Table 9-1 summarizes what you need for the hands-on activities in this chapter.

Table 9-1   Activity requirements

Activity	Requirements	Notes
Activity 9-1: Converting Decimal Numbers to Binary		
Activity 9-2: Converting Binary Numbers to Decimal		
Activity 9-3: Working with CIDR Notation		
Activity 9-4: Determining the Correct Prefix		
Activity 9-5: Using the `arp` Command	410Win8, 410Server1	Internet access needed
Activity 9-6: Using the `tracert` Command	410Win8, 410Server1	Internet access needed
Activity 9-7: Setting IPv6 Static Addresses	410Win8, 410Server1, 410Server2	
Activity 9-8: Working with IPv6	410Win8, 410Server1	

© 2015 Cengage Learning®

Transmission Control Protocol/Internet Protocol (TCP/IP) is a network protocol designed to deliver data packets to computers on any scale of network, from a small two-computer LAN to the worldwide Internet. TCP/IP is a suite of protocols, meaning it's composed of several protocols performing different functions but working together. The name comes from two of these protocols: Transmission Control Protocol (TCP) and Internet Protocol (IP).

Network operating systems now include two versions of IP, so you see TCP/IPv4 and TCP/IPv6 (or just IPv4 and IPv6) when examining a network interface's properties in Windows Server 2012/R2. The TCP part stays the same whether you're using IPv4 or IPv6, as do most other protocols in the suite, but the IP part of the suite is where big changes have occurred between versions. IP (both v4 and v6) is the focus of this chapter; later chapters discuss other components of the TCP/IP suite.

So why is a suite of protocols needed instead of just one protocol? The reason is that networking is a complex process, and all the components of TCP/IP have a specific job so that a single component doesn't become too big and unwieldy. It's because of this partitioning of responsibilities among protocols in the suite that TCP/IPv4 and TCP/IPv6 can run on the same system, with the changes mostly isolated to the functions IP performs. Just so you have an idea of the multitude of tasks a suite of networking protocols handles, here's a partial list, in no particular order:

- Logical addressing
- Logical to physical address resolution
- Name resolution

- Dynamic address assignment
- Efficient packet delivery
- Reliable packet delivery
- Packet sequencing
- Status messages
- File transfer
- Web page transfer
- Security

IP performs some of these functions alone, some are performed with a combination of IP and TCP, and others are performed by other protocols in the suite. So if you need to make a change to logical addressing, for example, which is handled by IP, you just need to change IP and leave the other protocols alone. In fact, the logical addressing shortcomings in IPv4 were the impetus for the development of IPv6. The next section lists some specific protocols in TCP/IP and their function.

This chapter refers to layers of the Open Systems Interconnect (OSI) model when discussing TCP/IP protocols, so make sure you understand the OSI model before studying the material in this chapter.

9

TCP/IP Components

TCP/IP is the default network protocol installed on Windows computers. Both Internet Protocol Version 4 (TCP/IPv4) and Internet Protocol Version 6 (TCP/IPv6) are installed on Windows computers starting with Windows Vista and Windows Server 2008. As mentioned, TCP/IP is a suite of protocols, so when it's installed on a computer, a number of protocols, services, and programs are usually installed with it. Some of the more common TCP/IP-related protocols are listed here with a brief description. Most of these protocols operate in a similar fashion in both IPv4 and IPv6; any differences are noted:

- *Domain Name System*—DNS is an Application-layer protocol that resolves domain names to addresses. When a network resource is requested by its name, such as \\server1\Shared or www.microsoft.com, DNS client software queries a DNS server to resolve the name of the server hosting the resource to its IP address. The DNS client protocol is installed automatically on Windows computers running TCP/IP. A DNS server, which is required to run a Windows domain, can be added as a server role in Windows Server 2012/R2 (discussed in Chapter 10).

- *Dynamic Host Configuration Protocol*—DHCP provides automatic IP address configuration and operates at the Application layer. By default, Windows computers are configured to request their IP address configuration from a DHCP server. The client portion of DHCP is installed by default on all computers with TCP/IP installed. IPv6 uses DHCPv6 and requires separate configuration from DHCPv4. The DHCP server role can be installed in Windows Server 2012/R2 and is discussed in Chapter 11.

- *Transmission Control Protocol*—TCP is a Transport-layer component of the TCP/IP suite that provides reliable data transfer between applications on computers. It handles flow control, packet sequencing, and data acknowledgments to help ensure that data transfers are completed without error. TCP is used by applications that require reliable transfer of large amounts of data. Because it's used to communicate between applications, it allows a single computer to run many applications that use TCP/IP and keep track of all the conversations.

- *User Datagram Protocol*—UDP is also a Transport-layer protocol used to communicate between applications, but it's a lightweight protocol. It's used by applications transferring only small amounts of data that don't require the reliability features of TCP.

- *Internet Protocol version 4*—IPv4, operating at the Network layer, is the TCP/IPv4 component that provides logical network addressing, efficient packet delivery, and routing. It's still the most commonly used version of IP, but the trend is moving toward IPv6.

- *Internet Protocol version 6*—IPv6 offers the same functions as IPv4, but it addresses some shortcomings of IPv4, as you learn in this chapter. Like IPv4, IPv6 is a Network-layer protocol and is installed by default on Windows Server 2012/R2. It's becoming more important in networking, especially in large networks and ISPs.

- *Address Resolution Protocol*—ARP resolves a computer's IPv4 address to its physical, or Media Access Control (MAC), address. When a computer or router must deliver a packet of data to another computer or router in the same network, ARP can be used to request the destination device's MAC address. ARP operates at the Network layer and is used only by IPv4.

- *Internet Control Message Protocol (ICMP)*—ICMP is a Network-layer protocol the ping program uses to test whether a computer can communicate with another computer. ICMP is also used by computers and network devices to send status messages to one another.

- *Internet Control Message Protocol (ICMPv6)*—ICMPv6 also operates at the Network layer and can be used to test connectivity. It's used for a host of other functions in an IPv6 network, including neighbor discovery, which replaces the function of ARP in an IPv4 network and performs router discovery and address autoconfiguration functions.

The TCP/IP suite has several other protocols, and not all these protocols are discussed at length in this book. This chapter focuses on IPv4 and IPv6 and some ancillary protocols, such as ICMP and ARP. Chapters 10 and 11 discuss DNS and DHCP in detail.

TCP/IP Communication

Before you get into the details of IP, you should make sure you have a solid understanding of the basic process of communication between two computers. Communication between two computers using TCP/IP often begins when one computer (the client) requires access to a resource or service on another computer (the server). When a user initiates the communication, the server's name is usually used. For example, a user wants to view the home page for *www.csmtech.local*. The user opens a Web browser and types "www.csmtech.local" in the address bar. For communication to proceed, the Web server's name (*www.csmtech.local*) must be resolved to its IP address, which involves a request to a DNS server.

After the client has the Web server's IP address, it must determine whether it's on the same network or a different network. The client finds this information by comparing its IP address with the Web server's IP address (discussed later in more detail in "IPv4 Addresses"). If the client and Web server are on the same network, the client must get the Web server's MAC address before the request can be sent. If they're on different networks, the client sends the request to its default gateway, or router. The router forwards the request until it gets to a router connected to the Web server's network. Understanding the basics of TCP/IP communication helps you better understand IP configuration and addressing, discussed throughout this chapter.

Before continuing, review the following general network terms:

- *MAC address*—The Physical-layer address that's an integral part of a network interface card (NIC). A NIC processes data it receives on the network only if the destination MAC address indicates the data is intended for that computer.

- *Frame*—A formatted unit of data that's ready to be transferred to the network medium. It contains a destination and source MAC address and an error-checking code called the frame check sequence (FCS). A frame is the unit of data used by the Data Link layer.

- *Packet*—The Network-layer unit of data used by IPv4 and IPv6. Its header contains the destination and source IP addresses along with other flags and parameters.

- *Segment*—The Transport-layer unit of data and is used by TCP and UDP. Among several other fields, it contains the destination and source port numbers used to identify Application-layer protocols.

The Role of TCP and UDP   TCP and UDP have a substantial role in most communication sessions between two computers. Have you ever wondered how your computer keeps track of the myriad network applications you run? At any time, you might be running a Web browser, an e-mail application, and a chat program and have a file open on a file server. When a computer receives data from the network, a frame is received by the NIC, which sends it as a packet up to the IP protocol, which then sends a segment to TCP or UDP. Now what? Eventually, data that's received usually goes to an application or a network service.

The TCP or UDP header provides the information needed to determine which application the received data should be sent to. TCP and UDP use port numbers to specify the source and destination Application-layer protocols. Using the analogy of sending a letter via the post office, if the IP address is the zip code and the street number is the MAC address, the port number specifies the person in the house who should read the letter. In other words, the MAC address and IP address get the packet to the computer, and the port number gets the data to the application or service.

The Internet Assigned Numbers Authority (IANA), a nonprofit agency responsible for Internet addressing and address management, assigns a dedicated port number to every well-known network service. For example, the HTTP protocol used by Web servers is assigned port 80, so when your computer formats a message to a Web server, the destination port number in the TCP header is 80. Similarly, when your e-mail application requests messages from your mail server, it sends the request to port 110, the Post Office Protocol (POP3) port number. Most client applications are assigned a random port number when they make a request to a server. So when you start a Web browser, for example, the Web browser window is assigned a port number. When the request for a Web page goes out, the source port number in the TCP header contains the number assigned to that Web browser window so that the Web server knows which port the reply should be sent to. If you open another Web browser window or tab, another port number is assigned, and so forth. The port number is a 16-bit value, so theoretically, you can open as many as 65,000 windows!

You can see the list of well-known port numbers at *www.iana.org/assignments/port-numbers.*

Some applications use TCP and some use UDP, depending on the requirements of the data being transmitted. If an application tends to send large amounts of data, such as a file transfer or Web browsing, TCP is usually used for reliability. If only small amounts of data are transferred, as with DNS queries and DHCP requests, UDP is usually used for its speed and low overhead. Table 9-2 lists common TCP/IP applications and the related port numbers and protocols.

Table 9-2   Common TCP and UDP port numbers

Application	TCP or UDP	Port number
FTP data transfer	TCP	20
FTP control	TCP	21
Telnet	TCP	23
SMTP	TCP	25
HTTP	TCP	80
POP3	TCP	110
LDAP	TCP	389
HTTPS	TCP	443
DNS	UDP	53
DHCP server	UDP	67
DHCP client	UDP	68
TFTP	UDP	69
SNMP	UDP	161

IP Operation

Before you get into the details of IP addressing and configuration, you need to look more closely at the functions of IP:

- Performs logical addressing
- Ensures efficient packet delivery
- Provides the information needed for packet routing

In this section, the term "IP" is used when the discussion refers to both IPv4 and IPv6. The version number is used when discussing features and functions that are specific to a version.

Logical Addressing   You might wonder why the term "logical address" is used. It's different from the MAC address, which is burned into a computer's NIC. It's called a "physical address" because it's actually part of the physical hardware and not easily changed.

Computers running TCP/IP use both a logical (IP) and physical (MAC) address to communicate. The physical address is used to deliver data to a computer after data gets to the network the computer is connected to. The IP address is used mainly to find the network a computer is connected to and to get data to that network. When an IP packet is constructed for delivery on the network, it always contains a source address and a destination address. The **source IP address** is the IP address of the computer that's sending the packet, and the **destination IP address** is the IP address of the computer the packet is being sent to. If the destination is a computer, the destination address is called a **unicast address**, which simply means that one (uni) computer is the intended recipient. As you see later in "IPv4 Addresses," there are also multicast and broadcast addresses.

Efficient Packet Delivery   IP is designed to deliver packets efficiently, so it doesn't have a lot of features for guaranteeing delivery of large amounts of data on a complex network. Its main job is to get data to the correct network and deliver it to the destination computer. If a large file consisting of hundreds or thousands of packets is transferred across the network, IP's only concern is delivering each packet making up the file, not delivering the file as a whole. If a packet gets lost or arrives at the destination out of order, fixing it isn't IP's job.

Returning to the mail delivery analogy, after you drop an envelope in a mailbox, you really have no way of knowing whether it made it safely to its destination. Certainly the mailman doesn't tell you. This process is like what happens with IP. If you want to know whether the letter arrived safely, you have to pay extra for certified mail, which is like using TCP as the Transport-layer protocol. With certified mail, an extra layer of complexity is added to send you an acknowledgement that your letter was delivered. The same is true of IP packets using TCP. IP just delivers packets, and TCP supplies the acknowledgement that a packet arrived at its destination. TCP can also assemble packets in the correct sequence if they arrive out of order. Most Internet data transfers use IP with TCP to ensure reliability.

Packet Routing   Routing packets is a key responsibility of IP. Routers use the destination IP address in each packet to determine which network the packet should be sent to and the best way (the route) to get it there. For example, in Figure 9-1, the networks are labeled Network 1 through Network 5, and the routers are labeled A to E. If Host 5.1 sends a packet to Host 2.1, the packet is first sent to Router C. Router C then determines the fastest way to get the packet to Network 2, which might mean sending it to Router A or Router B. Like traveling in a car, the shortest way isn't always the fastest way. For example, the link between Router C and Router B could be congested or a slow-bandwidth link, whereas the links from Router C to Router A to Router B might be fast and smooth sailing. It's the job of routers and the specialized IP-related protocols they run to make these decisions.

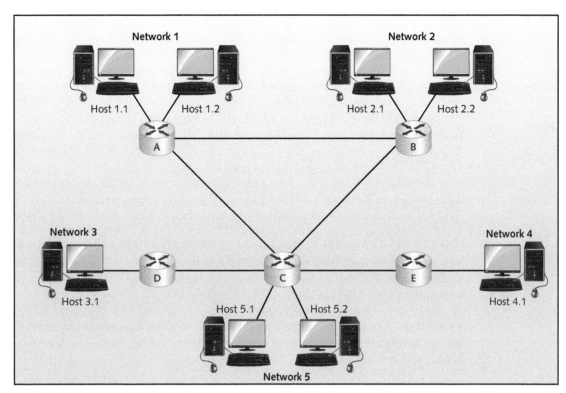

Figure 9-1   Routers in an IP network
© *2015 Cengage Learning®*

The addresses used in Figure 9-1 are simplified for the sake of illustration.

IPv4 Addresses

An IPv4 address is a 32-bit number divided into four 8-bit values called octets. Each **octet** can have a value from 0 to 255. IPv4 addresses are written in dotted decimal notation, yielding an address consisting of four decimal numbers, each in the range 0 to 255, separated by a period. For example, in the IPv4 address 10.255.0.100, 10 is the first octet and 100 is the fourth octet.

In this section, the term "IP" refers to IPv4.

Every IP address contains a network ID, which specifies the network on which the computer is found, and a host ID, which uniquely identifies the computer on that network. Determining which part of the IP address is the network ID and which part is the host ID depends on the **subnet mask**, another 32-bit dotted decimal number that consists of a contiguous series of binary 1 digits followed by a contiguous series of binary 0 digits. A contiguous series of eight binary 1s equals the decimal value 255. For example, a typical subnet mask is 255.0.0.0 or 255.255.0.0. In these two examples, for each 255 in the subnet mask, the corresponding octet of the IP address is part of the network ID.

Take a look at an example. In binary, the subnet mask 255.255.0.0 looks like 11111111.11 111111.00000000.00000000. (Binary math is discussed in the next section.) Say you configured a Windows computer with the IP address 10.1.221.101 and the subnet mask 255.0.0.0. Because the first octet of the subnet mask is 255 (a series of eight binary 1s), the first octet of the IP address is the network ID, which is 10. The network ID is written as 10.0.0.0, and the host ID is 1.221.101. Understand, however, that the network ID and host ID are used together when configuring a computer's IP address and when communicating with another computer. So the source address in a network packet being sent by the computer in this example is 10.1.221.101.

Now say the IP address is 172.31.100.6, and subnet mask is 255.255.0.0. The first two octets of the subnet mask are 255 (a total of 16 contiguous binary 1s), so the network ID is 172.31, which is written as 172.31.0.0. The host ID is 100.6. When referring to the network ID, you fill in the host part of the address with 0s.

Continuing with this pattern, say you have the IP address and subnet mask 192.168.14.250 and 255.255.255.0. They give you the network ID 192.168.14.0 and the host ID 250. You can't have the subnet mask 255.0.255.0 because the network ID must be contiguous. However, you can have an IP address and a subnet mask such as 172.16.67.5 and 255.255.192.0. What's going on in the third octet of this subnet mask? Even though this subnet mask doesn't look like the other examples, with only the values 255 and 0, it's still a contiguous series of 1s followed by a contiguous series of 0s. In binary, this subnet mask looks like this: 11111111.11111111.11000000.00000000.

In binary, the value 11000000 is the decimal number 192. The network ID in the previous example is 172.16.64.0, and the host ID is 3.5. How is this information determined? Before you go any further, it helps to understand a little about binary math and how to convert between binary and decimal.

Binary Math

An important part of IP addressing is how the subnet mask is used to determine the network ID. As you've seen, it's not as simple as stating that "Anywhere there's a 255 in the subnet mask, the corresponding octet in the IP address is part of the network ID." In addition, computers don't reason that way; they perform calculations, specifically in binary math. To determine the network ID of an IP address, computers use a **logical AND operation**, which is an operation between two binary values that you can think of as binary multiplication. Because there are only two unique digits in binary numbers, the multiplication is easy. There are only four possible results when you combine two binary numbers with AND, and three of these results are 0.

```
0 AND 0 = 0
1 AND 0 = 0
0 AND 1 = 0
1 AND 1 = 1
```

To determine the network ID based on the IP address and subnet mask, a computer simply performs a logical AND between the binary digits in the IP address and the binary digits in the subnet mask, which looks something like this:

```
10101100.00011111.01100100.00000110 (binary for 172.31.100.6)
                  AND
11111111.11111111.00000000.00000000 (binary for 255.255.0.0)
_____
10101100.00011111.00000000.00000000 (binary for 172.31.0.0)
```

You simply take the binary digit from the IP address (top number) and perform a logical AND with the corresponding digit in the subnet mask (bottom number). The result is the network ID 172.31.0.0. Take a look at the last example in the previous section:

```
10101100.00010000.01000011.00000101 (binary for 172.16.67.5)
                  AND
11111111.11111111.11000000.00000000 (binary for 255.255.192.0)
_____
10101100.00010000.01000000.00000000 (binary for 172.16.64.0)
```

After you do the AND operation, you can see the network ID 172.16.64.0 (that is, if you know how to convert binary to decimal, discussed next). The remaining bits in the IP address that are not part of the network ID are the host ID; in this case 3.5. So, essentially, what you can say is that anywhere there is a 1 bit in the subnet mask, the corresponding bits in the IP address are part of the network ID and anywhere there are 0 bits in the subnet mask, the corresponding bits are part of the host ID. This sure would be easier if you knew how to convert from decimal to binary and back, wouldn't it?

Converting Binary to Decimal   Before you start converting from binary to decimal and back, you need to review how the decimal number system works. It's based on powers of 10 (which is where the word "decimal" comes from, with "dec" meaning "ten"). Ten different symbols, 0 through 9, are used to represent any possible number. Each place in a decimal number can have one of 10 possible values: again, 0 through 9. Furthermore, each place in a decimal number can be expressed as a power of 10. The ones place can be expressed as a number, 0 through 9, multiplied by 10 raised to the 0 power, or 10^0. (Any number raised to the 0 power equals 1.) The tens place can be expressed as a number multiplied by 10 to the 1 power, or 10^1. The hundreds place can be expressed as a number multiplied by 10^2, and so on. For example, the decimal number 249 can be expressed as either of the following:

```
2 * 10² + 4 * 10¹ + 9 * 10⁰ = 249
2 * 100 + 4 * 10 + 9 * 1 = 249
```

When you see the number 249, you don't think of it in these terms because you grew up using the decimal number system, and recognizing the hundreds place, tens place, and ones place happens without conscious effort, as does the multiplication and addition that occurs. However, take a look at this number:

```
379420841249
```

A little more thought has to go into recognizing that the 3 represents 300 billion, the 7 represents 70 billion, and so forth. The binary number system works the same way, except everything is governed by twos. Two digits, 0 and 1, represent every possible number, and each place in a binary number is 0 or 1 multiplied by a power of 2. So instead of having the ones place, the tens place, the hundreds place, and so on, you have the ones place, the twos place, the fours place, and so on, based on 2^0, 2^1, 2^2, and so forth. For example, using the same method as for the decimal example, you can express the binary number 101 as either of the following. The numbers in bold are the binary digits.

```
1 * 2² + 0 * 2¹ + 1 * 2⁰ = 5
1 * 4 + 0 * 2 + 1 * 1 = 5
```

Converting Decimal to Binary   One way to convert from decimal to binary is shown in Table 9-3. The first two rows are the binary and exponent values of each bit position of an 8-bit number. You use 8 bits because in subnetting, most work can be done 8 bits at time. The third row is what you complete to determine the decimal number's binary representation.

Table 9-3   Decimal-to-binary conversion table

128	64	32	16	8	4	2	1
2^7	2^6	2^5	2^4	2^3	2^2	2^1	2^0
0	1	1	1	1	1	0	1

© 2015 Cengage Learning®

To use this method, start with the number you're trying to convert to binary: in this case, 125, which is referred to as the "test number." You compare the test number with the leftmost number in the preceding table (128). If it's equal to or greater than this number, you place a 1 in the column and subtract the number in the column from your test number; otherwise, place a 0 in the column. Remember: Eight binary places or 8 bits can represent only a value up to 255. If you're converting a number greater than 255, simply extend the table to the left (256, 512, and so on). Here's the sequence of steps:

1. 125 is less than 128, so you place a 0 in the column under the 128. The test number remains 125.

2. 125 is greater than 64, so you place a **1** in the column under the 64 and subtract 64 from 125, leaving your new test number as 61.

3. 61 is greater than 32, so you place a **1** in the column under the 32 and subtract 32 from 61, leaving your new test number as 29.

4. 29 is greater than 16, so you place a **1** in the column under the 16 and subtract 16 from 29, leaving your new test number as 13.

5. 13 is greater than 8, so you place a **1** in the column under the 8 and subtract 8 from 13, leaving your new test number as 5.

6. 5 is greater than 4, so you place a **1** in the column under the 4 and subtract 4 from 5, leaving your new test number as 1.

7. 1 is less than 2, so you place a 0 in the column under the 2.

8. 1 is equal to 1, so you place a **1** in the column under the 1 and subtract 1 from 1, leaving your new test number as 0. When your test number is 0, you're done.

Now try this with 199, 221, and 24. You should get the following results:

```
199 = 11000111
221 = 11011101
24 = 00011000
```

Converting Binary to Decimal   The easiest way to convert an 8-digit binary number (octet) is to use Table 9-3, as you did for the decimal-to-binary conversion. Of course, if your binary number is more than 8 bits, you can simply extend the table to the left as many places as necessary. Here's how to do it: Write your binary number in the third row of the table, as shown in Table 9-4. For every column with a 1 bit, write down the corresponding decimal number from the first row. For columns with a 0 bit, you can simply skip them or write down a 0. Using the binary number 11010011, you get the following:

```
128 + 64 + 0 + 16 + 0 + 0 + 2 + 1 = 211
```

Table 9-4   Converting 11010011 to 211

128	64	32	16	8	4	2	1
2^7	2^6	2^5	2^4	2^3	2^2	2^1	2^0
1	1	0	1	0	0	1	1

© 2015 Cengage Learning®

Plug in the binary values for 199, 221, and 24 to make sure you get the correct results.

Activity 9-1: Converting Decimal Numbers to Binary

Time Required: 20 minutes
Objective: Convert decimal numbers to binary.

Required Tools and Equipment: Paper and pencil
Description: Convert the following list of decimal numbers to binary without using a calculator. You can use Table 9-3 to help with the conversions or create your own table.

Decimal number	Binary number
167	
149	
252	
128	
64	
240	
255	
14	
15	
63	
188	
224	

Activity 9-2: Converting Binary Numbers to Decimal

Time Required: 20 minutes
Objective: Convert binary numbers to decimal.

9

Required Tools and Equipment: Paper and pencil
Description: Convert the following list of binary numbers to decimal without using a calculator. You can use Table 9-3 to help with the conversions or create your own table.

Binary number	Decimal number
00110101	
11111000	
00011111	
10101010	
01010101	
11111110	
11111100	
00111011	
11001100	
00110011	
00000111	
00111100	

IP Address Classes

When you enter an IP address in the Internet Protocol Version 4 (TCP/IPv4) Properties dialog box shown in Figure 9-2, Windows fills in a subnet mask automatically, which you can change if needed. Windows bases the suggested subnet mask on the class of the IP address you enter.

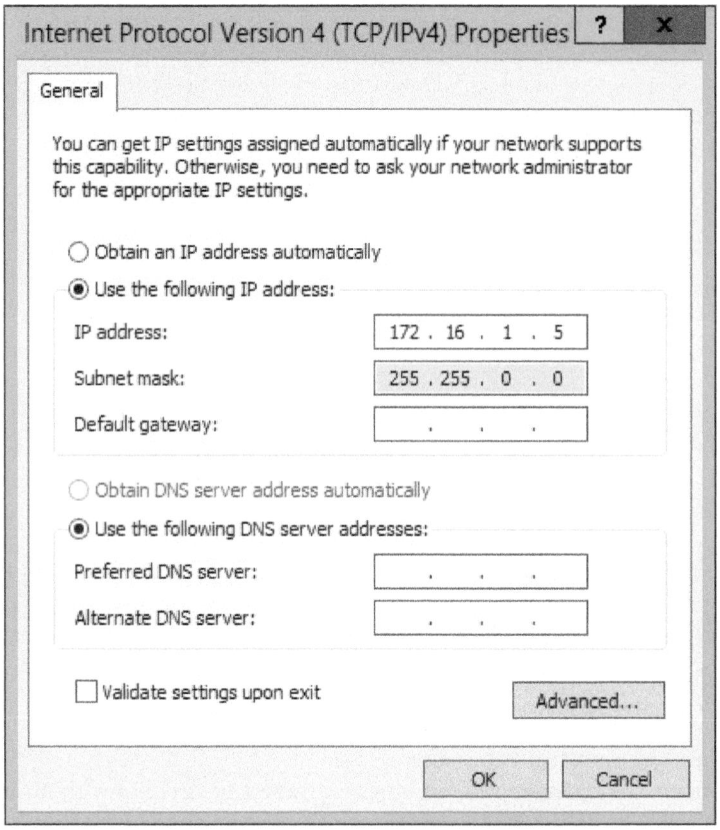

Figure 9-2 A subnet mask based on the address class

IP addresses are categorized in ranges referred to as Classes A, B, C, D, or E. Only IP addresses in the A, B, and C classes can be assigned to a network device (host). Although the IP address class system has been somewhat superseded by a more flexible way to manage IP addresses, called Classless Interdomain Routing (CIDR, discussed later in this chapter in "Classless Interdomain Routing"), the class system is a basis for determining which part of an IP address is the network ID and which part is the host ID. The first octet of an address denotes its class. Review the following facts about IP address classes:

- The value of the first octet for Class A addresses is between 1 and 127. Class A addresses were intended for use by large corporations and governments. An IP address registry assigns the first octet, leaving the last three octets for network administrators to assign to hosts. This allows 24 bits of address space or 16,777,214 hosts per network address. In a Class A IP address such as 10.159.44.201, for example, the network address is 10.0.0.0. So the first address in the 10.0.0.0 network is 10.0.0.1, and the last address is 10.255.255.254.

- Class B addresses begin with network IDs between 128 and 191 and were intended for use in medium to large networks. An IP address registry assigns the first two octets, leaving the third and fourth octets available for administrators to assign as host addresses. In the Class B address 172.17.11.4, for example, the network address is 172.17.0.0. Having two octets in the host ID allows 65,534 hosts per network address.

- Class C addresses were intended for small networks. An IP address registry assigns the first three octets, ranging from 192 to 223. In the Class C address 203.0.113.254, for example, the network address is 203.0.113.0. These networks are limited to 254 hosts per network.

- Class D addresses are reserved for **multicasting,** in which a packet is addressed so that more than one destination can receive it. Applications using this feature include videoconferencing and streaming media. In a Class D address, the first octet is in the range 224 to 239. Class D addresses can't be used to assign IP addresses to host computers.

- Class E addresses have a value from 240 to 255 in the first octet. This range of addresses is reserved for experimental use and can't be used for address assignment.

A couple of notes about this list: First, if you did your math, you would see that a Class C address provides 2^8 bits of address space, which yields 256 addresses, not 254. The number of addresses specified for Classes A and B are also two fewer than the address space suggests. This discrepancy happens because each network has two reserved addresses: the address in which all host ID bits are binary 0s and the address in which all host ID bits are binary 1s. For example, all the host bits in address 203.0.113.0 are binary 0s, and this address represents the network number and can't be assigned to a computer. The host bits in address 203.0.113.255 are binary 1s; this address is the broadcast address for the 203.0.113.0 network and can't be assigned to a computer.

The other note concerns the 127.0.0.0 network. Although technically a Class A address, it's reserved for the **loopback address,** which always refers to the local computer and is used to test the functioning of TCP/IP. A packet with a destination address starting with 127 is sent to the local device without reaching the network medium. Likewise, the reserved name **localhost** always corresponds to the IP address 127.0.0.1 so that a local machine can always be referenced by this name.

Even though localhost and the loopback address are usually associated with the address 127.0.0.1, any address in the 127.0.0.0 network (except 127.0.0.0 and 127.255.255.255) references the local machine in most OSs.

Table 9-5 summarizes address classes A, B, and C and the default subnet masks.

Table 9-5 IPv4 address class summary

Class	A	B	C
Value of first octet	0–127	128–191	192–223
Default subnet mask	255.0.0.0	255.255.0.0	255.255.255.0
Number of network ID bits	8	16	24
Maximum number of hosts/ network	16,777,214	65,534	254
Number of host bits	24	16	8

© 2015 Cengage Learning®

Private IP Addresses

Each device that accesses the Internet must do so by using a public IP address. Because of the popularity of TCP/IP and the Internet, unique IP addresses to assign to Internet-accessible devices are almost exhausted. To help alleviate this problem, TCP/IP's technical governing body reserved a series of addresses for private networks—that is, networks whose hosts can't be accessed directly through the Internet. The reserved addresses are as follows:

- Class A addresses beginning with 10 (one Class A network address)
- Class B addresses from 172.16 to 172.31 (16 Class B network addresses)
- Class C addresses from 192.168.0 to 192.168.255 (256 Class C network addresses)

The addresses in these ranges can't be routed across the Internet, which is why any organization can use them to assign IP addresses to their internal hosts. If access to the Internet is necessary, a process called Network Address Translation (NAT) is used, explained next in "Network Address Translation."

Another type of private IP address is a link-local address. It's not assigned manually or through DHCP; it's assigned automatically when a computer is configured to receive an IP address through DHCP but no DHCP service is available. Another term for this type of addressing is **Automatic Private IP Addressing (APIPA)**. APIPA addresses are assigned in the range 169.254.1.0 through 169.254.254.255 with a subnet mask of 255.255.0.0. Computers that are assigned a link-local address can communicate only on the local LAN, as packets containing these addresses shouldn't be forwarded by routers.

Link-local IPv4 addresses don't use the first and last subnets in the 169.254.0.0/16 range because these addresses are reserved for future use, according to RFC 3927.

Network Address Translation

Although subnetting can help alleviate the IP address shortage problem, it simply makes more efficient use of existing addresses. **Network Address Translation (NAT)** helps more by allowing an organization to use private IP addresses while connected to the Internet. As you learned, the three ranges of private IP addresses (one range for each class) can't be used as the source or destination address in a packet on the Internet.

Anyone can use private IP addresses for address assignment to internal computers and devices, and because the addresses aren't sent to the Internet, there's no address conflict. What if you want your computers to have access to the Internet, however? That's where NAT comes in. An organization can, for example, assign all its workstations' addresses in the 10.x.x.x private network. Say an organization has 1000 workstations. Although these addresses can't be used on the Internet, the NAT process translates a workstation address (as a packet leaves the network) into a valid public Internet address. When data returns to the workstation, the address is translated back to the original 10.x.x.x address. NAT is usually handled by a network device that connects the organization to the Internet, such as a router. As shown in Figure 9-3, when station 10.0.0.1 sends a packet to the Internet, the NAT router intercepts the packet and replaces its source address with 198.60.123.101 (a public Internet address). When a reply comes back addressed to 198.60.123.101, the NAT router replaces the destination address with 10.0.0.1.

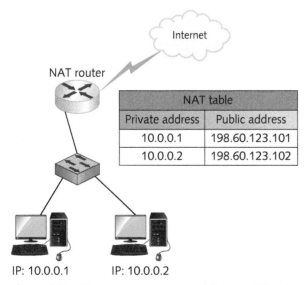

Figure 9-3   Private addresses are translated to public addresses with NAT

© Cengage Learning®

This process allows any company to use private IP addresses in its own network, requiring a public IP address only when a workstation attempts to access the Internet. An extension of NAT, called Port Address Translation (PAT), allows several hundred workstations to access the Internet with a single public Internet address.

 For an excellent tutorial on NAT, see *www.howstuffworks.com/nat.htm.*

Classless Interdomain Routing

If IP addresses have a default subnet mask assigned based on the value of the IP address's first octet, why do you even need to specify the subnet mask? The reason is the default subnet mask doesn't always suit the needs of your network. Address classes and default subnet masks were designed when TCP/IP was in its infancy, and computer networks and the Internet were almost unheard of. They met the needs of the few government agencies and universities using TCP/IP in the late 1970s and 1980s. The use of IP addresses with their default subnet masks is referred to as **classful addressing**.

After computer networks were being installed in every business, and users wanted access to the new information source called the Internet, classful addressing clearly needed some flexibility—hence, subnet masks that could be configured regardless of the address class. This type of IP address configuration became what's known as **Classless Interdomain Routing (CIDR)**. For example, assigning the IP address 172.31.210.10 with a subnet mask of 255.255.255.0 (instead of the default of 255.255.0.0) is perfectly acceptable. In this case, the network ID is 172.31.210, and the host ID is 10. Why would you want to assign a subnet mask different from the default? Aren't the default subnet masks good enough? In some cases, they are, but not in others.

Take, for instance, the address 172.31.0.0 with the default subnet mask 255.255.0.0. As Table 9-5 showed, this subnet mask allows a 16-bit host ID, making it possible to assign more than 65,000 host addresses, starting with 172.31.0.1 and ending with 172.31.255.254. (Remember that you can't assign an address with all 0 bits or all 1 bits in the host ID, so you have to exclude 172.31.0.0 and 172.31.255.255 from the possible IP addresses you can assign to a host.) The exact calculation for the number of hosts is $2^n - 2$; n is the number of bits in the host ID. Being able to assign this many addresses might seem like an advantage if you have a large network. However, having such a large address space assigned to a single network has two distinct disadvantages: If you're actually using the number of computers the address space affords (in this case, more than 65,000 computers), communication efficiency suffers, and if you aren't using the addresses, precious address space is wasted.

CIDR Notation   Writing IP addresses with their subnet masks can be tedious and takes up a lot of space. What's important is how many bits of the IP address constitute the network ID. To that end, you can specify an IP address and its subnet mask with CIDR notation. **CIDR notation** uses the format A.B.C.D/n; n is the number of 1 bits in the subnet mask, or expressed another way, the number of bits in the network ID. It's referred to as the "IP prefix" (or just "prefix"). For example, 172.31.210.10 with a 255.255.255.0 subnet mask is expressed as 172.31.210.10/24 in CIDR notation. The network ID is 24 bits, leaving 8 bits for the host ID. As another example, 10.25.106.12 with the subnet mask 255.255.240.0 is expressed as 10.25.106.12/20. In this case, the network ID is 20 bits, leaving 12 bits for the host ID.

Broadcast Domains   All computers and devices that share the same network ID in their IP address are said to be in the same broadcast domain. A **broadcast domain** defines which devices must receive a packet that's broadcast by any other device. A **broadcast** is a packet addressed to all computers on the network. TCP/IP communication relies heavily on broadcast packets to perform a variety of functions. For example, DHCP and ARP use broadcasts to perform their tasks. Every time a computer receives a broadcast packet, the NIC generates an interrupt, causing the CPU to stop what it's doing to read the packet. If the broadcast isn't relevant to the computer, the packet is usually discarded.

Now imagine 65,000 computers on the same broadcast domain; at any moment, probably several thousand are sending broadcast packets. The amount of traffic generated and the additional CPU utilization would likely bring the network to a screeching halt. Preventing this problem is where subnetting comes in.

Subnetting

If you do have 65,000 computers in your organization, instead of creating one large network with the network address 172.31.0.0/16, you can divide this very large network into many smaller subnetworks. For example, you can use 172.31.0.0/24, 172.31.1.0/24, and so forth up to 172.31.255.0/24. This strategy, called **subnetting**, makes 256 smaller subnetworks with a maximum of 2^8 - 2, or 254, devices per subnetwork. If a computer on one subnetwork needs to communicate with a computer on another subnetwork, the packets are sent to a router that locates the subnetwork and forwards the data. Now the maximum size of your broadcast domain is only 254 computers, which is more manageable.

When a classful network has been divided or subnetted into multiple smaller networks, the resulting networks are called "subnetworks." Functionally, however, there's no difference between a classful network and a subnetwork.

Another reason to subnet is to conserve IP addresses. Companies that maintain Internet-connected devices need public Internet addresses, which must be unique in the world—meaning a public address can be assigned to only one device on the Internet. In the past, if a company had four Web servers and two routers that needed public addresses, the only recourse an ISP had was to assign a class C network address consisting of 254 possible host addresses, thereby wasting 248 addresses. By subnetting a network, the ISP can assign an address such as 198.60.123.0/29 that uses only addresses 198.60.123.0 through 198.60.123.7, which satisfies the company's needs and still makes addresses 198.60.123.8 through 198.60.123.254 available for other customers.

Calculating a Subnet Mask

There are usually two approaches to subnetting, and they depend on the answer to these questions: Am I subnetting to provide a network with a certain number of host addresses? Or am I subnetting to provide a network with a certain number of subnets? If you're working for an ISP, the answer is usually yes to the first question, and if you're a network administrator for an organization, the answer is more likely to be yes to the second question. Sometimes the answer is a combination of both.

Say you have a large internetwork and need to break an IP address space into several subnets. Follow this process:

1. First, decide how many subnets you need. You can figure out the number of subnets needed by seeing how many network cable segments are or will be connected to router interfaces. Each router interface connection indicates a required subnet.

2. Next, decide how many bits you need to meet or exceed the number of required subnets. To calculate this value, use the formula 2^n, with n representing the number of bits you must reallocate from the host ID to the network ID. For example, if your starting network number is the Class B address 172.20.0.0, its default subnet mask is 255.255.0.0, which is your starting point. The number of subnets you create is always a power of 2, so if you need 20 subnets, you must reallocate 5 bits ($2^5 = 32$) because reallocating 4 bits gives you only 2^4, or 16, subnets.

3. Reallocate bits from the host ID, starting from the most significant host bit (that is, from the left side of the host ID).

4. You must also make sure you have enough host bits available to assign to computers on each subnet. To determine the number of host addresses available, use the formula discussed previously: 2^n - 2, with n representing the number of host (0) bits in the subnet mask.

Here's an example to help you put this formula to work: CSM Tech Publishing wants 60 subnets for its Class B address: 172.20.0.0/16. The nearest power of 2 to 60 is 64, which equals 2^6. This means you must reallocate 6 bits from the host portion of the original subnet mask (255.255.0.0) and make them subnet bits.

Reallocating 6 bits, starting from the leftmost bit of the third octet, creates a subnet mask with the bit pattern 11111100. The decimal value for this number is 252. This reallocating of bits changes the subnet mask from 255.255.0.0 to 255.255.252.0. Expressing it in CIDR notation gives you 172.20.0.0/22.

To calculate the number of host addresses for each subnet, just subtract the number of network ID bits from the total number of bits in an IP address: 32 - 22. The result is the number of bits left for the host ID. In this case, the number is 10. Again, the formula for determining the number of host addresses is 2^n - 2, so you have 2^{10} - 2 = 1022 addresses per subnet, which should be more than enough for most networks.

Now that you have a correct subnet mask, you need to determine what network numbers can be derived from using it. To do this, take the reallocated 6 bits, place them in the network number, and cycle the 6 bits through the possible combinations of values they represent. Table 9-6 shows the first 16 subnetwork numbers resulting from the preceding steps, with the third octet written in binary on the left and the resulting subnetwork address written in decimal on the right. The bits shown in bold are the 6 bits used to create the subnets. If you convert the third octet on the left side from binary to decimal, you'll see that it equals the third octet on the right.

Table 9-6   Subnetwork numbers and addresses

Subnetwork number in binary	Subnetwork address
172.20.**00000000**.0	172.20.0.0
172.20.**00000100**.0	172.20.4.0
172.20.**00001000**.0	172.20.8.0
172.20.**00001100**.0	172.20.12.0
172.20.**00010000**.0	172.20.16.0
172.20.**00010100**.0	172.20.20.0
172.20.**00011000**.0	172.20.24.0
172.20.**00011100**.0	172.20.28.0
172.20.**00100000**.0	172.20.32.0
172.20.**00100100**.0	172.20.36.0
172.20.**00101000**.0	172.20.40.0
172.20.**00101100**.0	172.20.44.0
172.20.**00110000**.0	172.20.48.0
172.20.**00110100**.0	172.20.52.0
172.20.**00111000**.0	172.20.56.0
172.20.**00111100**.0	172.20.60.0
...	...
172.20.**11111100**.0	172.20.252.0

© 2015 Cengage Learning®

A Pattern Emerges   Table 9-6 shows the first 16 of the possible 64 subnets and the last subnet created for network 172.20.0.0. As you can see, there's a pattern to the subnetwork numbers—they go in increments of 4. You can derive this pattern without having to list the subnets, however. Look at the octet where the subnet bits are reallocated, and then look at the rightmost reallocated bit. The subnet increment is determined by the binary place value of this bit: in this case, the 4s place.

You know when to stop counting subnets when all the subnet bits are binary 1s, as in the last entry in the table. You also know to stop counting when the subnet number equals the value of the changed octet in the subnet mask. In this case, the subnet mask 255.255.0.0 was changed to 255.255.252.0 after the bit reallocation. The 252 in the third octet of the subnet mask is the same value as the last subnet number.

Determining Host Addresses   Similarly, the host addresses in each subnet can be determined by cycling through the host bits. Therefore, the subnetwork 172.20.32.0 would have host addresses from 172.20.32.1 through 172.20.35.255. However, you can't use the IP address in which all host bits are 1s because it's the broadcast address for that network, so the actual range is 172.20.32.1 through 172.20.35.254, giving you 1022 host addresses. Table 9-7 shows this for the first five subnets and the last subnet.

Table 9-7   Host addresses per subnet

Subnetwork number	Beginning and ending host addresses in binary	Beginning and ending host addresses in decimal
172.20.0.0	172.20.00000000.00000001–172.20.00000011.11111110	172.20.0.1–172.20.3.254
172.20.4.0	172.20.00000100.00000001–172.20.00000111.11111110	172.20.4.1–172.20.7.254
172.20.8.0	172.20.00001000.00000001–172.20.00001011.11111110	172.20.8.1–172.20.11.254
172.20.12.0	172.20.00001100.00000001–172.20.00001001.11111110	172.20.12.1–172.20.15.254
172.20.16.0	172.20.00010000.00000001–172.20.00010011.11111110	172.20.16.1–172.20.19.254
...		...
172.20.252.0	172.20.11111100.00000001–172.20.11111111.11111110	172.20.252.1–172.20.255.254

© 2015 Cengage Learning®

Another Subnet Mask Example   In Figure 9-4, the network number is 192.168.100.0, which is a Class C network address with the default subnet mask 255.255.255.0.

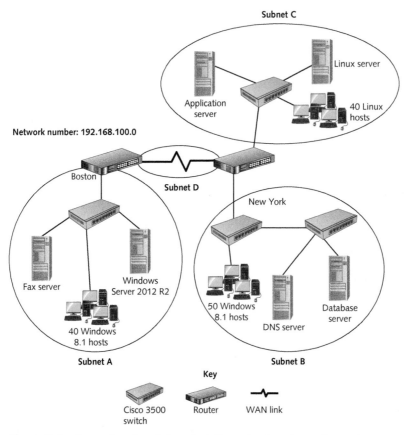

Figure 9-4   A sample network for calculating subnet mask requirements
© 2015 Cengage Learning®

The following steps show how to calculate a new subnet mask:

1. In this example, you can see that four cable segments are connected to router interfaces. The WAN cable segment between the two routers counts as a single cable segment and, therefore, a single subnet. You have to account for the WAN subnet even if the network has no hosts because the router interfaces require an IP address. As you can see, there are four subnetworks: Subnet A requires 43 IP addresses (40 for the Windows 7 hosts, 2 for the servers, and 1 for the router interface). Subnet B requires 53 IP addresses, subnet C requires 43 IP addresses, and subnet D requires only 2 IP addresses.

2. To accommodate the required number of subnets (4), you need a power of 2 that's equal to or greater than 4. Because $2^2 = 4$, you need to reallocate 2 bits from the host ID to the network ID.

3. Reallocating 2 bits from the leftmost part of the host portion of the original subnet mask (255.255.255.0) gives the last octet of your new subnet mask the bit pattern 11000000. Converting to decimal and putting the entire subnet mask together yields 255.255.255.192.

4. To be sure you have enough host bits per subnet, use the formula $2^n - 2$, where n is the number of 0 bits in the new subnet mask. The result is $2^6 - 2 = 62$. This number of host addresses satisfies your requirement of a maximum of 53 hosts per subnet.

Calculating a Subnet Mask Based on Needed Host Addresses Sometimes you need to know what prefix to assign an IP network based on the number of host addresses required for the network. This process is fairly straightforward. Suppose you're told that you need to determine the subnet mask to use with network ID 172.16.16.0, and the network will support 60 hosts. In this problem, simply determine how many host bits are needed to support the number of hosts specified, and subtract this number from 32, giving you the number of bits in the network ID. For this example of 60 hosts, you need 6 bits for the host ID because $2^6 = 64$, which is the closest power of 2 to 60. Therefore, the prefix is 26, so in CIDR notation, the network ID is 172.16.16.0/26. Examine the examples in Table 9-8 to become more comfortable with this process.

9

Table 9-8   Examples for determining the correct CIDR notation

Network ID	Required hosts	Host bits required	Network ID bits	CIDR notation
10.19.32.0	900	10 (2^{10}=1024)	22	10.19.32.0/22
172.25.110.0	505	9 (2^9=512)	23	172.25.110.0/23
192.168.100.32	28	5 (2^6=32)	27	192.168.100.32/27

To learn more about this topic and get plenty of subnetting practice, go to *www.subnetting.net*.

Activity 9-3: Working with CIDR Notation

Time Required: 20 minutes
Objective: Determine the subnet mask, number of host bits, and number of hosts for network numbers in CIDR notation.

Required Tools and Equipment: Paper and pencil
Description: Examine the IP addresses/prefixes specified in CIDR notation, and fill in the resulting subnet mask, number of host bits, and number of hosts possible in the network. The first row is completed for you. The next two rows include some of the information.

Network/prefix	Subnet mask	Host bits	Number of hosts
172.16.1.0/24	255.255.255.0	8	254
10.1.100.128/26	255.255.255.192	6	
10.1.96.0/19	255.255.224		8190
192.168.1.0/24			
172.31.0.0/16			
10.255.255.252/30			
172.28.240.0/20			
10.44.108.0/22			
192.168.100.24/21			
172.23.64.0/18			
192.168.5.128/25			

© 2015 Cengage Learning®

Activity 9-4: Determining the Correct Prefix

Time Required: 20 minutes

Objective: Determine the correct prefix, given the required number of hosts per network.

Required Tools and Equipment: Paper and pencil

Description: Given the IP address and number of hosts in the first two columns, determine the number of host bits required and write the network number with the correct prefix. The first one is completed for you, and the next two are partially completed.

Network ID	Required hosts	Host bits needed	Network ID/prefix
172.16.1.0	254	8	172.16.1.0/24
10.1.100.128	62	6	
10.1.96.0	8190		10.1.96.0/19
192.168.1.0	200		
172.31.0.0	65000		
10.255.255.252	2		
172.28.240.0	4000		
10.44.108.0	900		
192.168.240.0	2200		
172.23.64.0	16000		
192.168.5.128	110		

© 2015 Cengage Learning®

Supernetting

Although not practiced as commonly as subnetting, **supernetting** is sometimes necessary to solve certain network configuration problems and to make routing tables more streamlined. When talking about routing tables, supernetting is usually referred to as "route aggregation" or "route summarization."

Supernetting reallocates bits from the network portion of an IP address to the host portion, effectively making two or more smaller subnets a larger supernet. Supernets allow combining two or more consecutive IP network addresses and make them function as a single logical network. Here's how it works:

1. Suppose you have four Class C network addresses—192.168.0.0, 192.168.1.0, 192.168.2.0, and 192.168.3.0—available for your network design. You have a total of 900 hosts on your proposed network. You don't have four router interfaces that can use the four different

network numbers, however. You can combine the four networks into one by reallocating 2 bits ($2^2 = 4$) from the network portion of the address and adding them to the host portion. You then have a network address of 192.168.0.0 with the subnet mask 255.255.252.0. The 252 in the third octet is derived from setting the last 2 bits of the original Class C subnet mask (255.255.255.0) to 0, thereby making them part of the host portion.

2. Instead of supporting only 8 bits for the host address portion, the supernet now supports 10 bits (8 + 2) for host addresses. This number of bits provides 2^{10} - 2 host addresses on this supernet, or 1022, which satisfies your requirement for 900 hosts and allows you to assign all host addresses in a single network.

As mentioned, combining two or more small networks into one larger network is only one reason to supernet. Routers on the Internet can have enormous routing tables. The larger the routing table, the more work the router must do to determine where to send a packet. Route aggregation or summarization can combine multiple routing table entries into a single entry, which can drastically decrease the table's size on Internet routers. This reduction in routing table size increases routers' speed and efficiency. The procedure is similar to supernetting, except you configure routers.

Routing tables grow partly because routers communicate with one another by sending information about their routing tables to one another. If several networks can be represented by a single routing table entry, the routing tables are more efficient. Taking the previous example, suppose RouterA in a company network has the network addresses 192.168.0.0, 192.168.1.0, 192.168.2.0, and 192.168.3.0 in its routing table, and it communicates with RouterB (see Figure 9-5). Without supernetting/route summarization, RouterA sends all four network addresses to RouterB, each with its 255.255.255.0 subnet mask. Consequently, RouterB's routing table expands with these four additional routes. However, because all four routes lead to the same place (RouterA), these routes can be represented by a single entry. RouterA can summarize these routes by simply sending RouterB the address 192.168.0.0 with subnet mask 255.255.252.0, which tells RouterB that all networks from 192.168.0.0 through 192.168.3.0 can be reached through RouterA.

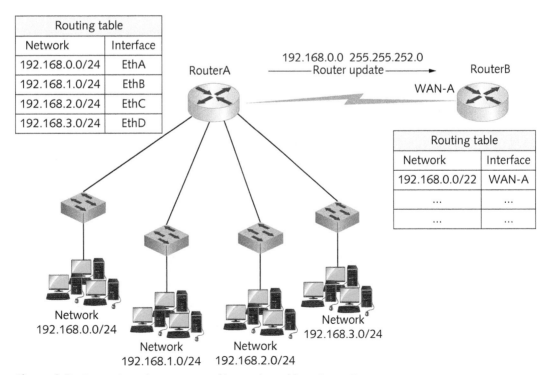

Figure 9-5   RouterA sends a summary of its routing table to RouterB
© *Cengage Learning®*

Configuring IPv4 Addresses

When you assign a computer an IP address, there are some rules to remember:

- Every IP address configuration must have a subnet mask.

- All hosts on the same network must share the same network ID in their IP addresses. The term "network" in this case means a grouping of computers connected to one or more switches (or access points), not separated by a router. Put another way, all computers are in the same broadcast domain.

- All host IDs on the same network must be unique.

- You can't assign an IP address in which all the host ID bits are binary 0. This type of IP address is reserved as the network ID. For example, IP address 10.1.0.0 with subnet mask 255.255.0.0 is reserved to identify network 10.1.

- You can't assign an IP address in which all the host ID bits are binary 1. This type of IP address is reserved as the network broadcast address. For example, IP address 10.1.255.255 with subnet mask 255.255.0.0 has all host ID bits set to binary 1 and is reserved as the broadcast address for the 10.1 network.

- Computers assigned different network IDs can communicate only by sending network packets to a router, which forwards the packets to the correct network.

Configuring Multiple IP Addresses

Windows OSs allow assigning multiple IP addresses to a single network connection in the Advanced TCP/IP Settings dialog box shown in Figure 9-6. As long as the address isn't assigned via DHCP, you can click the Add button and enter a new IP address and subnet mask. Multiple IP addresses can be useful in these situations:

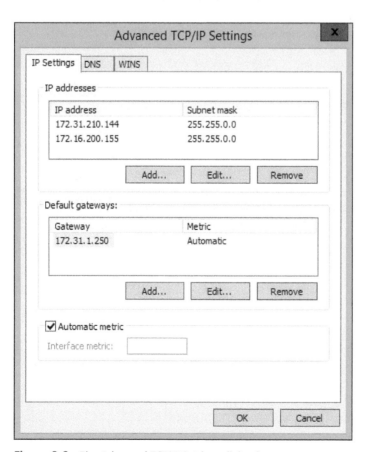

Figure 9-6   The Advanced TCP/IP Settings dialog box

- The computer is hosting a service that must be accessed by using different addresses. For example, a Web server can host multiple Web sites, each assigned a different IP address and domain name.

- The computer is connected to a physical network that hosts multiple IP networks. This situation can occur if your network addressing scheme is transitioning from one network ID to another, and you need a server to be available to both the old and the new IP networks until the transition is completed. It can also occur when you have multiple groups of computers (or hosts and virtual machines) connected to the same physical network but with different network addresses. If all the computers need access to server resources, the servers can be configured with IP addresses to serve all the IP networks.

 When multiple IP addresses are assigned to a Windows computer that uses a Windows DNS server supporting Dynamic DNS (the default DNS server configuration), the DNS server has a host entry for each IP address assigned to the computer.

You also have to configure more than one IP address on servers with multiple NICs, which are called multihomed servers. They're discussed in the next section.

Configuring the Default Gateway

Almost all IP address configurations require a default gateway address. The default gateway, which is usually a router or a computer configured to act as a router, tells the computer where packets destined for another network should be sent. By definition, the default gateway's address must have the same network ID as the host's network ID.

You can configure multiple default gateways in the Advanced TCP/IP Settings dialog box, and then Windows attempts to select the gateway with the best metric automatically. A **metric** is a value assigned to the gateway based on the speed of the interface used to access the gateway. Multiple gateways provide fault tolerance to a computer, so if the primary default gateway is no longer responding, Windows switches to another gateway. By using a feature called "fail-back," Windows attempts periodically to communicate with the original default gateway. If the original gateway comes back online, Windows switches back to it.

Using Multihomed Servers   A multihomed server has two or more NICs, each attached to a different IP network. Each NIC is assigned a network connection and requires its own IP address for the network it's connected to. This type of configuration can be used in the following situations:

- A server is accessed by internal clients (clients on the network) and external clients (clients on the Internet or an extranet). For example, you have a server for services such as file and printer sharing, DHCP, and DNS that also acts as a public Web server.

- A server provides resources for computers on multiple subnets of the network. Interfaces can be configured for each subnet, which provides more throughput than is possible with a single NIC.

- A server is configured as a router or virtual private network (VPN) server. Both functions often use multiple NICs.

For network connections to a LAN, Windows uses names such as Ethernet, Ethernet2, and so forth, which aren't very descriptive. Renaming each network connection to describe the network it connects to is recommended. For example, if a server is connected to internal and external networks, you might name one connection LAN-Internal and the other LAN-External. If the server is connected to two internal networks, you could use the network address in the names, such as LAN-172.31 and LAN-172.16. To rename a connection, right-click it in the Network Connections window and click Rename.

When a server is multihomed, it's usually connected to two physical as well as logical networks. Each physical network likely has a router. Simply configuring a default gateway for each interface might be tempting. However, Windows always chooses only one default gateway for sending packets to remote networks. For example, a server could receive a packet through an interface connected to the internal network and send the reply to the default gateway on the external network. You probably don't want this to happen. To solve this problem, you can use the route command, explained in the next section.

Using the route Command   Windows computers maintain a routing table that dictates where a packet should be sent, based on the packet's destination address. The route.exe command-line program enables you to display and alter the routing table's contents. Figure 9-7 shows partial results of the route print command, which displays the contents of the routing table.

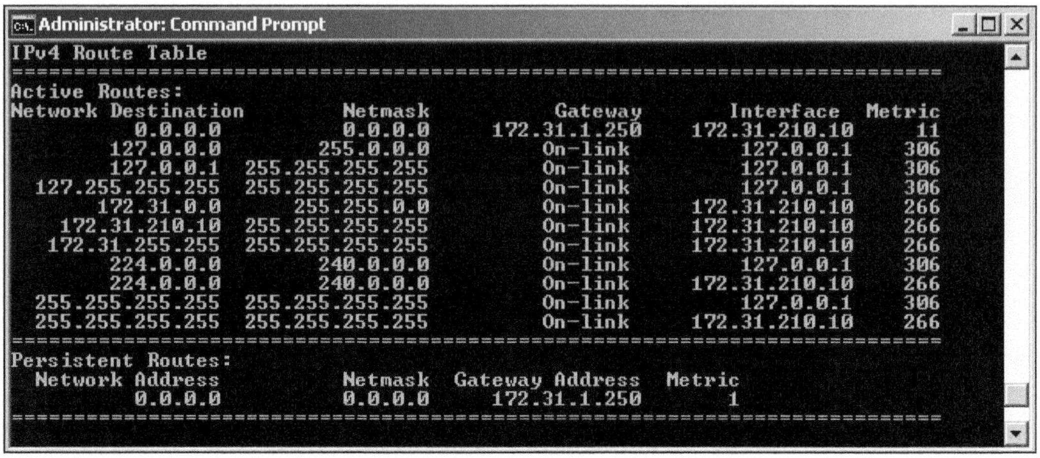

```
Administrator: Command Prompt                                                    _ □ ×
IPv4 Route Table
===========================================================================
Active Routes:
Network Destination        Netmask          Gateway       Interface  Metric
          0.0.0.0          0.0.0.0     172.31.1.250   172.31.210.10     11
        127.0.0.0        255.0.0.0         On-link        127.0.0.1    306
        127.0.0.1  255.255.255.255         On-link        127.0.0.1    306
  127.255.255.255  255.255.255.255         On-link        127.0.0.1    306
       172.31.0.0      255.255.0.0         On-link    172.31.210.10    266
    172.31.210.10  255.255.255.255         On-link    172.31.210.10    266
   172.31.255.255  255.255.255.255         On-link    172.31.210.10    266
        224.0.0.0        240.0.0.0         On-link        127.0.0.1    306
        224.0.0.0        240.0.0.0         On-link    172.31.210.10    266
  255.255.255.255  255.255.255.255         On-link        127.0.0.1    306
  255.255.255.255  255.255.255.255         On-link    172.31.210.10    266
===========================================================================
Persistent Routes:
  Network Address        Netmask  Gateway Address  Metric
          0.0.0.0        0.0.0.0     172.31.1.250       1
===========================================================================
```

Figure 9-7   Results of the route print command

These results are displayed in five columns. The first column, Network Destination, is a network number compared against an IP packet's destination address. The Netmask column displays the subnet mask associated with the network destination. The Gateway column is the address of the router where packets with a destination address matching the network destination should be forwarded. The Interface column is the address of the NIC the packet should be sent through to reach the gateway. The Metric column is the value assigned to the route. If the routing table contains two or more entries that can reach the same destination, the one with the lowest metric is chosen.

In Figure 9-7, notice the network destination of 0.0.0.0 with a netmask of 0.0.0.0. This entry indicates the default route or default gateway. A packet with a destination address that doesn't match any entries in the routing table is forwarded to the gateway address in the default route entry—in this case, 172.31.1.250. A gateway specified as "on-link" simply means the network destination is a network connected directly to one of the computer's interfaces. All Network Destination entries beginning with 127 indicate the computer's loopback address, which means "this computer." The Network Destination entries starting with 224 are multicast addresses, and entries starting with 255 are broadcast addresses. All packets with a multicast or broadcast destination address are sent to the local network, not to a router.

The route command can be used to change the routing table. For instance, a multihomed computer might have two or more possibilities for a default gateway. Best practices dictate configuring only one interface with a default gateway. However, suppose you have a server connected to two networks: 192.168.1.0/24 and 172.16.208.0/24, as shown in Figure 9-8. The 192.168.1.0 network connects to the Internet, and the 172.16.208.0 network is part of the internal network and is also connected to networks 172.16.200.0/24 through 172.16.207.0/24. In addition, the 192.168.1.0 network has no possible way to get to the 172.16 networks.

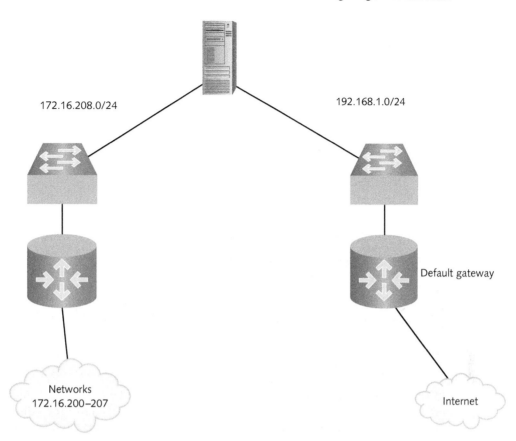

Figure 9-8 A multihomed server
© 2015 Cengage Learning®

If your default gateway is configured on the 192.168.1.0 network (as it should, because it's connected to the Internet), when your server replies to a packet from the 172.16.200.0 to 172.16.207.0 networks, it sends the reply out the 192.168.1.0 interface because that's where the default gateway is. Remember that by default, the routing table contains entries only for networks the computer is directly connected to plus the default route. So the server doesn't have an entry for the 172.16 networks, except 172.16.208.0. Any packets sent to these networks go to the default gateway, which can't deliver them to the destination network. To solve this problem, you can add routes to the routing table by using the following command:

```
route add 172.16.200.0 mask 255.255.255.0 172.16.208.250
```

This command creates a routing table entry for the 172.16.200.0 network with the subnet mask 255.255.255.0 and the gateway 172.16.208.250, which is the router on your server's network. You could make eight entries, one for each remote network, or a single entry, as shown:

```
route add 172.16.200.0 mask 255.255.248.0 172.16.208.250
```

This entry consolidates networks 172.16.200.0 through 172.16.207.0 into a single entry by using a modified subnet mask (the supernetting technique, discussed earlier).

IP Configuration Command-Line Tools

Several command-line tools are available to help you troubleshoot, display, and configure IP addresses and related TCP/IP settings on a Windows computer. This section examines the following tools:

- `netsh`
- PowerShell cmdlets
- `ipconfig`
- `ping`

- arp
- tracert
- nslookup

Other network configuration and troubleshooting tools are available, but they're typically used to verify correct IP configuration settings and connectivity.

Using `netsh`   You can use the `netsh.exe` command to perform a wide variety of network configuration tasks, such as firewall configuration and IP address configuration. To see a list of `netsh` commands, type `netsh /?` at the command prompt. To configure the IP address of an interface named Ethernet to 10.1.1.1/16, use this command:

```
netsh interface ipv4 set address "Ethernet"
    static 10.1.1.1 255.255.0.0
```

You can include the default gateway by adding the address to the end of the command:

```
netsh interface ipv4 set address "Ethernet"
    static 10.1.1.1 255.255.0.0 10.1.1.250
```

To set the primary DNS server for the computer to 10.1.1.100, use the following command:

```
netsh interface ipv4 set dns "Ethernet" static 10.1.1.100 primary
```

The `netsh` command has many options that are useful for network configuration tasks. You should spend some time with this command so that you have an understanding of what you can do with it.

Using PowerShell Cmdlets   Microsoft has expanded the number of cmdlets in PowerShell and made them easier to use for network configuration tasks. Microsoft certification exams place considerable emphasis on your ability to use PowerShell for everyday configuration tasks. This section describes some PowerShell cmdlets for viewing and configuring IP address settings.

The `Get-NetIPConfiguration` cmdlet displays IP configuration information about your network's interfaces. You use it to get the interface name you need for other commands. Figure 9-9 shows the output this command produces.

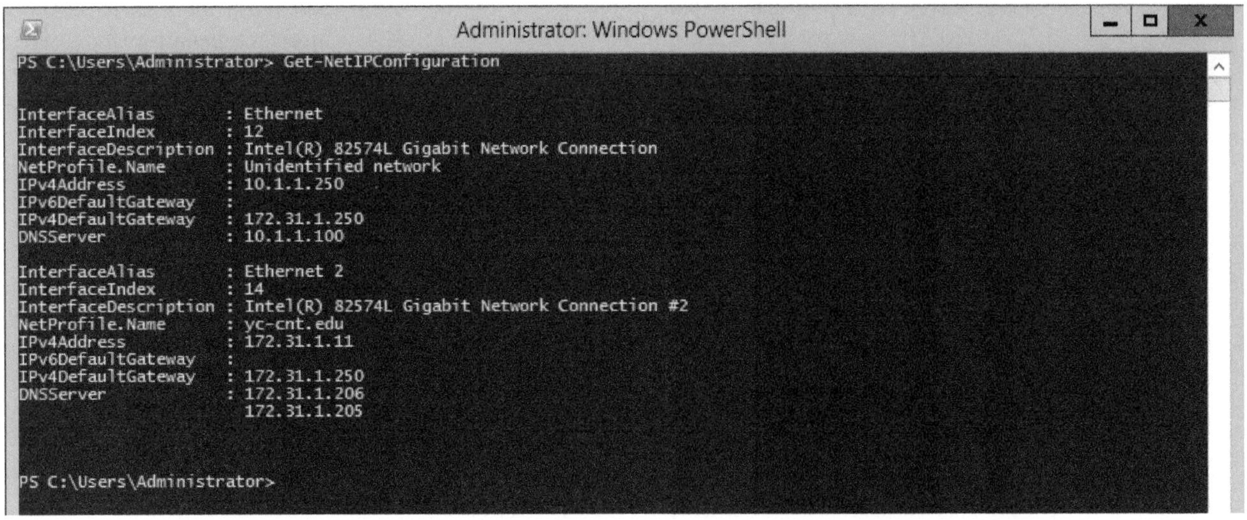

Figure 9-9   The `Get-NetIPConfiguration` cmdlet

You use the `Get-NetIPAddress` cmdlet to see detailed IP address configuration information on a specified interface. If no interface is specified, configuration information is shown for all interfaces.

The `Set-NetIPInterface` cmdlet is used to configure DHCP client settings, "wake on LAN" settings, and router settings. If it's used without specifying an interface, the settings apply to all interfaces. The first example disables DHCP on all interfaces, and the second example enables DHCP on the interface named Ethernet:

```
Set-NetIPInterface -DHCP disabled
Set-NetIPInterface -InterfaceAlias Ethernet -DHCP enabled
```

To get detailed help on this command, use `Get-Help Set-NetIPInterface -detailed`.

Use the `New-NetIPAddress` cmdlet to set new IP address configuration settings for an interface. You can also set the default gateway. To set the IP address to 172.16.1.10 with a subnet mask of 255.255.0.0 on the Ethernet interface, use the following command:

```
New-NetIPAddress -InterfaceAlias Ethernet -IPAddress 172.16.1.10
  -PrefixLength 16 -DefaultGateway 172.16.1.250
```

To modify the settings of an existing IP address, you use the `Set-NetIPAddress` cmdlet. For example, to change the prefix length (subnet mask) of the interface with IP addresses 172.16.1.10 to 24, use the following command:

```
Set-NetIPAddress -IPAddress 172.16.1.10 -PrefixLength24
```

The `Set-DnsClientServerAddress` cmdlet sets the DNS server addresses used by the DNS client on the specified interface, as shown in this example:

```
Set-DnsClientServerAddress -InterfaceAlias Ethernet
  -ServerAddress 172.16.1.100
```

There are many more options for these cmdlets. To get detailed help and see examples of using them, just use `Get-Help`.

Using `ipconfig` As you've learned, `ipconfig` is usually used to display a computer's IP address settings but can perform other tasks, depending on the options included:

- *No options*—Displays the basic IP configuration, including the IP address, subnet mask, and default gateway.

- `/all`—Displays extended IP configuration information, such as the computer name, domain name, network adapter description, physical (MAC) address, whether DHCP is used, and DNS address.

- `/release`—Releases its IP address back to the DHCP server if DHCP is used. If the address is released, the computer is assigned the invalid address of 0.0.0.0.

- `/renew`—Renews the IP address configuration lease.

- `/displaydns`—Windows caches the most recent DNS lookup request results, and this option displays the contents of the local DNS cache. If a computer recently did a DNS lookup for *www.yahoo.com*, for example, it keeps that information in local memory so that the next time the address is needed, a DNS query is unnecessary.

- `/flushdns`—Deletes cached DNS information from memory. This option can be useful if a computer's IP address or hostname was changed recently, and the cache contains obsolete information.

- `/registerdns`—Requests new DHCP leases and registers these names again with a DNS server.

Using `ping` You have used `ping` to test connectivity between two computers. It sends an ICMP Echo Request packet to the destination IP address specified in the command. If the destination computer receives the ICMP Echo Request, it replies with an ICMP Echo Reply packet. When the computer receives the reply packet, the `ping` program displays a message similar to this one:

```
reply from 192.168.100.201: bytes=32 time=<1ms TTL=128
```

In this output, the IP address is the address of the computer that sent the reply. The `bytes=32` parameter specifies how many data bytes are in the ICMP message. You can change the number of data bytes with options in the `ping` command. The `time=<1ms` parameter indicates that the reply took less than a millisecond from the time the ICMP Echo Request was sent. The `TTL=128` indicates the message's time to live, which specifies how many routers a packet can go through before the packet should be expired and discarded. At each router, the TTL is decremented. If the TTL reaches 0, the router sends the source computer a message indicating that the TTL expired before reaching its destination.

To see the options available with this command, type `ping /?` at a command prompt. Some of the options are as follows:

- `-t`—Sends ICMP Echo Request packets continually until you press Ctrl+C to stop. By default, `ping` sends four packets.

- `-a`—Tries to resolve the IP address to a hostname. If the name can be resolved, it's printed in the first line of the `ping` output.

- `-n count`—The *count* parameter is the number of Echo Request packets to send.

- `-l size`—The *size* parameter is the number of data bytes to send in each Echo Request packet. The default is 32 bytes.

- `-i TTL`—Time to live is the number of routers the packet can go through on the way to the destination before the packet should be expired.

Using arp   The `arp` command displays or makes changes to the Address Resolution Protocol (ARP) cache, which contains IP address–MAC address pairs. As discussed, when an IP packet is sent to a destination on the local network, the sending device must have the destination's MAC address. The source computer retrieves the MAC address by sending a broadcast ARP request packet to the local network. The ARP request packet essentially asks "Who has IP address A.B.C.D?" The computer on the local network that's assigned the IP address sends an ARP reply message containing its MAC address. When a computer learns another computer's MAC address, it keeps the address in its ARP cache temporarily so that it doesn't have to send another ARP request packet to communicate with that computer again. Entries in the ARP cache are kept for only a few minutes to prevent them from becoming obsolete. Some options for the `arp` command are as follows:

- `-a` or `-g`—Displays the contents of the ARP cache. These options perform the same function.

- `-d`—Deletes the entire contents of the ARP cache or a single entry specified by IP address. This option can be useful if a computer's NIC has changed recently, and the cache contains obsolete information.

- `-s`—Adds a permanent entry to the ARP cache by specifying a host's IP address and MAC address. This option should be used only if the address of a frequently accessed computer is unlikely to change. Remember: If the NIC is changed on a computer, its MAC address changes, too.

Using tracert   The `tracert` command is usually called "trace route" because it displays the route packets take between two computers. It displays the address or DNS name of each router a packet travels through to reach the specified destination. It then sends a series of three ICMP Echo Request packets with a TTL value starting at 1 and increases the value until the destination is reached. Each router a packet encounters along the way to the destination decrements the TTL value by 1. If the TTL value reaches 0, the router sends a TTL-expired message back to the sending computer and drops the packet. When `tracert` receives the TTL-expired message, it records the sending router's IP address and the time to receive a reply and displays this information. Next, a new series of three ICMP Echo Request packets are sent with an incremented TTL value. This procedure continues until all routers between the source and destination have been recorded.

Tracert is useful for troubleshooting the routing topology of a complex network and finding the bottleneck between a computer and a destination network. Because tracert displays the time it took to receive a reply from each router, a router (or the link to this router) showing an inordinately long delay might be where the bottleneck lies.

Using nslookup The nslookup command is used to test and troubleshoot DNS operation and can be used in command mode or interactive mode. In command mode, you type nslookup *host*; *host* is the name of a computer in the local domain or a fully qualified domain name. Nslookup replies with the specified host's IP address. By default, nslookup uses the DNS server address configured in the IP address settings. Following are some examples of using nslookup in command mode:

```
nslookup server99
nslookup www.yahoo.com
nslookup www.google.com 172.31.1.200
```

The first two commands query the default DNS server. The last command queries a DNS server at address 172.31.1.200.Because you can specify a different DNS server, you can compare the results of different DNS servers to verify correct DNS operation.

To use interactive mode, type nslookup at the command prompt, and the output shows which server it's using to perform lookups. You can type a question mark at the interactive mode prompt to get a list of available options and commands.

ACTIVITY

Activity 9-5: Using the arp Command

Time Required: 10 minutes
Objective: Use the arp command to display and delete ARP entries.

Required Tools and Equipment: 410Win8 and 410Server1; Internet access
Description: You want to see how the arp command works, so you display the ARP cache, and then delete its contents. Next, you use the ping and arp commands to see the difference between pinging a computer on a local and a remote network.

1. Start 410Server1. Log on to 410Win8 as **Administrator**. Click the **Desktop** tile, if necessary. Open a command prompt window by right-clicking **Start** and clicking **Command Prompt**.

2. Type **arp -a** and press **Enter**. You should see a few entries. Those listed as "static" in the Type column are created automatically by Windows. The dynamic entries are a result of your computer having recently sent an arp request message for the specified IP address. Note that these arp messages are sent automatically by your computer whenever it needs to get another computer's MAC address, such as when your Windows computer needs to contact the domain controller when you log on.

3. Type **arp -d** and press **Enter**. Type **arp -a** and press **Enter**. The -d option deletes the ARP cache. After the second command, you might get the message "No ARP Entries Found," or you might see an entry or two if your computer tried to contact another computer in the time between the two arp commands.

4. Type **arp -d** and press **Enter** to clear any recently acquired entries, and then immediately type **ping 410Server1** and press **Enter**. Type **arp -a** and press **Enter** again. You should see an ARP entry for 410Server1.

5. Type **arp -d** and press **Enter**, and then type **ping www.yahoo.com** and press **Enter**. Type **arp -a** and press **Enter**. The ARP cache should have at least two dynamic entries: One is your server's IP address, and the other should be for your default gateway address. Notice that there's no ARP entry for the address of www.yahoo.com. The entry for your server exists because your computer had to do a DNS lookup for www.yahoo.com and, therefore, had to get your server's MAC address because your server is also the DNS server. The entry for your default gateway exists because the ping packet had to be sent to your router to reach the network

where www.yahoo.com is located. Remember that the MAC address is used to deliver a packet to a device only on the local network, whether the device is a computer or a router.

6. Stay logged on to 410Win8, leave the command prompt window open, and leave 410Server1 running if you're continuing to the next activity.

ACTIVITY

Activity 9-6: Using the `tracert` Command

Time Required: 10 minutes
Objective: Use the `tracert` command.

Required Tools and Equipment: 410Win8 and 410Server1; Internet access
Description: Internet access has been slow, so you use the `tracert` command to try to determine where the bottleneck is.

1. Start 410Server1, if necessary. Log on to 410Win8 as **Administrator**, and open a command prompt window, if necessary.

2. Type **tracert 410server1** and press **Enter**. Because there are no routers between 410Win8 and 410Server1, you should get only one response line of output. Notice that three times are displayed because `tracert` sends three packets for each TTL value it uses. By sending three packets, you can average the times to get a more accurate picture of the response time.

3. Type **tracert www.yahoo.com** and press **Enter**. Some router hops include a name with the router's address, and you can sometimes use this name to get an idea of the router's geographical location or the name of the ISP that operates the router.

4. To speed up `tracert`'s results, you can tell it not to do router name lookups. Type **tracert -d www.yahoo.com** and press **Enter**. The results are displayed much faster, especially if you're several router hops away from www.yahoo.com.

5. Stay logged on to 410Win8, leave the command prompt window open, and leave 410Server1 running if you're continuing to the next activity.

Internet Protocol Version 6

IPv4 has been the driving force on the Internet for decades and continues to be the dominant protocol in use. However, it's starting to show its age as its address space becomes used up, and workarounds for security and quality of service must be put in place. IPv4 was developed more than 40 years ago, so it seems natural that as all other aspects of technology slowly get replaced, so will IPv4. This section discusses that replacement: IPv6. IPv6 addresses look very different from IPv4 addresses, and unlike IPv4, IPv6 addresses have a built-in hierarchy and fields with a distinct purpose. Configuring an IPv6 address is distinctly different from doing so for an IPv4 address. The transition from IPv4 to IPv6 is not going to happen overnight, so methods have been developed to allow IPv4 and IPv6 networks to coexist and communicate with one another.

This section doesn't attempt to give you a full explanation of IPv6 and its many complexities; there are entire books written on this topic. However, it addresses the key aspects of the IPv6 protocol and what you need to know to configure and support a Windows Server 2012/R2 server using IPv6.

IPv6 Overview

The Internet Engineering Task Force (IETF) started development on IPng (IP next generation) in 1994, and it was later named IPv6. IPv6 was developed to address IPv4's shortcomings. Some improvements and changes in IPv6 include the following:

- *Larger address space*—IPv4 addresses are 32 bits, which provide a theoretical four billion addresses. IPv6 addresses are 128 bits, so the number of possible addresses can be expressed as 34 followed by 37 0s, or 340 trillion trillion trillion. It's probably safe to say that running out of IPv6 addresses is unlikely.

- *Hierarchical address space*—Unlike IPv4, in which numbers in the address have little meaning other than the address class, and the network ID and host ID, IPv6 addresses have a more defined structure. For example, the first part of an address can indicate a particular organization or site.

- *Autoconfiguration*—IPv6 can be self-configuring or autoconfigured from a router or server running IPv6 or through DHCPv6.

- *Built-in Quality of Service (QoS) support*—IPv6 includes built-in fields in packet headers to support QoS strategies (used to prioritize data packets based on the type or urgency of information they contain) without having to install additional protocol components, as IPv4 does.

- *Built-in support for security*—From the ground-up, IPv6 is built to support secure protocols, such as Internet Protocol Security (IPsec), whereas IPv4's support for IPsec is an add-on feature.

- *Support for mobility*—With built-in support for mobility, routing IPv6 packets generated by mobile devices over the Internet is more efficient than with IPv4.

- *Extensibility*—IPv6 uses extension headers instead of IPv4's fixed-size 40-byte header. Extension headers allow adding features to IPv6 simply by adding a new header.

IPv6 Address Structure

The good news with IPv6 is that subnetting as it's done in IPv4 will be a thing of the past. The bad news is that you still need to work with binary numbers, and with 128 bits in the address, there are quite a few new things to learn. IPv6 addresses are written as eight 16-bit hexadecimal numbers separated by colons. There's no official name for each part of the address, so each 16-bit value is simply called a "field." A valid IPv6 address looks like this:

```
fe80:0:0:0:18ff:0024:8e5a:60
```

There are a few things to note in this address:

- IPv6 addresses often have several 0 values. One or more consecutive 0 values can be written as a double colon (::), so the preceding address can be written as `fe80::18ff:0024:8e5a:60`. However, you can have only one double colon in an IPv6 address.

- Leading 0s are optional. The value 0024 in the previous example could just as easily have been written as 24, and the value 60 could have been written as 0060.

- The hexadecimal numbering system was chosen to represent IPv6 addresses largely because it's much easier to convert to binary than decimal is. Each hexadecimal digit represents 4 bits, so to convert an IPv6 address to binary, simply convert each hexadecimal digit (accounting for leading 0s) to its binary equivalent. For example, the first field in the preceding address (`fe80`) can be written as follows:

```
1111 1110 1000 0000
  f    e    8    0
```

In Windows, when you view an IPv6 address in the network connection's Status dialog box or after using `ipconfig`, you see a percent sign (%) followed by a number at the end of the address. The number following the percent sign is the interface index, used to identify the interface in some `netsh` and PowerShell commands. You don't see a subnet mask or even the prefix length, as you do with an IPv4 address. However, IPv6 addresses have a prefix length; it's just that it's always 64 when discussing a host address. This is because in IPv6 host addresses, all IPv6 network IDs are 64 bits, so a typical IPv6 address can be written as follows:

```
fe80:0:0:0:18ff:0024:8e5a:60/64
```

However, because the prefix is always 64 for an IPv6 host address, the prefix is often omitted.

The IPv6 Interface ID Because the prefix length (network ID) of an IPv6 address is 64 bits, the interface ID (the host ID in IPv4) of an IPv6 address is 64 bits, too. So you can easily identify the network ID of an IPv6 address by looking at the first 64 bits (16 hex digits or four fields) and the interface ID by looking at the last 64 bits. For example, in the following address, the network ID is `fe80:0:0:0` and the interface ID is `18ff:0024:8e5a:60`:

`fe80:0:0:0:18ff:0024:8e5a:60`

Because the prefix isn't a variable length, working with IPv6 addresses is somewhat easier because you don't have to do a binary calculation with a subnet mask to determine the network and interface IDs.

An IPv6 interface ID can be assigned to a host in these ways:

- *Using the 48-bit MAC address*—Because a MAC address is only 48 bits, the other 16 bits come from the value `fffe` inserted after the first 24 bits of the MAC address. In addition, the first two zeros that compose most MAC addresses are replaced with 02. For example, given the MAC address 00-0C-29-7C-F9-C4, the host ID of an IPv6 address is `020c:29ff:fe7c:f9c4`. This autoconfigured 64-bit host ID is called an **Extended Unique Identifier (EUI)-64 interface ID**. This method is defined in RFC 4291.

- *A randomly generated permanent interface identifier*—The interface ID is generated randomly but is a permanent assignment maintained through system restarts. Windows Server 2008 and later use this method by default for permanent interfaces, such as Ethernet ports. However, you can have Windows use EUI-64 addresses with this `netsh` command or PowerShell cmdlet:

`netsh interface ipv6 set global randomizeidentifiers=disabled`
   or
`Set-NetIPv6Protocol -RandomizeIdentifiers Disabled`

- *A temporary interface identifier*—Some connections, such as dial-up Point-to-Point Protocol (PPP) connections, might use this method for interface IPv6 address assignment, defined in RFC 4941, whereby the interface ID is assigned randomly and changes each time IPv6 is initialized to maintain anonymity.

- *Via DHCPv6*—Addresses are assigned via a DHCPv6 server to IPv6 interfaces when they're initialized.

- *Manually*—Similar to IPv4 configuration, the IPv6 address is entered manually in the interface's Properties dialog box.

IPv6 Address Types

IPv4 defines unicast, multicast, and broadcast addresses, and IPv6 defines unicast, multicast, and anycast addresses. Unicast and multicast addresses in IPv6 perform much like their IPv4 counterparts, with a few exceptions. Anycast addresses are an altogether different animal.

IPv6 Unicast Addresses

A unicast address specifies a single interface on a device. To participate in an IPv6 network, every device must have at least one network interface that has been assigned a unicast IPv6 address. In most cases, each interface on a device is assigned a separate unicast address, but for load-balancing purposes, multiple interfaces on a device can share the same IPv6 unicast address. In the realm of IPv6 unicast addresses, there are three primary types: link-local, unique local, and global. In addition, there are addresses reserved for special purposes and transition addresses, which were developed to help with the transition from IPv4 to IPv6.

Link-Local Addresses Addresses starting with `fe80` are called **link-local IPv6 addresses** and are self-configuring. Link-local addresses can't be routed and are somewhat equivalent to Automatic Private IP Addressing (APIPA) in IPv4. Link-local addresses can be used for computer-to-computer communication in small networks where no routers are needed. In fact, a router doesn't forward packets with a link-local address destination or source address.

Most often, however, the use of link-local addresses is simply one step in the process toward autoconfiguration of a different type of address by a router or DHCPv6 server.

Link-local addresses are defined by RFC 4291, which you can read about at *http://tools.ietf.org/html/rfc4291*.

Unique Local Addresses
Unique local IPv6 addresses are analogous to the familiar private IPv4 addresses (refer back to "Private IP Addresses") that most companies use behind the network's firewall and are preconfigured on routers for use in small and medium networks. Unique local addresses, like private IPv4 addresses, can't be routed on the Internet (but can be routed inside the private network).

RFC 4193 at *http://tools.ietf.org/html/rfc4193* defines unique local addresses.

Unique local addresses begin with `fc` or `fd` and are usually expressed as `fc00::/7`. The format for a unique local address is as follows:

`fdgg:gggg:gggg:ssss:iiii:iiii:iiii:iiii`

In this example, the string of `g` characters after the `fd` represents a 40-bit global ID, which identifies a specific site in an organization. The string of four `s` characters represents the subnet ID field, giving each site 16 bits for subnetting its unique local address. The string of `i` characters represents the 64-bit interface ID. This address format allows a whopping 65,536 subnets, each with a 64-bit interface ID field. With more than 65,000 subnets per site and more than 18 quintillion hosts per subnet, you can see that IPv6 solves the address space problem with IPv4.

This global ID is supposed to be set to a pseudo-random 40-bit value. RFC 4193 provides an algorithm for generating the pseudo-random global ID. It's set to a random number to ensure that organizations whose networks are connected still have unique IPv6 address prefixes. In practice, you can assign the 40-bit global ID manually if you aren't concerned about a future conflict with another network.

As mentioned, unique local addresses can begin with `fc` or `fd`. The global IDs of unique local addresses beginning with `fd` are called "locally assigned" and are the only type RFC 4193 defines. Those starting with `fc` aren't defined as of this writing but might be used later, with an address registrar assigning the 40-bit global ID. For now, you should use `fd` when assigning unique local IPv6 addresses.

Unique local addresses effectively replace an older addressing format called "site-local addresses," which have the format `fec0::/10`. Site-local addresses were defined by RFC 3879 but have been deprecated, and the IETF considers them reserved addresses.

Global Addresses
Global unicast IPv6 addresses, defined by RFC 4291, are analogous to public IPv4 addresses. They are accessible on the public Internet and can be routed. Essentially, an IPv6 address is global if it doesn't fall into one of the other categories of address (special use, link-local, unique local, loopback, transition, and so forth).

IPv6 addresses have one sizable advantage over IPv4 addresses, aside from the much larger address space; a structure, or a hierarchy, can be built into IPv6 addresses that allows more efficient routing on the Internet. Global addresses have the following formats:

`2ggg:gggg:gggg:ssss:iiii:iiii:iiii:iiii`
    or
`3ggg:gggg:gggg:ssss:iiii:iiii:iiii:iiii`

In early specifications of the IPv6 standard, IPv6 addresses had a defined hierarchy built into the global ID. A top-level aggregator (TLA) was a 13-bit field allocated to Internet registries by the IANA, and a next-level aggregator was a 24-bit field to be used by ISPs to allocate addresses to its customers. These identifiers have been deprecated as specified by RFC 4147 and are no longer used. It's expected, however, that large ISPs and Internet registries will use the 45 bits of available global ID to form an address hierarchy for efficient routing.

As in the previous example, the g characters are the global ID or global routing prefix, the s characters are the subnet ID, and the i characters are the interface ID. As of this writing, only IPv6 addresses beginning with the binary bit pattern 0010 (decimal 2) or 0011 (decimal 3) are allocated for Internet use, which represent only one-eighth the total available address space. The rest of the address space is reserved. So the global unicast address space is often specified as 2000::/3, which means only the first three bits are a fixed value; the remaining part of the address is variable. Even with this constraint on the IPv6 address space, the 45 variable bits in the global ID allow more than 35 trillion different address prefixes, each with more than 65000 subnets.

The global ID is typically 48 bits, and the subnet ID 16 bits; however, this allocation is not fixed. A larger global ID with a smaller subnet ID (or vice versa) is possible but not likely to be common. The interface ID is fixed at 64 bits.

RFC 4147 lists IPv6 prefixes and their use. The table on this page shows that most of the address space is reserved by the IETF. The IPv6 address space has a tremendous amount of room to grow.

IPv6 Special-Purpose Addresses   There are a few IPv6 addresses and prefixes that have a special purpose:

- *Loopback address*—The loopback address in IPv6 is equivalent to 127.0.0.1 used in IPv4 and is written as ::1. Like its IPv4 counterpart, the IPv6 loopback is used only for testing local IPv6 protocol operation ; no packets actually leave the local computer.

- *Zero address*—The zero (or unspecified) address, which can be written simply as ::, is used as a placeholder in the source address field of an outgoing IPv6 packet when the sending computer doesn't yet have an IPv6 address assigned.

- *Documentation*—The global unicast address 2001:db8::/32 has been reserved for use in books and other documentation discussing IPv6. This address prefix can also be used for test labs, but it shouldn't be routed on a company network or the Internet.

- *IPv4-to-IPv6 transition*—A number of address prefixes are used for transitioning from IPv4 to IPv6 and to support both IPv4 and IPv6 on the same network. These addresses are discussed later in "Transitioning from IPv4 to IPv6."

Subnetting with IPv6   Although subnetting as done in IPv4 will be a thing of the past, it doesn't mean subnetting won't be used at all in IPv6 networks. Typically, ISPs allocated IPv4 addresses to businesses in groups specified by a network address and IP prefix. ISPs try to give a business only the number of addresses it requires. However, with IPv6 having such a large address space, most address allocations will have a /48 prefix, even for small home networks. This means the network ID is 48 bits, and the network administrator has 80 bits for assigning subnets and host IDs. Because the host ID is 64 bits, 16 bits are left for creating subnets. This number of bits allows for 65,536 subnets, more than enough for all but the largest organizations. Large conglomerates can get multiple /48 prefix addresses or /47 prefix addresses, which provide more than 130,000 subnets. A typical IPv6 address assigned by an ISP looks like Figure 9-10.

| Global routing prefix (48 bits) | Subnet ID (16 bits) | Interface ID (64 bits) |

Figure 9-10   Structure of a typical IPv6 address
© 2015 Cengage Learning®

With 16 bits available to subnet, there are many strategies you can use. A small network that doesn't have multiple subnets can simply leave the subnet ID as all 0s, for example, and an address in this situation might look like this:

`2001:DB8:A00:0000:020C:29FF:FE7C:F9C4/64`

The first two fields (`2001:DB8`) of this address use the reserved documentation prefix mentioned previously. The `A00` in the address is the last 16 bits of the network prefix and was randomly chosen for this example. The 0s following the `A00` are the subnet ID, and the last 64 bits are the computer's interface ID. The `/64` just indicates that the network portion of the address is the first 64 bits (network prefix plus subnet ID), although the prefix for an interface ID is unnecessary.

A network that does need to subnet could just take the 16 bits for the subnet ID and start counting. For example, a company could make the first three subnets as follows; the bold part of the address is the subnet ID, and the 64-bit interface ID has been omitted.

`2001:DB8:A00:`**`0000`**
`2001:DB8:A00:`**`0001`**
`2001:DB8:A00:`**`0002`**

Large organizations with multiple locations could take a more structured approach and assign each location a bank of subnets as in the following:

- `2001:DB8:A00:0000`—Assigned to New York location
- `2001:DB8:A00:4000`—Assigned to London location
- `2001:DB8:A00:8000`—Assigned to Shanghai location

With this strategy, each location has 4000 hexadecimal subnet IDs to work with. For example, New York can make subnets `2001:DB8:A00:0000`, `2001:DB8:A00:0001`, `2001:DB8:A00:0002`, and so forth, up to `2001:DB8:A00:3FFF`. Put another way, each location can configure up to 16,384 subnets. As you can see, subnetting does still exist in IPv6, but it's a more straightforward process than in IPv4.

Multicast Addresses

A multicast address in IPv6 performs the same function as its IPv4 counterpart. A multicast address isn't assigned to an interface, but a node can listen for packets with multicast addresses to participate in a multicast application. Multicast addresses are easily identified because they begin with `ff` (first 8 bits of the address set to 1). Beyond that, multicast addresses have the following structure:

`ffxy:zzzz:zzzz:zzzz:zzzz:zzzz:zzzz:zzzz`

- *Flags*—The 4-bit flags field, indicated by the x, uses the three low-order bits. The high-order bit is reserved and must be 0. The next high-order bit is the R (rendezvous point) flag; when set, it indicates that the address contains a rendezvous point. The next high-order bit is the P (prefix) flag; when set, it indicates that the multicast address is based on the network prefix. The last bit, called the T (transient) bit, indicates a permanently assigned or well-known address assigned by IANA when it's 0. If the T bit is 1, the multicast address isn't permanently assigned—in other words, "transient." If the R flag is set to 1, the P and T flags must also be set to 1. If the P flag is set to 1, the T bit must also be set. Common values for this field, therefore, are 0, 1, 3, and 7.

- *Scope*—The scope field, indicated by the y, specifies whether and where the multicast packet can be routed. Common values and scopes for this field are as follows:

  o 1: Interface-local scope, which is essentially a multicast loopback address because the packet can't be sent across the network; it must stay with the current node.

  o 2: Link-local scope, which means the packet must stay on the current network and can't be routed.

o 5: Site-local scope, meaning this scope can be targeted at specific devices on the network, such as routers and DHCP servers.

o 8: Organization-local, which means the packet can't be routed beyond the organization's network.

o E: Global scope, meaning these multicast packets can be routed on the public Internet.

- *Group ID*—This field, represented by the z characters, identifies a multicast group, which is the group of computers listening to the stream of multicast packets. In essence, this 112-bit field identifies the unique multicast application that's transmitting the multicast packets. RFC 2375 lists the well-known multicast address assignments.

Anycast Addresses

Anycast addresses are unique, in that they can be assigned to multiple interfaces on different nodes and are recognized as anycast addresses only by the devices that use them. Specifically, anycast addresses are assigned to routers and are used to allow other IPv6 nodes to deliver internetwork packets to the nearest router on a subnet. They're typically used when more than one router exists on a subnet. Each router interface on the subnet can be assigned the anycast address. When a node sends a packet to the anycast address, the packet is delivered to the "nearest" router as defined by the routing protocols. It's often defined as a one-to-one-of-many association because there are potentially many destinations, but the packet is delivered to only one.

Anycast addresses don't have a special format because they're just unicast addresses used in a special way. Just assigning an address to multiple interfaces makes a unicast address an anycast address. However, the node that's assigned the anycast address must be configured to recognize these addresses. Currently, only router interfaces should be assigned an anycast address, and the router must be configured to recognize that the interface has been assigned this type of address.

IPv6 Autoconfiguration

IPv6 autoconfiguration occurs by two methods: stateless and stateful. With Windows Vista/ Windows Server 2008 and later computers, these methods can actually be used together.

- *Stateless autoconfiguration*—The node listens for router advertisement messages from a local router. If the Autonomous flag in the router advertisement message is set, the node uses the prefix information contained in the message. In this case, the node uses the advertised prefix and its 64-bit interface ID to generate the IPv6 address. If the Autonomous flag isn't set, the prefix information is ignored, and the node can attempt to use DHCPv6 for address configuration or an automatically generated link-local address.

- *Stateful autoconfiguration*—The node uses an autoconfiguration protocol, such as DHCPv6, to obtain its IPv6 address and other configuration information. A node attempts to use DHCPv6 to get IPv6 address configuration information if there are no routers on the network providing router advertisements or if the Autonomous flag in router advertisements isn't set.

Autoconfiguration on Windows Hosts

The Windows autoconfiguration process involves the following steps:

1. At initialization, a link-local address is determined.

2. The link-local address is verified as unique by using duplicate address detection.

3. If the address is verified as unique, the address is assigned to the interface; otherwise, a new address is generated and Step 2 is repeated.

4. The host transmits a router solicitation message. This message is addressed to the `all-routers` multicast address.

5. If no router advertisement messages are received in response to the solicitation message, the host attempts to use DHCPv6 to get an address.

6. If a router advertisement message is received and has an Autonomous flag set, the prefix in the router advertisement is used along with the interface ID to configure the IPv6 address on the interface. The host can also use a DHCPv6 server to acquire other IPv6 configuration parameters if specified in the router advertisement. If the Autonomous flag isn't set, the host uses DHCPv6 to acquire the address.

These steps are for Windows 8/8.1 and Windows Server 2012/R2 hosts. Windows Server 2008 and Windows 7 hosts don't attempt to use DHCPv6 if no router advertisements are received; otherwise, the process is the same.

Note that the IPv6 client maintains its link-local address even if it successfully gets an address via autoconfiguration or DHCPv6. Also, it's possible for the router advertisement to have the Autonomous flag set, causing the IPv6 client to autoconfigure an address *and* specify that the client should use DHCPv6 to get an address. In this case, the client does both and ends up with two addresses. It's also possible for more than one router to advertise an IPv6 prefix, causing the client to autoconfigure multiple addresses.

Windows Server 2012/R2 and Windows 8/8.1 can be configured to send router advertisements, so you don't need to configure a router to do so. You can use the following commands to make Windows Server 2012/R2 send out router advertisements so that IPv6 clients can autoconfigure their IPv6 addresses. These examples use the IPv6 prefix `2001:db8:1234:1::/64`, and the network interface is named "Ethernet." You replace the prefix with your own and "Ethernet" with the name of your network interface, if it's different.

To configure Windows Server 2012/R2 to send router advertisements, use the following command at a PowerShell or command prompt. Notice that both the `routerdiscovery` and `advertise` flags must be set in the same command:

```
netsh interface ipv6 set interface "Ethernet" routerdiscovery=enabled
   advertise=enabled
```

To configure the router advertisements with the Managed Address Configuration and Other Stateful Configuration flags disabled, which tells the client not to use a DHCPv6 server for its address or other IPv6 configuration parameters, use the following command:

```
netsh interface ipv6 set interface "Ethernet" managedaddress=disabled
   otherstateful=disabled
```

To configure the router advertisement with the address prefix you want to advertise:

```
netsh interface ipv6 add route
   interface="Ethernet" prefix=2001:db8:1234:1::/64 publish=yes
```

To view the IPv6 routes that are "published," meaning the IPv6 prefix is sent in router advertisements, use the following command:

```
netsh interface ipv6 show route
```

To see the detailed configuration of your interface, which includes a listing of all the configuration options, use the following command:

```
netsh interface ipv6 show interfaces interface="Ethernet"
   level=verbose
```

The output of the two preceding commands are shown in Figure 9-11 and 9-12, with the relevant lines highlighted.

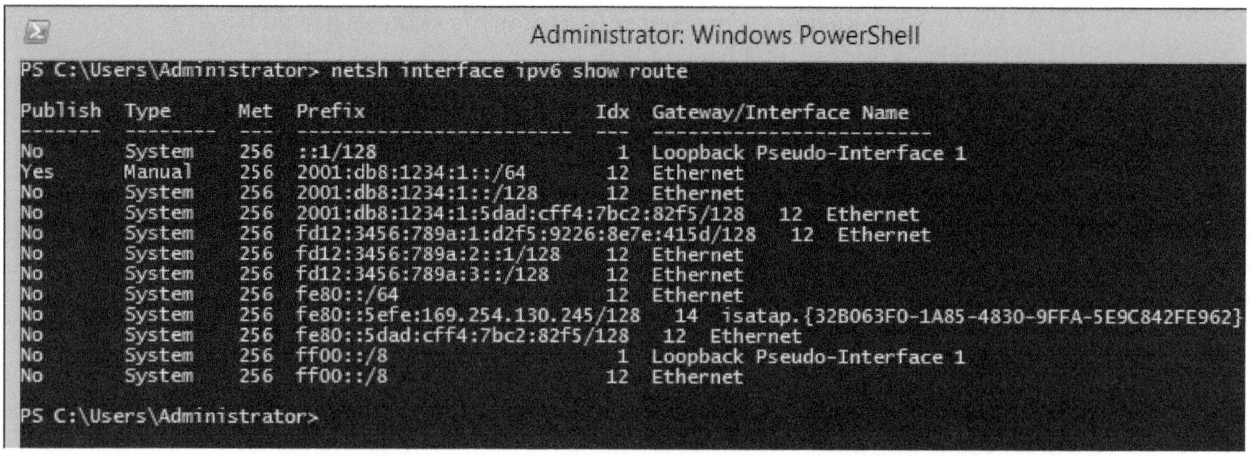

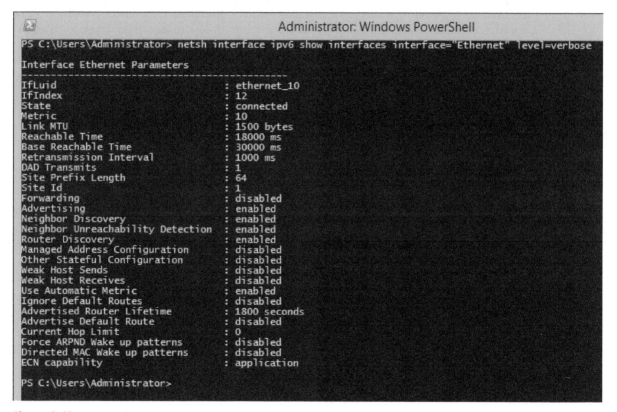

Figure 9-11 Output from `netsh interface ipv6 show route`

Figure 9-12 Output from `netsh interface ipv6 show interfaces interface="Ethernet" level=verbose`

Transitioning from IPv4 to IPv6

The move from IPv4 to IPv6 isn't happening on a particular date worldwide; rather, the transition is under way and will continue over several years. However, whether it's a small business with just a few Internet-connected computers or a 100,000-computer global enterprise, the switch to IPv6 is inevitable. Thankfully, both protocols can coexist easily on the same computer and the same network, allowing network administrators to ease into the transition instead of having to change from IPv4 to IPv6 instantly.

Starting with Windows Server 2008 and Vista, the Windows OS has maintained a **dual IP layer architecture** by default, meaning that both IPv4 and IPv6 are installed and enabled by default in current Windows OSs, as you probably noticed when you examined the network connection properties earlier. So in one sense, Windows is IPv6 ready, with no additional configuration required. However, transitioning an entire network from IPv4 to IPv6 successfully while maintaining compatibility with IPv4 requires a variety of transition technologies. Most of these technologies are built into Windows, but some you configure as needed. These technologies and special address types, discussed in the following sections, help ease the transition to IPv6 while maintaining compatibility with IPv4:

- Dual IP layer architecture
- IPv6-over-IPv4 tunneling
- Intra-Site Automatic Tunnel Addressing Protocol (ISATAP)
- 6to4
- Teredo

Dual IP Layer Architecture

A dual IP layer architecture means that both IPv4 and IPv6 are running, and the computer can communicate directly with both IPv4 and IPv6 devices by using the native packet types. A variation of dual IP layer architecture is dual-stack architecture. With dual IP layer architecture, there are two versions of the IP component of the TCP/IP stack and only one version of all the other components (TCP, UDP, Application-layer protocols). With the dual-stack architecture, there are two versions of the entire TCP/IP protocol suite: one for IPv4 and one for IPv6. Windows XP and Windows Server 2003 use this architecture. The dual IP layer is slightly more efficient, but both architectures achieve the same objective: the capability to communicate with both IPv4 and IPv6 devices. In addition, computers running either architecture can encapsulate IPv6 packets in an IPv4 header; a process called tunneling.

IPv6-over-IPv4 Tunneling

Tunneling is a network protocol technique that allows transmitting a packet in a format that's otherwise incompatible with the network architecture by encapsulating the packet in a compatible header format. For example, VPNs use tunneling to send encrypted data across the Internet by encapsulating an encrypted packet in a standard unencrypted IP header (see Figure 9-13).

IPv4 header	IPv6 headers and extensions	Upper-layer protocol data unit (PDU)

Figure 9-13   IPv6 packet encapsulated in an IPv4 header
© 2015 Cengage Learning®

IPv6-over-IPv4 tunneling allows a host to send an IPv6 packet over an IPv4 network to an IPv6 device. How is this feature useful? Suppose your network runs a dual IP layer architecture, and you need to access a server across the Internet that's running an IPv6-only application. Unfortunately, your ISP is still using IPv4-only routers. The only way to get IPv6 packets to the IPv6 application is to encapsulate them in IPv4 headers, allowing them to traverse the Internet as IPv4 packets. At the destination network, the packets are de-encapsulated and delivered to the server as IPv6 packets. Figure 9-14 illustrates this process.

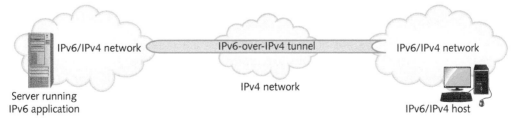

Server running
IPv6 application

IPv6/IPv4 network

IPv6-over-IPv4 tunnel

IPv4 network

IPv6/IPv4 network

IPv6/IPv4 host

Figure 9-14   IPv6-over-IPv4 tunneling
© 2015 Cengage Learning®

Some details are left out of Figure 9-14 because a variety of methods are used to create tunnels. A common method is creating the tunnel from router to router so that the IPv6 packet is encapsulated when it gets to a router in the source network and de-encapsulated at the router connected to the destination network. Tunnels can also be created between two hosts and between a host and a router.

Manually Creating an IPv6-over-IPv4 Tunnel An IPv6-over-IPv4 tunnel can be created in Windows Server 2012/R2 when it's configured as a router by using the following command:

```
netsh interface ipv6 add v6v4tunnel tunnelToNet1 192.168.2.250
   192.168.1.250
```

Figure 9-15 shows a network in which Windows Server 2012 is used as a router on both sides of the tunnel. In the preceding command, the parameter *tunnelToNet1* represents the name of the tunnel interface you're creating. The two IPv4 addresses are the addresses on the servers connected to the Internet. The first IP address is the address of the local server, and the second address is the address of the remote server interface that's connected to the Internet. This command runs on the server in the `2001:db8:2::/64` network. You repeat the command on the server on both sides of the tunnel, interchanging the IP addresses and changing the tunnel name, if you like:

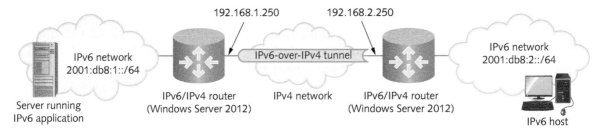

Figure 9-15 A router-to-router IPv6-over-IPv4 tunnel
© *2015 Cengage Learning®*

Next, you need to create a route to the remote IPv6 network, specifying the tunnel as the interface to use to reach the IPv6 network:

```
netsh interface ipv6 add route 2001:db8:1::/64 tunnelToNet1
```

This command runs on the server in the `2001:db8:2::/64` network. You use the same command on the other server but change the destination IPv6 network and tunnel name, if necessary.

Intra-Site Automatic Tunnel Addressing Protocol

Intra-Site Automatic Tunnel Addressing Protocol (ISATAP) is used to transmit IPv6 packets between dual IP layer hosts across an IPv4 network. This automatic tunneling protocol doesn't require manual configuration, as IPv6-over-IPv4 tunneling does. ISATAP is enabled by default on Windows Server 2012/R2 as well as Windows 8/8.1, Windows Server 2008, Windows 7, and Vista with SP1.

In Windows, ISATAP interfaces are created for each LAN interface. ISATAP addresses have the following format:

```
fe80::5efe:n:n:n:n
```

The first 64 bits of an ISATAP address are the link-local IPv6 address `fe80` followed by 48 0 bits. The next 16 bits are typically 0 unless the globally unique flag is set, in which case the next 16 bits in hexadecimal are `0200`. The next 16 bits are `5efe`. ISATAP embeds the IPv4 address in the last 32 bits of the IPv6 address. For example, if a LAN interface has the IPv4 address 172.31.210.200, the ISATAP address is as follows:

```
fe80::5efe:172.31.210.200
```

Even though ISATAP is enabled by default in Windows Server 2012/R2, the media state is disconnected, so you don't see the ISATAP address. To solve this problem, add a DNS A record entry for the ISATAP interface or add a hosts file entry. You can get the ISATAP interface's name with `ipconfig`. It's in the format `isatap.DNSsuffix`. For example, if your computer is in the mydomain.local domain, the name of the ISATAP adapter is isatap.mydomain.local. Your hosts file entry would look like the following:

```
172.31.210.200 isatap.mydomain.local
```

After you have an entry in the hosts file (or DNS server), the ISATAP interface name can be resolved, and the address is assigned as shown in Figure 9-16. Notice that the ISATAP address includes `%13` at the end to indicate the interface index, which is part of a link-local IPv6 address.

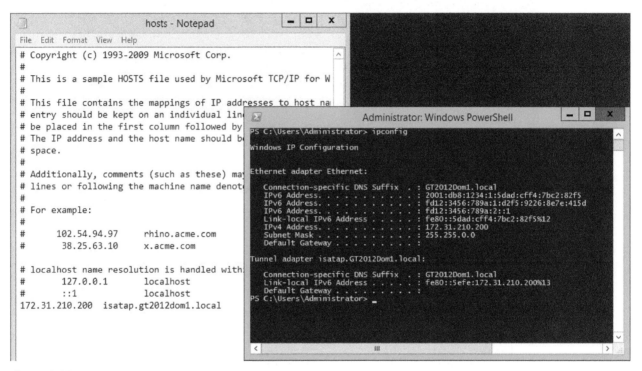

Figure 9-16   The hosts file entry and ISATAP interface

You can test an ISATAP interface by using `ping`. Suppose you have two computers with the IPv4 addresses 172.31.210.200 and 172.31.210.102 configured. Their ISATAP addresses are `fe80::5efe:172.31.210.200` and `fe80::5efe:172.31.210.102`. You must include the interface index of the source computer's ISATAP address in the `ping` command so that it knows the ISATAP address should be used as the source address. For example, to ping from `fe80::5efe:172.31.210.200%13`, use the following command:

```
ping fe80::5efe:172.31.210.102%13
```

You use the interface index of the source computer—the one you're sending the `ping` from, not the destination computer's. Figure 9-17 shows the results of this command.

Even though the ISATAP address begins with `fe80`, making it a link-local address, the packets get tunneled inside an IPv4 header, making the packets capable of traversing an IPv4-only routed network. Although ISATAP is an effective tunneling interface to carry IPv6 traffic across IPv4 networks, Microsoft recommends using it for testing while transitioning to a native IPv6 environment for a production network.

```
Windows IP Configuration

Ethernet adapter Ethernet:

   Connection-specific DNS Suffix  . : GT2012Dom1.local
   IPv6 Address. . . . . . . . . . . : 2001:db8:1234:1:5dad:cff4:7bc2:82f5
   IPv6 Address. . . . . . . . . . . : fd12:3456:789a:2::1
   Link-local IPv6 Address . . . . . : fe80::5dad:cff4:7bc2:82f5%12
   IPv4 Address. . . . . . . . . . . : 172.31.210.200
   Subnet Mask . . . . . . . . . . . : 255.255.0.0
   Default Gateway . . . . . . . . . :

Tunnel adapter isatap.GT2012Dom1.local:

   Connection-specific DNS Suffix  . : GT2012Dom1.local
   Link-local IPv6 Address . . . . . : fe80::5efe:172.31.210.200%13
   Default Gateway . . . . . . . . . :
PS C:\Users\Administrator> ping fe80::5efe:172.31.210.102%13

Pinging fe80::5efe:172.31.210.102%13 with 32 bytes of data:
Reply from fe80::5efe:172.31.210.102%13: time=595ms
Reply from fe80::5efe:172.31.210.102%13: time<1ms
Reply from fe80::5efe:172.31.210.102%13: time<1ms
Reply from fe80::5efe:172.31.210.102%13: time<1ms

Ping statistics for fe80::5efe:172.31.210.102%13:
    Packets: Sent = 4, Received = 4, Lost = 0 (0% loss),
Approximate round trip times in milli-seconds:
    Minimum = 0ms, Maximum = 595ms, Average = 148ms
PS C:\Users\Administrator>
```

Figure 9-17   Using `ping` to test ISATAP interfaces

6to4 Tunneling

6to4 provides automatic tunneling of IPv6 traffic over an IPv4 network. It can provide host-to-router or router-to-host tunneling but is most often used to create a router-to-router tunnel. The key to 6to4 tunneling is the `2002::/16` prefix. Routers configured to perform 6to4 tunneling recognize the `2002` prefix as a 6to4 address, just as `fe80::5efe` is recognized as an ISATAP address. When an IPv6 packet with addresses using the `2002` prefix arrives at a 6to4 configured router, the router knows to encapsulate the packet in an IPv4 header. A 6to4 address has the following format:

`2002:xxxx:xxxx::/48`

The first 16 bits are always `2002`, and the next 32 bits, represented by the x characters, are the hexadecimal representation of the 32-bit IPv4 address. The remaining bits are the subnet ID and 64-bit interface ID. The IPv4 address embedded in the 6to4 address must be a public address, which limits the use of this tunneling technology because it can't traverse a router interface that uses NAT.

Teredo Tunneling

Teredo is an automatic IPv6-over-IPv4 tunneling protocol that solves the problem of 6to4's requirement of a public IPv4 address and the inability to traverse NAT routers. Teredo allows the tunnel endpoints to exist behind a NAT firewall by tunneling IPv6 packets between hosts instead of requiring a router as an endpoint.

Teredo achieves NAT traversal by encapsulating IPv6 packets in IPv4 UDP messages, which can traverse most NAT routers. It has the added benefit of allowing IPv4 applications to communicate through a NAT router that otherwise might not be able to. Teredo has three components:

- *Teredo client*—A host device behind a NAT router that's running IPv4 and IPv6 and wants to use Teredo tunneling to access IPv6 devices or other Teredo clients across an IPv4 network. Windows Server 2012/R2, Windows Server 2008 R2, Windows 8/8.1, and Windows 7 include the Teredo client.

- *Teredo server*—A node on the Internet running IPv4 and IPv6 that's connected to both IPv4 and IPv6 networks. A Teredo server facilitates communication between Teredo clients. Windows Server 2012/R2, Windows Server 2008 R2, Windows 8/8.1, and Windows 7 include the Teredo server. Teredo servers are most useful for an ISP that wants to provide Teredo services for its customers.

- *Teredo relay*—A router running IPv6 and IPv4 that forwards packets between Teredo clients and hosts on IPv6 networks. A Teredo relay advertises the 2001::/32 network (discussed next) to let hosts know that it provides Teredo relay services. Teredo relays are most useful for IPv6 content providers so that IPv4/IPv6 hosts can access their services across the IPv4 Internet.

A Teredo address can be identified by the Teredo prefix 2001::/32 and has the following format:

```
2001:tttt:tttt:gggg:pppp:xxxx:xxxx
```

The first 16 bits are always the Teredo prefix 2001. The next 32 bits, represented by t characters, are the Teredo server's IPv4 public address. The next 16 bits, shown as g characters, are Teredo flags that specify processing options. The p characters represent an obscured UDP port the client uses for Teredo traffic. The port is obscured to prevent certain types of NATs from attempting to translate the port. The last 32 bits are the obscured IPv4 address the client uses for Teredo traffic.

For more information on IPv6 transition technologies, see *http://technet. microsoft.com/en-us/library/dd379548(v=ws.10).aspx*.

Activity 9-7: Setting IPv6 Static Addresses

Time Required: 10 minutes
Objective: Set IPv6 static addresses.

Required Tools and Equipment: 410Win8, 410Server1, 410Server2
Description: Before you begin using common tools with IPv6, such as ipconfig and ping, you configure static IPv6 addresses to work with.

1. Log on to 410Server1 as **Administrator,** if necessary. Open a PowerShell prompt window.

2. Type **New-NetIPAddress -InterfaceAlias Ethernet -IpAddress 2001:db8:10::1 -PrefixLength 64** and press Enter. Type **Get-NetIPConfiguration** and press **Enter** to see information similar to what ipconfig /all shows.

3. On 410Win8, open the Network and Sharing Center, and click **Change adapter settings.**

4. Right-click **Ethernet** and click **Properties.** Double-click **Internet Protocol Version 6 (TCP/IPv6).**

5. Click **Use the following IPv6 address.** In the IPv6 address text box, type **2001:db8:10::10.** In the Subnet prefix length text box, type **64.** Click **OK** twice.

6. Start 410Server2, if necessary and log on as **Administrator.** Open a command prompt window, if necessary, and then type **netsh interface ipv6 set address "Ethernet" 2001:db8:10::2** and press Enter.

7. Type **netsh interface ipv6 show interfaces interface="Ethernet" level=verbose** and press Enter. This command shows you detailed information about the IPv6 status on the interface.

8. Close the command prompt window, and shut down 410Server2. Stay logged on to 410Win8 and 410Server1.

Activity 9-8: Working with IPv6

Time Required: 15 minutes
Objective: Use `ipconfig` and `ping` with IPv6 and change an IPv6 interface address.

Required Tools and Equipment: 410Win8 and 410Server1
Description: Your company has plans to move to IPv6. Because you haven't used IPv6, you want to become comfortable with using common tools, such as `ipconfig` and `ping`.

1. Log on to 410Win8 as **Administrator** and open a command prompt window, if necessary. Make sure 410Server1 is running.

2. Type **ipconfig** and press **Enter**. Find the output line starting with "Link-local IPv6 Address." Notice that the assigned address starts with `fe80::`. The `fe80` indicates a link-local IPv6 address, and the `::` indicates a string of 0 values—in this case, a string of three consecutive 0 values. The rest of the address (64 bits) has been randomly assigned by Windows.

3. Type **ping ::1** and press **Enter**. Windows replies because you just pinged your own computer. Type **ping -a ::1** and press **Enter**. The `-a` option tells Windows to display the hostname for the `::1` address, which is the name of your 410Win8 computer.

4. Type **ping -6 410Server1** and press **Enter**. The `-6` option tells `ping` to use IPv6 addresses. You should receive a reply from 410Server1 from the address you assigned in the previous activity.

5. Type **getmac** and press **Enter** to display your computer's MAC address. Make a note of this address.

6. Type **netsh interface ipv6 set global randomizeidentifiers=disabled** and press **Enter**. Your interface is now using the EUI-64 format to assign the link-local IPv6 address.

7. Type **ipconfig** and press **Enter**. Notice that the last 64 bits of the IPv6 address now look like your MAC address, with the addition of `fffe` after the first 24 bits and `02` instead of the first `00` of your MAC address.

8. Close the command prompt window, and log off.

Chapter Summary

- TCP/IP is a network protocol designed to deliver data packets to computers on any scale of network, from a small two-computer LAN to the worldwide Internet. TCP/IP is a suite of protocols, meaning it's composed of several protocols performing different functions but working together.

- Both Internet Protocol Version 4 (TCP/IPv4) and Internet Protocol Version 6 (TCP/IPv6) are installed on Windows Server 2012/R2. IP provides logical addressing, efficient packet delivery, and the information needed for packet routing.

- An IPv4 address is a 32-bit dotted decimal number broken into four octets. Every IP address must have a subnet mask to indicate which part of the IP address is the network ID and which part is the host ID. There are three IP address classes—A, B, and C—each with a default subnet mask.

- CIDR notation uses the format A.B.C.D/*n*; *n* is the number of 1 bits in the subnet mask.

- Subnetting uses a modified subnet mask to divide a large network into two or more smaller, more manageable networks. It's used to reduce the adverse effect of the many broadcast messages found in a large broadcast domain (another name for an IP network) and to conserve IP addresses by assigning to a company only the number of public IP addresses it requires.

- Supernetting reallocates bits from the network portion of an IP address to the host portion, effectively combining two or more smaller subnets into a larger supernet.

- When you assign a computer an IP address, there are some rules to remember: Every IP address configuration must have a subnet mask, all hosts on the same network must share the same network ID in their IP addresses, and all host IDs on the same network must be unique.

- Several command-line tools are available for checking the status of and troubleshooting IP configuration, including `ping`, `ipconfig`, `arp`, `tracert`, and `nslookup`.

- IPv6 uses a 128-bit address expressed by eight 16-bit hexadecimal numbers separated by a colon. Some reasons for this new IP version are a larger address space, a hierarchical address space, autoconfiguration, built-in QoS, and built-in security.

- IPv6 defines unicast, multicast, and anycast addresses. IPv6 autoconfiguration occurs by two methods: stateless and stateful. With current Windows versions, both methods can be used together.

- Several transition technologies and special address types are available to help ease the transition to IPv6 yet maintain compatibility with IPv4: dual IP layer architecture, IPv6-over-IPv4 tunneling, Intra-Site Automatic Tunnel Addressing Protocol, 6to4, and Teredo.

Key Terms

6to4   An IPv4-to-IPv6 transition protocol that provides automatic tunneling of IPv6 traffic over an IPv4 network. It can handle host-to-router or router-to-host tunneling but is most often used to create a router-to-router tunnel.

Automatic Private IP Addressing (APIPA)   A method of automatic IP address assignment that occurs when a computer can't contact a DHCP server; uses the range 169.254.1.0 through 169.254.254.255.

broadcast   A packet addressed to all computers on the network.

broadcast domain   The bounds of a network that defines which devices must receive a packet that's broadcast by any other device; usually an IP subnet.

CIDR notation   A method of expressing an IP address in the format A.B.C.D/*n*; *n* is the number of 1 bits in the subnet mask or the number of bits in the network ID. *See also* Classless Interdomain Routing (CIDR).

classful addressing   The use of IP addresses with their default subnet masks according to their address class: A, B, or C.

Classless Interdomain Routing (CIDR)   The use of IP addresses without requiring the default subnet mask. *See also* subnet mask.

destination IP address   The IP address of the computer a packet is sent to.

dual IP layer architecture   The current architecture of the IPv6 protocol in Windows, in which both IPv4 and IPv6 share the other components of the stack.

Extended Unique Identifier (EUI)-64 interface ID   An autoconfigured IPv6 host address that uses the MAC address of the host plus an additional 16 bits.

Intra-Site Automatic Tunnel Addressing Protocol (ISATAP)   An automatic tunneling protocol used to transmit IPv6 packets between dual IP layer hosts across an IPv4 network. *See also* dual IP layer architecture.

link-local IPv6 address   Similar in function to the IPv4 APIPA addresses, link-local IPv6 addresses begin with `fe80`, are self-configuring, and can't be routed. *See also* Automatic Private IP Addressing (APIPA).

localhost   A reserved name that corresponds to the loopback address, 127.0.0.1. *See also* loopback address.

logical AND operation   A binary operation in which there are two operands; the result is 0 if either operand is 0 and 1 if both operands are 1.

loopback address   The IP address 127.0.0.1, which always refers to the local computer and is used to test the functioning of TCP/IP.

metric   A value assigned to the gateway based on the speed of the interface used to access the gateway.

multicasting   A network communication in which a packet is addressed so that more than one destination can receive it.

Network Address Translation (NAT)   A process that translates the source or destination IP address in a packet to a different value; often used to allow using private IP addresses while connected to the Internet.

octet   An 8-bit value; a number from 0 to 255 that's one of the four numbers in a dotted decimal IP address.

source IP address   The IP address of a computer that's sending a packet.

subnet mask   A 32-bit dotted decimal number consisting of an unbroken series of binary 1 digits followed by an unbroken series of binary 0 digits. Used with an IP address to determine the network ID.

subnetting   A process that reallocates bits from an IP address's host portion to the network portion, creating multiple smaller address spaces.

supernetting   A process that reallocates bits from an IP address's network portion to the host portion, effectively combining smaller subnets into a larger supernet.

Teredo   An automatic IPv6-over-IPv4 tunneling protocol that solves the problem of 6to4's requirement of a public IPv4 address and the inability to traverse NAT routers. *See also* 6to4.

Transmission Control Protocol/Internet Protocol (TCP/IP)   A network protocol suite designed to deliver data packets to computers on any scale of network, from a small two-computer LAN to the worldwide Internet.

tunneling   A common network protocol technique that allows transmitting a packet in a format that would otherwise be incompatible for the network architecture by encapsulating the packet in a compatible header format.

unicast address   An address in a unit of network data intended for a single destination computer.

unique local IPv6 address   An address for devices on a private network that can't be routed on the Internet.

Review Questions

1. Which of the following is needed if a computer with the IP address 172.31.210.10/24 wants to communicate with a computer with the IP address 172.31.209.122/24?

   a. Hub

   b. Router

   c. Switch

   d. Server

2. You have just typed the commands `ipconfig /flushdns` and `ping server1`. Which of the following protocols is used first as a result of these commands?

   a. TCP

   b. DNS

   c. ICMP

   d. DHCP

3. Which command should you use with a dual-homed server to make sure the server sends packets out the correct interface?

   a. `ipconfig`

   b. `ping`

   c. `tracert`

   d. `route`

4. Which command should you use to determine whether there's a bottleneck between your computer and a computer on another network?

   a. `ipconfig`

   b. `ping`

   c. `tracert`

   d. `route`

5. Which command should you use to configure the primary DNS server on your computer?

   a. `ipconfig`

   b. `netsh`

   c. `nslookup`

   d. `arp`

6. Which IP address expressed in CIDR notation has the subnet mask 255.255.255.0?

   a. 10.100.44.123/24

   b. 172.16.88.222/16

   c. 192.168.100.1/26

   d. 172.29.111.201/18

7. Which IP network address expressed in CIDR notation can support a maximum of 1022 hosts?

   a. 10.100.44.0/24

   b. 172.16.4.0/22

   c. 192.168.100.64/26

   d. 172.29.128.0/18

8. You have just finished a default installation of Windows Server 2012. You know that TCP/IP is installed. How does the server get assigned an IP address?

   a. TCP

   b. DNS

   c. ARP

   d. DHCP

9. Your DNS server is on the same network as the computer where you enter the following commands:

```
arp -d
ipconfig /flushdns
nslookup server1
```

Which of the following protocols is used first as a result of these commands?

   a. TCP

   b. DNS

   c. ARP

   d. DHCP

10. The IP address 10.240.0.0/8 can't be assigned to a host. True or False?

11. Which of the following is a good reason to subnet an IPv4 network? (Choose all that apply.)

   a. Eliminate the need for ARP requests.

   b. Decrease the size of the broadcast domain.

   c. Allow broadcasts to reach more computers.

   d. Conserve IP addresses.

12. Which of the following IP addresses has 12 bits in the host ID?

    a.   172.31.21.12/16

    b.   172.31.89.100/12

    c.   12.49.127.88/8

    d.   12.156.109.252/20

13. You have set up an e-mail server that needs to respond to e-mail requests, using mail.coolgadgets.com and mail.niftytools.com in the request URL. How can you do this?

    a.   Install two NICs, and assign the same IP address to both NICs. Configure DNS to map one MAC address to mail.coolgadgets.com and the other MAC address to mail.niftytools.com.

    b.   Configure two IP addresses on one NIC. Configure DNS to map one IP address to mail.coolgadgets.com and the other IP address to mail.niftytools.com.

    c.   Install two NICs, and connect each one to a different network. Set up the router on each network to forward mail packets to the NIC bound to the correct URL.

    d.   Install two NICs, and assign different IP addresses to each NIC, but make sure both IP addresses use the same network ID. Configure the NICs to use default gateways on different networks.

14. You have a server with two NICs, each attached to a different IP network. You're having problems communicating with devices on remote networks that send packets to one of the interfaces. The server receives the packets fine, but the server's replies never reach the intended destination network. Replies to packets that come in through the other interface seem to reach their destination without any problems. What can you do that will most likely solve the problem?

    a.   Configure a second default gateway on the interface exhibiting problems.

    b.   Change the default gateway to use the router that's on the network of the interface exhibiting problems.

    c.   Use the `route` command to add routes to the networks that aren't receiving replies.

    d.   Replace the NIC that's having problems replying to packets.

15. You have just changed the IP address on a computer named computer5 in your domain from 172.31.1.10/24 to 172.31.1.110/24. You were communicating with this computer from your workstation fine right before you changed the address. Now when you try the command `ping computer5` from your workstation, you don't get a successful reply. Other computers on the network aren't having a problem communicating with the computer. Which command might help solve the problem?

    a.   `arp -d`

    b.   `ipconfig /flushdns`

    c.   `tracert computer5`

    d.   `ping -6 172.31.1.110`

16. Which command can cause an address of 0.0.0.0 to be assigned to a host?

    a.   `nslookup 0.0.0.0`

    b.   `netsh set IPv4 address=Null`

    c.   `Set-NetIPInterface -InterfaceAlias Ethernet -DHCP enabled`

    d.   `ipconfig /release`

17. Which address can't be assigned to a host computer?

    a. 10.100.44.16/24

    b. 172.16.7.255/22

    c. 192.168.100.66/26

    d. 172.29.132.0/18

18. Which of the following is a benefit of using IPv6 rather than IPv4? (Choose all that apply.)

    a. You can assign four times the number of addresses in IPv6.

    b. Subnetting to conserve IP addresses is less of a concern.

    c. Features to improve communication security and quality are built into IPv6.

    d. IPv6 addresses are expressed as 16 8-bit numbers separated by colons, which are easier to read than dotted decimal notation.

19. Which of the following is a valid IPv6 address? (Choose all that apply.)

    a. `fe80:0:0:FEED::1`

    b. `2001:DB8:00AB:11:3344`

    c. `fe80:DB8::EE::8901`

    d. `2001:DB8:BAD:F00D:0020:3344:0:e4`

20. Which IPv6 transition technology can be used with NAT routers and has the address prefix `2001::/32`?

    a. Teredo

    b. ISATAP

    c. 6to4

    d. IPv6-over-IPv4

21. Which IPv6 transition technology requires the `netsh` command to manually create the tunnel to carry IPv6 traffic over the IPv4 Internet?

    a. Teredo

    b. ISATAP

    c. IPv6-over-IPv4

    d. 6to4

22. Which IPv6 transition technology embeds an IPv4 address in a link-local IPv6 address?

    a. Teredo

    b. ISATAP

    c. IPv6-over-IPv4

    d. 6to4

23. How many bits are in the interface ID of an IPv6 address?

    a. 32

    b. 64

    c. 16

    d. 48

24. What type of IPv6 address should you use when you have multiple routers on a subnet and want hosts to use the nearest router for packets that should be delivered to remote networks?

    a. Multicast

    b. Broadcast

    c. Anycast

    d. Unicast

25. What address should you ping if you want to test local IPv6 operation but don't want to actually send any packets on the network?

    a. `1::f`

    b. `2001::db8`

    c. `fe80::ffff`

    d. `::1`

Case Projects

Case Project 9-1: Creating a List of MAC Addresses

You have been asked to create a list of all MAC addresses and corresponding IP addresses and computer names in your network. Propose at least two methods for performing this task. Your network has almost 100 computers in a Windows Server 2012 R2 domain network with statically assigned IP addresses. Using the tools available in Windows Server 2012 R2, carry out the procedure you think will work best. Write a short report of your results and submit it to your instructor.

Case Project 9-2: Calculating a Subnet Mask

You're the network administrator for a growing ISP. One of the networks the IANA assigned to you is 198.60.123.0/24. You have decided to use this address to satisfy the requirements of 16 corporate customers, each needing between 10 and 14 public addresses. Without using a subnet calculator, calculate a subnet mask that meets the requirements. In the following chart, write the subnet mask along with the 16 subnetworks in CIDR notation, and list the range of host addresses each subnetwork will have available:

Subnet Mask:	
Subnetwork	Range of host addresses

Case Project 9-3: Using IPv6 Subnetting

You're the head network administrator for a large manufacturing enterprise that's completing its support for IPv6. The company has six major locations with several thousand users in each location. You have network administrators in each location. You're using a base IPv6 address of 2001:DB8:FAB/48 and want network administrators to be able to subnet their networks however they see fit. You want to maintain a reserve of address spaces for a possible 6 to 10 additional locations in the future. Each network administrator should be able to construct at least 200 subnets from the address you supply, and each location should have the same amount of available address space. What IPv6 addresses should you assign to each location? When constructing your answer, list each location as Location 1, Location 2, and so forth.

Case Project 9-4: Using Additional Networking Tools

A number of network tools, such as protocol analyzers and scanners, can help you troubleshoot a network. Find, download, and install the following tools on your 410Win8 computer:

- Wireshark network analyzer
- Netinfo (trial version of a suite of networking tools, including a ping and port scanner)

If necessary, use the help documentation that comes with these tools to understand how they work and what you can do with them. Write a brief report explaining how these tools can be useful in understanding and troubleshooting network communication. Use Wireshark to capture all the packets generated by pinging 410Server1 from 410Win8 (using the command ping 410Server1). Make sure you clear ARP and DNS caches first. Print the first 10 packets captured.

9

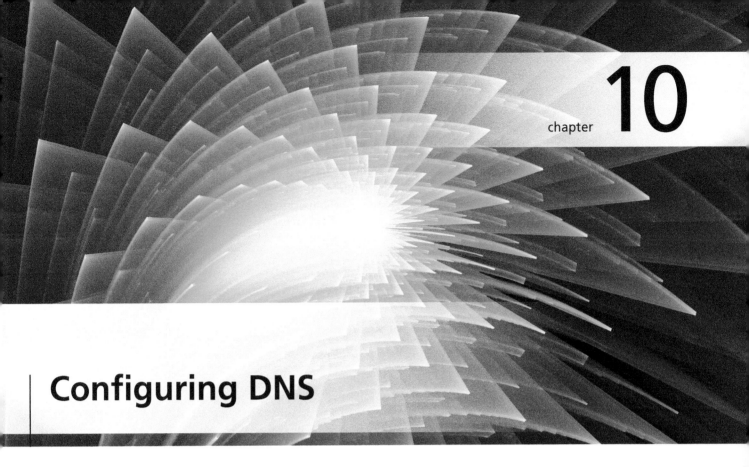

chapter 10

Configuring DNS

After reading this chapter and completing the exercises, you will be able to:

- Describe the structure of Domain Name System
- Install and configure DNS
- Configure DNS zones
- Configure advanced DNS server settings
- Monitor and troubleshoot DNS

To function correctly, most applications and services that use TCP/IP depend on a service to resolve computer names to addresses and to find computers that offer specific services. In fact, most network systems today would be almost unusable without a name-to-address translation system; without one, users and computers would need to know the address of each computer they communicate with. Because the TCP/IP suite is the default protocol for Windows, Domain Name System (DNS) is the default name resolution protocol for Windows computers. For Windows domain networks, DNS is required for operation because Active Directory depends on it. This chapter describes the structure of the worldwide DNS system and explains how to configure and maintain DNS in a Windows domain environment.

Introduction to Domain Name System

Table 10-1 describes what you need for the hands-on activities in this chapter.

Table 10-1   Activity requirements

Activity	Requirements	Notes
Activity 10-1: Using DNS Manager	410Server1	
Activity 10-2: Installing DNS and Creating a New Zone	410Server2	
Activity 10-3: Working with Reverse Lookup Zones	410Server1, 410Win8	
Activity 10-4: Creating Static DNS Entries	410Server2	
Activity 10-5: Creating a Secondary Zone and Configuring Zone Transfers	410Server1, 410Server2	
Activity 10-6: Configuring and Testing Forwarders	410Server1, 410Server2	
Activity 10-7: Working with Root Hints	410Server1, 410Server2	Internet connection required
Activity 10-8: Uninstalling DNS	410Server2	

© 2015 Cengage Learning®

Domain Name System (DNS) is a distributed hierarchical database composed mainly of computer name and IP address pairs. A distributed database means no single database contains all data; instead, data is spread out among many different servers. In the worldwide DNS system, data is distributed among thousands of servers throughout the world. A hierarchical database, in this case, means there's a structure to how information is stored and accessed in the database. In other words, unless you're resolving a local domain name for which you have a local server, DNS lookups often require a series of queries to a hierarchy of DNS servers before the name can be resolved.

The Structure of DNS

To better understand the DNS lookup process, reviewing the structure of a computer name on the Internet or in a Windows domain is helpful. Computer names are typically expressed as *host.domain.top-level-domain*; the *top-level-domain* can be com, net, org, us, edu, and so forth. As you learned in Chapter 6, this naming structure is called the fully qualified domain name (FQDN). The DNS naming hierarchy can be described as an inverted tree with the root at the top (named "."), top-level domains branching out from the root, and domains and subdomains branching off the top-level domains (see Figure 10-1).

The entire DNS tree is called the **DNS namespace**. When a domain name is registered, the domain is added to the DNS hierarchy and becomes part of the DNS namespace. Every domain has one or more servers that are authoritative for the domain, meaning the servers contain a master copy of all DNS records for that domain. A single server can be authoritative for multiple domains.

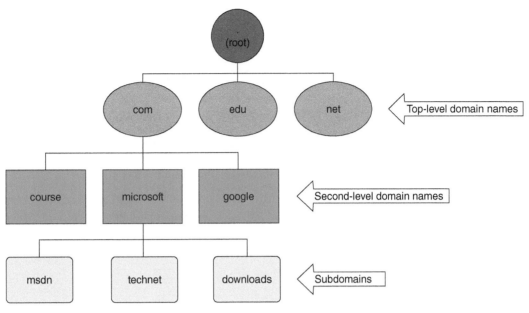

Figure 10-1   A partial view of the DNS naming hierarchy
© *Cengage Learning*®

10

Each shape in Figure 10-1 has one or more DNS servers managing the names associated with it. For example, the root of the tree has 13 DNS servers called **root servers** scattered about the world that keep a database of addresses of other DNS servers managing top-level domain names. These other servers, aptly named, are called **top-level domain (TLD) servers**. Each top-level domain has servers that maintain addresses of other DNS servers. For example, the com TLD servers maintain a database containing addresses of DNS servers for each domain name ending with com, such as tomsho.com and microsoft.com. Each second-level DNS server can contain hostnames, such as www or server1. Hostnames are associated with an IP address, so when a client looks up the name www.microsoft.com, the DNS server returns an IP address. Second-level domains can also have subdomains, such as the technet in technet.microsoft.com.

The DNS Database   DNS servers maintain a database of information that contains zones. A **zone** is a grouping of DNS information that belongs to a contiguous portion of the DNS namespace, usually a domain and possibly one or more subdomains. Each zone contains a variety of record types called **resource records** containing information about network resources, such as hostnames, other DNS servers, domain controllers, and so forth; they're identified by letter codes. Table 10-2 lists resource record types, the identifying codes, and a description of the resource record.

Table 10-2   DNS resource record types

Record type (code)	Description
Start of Authority (SOA)	Less a resource than an informational record, the SOA identifies the name server that's authoritative for the domain and includes a variety of timers, dynamic update configuration, and zone transfer information.
Host (A)	The most common resource record; consists of a computer name and an IPv4 address.
IPv6 Host (AAAA)	Like an A record but uses an IPv6 address.
Name Server (NS)	The FQDN of a name server that has authority over the domain. NS records are used by DNS servers to refer queries to another server that's authoritative for the requested domain.

(continues)

Record type (code)	Description
Canonical Name (CNAME)	A record containing an alias for another record that enables you to refer to the same resource with different names yet maintain only one host record. For example, you could create an A record for a computer named "web" and a CNAME record that points to the A record but allows users to access the host with the name "www."
Mail Exchanger (MX)	Contains the address of an e-mail server for the domain. Because e-mail addresses are typically specified as *user@domain*.com, the mail server's name is not part of the e-mail address. To deliver a message to the mail server, an MX record query supplies the address of a mail server in the specified domain.
Pointer (PTR)	Used for reverse DNS lookups. Although DNS is used mainly to resolve a name to an address, it can also resolve an address to a name by using a reverse lookup. PTR records can be created automatically on Windows DNS servers.
Service Records (SRV)	Allows DNS clients to request the address of a server that provides a specific service instead of querying the server by name. This type of record is useful when an application doesn't know the name of the server it needs but does know what service is required. For example, in Windows domains, DNS servers contain SRV records with the addresses of domain controllers so that clients can request the logon service to authenticate to the domain.

© 2015 Cengage Learning®

DNS records can be added to a zone and changed by using one of two methods:

- *Static updates*—With this method, an administrator must enter DNS record information manually. Using this method is reasonable with a small network of only a few resources accessed by name, but in a large network, static updates can be an administrative burden.

- *Dynamic updates*—Referred to as **Dynamic DNS (DDNS)**, computers in the domain can register or update their own DNS records, or DHCP can update DNS on the clients' behalf when a computer leases a new IP address. Both the client computer and the DHCP server must be configured to use this feature.

The DNS Lookup Process   When a computer needs to acquire information from a DNS server, it sends a lookup or query to the server. A computer making a DNS query is called a "DNS client" or "DNS resolver." Two types of DNS queries can be made:

- *Iterative query*—When a DNS server gets an **iterative query**, it responds with the best information it currently has in its local database to satisfy the query, such as the IP address of an A record it retrieves from a local zone file or cache. If the DNS server doesn't have the specific information, it might respond with the IP address of a name server that *can* satisfy the query; this type of response is called a **referral** because the server is referring the DNS client to another server. If the server has no information, it sends a negative response that essentially says "I can't help you." DNS servers usually query each other by using iterative queries.

- *Recursive query*—A **recursive query** instructs the DNS server to process the query until it responds with an address that satisfies the query or with an "I don't know" message. A recursive query might require a DNS server to contact several other DNS servers before it finally sends a response to the client. Most queries made by DNS clients are recursive queries, and DNS servers also use recursive queries when using a forwarder.

A typical DNS lookup made by a DNS client can involve both recursive and iterative queries. A sample query demonstrating the hierarchical nature of DNS (see Figure 10-2) is outlined in the following steps:

1. A user types www.microsoft.com in the Web browser's address bar. The computer running the Web browser, called the DNS client or **resolver**, sends a recursive query to the DNS server's address in its IP configuration. Typically, this DNS server, called the "local DNS server," is maintained on the network or at the client's ISP.

2. The local DNS server checks its local zone data and cache. If the name isn't found locally, it sends an iterative query to a DNS root server.

3. The root server sends a referral to the local DNS server with a list of addresses for the TLD servers handling the com top-level domain.

4. The local DNS server sends another iterative query to a com TLD server.

5. The com TLD server responds with a referral to DNS servers responsible for the microsoft. com domain.

6. The local DNS server then sends another iterative query to a microsoft.com DNS server.

7. The microsoft.com DNS server replies with the host record IP address for www.microsoft. com.

8. The local DNS server responds to the client with the IP address for www.microsoft.com.

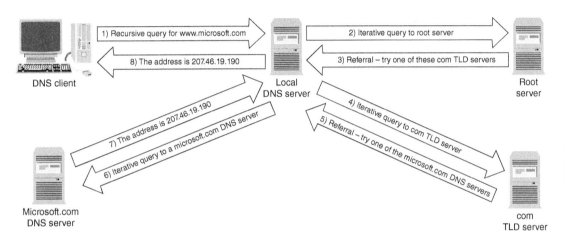

Figure 10-2 A DNS hierarchical lookup

© *Cengage Learning*®

Thankfully, the process shown in Figure 10-2 doesn't occur with every DNS lookup. Computers cache information they get from DNS, as you learned in Chapter 9. Furthermore, the local DNS server also caches recent lookups. So the entire process occurs only when neither the computer doing the lookup nor the local DNS server has a cached copy of the requested name resolution.

To add another wrinkle to the DNS lookup process, DNS clients maintain a text file called Hosts that can contain static DNS entries. On Windows, this file is stored in *%systemroot%* System32\drivers\etc. By default, it contains only sample entries. In versions of Windows before Windows Server 2008 R2 and Windows 7, it contained records for resolving the local loopback address for both IPv4 and IPv6. These records are now commented out with an explanation that the DNS service handles localhost name resolution. The file's format is simply IP address and hostname separated by one or more spaces. A typical Hosts file entry looks like this:

```
127.0.0.1 localhost
::1 localhost
```

You see these two entries in the Hosts file in Windows Server 2012/R2, but they have the # character in front of them, indicating that they're comments.

The entries in the Hosts file are cached at system startup and each time the file is changed. You can add as many entries as you like to this file. Usually, however, it's left as it is because in a dynamic network, static DNS entries are likely to cause more harm than good. Some people use the Hosts file as a sort of Web filter. For example, you can add entries to this file for hosts on domains that create pop-up ads and fill your Web pages with advertisements. For each entry, simply use the address 127.0.0.1. Unless you're running a Web server locally, your browser won't get a response from this address, and the Web site supplying the ad will be blocked. You can even download a Hosts file that's already loaded with hundreds of entries for well-known Web advertisers, such as *http://doubleclick.net*.

DNS Server Roles

DNS servers can perform one or more of the following roles for a zone:

- *Authoritative server*—As discussed, an **authoritative server** for a domain holds a complete copy of a zone's resource records.

- *Forwarder*—A **forwarder** is a DNS server to which other DNS servers send requests they can't resolve themselves. It's commonly used when a DNS server on an internal private network receives a query for a domain on the public Internet. The internal DNS server forwards the request recursively to a DNS server connected to the public Internet. This method prevents the internal DNS server from having to contact root servers and TLD servers directly because the forwarder does that on its behalf.

- *Conditional forwarder*—A **conditional forwarder** is a DNS server to which other DNS servers send requests targeted for a specific domain. For example, computers in the csmtech.local domain might send a DNS query for a computer named server1.csmpub. local. The DNS server in the csmtech.local domain can be configured with a conditional forwarder that in effect says "If you receive a query for csmpub.local, forward it to the DNS server handling the csmpub.local domain." Servers that are forwarders or conditional forwarders require no special configuration, but the servers using them as forwarders must be configured to do so.

- *Caching-only server*—A **caching-only DNS server** isn't configured with any zones. Its sole job is to field DNS queries, do recursive lookups to root servers or send requests to forwarders, and then cache the results. After the query results are cached, the caching server can respond to a similar query directly. Caching servers are ideal for branch offices so that local computers' queries are forwarded to an authoritative server at a main office.

Activity 10-1: Using DNS Manager

Time Required: 15 minutes
Objective: Explore DNS Manager.

Required Tools and Equipment: 410Server1
Description: You're unfamiliar with DNS. Your network is growing, and you need to manage and monitor your DNS database and settings. You start by familiarizing yourself with the DNS Manager console.

1. Log on to 410Server1 as **Administrator**.

2. Open Server Manager, and click **Tools, DNS** to open the DNS Manager console.

3. Click to expand **410Server1** in the left pane, if necessary, and click to expand **Forward Lookup Zones**. Then click **Forward Lookup Zones** again to see a window similar to Figure 10-3.

4. In the left pane, click **410Server2012.local** to see folders and resource records in the right pane. Scroll to the right to see the Timestamp column. Records that were created dynamically have a timestamp; records created by an administrator or generated by the system are shown as static.

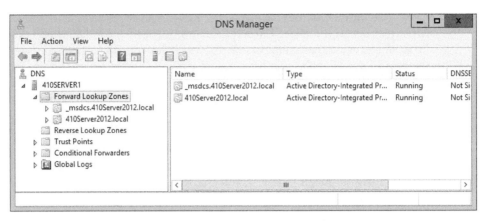

Figure 10-3   The DNS Manager console

5. The first few entries show "(same as parent folder)" in the Name column, which means they take on the domain's name. If DNS gets an A record query for 410Server2012.local without a hostname, it returns the IP addresses shown for the "(same as parent folder)" A record entry. Double-click the **Start of Authority (SOA)** record. In the 410Server2012.local Properties dialog box, review the information available in all the tabs. The SOA record is discussed in more detail later in "Start of Authority Records." Click **Cancel**.

6. Double-click the **410server1** A record entry. Figure 10-4 shows the Properties dialog box for an A record. You can't change the Host or FQDN fields of an A record, but you can change the IP address. If you make a change, you can click the "Update associated pointer (PTR) record" check box to have the PTR record reflect the address change.

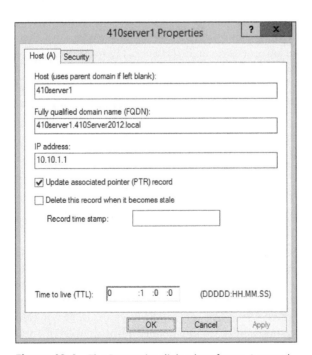

Figure 10-4   The Properties dialog box for an A record

7. Click the **Security** tab. DNS records stored in Active Directory have the same type of permission settings as other Active Directory and NTFS objects, including permission inheritance and special permissions. You can assign permissions to users to allow them to manage DNS records, if necessary. Click **Cancel**.

8. Click **View, Advanced** from the menu. The Advanced view shows additional information in DNS Manager, such as the folder Cached Lookups. Click to expand **Cached Lookups** and then the .(root) folder, which has subfolders named for TLDs (com, local, net, and so on). Click to expand the **com** folder. Domains you have visited with any computer using this DNS server for DNS lookups have a folder containing A, NS, and other resource records. Cached entries save time and bandwidth because the local DNS server can respond to queries for records it has in its cache.

9. Browse through the folders until you find an A or a CNAME record. (If you can't find one, start your Web browser and go to **www.microsoft.com** to create a record in the microsoft folder. Close your browser and refresh DNS Manager.) Double-click the **A or CNAME** record. In the Properties dialog box, you see a time to live (TTL) value, which tells DNS how long to keep the cached entry. The referring DNS server (an authoritative DNS server for the domain the record came from) sends the TTL value, which prevents a DNS server from caching out-of-date information. Click **Cancel**.

10. Click the **com** folder. You should see several NS entries with names in the Data column, such as a.gtld-servers.net, b.gtld-servers.net, and so on, referred to as "generic top-level domain (GTLD) servers." These servers are responsible for com domains throughout the Internet. Double-click **a.gtld-servers.net**. Notice that no IP address is associated with the entry. When your DNS server needs to find the address of a com name server, it must query to find a TLD server's address first. Click **Cancel**.

11. Right-click **Cached Lookups** and click **Clear Cache** to delete the cache. There are no entries in the cache now, except some folders and an entry for localhost. Clear the local DNS cache by opening a command prompt window, typing **ipconfig/flushdns**, and pressing **Enter**. Close the command prompt window.

12. Start your Web browser, go to any com domain, and then exit your Web browser. Refresh the DNS Manager console. Under Cached Lookups, click to expand the .(root) folder, and then click the **com** folder. You should see the list of GTLD servers and a folder for the domain you visited (possibly more than one folder). Click the **net** folder, and then double-click the **gtld-servers** folder. You see several A records for the GTLD servers listed and perhaps some AAAA entries with IPv6 addresses.

13. Right-click **410Server1** in the left pane and click **Properties**. Click the **Forwarders** tab. If a forwarder is listed, it's because Windows installs the DNS server configured for this computer as a forwarder when DNS is installed. If there's a forwarder, click the **Edit** button, click the forwarder address, click **Delete**, and then click **OK**. Examine the other tabs in the Properties dialog box, and then click **Cancel**.

14. Leave the DNS Manager console open and stay logged on for the next activity.

Installing and Configuring DNS

DNS is an integral part of most network communication sessions between computers. Each time an application or app (as it's called on mobile devices) communicates with the Internet or another device, it uses DNS to resolve a network device's name to an IP address. A correctly configured and efficiently functioning DNS service, therefore, is essential for a well-functioning network.

Windows domains and Active Directory rely exclusively on DNS for resolving names and locating services. When a workgroup computer attempts to join a domain, it contacts a DNS server to find records that identify a domain controller for the domain. When a member computer or server starts, it contacts a DNS server to find a domain controller that can authenticate it to the domain. When domain controllers replicate with one another and when trusts are created between domains in different forests, DNS is required to resolve names and services to IP addresses.

Installing DNS

During Active Directory installation, Windows attempts to find a DNS server and, if it's unsuccessful, asks whether you want to install DNS. When a new forest is created, it's best to have Windows install DNS during Active Directory installation because Windows automatically creates all the initial zone records that Active Directory needs. If DNS is installed later, you have to create the zone database manually.

You might need to install DNS manually on a domain controller, member server, or stand-alone server. In any case, you start by installing the DNS Server role with Server Manager or PowerShell. If the DNS server is intended to manage domain name services for Active Directory, you should install the DNS Server role on a domain controller so that you gain the benefits of Active Directory integration. If you're installing DNS on a domain controller, Windows detects the installation and informs you that DNS zones will be integrated with Active Directory.

When you install the DNS Server role, there are no choices to make—just a couple of clicks, and you're finished. DNS Manager, shown previously, is then available from the Tools menu in Server Manager. Unless DNS was installed as part of an Active Directory installation, your first step in configuring DNS is usually to create a zone.

Creating DNS Zones

Although DNS zones are created automatically during Active Directory installation, you might need to create a zone manually in the following situations:

- When you don't install DNS at the time you install Active Directory
- When you install DNS on a server that's not a domain controller
- When you create a stub zone
- When you create a secondary zone for a primary zone
- When you create a primary or secondary zone for an Internet domain

When you create a zone in DNS Manager, you must answer the following questions about it:

- Will it be a forward or reverse lookup zone?
- What type of zone do you want to create: primary, secondary, or stub?
- Should the zone be Active Directory–integrated?
- What's the replication scope of the zone?
- What's the name of the zone?
- How should the zone handle dynamic updates?

Forward and Reverse Lookup Zones Before you begin creating a zone, you must decide whether it's a forward or reverse lookup zone:

- *Forward lookup zone*—A **forward lookup zone (FLZ)**, the type you work with most often, contains records that translate names to IP addresses, such as A, AAAA, and MX records. It's named after the domain whose resource records it contains, such as csmtech.local.

- *Reverse lookup zone*—A **reverse lookup zone (RLZ)** contains PTR records that map IP addresses to names and is named after the IP network address (IPv4 or IPv6) of the computers whose records it contains.

To create one of these zones, right-click the Forward Lookup Zones folder or the Reverse Lookup Zones folder in the DNS Manager console and click New Zone to start the New Zone Wizard.

Zone Type After you have decided whether to install a FLZ or RLZ and started the New Zone Wizard, you select the type of zone you want to create, as shown in Figure 10-5. As mentioned, a zone is a database containing resource and information records for a domain and possibly subdomains. There are three different zone types:

- *Primary zone*—A **primary zone** contains a read/write master copy of all resource records for the zone. Updates to resource records can be made only on a server configured as a primary zone server, referred to as the "primary DNS server." A primary DNS server is considered authoritative for the zone it manages. A primary zone can be an Active Directory–integrated or a standard zone.

Figure 10-5 Selecting the zone type

- *Secondary zone*—A **secondary zone** contains a read-only copy of all resource records for the zone. Changes can't be made directly on a secondary DNS server, but because it contains an exact copy of the primary zone, it's considered authoritative for the zone. Although a secondary zone can be only a standard zone, not an Active Directory–integrated zone, a file-based secondary zone can be created on a server that's not a DC or on a DC in another Active Directory domain or forest. Secondary zones can be used in this way to resolve names for domain-based resources outside the domain.

- *Stub zone*—A **stub zone** contains a read-only copy of only the SOA and NS records for a zone and the necessary A records to resolve NS records. A stub zone forwards queries to a primary DNS server for the zone it holds SOA and NS records for and isn't authoritative for the zone. A stub zone can be an Active Directory–integrated or a standard zone.

Active Directory–Integrated Zones The "Store the zone in Active Directory" check box in Figure 10-5 means you want the zone to be stored in an Active Directory partition; in this case, it's called an **Active Directory–integrated zone.** It's not a new zone type; it's just a primary or stub zone with the DNS database stored in an Active Directory partition. The server where you're creating the new zone must be a writeable domain controller (as opposed to a read only domain controller). When you're storing the zone in Active Directory, the only valid zone type options are primary and stub zones. If you select a secondary zone, the option to store the zone in Active Directory is disabled.

Standard Zones A zone that isn't Active Directory integrated is referred to as a **standard zone,** and the zone data is stored in a text file that can be opened and edited with a simple text editor (although using DNS Manager is preferable on a Windows system). This text file is named *zone-name*.dns (with *zone-name* typically the domain name) and is in the %*systemroot*%\ system32\dns folder on the DNS server. A standard zone can be a primary, secondary, or stub zone. Standard zones are mostly installed on stand-alone servers that need to provide name resolution services for network resources outside the domain or in networks that don't use Active Directory at all, such as Linux or UNIX-based networks. In addition, standard zones are used for Internet name resolution.

Zone Replication Zone replication is the transfer of zone changes from one DNS server to another. For a standard zone, zone replication is called "zone transfer" (discussed later in "Zone Transfers"). If DNS is installed on a domain controller that's part of an existing domain, zone information is copied to the new DC by default when Active Directory replication occurs. No administrator action is necessary to create zones; they're replicated from other DCs in the domain. If you create a zone manually and configure it as an Active Directory–integrated zone, the zone information is copied automatically to other DNS servers running Active Directory.

For the purposes of zone replication, an Active Directory–integrated zone has the following advantages over a standard zone:

- *Automatic zone replication*—When DNS is installed on a new domain controller, zones are replicated to the new DNS server automatically. Standard zones require manual configuration of zone transfers.

- *Multimaster replication and update*—Multiple domain controllers can be configured as primary DNS servers, and changes can be made on any of these domain controllers. Multimaster replication provides fault tolerance because no single server is relied on to make DNS changes. Changes to DNS are replicated to all other DCs in the domain configured as DNS servers. In contrast, a standard zone has a single primary DNS server (and possibly one or more secondary servers), which is the only server where changes to the database can be made. If a standard primary server fails, DNS changes can't be made until another primary server is brought online.

- *Secure updates*—DNS can be configured to allow dynamic DNS updates only from DNS clients that have authenticated to Active Directory. This option prevents rogue clients from introducing false information into the DNS database.

- *Efficient replication*—Replication of Active Directory–integrated zones can target only the DNS record properties that have changed. This option conserves bandwidth, compared with standard zones, which transfer the entire zone database by default.

10

Active Directory Zone Replication Scope   After you have chosen the zone type, the next step depends on whether the zone is Active Directory integrated. If it is, you're asked to select the zone replication scope (see Figure 10-6). The zone replication scope determines which partition the zone is stored in and which DCs the zone information is replicated to.

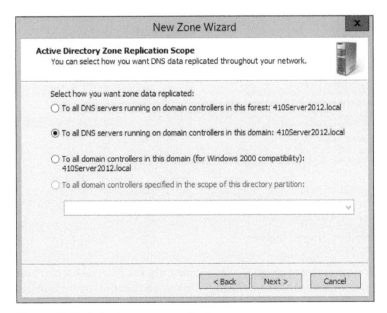

Figure 10-6   Selecting a zone replication scope

- *To all DNS servers running on domain controllers in this forest*—Stores the zone in the forest-wide DNS application directory partition ForestDNSZones. This partition is created when DNS is installed on the first DC in the forest.

- *To all DNS servers running on domain controllers in this domain*—Stores the zone in the domain-wide DNS application directory partition DomainDNSZones. It's the default option for new zones.

- *To all domain controllers in this domain (for Windows 2000 compatibility)*—Stores the zone in the domain partition, which is used to store most Active Directory objects. DNS zone information is replicated to all other DCs in the domain, regardless of whether the DNS Server role is installed. This option is the only one available for Windows 2000 DCs and should be selected if DNS information must be replicated to Windows 2000 DNS servers.

- *To all domain controllers specified in the scope of this directory partition*—A custom DNS application partition must be created before selecting this option, and the partition must use the same name on each DC hosting DNS that should participate in replication. Use this option to limit which DNS servers receive zone data to control replication traffic. Custom DNS application partitions are created by using the `Add-DnsServerDirectoryPartition` PowerShell cmdlet or `dnscmd.exe` (which might be deprecated in future versions of Windows Server).

Zone Name   The next step is to give the zone a name. For an FLZ, it's the FQDN, such as csmtech.local. For an RLZ, specify whether it's an IPv4 or IPv6 zone, and then enter the network ID portion of the zone. The zone name is created automatically by using the network ID's octets in reverse order and appending "in-addr.arpa" to the name. For example, if the IP network the RLZ is being created for is 10.1.0.0, you enter 10.1 in the Zone Name window, and Windows creates a zone named 1.10.in-addr.arpa.

Dynamic Updates   The final step in creating a new zone is to select whether and how to use dynamic updates, shown in Figure 10-7. Dynamic updates can be configured in one of three ways:

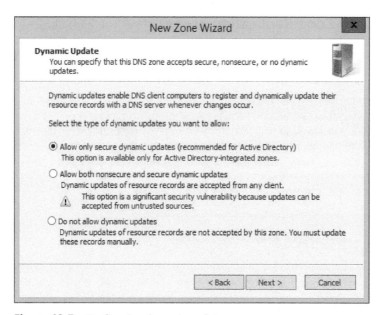

Figure 10-7   Configuring dynamic updates

- *Allow only secure dynamic updates*—Available only for Active Directory–integrated zones, this option ensures that the host initiating the record creation or update has been authenticated by Active Directory.

- *Allow both nonsecure and secure dynamic updates*—Both authenticated Active Directory clients and non–Active Directory clients can create and update DNS records. This option isn't recommended because it allows rogue clients to create DNS records with false information. A rogue DNS client can impersonate a server by updating the server's A record with its own IP address, thereby redirecting client computers to a fraudulent server.

- *Do not allow dynamic updates*—All DNS records must be entered manually. This option helps secure the environment, but on a network with many hosts that must be accessed by name and on networks using DHCP, it's an administrative nightmare. However, this option does work well for a DNS server that manages names for public resources, such as Web and mail servers with addresses that are usually assigned statically and don't change often.

PowerShell Commands for DNS Management A number of PowerShell commands are available for installing and configuring DNS. The following commands cover installing DNS and creating a new zone:

- `Install-WindowsFeature DNS -IncludeManagementTools`—Installs DNS and the DNS management tools.
- `Add-DnsServerPrimaryZone csmtech.local -ReplicationScope Domain`—Creates an Active Directory–integrated FLZ named csmtech.local with domain-wide replication scope.
- `Add-DnsServerPrimaryZone csmtech.local -ZoneFile csmtech.local.dns`—Creates a standard FLZ named csmtech.local and stores it in a zone file named `csmtech.local.dns`.
- `Add-DnsServerPrimaryZone -NetworkID 10.10.0.0/16 -ReplicationScope Forest`—Creates an Active Directory–integrated RLZ for network ID 10.10.0.0/16 with forest-wide replication scope. The name of the RLZ is 11.10.in-addr.arpa.
- `Add-DnsServerPrimaryZone -NetworkID 10.10.0.0/16 -ZoneFile 10.10.in-addr.arpa.dns`—Creates a standard RLZ for network ID 10.10.0.0/16 and stores it in a zone file named `10.10.in-addr.arpa.dns`.

To create secondary or stub zones, the relevant commands are `Add-DnsServerSecondaryZone` and `Add-DnsServerStubZone`. Remember that secondary zones can't be Active Directory integrated.

You can use the command-line tool `dnscmd.exe` to create zones and perform other DNS management tasks. However, this command might be deprecated in the future, and Microsoft recommends using PowerShell to manage DNS from the command line. Remember: To get help and examples for using PowerShell cmdlets, type `get-help` *CmdletName* `-detailed` at a PowerShell prompt.

Activity 10-2: Installing DNS and Creating a New Zone

Time Required: 20 minutes
Objective: Install DNS on a workgroup server.

Required Tools and Equipment: 410Server2
Description: You want to work with DNS zones and explore DNS server features. You install DNS on a workgroup server and create a test zone.

Remember that 410Server2 is still operating in Minimal Server Interface mode, so if you close the command prompt window or Server Manager, you need to press Ctrl+Alt+Del to open Task Manager and start a task. You can also log off and log back on to start both Server Manager and a command prompt window.

1. Start 410Server2, log on as **Administrator**, and open Server Manager.

2. Start the Add Roles and Features Wizard. In the Server Roles window, click to select **DNS Server**. Click **Add Features**, and accept the remaining default options. When the role is installed, close the wizard.

3. In Server Manager, click **Tools, DNS** from the menu to open DNS Manager. In the left pane, click to expand **410Server2** and then **Forward Lookup Zones**. No zones are listed yet.

4. Right-click **Forward Lookup Zones** and click **New Zone** to start the New Zone Wizard. In the welcome window, click **Next**.

5. In the Zone Type window, notice that the option to store the zone in Active Directory is grayed out because the server isn't a DC. Accept the default **Primary zone** setting, and then click **Next**.

6. Type **Testdom1.local** in the Zone name text box, and then click **Next**. In the Zone File window, accept the default filename **Testdom1.local.dns**, and then click **Next**.

7. In the Dynamic Update window, click the **Allow both nonsecure and secure dynamic updates** option, and then click **Next**. Click **Finish**.

8. In the DNS Manager console, click **Testdom1.local** in the left pane. You see two resource records: the SOA record created for every zone and an NS record. Double-click the SOA record to open the domain Properties dialog box to the Start of Authority (SOA) tab. Most of the settings for the SOA are discussed later in "Start of Authority Records." Click **Cancel**.

9. Double-click the NS record. The same Properties box is opened as for the SOA record, but it opens to the Name Servers tab. Click **Cancel**, and close the DNS Manager console.

10. Now that 410Server2 is a DNS server, you're going to change its IP address configuration so that it uses itself for DNS lookups and DNS registration. Open a command prompt window, and type **powershell** and press Enter. Type **Set-DNSClientServerAddress Ethernet -ServerAddresses 127.0.0.1** and press Enter.

11. To set the DNS suffix for the Ethernet interface to testdom1.local so that the server registers its name with the zone you just created, type **Set-DnsClient Ethernet -ConnectionSpecificSuffix testdom1.local -UseSuffixWhenRegistering $true** and press Enter.

12. Before you register the name with DNS, type **nslookup 410Server2.testdom1.local** and press Enter. You see a message that localhost can't find 410Server2, which means there's no A record yet for 410Server2.

13. To register the server name with DNS, type **ipconfig /registerdns** and press Enter. Try the lookup again by typing **nslookup 410Server2.testdom1.local** and pressing Enter. The lookup is successful this time.

14. Open the DNS Manager console, **expand Forward Lookup Zones**, and click the **Testdom1. local** zone to verify that the A record for 410Server2 has been created.

15. You use 410Server2 for Activity 10-4, so stay logged on to it.

Activity 10-3: Working with Reverse Lookup Zones

Time Required: 15 minutes
Objective: View the properties of reverse lookup zones and create an RLZ.

Required Tools and Equipment: 410Server1 and 410Win8
Description: You're unfamiliar with reverse lookup zones, so you create one on 410Server1 so that reverse lookups work for your domain resources.

1. Log on to 410Server1 as **Administrator**, if necessary. Start 410Win8 and log on to the domain as **Administrator**.

2. On 410Win8, open a command prompt window. Type **nslookup 10.10.1.5** (the address for 410ServerCore) and press Enter. You see a response stating that the address can't be found.

3. On 410SServer1, open a PowerShell prompt. To create an RLZ named 10.10.in-addr.arpa, type
`Add-DnsServerPrimaryZone -NetworkID 10.10.0.0/16`
`-ReplicationScope Domain` and press **Enter**.

4. Open the DNS Manager console, and click to expand **Reverse Lookup Zones** to verify that the zone has been created. Click **10.10.in-addr.arpa**. You see the SOA and NS records.

5. You can use `ipconfig /registerdns` on each computer to create PTR records, but there's another method that can be done from the server. Click to expand **Forward Lookup Zones**, and then click **410Server2012.local**. Double-click **410ServerCore** in the right pane. Click to select the **Update associated pointer (PTR) record** check box, and then click **OK**.

6. Click the **10.10.in-addr.arpa** RLZ in the left pane again. If the PTR record isn't there, click the **Refresh** icon in DNS Manager to see the 10.10.1.5 PTR record. Repeat Step 5 for 410Server1 and 410Win8, making sure you click the Host (A) record, not the IPv6 Host (AAAA) record. Check the RLZ to verify that the records have been created.

7. On 410Win8, type `nslookup 10.10.1.5` and press **Enter** to verify that you can do a reverse lookup.

8. Shut down 410Win8, but stay logged on to 410Server1 for the next activity.

Creating Resource Records in Zones

As discussed, resource records can be created dynamically or as static records. Dynamic records are created by the resource or with a DHCP server. Static records are created manually by an administrator or automatically by Windows.

Creating Dynamic DNS Records Dynamic DNS records are created and updated by the resource or, when using DHCP to assign IP addresses, by the DHCP server when an IP address is leased or renewed. When a device is assigned an IP address, it registers its name with the DNS server configured in its IP address settings. If the device has an IPv4 address, an A record is created; if it has an IPv6 address, an AAAA record is created. If the device gets its IP address settings from a DHCP server, the DHCP server can be configured to register the computer's name and address on its behalf. Whenever a computer's IP address changes or it renews its IP address lease from the DHCP server, the DNS records are updated. Each time a dynamic record is created or updated, a time-to-live (TTL) value and timestamp are added to the record. The TTL specifies how long the record should remain in the DNS database. If the record expires, it's deleted from the database.

You can also force a client to register its address by using the `ipconfig /registerdns` command.

If a reverse lookup zone exists for the host's IP address, PTR records are created dynamically in the same manner as host records. PTR records can also be created by opening a host record's properties and selecting the "Update associated pointer (PTR) record" check box.

Creating Static DNS Records Static DNS records are called "static" because they don't expire. They stay in the DNS database until someone removes them. Unlike dynamically created records, which have a timestamp, static records have no timestamp, by default. Static records are created manually by an administrator or automatically by Windows under some circumstances. To create a static record in DNS Manager, you right-click the zone, and select the record type. In an FLZ, the most common type of record to create is a New Host record, which can be an IPv4 (A) record or an IPv6 (AAAA) record (see Figure 10-8). Enter a name in the Name text box to create the FQDN automatically. DNS Manager creates an A or AAAA record automatically,

10

Figure 10-8   Creating a new host record

depending on whether an IPv4 or IPv6 address is entered. If you select the "Create associated pointer (PTR) record" check box, a PTR record is created if a suitable RLZ exists for the IP address entered.

To create a PTR record, right-click the RLZ and click New Pointer (PTR). Type the host IP address, and then type or browse for the hostname (see Figure 10-9).

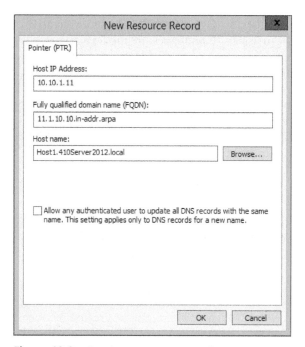

Figure 10-9   Creating a new PTR record

As mentioned, Windows can create a static resource record automatically. When a new zone is created, SOA and NS static records are created for the zone, and in Active Directory–integrated zones, SRV, PTR, and A records are created automatically for domain controllers.

This section has given you an overview of creating DNS records. This topic is covered in more detail in *MCSA Guide to Administering Windows Server 2012/R2, Exam 70-411* (Cengage Learning, 2015).

PowerShell Commands for Creating DNS Resource Records The following PowerShell cmdlets are used to create DNS resource records:

- `Add-DnsServerResourceRecord -A -ZoneName csmtech.local -Name host1 -IPv4Address 192.168.1.11`—Adds an A record named host1 to the csmtech.local zone.

- `Add-DnsServerResourceRecord -AAAA -ZoneName csmtech.local -Name host1 -IPv6Address 2001:DB8::11`—Adds an AAAA record named host1 to the csmtech.local zone.

- `Add-DnsServerResourceRecord -CName -ZoneName csmtech.local -Name h1 -HostNameAlias host1.csmtech.local`—Adds a CNAME (alias) record named h1 with the target host1.csmtech.local.

- `Add-DnsServerResourceRecord -Ptr -ZoneName 1.168.192.in-addr.arpa -Name 11.1 -PtrDomainName host1.csmtech.local`—Adds a PTR record named host1.csmtech.local with the IP address 192.168.1.11 to the 1.168.192.in-addr.arpa RLZ.

Activity 10-4: Creating Static DNS Entries

Time Required: 15 minutes
Objective: Create static A, CNAME, and PTR records.

Required Tools and Equipment: 410Server2
Description: You want to experiment with creating static DNS records, so you use the test zone you created on 410Server2.

1. Log on to **410Server2** as Administrator, if necessary.

2. Open the DNS Manager console, if necessary, and click to expand **Forward Lookup Zones.** Right-click **Testdom1.local** and click **New Host (A or AAAA).**

3. In the New Host dialog box, type **webserver1** in the Name text box and **10.10.1.11** in the IP address text box. Click to select **Create associated pointer (PTR) record.** Click the **Add Host** button. Click **OK** and then **Done.**

4. Open a command prompt window, type **nslookup webserver1.testdom1.local**, and press **Enter.** The name is resolved. Type **nslookup 10.10.1.11** and press **Enter.** You haven't created an RLZ on this DNS server, so the reverse lookup isn't successful.

5. In the DNS Manager console, right-click **testdom1.local** and click **New Alias (CNAME).** In the New Resource Record dialog box, type **www** in the Alias name text box. In the "Fully qualified domain name (FQDN) for target host" text box, type **webserver1.tesdom1.local,** and then click **OK.**

6. At the command prompt, type **nslookup www.testdom1.local** and press **Enter.** The command returns the address webserver1.testdom1.local and lists the alias name www.

7. In the DNS Manager console, click to select **Reverse Lookup Zones,** and then right-click it and click **New Zone.** In the welcome window of the New Zone Wizard, click **Next.** Accept the default setting **Primary zone,** and then click **Next.** Accept the default **IPv4 Reverse Lookup Zone,** and then click **Next.**

8. In the Network ID text box, type **192.168.** Notice in the "Reverse lookup zone name" text box that the octets of the network ID are reversed to form the reverse lookup zone name (see Figure 10-10).

9. Backspace over the network ID, and type **10.10.** The reverse lookup zone name is now 10.10.in-addr.arpa. Click **Next.** In the Zone File window, accept the default filename, and click **Next.**

10. In the Dynamic Update window, click **Allow both nonsecure and secure dynamic updates.** Click **Next** and then **Finish.**

11. In the DNS Manager console, expand **Reverse Lookup Zones,** if necessary. Click to select the **10.10.in-addr.arpa** RLZ, and then right-click it and click **New Pointer (PTR).** In the Host IP Address text box, the address is started for you with 10.10. Type **1.11,** and in the Host name text box, type **www.testdom1.local,** and then click **OK.**

10

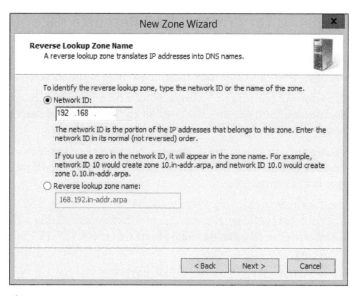

Figure 10-10   Identifying the reverse lookup zone name

12. At the command prompt, type **nslookup 10.10.1.11** and press **Enter**. You should see the www.testdom1.local record returned. Close the command prompt window.

13. Stay logged on to 410Server2 if you're continuing to the next activity.

Configuring DNS Zones

After a zone is created, you can view and change its properties in DNS Manager by right-clicking the zone and clicking Properties. In the General tab (see Figure 10-11), you can view and change the following options:

Figure 10-11   A zone's Properties dialog box

- *Status*—Pause a running DNS zone or start a paused DNS zone. When a zone is paused, queries made to it are refused.

- *Type*—Change the zone type (primary, secondary, or stub) and choose whether the zone should be Active Directory integrated.

- *Replication*—Change the replication scope. This button is grayed out for a standard zone.

- *Dynamic updates*—On an Active Directory–integrated zone, choose Secure only, Nonsecure and secure, or None. Standard zones don't have the Secure only option.

- *Aging*—Click this button to configure aging and scavenging options, which specify how often stale resource records are removed from the zone database. Aging and scavenging are covered in *MCSA Guide to Administering Windows Server 2012/R2, Exam 70-411* (Cengage Learning, 2015).

Start of Authority Records

The SOA record, found in every zone, contains information that identifies the server primarily responsible for the zone as well as some operational properties for the zone. Shown in Figure 10-12, the SOA record contains the following information:

- *Serial number*—A revision number that increases each time data in the zone changes. This number is used to determine when zone information should be replicated.

- *Primary server*—On a primary Active Directory–integrated zone, this field displays the name of the server where DNS Manager is currently running. For a standard zone, it displays the primary DNS server's name.

- *Responsible person*—The e-mail address of the person responsible for managing the zone. A period rather than an @ sign is used to separate the username from the domain name (according to RFC 1183, which defines DNS resource record types).

- *Refresh interval*—Specifies how often a secondary DNS server attempts to renew its zone information. When the interval expires, the server requests the SOA record from the primary DNS server. The serial number in the retrieved SOA record is then compared with the serial number in the secondary server's SOA record. If the serial number has changed, the secondary server requests a new copy of the zone data. After the transfer is completed, the refresh interval begins anew. The default value is 15 minutes.

- *Retry interval*—The amount of time a secondary server waits before retrying a zone transfer that has failed. This value should be less than the refresh interval and defaults to 10 minutes. The retry interval begins after the refresh interval expires, and the primary server can't be contacted or the zone transfer fails.

10

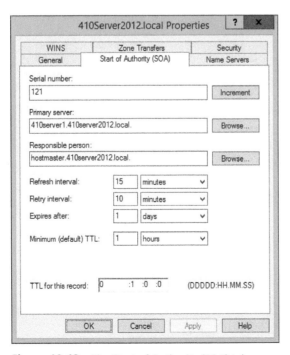

Figure 10-12   The Start of Authority (SOA) tab

- *Expires after*—The amount of time before a secondary server considers its zone data obsolete if it can't contact the primary DNS server. If the refresh interval expires without a successful zone transfer, this timer begins. If it expires without an update to the zone data (or an indication that the zone data hasn't changed), the DNS server stops responding to queries. This value must be higher than the refresh and retry intervals combined; the default is 1 day.

- *Minimum (default) TTL*—This setting specifies a default TTL value for zone data when a TTL isn't supplied. The TTL value tells other DNS servers that cache records from this zone how long to keep cached data; it should be adjusted according to how often data in the zone is likely to change. For example, a zone that maintains only static entries for resources that aren't changed, added, or removed can often specify a high TTL value. If a zone maintains dynamic records or records for resources that are going online and offline constantly, this value should be lower. If a redesign of your network will cause many changes to zone data, this value can be lowered temporarily. Then wait until the previous TTL time has elapsed before making the changes. This way, servers caching records that will be changed don't store them very long. The TTL set on resource records overrides this default value, which is 1 hour.

Name Server Records

NS records specify FQDNs and IP addresses of authoritative servers for a zone. A typical configuration with Active Directory–integrated zones has an NS record for each domain controller configured as a DNS server in the domain or forest, depending on the scope of zone replication.

NS records are also used to refer DNS queries to a name server that has been delegated authority for a subdomain. For example, com TLD servers refer queries for resources in the technet.microsoft.com subdomain to a DNS server that's authoritative for the microsoft.com domain. The microsoft.com domain name server can then refer the query to another DNS server that has been delegated authority for the technet subdomain of microsoft.com. Subdomains need not be delegated; they can simply be created under the zone representing their parent domain. If the subdomain has many resources and traffic on it is heavy, however, zone delegation is a wise approach. Zone delegation is covered in *MCSA Guide to Administering Windows Server 2012/R2, Exam 70-411* (Cengage Learning, 2015).

An NS record technically consists of just the name server's FQDN, but for the name to be useful, there must be a way to resolve it to an IP address. DNS does this with a **glue A record**, which is an A record containing the name server's IP address. On Windows DNS servers, glue records are created automatically, if possible, by a DNS lookup on the NS record's FQDN; they don't appear as an A record anywhere in the zone database. Figure 10-13 shows the interface for

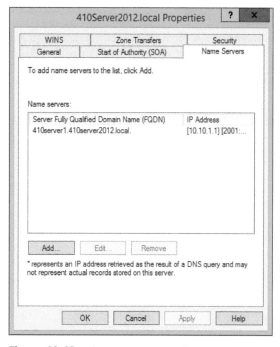

Figure 10-13   The Name Servers tab

creating and editing NS records. If Windows fails to resolve the name server's FQDN, you can edit the record and add an IP address manually.

Using Stub Zones

Stub zones, as discussed, are a special type of zone containing only an SOA record, one or more NS records, and the necessary glue A records to resolve NS records. Essentially, a stub zone points to another DNS server that's authoritative for the zone. The records in a stub zone, like other Active Directory–integrated zones and secondary zones, are updated regularly through Active Directory replication and zone transfers. Reasons for using stub zones include the following:

- *Maintenance of zone delegation information*—If changes are made to addresses of the name servers hosting a delegated zone, the NS records on the parent DNS server must be updated manually. If a stub zone is created for the delegated zone on the parent DNS server, the NS records are updated automatically. The use of a stub zone effectively eliminates manual maintenance of the delegated zone's NS records.

- *In lieu of conditional forwarders*—If changes are made to addresses of domain name servers that are conditionally forwarded, the IP addresses for the conditional forwarder records must be changed manually. If a stub zone is created instead of using a conditional forwarder, the NS records in the stub zone are updated automatically.

- *Faster recursive queries*—When a DNS server receives a query for a resource record in the stub zone, it can make a recursive query by using the stub zone's NS records rather than accessing a root server.

- *Distribution of zone information*—When a network consists of many zones, distribution of these zones is necessary to make the entire DNS namespace accessible throughout the network. Typically, this distribution requires secondary zones or Active Directory–integrated zones. Stub zones can be used strategically to reduce the number of secondary zones or full Active Directory–integrated zones; reducing the number of these zones cuts down network traffic caused by zone transfers and replication.

Zone Transfers

A **zone transfer** copies all or part of a zone from one DNS server to another and occurs as a result of a secondary server requesting the transfer from another server. The server requesting the zone transfer is sometimes called the "slave," and the server providing the zone information is sometimes called the "master." The master server can host a primary or secondary zone, but the slave server always hosts a secondary zone. Although Active Directory–integrated zones use Active Directory replication to transfer zone information, you can configure standard zone transfers if the target is a standard secondary zone. Zone transfers can be initiated in two ways:

- *Refresh interval*—As discussed, a secondary zone server requests zone information from another server (a primary or another secondary master) when the zone's refresh interval expires, which is every 15 minutes by default.

- *DNS notify*—A master server can be configured to send a DNS notify message to secondary servers when zone information changes. The secondary server can then request the zone transfer immediately without waiting for the refresh interval to expire.

Zone transfers are configured in the Zone Transfers tab of a zone's Properties dialog box (see Figure 10-14), which has the following options:

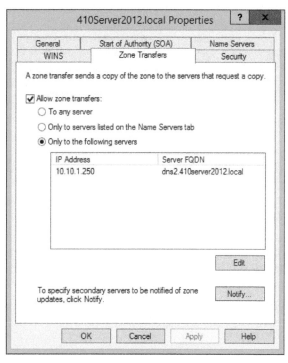

Figure 10-14 The Zone Transfers tab

- *Allow zone transfers*—Selecting this check box enables zone transfers. By default, zone transfers in Active Directory–integrated zones are disabled. In standard zones, zone transfers are enabled for all other name servers listed for that zone. Options for configuring zone transfers are as follows:

  o To any server: Allows any server to request a zone transfer. This option isn't recommended for most environments, as it allows any host to request network information, which is not secure.

  o Only to servers listed on the Name Servers tab: This option is the default for standard zones.

  o Only to the following servers: You can specify servers to which zone information can be transferred.

- *Notify*—Clicking this button opens a dialog box where you can specify servers that should receive notifications of changed zone information. By default, the notify option is enabled in standard zones for servers listed in the Name Servers tab.

If all zones are hosted on Windows domain controllers and are Active Directory integrated, there's no need to configure zone transfers because Active Directory replication handles this process.

Incremental Zone Transfers   There are two types of zone transfer: full zone transfers and incremental zone transfers. A full zone transfer was the only transfer method in earlier DNS versions. As DNS databases grew larger and zone files became more numerous and much bigger, incremental zone transfers were defined. Both the master and slave DNS servers must support incremental zone transfers to use them.

When a secondary server requests a zone transfer, it can request an incremental transfer. (If the secondary zone is newly configured on the server, it requests a full zone transfer.) If the serial number of the slave's zone is lower than the master's, the master determines the differences between its current zone data and the slave's zone data. The master then transfers only the resource records that have changed. For incremental zone transfers to work, the master must keep a record of incremental changes with each serial number change. For example, if a slave server requests an incremental zone transfer, and its zone serial number is 500 and the master's zone serial number is 502, the master sends all changes that have occurred to the zone between serial number 500 and 502. Even if an incremental transfer is requested, the master can still respond with a full zone transfer if it doesn't support incremental transfers or have enough change history to respond accurately with an incremental transfer.

Activity 10-5: Creating a Secondary Zone and Configuring Zone Transfers

Time Required: 15 minutes
Objective: Create a secondary zone and configure zone transfers.

Required Tools and Equipment: 410Server1 and 410Server2
Description: You want a backup for fault tolerance and load sharing of the standard primary zone you created in Activity 10-2, so you decide to create a secondary zone on 410Server1 and configure zone transfers.

1. Log on to 410Server1 as **Administrator**, and open the DNS Manager console, if necessary.

2. Right-click **Forward Lookup Zones** and click **New Zone.** In the New Zone Wizard's welcome window, click **Next.**

3. In the Zone Type window, click the **Secondary zone** option button, and then click **Next.** Type **Testdom1.local** in the Zone name text box, and then click **Next.**

4. In the Master DNS Servers window type **10.10.1.2** (the address of 410Server2) in the Master Servers text box, and press **Enter.** You should see that the address is validated. Click **Next,** and then click **Finish.**

5. Log on to 410Server2 as **Administrator**, and open the DNS Manager console, if necessary.

6. Right-click **Testdom1.local** and click **Properties.** Click the **Zone Transfers** tab.

7. Make sure the **Allow zone transfers** check box is selected, and then click the **Only to the following servers** option button.

8. Click the **Edit** button. Click in the "IP addresses of the secondary servers" text box, type **10.10.1.1** (the address of 410Server1), press **Enter,** and then click **OK.** Click **OK** again to close the zone's Properties dialog box.

9. On 410Server1, click **Testdom1.local** in the left pane of DNS Manager, and then click the **Refresh** toolbar button. The zone data should have been transferred successfully, and you should see the SOA, NS and A records for Testdom1.local.

10. Test the zone by opening a command prompt window on 410Server1, typing `nslookup www.testdom1.local`, and pressing **Enter.** You should get a successful reply. Close the command prompt window.

11. Stay logged on if you're continuing to the next activity.

Using WINS with DNS

Windows Internet Name Service (WINS) is a legacy name service used to resolve NetBIOS names, sometimes referred to as "single-label names." WINS has similarities to DDNS, in that a central database of name-to-address mappings is maintained on a server where client computers update their own records dynamically. Windows clients do a WINS lookup by contacting the server with the name of the host whose IP address is required. WINS supports only IPv4 and is slowly becoming obsolete. You should configure your DNS server to use WINS only if you have older Windows clients, such as Windows 9x, and non-Windows clients that use only DNS. DNS/WINS integration allows non-Windows clients to resolve the names of older Windows clients that require NetBIOS name resolution. WINS might also be a part of your network if you're running older applications that depend on NetBIOS name resolution. The WINS tab in a zone's Properties dialog box has the following configuration options:

- *Use WINS forward lookup*—When this option is enabled for the zone, the DNS server attempts to contact a WINS server to resolve the name, if it couldn't be resolved through DNS. WINS forward lookup is disabled by default.

- *Do not replicate this record*—If WINS forward lookups are enabled, selecting this check box prevents the WINS resource record from being replicated to other DNS servers. This option should be selected if you have non-Windows DNS servers in your environment because WINS resource records are Windows specific, and including them in a zone transfer could corrupt the zone or prevent its transfer.

- *IP address*—Enter the IP addresses of WINS servers that should be contacted for name resolution.

- *Time to live (TTL)*—This text box specifies how long a cached WINS resource record is kept.

Using the GlobalNames Zone   Although WINS is still supported in Windows, a feature to help IT administrators migrate away from WINS was introduced in Windows Server 2008. This feature, the **GlobalNames zone (GNZ)**, provides a method for IT administrators to add single-label names (computer names that don't use a domain suffix) to DNS, thereby allowing client computers to resolve these names without including a DNS suffix in the query. The GNZ is not a replacement for a dynamically created WINS database because records in this zone must be added manually. For important servers with names currently being resolved by WINS, however, a GNZ is an option worth considering, especially if only a few hosts are the sole reason for maintaining WINS.

The GNZ feature isn't just a partial replacement for WINS, however. If your network supports mobile users whose laptops and other mobile devices are unlikely to have the correct DNS suffixes configured, GNZ can make access to servers these users need more convenient. Instead of mobile users having to remember resource FQDNs, they can simply access them by using a single-label name, such as Web1.

You must enable the GNZ feature on servers hosting this zone before you create a GNZ. Use the following command to enable GNZ at a PowerShell prompt:

```
Set-DnsServerGlobalNameZone -Enable $true
```

After GNZ support is enabled, you create a new zone that can be (but need not be) Active Directory integrated and named GlobalNames (not case sensitive). Dynamic updates should be disabled because GNZ doesn't support DDNS. For each host to be accessed with a single-label name, create a CNAME record in the GNZ that references the host's A record. You must enable GNZ support on each server the zone is replicated to.

Advanced DNS Server Settings

So far, you have focused on DNS zone creation and configuration—and rightly so because zones are where all the data is and where most DNS configuration takes place. However, you should be familiar with several DNS server settings to configure an optimal DNS environment and solve DNS problems when they occur. These settings are discussed in the following sections:

- Forwarders
- Root hints
- Round robin
- Recursion
- Debug logging

DNS Forwarders

Forwarders were defined previously in "DNS Server Roles," but this section goes into more detail on when to configure and use them. Recall how a typical DNS query is processed: A DNS server receives a lookup request from a client and, if it's unable to satisfy the request, a recursive query ensues, starting with a root server. This process works well, but in situations such as the following, referring the query to a forwarder is more efficient:

- *When the DNS server address for the target domain is known*—Suppose a company has a department working on highly confidential research, and this department is segmented from the rest of the network by routers and firewalls. This department maintains its own domain controllers and DNS servers that aren't part of the organization's domain. However, department members often need access to resources on the network servers. In addition, the research department's DNS servers aren't permitted to contact the Internet. For computers in this department network to resolve names for company resources, a forwarder can be configured on its DNS server that points to a company DNS server. The company DNS server not only resolves queries for company domain resources, but also performs recursive lookups for external domains on behalf of the research department's DNS server.

- *When only one DNS server in a network should make external queries*—A network consisting of several DNS servers might want to limit external queries to a single DNS server. This strategy has several benefits. First, network security can be enhanced by limiting exposure to the Internet to only one server. Second, because a single server is making all the queries to Internet domains, overall DNS performance can be enhanced because the server builds an extensive cache of Internet names. To use this strategy, all DNS servers on the network, except the actual forwarder, should be configured with the forwarder.

- *When a forest trust is created*—Windows requires DNS name resolution between the two forests involved in a trust relationship. Configuring conditional forwarders in the forest root name servers of both forests that point to each other is a good way to accomplish this.

- *When the target domain is external to the network and an external DNS server's address is known*—A company running a small network with limited bandwidth might find that the traffic caused by an internal DNS server's recursive lookups is excessive. The internal DNS server can provide name resolution for all internal resources and forward queries for external names to the DNS server of the company's ISP.

Starting with Windows Server 2003, Microsoft introduced conditional forwarding. Traditional forwarding means "If you can't resolve the query, forward it to this address." Conditional forwarding enables administrators to forward queries for particular domains to particular name servers and all other unresolved queries to a different server.

Configuring Traditional Forwarders Configuring a traditional forwarder is straightforward. Right-click the server node in DNS Manager, click Properties, and click the Forwarders tab (see Figure 10-15).

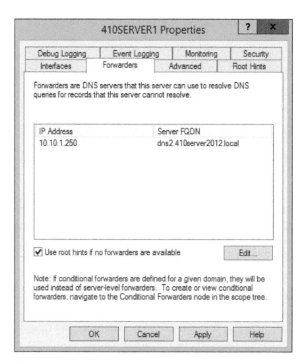

Figure 10-15   Configuring traditional forwarders

After clicking the Edit button, you can enter the IP address or FQDN of DNS servers that unresolved requests should be sent to. If more than one server is specified, they're queried in the order in which they're listed. Additional servers are queried only if no response is received from the first server. If no response is received from any forwarder, by default, the normal recursive lookup process is initiated, starting with a root server. If the "Use root hints if no forwarders are available" check box is not selected and no forwarders respond, the DNS server sends a failure reply to the client.

Configuring Conditional Forwarders   Conditional forwarders are configured in the Conditional Forwarders node in DNS Manager. To create a conditional forwarder, expand the Conditional Forwarders node, and then right-click Conditional Forwarders and click New Conditional Forwarder.

Enter the domain name for which you want to forward queries, and then add IP addresses for DNS servers that are authoritative for the domain. After you enter the IP address, Windows attempts to resolve the IP address to the server's FQDN. You can store the forwarder in Active Directory and have it replicated forest-wide or domain-wide. With forwarders and/or conditional forwarders configured, the DNS server attempts to resolve DNS queries in this order:

1. From locally stored zone resource records

2. From the DNS cache

3. From conditional forwarders (if configured and the domain name matches)

4. From traditional forwarders (if configured)

5. Recursively by using root hints (only if no traditional forwarder is configured)

Root hints aren't used if a traditional forwarder is configured because after the forwarder is queried, the recursive lookup process is complete.

Root Hints

Root hints consist of a list of name servers preconfigured on Windows DNS servers that point to Internet root servers, which are DNS servers located on the Internet and managed by the Internet Assigned Numbers Authority (IANA). These servers contain lists of name servers that are responsible for top-level domains. Root hints are configured in the Root Hints tab of a DNS server's Properties dialog box.

The root hints data comes from the `Cache.dns` file in the *%systemroot%* System32\DNS folder on a DNS server. Why is this file called the root hints file? As you can imagine, if the file is loaded during DNS installation, its data (root server IP addresses, for the most part) can become obsolete quickly. Instead of using the addresses in `Cache.dns` to perform recursive lookups, Windows selects one of the addresses randomly to request an up-to-date list of root server addresses. Windows then caches this list to use for queries to TLD servers. The `Cache.dns` file is also updated with this list. The query for the list of root servers occurs each time the DNS server is started. The root hints file can also be copied from another DNS server by clicking the Copy from Server button in the Root Hints tab. In addition, root hints can be updated through the Windows Update service.

You can configure an internal DNS server as a root server if your network is isolated from the public Internet. You do this by creating an FLZ with the "." name. This server is then considered authoritative for all domains. After you create this root zone, your root hints file is disabled, and you can't create any forwarders. Next, configure your other DNS servers to point to your new root server by removing the existing root hints entries and adding an entry that points to your new root server. If you ever decide to remove the root server, simply delete the root FLZ, and Windows prompts you to reload the root hints file.

Round Robin

You can configure load sharing among servers running mirrored services. With a mirrored service, data for a service running on one server is duplicated on another server (or servers). For example, you can set up an FTP server or a Web server on servers that synchronize their content with one another regularly. Then configure DNS with multiple A records, using the server's name in both records, but with each entry configured with a different IP address.

For example, suppose you have a Web server with the FQDN www.csmtech.local that's heavily used, responding slowly, and dropping connections. You can set up two additional Web servers and configure a mechanism for synchronizing files between the servers, such as DFSR or a third-party file synchronization service. Next, you create two additional DNS A records (you already have one for the existing Web server) in the csmtech.local domain that use the same hostname, www, but different IP addresses. The Windows DNS service responds to queries for the www host by sending all three IP addresses in the response but varying the order of IP addresses each time.

This process is called **round robin** because each IP address is placed first in the list an equal number of times. Hosts receiving the DNS response always attempt to use the first address listed. You can improve the results of round robin DNS by configuring a shorter TTL on the three A records so that remote DNS servers don't cache IP addresses for an extended period. By default, the round robin option is enabled on Windows DNS servers, but you can disable it in the Advanced tab of the DNS server's Properties dialog box (see Figure 10-16 in the next section).

Recursive Queries

Recursive queries, used in DNS queries, were defined earlier in "The DNS Lookup Process." Typically, resolving DNS queries involves iterative queries to a root server first, then to a TLD server, and finally to an authoritative server for the domain name being resolved. However, a recursive query might involve a forwarder instead, in which the DNS server sends a recursive query to the forwarder. The forwarder resolves the query and responds to the DNS server or performs a recursive query starting with a root server.

Recursion is enabled on Windows DNS servers by default, but there are two ways to change this setting. The first involves configuring forwarders. As shown previously in Figure 10-15, there's the check box "Use root hints if no forwarders are available." If this check box isn't selected, recursion is disabled, but only if forwarders don't respond. The second is the "Disable recursion (also disables forwarders)" option in the Advanced tab of the DNS server's Properties dialog box (see Figure 10-16). If this check box is selected, the DNS server doesn't attempt to contact any other DNS servers, including forwarders, to resolve a query.

Figure 10-16   The Advanced tab of a DNS server's Properties dialog box

For example, you might want to disable recursion when you have a public DNS server containing resource records for your publicly available servers (Web, e-mail, and so forth). The public DNS server is necessary to resolve iterative requests from other DNS servers for your public domain, but you don't want unauthorized Internet users using your DNS server to field recursive client requests.

Event and Debug Logging

When DNS is installed, a new event log is created to record informational, error, and warning events generated by the DNS server. You can configure which event types should be logged in the Event Logging tab of the server's Properties dialog box (shown in Figure 10-17). Events you're likely to find in the DNS Server log include zone serial number (referred to as "version number" in the DNS Server log) changes, zone transfer requests, and DNS server startup and shutdown events. The event log can help you diagnose problems, such as when an error causes the server to stop or keeps it from starting or when communication between servers for replication or zone transfers has failed. When DNS problems are evident and can't be traced easily to misconfiguration, the event log is the first place to look.

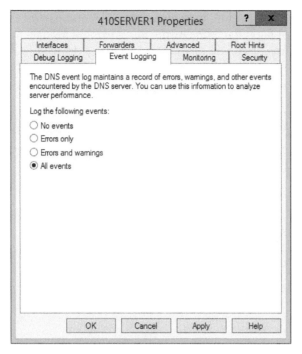

Figure 10-17   The Event Logging tab

When serious DNS debugging is warranted, you can enable debug logging in the server's Properties dialog box. Debug logging records selected packets coming from and going to the DNS server in a text file. Figure 10-18 shows the packet-capturing options for debug logging.

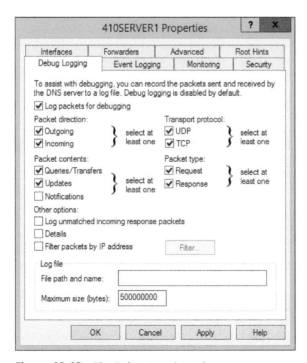

Figure 10-18   The Debug Logging tab

Figure 10-19 shows a sample of debug logging output. The first part of the file is a key to help you interpret the captured data. Each line of the file starting with date and time is a summary of a captured packet. If necessary, you can enable logging of detailed packet contents. The information from debug logging can help you solve problems related to "Web page not found" errors, zone transfer problems, redirect errors, and other DNS operational errors that aren't easy to find by examining the DNS configuration and event logs alone.

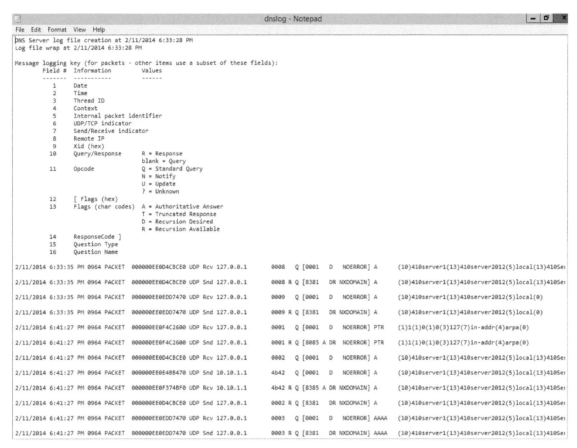

Figure 10-19 Debug logging output

PowerShell Commands for Advanced DNS Server Settings

Table 10-3 lists PowerShell cmdlets you can use to configure some DNS server settings discussed in the preceding sections.

Table 10-3 PowerShell cmdlets for DNS server settings

PowerShell cmdlet	Description	Example
Add-DnsServerForwarder	Adds forwarders to the DNS server's forwarders list	Add-DnsServerForwarder -IPAddress 10.10.1.2
Set-DnsServerForwarder	Changes the settings of an existing forwarder or overwrites the existing list of forwarders	Set-DnsServerForwarder -IPAddress 10.10.1.5
Add-DnsServerRootHint	Adds a root hint to the DNS server	Add-DnsServerRootHint root.mydomain.local -IPAddress 10.10.1.50
Import-DnsServerRootHint	Imports root hints from another DNS server	Import-DnsServerRootHint 410server2.testdom1.local
Set-DnsServerRecursion	Sets the recursion settings for the DNS server	Set-DnsServerRecursion -Enable $true
Set-DnsServerDiagnostics	Sets debugging and logging parameters	Set-DnsServerDiagnostics -All $true

ACTIVITY

Activity 10-6: Configuring and Testing Forwarders

Time Required: 10 minutes

Objective: Create and test a conditional forwarder and a regular forwarder.

Required Tools and Equipment: 410Server1 and 410Server2

Description: You want 410Server2 to be able to resolve host names for clients that want to access hosts in the 410Server2012.local domain. You could create a secondary zone on 410Server2 and configure zone transfers on 410Server1 for the 410Server2012.local domain, but you decide that configuring a conditional forwarder is more suitable. Next, you create a standard forwarder to test the feature.

1. Log on to 410Server2 as **Administrator,** and open the DNS Manager console and a command prompt window, if necessary. Make sure 410Server1 is running.

2. At the command prompt, type **nslookup 410Server1.410server2012.local** and press **Enter.** The lookup is not successful.

3. In DNS Manager, click to select **Conditional Forwarders,** and then right-click it and click **New Conditional Forwarder.** The New Conditional Forwarder dialog box opens. In the DNS Domain text box, type **410server2012.local.** Click in the "IP addresses of master servers" list box, type **10.10.1.1,** and press **Enter** (see Figure 10-20). Click **OK.**

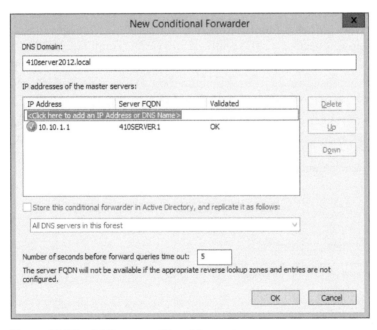

Figure 10-20   Adding a conditional forwarder

4. At the command prompt, type **nslookup 410server1.410server2012.local** and press **Enter.** The lookup is successful.

5. Next, you remove the conditional forwarder that's considered a zone. On 410Server2, type **powershell** at the command prompt and press **Enter** to start PowerShell, if necessary. Type **Remove-DnsServerZone 410Server2012.local** and press **Enter.** Press **Enter** to confirm.

6. Type **nslookup 410server1.410server2012.local** and press **Enter.** The lookup is still successful because the local DNS server cached the information for 410Server1 from the previous successful lookup. Eventually, the cached information expires, but you delete it in the next step.

7. Type **Clear-DnsServerCache** and press **Enter.** Press **Enter** to confirm. Type **nslookup 410server1.410server2012.local** and press **Enter.** The lookup is no longer successful.

8. To create a standard forwarder, type **Add-DnsServerForwarder 10.10.1.1** and press **Enter.**

9. In DNS Manager, right-click **410Server2** in the left pane and click **Properties**. Click the **Forwarders** tab. You see the forwarder you created in Step 8. (If you don't see the forwarder, close the Properties dialog box, click **410Server2**, click the **Refresh** icon, and repeat this step.) Click **Cancel**.

10. Type **nslookup 410server1.410server2012.local** and press **Enter**. The lookup is successful.

11. To remove the forwarder, type **Remove-DnsServerForwarder 10.10.1.1** and press **Enter** to confirm.

12. Stay logged on if you're continuing to the next activity. Leave the DNS Manager console and the command prompt window open.

Activity 10-7: Working with Root Hints

Time Required: 15 minutes
Objective: View the root hints file and transfer root hints.

Required Tools and Equipment: 410Server1, 410Server2, Internet connection
Description: In this activity, you work with the root hints file. Verify that you can contact root servers for DNS lookups, and then delete the root hints file, delete the DNS cache, and verify that you can no longer contact root servers for DNS lookups. Finally, you view the contents of the root hints file.

1. Log on to 410Server2 as **Administrator**, and open the DNS Manager console and a command prompt window, if necessary. Make sure 410Server1 is running.

2. At the command prompt, type **nslookup www.yahoo.com** and press **Enter**. The lookup is successful because root hints are configured on 410Server2, and it performed a recursive lookup by contacting root servers and then TLD servers.

3. In the DNS Manager console, right-click **410Server2** and click **Properties**. Click the **Root Hints** tab (see Figure 10-21). In the list of 13 root servers, click any server and click **Edit**. DNS attempts to validate the root server. If it can be validated, you see a green check box and an OK. Click **Cancel**.

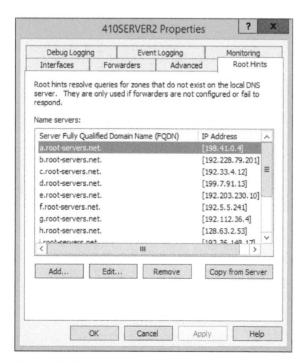

Figure 10-21   Configuring root hints

4. Click the **Remove** button until all root servers are deleted, and then click **OK**.

5. Type **nslookup www.yahoo.com** and press **Enter**. The lookup is still successful because the record for www.yahoo.com is cached on the server.

6. Type **powershell** and press **Enter**, if necessary, to start a PowerShell prompt. Type **Clear-DnsServerCache** and press **Enter**. Press **Enter** to confirm.

7. Type **nslookup www.yahoo.com** and press **Enter**. The lookup is no longer successful because your server can't contact the root servers.

8. In the DNS Manager console, right-click **410Server2** and click **Properties**. Click the **Root Hints** tab, and then click the **Copy from Server** button. In the IP address or DNS name text box, type **10.10.1.1** (the address of 410Server1), and then click **OK** to repopulate the root server list. Click **OK**.

9. At the command prompt, type **nslookup www.yahoo.com** and press **Enter**. The lookup is successful.

10. To see the file where root hints are stored, type **notepad c:\windows\system32\ dns\cache.dns** at the command prompt and press **Enter** to see the list of root servers. (*Note:* You can also update this file manually by going to *www.internic. net/domain/named.root* and copying the contents of the file you see there into the cache.dns file.)

11. Log off 410Server1, but stay logged on to 410Server2.

Activity 10-8: Uninstalling DNS

10

Time Required: 10 minutes
Objective: Uninstall DNS from 410Server2.

Required Tools and Equipment: 410Server2
Description: You're done working with DNS, so you uninstall DNS from 410Server2 and reset its DNS server address to point to 410Server1 again.

1. Log on to 410Server2 as **Administrator**, if necessary.

2. Open Server Manager, and click Tools, Windows PowerShell from the menu to open a PowerShell prompt.

3. Type **Uninstall-WindowsFeature DNS -restart** and press **Enter**. If prompted to continue, type **y** and press **Enter**. The server uninstalls DNS and restarts.

4. When 410Server2 restarts, log on as **Administrator**, and open a PowerShell prompt. Type **Set-DnsClientServerAddress -InterfaceAlias Ethernet -ServerAddresses 10.10.1.1** and press **Enter**.

5. Log off 410Server2.

Monitoring and Troubleshooting DNS

A network's DNS structure can range from a basic single-domain, single-server scheme to a complex multidomain scheme with subdomains, secondary zones, forwarders, and stub zones. In addition, many environments use more than one name resolution service; for example, some Windows applications and services depend on WINS and NetBIOS lookups. To troubleshoot a DNS problem, such as a failed name resolution, first you need to know that DNS is actually used for name resolution. After determining that DNS is part of the process, you can begin monitoring DNS, if the problem is performance related, or troubleshooting DNS queries and zone activities when there are query failures.

DNS Troubleshooting

Windows has several tools to administer, monitor, and troubleshoot DNS server operation, including the following commonly used tools:

- *DNS Manager*—The main DNS configuration tool, used to perform most DNS configuration tasks, monitor zone data and the DNS cache's contents, and configure event logging and debug logging.

- dcdiag /test:dns—Test DNS operation on domain controllers and solve problems with DNS forwarders, delegation, dynamic updates, and record registration. Particularly useful for checking that SRV resource records are registered by using dcdiag /test:dns /DnsRecordRegistration.

- dnscmd.exe—A command-line tool that enables administrators to perform basic to advanced configuration and monitoring. Although dnscmd is still available in Windows Server 2012/R2, Microsoft recommends transitioning to PowerShell. Some available command options are as follows:

  o /info: Displays server information

  o /statistics: Displays or clears server statistics

  o /clearcache: Clears the server cache

  o /zoneinfo: Displays zone information

  o /directorypartitioninfo: List information about the DNS application directory partition

  o /enumrecords: Lists all resource records for a zone

  o /enumzones: Lists all zones on the server

  o /ipvalidate: Validates a remote DNS server

- *PowerShell*—Dozens of PowerShell commands are available for managing DNS. To see a list of all cmdlets for working with DNS, type Get-Command -Module DnsServer at a PowerShell prompt. Here are a few cmdlets that are useful for DNS troubleshooting:

  o Clear-DnsServerCache: Clears the DNS server cache

  o Get-DnsServer: Displays the DNS server configuration

  o Get-DnsServerDiagnostics: Displays details about DNS event logging

  o Get-DnsServerForwarder: Displays DNS forwarder configuration

  o Get-DnsServerStatistics: Shows statistics for the server or a specified zone

  o Show-DnsServerCache: Shows the cache records

  o Test-DnsServer: Tests the specified DNS server

- *Event Viewer*—Used to view the DNS Server event log (can also be viewed in the Global Logs node in DNS Manager).

- dnslint—A command-line program used to check for resource records on a server, verify delegations, verify resource records needed for Active Directory replication, and perform e-mail connectivity tests. You can download dnslint from the Microsoft Web site and find information on using it at *http://support.microsoft.com/kb/321045*.

- nslookup—Used to test DNS queries with the default DNS server or a specific DNS server.

- ipconfig—Used to check DNS client configuration and the DNS suffix search list; also used to cause a client to register its DNS name and display and delete locally cached DNS records.

- *Performance Monitor*—Found in the Tools menu of Server Manager; you can monitor more than 60 performance counters related to DNS. It's used to create a baseline of performance data that you can use for comparison with future readings if DNS performance degrades.

- *Protocol analyzer*—This type of tool provides information similar to debug logging but with more flexibility. You can download Network Monitor, or its successor Microsoft Message Analyzer, from the Microsoft Download Center. An excellent free protocol analyzer, Wireshark, can be downloaded from *www.wireshark.org*.

Before you can begin troubleshooting DNS queries efficiently, you need a clear picture in your mind of the DNS lookup process. Earlier in the chapter, an example was given but didn't factor in variables such as the Hosts file, cache, and forwarders. Taking these factors into account, a DNS lookup involves the following steps, starting with the DNS client:

1. Check the local DNS cache, which contains the contents of the Hosts file.
2. Query the DNS server with a recursive lookup.

If the address is resolved in Step 1, it's returned to the requesting application, and the process is completed. After Step 2 has been initiated, the query is in the hands of the DNS server being queried, and the following steps occur on this server:

3. Check local zone data.
4. Check locally cached data.
5. Query root server or configured forwarders.

Remember that Step 3 can include primary zones, secondary zones, and stub zones as well as delegated zones. At Step 5, the recursive query process continues until the name is resolved or a "lookup failed" message is returned. At this point, however, the lookup process is largely out of the local administrator's hands.

When troubleshooting a query, you want to eliminate the easy things first, which usually means verifying the client configuration. To verify DNS configuration, use these ipconfig options:

- /all—Displays IP addresses of the configured DNS servers as well as the DNS suffix search list.

- /displaydns—Displays the local DNS cache, which also has the contents of the Hosts file.

- /flushdns—Deletes the local DNS cache. Sometimes the local cache is big, and spotting a problem could be difficult. Deleting the cache is harmless and can save you from wading through dozens of cached entries.

After these steps, double-check the Hosts file to make sure you didn't miss something when you displayed the local cache.

If everything checks out on the client, your job just got tougher. You'll probably want to proceed with analyzing the DNS server the client uses, including examining the following:

- *Locally cached data*—Stale records can return incorrect results. If you suspect records are stale, delete the cache or the suspect domains in the cache.

- *DNS Server log*—Use Event Viewer to view the DNS Server log, or use DNS Manager to view the DNS Events node under the Global Logs node. Both applications record the same information. Look for warning or error messages indicating service failures or zone transfer or replication failures.

- *Verify Active Directory replication*—You can use dcdiag or dnslint to verify that the correct resource records exist for Active Directory replication. The dnslint /ad /s localhost /v command generates a report in HTML format and opens the report in Internet Explorer. Warnings and errors are color-coded in the report.

- *Verify SRV records*—Use dcdiag /test:dns /dnsrecordregistration to be sure that SRV and other resource records are registered correctly. If SRV records for a DC aren't registered, start and stop the Netlogon service by entering net stop netlogon and then net start netlogon on the DC. Registered SRV records are stored in *%systemroot%*System32\Config\netlogon.dns.

- *Verify zone transfers*—The `nslookup` command can request records from an entire zone. On a server hosting secondary zones, use `nslookup` in interactive mode by typing `nslookup` and pressing Enter. Change the server to the primary DNS server for the zone with the `server servername` command, and then use `ls -d domain` (substituting the name of the zone you want to verify for `domain`). If zone transfers aren't working, you get a "query refused" message. Otherwise, the zone data is displayed. Also, verify the settings in the Zone Transfer tab on the primary server to make sure the secondary server is in the server list or that any server can request zone transfers.

- *Verify zone delegations*—Use the `dnslint /d delegatedzone /s IP_of_authoritative_server` command to produce a report to verify the delegation.

- `ping`—Use `ping` to verify connectivity to remote DNS servers that might be part of the lookup process.

- *Verify PTR records*—It's easy to forget to create the zones needed for PTR records and make sure PTR records are created when entering a new A record manually. Certain processes require reverse lookups, so make sure critical servers have PTR records as well as A records. To do this, check for the reverse lookup zone in DNS Manager, or use `nslookup` to do a forward lookup for the host's IP address first, and then do a reverse lookup, using the returned IP address. If the lookup fails, the PTR record doesn't exist.

The procedures and tools described in this section should arm you with the knowledge you need to start the DNS troubleshooting process and solve at least minor problems. More complex problems take some perseverance with these tools and perhaps debug logging and protocol analysis. The better you understand the DNS process, the more quickly you can solve problems. Use debug logging and a protocol analyzer periodically to examine DNS operation when it's working correctly, and save these results. This way, you have something to compare with troubleshooting output when problems happen.

Chapter Summary

- DNS is based on a hierarchical naming structure and a distributed database. DNS names use the structure *host.domain.top-level-domain* or perhaps *host.subdomain.domain. top-level-domain*. This naming structure is the fully qualified domain name (FQDN).

- DNS can be described as an inverted tree with the root domain at the top, top-level domains branching off the root, and domains and subdomains branching off top-level domains. The entire DNS tree is called the DNS namespace. Every domain has one or more authoritative name servers.

- The DNS database is composed of zones containing resource records, such as Start of Authority (SOA), Host (A), and Service (SRV) records. Host (A) resource records can be updated with static or dynamic updates.

- DNS lookups involve iterative and recursive queries. Most lookups start from the DNS resolver with a recursive query to a DNS server. The DNS server satisfies the query or performs a series of iterative queries, starting with a root server.

- DNS servers can perform one or more of the following roles: authoritative server, forwarder, conditional forwarder, and caching-only server.

- DNS is an integral part of most network communication sessions between computers. A properly configured and efficiently functioning DNS, therefore, is essential for a well-functioning network. DNS can be installed automatically during Active Directory installation or as a separate server role.

- You might need to install a new zone manually if the DNS server isn't a DC, when you create a stub zone, when you create a secondary zone, and when you create a zone for an Internet domain.

- A zone can be a forward lookup zone or a reverse lookup zone. FLZs contain host records primarily. Reverse lookup zones contain PTR records.

- DNS databases consist of the following zone types: primary zone, secondary zone, and stub zone. Primary and stub zones can also be Active Directory–integrated zones.

- Active Directory–integrated zones have the advantages of automatic replication, multimaster replication and update, secure updates, and efficient replication. The scope of Active Directory zone replication can be forest-wide, domain-wide, or custom.

- Resource records can be dynamically created or static records. Dynamic records are often created with a DHCP server. Static records can be created by using DNS Manager or PowerShell cmdlets.

- SOA records contain information about a zone, including its serial number and timers used for zone transfers. NS records specify the name of a server that's authoritative for the zone.

- Advanced DNS settings include configuring forwarders, root hints, round robin, recursive queries, and logging.

- Tools for monitoring and troubleshooting DNS include `dcdiag`, `dnscmd`, `dnslint`, `nslookup`, `ipconfig`, PowerShell cmdlets, Performance Monitor, and protocol analyzers. You need to understand the DNS query process to troubleshoot DNS problems efficiently.

Key Terms

Active Directory–integrated zone   A primary or stub zone with the DNS database stored in an Active Directory partition rather than a text file. Because Active Directory zones are replicated to other domain controllers automatically, only primary and stub zones can be Active Directory integrated.

authoritative server   A DNS server that holds a complete copy of a zone's resource records (typically a primary or secondary zone).

caching-only DNS server   A DNS server with no zones. Its sole job is to field DNS queries, do recursive lookups to root servers, or send requests to forwarders, and then cache the results.

conditional forwarder   A DNS server to which other DNS servers send requests targeted for a specific domain.

DNS namespace   Defines the structure of names used to identify resources in Internet domains. It consists of a root name (defined as a period), top-level domains, second-level domains, optionally one or more subdomains, and hostnames separated by periods.

Dynamic DNS (DDNS)   A DNS name-registering process whereby computers in the domain can register or update their own DNS records.

forwarder   A DNS server to which other DNS servers send requests they can't resolve themselves.

forward lookup zone (FLZ)   A DNS zone containing records that translate names to IP addresses, such as A, AAAA, and MX records. It's named after the domain whose resource records it contains.

GlobalNames zone (GNZ)   A feature that provides a way for IT administrators to add single-label names (computer names that don't use a domain suffix) to DNS, thereby allowing client computers to resolve these names without including a DNS suffix in the query.

glue A record   An A record used to resolve the name in an NS record to its IP address.

iterative query   A type of DNS query to which a DNS server responds with the best information it has to satisfy the query. The DNS server doesn't query additional DNS servers in an attempt to resolve the query.

primary zone   A DNS zone containing a read/write master copy of all resource records for the zone; this zone is authoritative for the zone.

recursive query   A query in which the DNS server processes the query until it responds with an address that satisfies the query or with an "I don't know" message. The process might require the DNS server to query several additional DNS servers.

referral   A response to an iterative query in which the address of another name server is returned to the requester.

resolver   A DNS client that sends a recursive query to a DNS server. *See also* recursive query.

resource records   Data in a DNS database containing information about network resources, such as hostnames, other DNS servers, and services; each record is identified by a letter code.

reverse lookup zone (RLZ)   A DNS zone containing PTR records that map IP addresses to names; it's named with the IP network address (IPv4 or IPv6) of the computer whose records it contains.

root hints   A list of name servers preconfigured on Windows DNS servers that point to Internet root servers, which are DNS servers located on the Internet and managed by IANA.

root servers   DNS servers that keep a database of addresses of other DNS servers managing top-level domain names.

round robin   A method of responding to DNS queries when more than one IP address exists for the queried host. Each IP address is placed first in the list of returned addresses an equal number of times so that hosts are accessed alternately.

secondary zone   A DNS zone containing a read-only copy of all resource records for the zone. Changes can't be made directly on a secondary DNS server, but because it contains an exact copy of the primary zone, it's considered authoritative for the zone.

standard zone   A primary, secondary, or stub zone that isn't Active Directory integrated.

stub zone   A DNS zone containing a read-only copy of only the zone's SOA and NS records and the necessary A records to resolve NS records. A stub zone forwards queries to a primary DNS server for that zone and is not authoritative for the zone.

top-level domain (TLD) servers   DNS servers that maintain addresses of other DNS servers that are authoritative for second-level domains that use the top-level domain. For example, a TLD server for the com top-level domain contains NS records for authoritative DNS servers for all domains ending in com.

zone   A grouping of DNS information that represents one or more domains and possibly subdomains.

zone replication   The transfer of zone changes from one DNS server to another.

zone transfer   An operation that copies all or part of a zone from one DNS server to another and occurs as a result of a secondary server requesting the transfer from another server.

Review Questions

1. Which of the following best describes DNS? (Choose all that apply.)

    a.   Hierarchical database

    b.   Flat database

    c.   Monolithic database

    d.   Distributed database

2. Which of the following accurately represents an FQDN?

    a.   host.top-level-domain.subdomain.domain

    b.   domain.host.top-level-domain

    c.   host.subdomain.domain.top-level-domain

    d.   host.domain.top-level-domain.subdomain

3. A DNS server that can't resolve a query from its local data sends a recursive query to a root server. True or False?

4. A resource record containing an alias for another record is which of the following record types?

   a. A

   b. CNAME

   c. NS

   d. PTR

5. What type of resource record is necessary to get a positive response from the command `nslookup 192.168.100.10`?

   a. A

   b. CNAME

   c. NS

   d. PTR

6. When a DNS server responds to a query with a list of name servers, what is the response called?

   a. Iterative

   b. Recursive

   c. Referral

   d. Resolver

7. You're scanning the local cache on a DNS client, and you come across the notation `::1`. What does it mean?

   a. The cache is corrupt.

   b. It's the IPv6 localhost address.

   c. It's the link-local address.

   d. It's a reverse lookup record.

8. Your company just opened a small branch office where 10 computer users will work. You have installed a single Windows Server 2012 R2 computer configured as a member server for basic file and print server needs. Users require DNS for Internet access and to resolve names of company resources. You decide to install DNS on the existing server. Which of the following types of installations makes the most sense?

   a. A primary server hosting a standard zone

   b. An Active Directory–integrated zone hosting the zone in which the server is a member

   c. A caching-only DNS server

   d. A server that's a forwarder

9. You have a DNS server outside your corporate firewall that's a stand-alone Windows Server 2012 R2 server. It hosts a primary zone for your public Internet domain name, which is different from your internal Active Directory domain names. You want one or more of your internal servers to be able to handle DNS queries for your public domain and to serve as a backup for the primary DNS server outside the firewall. Which configuration should you choose for internal DNS servers?

   a. Configure a standard secondary zone.

   b. Configure a standard stub zone.

   c. Configure a forwarder to point to the primary DNS server.

   d. Configure an Active Directory–integrated stub zone.

10. DNS ServerA forwards a query to ForwarderB, which replies with a "not found" message. DNS ServerA continues the lookup by querying a root server. True or False?

11. Which of the following is true about stub zones? (Choose all that apply.)

    a. They're authoritative for the zone.

    b. Their records are updated by the primary server automatically.

    c. They can't be Active Directory integrated.

    d. They contain SOA and NS records.

12. You have Windows Server 2012 R2 DNS servers, Windows Server 2008 DNS servers, and two old Windows 2000 DNS servers in a Windows domain. You just created a new zone, newzone.com, that you want replicated by Active Directory to all DNS servers. Where should you store the zone?

    a. ForestDNSZones partition

    b. Newzone.com.dns

    c. DomainDNSZones partition

    d. Domain partition

13. The DNS server at your headquarters holds a standard primary zone for the abc.com domain. A branch office connected by a slow WAN link holds a secondary zone for abc. com. Updates to the zone aren't frequent. How can you decrease the amount of WAN traffic caused by the secondary zone checking for zone updates?

    a. In the SOA tab of the zone's Properties dialog box, increase the minimum (default) TTL.

    b. In the Advanced tab of the DNS server's Properties dialog box, increase the expire interval.

    c. In the SOA tab of the zone's Properties dialog box, increase the refresh interval.

    d. In the Zone Transfers tab of the SOA Properties dialog box, decrease the retry interval.

14. What type of record does DNS create automatically to resolve the FQDN of an NS record?

    a. PTR records

    b. CNAME records

    c. Glue A records

    d. Auto SRV records

15. You want a DNS server to handle queries for a domain with a standard primary zone hosted on another DNS server, and you don't want the server to be authoritative for that zone. How should you configure the server? (Choose all that apply.)

    a. Configure a secondary zone on the DNS server.

    b. Configure a stub zone on the DNS server.

    c. Configure a forwarder on the DNS server.

    d. Configure zone hints for the primary zone.

16. You're in charge of a standard primary zone for a large network with frequent changes to the DNS database. You want changes to the zone to be transmitted as quickly as possible to all secondary servers. What should you configure and on which server?

    a. Configure DNS notifications on the primary zone server.

    b. Configure DNS recursion on the secondary zone servers.

    c. Configure round robin on the primary zone server.

    d. Configure a smaller default TTL for the primary zone server.

17. You have several hundred client computers using WINS to resolve names of some enterprise servers. Many of the client computers are laptops used to connect to the network remotely. You're trying to eliminate WINS from your network to reduce the number of protocols and services you must support. What can you do, with the least administrative effort, that allows you to stop using WINS yet still allows clients computers to use a single-label name for accessing enterprise servers?

    a. Create a GlobalNames zone and add CNAME records for enterprise servers.

    b. Create a Hosts file containing servers' names and addresses and upload this file to each client that needs it.

    c. Configure each client computer with the correct domain suffix.

    d. Create a stub zone and add CNAME records for each enterprise server.

18. You manage the DNS structure on your network. The network security group has decided that only one DNS server should contact the Internet. Under no circumstances should other servers contact the Internet for DNS queries, even if the designated server is down. You have decided that the DNS server named DNS-Int should be the server allowed to contact the Internet. How should you configure your DNS structure to accommodate these requirements?

    a. On each DNS server except DNS-Int, configure a forwarder pointing to DNS-Int. Configure DNS-Int as a forwarder by enabling forwarded requests in the Forwarders tab of the server's Properties dialog box.

    b. On each DNS server except DNS-Int, configure a root hint to point to DNS-Int and delete all other root hints. Configure a root zone on DNS-Int.

    c. On each DNS server except DNS-Int, configure a forwarder pointing to DNS-Int. Disable the use of root hints if no forwarders are available. No changes are necessary on DNS-Int.

    d. On each DNS server except DNS-Int, in the Advanced tab of the server's Properties dialog box, disable recursion. No changes are necessary for DNS-Int.

19. You have a zone containing two A records for the same hostname, but each A record has a different IP address configured. The host records point to two servers hosting a high-traffic Web site, and you want the servers to share the load. After some testing, you find that you're always accessing the same Web server, so load sharing isn't occurring. What can you do to solve the problem?

    a. Enable the load sharing option on the zone.

    b. Enable the round robin option on both A records.

    c. Enable the load sharing option on both A records.

    d. Enable the round robin option on the server.

20. Which is the correct order in which a DNS client tries to resolve a name?

    a. Cache, DNS server, Hosts file

    b. Hosts file, cache, DNS server

    c. Cache, Hosts file, DNS server

    d. DNS server, cache, Hosts file

10

21. You want to verify whether a PTR record exists for the server1.csmtech.local host, but you don't know the server's IP address. Which of the following commands should you use to see whether a PTR record exists for server1.csmtech.local?

    a. `ping -a server1.csmtech.local`, and then `ping IPAddress` returned from the first `ping`

    b. `nslookup server1.csmtech.local`, and then `nslookup IPAddress` returned from the first `nslookup`

    c. `dnscmd /PTR server1.csmtech.local`

    d. `dnslint /PTR server1.csmtech.local`

22. You have two DCs, each with three Active Directory–integrated zones. You're getting inconsistent DNS lookup results and suspect a problem with Active Directory replication. What tool can you use to investigate the problem? (Choose all that apply.)

    a. `nslookup`

    b. `dnscmd`

    c. `dcdiag`

    d. `ipconfig`

23. To resolve a query, a DNS server looks in its local cache first. True or False?

24. You have just finished setting up your DNS infrastructure, and the DNS process seems to be working well. You want to be able to create a baseline of performance data so that if slowdowns occur later, you have information for comparison purposes. Which tool should you use?

    a. `dnscmd.exe`

    b. Debug logging

    c. Performance Monitor

    d. Event logging

25. You're having trouble with logons and other domain operations in your domain named csmtech.local. You want to verify that your domain clients can find domain controllers. Which of the following can you do? (Choose all that apply.)

    a. Use the `dcdiag /test:dns /DnsRecordRegistration` command.

    b. Look at the %*systemroot*%\System32\Config\netlogon.dns file.

    c. Look at the %*systemroot*%\System32\dns\cache.dns file.

    d. Use the `nslookup -type = CNAME -domain=csmtech.local` command.

Case Projects

Case Project 10-1: Resolving Names of Internet Resources

You have an Active Directory–integrated domain named csmtech.local with two DCs that are DNS servers. You also have an Internet presence with its own domain name, csmpub.com, and a DNS server that's not part of an Active Directory domain. You want the DCs to be able to resolve the names of csmpub.com resources and to act as backup for the csmpub.com DNS database. What can you do to achieve these goals? Describe the steps you would take.

Case Project 10-2: Restricting Registration

You manage an Active Directory domain named csmtech.local. The DNS server is a DC for csmtech.local and hosts a standard primary DNS zone for csmtech.local. You have noticed resource records in the zone from computers that aren't domain members. What can you do to ensure that only domain members can update resource records in the zone?

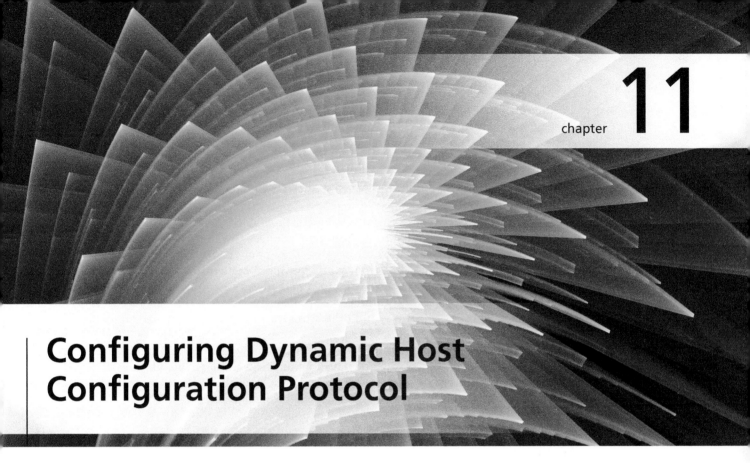

chapter 11

Configuring Dynamic Host Configuration Protocol

After reading this chapter and completing the exercises, you will be able to:

- Describe the DHCP protocol and process
- Install and configure a DHCP server
- Configure DHCP server settings
- Configure a DHCP relay agent

Transmission Control Protocol/Internet Protocol (TCP/IP) is the standard networking protocol for all types and sizes of networks. As you know, every device on a TCP/IP network needs an IP address to communicate with other devices. Two methods are available for IP address assignment: static and dynamic. Although static IP addressing has its merits, managing static addresses on networks of more than a few dozen computers can descend into chaos quickly.

After Dynamic Host Configuration Protocol (DHCP) has been configured, it relieves many of the administrative headaches of managing static IP addressing on large networks. Small office and home networks typically use a Wi-Fi-enabled router, which is configured to assign an IP address via DHCP to devices that connect to the network. These routers might require little to no configuration because they come configured for DHCP. On a larger Windows-based network, however, you want more control over IP addressing and the ability to use features such as authorization and filters to enhance security, reservations, exclusions, IPv6 compatibility, and server policies. Windows Server 2012/R2 has the DHCP Server role with these features and others to give you an enterprise-scale dynamic IP addressing solution.

This chapter discusses how DHCP works, and you learn how to install and configure DHCP, including server authorization, scopes, and DHCP options. You also learn about some advanced features, such as reservations, exclusions, server policies, and filters. Last, you learn how to configure DHCP on a multi-subnet network by using DHCP relay.

 There are two versions of DHCP: DHCPv4 and DHCPv6. This chapter covers DHCPv4. DHCPv6 is covered in *MCSA Guide to Configuring Advanced Windows Server 2012 Services, Exam 70-412* (Cengage Learning, 2015).

An Overview of Dynamic Host Configuration Protocol

Table 11-1 describes what you need for the hands-on activities in this chapter.

Table 11-1   Activity requirements

Activity	Requirements	Notes
Activity 11-1: Installing and Authorizing a DHCP Server	410Server1, 410Server2	
Activity 11-2: Creating and Testing a DHCP Scope	410Server2, 410Win8	
Activity 11-3: Working with Exclusions and Reservations	410Server2, 410Win8	
Activity 11-4: Configuring DHCP Options	410Server2, 410Win8	
Activity 11-5: Creating a DHCP Filter	410Server2, 410Win8	
Activity 11-6: Creating a DHCP Policy	410Server2, 410Win8	
Activity 11-7: Uninstalling the DHCP Server Role	410Server2, 410Win8	

© 2015 Cengage Learning®

Dynamic Host Configuration Protocol (DHCP) is a component of the TCP/IP protocol suite, which is used to assign an IP address to a host automatically from a defined pool of addresses. IP addresses assigned via DHCP are usually leased, not permanently assigned. When a client receives an IP address from a server, it can keep the address until the lease expires, at which point the client can request a new IP address. However, to prevent a disruption in communication, the client attempts to renew the lease when the lease interval is 50% expired. DHCP is based on broadcast packets, so there must be a DHCP server or DHCP relay agent (discussed later in "DHCP Relay Agents") in the same subnet as the client. Recall that broadcast packets are forwarded by switches but not by routers, so they're heard only by devices on the same LAN. DHCP is a fairly simple protocol, consisting of just eight message types. These message types and the DHCP address assignment and renewal processes are discussed in the following sections.

The DHCP Address Assignment Process

Like most TCP/IP protocols, DHCP is a client/server protocol. A client makes a request for an IP address, and the server responds. The process of a DHCP client requesting an IP address and a DHCP server fulfilling the request is actually a four-packet sequence. All four packets are broadcast packets. DHCP was designed to use broadcast packets because a client that doesn't have an IP address can't be sent a unicast packet; it can, however, receive and respond to a broadcast packet. DHCP uses the UDP Transport-layer protocol on ports 67 and 68. Port 67 is for sending data from the client to the server, and port 68 is for sending data from the server to the client. The four-packet sequence is explained in the following list and illustrated in Figure 11-1:

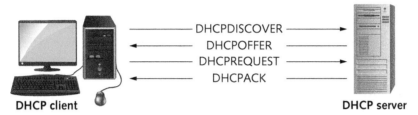

DHCP client   **DHCP server**

Figure 11-1   The packet sequence for DHCP address assignment
© 2015 Cengage Learning®

1. *DHCPDISCOVER*—The client transmits a broadcast packet via UDP source port 68 and UDP destination port 67 to the network, asking for an IP address from an available DHCP server. The client can request its last known IP address and other IP address parameters, such as the subnet mask, router (default gateway), domain name, and DNS server.

2. *DHCPOFFER*—A DHCP server receives the DHCPDISCOVER packet and responds with an offer of an IP address and subnet mask from the pool of addresses, along with the lease duration. The broadcast packet is transmitted via UDP source port 67 and UDP destination port 68. Because the packet is a broadcast, all computers on the subnet get it. The packet contains the MAC address of the client computer that sent the DHCPDISCOVER packet, so other computers disregard it.

3. *DHCPREQUEST*—The client responds by requesting the offered address. Because it's possible that multiple DHCP servers responded to the DHCPDISCOVER, the client might get multiple offers but accepts only one offer. The DHCPREQUEST packet includes a server identifier, which is the IP address of the server the offer is accepted from. Any other DHCP servers that made an offer see the server identifier and return the offered IP address to the pool.

4. *DHCPACK*—The server the offer was accepted from acknowledges the transaction and sends any other requested IP parameters to the client. The transaction is now complete, and the client binds the IP address and other parameters to its network interface.

DHCP Address Renewal   The DHCPDISCOVER broadcast packet is sent only when the client currently has no IP address configured on the interface the packet is transmitted from or after its current address has expired. As mentioned, a client attempts to renew the address lease when it's 50% expired. The **lease renewal** process is somewhat different, and because the client already has an IP address and the address of the DHCP server, the client uses unicast packets rather than broadcast packets. A successful renewal is a two-packet sequence:

1. *DHCPREQUEST*—When the lease is 50% expired, the client sends a unicast packet to the DHCP server, requesting a renewal lease for its current IP address. If the server doesn't respond, the client retries the renewal request up to three more times, occurring at 4, 8, and 16 seconds after the first renewal request.

2. *DHCPACK*—If the server responds and can honor the renewal request, the server sends a unicast packet to the client granting and acknowledging the renewal request.

The two-packet sequence for a lease renewal occurs when a server is available to service the request and the server can honor the renewal request. The renewal request might fail in these common situations:

- The server responds but can't honor the renewal. This situation can occur if the requested address has been deleted or deactivated from the scope or the address has been excluded from the scope since the time the client received it. The server sends a DHCPNAK to the client, and the client unbinds the address from its network interface and begins the process anew with a broadcast DHCPDISCOVER packet.

- The server doesn't respond. If the server has been taken offline, moved to another subnet, or can't communicate (perhaps because of a hardware failure), the DHCPREQUEST packet can't be serviced. In this case, the following steps occur:

1. The client keeps its current address until 87.5% of the lease interval has expired. At that time, the client sends a broadcast DHCPREQUEST requesting a lease renewal from any available DHCP server.

2. There are two possible results from the DHCPREQUEST broadcast:

   o A DHCP server responds to the request. If it can provide the requested address, it replies with a DHCPACK and the address is renewed; otherwise, it replies with a DHCPNAK (negative acknowledgement) indicating that it can't supply the requested address. In this case, the client immediately unbinds the address from the network interface and starts the DHCP sequence over, beginning with a DHCPDISCOVER broadcast packet.

   o No DHCP server responds. In this case, the client waits until the lease period is over, unbinds the IP address, and starts the sequence over with a DHCPDISCOVER broadcast packet. If no server responds, a Windows client (other client OSs might behave differently) binds an Automatic Private IP Addressing (APIPA) address to the network interface and sends a DHCPDISCOVER every 5 minutes in an attempt to get a DHCP-assigned address. If an alternate IP address configuration has been configured on the interface, it's used instead of an APIPA address, and no further attempts are made to get a DHCP-assigned address until the interface is reset or the computer restarts.

DHCP Messages   You've learned about the most common DHCP message types for lease request and renewal. Table 11-2 describes all the message types exchanged between a DHCP server and client. The first column includes the message type number found in the DHCP packet. Message types that have been covered already are described briefly.

Table 11-2   DHCP message types

Message number	Message name	Description
1	DHCPDISCOVER	Sent by a client to discover an available DHCP server and request a new IP address.
2	DHCPOFFER	Sent by the server in response to a DHCPDISCOVER with an offer of an IP address.
3	DHCPREQUEST	Sent by a client to request a lease on an offered IP address in response to a DHCPOFFER or to renew an existing lease.
4	DHCPDECLINE	Sent by a client in response to a DHCPOFFER to decline an offered IP address. Usually occurs when the client has determined that the offered address is already in use on the network.
5	DHCPACK	Sent by the server to acknowledge a DHCPREQUEST or DHCPINFORM. This message also contains DHCP options requested by the client.

(continues)

Message number	Message name	Description
6	DHCPNAK	Sent by the server in response to a DHCPREQUEST. Indicates that the server can't fulfill the request. Usually occurs when a client is attempting a renewal, and the requested address is no longer available for lease.
7	DHCPRELEASE	Sent by a client to release a leased address. Usually occurs when a user runs the `ipconfig /release` command or a command of a similar function. However, it can also occur if a client is configured to release its address when the computer is shut down. (By default, Windows clients don't release an address when they are shut down.)
8	DHCPINFORM	Sent by a client to request additional configuration. The client must already have an IP address and a subnet mask. Can be used by a client that has a static IP address but has been configured to get a DNS address or router address via DHCP.

© 2015 Cengage Learning®

Installing and Configuring a DHCP Server

The DHCP service is installed as a server role, aptly named DHCP Server. There are no role service components for this server role; the DHCP management tool is the only additional component installed. DHCP Server can be installed by using the Add Roles and Features Wizard via Server Manager or the following PowerShell cmdlet:

```
Install-WindowsFeature DHCP -IncludeManagementTools
```

After you install this role, the DHCP console (see Figure 11-2) is available on the Tools menu in Server Manager. The red down arrow on the IPv4 and IPv6 nodes indicates that the server isn't currently providing services. In a Windows domain network, the DHCP server must be authorized, and a scope must be created before the server can begin providing DHCP services. In a workgroup network, authorization is automatic.

11

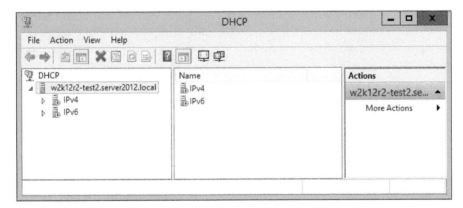

Figure 11-2 The DHCP console

DHCP Server Authorization

A DHCP server must be authorized on a domain network before it can begin providing services. The reason is that DHCP clients have no way of determining whether a DHCP server is valid. When a client transmits a DHCPDISCOVER packet, any DHCP server receiving the broadcast can respond. The client accepts the first offer it gets that meets the requirements in the DHCP-DISCOVER packet. If a rogue DHCP server is installed on a network, whether accidentally or on purpose, incorrect IP address settings could be configured on client computers. These settings likely include the DNS server and default gateway the client uses in addition to the IP address and subnet mask. At best, incorrect IP address settings cause the client to stop communicating correctly. At worst, servers set up by an attacker to masquerade as legitimate network resources can capture passwords and other sensitive information.

On a domain network, a DHCP server can be installed on a domain controller, a member server, or a stand-alone server. However, for authorization to work correctly, installing DHCP on a stand-alone server in a domain network isn't recommended. If you use this setup in a network that already has an authorized server, the stand-alone server can't lease addresses.

After a DHCP server is installed, you authorize it by right-clicking the server name in the DHCP console and clicking Authorize. **DHCP server authorization** requires Enterprise Administrator credentials, so if you aren't logged on as an Enterprise Administrator (the Administrator account in the forest root domain or a member of the Enterprise Administrators universal group), you're prompted for credentials. To authorize a DHCP server with PowerShell, use the Add-DhcpServerInDC cmdlet.

Activity 11-1: Installing and Authorizing a DHCP Server

Time Required: 10 minutes
Objective: Install and authorize a DHCP server.

Required Tools and Equipment: 410Server1 and 410Server2
Description: You want to assign IP addresses dynamically to client computers, so you install the DHCP Server role on a stand-alone server, and then join the server to a domain and authorize it.

1. Start 410Server1 and 410Server2, if necessary. Log on to 410Server2 as **Administrator**.

2. On 410Server2, open Server Manager, and open a PowerShell prompt by clicking **Tools, Windows PowerShell** from the menu. Type **Install-WindowsFeature DHCP -IncludeManagementTools** and press **Enter**.

3. When the DHCP Server installation finishes, click **Tools, DHCP** from the Server Manager menu to open the DHCP console.

4. Click to expand the server node in the left pane. Notice that both the IPv4 and IPv6 nodes show check marks inside green circles, indicating that they're ready to provide DHCP services. Right-click the server node. There's no option to authorize the server because it was authorized automatically, as the server isn't a domain member.

5. Point to **All Tasks**, where you see options for starting, stopping, pausing, resuming, and restarting the DHCP service.

6. Click the **IPv4** node. Read the information in the middle pane about adding a scope, which you do in the next activity. Close the DHCP console.

7. Next, add 410Server2 to the domain by typing **Add-Computer -DomainName 410Server2012.local -Restart** and pressing **Enter**.

8. When prompted for your credentials, type **administrator** in the User name text box and **Password01** in the Password text box. The computer restarts.

9. Log on to the domain as **Administrator** (by clicking the back arrow, clicking **Other user**, and logging on as **410Server2012\administrator**), and open the DHCP console.

10. Click to expand the server node. Notice that the IPv4 and IPv6 nodes have a red down arrow, indicating that the service is disabled. To authorize the server, right-click the server node and click **Authorize**.

11. Click the server node, and click the **Refresh** toolbar icon. You see a check mark in a green circle on the IPv4 and IPv6 nodes. Right-click the server node. If you need to, you can unauthorize a server after it's authorized.

12. Stay logged on to 410Server2 if you're continuing to the next activity. You can leave 410Server1 running or shut it down.

DHCP Scopes

A **DHCP scope** is a pool of IP addresses and other IP configuration parameters that a DHCP server uses to lease addresses to DHCP clients. A scope consists of the following required parameters:

- *Scope name*—A descriptive name for the scope. You can define multiple scopes on a DHCP server, so you might name the scope based on the range of IP addresses in it. For example, a scope that services the 10.10.0.0 network might be named "10.10-subnet."

- *Start and end IP addresses*—The start and end IP addresses define the address pool. You can't specify a start address that's the network ID or an end address that's the broadcast address for the subnet.

- *Prefix length or subnet mask*—Specify a prefix length or subnet mask that's assigned with each IP address. For example, you can specify 16 for the prefix length or 255.255.0.0 for the subnet mask. Windows fills in the prefix and subnet mask automatically based on the class of the start and end IP addresses, but you can change this information.

- *Lease duration*—The **lease duration** specifies how long a DHCP client can keep an address. As discussed, a client tries to renew the address long before the lease expires but must release the address if it can't renew it before it expires. The lease duration is specified in days, hours, and minutes, with a minimum lease of 1 minute and a maximum lease of 999 days, 23 hours, and 59 minutes. The default lease duration is 8 days. The lease can also be set to unlimited, but this setting isn't recommended because if the client is removed from the network or its NIC is replaced, the address is never returned to the pool for lease to other clients. An unlimited duration can also cause DNS records to become stale when DHCP is configured to update DNS records on behalf of the client.

You can configure other options when you create a scope with the New Scope Wizard or PowerShell or change the scope's properties after it's created.

Exclusion Ranges   A DHCP scope contains a continuous range of IP addresses that are leased to DHCP clients. You might want to exclude certain addresses or a range of addresses from the scope for use in static address assignments. Static addresses are usually assigned to servers, routers, and other critical infrastructure devices to make sure they always have an address that never changes. So to avoid IP address conflicts, you need to exclude addresses that are assigned statically. Addresses can be excluded in two ways:

- *De facto exclusion*—You don't actually create an exclusion with this method; you simply set the start and end IP addresses in the scope so that several addresses in the subnet fall outside the scope's range. For example, if you set a scope's start address to 10.1.1.10 and end address to 10.1.1.240 with a 24-bit prefix, you have addresses 10.1.1.1 through 10.1.1.9 and addresses 10.1.1.241 through 10.1.1.254 to use for static address assignments. You might not need to create an exclusion range unless you use all these addresses.

- *Create an exclusion range*—Sometimes a scope is created after static address assignments have been made, and the static addresses occupy several ranges of addresses throughout the subnet (instead of at the beginning or end). For example, if your subnet is 10.1.1.0/24, and you have devices with static addresses in the range 10.1.1.100 through 10.1.1.110, you probably need to create one or more exclusion ranges because these addresses fall right in the middle of the subnet. An **exclusion range** consists of one or more addresses in the scope that the DHCP server doesn't lease to clients. They can be created when the scope is created with the New Scope Wizard or afterward by right-clicking the Address Pool node under the scope and clicking New Exclusion Range. In the Add Exclusion dialog box, type the start and end IP addresses. You can exclude a single IP address by specifying only the start address. You can create as many exclusion ranges as you need.

Reservations   A reservation is an IP address associated with the MAC address of a DHCP client to ensure that when the client requests an IP address, it always gets the same one, along with any configured options. The IP address in the reservation must fall within the same subnet as the scope and uses the same subnet mask that's configured for the scope. If options are configured for the reservation, they take precedence over options configured at the scope or server level (discussed later in "DHCP Options"). A reservation address can be any address in the subnet defined by the scope's address range and can even be within an exclusion range.

If the IP address you want to use in the reservation is already in use by another DHCP client, the client using the address continues to use it until it attempts to renew it. You can force the client to release the address and get a different address by entering `ipconfig /release` and `ipconfig /renew` at a command prompt. The client the reservation is made for can be forced to start using the reserved address by entering `ipconfig /renew` at the command prompt, or you can wait until it attempts to renew its current address.

Multiple Subnets, Multiple Scopes   A DHCP scope can service a single subnet. When a DHCP server receives a DHCPDISCOVER message on an interface, it offers an IP address from the scope for which the address pool is in the same subnet as the interface's address. For example, suppose a DHCP server has a single network interface configured for address 10.10.1.1/16. When a DHCPDISCOVER is received on that interface, the server offers an address from the scope containing addresses in the 10.10.0.0/16 network. Likewise, if the DHCP server receives a DHCPREQUEST for a particular IP address, as when a client renews a lease, the server can fulfill the request only if the requested address is on the same subnet as the server's interface and there's a matching scope.

You can't create overlapping scopes. In other words, you can't create multiple scopes with address pools in the same subnet. For example, suppose you create a scope with the start address 10.10.0.1, end address 10.10.0.100, and prefix length 16. You can't create another scope with the start address 10.10.5.1 and end address 10.10.5.100 with prefix length 16 because both address pools are in the 10.10.0.0 subnet.

What do you do when your network has multiple subnets? Because DHCP is based on broadcasts, which can't traverse routers, there are three main methods for handling a network with multiple subnets:

- Configure a DHCP server in each subnet, each configured with a scope to service that subnet.

- Configure a single DHCP server with network interfaces connected to each subnet and scopes defined for each subnet. This setup is shown in Figure 11-3. This method obviously becomes untenable when the number of subnets increases because you need an interface for each subnet.

- Configure DHCP relay agents on subnets that don't have a DHCP server. DHCP relay agents forward DHCP requests to a central DHCP server configured with scopes for each subnet. DHCP relay agents are discussed later in "DHCP Relay Agents."

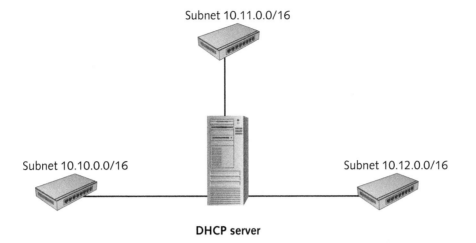

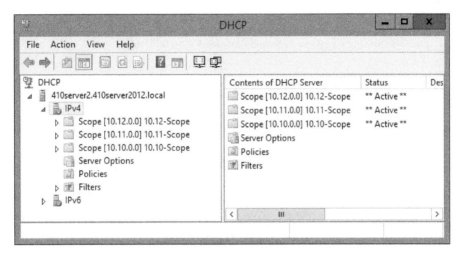

Figure 11-3 A server configured with multiple scopes

Courtesy of Microsoft Corporation and © 2015 Cengage Learning®

Split Scopes A **split scope** is a fault-tolerant DHCP configuration in which two DHCP servers share the same scope information, allowing both servers to offer DHCP services to clients. One server is configured as the primary DHCP server and the other as the secondary. In most cases, the secondary server leases addresses only if the primary server is unavailable. With Windows Server versions before Windows Server 2008 R2, you had to configure a split scope manually. Starting with Windows Server 2008 R2, however, the DHCP Server role has the Dhcp Split-Scope Configuration Wizard to automate the process. You create a split scope by using the wizard as follows:

1. Install the DHCP Server role on two servers designated DHCP1 and DHCP2 for this example. DHCP1 is the primary DHCP server, and DHCP2 is the secondary.

2. Create a scope on DHCP1, including any options, and activate.

3. Run the wizard on DHCP1. To do so, right-click the scope in the DHCP console and click Advanced, and then click Split-Scope. The wizard prompts you for the following information:

   o The name or address of the secondary DHCP server.

   o The percentage of split (see Figure 11-4). A typical split percentage is 80/20, meaning the primary server can lease 80% of the addresses and the secondary server has 20%, but you can configure the split as needed for your environment. If you're configuring the split scope for load balancing rather than fault tolerance, you can set the split to 50%.

Dhcp Split-Scope Configuration Wizard

Percentage of Split
Select the percentage of IP addresses that will be allocated to each of the split-scope servers.

Scroll the slider to choose the percentage of split of IPv4 address range of this scope:

10.1.1.1   10.1.1.254

0   '   '   '   '   50   '   '   '   100
                          Percentage of IPv4 Addresses

	Host DHCP Server	Added DHCP Server
Percentage of IPv4 Addresses Serviced:	80	20

Following is the Exclusion IPv4 Address Range:

Start IPv4 Address: 10 . 1 . 1 . 204   10 . 1 . 1 . 1

End IPv4 Address: 10 . 1 . 1 . 254   10 . 1 . 1 . 203

Note: The existing exclusions will also be configured appropriately on the DHCP Servers.

[< Back]   [Next >]   [Cancel]

Figure 11-4   Setting the percentage of split

o Delay in DHCP offer. Specify the number of milliseconds each server should delay between receiving a DHCPDISCOVER and sending a DHCPOFFER. You usually set the primary server for a 0 delay. You want the secondary server to delay long enough that the primary server services most client requests. You might have to adjust this value until you get the intended results. A value of 1000 is a good place to start. If you're configuring a split scope for load balancing, leave the delay at 0 for both servers.

4. The wizard creates the scope on the secondary server and creates the necessary exclusion range, according to the split percentage on both servers, to ensure that IP addresses aren't duplicated.

5. Create reservations on both servers. If you're using reservations, you need to create them manually on both servers so that either server can offer reserved addresses; the split scope function doesn't replicate reservations.

Split scopes are covered in more detail in *MCSA Guide to Configuring Advanced Windows Server 2012/R2 Services, Exam 70-412* (Cengage Learning, 2015).

Superscopes   A **superscope** is a special type of scope consisting of one or more member scopes that allows a DHCP server to service multiple IPv4 subnets on a single physical network. (Superscopes aren't supported in IPv6.) Although it isn't a common configuration for a network, it can and does occur. A superscope directs the DHCP server to draw addresses from both scopes, even though it has only a single interface configured for one of the IP subnets. This configuration can be useful if the number of computers on a physical network exceeds the size of the original subnet. To configure a superscope, first configure two or more scopes to include in the super-scope; each scope that's part of a superscope is referred to as a "member scope." Then create the superscope and add the member scopes.

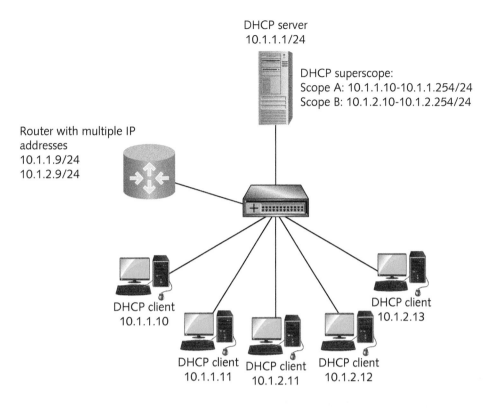

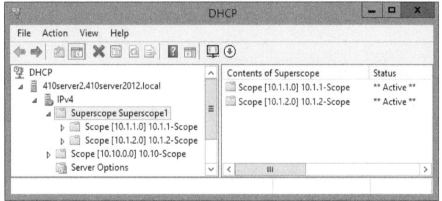

Figure 11-5   A network that uses a superscope

Courtesy of Microsoft Corporation and © 2015 Cengage Learning®

An example of a network with a superscope is shown in Figure 11-5. There are two subnets configured: 10.1.1.0/24 and 10.1.2.0/24. The router interface is configured with two IP addresses and can route between the two subnets. The DHCP server is configured with a superscope named Superscope1 with two member scopes—one for each subnet. Superscopes are covered in more detail in *MCSA Guide to Configuring Advanced Windows Server 2012/R2 Services, Exam 70-412* (Cengage Learning, 2015).

Activity 11-2: Creating and Testing a DHCP Scope

Time Required: 15 minutes
Objective: Create a DHCP scope and test it.

Required Tools and Equipment: 410Server2 and 410Win8
Description: You have installed the DHCP Server service and authorized it. Before it can start leasing addresses, you need to define a scope and then test it by leasing an address with 410Win8.

1. Log on to 410Server2 as **Administrator**, and open the DHCP console, if necessary.

2. Click to expand the server node, if necessary. Click the **IPv4** node, and then right-click it and click **New Scope** to start the New Scope Wizard. In the welcome window, click **Next**.

3. In the Scope Name window, type **10.10-Scope** in the Name text box, add a description, if you like, and then click **Next**.

4. In the IP Address Range window, type **10.10.1.100** in the Start IP address text box and **10.10.1.255** in the End IP address text box. In the Length text box, type **16** (see Figure 11-6), and then click **Next**.

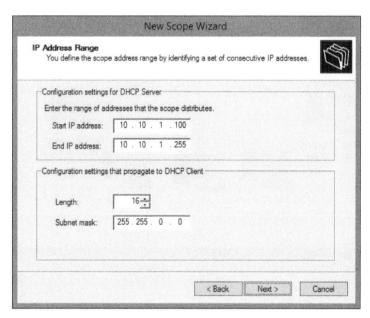

Figure 11-6   Specifying the IP address range

5. In the Add Exclusions and Delay window, click **Next**.

6. In the Lease Duration window, type 0 in the Days text box, **1** in the Hours text box, and 0 in the Minutes text box (see Figure 11-7). One hour is a short lease time, but it's adequate for testing. Click **Next**.

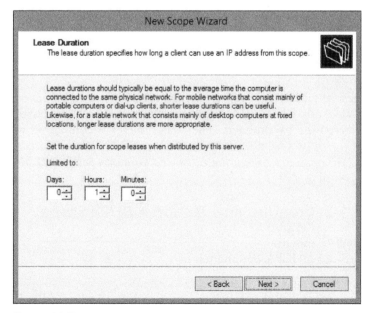

Figure 11-7   Setting the lease duration

7. In the Configure DHCP Options window, click **No, I will configure these options later**, and then click **Next**.

8. In the Completing the New Scope Wizard window, click **Finish**.

9. In the DHCP console, you see the new scope, but a red down arrow indicates it's not activated. Click the scope you just created. You see additional nodes under it, which you work with later. Right-click the scope and click **Activate**. The scope is now activated (see Figure 11-8).

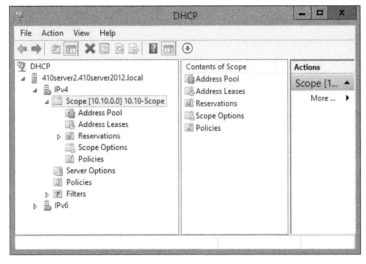

Figure 11-8   The DHCP console with a scope activated

10. Start 410Win8, if necessary, and log on to the domain as **Administrator**.

11. Open a command prompt window on 410Win8, and then type **powershell** and press **Enter**. Type **Set-NetIPInterface -InterfaceAlias Ethernet -Dhcp Enabled** and press **Enter**. To set the DNS server address for DHCP, type **Set-DnsClientServerAddress -InterfaceAlias Ethernet -ResetServerAddresses** and press **Enter**.

12. Type **ipconfig /all** and press **Enter**. You see that the address 10.10.1.100 with subnet mask 255.255.0.0 was assigned. Look for the line starting with "DHCP Server"; the address is 10.10.1.2, the address of 410Server2.

13. On 410Server2, in the DHCP console, click **Address Leases**. You see the address leased to 410Win8 (see Figure 11-9).

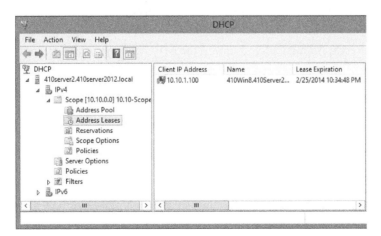

Figure 11-9   Viewing address leases

14. Stay logged on to 410Server2 and 410Win8 if you're continuing to the next activity.

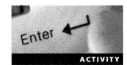

Activity 11-3: Working with Exclusions and Reservations

Time Required: 20 minutes

Objective: Create exclusion ranges and reservations and test them.

Required Tools and Equipment: 410Server2 and 410Win8

Description: In this activity, you create an exclusion range and verify that the address can't be leased. You also create a reservation for 410Win8 and verify that the reserved address is leased by 410Win8.

1. Log on to 410Win8 as **Administrator**, and open a command prompt window, if necessary. Type **ipconfig /renew** and press **Enter** to get a fresh lease on the IP address. The leased address should still be 10.10.1.100.

2. Log on to 410Server2 as **Administrator**, and open the DHCP console, if necessary. Click to expand the server node and the **IPv4** node, if necessary.

3. If necessary, click to expand the **10.10-Scope** scope you created earlier. Right-click **Address Pool** and click **New Exclusion Range**.

4. In the Start IP address text box, type **10.10.1.100**, and in the End IP address text box, type **10.10.1.105**. Click **Add** and then **Close**. Click **Address Pool** to see the exclusion range listed. You see an icon with a red ×.

5. On 410Win8, type **ipconfig /all** at the command prompt and press **Enter**. In the output, look for the "Lease Obtained" and "Lease Expires" lines under the Ethernet connection to see your lease information.

6. Type **ipconfig /renew** and press **Enter**. You'll probably see an error message indicating an error while renewing the interface. Because you excluded the address 410Win8 was using, it was unable to renew the address, but it leased a new one. Type **ipconfig** and press **Enter**. You should see that you now have the address 10.10.1.106.

7. On 410Server2, click **Address Leases** in the DHCP console. Click the **Refresh** icon if you don't see any address leases. You should see the lease for 410Win8. In the right pane, scroll to the right until you see the Unique ID column, which is the MAC address of 410Win8.

8. You can create a reservation manually or from an existing lease. To create a reservation from 410Win8's existing lease, right-click the lease in the right pane and click **Add to Reservation**. You see a message stating that the lease was converted to a reservation successfully. Click **OK**.

9. In the left pane, click **Reservations**. Right-click the new reservation in the right pane and click **Properties**. You can change the name of the reservation and the MAC address and add a description, but you can't change the IP address. If you need to change the IP address, you must delete the reservation and create a new one.

10. To create a reservation manually, you need the MAC address of the computer you're creating the reservation for. Select the MAC address of the 410Win8 reservation and copy it. Change the last character to a different hexadecimal value. This reservation no longer applies to 410Win8 because you changed the MAC address. Click **OK**.

11. In the right pane, click empty space and click **New Reservation**. In the Reservation name text box, type **410Win8**. (The reservation name is just a label and doesn't affect a reservation's function, but you can't have two reservations with the same name.)

12. In the IP address text box, Windows starts the address. Finish it by typing **1.100**. Right-click the MAC address text box and click **Paste** to paste the MAC address of 410Win8 you copied in Step 10 (see Figure 11-10, although your address will be different from the one in the figure). Click **Add** and then **Close**. Remember that 10.10.1.100 is in the excluded range you created earlier, but as you see in the next step, reservations still work even if they're in the excluded range.

Figure 11-10   Creating a reservation

13. On 410Win8, type `ipconfig /renew` at the command prompt and press **Enter**. An error message is displayed. Type `ipconfig` and press **Enter**. 410Win8 now has the address 10.10.1.100.

14. Stay logged on to 410Server2 and 410Win8 if you're continuing to the next activity.

DHCP Options

An IP address and subnet mask are the minimum settings needed for a computer to communicate on a network. However, almost every network requires a DNS server IP address for name resolution and a default gateway to communicate with other subnets and the Internet. The DHCP server can be configured to send both these addresses to DHCP clients along with the IP address and subnet mask. Many other options can be configured and might be necessary, depending on the network environment. DHCP options can be assigned at the following levels:

- *Server options*—Options configured at the server level affect all scopes but can be overridden by a scope, policy, or reservation option.

- *Scope options*—Scope options affect clients that get a lease from the scope in which the option is configured. Scope options can be overridden by reservation options or DHCP policies.

- *Policy options*—DHCP policies, a new feature in Windows Server 2012/R2, allow an administrator to assign IP address options to clients based on client properties, such as device type, MAC address, or OS. DHCP policies are discussed later in "Configuring Policies." Options specified at the policy level can be overridden only by reservation options.

- *Reservation options*—A reservation is an address associated with a computer's MAC address. When the computer with the specified MAC address requests an IP address, the DHCP server offers the reserved address and any configured options, thus ensuring that the computer is always assigned the same IP address settings. Options set on a reservation take precedence over any conflicting options set at any other level.

Common DHCP Options   DHCP options are specified in the format *NNNOptionName*, with *NNN* representing a three-digit number that uniquely identifies the option in the DHCP packet, and *OptionName* being the option's user-friendly name. Some of the most common options include the following:

- *003 Router*—This option is almost always requested by the DHCP client and supplied by the DHCP server because it configures the client's default gateway setting, which is needed for the client to communicate with other networks. This option is usually configured at the scope level because each scope has a different default gateway associated with it. If you have only one scope, you can configure it at the server level. If you use policies or reservations, you can configure the router option at these levels so that selected computers can use a different default gateway than the rest of the scope does, if needed.

- *006 DNS Servers*—This option might or might not be configured as a scope option because DNS servers often provide services for an entire internetwork. This option is often configured as a server option that applies to all scopes. However, if the option is configured on a scope, the scope option takes precedence. The DNS Servers option consists of a list of IP addresses of DNS servers the client can use for name resolution.

- *015 DNS Domain Name*—This option can also be configured as a server or scope option. It provides a domain name, such as csmtech.local, to DHCP clients. The DNS Domain Name option configures the client domain name, which a client needs when performing a DNS query with a single-label name. For example, if a user types \\Server1 in the Run dialog box, the DNS client attempts to resolve Server1 to an IP address. If no domain name is configured, the client sends the query to the DNS server as just Server1. Without a domain name, the lookup fails. However, if a domain name is configured, the DNS client software adds the domain name to the query so that the actual DNS query is sent as Server1.csmtech.local. The domain name is also used by the client when registering its computer name with the DNS server. Without a domain name that matches a zone name on the server, the registration fails. Domain members configure their DNS domain names automatically with the name of the domain they're a member of, so this option is unnecessary if all computers receiving DHCP addresses are domain members.

- *044 WINS/NBNS Servers*—This option is used only on networks with WINS servers.

- *046 WINS/NBT Node Type*—This option is used with option 044 to specify the WINS node type.

Configuring Options   Server options are configured by clicking the IPv4 or IPv6 node in the DHCP console, right-clicking Server Options, and clicking Configure Options. The Server Options dialog box has two tabs. The General tab has a list of available options in the upper pane. If you click the check box for an option, the lower pane is enabled so that you can enter information for the selected option. For example, in Figure 11-11, the 003 Router option is selected. For this option, you add one or more router addresses that clients use for their default gateway configuration.

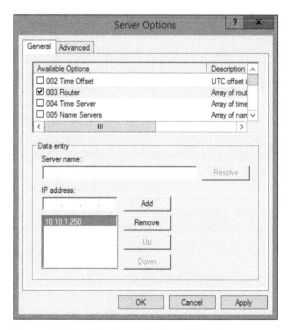

Figure 11-11   The Server Options dialog box

The Advanced tab of the Server Options dialog box has the same list of options as well as a list box to choose the **Vendor Class,** a field in the DHCP packet that device manufacturers or OS vendors use to identify a device model or an OS version. You can use this field to set different DHCP options. Starting with Windows Server 2012, the Vendor Class options should be used only when creating DHCP policies, discussed later in "Configuring Policies."

Scope and reservation options are set the same way as server options. To configure scope options, click the scope in the DHCP console, and then right-click Scope Options in the right pane and click Configure Options. To configure reservation options, right-click a reservation and click Configure Options. You can configure different options for each reservation.

Activity 11-4: Configuring DHCP Options

Time Required: 10 minutes
Objective: Configure router and DNS server options.

Required Tools and Equipment: 410Server2 and 410Win8
Description: You have the scope configured and tested. Now you need to add router and DNS server options so that clients are fully functional. First, you configure the 003 Router and 006 DNS Servers options in the scope, and then you configure a different value for the 006 DNS Servers option in the reservation so that you can see reservation options take precedence over scope options.

1. Log on to 410Server2 as **Administrator,** and open the DHCP console, if necessary. Click to expand the server node and the **IPv4** node, if necessary.

2. Click the **10.10-Scope** scope. In the right pane, right-click **Scope Options** and click **Configure Options.**

3. In the Scope Options dialog box, click the **003 Router** check box. In the lower pane, type **10.10.1.250** (or another value if required for your network) in the IP address text box, and click **Add.**

4. In the upper pane, click the **006 DNS Servers** check box. Type **10.10.1.1** in the IP address text box, and click **Add.** Windows attempts to validate the address. (If 410Server1 isn't running, you see a message stating that the address is not a valid DNS address and asking whether you still want to add it. Click **Yes.**) Click **OK.**

5. In the DHCP console, double-click **Scope Options** in the right pane. You see the two options you just configured.

6. On 410Win8, log on as **Administrator,** and open a command prompt window, if necessary. Type **ipconfig /renew** and press **Enter.** You see that the default gateway is set to 10.10.1.250. Type **ipconfig /all** and press **Enter.** The DNS Servers line under the Ethernet connection should be set to 10.10.1.1.

7. On 410Server2, click to expand **Reservations,** if necessary. Right-click the **410Win8** reservation and click **Configure Options.**

8. Click the **006 DNS Servers** check box. Type **10.10.1.2** in the IP address text box, and click **Add.** Click **Yes** in the message box, and click **OK.**

9. On 410Win8, type **ipconfig /renew** and press **Enter,** and then type **ipconfig /all** and press **Enter.** The DNS Servers line under the Ethernet connection should be set to 10.10.1.2 because the reservation option takes precedence over the scope option.

10. On 410Server2, click **Reservations** in the left pane, if necessary. For each of the two reservations, right-click the reservation and click **Delete,** and then click **Yes** to confirm.

11. Stay logged on to 410Server2 and 410Win8 if you're continuing to the next activity.

DHCP Server Configuration

You can perform several DHCP server configuration tasks in the DHCP console. The options you can change depend on whether you right-click the topmost node with the server name or the IPv4 or IPv6 nodes. If you right-click the server node, you see a menu listing the tasks you can perform, most of which are described in the following list:

- *Add/Remove Bindings*—This option is useful on multihomed servers. If the DHCP server has two or more network connections, you might not always want it to respond to DHCP packets from all networks, as when one network is connected to the Internet. You can enable or disable the binding for each interface (see Figure 11-12). When a binding is disabled, it prevents the server from listening on DHCP server port UDP 67.

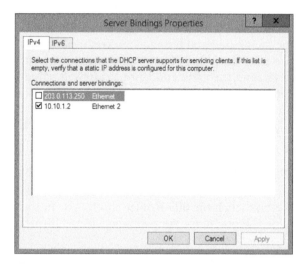

Figure 11-12   The Server Bindings Properties dialog box

- *Backup*—You can back up the DHCP database, which is stored in %*systemroot*%\System32\dhcp\dhcp.mdb. The backup is stored in %*systemroot*%\System32\dhcp\backup\DhcpCfg by default, but you're prompted to change the path if needed. After you select a path, the DHCP database is backed up, including all scopes, options, exclusion ranges, reservations, and leases.

- *Restore*—If you need to restore a backup of the DHCP database, perhaps after database corruption caused by a system crash, choose this option and the path to the most current backup. When you restore the database, the DHCP server is stopped and restarted after the restore is finished. You should then reconcile the scopes, which you do by right-clicking the IPv4 or IPv6 node in the DHCP console and clicking Reconcile All Scopes. You can also reconcile a scope separately by right-clicking it and clicking Reconcile.

- *All Tasks*—If you point to All Tasks, you have the option to start, stop, pause, resume, or restart the DHCP server service.

- *Delete*—Deletes the server from the console but doesn't actually uninstall the DHCP Server role.

- *Refresh*—Refreshes the view.

- *Properties*—Opens the Properties dialog box for the DHCP server, where you can change the default database path and backup path.

The IPv4 and IPv6 nodes have many of the same options, but several are found only in the IPv4 mode. Right-click the IPv4 node to see the menu options described in the following list:

- *Display Statistics*—This option displays statistics about the server and DHCP transactions (see Figure 11-13) that can be useful in troubleshooting problems. For example, a lot of Nacks can indicate an incorrect configuration, such as a corrupt or deactivated scope. A lot of Declines can indicate IP address conflicts. If a DHCP client finds that the leased IP address is in use, it sends a DHCPDECLINE and requests another address.

Figure 11-13   Server statistics

- *New Scope*—Starts the New Scope Wizard.

- *New Superscope*—Starts the New Superscope Wizard. This option is available only under the IPv4 node because IPv6 doesn't support superscopes.

- *New Multicast Scope*—Starts the New Multicast Scope Wizard. A multicast scope assigns multicast addresses to client applications that require multicast addresses. This option is available only under the IPv4 node because IPv6 doesn't support multicast scopes. Configuring multicast scopes is covered in *MCSA Guide to Configuring Advanced Windows Server 2012/R2 Services, Exam 70-412* (Cengage Learning, 2015).

- *Configure Failover* and *Replicate Failover Scopes*—These options configure high availability for DHCP services. You can configure fault tolerance and load balancing of DHCP services by allowing two DHCP servers to provide IP address and DHCP option information for the same scopes. The servers replicate configuration and lease information with each other to ensure that both servers have current data for leasing IP addresses to clients. Configuring high availability for DHCP is covered in *MCSA Guide to Configuring Advanced Windows Server 2012/R2 Services, Exam 70-412* (Cengage Learning, 2015). Failover isn't an option in IPv6.

- *Define User Classes* and *Define Vendor Classes*—These options are used to define User Class and Vendor Class values that can be used in DHCP policies.

- *Reconcile All Scopes*—If the lease information shown in the DHCP console doesn't seem to reflect the actual client leases or if the database appears corrupted, use this option to try to solve the problem. It attempts to fix inconsistencies between DHCP summary lease information stored in the Registry and detailed lease information stored in the DHCP database. If no problems are found, DHCP reports that the database is consistent. If inconsistencies are found, the inconsistent addresses are listed in the Reconcile All Scopes dialog box (see Figure 11-14). Select the addresses listed and click Reconcile. The reconcile process restores an inconsistent address to the original DHCP client or creates a temporary reservation for the address. With a temporary reservation, when the lease time expires or a renewal attempt is made, the address is returned to the scope. This option isn't available for IPv6 scopes.

Figure 11-14 Viewing inconsistent addresses in the DHCP database

- *Set Predefined Options*—Using this selection, you can create custom DHCP options. One use is to create the 060 PXEClient option required for some configurations of Windows Deployment Services (WDS), discussed later in "Configuring DHCP for PXE Boot." Some specialized IP devices, such as Voice over IP (VoIP) phones, might also require custom options.

- *Properties*—This option opens the Properties dialog box for the IPv4 server, discussed next.

Configuring IPv4 Server Properties

The IPv4 Properties dialog box has these six tabs:

- *General*—Specify statistics and logging parameters (see Figure 11-15). In addition, if you enable the "Show the BOOTP table folder" option, a new folder is added under the IPv4 node in the DHCP console so that you can configure BOOTP support. BOOTP is a remote boot protocol that devices use to boot from an image stored on a server.

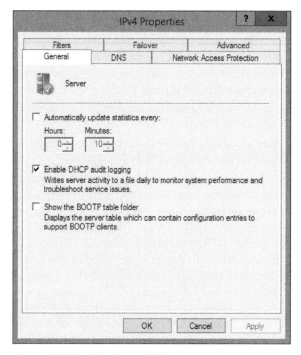

Figure 11-15 The General tab

- *DNS*—Configure how DHCP interacts with a DNS server for making dynamic updates on behalf of DHCP clients (see Figure 11-16). You can configure the following settings:

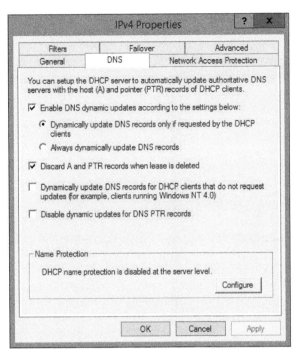

Figure 11-16   The DNS tab

> o Dynamically update DNS records only if requested by the DHCP clients: This option is the default. When a client leases an IP address or renews a lease and sends option 81 in the DHCPREQUEST packet, the DHCP server attempts to register records dynamically with the DNS server on behalf of the client. Option 81 in the DHCPREQUEST packet contains the client's FQDN. By default, Windows clients configure option 81 so that the client updates its own A record and requests that the server update the PTR record.
>
> o Always dynamically update DNS records: If this option is set, the DHCP server always attempts to register A and PTR records for the client as long as the client supports option 81.
>
> o Discard A and PTR records when lease is deleted: If a lease is deleted and this option is selected (the default), the DHCP server attempts to contact the DNS server to delete the A and PTR records associated with the lease.
>
> o Dynamically update DNS records for DHCP clients that do not request updates: If a client doesn't support option 81 (you have to go all the way back to Windows NT 4.0 for Windows clients that don't support it), and this option is set, the server attempts to register DNS records on the client's behalf.
>
> o Disable dynamic updates for DNS PTR records: If set, the DHCP server doesn't attempt to register PTR records for DHCP clients.
>
> o Name Protection: Click the Configure button to enable name protection. When enabled, the DHCP server doesn't register A and PTR records if a DNS record with a different name already exists. Secure dynamic updates on the DNS server must be enabled for name protection to work.

- *Network Access Protection*—Enable or disable Network Access Protection (NAP) on all scopes. NAP is discussed in *MCSA Guide to Administering Windows Server 2012/R2, Exam 70-411* (Cengage Learning, 2015).

- *Filters*—In this tab (see Figure 11-17), you can configure MAC address filters to allow or deny DHCP services to computers based on their MAC addresses. You can only enable or disable the allow or deny list. To configure the lists, you use the Filters node under the IPv4 node. If you click the Advanced button, you can select from a list of hardware types to exempt from filtering.

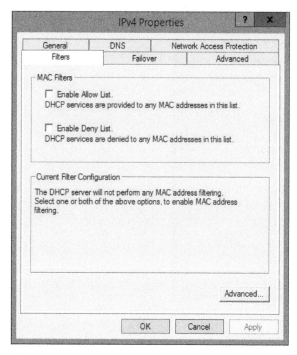

Figure 11-17   The Filters tab

- *Failover*—Configure and view failover status, if configured.
- *Advanced*—In this tab (see Figure 11-18), you configure the following options:

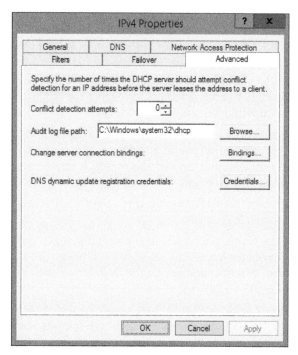

Figure 11-18   The Advanced tab

o Conflict detection attempts: If enabled, **conflict detection** causes the DHCP server to attempt to ping an IP address before it offers an address to a client to ensure that the address isn't already in use. Conflict detection attempts can be set between 0 and 5, which specifies how many `ping` packets the server should send before assuming the address isn't in use. By default, conflict detection attempts are set to 0, which disables conflict detection. In most cases, the server never sends a `ping` packet because it must first send an ARP to get a MAC address, unless it has an entry for the IP address in its ARP cache already. In any case, the DHCP server must time out between attempts before trying another attempt or proceeding with the release, which slows down the DHCP lease process. Because most client computers do conflict detection before accepting an offered address, conflict detection should be enabled on the DHCP server only if the server is receiving many DHCPDECLINE messages. After the problem is remedied, conflict detection should be disabled.

o Audit log file path: You can change the default path for the audit log file.

o Change server connection bindings: Clicking the Bindings button performs the same function as the Add/Remove Bindings option you see when you right-click the server node, discussed earlier.

o DNS dynamic update registration credentials: If you click the Credentials button, you can enter the username, domain name, and password for a domain account that has permission to send dynamic updates. Configuring credentials is needed only if the DHCP service is running on a domain controller and secure dynamic DNS update is enabled.

The IPv6 Properties dialog box has only the General, DNS, and Advanced tabs, with largely the same configuration options as these tabs in the IPv4 Properties dialog box.

Configuring Scope Properties

To access a scope's properties, right-click it and click Properties. The Scope Properties dialog box has four tabs:

- *General*—In the General tab (see Figure 11-19), you can change the scope name and the start and end IP addresses, but you can't change the subnet mask (prefix length). You can also change the lease duration, which by default is 8 days. This duration is fine for a typical office environment, where the same computers are used each day. Having a long lease

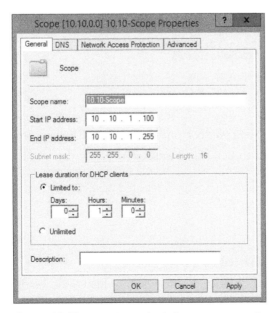

Figure 11-19 The General tab for scope properties

duration prevents unnecessary traffic from frequent lease renewals. However, you might want a shorter lease time in a less predictable environment where lots of computers are used for brief periods and then not used again for long periods or ever, as in a testing or training environment that uses a lot of virtual machines. Another example is a wireless network in a public setting, where mobile devices come and go constantly. Another reason to set a short lease duration is that you're planning to make changes to the IP addressing scheme that require a major scope change. As the time for the change approaches, you can make the lease time shorter and shorter until it's less than a day. You can make the scope change overnight or over a weekend, and the short lease time ensures that all clients need to renew their lease in a short period. Renewal requests are denied; instead, clients are assigned addresses from the new scope.

- *DNS*—This tab contains the same dynamic DNS configuration options as the DNS tab in the IPv4 Properties dialog box, discussed earlier, but it pertains to only a single scope rather than all scopes.

- *Network Access Protection*—Enable or disable NAP on the scope.

- *Advanced*—Configure which type of clients the server responds to (see Figure 11-20):

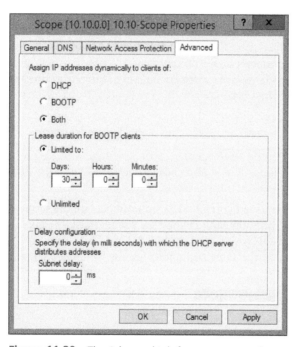

Figure 11-20   The Advanced tab for scope properties

  o DHCP: The default setting; the server responds only to DHCP client requests.

  o BOOTP: The server responds to BOOTP clients.

If the BOOTP or Both option is selected, you can choose a maximum lease duration for BOOTP clients.

  o Both: The server responds to DHCP and BOOTP clients.

  o Delay configuration: You can set a delay, specified in milliseconds, before the server responds to DHCPDISCOVER messages. This option is useful in split scope configurations, discussed earlier, and is configured automatically by the split scope wizard.

Configuring Filters

DHCP filters allow administrators to restrict which computers on a network are leased IP addresses. Filters use MAC addresses as the filtering criteria, so it's a simple allow or deny permission based on a client's MAC address. Filters are configured under the IPv4 node and aren't available for IPv6 DHCP. To set a filter, click Filters under the IPv4 node, and then right-click Allow or Deny and click New Filter. In the New Filter dialog box, you add each MAC address you want to allow or deny, along with an optional description for each address. After the addresses are added, you enable the filter.

If you create an allow filter, only a device with a MAC address in the filter list can lease an IP address from the DHCP server. All other devices are denied. If you create a deny filter, all devices except those with a MAC address in the filter list can lease an address from the DHCP server.

You can add addresses to the allow or deny filter from the list of current address leases, instead of manually adding each address. To do so, click Address Leases under a scope, select one or more addresses you want to add to a filter, right-click a selected address, point to Add to Filter, and click Allow or Deny to add the selected addresses to the filter.

Activity 11-5: Creating a DHCP Filter

Time Required: 10 minutes
Objective: Create a DHCP filter.

Required Tools and Equipment: 410Server2 and 410Win8
Description: You need to lock down your DHCP server so that only known computers can receive an IP configuration, so you decide to configure DHCP allow and deny filters. First, you create an allow filter manually, and then you create a deny filter from an existing lease.

1. Log on to 410Server2 as **Administrator**, and open the DHCP console, if necessary. Click to expand the server node and the **IPv4** node, if necessary.

2. Click **Filters**. In the right pane, right-click **Allow** and click **New Filter**. In the New Filter dialog box, type **123456789012** in the MAC address text box. In the Description text box, type **Sample filter**, and then click **Add**. Click **Close**.

3. In the left pane, click **Allow** to see the new filter. Notice that the Allow node has a red down arrow, indicating the scope isn't enabled.

4. Click to expand the **10.10-Scope** scope, and then click **Address Leases**. In the right pane, right-click the lease for 410Win8, point to **Add to Filter**, and click **Deny** to add 410Win8's MAC address to the deny filter.

5. Click the **Deny** filter to see the new entry for 410Win8. (You might need to click the Refresh icon.) Right-click the **Deny** filter and click **Enable**.

6. On 410Win8, log on as **Administrator**, and open a command prompt window, if necessary. Type **ipconfig /renew** and press Enter. After a while, you see an error message stating that the address couldn't be renewed. Type **ipconfig** and press Enter. Because the lease hasn't expired, 410Win8 still has its IP address. The deny filter keeps clients from getting a new address or renewing an address, but it doesn't prevent them from keeping an address already leased.

7. Type **ipconfig /release** and press Enter, and then type **ipconfig /renew** and press Enter. 410Win8 is unable to lease an IP address.

8. On 411Server1, in the DHCP console, right-click the **Deny** filter and click **Disable**. Right-click the **Allow** filter and click **Disable**.

9. On 410Win8, type **ipconfig /renew** and press Enter. 410Win8 can lease an address again.

10. Stay logged on to 410Server2 and 410Win8 if you're continuing to the next activity.

Configuring Policies

DHCP policies, a new feature in Windows Server 2012, give administrators more fine-tuned control over address lease options with conditions. A policy contains conditions that specify one or more clients that IP address settings should be delivered to. Conditions can be based on a number of criteria, and more than one criteria can be used in a condition with AND and OR operators. You can create policy conditions with any combination of the following criteria:

- *Vendor Class*—Defined earlier, the Vendor Class is most often used by device or OS manufacturers to identify a type of device or OS. Vendor Classes can be used to identify VoIP phones, printers, mobile devices, and so forth. For example, you can create the condition "Vendor Class equals Hewlett-Packard JetDirect" to identify all HP printers.

 Finding the Vendor Class in a device's documentation can be difficult. One way to discover this information is to set up the device on the network, configure it to use DHCP, and then capture the DHCP packets it transmits with a protocol analyzer, such as Wireshark. The Vendor Class is in the DHCPDISCOVER packet in the Option 60 field.

- *User Class*—Similar to the Vendor Class, except a **User Class** can be a custom value you create on the DHCP server and then configure on a DHCP client. For example, if you have special settings you want the DHCP server to deliver to all computers in the Engineering Department, you can create a User Class named "Engineering," and then configure the network interface on the relevant computers with this User Class. To configure a User Class on a Windows computer, type ipconfig /setclassid Ethernet "Engineering", which sets the User Class on the Ethernet network connection to "Engineering."

- *MAC address*—You can use wildcards with a list of MAC addresses so that you can use the organizationally unique identifier (OUI) part of the MAC address to specify a manufacturer. The OUI is the first 24 bits of a MAC address. For example, you can create the condition "MAC address equals 000F34*" to identify certain types of Cisco routers.

- *Client identifier*—The client identifier (ClientID) is usually the MAC address but can also be the GUID of the NIC on a PXE client.

- *Fully qualified domain name*—You can use an FQDN in a condition, starting with Windows Server 2012 R2. An FQDN can be used only to configure DNS-related configuration information, such as dynamic DNS registration. You can use this criterion to match computers based on their FQDNs and use wildcards to group computers based on their hostnames or DNS suffixes. For example, you can create a condition such as "Fully qualified domain name equals *.csmtech.local," which matches computers with an FQDN ending with csmtech.local. You can also use this criterion to identify workgroup computers (computers that aren't domain members).

- *Relay agent information*—This criterion is useful when a wireless access point acts as a DHCP relay, sending DHCP requests to the DHCP server on behalf of wireless clients. You can assign wireless clients' IP addresses with a shorter lease time and perhaps a different default gateway and DNS server. To create a condition based on relay agent information (DHCP option 82), you enter a hexadecimal code provided by the relay agent's manufacturer.

Policies can be configured at the server level or the scope level. Scope-level policies take precedence over server-level policies if both are configured and there's a conflict. Server-level policies are limited to assigning DHCP options and lease duration to clients matching the policy conditions. Scope-level policies can also issue IP addresses from a specified range to matching clients. For example, if the scope has the start address 10.1.1.1 and end address 10.1.1.254 with the prefix length 24, the policy can specify that all matching clients are issued an address in the range 10.1.1.100 through 10.1.1.150. To create a policy, just right-click the Policies node under the IPv4 node or the scope and click New Policy to start the DHCP Policy Configuration Wizard. Then follow these steps:

1. Give the policy a name and optionally a description.
2. Create one or more conditions that identify devices.

3. Configure settings for the policy, such as router and DNS servers.

4. Configure additional settings in the policy's Properties dialog box. You can configure lease time and DNS settings and make changes to other settings that were configured in the wizard.

Activity 11-6: Creating a DHCP Policy

Time Required: 10 minutes
Objective: Create a DHCP policy.

Required Tools and Equipment: 410Server2 and 410Win8
Description: You have new Cisco VoIP phones that require different IP address settings than the rest of the devices on the network do. You decide to create a policy to deliver different options to these phones. In this activity, you create a new User Class so that you can test the policy with your 410Win8 computer. In a real situation, the phones would have a defined Vendor Class, so if you were doing this for actual Cisco IP phones, you would replace User Class with Vendor Class wherever you see it in this activity.

1. Log on to 410Server2 as **Administrator**, and open the DHCP console, if necessary. Click to expand the server node and the **IPv4** node, if necessary.

2. To create a new User Class, right-click the **IPv4** node and click **Define User Classes**. In the DHCP User Classes dialog box, click **Add**. In the New Class dialog box, type **Cisco IP Phone** in the Display name text box and **Cisco Voice over IP phones** in the Description text box.

3. In the lower pane of the New Class dialog box, click in the box under ASCII and type **Cisco IP Phone** (see Figure 11-21). This is the actual Vendor Class ID used by DHCP; the display name might not be the same. Click **OK** and then **Close**.

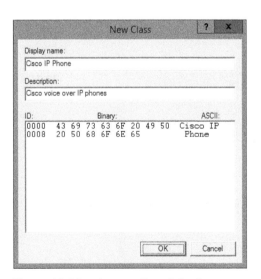

Figure 11-21   The New Class dialog box

4. Under the IPv4 node, right-click **Policies** and click **New Policy**. In the DHCP Policy Configuration Wizard, type **Cisco VoIP Policy** and click **Next**.

5. In the "Configure Conditions for the policy" window (see Figure 11-22), click **Add**.

6. In the Add/Edit Condition dialog box, click the arrow to see the available criteria in the Criteria list box, and click **User Class**. In the Operator list box, you have the choice of Equals or Not Equals. Leave the default setting **Equals**.

Figure 11-22 The "Configure Conditions for the policy" window

7. In the Value(s) section, click the **Value** list arrow and click **Cisco IP Phone**. Because there might be different models of Cisco IP phones, click the **Append wildcard** check box so that the condition is "User Class Equals Cisco IP Phone*," meaning any string can come after "Phone," and the User Class will match (see Figure 11-23). Click **Add,** and then click **Ok.**

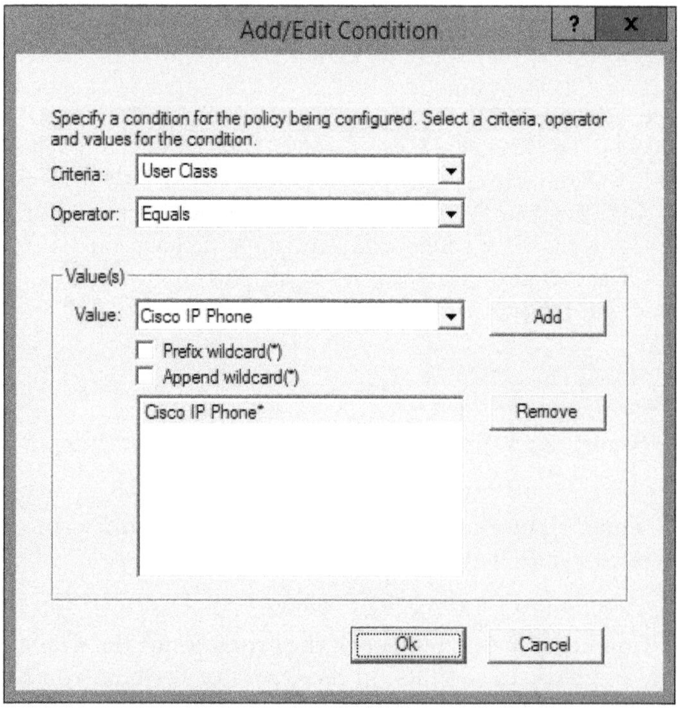

Figure 11-23 Adding a condition

8. In the "Configure Conditions for the policy" window, you see the line "User Class Equals Cisco IP Phone*." You can add conditions, if needed. Leave the **OR** option button selected, and click **Next**. In the next window, where you're asked whether you want to configure an IP address range for the policy, click the **No** option button, and then click **Next**.

9. In the "Configure settings for the policy" window, you select the DHCP options you want to apply to the selected devices. You might want a different default gateway for these devices, so click the **003 Router** check box. Type **10.10.1.251** in the IP address text box, and click **Add**. Click **Next**.

10. In the Summary window, check your settings and click **Finish**.

11. If necessary, click **Policies** in the DHCP console. In the right pane, right-click the **Cisco VoIP Policy** and click **Properties**. In this dialog box, you can change existing settings and configure lease duration and dynamic DNS settings. Click **Set lease duration for the policy**. Because phones are on all the time, you might want a longer lease duration for these devices. Type **30** in the Days text box, and click **OK**. Policies are enabled by default, so it's ready to start serving options for Cisco IP phones.

12. On 410Win8, open a command prompt window, if necessary. Type `ipconfig /setclassid Ethernet "Cisco IP Phone 2640"` and press **Enter** to set the User Class ID on the Ethernet interface to Cisco IP Phone 2640. Because the policy says to match Cisco IP Phone*, it should match.

13. When you change the class ID on a PC, it attempts to renew IP address settings automatically, so type `ipconfig /all` and press **Enter** to see the new settings. Look for the Default Gateway line, which should now be 10.10.1.251. The Lease Expires line should be 30 days from now, and the DHCPv4 Class ID line should be set to Cisco IP Phone 2640.

14. To delete the class ID and get IP settings from the regular scope, type `ipconfig /setclassid Ethernet` and press **Enter**. Because you didn't enter a class ID, it's set to blank. Type `ipconfig /all` and press **Enter** to see that your settings are back to normal.

15. Log off or shut down 410Server2 and 410Win8.

Configuring DHCP for PXE Boot

If you're using Windows Deployment Services (WDS) to install Windows OSs on computers, you might need to configure DHCP to respond to **Preboot Execution Environment (PXE)** network interfaces. PXE is a network environment built into many NICs that allows a computer to boot from an image stored on a network server. WDS uses this feature to install the Windows OS remotely. In many cases, when you configure the WDS role service, the DHCP configuration is handled by the WDS configuration wizard, but in some circumstances, you need to configure DHCP options manually.

If a Microsoft DHCP server and WDS are on the same server and all potential WDS clients are on the same network as the WDS server, you don't have to change any DHCP settings. However, if the DHCP server is on a different server or a different subnet, you do. Here are the most commons setups that require special DHCP configuration:

- *The DHCP server is on a different server or a different subnet from the WDS server*—You must configure two DHCP server options. For Option 066 Boot Server Host Name, you can supply the WDS server's IP address or server name. Option 067 Bootfile Name is the name and path of the boot file WDS clients need to start remote OS installation.

- *DHCP is installed on the same server as WDS, but it's not a Microsoft DHCP server or the Microsoft DHCP server is installed after WDS was installed*—In this case, you need to configure a predefined DHCP option (discussed earlier in "DHCP Server Configuration") with code 060. Add the 060 PXEClient option to the DHCP server by right-clicking the IPv4 node in the DHCP console and clicking Set Predefined Options. Click Add, and then fill in the dialog box as shown in Figure 11-24. Type the WDS server's IP address or name in the String text box, and click OK. Under the IPv4 node, right-click Server Options and click Configure Options, and then click 060 PXEClient. When PXE clients request an IP address, this option instructs them to contact the specified WDS server to get their boot configuration.

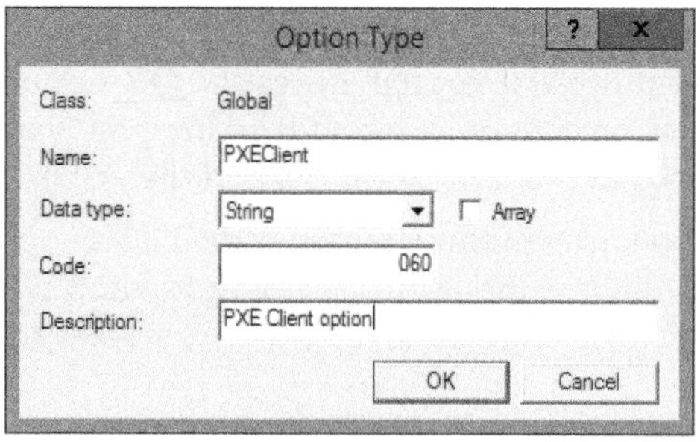

Figure 11-24   Creating the PXEClient option

DHCP Relay Agents

A **DHCP relay agent** is a device that listens for broadcast DHCPDISCOVER and DHCPREQUEST messages and forwards them to a DHCP server on another subnet. You configure a DHCP relay agent on a subnet that doesn't have a DHCP server so that you can still manage DHCP addresses from a central server without having to configure the DHCP server with network interfaces in each subnet. In this setup, a DHCP server is configured on one subnet and has multiple scopes configured, one for each subnet in the internetwork that has DHCP clients (as shown in Figure 11-25). This figure shows three subnets. The DHCP server in the 10.1.1.0/24 subnet has three scopes configured, one for each of the three subnets. When a DHCP client in the 10.1.2.0 or 10.1.3.0 subnet requests an IP address, the DHCP relay agent in the same subnet forwards the request to the DHCP server on the 10.1.1.0 subnet.

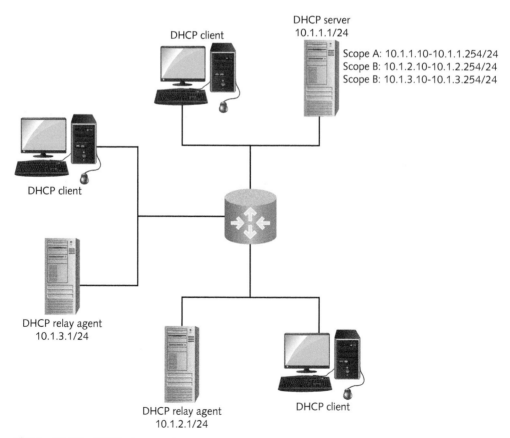

Figure 11-25   DHCP relay agents

Most commercial routers can be configured as DHCP relay agents, eliminating the need to configure a Windows server as a relay agent in each subnet.

The details of the DHCP relay process are as follows:

1. A client on the same subnet as the DHCP relay agent sends a DHCPDISCOVER broadcast requesting an IP address.

2. The relay agent forwards the message to the DHCP server's IP address as a unicast.

3. The DHCP server receives the unicast DHCPDISCOVER. The relay agent's address is contained in the message, so the DHCP server knows to draw an address from the scope matching the relay agent's IP address. For example, if the relay agent has the address 10.1.2.10, the DHCP server looks for a scope containing a range of addresses that includes 10.1.2.10.

4. The DHCP server sends a unicast DHCPOFFER message to the relay agent.

5. The relay agent forwards the DHCPOFFER as a broadcast to the subnet the DHCPDISCOVER was received from. Because the client doesn't yet have an IP address, the agent must forward the DHCPOFFER as a broadcast message.

6. The DHCP client broadcasts a DHCPREQUEST.

7. The relay agent receives the DHCPREQUEST and forwards it to the DHCP server.

8. The DHCP server replies with a DHCPACK to the relay agent.

9. The relay agent forwards the DHCPACK to the client, and the client binds the address to its interface.

10. Renewal requests are unicast packets, so the DHCP client can communicate directly with the DHCP server for renewals.

Installing a DHCP Relay Agent

The DHCP relay agent function is configured as part of the Routing role service under the Remote Access server role. To make a Windows Server 2012/R2 server a DHCP relay agent, follow these steps:

1. Install the Remote Access server role and include the Routing role service.

2. In the Routing and Remote Access console, right-click the server node and click Configure and Enable Routing and Remote Access.

3. In the Routing and Remote Access Server Setup Wizard, click Next, and then click Custom configuration.

4. In the Custom Configuration window, click the LAN routing check box (see Figure 11-26). Click Next and then Finish. Click Start service when prompted.

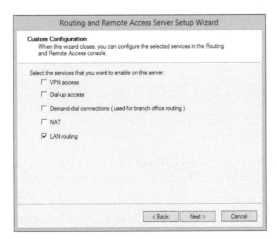

Figure 11-26   The Custom Configuration window

5. In the Routing and Remote Access console, expand the IPv4 node, and then right-click the General node and click New Routing Protocol. If necessary, click DHCP Relay Agent. If you have more than one interface, you see other options in addition to DHCP Relay Agent. Click OK.

6. In the Routing and Remote Access console, right-click DHCP Relay Agent and click New Interface. Click the interface you want the server to provide relay services on, and click OK. If the server has more than one network connection, you can add interfaces.

7. In the DHCP Relay Properties dialog box, accept the default settings (see Figure 11-27), and click OK.

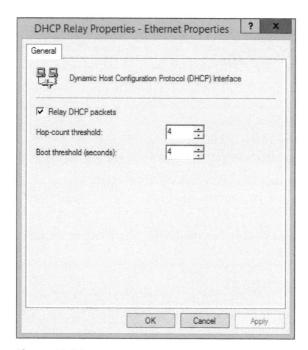

Figure 11-27   Setting DHCP relay properties

8. In the Routing and Remote Access console, right-click DHCP Relay Agent and click Properties. Type the address of the DHCP server the relay agent should forward DHCP messages to, and then click Add. You can add more than one address if you're using load balancing. Click OK. The relay agent is configured to send DHCP messages to the specified IP address.

   A DHCP server can't be configured as a DHCP relay agent.

Activity 11-7: Uninstalling the DHCP Server Role

Time Required: 10 minutes
Objective: Uninstall the DHCP server role.

Required Tools and Equipment: 410Server2 and 410Win8
Description: You're finished working with DHCP, so you uninstall the role and set 410Win8's IP address back to a static address.

1. Log on to 410Server2 as **Administrator**, if necessary. Open Server Manager, and uninstall the DHCP Server role with the default options.

2. Log on to 410Win8 as **Administrator**, if necessary. Configure 410Win8's network interface to use the following IP address settings:

IP address: 10.10.1.10
Subnet mask: 255.255.0.0
Default gateway: 10.10.1.250 (or an address that works for your network)
Primary DNS server: 10.10.1.1

3. Log off or shut down 410Win8 and 410Server2.

Chapter Summary

- Dynamic Host Configuration Protocol (DHCP) is a component of the TCP/IP protocol suite that's used to assign an IP address to a host automatically from a defined pool of addresses. IP addresses assigned via DHCP are usually leased, not permanently assigned. DHCP is a client/server protocol.

- The process of a DHCP client requesting an IP address and a DHCP server fulfilling the request is actually a four-packet sequence of broadcasts: DHCPDISCOVER, DHCPOFFER, DHCPREQUEST, and DHCPACK. DHCP uses the UDP Transport-layer protocol on ports 67 and 68. Port 67 is used for sending data from the client to the server, and port 68 is for sending data from the server to the client. There are eight DHCP message types.

- The DHCP service is installed as a server role named DHCP Server; it has no role service components. A DHCP server must be authorized on a domain network before it can begin providing services.

- A DHCP scope is a pool of IP addresses and other IP configuration parameters that a DHCP server uses to lease addresses to DHCP clients. An exclusion range consists of one or more addresses in the scope that the DHCP server doesn't lease to clients. A reservation is an IP address associated with the MAC address of a DHCP client to ensure that when the client requests an IP address, it always gets the same one, along with any configured options.

- A split scope is a fault-tolerant DHCP configuration in which two DHCP servers share the same scope information, allowing both servers to offer DHCP services to clients. A superscope is a special type of scope consisting of one or more member scopes that allows a DHCP server to service multiple IPv4 subnets on a single physical network.

- Almost every network requires a DNS server's IP address for name resolution and a default gateway to communicate with other subnets and the Internet. The DHCP server can be configured to send both these addresses to DHCP clients along with the IP address and subnet mask. DHCP options can be assigned at these levels: server, scope, policy, and reservation.

- Server options are configured in the DHCP console. Scope and reservation options are the same as server options.

- You can perform several DHCP server configuration tasks in the DHCP console. The options you can change depend on whether you right-click the topmost node with the server name or the IPv4 or IPv6 nodes. Server configuration tasks include adding or removing bindings, backing up and restoring, creating scopes, configuring failover, reconciling scopes, setting predefined options, and configuring properties.

- The IPv4 server properties include statistics and logging parameters, dynamic DNS configuration, NAP configuration, filters, conflict detection, and configuration of DNS registration credentials. Configuring scope properties includes scope name and address range, dynamic DNS configuration, and DHCP/BOOTP configuration.

- DHCP filters allow administrators to restrict which computers on a network are leased an IP address based on the client MAC address.

- DHCP policies, a new feature in Windows Server 2012, give you more fine-tuned control of address lease options than you have with server, scope, and reservation options. Policies can be configured based on criteria such as Vendor Class, User Class, MAC address, client identifier, FQDN, and relay agent information.

■ If you're using Windows Deployment Services to install Windows OSs on computers, you might need to configure DHCP to respond to Preboot Execution Environment network interfaces.

■ A DHCP relay agent is a device that listens for broadcast DHCPDISCOVER and DHCPREQUEST messages and forwards them to a DHCP server on another subnet. It's configured as part of the Routing role service under the Remote Access server role.

Key Terms

conflict detection   A DHCP server property that causes the DHCP server to attempt to ping an IP address before it's offered to a client to make sure the address isn't already in use.

DHCP filter   A DHCP server feature that allows administrators to restrict which computers on a network are leased IP addresses.

DHCP policies   A new feature in Windows Server 2012 that gives administrators more fine-tuned control over address lease options with conditions based on criteria.

DHCP relay agent   A device that listens for broadcast DHCPDISCOVER and DHCPREQUEST messages and forwards them to a DHCP server on another subnet.

DHCP scope   A pool of IP addresses and optionally other IP configuration parameters from which a DHCP server leases addresses to DHCP clients.

DHCP server authorization   The process of enabling a DHCP server in a domain environment to prevent rogue DHCP servers from operating on the network.

Dynamic Host Configuration Protocol (DHCP)   A component of the TCP/IP protocol suite used to assign an IP address to a host automatically from a defined pool of addresses.

exclusion range   A range of addresses in the scope that the DHCP server doesn't lease to clients.

lease duration   A parameter of a DHCP IP address lease that specifies how long a DHCP client can keep an address.

lease renewal   The process of a DHCP client renewing its IP address lease by using unicast DHCPREQUEST messages.

Preboot Execution Environment (PXE)   A network environment built into many NICs that allows a computer to boot from an image stored on a network server.

reservation   An IP address associated with a DHCP client's MAC address to ensure that when the client requests an IP address, it always gets the same one, along with any configured options.

split scope   A fault-tolerant DHCP configuration in which two DHCP servers share the same scope information, allowing both servers to offer DHCP services to clients.

superscope   A special type of scope consisting of one or more member scopes; it allows a DHCP server to service multiple IP subnets on a single physical network.

User Class   A custom value you create on the DHCP server and then configure on a DHCP client; used much like the Vendor Class value.

Vendor Class   A field in the DHCP packet that device manufacturers or OS vendors can use to identify a device model or an OS version.

Review Questions

1. Which of the following is true about the DHCP protocol? (Choose all that apply.)

   a. There are eight message types.

   b. DHCPDISCOVER messages sent by clients traverse routers.

   c. It uses the UDP Transport-layer protocol.

   d. An initial address lease involves three packets.

2. You have a DHCP server set up on your network and no DHCP relay agents. You're capturing DHCP packets with a protocol analyzer and see a broadcast packet with UDP source port 68 and UDP destination port 67. Which of the following DHCP message types can the packet be?

    a. A DHCPREQUEST to renew an IP address lease

    b. A DHCPACK to acknowledge an IP address lease request

    c. A DHCPDISCOVER to request an IP address

    d. A DHCPOFFER to offer an IP address lease

3. In the DHCP server's statistics, you notice that a lot of DHCPNAK packets have been transmitted. What's the most likely reason?

    a. You changed the range of addresses in a scope recently.

    b. The DHCP server has been taken offline.

    c. The server is offering a lot of addresses that are already in use.

    d. Client computers are getting multiple offers when they request an address.

4. You have configured your computers with static IP addresses but want them to get the DNS server and default gateway settings via DHCP. What type of DHCP message do you see as a result?

    a. DHCPREQUEST

    b. DHCPRELEASE

    c. DHCPNAK

    d. DHCPINFORM

5. After you install the DHCP Server role on a member server, what must you do before the server can begin providing DHCP services?

    a. Configure options.

    b. Activate the server.

    c. Authorize the server.

    d. Create a filter.

6. Which of the following is a required element of a DHCP scope? (Choose all that apply.)

    a. Subnet mask

    b. Scope name

    c. Router address

    d. Lease duration

7. What's the default lease duration on a Windows DHCP server?

    a. 8 hours

    b. 16 minutes

    c. 8 days

    d. 16 hours

8. IP addresses can be leased for an unlimited period. True or False?

9. What should you define in a scope to prevent the DHCP server from leasing addresses that are already assigned to devices statically?

    a. Reservation scope

    b. Exclusion range

    c. Deny filters

    d. DHCP policy

10. You have four printers that are accessed via their IP addresses. You want to be able to use DHCP to assign addresses to the printers, but you want to make sure they always have the same address. What's the best option?

    a. Create reservations.

    b. Create exclusions.

    c. Configure filters.

    d. Configure policies.

11. A DHCP server can serve clients from only one subnet. True or False?

12. You have defined a scope on your DHCP server with the start address 172.16.1.1, end address 172.16.1.200, and prefix length 16. You want to create another scope on the server. Which of the following is a valid scope you can create on this server?

    a. Start address 172.19.1.1, end address 172.19.1.255, prefix length 24

    b. Start address 172.17.1.1, end address 172.17.1.200, prefix length 16

    c. Start address 172.16.2.1, end address 172.19.2.100, prefix length 16

    d. Start address 172.31.0.1, end address 172.31.1.254, prefix length 8

13. You want high availability for DHCP services, a primary server to handle most DHCP requests, and a secondary server to respond to client requests only if the primary server fails to in about a second. The primary server has about 85% of the IP addresses to lease, leaving the secondary server with about 15%. You don't want the servers to replicate with each other. What should you configure?

    a. Multicast scope

    b. Failover

    c. Superscope

    d. Split scope

14. A subnet on your network uses DHCP for address assignment. The current scope has start address 192.168.1.1 and end address 192.168.1.200 with the subnet mask 255.255.255.0. Because of network expansion, you have added computers, bringing the total number that needs DHCP for address assignment to 300. You don't want to change the IP addressing scheme or the subnet mask for computers already on the network. What should you do?

    a. Create a new scope with start address 192.168.2.1 and end address 192.168.2.200 with prefix length 24 and add the existing scope and new scope to a superscope.

    b. Add a scope with start address 192.168.1.1 and end address 192.168.2.200 with the subnet mask 255.255.255.0. Then delete the existing scope.

    c. Create a new scope with start address 192.168.1.1, end address 192.168.2.200, and prefix length 16.

    d. Add another DHCP server. Using the split scope wizard, split the existing scope with the new server and assign each server 100% of the addresses.

15. Server options take precedence over scope options. True or False?

16. You want mobile devices on your network to have a shorter lease time than other devices without having a different scope. You don't have detailed information about the mobile devices, such as MAC addresses, because they are employees' personal devices. What DHCP feature might you use to assign a shorter lease to these mobile devices?

    a. Reservation options

    b. Scope options

    c. Policy options

    d. Filter options

17. You have DHCP clients on the network that aren't domain members. You want to be sure these computers can register their hostnames with your DNS servers. Which option should you configure?

    a. 003 Router

    b. 044 WINS/NBNS Servers

    c. 006 DNS Servers

    d. 015 DNS Domain name

18. You want all computers in the Management Department to use a default gateway that's different from computers in other departments. All departments are on the same subnet. What should you do first on the server?

    a. Create a User Class.

    b. Create a new scope.

    c. Create an allow filter.

    d. Create a Vendor Class.

19. You have a DHCP server with two NICs: NIC1 and NIC2. NIC1 is connected to a subnet with computers that use DHCP for address assignment. NIC2 is connected to the data center subnet, where all computers should use static addressing. You want to prevent the DHCP server from listening for DHCP packets on NIC2. What should you do?

    a. Configure bindings.

    b. Disable the scope.

    c. Create a filter for NIC2.

    d. Configure failover.

20. You notice that some information shown in the DHCP console for DHCP leases doesn't agree with lease information you see on some client computers where you used `ipconfig /all`. What should you do to make DHCP information consistent?

    a. Back up and restore the database.

    b. Reconcile the scopes.

    c. Create a deny filter for the leases that look wrong.

    d. Delete the `dhcp.mdb` file and click Refresh.

21. Some of your non-Windows clients aren't registering their hostnames with the DNS server. You don't require secure updates on the DNS server. What option should you configure on the DHCP server so that non-Windows clients names are registered?

    a. Update DNS records dynamically only if requested by the DHCP clients.

    b. Always dynamically update DNS records.

    c. Update DNS records dynamically for DHCP clients that don't request updates.

    d. Configure name protection.

22. You're reviewing DHCP server statistics and notice that the server has received many DHCPDECLINE messages. What should you configure on the server to reduce the number of DHCPDECLINE messages?

    a. DHCP policies

    b. Conflict detection

    c. Connection bindings

    d. DNS credentials

23. You have a network of 150 computers and notice that a computer you don't recognize has been leasing an IP address. You want to make sure this computer can't lease an address from your server. What's the best solution that takes the least administrative effort?

    a. Create an allow filter.

    b. Create a new policy.

    c. Create a deny filter.

    d. Create a Vendor Class.

24. Which of the following is a criterion you can use with conditions in DHCP policies? (Choose all that apply.)

    a. Vendor Class

    b. MAC address

    c. OS version

    d. SSID

25. Why might you need to create predefined options with code 060?

    a. To support WSUS clients

    b. To support Linux clients

    c. To support WDS clients

    d. To support mobile clients

Case Projects

CASE PROJECTS

Case Project 11-1: Configuring DHCP for a New Subnet

CSM Tech Publishing has expanded its network from one subnet to two subnets and is putting 200 computers on the new subnet, with plans for adding up to 100 more computers over the next few years. Currently, it's using DHCP for the existing subnet and has a scope configured with start address 172.16.1.1 and end address 172.16.1.200 with a prefix length of 24. The DHCP server is in the main distribution facility where the router is placed to route between the subnets. The current DHCP server runs Windows Server 2012 R2, is performing well, and has plenty of unused computing resources (CPU, memory, and so forth). You need to configure DHCP for the new subnet at the lowest cost possible. What do you recommend for adding DHCP services to the new subnet? Propose a DHCP configuration and the scope's start and end addresses and prefix length for the new subnet.

Case Project 11-2: Supporting New Mobile Devices

You're called in to consult for a company that's issuing about 100 new wireless mobile devices to selected employees. There are two subnets, each with a DHCP scope that has about 150 unused addresses and an access point that relays DHCP requests from wireless clients to the DHCP server. The mobile devices will be equally distributed between the subnets. Both scopes are served by a dual-homed server. You want these mobile devices to be issued IP addresses, using the last 75 addresses of both scopes, and have a shorter lease time for addresses. What do you propose? What information do you need to carry out the proposal?

chapter 12

Configuring Virtualization with Hyper-V

After reading this chapter and completing the exercises, you will be able to:

- Install the Hyper-V server role
- Create and use virtual machines
- Configure virtual networks
- Work with virtual hard disks
- Manage and configure virtual machines

Virtualization has become a mainstream technology in both small and large networks. Server virtualization can be used to achieve a variety of goals, including consolidating servers, increasing server availability, creating virtual desktops, isolating applications for testing, and more. For these reasons and more, the Hyper-V role is likely to be a part of most Windows Server 2012/R2 deployments.

This chapter focuses on how to use the Hyper-V server role for a virtualization platform. You learn the requirements for installing Hyper-V and how to install and configure the Hyper-V role, create virtual machines, manage virtual hard disks and virtual networks, and manage and optimize virtual machines.

Installing Hyper-V

Table 12-1 describes what you need for the hands-on activities in this chapter.

Table 12-1   Activity requirements

Activity	Requirements	Notes
Activity 12-1: Installing the Hyper-V Server Role	410Server2	
Activity 12-2: Creating a Virtual Machine	410Server2	
Activity 12-3: Installing Windows Server 2012 R2 as a Guest OS	410Server2	
Activity 12-4: Working with Virtual Machines in Hyper-V Manager	410Server2	
Activity 12-5: Exporting and Importing a VM	410Server2	
Activity 12-6: Working with External Virtual Switches	410Server2	
Activity 12-7: Working with Internal Virtual Networks	410Server2	
Activity 12-8: Creating a Dynamically Expanding Virtual Disk	410Server2	
Activity 12-9: Converting a Dynamic Disk to a Fixed-Size Disk	410Server2	
Activity 12-10: Creating a VM and Attaching a Differencing Disk	410Server2	
Activity 12-11: Enabling Enhanced Session Mode	410Server2	

© 2015 Cengage Learning®

NOTE   The Hyper-V role isn't supported in virtual environments. If you're using virtual machines for the activities, the Hyper-V activities might not work. It's possible to install and use the Hyper-V role on a virtual machine running in VMware Workstation 9 and later, but additional configuration steps are necessary. See the lab setup guide in the "Before You Begin" section of this book for details on installing Hyper-V on a VMware virtual machine.

As you learned in Chapter 1, virtualization creates a software environment to emulate a computer's hardware and BIOS, allowing multiple OSs to run on the same physical computer at the same time. In Windows Server 2012/R2, you use the Hyper-V server role to create this environment. Before jumping into installing Hyper-V, review the following virtualization terms:

- A virtual machine (VM) is the virtual environment that emulates a physical computer's hardware and BIOS.

- A guest OS is an operating system installed in a VM in the same way you install an operating system on a physical computer. Hyper-V supports a wide variety of guest OSs, discussed later in "Creating Virtual Machines in Hyper-V."

- A host computer is the physical computer on which VMs run, and a host OS is the operating system running on the host.

- Virtualization software is the software for creating and managing VMs and creating the virtual environment in which a guest OS is installed. Examples are VMware Workstation, Oracle VirtualBox, and, of course, Hyper-V.

- The hypervisor is the virtualization software component that creates and monitors the virtual hardware environment, which allows multiple VMs to share physical hardware resources. The hypervisor on a host computer acts somewhat like an OS kernel, but instead of scheduling processes for access to the CPU and other devices, it schedules VMs. It's sometimes called the "virtual machine monitor (VMM)." There are two types of hypervisors:

  o A type 1 hypervisor implements OS virtualization by running on the host computer's hardware, and it controls and monitors guest OSs. It bypasses the need to install a host OS. Instead, it controls access to the host's hardware and provides device drivers for guest OSs. Also called **bare-metal virtualization**, it's used mainly for server virtualization in data centers. Examples include VMware ESX Server, Citrix XenServer, and Hyper-V Server.

  o A type 2 hypervisor implements OS virtualization by being installed in a general-purpose host OS, such as Windows 8 or Linux, and the host OS accesses host hardware on behalf of the guest OS. Also called **hosted virtualization**, it's used mostly for desktop virtualization solutions. Examples include VMware Player and Workstation, Microsoft Virtual PC, and Oracle VirtualBox.

- A **virtual disk** consists of files on the host computer that represent a virtual machine's hard disk.

- A **virtual network** is a network configuration created by virtualization software and used by virtual machines for physical and virtual network communication.

- A **checkpoint** is a partial copy of a VM made at a particular moment; it contains changes made since the VM was created or since the last checkpoint and can be used to restore the VM to its state when the checkpoint was taken. A checkpoint is also referred to as a "snapshot."

As a type 1 hypervisor, the Hyper-V virtualization environment sits between the hardware and virtual machines. Each virtual machine is a child partition on the system, and Windows Server 2012/R2 with Hyper-V installed is the parent or management partition. The Hyper-V Manager console runs on Windows Server 2012/R2 in the parent partition and serves as an interface for managing the VMs running in child partitions, as shown in Figure 12-1.

12

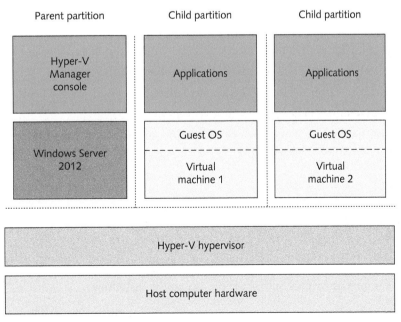

Figure 12-1   The Hyper-V architecture

Hyper-V Server, a free download, can be installed on a server without having Windows Server 2012/R2 installed. Hyper-V is then managed by another server running Windows Server 2012/R2.

Figure 12-2 shows the Hyper-V Manager console in Windows Server 2012 R2 with four VMs running. At the bottom of the middle pane is a thumbnail of the currently selected VM, named 410Server1. You can double-click the thumbnail to connect to the VM and use it like a physical computer.

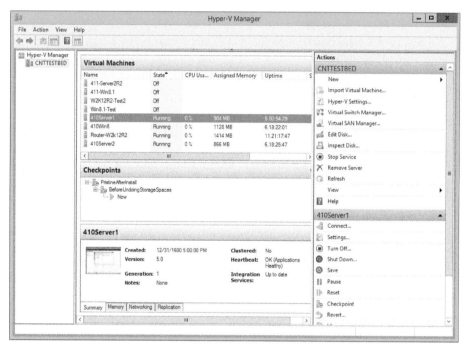

Figure 12-2   The Hyper-V Manager console

Hyper-V is a server role that's installed like any server role in Windows Server 2012/R2, using the Add Roles and Features Wizard in Server Manager. However, unlike some other roles you can install, your system must meet a few prerequisites to install and use Hyper-V:

- Windows Server 2012/R2 Standard or Datacenter Edition installed
- A 1.4 GHz or faster 64-bit CPU with virtualization extensions (AMD-V or Intel-VT)
- A CPU that supports Data Execution Prevention (DEP)
- Free disk space at least equal to the minimum requirement for the OS you're going to install as a virtual machine

Remember that the amount of space required by a guest OS is no different from the space required of an OS installed on physical hardware.

- RAM at least equal to the minimum amount required for Windows Server 2012/R2 plus the minimum amount required for the OS you're installing

For example, the minimum amount of RAM required by Windows Server 2012/R2 is 512 MB. If you plan to install a Windows Server 2012/R2 guest OS, you need another 512 MB for the guest for a total of 1 GB. For all practical purposes, however, 2 to 4 GB of RAM should be considered the minimum amount on a Hyper-V host machine.

After you have an adequately configured system running a 64-bit version of Windows Server 2012/R2, you can install the Hyper-V role. Keep in mind that you can't install Hyper-V on Windows Server 2012/R2 running as a virtual machine.

You can run the Hyper-V role in a virtual machine on VMware Workstation 9 and later; however, the feature isn't officially supported.

Hyper-V Licensing

When you install a guest OS in a virtual machine, you must have a valid license for the guest OS. Windows Server 2012/R2 with Hyper-V includes licenses for **virtual instances** of Windows Server 2012/R2 with the Standard and Datacenter editions:

- Standard Edition includes one license for a virtual instance of Windows Server 2012/R2, which means you can install Windows Server 2012/R2 as a guest OS on a single VM without having to purchase an additional Windows Server 2012/R2 license key.

- Datacenter Edition includes a license for unlimited virtual instances of Windows Server 2012/R2.

Now it's time to install the Hyper-V role so that you can begin creating and working with virtual machines.

Activity 12-1: Installing the Hyper-V Server Role

Be sure your computer meets the requirements described earlier for supporting Hyper-V.

Time Required: 15 minutes
Objective: Install the Hyper-V server role.

Required Tools and Equipment: 410Server2
Description: You want to start working with virtualization, so you install the Hyper-V server role on 410Server2, which must meet the minimum requirements. Because 410Server2 is still using the Minimal Server Interface, you change it to using the full GUI so that you can use the GUI tools in the subsequent activities.

1. Log on to 410Server2 as **Administrator**, if necessary. Open Server Manager, and click **Tools, Windows PowerShell** from the menu. At the PowerShell prompt, type **Install-WindowsFeature Server-GUI-Shell -Restart** and press **Enter**. After the server restarts, log on as **Administrator**.

2. In Server Manager, start the Add Roles and Features Wizard, and install the Hyper-V server role. Accept the default choices until you get to the Virtual Switches window (see Figure 12-3). Read the information about virtual switches, click the **Ethernet** check box, and then click **Next**.

3. In the Migration window, you can enable live migration for this Hyper-V host. Accept the default setting (migration isn't enabled), and then click **Next**. In the Default Stores window, you can choose the drives to store virtual hard disks and virtual machine configuration files. Accept the default settings, and then click **Next**.

4. In the Confirmation window, click **Install**. When the installation is finished, click **Close** and restart 410Server2.

5. When the server restarts, log on as **Administrator**. Open Server Manager, and click **Tools, Hyper-V Manager** from the menu.

6. In Hyper-V Manager, click the server node in the left pane.

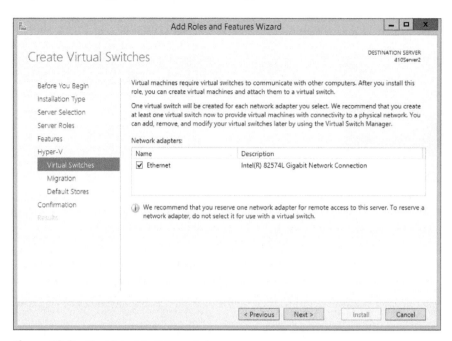

Figure 12-3   The Virtual Switches window

7. In the Actions pane, click **Hyper-V Settings**. In the Hyper-V Settings window, you can change server settings, such as default storage paths, virtual machine migrations, replication, and the behavior of the mouse and keyboard. Click **Cancel**.

8. Stay logged on to 410Server2 for the next activity.

Creating Virtual Machines in Hyper-V

With Hyper-V installed, the Hyper-V Manager console is available in Server Manager's Tools menu. You use it to create and manage virtual machines, configure virtual networks, and configure the Hyper-V server. To begin using Hyper-V, click the name of the server in the left pane.

To use virtualization, you must create a virtual machine first. In Hyper-V Manager, all tasks related to creating and managing virtual machines are listed in the Actions pane. For Hyper-V server configuration tasks, you can right-click the server in the left pane and select a task, and for VM configuration tasks, you can right-click a VM in the middle pane.

Hyper-V VMs consist of these files stored on the Hyper-V server:

- *Configuration file*—This XML file containing the details of a VM's virtual hardware configuration is stored by default in the Virtual Machines folder in %*systemroot*%\ ProgramData\Microsoft\Windows\Hyper-V. Each checkpoint created for a VM also has an XML configuration file associated with it stored by default in the same path in the Snapshots folder. These files have an .xml extension.

- *Virtual hard disk files*—Each virtual hard disk assigned to a VM has an associated VHD or VHDX file that holds the hard disk's contents. By default, these files are stored in C:\Users\Public Documents\Hyper-V\Virtual hard disks and have a .vhd or .vhdx extension. VHDX is the newer and preferred virtual hard disk format. VHDX disks provide better performance than VHD disks do and have a 64 TB capacity compared with 2 TB for VHD disks.

In addition, you might also find the following types of files associated with a VM:

- *Differencing or checkpoint files*—These files are similar to virtual hard disk files, but they're associated with a parent VHD or VHDX file and are created when you create a differencing disk or checkpoint. Differencing disks are discussed in "Working with Virtual Hard Disks," and checkpoints are discussed in "Managing Checkpoints" later in this chapter. These files have an .avhd or .avhdx extension, depending on whether they're associated with a VHD or VHDX virtual hard disk.

- *Saved state files*—If you save a VM's state, two files are created. A file with a `.bin` extension contains the contents of the saved VM's memory, and a file with a `.vsv` extension contains the saved state of the VM's devices. Both files are in a folder named with the GUID of the VM located where the VM's configuration file is stored.

The process of creating a VM involves just a few general steps:

1. Start the New Virtual Machine Wizard in Hyper-V Manager.

2. Give the new VM a descriptive name.

3. Choose a location for the VM. Storing virtual machines on a hard disk that's separate from your Windows Server 2012/R2 installation is usually best. In data center applications, VMs are often stored on storage area networks (SANs) for enhanced reliability and management. With this setup, if a host server goes down or is taken out of service for maintenance, another Hyper-V host can be assigned to run its VMs without having to physically move VM files.

4. Choose a generation 1 or generation 2 virtual machine. A generation 1 virtual machine creates a virtual hardware environment compatible with Hyper-V versions before Windows Server 2012. A generation 2 virtual machine requires at least a Windows Server 2012 or Windows 8 guest OS and supports features such as secure boot, PXE boot, and SCSI boot.

5. Assign the amount of memory the VM requires. Memory requirements for virtual machines are the same as requirements for installing the OS on a physical computer. With Hyper-V, you can take advantage of dynamic memory allocation, in which the hypervisor allocates only as much memory as the VM needs, up to a maximum.

6. Configure networking. You have the choice of connecting with an external switch, which uses one of the host network adapters; using a private switch or an internal switch; or leaving the VM disconnected from the network. This option can be changed later.

7. Create a virtual hard disk. You can give the virtual disk a name or accept the default, and you can choose the virtual disk's size and location. Putting virtual disk files on a drive separate from the Windows Server 2012/R2 host's boot drive results in the best performance. You can also use an existing virtual hard disk or attach a hard disk later.

8. Install an OS. In this step, you can install an OS from media inserted in the host's physical CD/DVD drive (generation 1 VM only), from a CD/DVD image file (an `.iso` file), from a boot floppy disk image (generation 1 VM only), or over the network by using PXE boot. You can also install an OS later.

Activity 12-2: Creating a Virtual Machine

Time Required: 10 minutes
Objective: Create a virtual machine and install Windows Server 2012 R2 on it.

Required Tools and Equipment: 410Server2
Description: You have installed the Hyper-V role on your server and are ready to create a virtual machine. You have the installation DVD for Windows Server 2012 R2.

1. Log on to 410Server2 as **Administrator**, and open Hyper-V Manager, if necessary.

2. If necessary, click **410Server2** in the left pane of Hyper-V Manager. In the Actions pane, click **New**, and then click **Virtual Machine**.

3. Read the information in the Before You Begin window. You can create a default virtual machine simply by clicking Finish in this window, but for this activity, click **Next**.

4. In the Name text box, type **VMTest1**. You can choose a location to store the virtual machine configuration, but for this activity, accept the default location C:\ProgramData\Microsoft\ Windows\Hyper-V by clicking **Next**.

5. In the Specify Generation window, you choose whether to create a generation 1 or generation 2 virtual machine. Leave the default **Generation 1**, and click **Next**.

6. In the Assign Memory window, verify that the value in the Startup memory text box is **512 MB** (the minimum requirement for Windows Server 2012 R2), and then click **Next**.

7. In the Configure Networking window, leave the default option **Not Connected**. You configure virtual networks and connect the VM to a network later. Click **Next**.

8. In the Connect Virtual Hard Disk window, you can enter the virtual hard disk's name, size, and location. By default, the size is 127 GB, and Hyper-V names the hard disk the same as the VM with the extension .vhdx. You can also use an existing virtual disk or attach one later. Write down the location where Hyper-V stores the virtual hard disk by default in case you want to access the virtual disk later. Click **Next** to accept the default settings.

9. In the Installation Options window, click the **Install an operating system from a bootable CD/DVD-ROM** option button. This option causes your VM to boot from an installation DVD inserted in the host machine's DVD drive. You can also boot the VM from an image file (.iso) of the installation DVD. Check with your instructor as to whether you should use the physical DVD drive or an image file. Click **Next**.

10. The Summary window displays a summary of your virtual machine configurations. Click **Finish**. After the virtual machine is created, you return to Hyper-V Manager.

11. Leave Hyper-V Manager open if you're continuing to the next activity.

Activity 12-3: Installing Windows Server 2012 R2 as a Guest OS

Time Required: 30 to 60 minutes, depending on the host computer's performance
Objective: Install Windows Server 2012 R2 on a virtual machine.

Required Tools and Equipment: 410Server2 and the Windows Server 2012 R2 installation DVD
Description: You have created a virtual machine and are ready to install Windows Server 2012 R2 as a guest OS, using the installation DVD.

This activity covers only the steps to get the installation started. The actual installation on a virtual machine is identical to installing Windows Server 2012 R2 on a physical server.

1. Log on to 410Server2 as **Administrator**, if necessary.

2. Insert the Windows Server 2012 R2 installation DVD. (If Autorun is enabled on your DVD drive, the Windows Server 2012 R2 Setup program runs. If it does, exit it.)

3. If necessary, open Hyper-V Manager. In the center pane, right-click the **VMTest1** virtual machine you created in Activity 12-2 and click **Connect**. You see a window similar to the one in Figure 12-4.

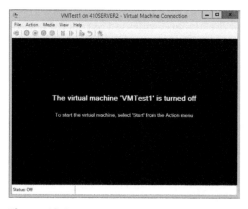

Figure 12-4   The Virtual Machine Connection console before starting the VM

4. The virtual machine isn't started yet, so click **Action, Start** from the menu. (You can also start the VM by clicking the blue-green Start icon on the toolbar.)

5. From this point, the installation is identical to the Windows Server 2012 R2 installation steps in Activity 2-1, until you need to press Ctrl+Alt+Delete to log on. For a Hyper-V virtual machine, you press **Ctrl+Alt+End** instead. (You can also click the Ctrl+Alt+Delete icon on the toolbar or click Action, Ctrl+Alt+Delete from the menu, and Hyper-V sends the keystroke combination to the virtual machine.) Install the **Server with a GUI** option. Use the default options for the remainder of the installation.

If you press Ctrl+Alt+Delete, the host machine intercepts the keystroke instead of the VM.

6. After the installation is finished, set the password to **Password01** and log on. After you're logged on to the VM, shut it down by right-clicking **Start**, pointing to **Shut down or sign out**, and clicking **Shut down**.

7. Stay logged on to 410Server2 if you're continuing to the next activity.

Basic Virtual Machine Management with Hyper-V Manager

With Hyper-V, a virtual machine runs in the background until you connect to it in Hyper-V Manager. A running VM doesn't require using Hyper-V Manager, nor does it require anyone to be logged on to the server. Furthermore, you can configure a VM to start and shut down automatically when the host server starts and shuts down. In addition, like any OS, you can manage a VM remotely by using tools such as Remote Desktop and MMCs if the VM is configured to communicate with the host network.

When you want to configure and manage a VM's properties or access it locally, you do need to use Hyper-V Manager. The middle pane shows all installed virtual machines at the top (see Figure 12-5) and displays each VM's name, state, CPU use, assigned memory, uptime, and status. Normally, the Status column doesn't display anything unless you perform a task such as exporting a VM or creating a checkpoint. When you select a VM, the Checkpoints section shows a list of checkpoints created for it. If you click the VM's name in this section, you see a screenshot of the VM at the time the checkpoint was taken along with the time and date it was taken. The bottom section shows a real-time screenshot of a running VM. When a running VM's screen changes, the screenshot in Hyper-V Manager reflects the change with a slight delay.

Figure 12-5   Hyper-V Manager showing a virtual machine

Connecting to a virtual machine opens a window that serves as the user interface to the VM and looks similar to a Remote Desktop connection. You can connect to a VM by using any of the following methods:

- Right-click the VM and click Connect.
- Double-click the VM.
- Select the VM and double-click its screenshot in the bottom section.
- Select the VM and click Connect in the Action menu or Actions pane.

After you're connected, you see the Virtual Machine Connection console, shown in Figure 12-6. The toolbar icons from left to right are as follows:

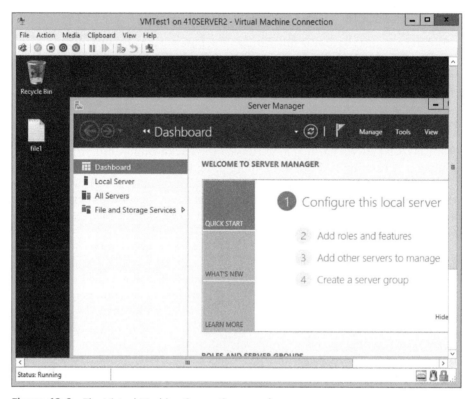

Figure 12-6   The Virtual Machine Connection console

- Ctrl+Alt+Delete (sends a Ctrl+Alt+Delete keystroke to the VM)
- Start (starts the VM)
- Turn Off (turns off the VM)
- Shut Down (sends a signal to the OS to perform a shutdown)
- Save (saves the VM's state, similar to Windows hibernation mode)
- Pause (pauses the VM, similar to Windows sleep mode)
- Reset (resets the VM)
- Checkpoint (creates a checkpoint of a VM)
- Revert (reverts to a VM's checkpoint)
- Session mode (changes the session mode)

Most of the options on the toolbar are self-explanatory, but checkpoints are discussed later in "Managing Virtual Machines," and Enhanced Session mode is discussed in the "Enhanced

Session Mode" section. You can access all these toolbar options from the Action menu, too. The following list summarizes some tasks you can perform with other menus:

- *File*—Access the VM's settings and exit the VM.
- *Media*—Specify a CD/DVD drive the VM should connect to, specify an .iso file the VM mounts as a virtual CD/DVD drive, or specify a floppy disk image that can be mounted as a virtual floppy disk.
- *Clipboard*—Copy a screenshot of the VM to the Clipboard or paste Clipboard text into the VM. You can also copy and paste between the host computer and virtual machines or between virtual machines.
- *View*—Toggle the display of the toolbar and switch to full-screen mode.

If you want to disconnect from a virtual machine, which closes the Virtual Machine Connection console but doesn't shut down the VM, simply click File, Exit from the menu or close the window.

Activity 12-4: Working with Virtual Machines in Hyper-V Manager

Time Required: 25 minutes
Objective: Explore Hyper-V Manager.

Required Tools and Equipment: 410Server2
Description: You have installed a test VM that you can use to become familiar with managing virtual machines in Windows Server 2012 R2. You create a checkpoint, make some changes to the OS, and revert to the checkpoint.

1. Log on to 410Server2 as **Administrator**, if necessary.
2. Open Server Manager, and click **Tools, Hyper-V Manager** from the menu.
3. Right-click the **VMTest1** virtual machine you created in Activity 12-2 and click **Connect**.
4. Power on VMTest1 by clicking the **Start** toolbar icon or clicking **Action, Start** from the menu. While Windows is booting, close the Virtual Machine Connection console. Notice that in Hyper-V Manager, the VM's CPU use changes as Windows boots, and the VM's screenshot in the bottom pane changes periodically.
5. Double-click the VM's screenshot at the bottom of Hyper-V Manager to open the Virtual Machine Connection console for the VM. After Windows finishes booting, click the **Ctrl+Alt+Delete** toolbar icon (the leftmost icon) to send a Ctrl+Alt+Delete keystroke to the VM, and log on as **Administrator**.

To see a description of any toolbar icon, hover your mouse pointer over it.

6. Start Notepad, and type your name in a new text document. Don't close Notepad or save the file yet. Click the **Save** toolbar icon or click **Action, Save** from the menu of the Virtual Machine Connection console.
7. Close the Virtual Machine Connection console. In Hyper-V Manager, notice that the State column for the VM shows "Saved" (or "Saving" if it hasn't finished saving). After it has finished saving, open the Virtual Machine Connection console by double-clicking **VMTest1**. Start the VM by clicking the **Start** toolbar icon. You're right where you left off in Notepad.
8. Save the Notepad file to your desktop as **file1.txt**, and then exit Notepad.

12

9. Click the **Checkpoint** toolbar icon or click **Action, Checkpoint** from the menu. When you're prompted to enter a name, type **BeforeDeletingFile1**, and then click **Yes**. In the status bar of the Virtual Machine Connection console, you see a progress bar that says "Taking checkpoint."

10. After the checkpoint is finished, minimize the VM, and note that the checkpoint is listed in Hyper-V Manager in the Checkpoints section. Maximize the VM, and delete the Notepad file you created. Empty the Recycle Bin so that you know the file is really gone.

11. Click the **Revert** toolbar icon or click **Action, Revert** from the menu.

12. Click **Revert** when prompted. The VM displays a message that it's reverting. When the desktop is displayed again, you should see the Notepad file back on the desktop. Close the Virtual Machine Connection console.

13. In Hyper-V Manager, right-click **VMTest1** and click **Shutdown**. When prompted, click the **Shut Down** button. The Status column displays "Shutting Down Virtual Machine." Close the Virtual Machine Connection console.

14. After the VM state changes to Off, delete the checkpoint by right-clicking **BeforeDeletingFile1** in the Checkpoints section and clicking **Delete Checkpoint**. Click **Delete** to confirm.

15. Stay logged on to 410Server2 if you're continuing to the next activity.

Advanced VM Creation Methods

Virtual machines can be created by using other methods besides the New Virtual Machine Wizard, including the following:

- Importing an exported VM
- Copying the virtual disk
- Converting a physical machine to a virtual machine

Exporting VMs   Virtual machines can be exported and then imported to create one or more virtual machines. Starting with Windows Server 2012 R2, you can even export a running VM. In previous versions of Hyper-V, the VM had to be shut down. Because you can export a VM while it's running, this feature allows you to back up a VM without shutting it down first. You can use an exported VM as a backup or to make a copy of an existing VM. When you choose the Export option for a VM, you're prompted to enter a path for storing the exported VM. Starting with Windows Server 2012, you can enter a path to a network share; previous versions required a path to local storage. After a VM is exported, it can be moved to archival storage as a backup, imported on another server running Hyper-V, or imported on the same server.

Importing VMs   In previous versions of Windows Server, you had to export a VM before you could import it. Starting with Windows Server 2012 R2, you can import a VM that hasn't been exported first. This new feature can come in handy if, for example, your Hyper-V host suffers a hardware or software failure; you can simply move the hard disk containing VMs to another host and import them in place. When you import a virtual machine, you have three options for the type of import:

- *Register the virtual machine in-place (use the existing unique ID)*—This option registers the exported VM in Hyper-V from its current location. No copy of the exported VM is made. Use this option only if you're restoring a failed or corrupt VM or rebuilding a Hyper-V host, and the files are already where you want them. The advantage of this option is that the import process is fast.

- *Restore the virtual machine (use the existing unique ID)*—This option is usually best for restoring VMs. It copies the VM files to their original location on the host, leaving the exported files unchanged and available for future restoration if needed. You can't use this option if the original exported VM is already running on the Hyper-V host.

- *Copy the virtual machine (create a new unique ID)*—Use this option to make a copy or clone of a virtual machine and register it in Hyper-V. For example, use this option if you want to use a VM as a template for additional VMs that you can run on the same Hyper-V host or another Hyper-V host. Because a new unique ID is created, the VMs can run on the same Hyper-V host as the exported VM.

Exporting a VM doesn't change the original VM in any way. You can continue to use the original VM as before.

Activity 12-5: Exporting and Importing a VM

Time Required: 30 minutes
Objective: Export a VM and then import it.

Required Tools and Equipment: 410Server2
Description: You want to make a copy of a VM so that you have two VMs to work with, so you export your current VM, rename it, and then import it as a new VM.

1. Log on to 410Server2 as **Administrator**, and start Hyper-V Manager, if necessary.

2. Click **VMTest1**, if necessary. In the Actions pane, under VMTest1, click **Export**. In the Export Virtual Machine dialog box, click **Browse** to select an export path.

3. In the Select Folder window, navigate to the C drive or another location of your choice, click **New folder**, and name it **VMExport**. Click **Select Folder**.

4. In the Export Virtual Machine dialog box, click **Export**.

5. In Hyper-V Manager, the Status column displays "Exporting" and shows the percentage completed. The export operation takes a while. Wait until it's finished before continuing to the next step.

6. Now that the VM is exported, you import it to create a second VM. Click **Import Virtual Machine** in the Actions pane to start the Import Virtual Machine Wizard. In the Before You Begin window, click **Next**.

7. In the Locate Folder window, click **Browse**. Browse to the **VMExport** folder and then click **VMTest1**. Click **Select Folder**, and then click **Next**. In the Select Virtual Machine window, VMTest1 is selected because it's the only option, so click **Next**.

8. In the Choose Import Type window, click **Copy the virtual machine (create a new unique ID)**, and then click **Next**.

9. In the Choose Destination window, you can accept the default locations for the VM configuration files or specify different paths. Accept the default settings and click **Next**.

10. In the Choose Storage Folders window, you can change the default location for the virtual hard disk files. If you accept the default, you get an error message stating the file already exists. Click **Browse**. In the Select Folder dialog box, create a folder named **VMTest2**, and then click **Select Folder**. Click **Next**.

11. In the Summary window, verify your choices and click **Finish**. After the import is finished, another VM named VMTest1 is listed in Hyper-V Manager. Rename the new VM (listed second in Hyper-V Manager) **VMTest2**.

12. Stay logged on if you're continuing to the next activity.

Copying a Virtual Disk   Copying a virtual disk doesn't actually create a new VM, but it means you don't have to install a guest OS on a new VM. The result isn't much different from an export operation followed by an import with the "Copy the virtual machine" option, but the procedure is different:

1. Copy the virtual hard disk from an existing VM to a new folder or rename the copied file, and you can leave it in the same folder as the original virtual disk. Hyper-V virtual hard disks have the extension .vhdx and are usually placed in the location you select when you

12

create a virtual hard disk in the New Virtual Machine Wizard (as you did in Activity 12-2). The VM that's currently using the virtual disk should be shut down before you copy it.

2. Create a virtual machine with the New Virtual Machine Wizard, but in the Connect Virtual Hard Disk window, select the "Use an existing virtual hard disk" option, and browse to the copied virtual hard disk.

3. Finish the New Virtual Machine Wizard.

Because the guest OS is on the virtual hard disk, you have a new VM with the same guest OS as the original virtual hard disk. The only real difference between this method and the export/import method is that you must create the virtual machine and can change the VM name and configuration in the New Virtual Machine Wizard.

Converting a Physical Machine to a Virtual Machine
Hyper-V has no built-in tools to create a virtual machine from a physical computer, but other tools are available for this task. One comes with the Microsoft System Center Virtual Machine Manager (SCVMM), which is a tool for managing multiple Hyper-V hosts. It has the Convert Physical Server Wizard that walks you through the conversion process.

A less expensive and less complex option is to download the free `disk2vhd` utility from *http://technet.microsoft.com/sysinternals/*. This utility runs on the physical server and creates a virtual hard disk file from the disk on the physical server. You can then create a VM in Hyper-V and choose the option to use an existing virtual hard disk to convert your physical computer to a virtual machine. Be aware that the OS on the physical disk was originally meant for a particular hardware configuration, so you might have to change other settings. The original physical disk is unaltered and can be used as always.

 You can create a virtual disk by copying the contents of one of the host machine's physical disks. In Hyper-V Manager, just click New, Hard Disk. If you remove a computer's OS disc and install it in the Hyper-V host machine, you can essentially create a VM from a physical disk. Using the `disk2vhd` utility is usually an easier solution, however.

Creating and Configuring VMs with PowerShell
You can also create and manage VMs with PowerShell cmdlets and create PowerShell scripts to automate VM management. Table 12-2 describes the cmdlets you use most often when working with VMs.

Table 12-2   PowerShell cmdlets for working with VMs

Cmdlet	Use	Example
New-VM	Create a virtual machine.	To create a VM named VMTest1 with 2 GB RAM and a blank virtual disk named VMTest1.vhdx stored in the V:\VMs\VMTest1 folder, enter: `New-VM -Name VMTest1 -MemoryStartupBytes 2GB -NewVHDPath V:\VMs\VMTest1\ VMTest1.vhdx`
Start-VM	Start a VM.	To start all VMs with a name starting with "VMTest," enter: `Start-VM -Name VMTest*`
Stop-VM	Shut down a VM. Use the -Force option to force the shutdown even if running applications have unsaved data or the screen is locked. Loss of data can result if a running application doesn't automatically save data.	To shut down all VMs with a name starting with "VMTest," enter: `Stop-VM -Name VMTest*`

(continues)

Cmdlet	Use	Example
Get-VM	Display information about a VM. Can also be used to pipe information to other cmdlets.	To display a list of running VMs, enter: `Get-VM	Where-Object {$_.State -eq 'Running'}`
Suspend-VM	Pause a running VM.	`Suspend-VM -Name VMTest1`
Save-VM	Save the state of a VM.	`Save-VM -Name VMTest1`
Restart-VM	Shut down and restart a VM.	`Restart-VM -Name VMTest1`
Checkpoint-VM	Create a VM checkpoint (snapshot).	To create a checkpoint for VMTest1 named "BeforeInstallingAD," enter: `Checkpoint-VM -Name "VMTest1" -SnapshotName "BeforeInstallingAD"`
Restore-VMSnapshot	Restore a VM to a previous checkpoint.	To restore the VMTest1 VM to a snapshot named "BeforeInstallingAD," enter: `Restore-VMSnapshot -Name "BeforeInstallingAD" -VMName VMTest1`
Export-VM	Export a VM.	To export the VMTest1 VM to the V:\VMExport folder, enter: `Export-VM -Name VMTest1 -Path V:\VMExport`
Import-VM	Import a VM.	To import the previously exported VMTest1 with the copy and create new ID option, enter: `Import-VM -Path "V:\VMExport\VMTest1" -Copy GenerateNewID`

As with all PowerShell cmdlets, you can use `Get-Help cmdletname -detailed` to get detailed help with examples. To see a list of all VM-related cmdlets, use `Get-Command *-vm*`, and to see a list of VHD-related cmdlets, use `Get-Command *-vhd` at a PowerShell prompt.

Generation 1 and Generation 2 VMs

Starting with Windows Server 2012 R2, when you create a VM with the New Virtual Machine Wizard or the `New-VM` PowerShell cmdlet, you have the option of creating a generation 1 or generation 2 VM. Generation 2 VMs are based on revised virtual hardware specifications, so they have enhanced VM capabilities and support for newer standards:

- *Unified Extensible Firmware Interface (UEFI) firmware instead of traditional PC BIOS*—Enhances the VM's hardware environment and removes the 2.2 TB partition limit for the boot volume. Also supports PXE boot with synthetic device drivers as well as booting from a SCSI virtual disk. The guest OS must be 64-bit.

- *Device support*—Removes support for legacy network adapters, IDE controllers, legacy keyboards, and floppy disk controllers. Adds support for booting from software-based devices, using virtual machine bus (VMBus), SCSI devices, and a new software-based DVD drive. Generation 2 VMs don't support booting from a physical DVD device; you must use an ISO file or a network boot to start an installation.

- *Network boot with IPv6*—Generation 1 VMs could network boot only with IPv4.

- *VHDX-only support*—Generation 2 VMs support only VHDX hard disk files, but you can convert a VHD file to VHDX with the `Convert-VHD` PowerShell cmdlet.

- *GPT boot*—Generation 2 VMs can boot to a boot disk that uses a GUID Partitioning Table (GPT) partitioning scheme.

- *Disk expansion*—A VHDX disk can be expanded while the VM is online, including the boot volume.

- *Reduced attack surface*—By removing legacy devices and adding the secure boot feature, security is improved for generation 2 VMs.

- *Secure boot*—Prevents unauthorized code from running during a system boot.

There are other changes, but this list contains the most important improvements. Converting a generation 1 VM to generation 2 is possible, but you can't use a generation 2 VM on Hyper-V versions before Windows Server 2012 R2. In addition, generation 2 VMs support only Windows 8 or Windows Server 2012 and later guest OSs.

Hyper-V Virtual Networks

Hyper-V virtual machines are used for a variety of reasons, and how a particular VM is used usually dictates how you configure the VM's network connection. VMs are connected to a virtual network through a Hyper-V virtual switch created in Hyper-V Manager or with a PowerShell cmdlet. Each virtual switch you create is a separate virtual network. You can create three types of virtual switches and, by extension, virtual networks: external, internal, and private.

To create, delete, and modify virtual switches in Hyper-V, click Virtual Switch Manager in the Actions pane or use the PowerShell cmdlets listed when you enter `Get-Command *-VMSwitch*`. The following sections describe the types of virtual networks you can create.

 Another option is to not connect a VM to a virtual switch at all.

External Virtual Switches

An **external virtual switch** binds a virtual switch to one of the host's physical network adapters, allowing virtual machines to access a LAN connected to the host. During installation of the Hyper-V role, you have the option of creating an external virtual switch by binding one or more of the host's physical adapters to a virtual switch (as you did in Activity 12-1). Only one external switch can be created per physical network adapter. When a VM is connected to an external switch, it acts like any other device on the LAN. For example, the VM can get an IP address from a DHCP server on the external network and use the network's default gateway to access other networks and the Internet.

You use an external virtual switch when external computers must have direct access to the VM or when the VM must have access to external network resources, such as when a VM is configured as a Web server, DNS server, or domain controller.

 In earlier Hyper-V versions, you couldn't bind a wireless NIC to an external virtual switch. Starting with Hyper-V in Windows Server 2012, you can use a wireless NIC. Hyper-V creates an additional network bridge adapter on the host computer for this purpose.

If you're using external virtual switches, having more than one physical NIC installed on the host computer is highly recommended. This way, you can dedicate one of the NICs to host communication, and the other NIC or NICs can be bound to external virtual switches.

When a NIC is designated for use in an external virtual switch, Windows binds the Hyper-V Extensible Virtual Switch protocol to the physical NIC and unbinds all other protocols. This process creates a virtual switch through which VMs and the host can communicate with the physical network and each other. A new virtual network adapter (virtual NIC) is created on the host computer that has all the usual protocol bindings enabled. The VMs configured to use the external virtual switch are bound to the virtual NIC, which communicates through the virtual switch.

To help you understand virtual networks better, Figure 12-7 shows a host computer without any virtual networks configured, and Figure 12-8 shows the host and virtual machines connected to an external virtual network. In Figure 12-8, the host's physical NIC is bound only to the Hyper-V Extensible Virtual Switch protocol and has a physical connection to the external network. The host's physical NIC has a virtual connection to the virtual switch and facilitates

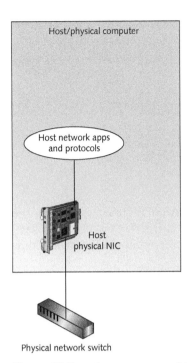

Figure 12-7   A host computer with no virtual networks configured
© 2015 Cengage Learning®

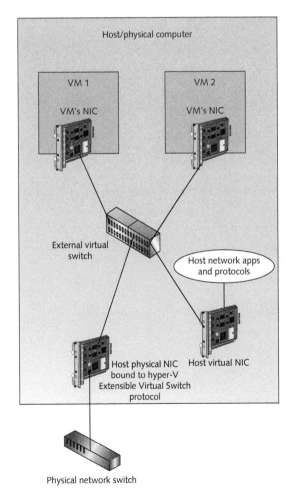

Figure 12-8   A host and VM connected through an external virtual network
© 2015 Cengage Learning®

12

communication between VMs and the external network. The new virtual NIC created on the host has all the usual network protocol bindings (Client for Microsoft Networks, File and Printer Sharing for Microsoft Networks, TCP/IP, and so forth), allowing host applications and protocols to communicate through the virtual switch to the external network and VMs.

Activity 12-6: Working with External Virtual Switches

Time Required: 20 minutes

Objective: Delete the external virtual switch created during the Hyper-V installation, and then re-create it.

Required Tools and Equipment: 410Server2

Description: You want to see how external virtual switches affect the settings of the host computer's network connections. You delete the current external virtual switch and view your network connection's properties. Next, you re-create the virtual switch and see how the host network connections are changed.

If you're connected to the host computer via Remote Desktop when you perform this activity, you lose your connection and have to reconnect.

1. Log on to 410Server2 as **Administrator**, and open Hyper-V Manager, if necessary.

2. Click **Virtual Switch Manager** in the Actions pane. In the left pane, click the virtual switch listed under "New virtual network switch" (see Figure 12-9).

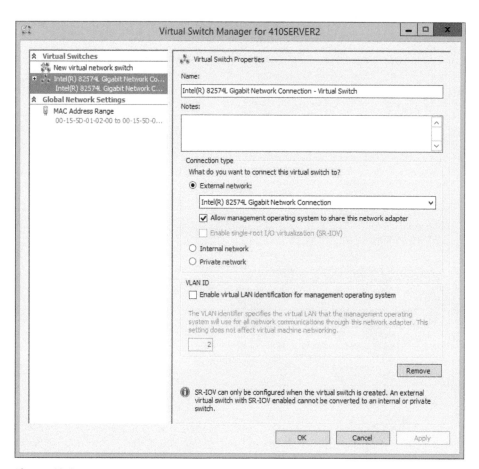

Figure 12-9 The Virtual Switch Manager

3. Click **Remove** to delete the virtual switch, and then click **OK**. In the warning message that you'll lose your network connection temporarily, click **Yes** to apply the network changes. (If you're connected to the Hyper-V host remotely, you lose your connection and might have to reconnect to the host.)

4. Open Network Connections by right-clicking **Start** and clicking **Network Connections**. Right-click the **Ethernet** connection and click **Properties**. Notice that the Hyper-V Extensible Virtual Switch protocol is installed but isn't checked, which means it isn't bound to the adapter. Close the Properties dialog box.

5. In Hyper-V Manager, click **Virtual Switch Manager** in the Actions pane. In the left pane, click **New virtual network switch**, if necessary, click **External**, and then click the **Create Virtual Switch** button to create an external virtual network.

6. Type **External10.10** in the Name text box and click **OK**. Click **Yes** in the Apply Networking Changes message box.

7. Look in the Network Connections window. You see a new connection named vEthernet (External10.10). Next, open the Properties dialog box for the connection named "Ethernet." Notice that only the Hyper-V Extensible Virtual Switch protocol is selected. This is the physical NIC that creates the virtual switch for the external network. Click **Cancel**. Open the Properties dialog box for the vEthernet connection. All the protocols are selected except Hyper-V Extensible Virtual Switch and Microsoft Network Adapter Multiplexor Protocol. This is a virtual NIC that VMs and the host computer use to communicate with the virtual switch and, therefore, the physical network. Figure 12-10 shows both network connections side by side.

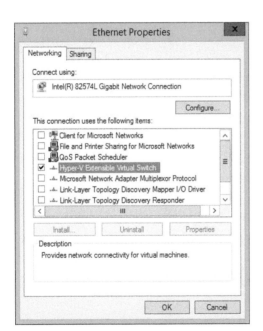
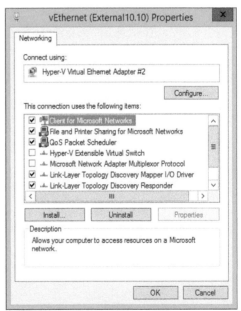

Figure 12-10 The physical NIC bound to the Hyper-V Extensible Virtual Switch protocol (left) and the new virtual NIC (right)

8. Because you deleted the original virtual switch, you must reassign the VM's network connections to the new virtual switch. In Hyper-V Manager, right-click **VMTest1** and click **Settings**.

9. In the Settings for VMTest1 window, click **Network Adapter** in the left pane under **Hardware**. In the right pane, click the **Virtual switch** list arrow (which displays "Not connected") and click **External10.10**. Click **OK**. Follow the same procedure for **VMTest2**.

10. Start and connect to both **VMTest1** and **VMTest2**. Try to ping the default gateway or another device on the physical network. You should be successful. If you get an error starting one of the VMs because of a conflict, you might need to change the settings on one of the VMs so that the DVD drive isn't connected to the physical drive.

11. Close the Virtual Machine Connection consoles, but stay logged on to the Windows host if you're continuing to the next activity.

Internal Virtual Switches

An **internal virtual switch** allows virtual machines and the host to communicate with one another but doesn't give VMs access to the physical network. An internal switch isn't bound to any of the host's physical NICs. When an internal virtual switch is created, a new virtual NIC is created on the host computer that's bound to the name of the new switch. The new virtual NIC allows the host to communicate with the VMs on that internal switch. A virtual switch is created, but it's internal to Hyper-V, so it can't be seen on the host computer. By default, the new virtual NIC attempts to get an address via DHCP, but because it doesn't have a connection to the physical network, it's assigned an APIPA address. Any VMs connected to the internal switch are also assigned an APIPA address if you don't assign a static IP address or have a VM configured as a DHCP server on the virtual switch. Figure 12-11 shows how an internal virtual switch

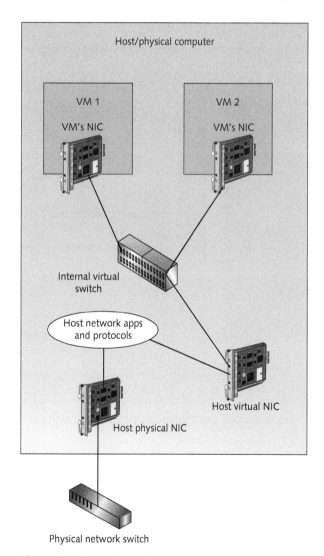

Figure 12-11 An internal virtual network

© 2015 Cengage Learning®

works. The difference between an external and internal virtual switch is that the host virtual NIC doesn't have a connection to the physical switch, which prevents VMs from communicating with the physical network. In addition, the host physical NIC and host virtual NIC have all the normal bindings, allowing network applications and protocols to communicate with both NICs. Only the host can communicate with the virtual machines.

An internal virtual switch is used when devices on the physical network don't need direct access to the VMs, and vice versa. Examples include test and lab environments where you want VMs to be isolated from the physical network but still want to communicate with VMs from the host. You can also use an internal virtual switch to isolate applications from the external network but allow communication between the networks by using a router. This configuration is discussed later in "Communicating Between Hyper-V Switches."

Activity 12-7: Working with Internal Virtual Networks

Time Required: 20 minutes
Objective: Create an internal virtual network and connect a VM to it.

Required Tools and Equipment: 410Server2
Description: You want to see how internal virtual networks affect communication between VMs and the host computer, so you create an internal virtual network and connect one of the VMs to this network.

1. Log on to 410Server2 as **Administrator**, and open Hyper-V Manager, if necessary.

2. Click **Virtual Switch Manager** in the Actions pane. In the middle pane, click **Internal**, and then click the **Create Virtual Switch** button.

3. Type **InternalNet1** in the Name text box, and click **OK**.

4. Open Network Connections. You see a new connection named vEthernet (InternalNet1). Open its Properties dialog box, and you see that all the standard protocols are bound to this virtual NIC. Close the Properties dialog box.

5. Right-click **vEthernet (InternalNet1)** and click **Status**, and then click **Details**. Notice that the value of the IPv4 IP address is an APIPA address. Write down the IP address, and then click **Close** twice. Close Network Connections.

6. In Hyper-V Manager, right-click **VMTest1** and click **Settings**. Under Hardware, click **Network Adapter**. Click the **Virtual switch** list arrow, click **InternalNet1** in the list of options, and then click **OK**.

7. Double-click **VMTest1** to connect to it. If the VM isn't running, start it now. Log on to VMTest1 as **Administrator**.

8. Open a command prompt window on VMTest1. Type **ipconfig** and press **Enter**. Notice that the IP address is an APIPA address.

9. Type **ping *host-address*** (replacing *host-address* with the IP address you wrote down in Step 5) and press **Enter**. The ping should be successful. Start and connect to **VMTest2**, and determine its IP address. From VMTest1, try to ping VMTest2. Your ping isn't successful because these VMs are no longer connected to the same virtual network.

10. Follow Step 6 to connect **VMTest2** to **InternalNet1**. Verify that you can ping VMTest2 from VMTest1, and vice versa. (If the pings aren't successful, turn off the firewall for Public networks on VMTest1 and VMTest2, and try again.)

11. Close the Virtual Machine Connection consoles, but stay logged on to 410Server2 if you're continuing to the next activity.

12

Private Virtual Switches

A **private virtual switch** isn't much different from an internal virtual switch except that the VMs connected to the private virtual switch can't communicate with the host computer. Creating a private virtual switch doesn't create a network connection on the host computer because there's no connection between the host computer and the VMs. Figure 12-12 shows this configuration. Notice that there's no virtual NIC on the host in this configuration because there's no communication between the host and the VMs.

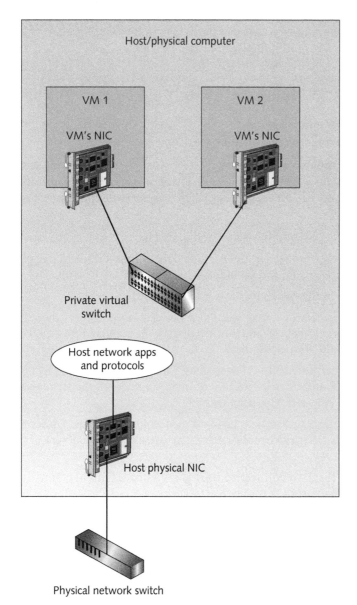

Figure 12-12   A private virtual network
© 2015 Cengage Learning®

A private virtual switch is used when you want to isolate the VMs connected to the network from all outside communication. You might use this setup as a domain testing environment or a development network in which you need to isolate virtual network traffic.

Communicating Between Hyper-V Switches

What if you want to isolate VMs in their own private network, but you want them to be able to access other private networks or an external network? With a physical network, you do this by creating subnets and using a router to route traffic between them. Hyper-V networks are no different. You can do this in two different ways:

- Create an external and a private virtual switch, and then configure one VM with two NICs and have one NIC connected to each virtual switch (see Figure 12-13). Because you can configure a Windows Server 2012/R2 server as a network router, install RRAS on the VM and enable routing. This VM can route packets between the private switch and the external switch.

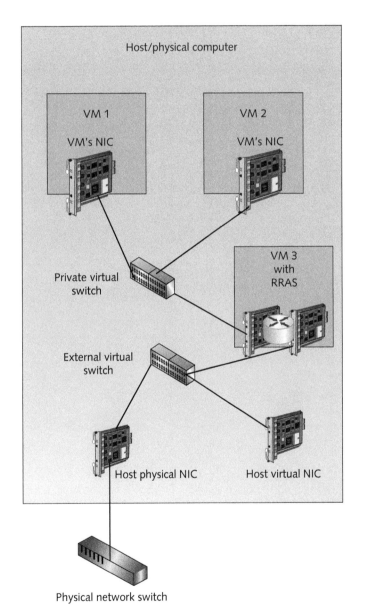

Figure 12-13   Routing between a private and an external virtual switch
© 2015 Cengage Learning®

- Create an internal virtual switch and enable routing on the host machine so that it routes between the internal and physical switches (see Figure 12-14).

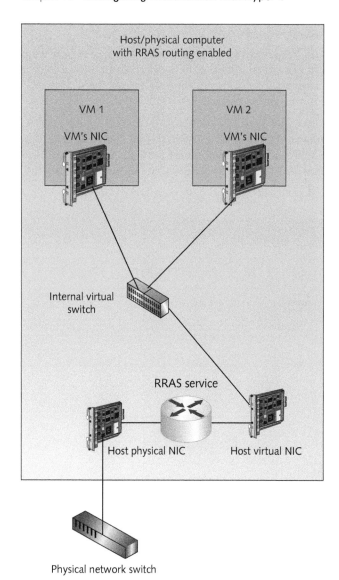

Figure 12-14 Routing between an internal network and the physical network
© *2015 Cengage Learning*®

Using Virtual LAN IDs

Virtual LANs (VLANs) enable you to create subnets, or broadcast domains, on a single external or internal virtual switch. Each VLAN effectively creates an isolated network, much like a private virtual switch. To enable VLANs on a virtual switch, click the "Enable virtual LAN identification for management operating system" check box in the Virtual Switch Manager (see Figure 12-15). The physical NIC on the host must support VLANs (also called "VLAN tagging") for this option to work.

When you enable **VLAN identification,** you choose an ID number in the Virtual Network Manager (the 2 shown in Figure 12-15), which is the VLAN identifier for the host network. When you connect a VM's network interface to a virtual switch that has VLAN IDs enabled, you specify the VLAN ID for this VM. All machines (VMs and hosts) that share a VLAN ID can communicate with one another as though they were on the same subnet. The machines sharing a VLAN ID must be configured with IP addresses that have a common network ID. Machines with different VLAN IDs can't communicate directly with one another but can communicate if a router is configured to route between the VLANs. You configure a router to route between VLANs just as you configure one to route between separate virtual networks, as discussed in the previous section.

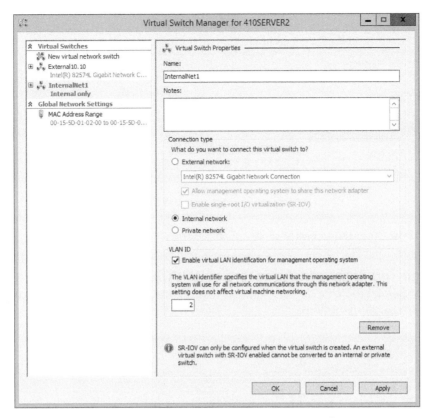

Figure 12-15   Enabling VLAN identification on a virtual network

Advanced Virtual Network Adapter Configuration

Aside from connecting a VM's network adapter to a virtual switch, you might need to perform other configuration tasks related to a VM's network connections. The following sections cover these advanced configuration tasks: configuring MAC addresses, configuring advanced features on network adapters, and enabling single-root I/O virtualization.

Configuring MAC Addresses   Every network adapter must have a unique MAC address on the network, and the network adapters on VMs are no different. Because the network adapter on a VM is virtual and, therefore, can't have a true burned-in-address, Hyper-V must assign a MAC address to each network adapter connected to a virtual network, using a pool of addresses it maintains. When a new network adapter is connected to a virtual network, a MAC address is assigned dynamically to the adapter from the pool. The MAC address pool contains 256 addresses by default, but this number can be changed. To view or change the MAC address pool in Hyper-V Manager, click Virtual Switch Manager, and then click MAC Address Range in the left pane (see Figure 12-16).

If you want to expand or change the pool, be aware that the first three bytes are the organizationally unique identifier (OUI) assigned to Microsoft and shouldn't be changed. The fourth and fifth bytes are the hexadecimal equivalent of the last two octets of the MAC address of the server's physical NIC. To expand the pool, changing the second to last byte of the maximum address is best. For example, in Figure 12-16, if you change the 02 to 03 in the Maximum text boxes, your range of available addresses is now 00-15-5D-01-02-00 to 00-15-5D-01-03-FF, doubling the number of addresses from 256 to 512. If you have more than one Hyper-V server on the network and are connecting VMs to an external network, you must be careful that you don't overlap the MAC address range with another server's range. The problem with overlapping ranges is important only if the VMs are connected to the external network. To view or change the assigned MAC address to a VM's network adapter, open the VM's settings and click to expand the network adapter, and then click Advanced Features.

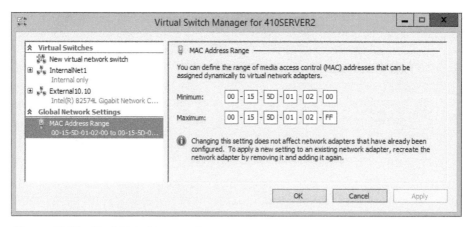

Figure 12-16   The MAC address pool

Configuring Network Adapters with Advanced Features   In the Advanced Features dialog box for a network adapter (see Figure 12-17), you can configure the following features and security options:

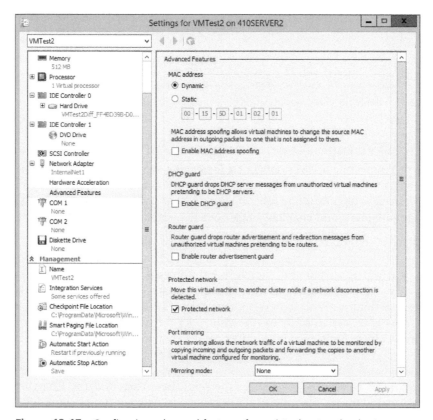

Figure 12-17   Configuring advanced features for a virtual network adapter

- *MAC address*—By default, network adapters are assigned a MAC address dynamically, but you can assign a static MAC address, if necessary. You must be careful not to duplicate a MAC address, and changing the OUI portion of the address isn't recommended. If you do change it, make sure bit 2 of the first byte is set, indicating that the address is locally administered and doesn't contain an OUI. For example, you can change the first byte to 02. You might want to use a static MAC address if the VM moves between host computers, and you want its MAC address to remain the same. For example, if you're using DHCP reservations, the reservation is based on the MAC address, so the VM's MAC address must stay the same for the reservation to work.

- *Enable MAC address spoofing*—If this option is enabled, the VM can change the source MAC address on outgoing packets, and the virtual switch is allowed to "learn" addresses other than the one assigned to the virtual adapter. This feature makes the virtual network less secure, but it might be necessary for network load balancing and clustering.

- *Enable DHCP guard*—If this option is enabled, the VM doesn't accept DHCP server messages from unauthorized VMs. With this option enabled, you use the following PowerShell command to authorize a DHCP server for this VM:

```
Set-VMNetworkAdapter -VMName MyDhcpServer1 -DhcpGuard Off
```

- *Enable router advertisement guard*—Similar to the Enable DHCP guard option, it prevents a VM from receiving router advertisements and redirection messages from unauthorized VMs. You use the following PowerShell command to authorize a router for a VM with this option enabled:

```
Set-VMNetworkAdapter -VMName MyRouter1 -RouterGuard Off
```

- *Protected network*—This new feature in Windows Server 2012 R2 is enabled by default. If Hyper-V detects that the VM's network adapter becomes disconnected from the network, it attempts to move the VM to another server where the network is available. This option is applicable only on Hyper-V failover clusters.

- *Port mirroring*—Traffic from the virtual switch port the adapter is connected to is copied and sent to another VM's virtual switch port for the purposes of monitoring and capturing network traffic.

Enabling Single-Root I/O Virtualization   Single-root I/O virtualization (SR-IOV) is an advanced feature that enhances the virtual network adapter's performance. It allows a virtual adapter to bypass the virtual switch software on the parent partition (the Hyper-V host) and communicate directly with the physical hardware, thereby lowering overhead and improving performance. The performance advantage is most obvious on high-speed NICs, such as 10 GB Ethernet and higher.

SR-IOV must be supported by a PCI Express NIC installed on the host, and installing drivers on the guest OS might be necessary. If you enable SR-IOV and resources to support it aren't available, the virtual network adapter connects by using the virtual switch as usual. To enable SR-IOV for a virtual network adapter, in the Settings window for the VM, click to expand the network adapter, click Hardware Acceleration, and click Enable SR-IOV. You must also enable SR-IOV in the Virtual Switch Manager when you create the external virtual switch. If you enable SR-IOV and it's supported, you can check Device Manager on the VM and see the actual NIC make and model listed under network adapters. For adapters with SR-IOV not enabled or not supported, you see only the Microsoft Hyper-V network adapter.

Configuring NIC Teaming on VMs

You learned about NIC teaming in Chapter 3, but this section gives you a review. NIC teaming allows multiple network interfaces to work in tandem to increase available bandwidth and provide load balancing and fault tolerance. You can configure NIC teaming on VMs as well as physical computers. On VMs, you use the same procedure as on physical computers, but for the most reliability, you should enable the feature first in the network adapter's Advanced Features dialog box (in the "Port mirroring" section). If you don't enable it, you can still create a NIC team on the VM, but if one of the physical NICs in the team fails, the team stops working instead of providing failover protection. The requirements for configuring a NIC team on a VM are similar to those for creating one on a physical computer: Windows Server 2012 or later and two or more physical Ethernet NICs to be members of the NIC team. In addition, NIC teaming can be configured only on VMs connected to external virtual switches.

If you have already configured NIC teaming on the Hyper-V host server, configuring it on VMs running on the host isn't necessary. Any VM connected to an external virtual switch that's mapped to the host's NIC team gets the benefits of NIC teaming on the host. However, if you have a VM that you want a dedicated NIC team for, you should configure NIC teaming on the VM, too. In this case, NIC teaming must be enabled on each virtual network adapter that's part of the team, and each virtual network adapter must be connected to a separate external virtual switch. You can have NIC teams configured on the host computer and on VMs, but they must use separate physical NICs. That is, the NICs on the host that are part of a NIC team can't be used in a NIC team on a VM, and vice versa. Likewise, an external virtual switch can be mapped only to a NIC team on the host or to a physical NIC on the host; it can't be mapped to a NIC that's a member of a NIC team. You must plan physical and virtual network configurations carefully to be sure you have enough physical NICs to accommodate the host's physical network needs and the virtual network needs.

 Although NIC teaming on physical computers can use up to 32 NICs in a team, Microsoft supports VM NIC teams with only two team members. You can create a team with more members, but it's not officially supported.

Synthetic Versus Legacy Network Adapters

On generation 1 VMs, you have the option of using synthetic network adapters or legacy network adapters. **Synthetic network adapters** are available on generation 1 VMs only if Integration Services is installed. On generation 2 VMs, legacy network adapters have been deprecated, and you must have Integration Services installed to add a network adapter.

In general, you should always use synthetic network adapters (shown as just "Network Adapters" in the Add Hardware section of the Settings window for a VM) because they produce much better performance than legacy adapters do. However, with a generation 1 VM, you should use a legacy network adapter in the following situations:

- The guest OS doesn't support synthetic network adapters, such as some non-Windows OSs that don't support Integration Services.

- You need to PXE boot, or the VM needs to access the network for some other reason before the OS starts.

Note that generation 2 VMs don't support legacy network adapters, and the synthetic adapters on generation 2 VMs do support PXE boot, so there's no reason to use a legacy adapter. However, generation 2 VMs support only Windows Server 2012/R2 and later and 64-bit versions of Windows 8/8.1 and later.

Configuring Fibre Channel Adapters

A Fibre Channel adapter allows a VM to access Fibre Channel storage directly from a VM. For example, a VM can access a Fibre Channel SAN to gain access to large amounts of high-performance storage. Access to shared Fibre Channel storage also enables administrators to cluster VMs to provide application and node-level fault tolerance across multiple Hyper-V servers.

To use Fibre Channel on a VM to connect to a SAN, you must first create a virtual Fibre Channel SAN in Hyper-V Manager. To do so, click Virtual SAN Manager in the Actions pane. In the Virtual SAN Manager, click Create to add a virtual Fibre Channel SAN (see Figure 12-18).

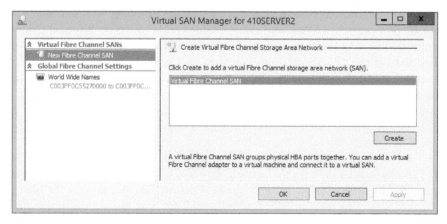

Figure 12-18   Adding a virtual Fibre Channel SAN

Before you can add a virtual Fibre Channel SAN, the host computer must have the necessary Fibre Channel host bus adapters and drivers installed and configured. After creating a virtual Fibre Channel SAN, you add a Fibre Channel adapter to the VM by using the Add Hardware option in the VM's Settings window. In the Fibre Channel Adapter dialog box (see Figure 12-19), you connect the adapter to the virtual SAN you created in the Virtual SAN Manager and configure additional options. Configuring Fibre Channel SANs is beyond the scope of this book, but you should know about this option for VMs if Fibre Channel SANs are already part of your storage configuration.

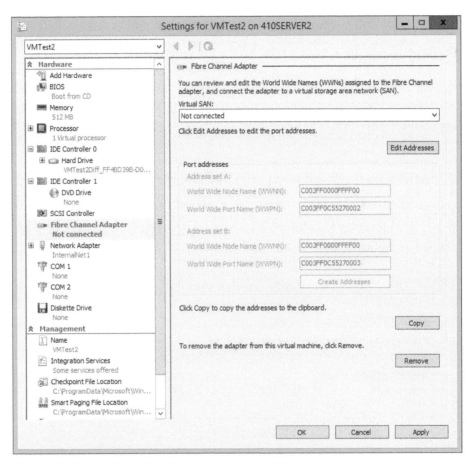

Figure 12-19 Adding a Fibre Channel adapter to a VM

Working with Virtual Hard Disks

As you've learned, a virtual hard disk is a file on the host computer with the `.vhd` or `.vhdx` extension. From a VM's standpoint, a virtual hard disk is no different from a physical hard disk. However, from the perspective of an IT manager using Hyper-V, virtual hard disks are more flexible than physical disks. Virtual hard disks can be one of three types:

- *Fixed size*—The full amount of space required for a fixed-size disk, as the name implies, is allocated on the host's storage when the virtual disk is created. **Fixed-size disks** are recommended when the VM needs to run disk-intensive (a lot of disk I/O operations) applications.

- *Dynamically expanding*—The virtual hard disk file grows as data is written to it, up to the size you specify when the disk is created. The dynamic aspect of this type of disk goes only one way; the file doesn't shrink when data is deleted from the virtual disk. This option saves host disk space until the disk grows to its maximum size but at the expense of performance. **Dynamically expanding disks** are somewhat slower than fixed-size disks, and there are some concerns about host disk fragmentation when using them. However, with the VHDX format, Microsoft has made strides toward performance parity between fixed-size and dynamically expanding disks. Unless the VM is running disk-intensive applications, dynamically expanding disks are a good choice. Additionally, VMs that use dynamic disks can be backed up faster because a virtual disk's file size is smaller than a fixed-disk's file size.

- *Differencing*—A **differencing disk** uses a parent/child relationship. A parent disk is a dynamically expanding or fixed-size disk with an OS installed, possibly with some applications and data. It becomes the baseline for one or more child (differencing) disks. A VM with a differencing disk operates normally, but any changes made to its hard disk are made only to the differencing disk, leaving the parent disk unaltered. The parent disk shouldn't be connected to a VM because it must not be changed in any way. With differencing disks, several VMs can be created by using the parent disk as the baseline but using only the additional host disk space of the differencing disk. Differencing disks are an ideal way to provision (make available) several VMs quickly without having to install an OS and applications or copy an entire virtual disk. Differencing disks work like dynamically expanding disks, in that they start very small and grow as data is written to them. All child disks must use the same format (VHD or VHDX) as the parent disk.

Creating and Modifying Virtual Disks

Virtual disks can be created when a VM is created or with the New Virtual Hard Disk Wizard. During VM creation, the disk is created as a dynamically expanding disk, but you can change it to a fixed-size disk later. When you use the wizard, you choose the type of disk you want to create (see Figure 12-20).

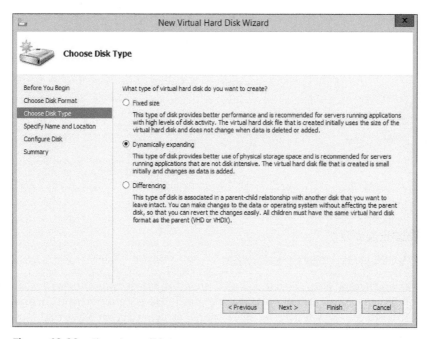

Figure 12-20   Choosing a disk type

Virtual disks are created in a default location (C:\Users\Public Documents\Hyper-V\Virtual hard disks), unless you specify a different path. You can view and change the default location by clicking Hyper-V Settings in the Actions pane in Hyper-V Manager. After a virtual disk is created, you can attach it to a new or existing VM.

One thing that makes virtual disks so flexible is being able to modify certain aspects of them in the Edit Virtual Hard Disk Wizard. To start this wizard, click Action, Edit Disk from the Hyper-V menu. After selecting the virtual hard disk you want to edit, you can select actions that vary depending on the type of disk you select. Figure 12-21 shows the options for a dynamically expanding disk.

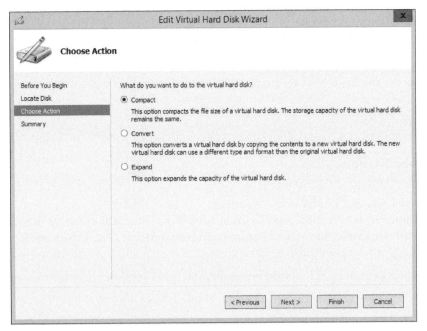

Figure 12-21 Selecting an action for a dynamically expanding disk

The following list describes the available disk-editing options:

- *Compact*—Reduces the size of a dynamically expanding disk by eliminating the space used by deleted files.
- *Convert*—Converts a dynamically expanding disk to a fixed-size disk, and vice versa. You can also change the format from VHD to VHDX, and vice versa.
- *Expand*—Allows you to make a fixed-size or dynamically expanding disk larger.
- *Merge*—This option is available only for differencing disks. You can merge a differencing disk's contents into its parent disk or merge the differencing disk with the parent disk to create a new disk while leaving the original parent disk unchanged.
- *Reconnect*—Reconnects a differencing disk with its parent disk.

Before performing any of the disk-editing tasks, you must shut down the VM connected to the target disk.

A little explanation is needed for a few of these disk-editing tasks. When you convert a dynamic disk to a fixed-size disk, a new fixed-size virtual disk is created, and you supply a new name. After the conversion is finished, you disconnect the original dynamic disk from the VM and connect the new fixed-size disk. Alternatively, you can rename the dynamic disk (or delete it), and then rename the new fixed-size disk the same as the original dynamic disk. With this method, the VM connects to the new fixed-size disk automatically when you restart it. For example, if the original dynamically expanding disk is named VMTest1.vhdx, you can name the new fixed-size disk VMTest1fixed.vhdx when you do the conversion. When the conversion is finished, rename VMTest1.vhdx as VMTest1dyn.vhdx and rename VMTest1fixed.vhdx as VMTest1.vhdx.

If you rename the fixed-size disk instead of connecting the new fixed-size disk in the VM's settings, you must make sure the VM has at least Modify permissions to the new virtual hard disk. In most cases, the Authenticated Users group is assigned the Modify permission automatically, which is adequate, but if the VM fails to start and displays an "Access denied" error, check the permissions for the .vhdx file.

There are a few caveats for expanding a disk. First, no checkpoints can be associated with the VM attached to the virtual disk you're expanding. Second, the new space on the hard disk appears in Windows as unallocated space. You must extend the adjacent volume to make the existing volume larger or create a volume from the unallocated space. In current Windows OSs, you can use the Disk Management MMC or the `diskpart` command to extend an existing volume, including the system partition, or create a new volume.

Activity 12-8: Creating a Dynamically Expanding Virtual Disk

Time Required: 20 minutes

Objective: Create a dynamically expanding virtual disk and attach it to a VM.

Required Tools and Equipment: 410Server2

Description: Your VM needs a new virtual hard disk where you can store data files, so you create a dynamically expanding virtual disk, attach it to VMTest1, and then create a new volume on the disk.

1. Log on to 410Server2 as **Administrator**, and open Hyper-V Manager, if necessary.

2. In the Actions pane, click **New** and then **Hard Disk**. In the Before You Begin window, click **Next**.

3. In the Choose Disk Format window, accept the default setting **VHDX**, and click **Next**.

4. In the Choose Disk Type window, accept the default setting **Dynamically expanding**, and click **Next**.

5. In the Specify Name and Location window, type **VMTest1-2.vhdx**. (Although the name isn't critical, you're attaching VMTest1 to this new virtual disk and the -2 in the name indicates it's the second disk.) Click **Next**.

6. In the Configure Disk window, type **2** in the **Size** text box (see Figure 12-22). You're creating a small 2 GB virtual disk because you convert it to a fixed-size disk later; the larger the disk, the longer it takes to convert and the more storage on the host it takes. Notice that you can copy the contents of an existing physical disk or virtual disk to the new disk, if needed. Click **Next**.

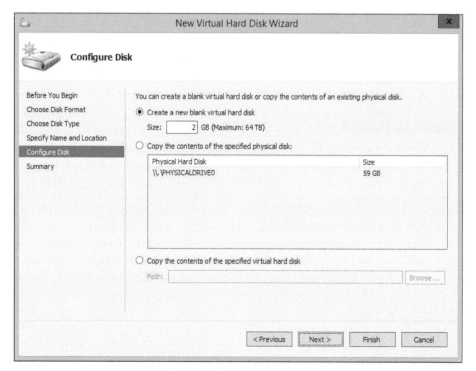

Figure 12-22   The Configure Disk window

7. In the Summary window, review the options for the new disk, and click **Finish**.

8. Next, you connect VMTest1 to the new virtual disk. Make sure VMTest1 is powered off. If it isn't, shut it down now. In Hyper-V Manager right-click **VMTest1** and click **Settings**.

9. In the Settings for VMTest1 window, click **SCSI Controller**, and click **Add** to add a hard disk. Notice that you can create a new virtual disk at this time, but because the disk you want is already created, click **Browse**. VMTest1-2 should be only about 4 MB. Click **VMTest1-2** and click **Open**. Click **OK**.

10. In Hyper-V Manager, double-click **VMTest1** and click the **Start** icon. Log on to **VMTest1**, open File Explorer, and click **This PC**. The new virtual disk isn't shown because you need to initialize it and create a new volume first.

11. On VMTest1, right-click **Start** and click **Disk Management**. Right-click **Disk 1** and click **Online** to bring the disk online. Right-click it again and click **Initialize Disk**. Click **OK**.

12. Right-click the **Unallocated** box next to Disk 1 and click **New Simple Volume**. Finish the New Simple Volume Wizard by accepting the default options. After the disk is finished formatting, close Disk Management.

13. In File Explorer, you should see the new volume with drive letter E assigned. (If you get a message stating that you need to format the disk, click **Cancel**.) Create a folder on the E drive, and create a text file in this folder.

14. Shut down VMTest1. Stay logged on to 410Server2 if you're continuing to the next activity.

Activity 12-9: Converting a Dynamic Disk to a Fixed-Size Disk

Time Required: 15 minutes

Objective: Convert a dynamically expanding disk to a fixed-size disk.

Required Tools and Equipment: 410Server2

Description: You want to get the most performance possible from the virtual disk you created for VMTest1. You decide that converting the dynamic disk to a fixed-size disk will increase the performance to the level you need.

1. Log on to 410Server2 as **Administrator**, and open Hyper-V Manager, if necessary.

2. Right-click **VMTest1** and click **Settings**. In the left pane, click the **VMTest1-2.vhdx** hard disk under SCSI Controller, and in the right pane, click **Edit**.

3. In the Locate Disk window, read the information about editing virtual hard disks. Note that editing differencing disks, disks with checkpoints, and disks involved in replication might result in data loss. Click **Next**.

4. In the Choose Action window, click the **Convert** option button, and then click **Next**. In the Choose Disk Format window, accept the default **VHDX**, and click **Next**.

5. In the Choose Disk Type window, click **Fixed size**, and then click **Next**. In the Configure Disk window, leave the current path, and type **VMTest1-2Fixed.vhdx** at the end of it. Click **Next**.

6. In the Summary window, click **Finish**. The conversion takes a few minutes.

7. When the conversion is finished, click **Browse** in the Settings for VMTest1 window. The fixed-size disk is shown with the size 2 GB (actually, similar to 2,101,248 KB). Click **VMTest1-2Fixed** and click **Open** to attach this disk to VMTest1. Click **OK**.

8. In Hyper-V Manager, double-click **VMTest1** and click the **Start** icon. Log on to VMTest1, and open File Explorer. Explore the E drive to verify that the files you created in Activity 12-8 are still there.

9. Normally, you test a new fixed-size disk for a while before deleting the old dynamic disk, but deleting it should be safe now. Unless you're low on disk space, however, there's no need to do it now. Shut down VMTest1, and stay logged on to 410Server2 if you're continuing to the next activity.

Activity 12-10: Creating a VM and Attaching a Differencing Disk

Time Required: 20 minutes
Objective: Create a VM and attach a differencing disk.

Required Tools and Equipment: 410Server2
Description: You have a baseline VM with Windows Server 2012 R2 installed. You want to create a VM and attach a differencing disk, using the original VM's disk as a baseline.

1. Log on to 410Server2 as **Administrator**, and open Hyper-V Manager, if necessary.

2. Right-click **VMTest2** and click **Settings**. Write down the name and location of the virtual hard disk attached to VMTest2, or paste this information into Notepad. (*Note:* Because you imported VMTest1 to create VMTest2, the name of the hard disk file is VMTest1.)

3. Click to select the virtual hard disk, click **Remove** to detach the virtual hard disk from VMTest2, and then click **OK**. Click **Continue** when prompted.

4. Open File Explorer, and browse to the location of the virtual hard disk you noted in Step 2. (The path should be C:\Users\Public\Documents\Hyper-V\Virtual hard disks\VMTest2\.) Rename the virtual hard disk **VMParent.vhdx.**

5. In Hyper-V Manager, click **New**, and then click **Hard Disk**. In the Before You Begin window, click **Next**. In the Choose Disk Format window, click **Next** to accept the default setting **VHDX.**

6. In the Choose Disk Type window, click **Differencing**, and then click **Next**.

7. You're using this differencing disk for VMTest2, so in the Specify Name and Location window, type **VMTest2Diff.vhdx** in the Name text box, and click **Next**.

8. In the Configure Disk window, click **Browse**, double-click **VMTest2**, and click **VMParent**. Click **Open**, and then click **Next**. In the Summary window, click **Finish**.

9. Follow Steps 5 through 8 again, but in Step 7, type the name **VMTest3Diff.vhdx**.

10. In Hyper-V Manager, right-click **VMTest2** and click **Settings**. Click **IDE Controller 0**, and then click **Add**.

11. Click **Browse**. Click **VMTest2Diff.vhdx**, click **Open**, and then click **OK**.

12. Create another virtual machine by clicking **New** and then **Virtual Machine**. In the Before You Begin window, click **Next**.

13. Type **VMTest3** in the Name text box, and then click **Next**. Click **Next** to accept the default **Generation 1**. Click **Next** to accept the default amount of memory. In the Configure Networking window, click **InternalNet1** for the network connection, and then click **Next**.

14. In the Connect Virtual Hard Disk window, click **Use an existing virtual hard disk**. Click **Browse**, click **VMTest3Diff.vhdx**, and click **Open**. Click **Next** and then **Finish**.

15. Start and connect to **VMTest2** to be sure it works, and then do the same with **VMTest3**. You now have two VMs sharing the same parent virtual disk, but each VM uses a separate and much smaller differencing disk. To verify the differencing disks' sizes, open File Explorer on 410Server2, and browse to the location of the virtual hard disks. The differencing disks are about 200 MB each, and the parent disk is around 8 to 10 GB. By using a differencing disk for two VMs, you saved 8 to 10 GB of disk space on the host. For each VM you configure to use the same parent disk, you save an additional 8 to 10 GB of host disk space.

16. Shut down the VMs, but stay logged on to 410Server2 if you're continuing to the next activity.

Pass-Through Disks

A **pass-through disk** isn't a virtual disk; it's a physical disk in the offline state that's attached to the host. It can be connected to a VM only if it has been set to offline status. If you have an offline physical disk on the host, you can attach it to a VM in the VM's Settings window (see Figure 12-23). If the disk already has data on it, the data is retained and available to the VM.

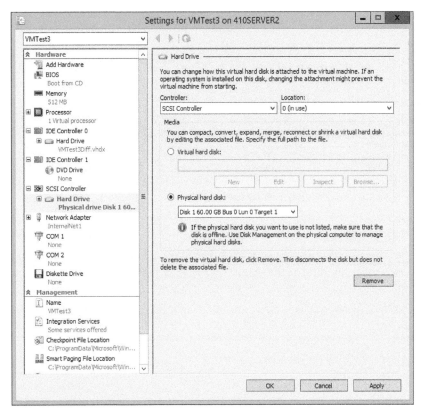

Figure 12-23   Adding a pass-through disk to a VM

From the VM's standpoint, a pass-through disk works just like a virtual disk except you can't use any of the disk-editing options on it, you can't take checkpoints, and you can't use a differencing disk with it. A pass-through disk has modest performance advantages over virtual disks, but unless you really need the extra bit of performance, a pass-through disk's lack of flexibility makes it less attractive as a VM storage option. Pass-through disks do have an advantage over VHD disks because VHD disks are limited to 2 TB. However, the VHDX format doesn't have the 2 TB limitation, so using pass-through disks is a benefit only when direct access to the physical drive improves performance. Some applications that might benefit from the VM using a pass-through disk include SQL servers and high-performance cluster servers.

For high-performance disk storage, many administrators prefer using SAN storage through Fibre Channel or iSCSI instead of pass-through disks.

Storage Quality of Service

Storage Quality of Service (QoS) is a new feature in Windows Server 2012 R2 that enables administrators to specify minimum and maximum performance values for virtual hard disks. The maximum specified value actually limits a VM's access to a virtual hard disk to prevent it from consuming too many storage resources, which can affect other VMs' access to storage. Setting a minimum specified value generates a notification if access to a virtual hard disk falls below the specified threshold.

Storage QoS can be set on IDE and SCSI virtual hard disks. In Hyper-V Manager, open a VM's Settings window, click to expand the hard disk where you want to set QoS, and click Advanced Features (see Figure 12-24). Click the "Enable Quality of Service management" check box. You can set minimum and maximum I/O operations per second (IOPS). Each 8 KB of data read or written per second is considered one I/O operation. For example, if you want to be notified when the hard disk falls below 8000 KB of input or output per second, set the minimum to 1000. If you want to prevent the disk from exceeding 80,000 KB per second, set the maximum to 10,000.

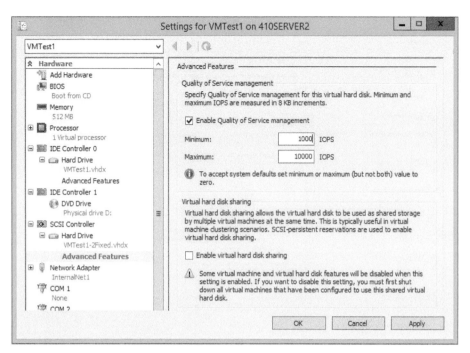

Figure 12-24   Enabling storage QoS

Figure 12-24 also shows an option for virtual hard disk sharing, which allows multiple VMs in a cluster configuration to share a virtual hard disk. This option is available only for SCSI virtual hard disks, and if it's enabled, storage QoS can't be enabled for that virtual hard disk.

Managing Virtual Machines

Now that you have a general understanding of how Hyper-V works and how to configure virtual networks and virtual hard disks, this section covers additional features you can use to manage and configure the virtual environment. In particular, you examine the following:

- Virtual machine hardware settings
- Integration Services
- Automatic start and stop actions
- Managing checkpoints
- Resource metering
- Enhanced Session mode

Virtual Machine Hardware Settings

Virtual machines have a number of hardware settings that can be configured. You have already looked at how to configure the network and hard disk settings. In this section, you look at options for changing BIOS settings, modifying the amount of memory allocated to a VM, and configuring virtual processor settings. Most settings can't be changed unless the VM is powered off. All these settings are accessed by right-clicking a VM and clicking Settings.

BIOS and Firmware Settings   The BIOS settings for a generation 1 VM enable you to change the order in which the VM's BIOS searches for boot devices (see Figure 12-25). To do this, click a device in the Startup order list box and click the Move Up or Move Down button to change its order. For example, if you already have an OS installed on the VM's hard disk, you might want to set the boot order to list the IDE disk first so that the VM doesn't attempt to boot from a CD.

Managing Virtual Machines

Figure 12-25 BIOS settings for a generation 1 VM

On a generation 2 VM, the hardware category is Firmware instead of BIOS (see Figure 12-26). You can enable the Secure Boot feature and set the boot order. Secure Boot is enabled by default and is recommended because it prevents unauthorized code from running at startup. The boot

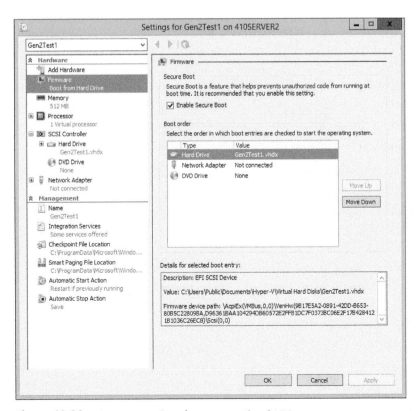

Figure 12-26 Firmware settings for a generation 2 VM

order options are simplified because you have options only for the network adapter and hard disks. On generation 2 VMs, the disk controllers are SCSI only; IDE and CD drives are no longer supported. However, you can boot from a DVD ISO image. To do so, first add a DVD drive and connect it to an ISO image stored on the host. You can't boot from a physical DVD drive with generation 2 VMs.

Memory Allocation   When you create a VM, you can configure the amount of memory it's allocated from the host computer, and you can change this amount at any time later. The amount of memory you allocate must take into account other VMs running simultaneously and enough memory left over for the host server. Windows Server 2012/R2 running Hyper-V needs about 800 MB RAM (512 MB for Windows Server 2012/R2 and 300 MB for Hyper-V) plus 32 MB for each running VM that has been assigned up to 1 GB RAM. For example, if you plan to run three virtual machines, each with 1 GB RAM, you need 3 times 1 GB for the VMs plus 32 MB times 3 plus 800 MB for the host, for a total of a little less than 4 GB. If the VMs are allocated more than 1 GB, add 8 MB to the host for each additional GB.

Dynamic Memory   Dynamic Memory, a feature that became available with Windows Server 2008 R2 Service Pack 1, allows an administrator to set startup, minimum, and maximum memory allocation values for each VM. Hyper-V adjusts the memory allocation for a VM up or down, based on its actual memory needs, between the minimum and maximum value you specify. Dynamic Memory isn't enabled by default; you enable it by choosing Memory in the VM's settings (see Figure 12-27). The following list describes the settings for this feature:

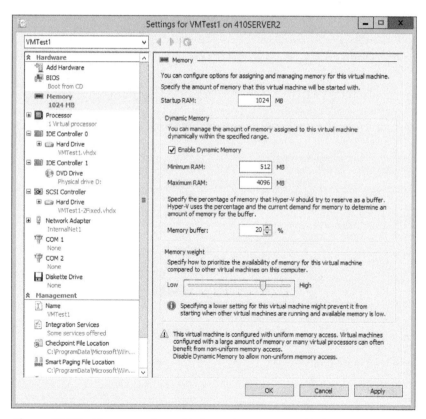

Figure 12-27   Memory settings with Dynamic Memory enabled

- *Startup RAM*—This setting specifies the amount of RAM allocated to a VM when it starts. When a computer starts, it often consumes more RAM because of all the processes loaded into memory and started. Some processes look for a minimum amount of available RAM when they're started, and if this amount isn't available, they don't start. After all the initial processes have started, the system might require less than the startup RAM.

- *Minimum RAM*—The least RAM the VM can ever be allocated.

- *Maximum RAM*—The most RAM the VM can ever be allocated.

- *Memory buffer*—The amount of extra memory Hyper-V attempts to assign to a VM above the VM's current requirements. For example, if the memory buffer is set to 20% and the VM currently needs 1 GB RAM, Hyper-V attempts to allocate 1 GB plus 20%, or 1.2 GB. The memory buffer amount is allocated to a VM only if there's enough physical memory to support the requested amount.

- *Memory weight*—This slider represents a priority. If there's not enough physical memory to allocate the requested amount of RAM to all VMs, the VMs with the highest memory weight are given the highest priority. By default, the memory weight slider is set in the middle of the scale.

Smart Paging   **Smart paging** works with Dynamic Memory. It's a file on the host computer used for temporary memory storage when a sudden surge in memory requirements exceeds the physical amount of memory available. Smart paging is used only when a VM is restarting, there's no available physical memory, and the host can't reclaim any memory from other running VMs. In fact, the smart paging file is created only when it's needed, and it's deleted after the VM no longer needs it. So this file is a sort of failsafe to bridge the gap between a VM's required startup memory and its minimum memory when physical memory is low.

No configuration is needed for smart paging other than its location on the host, which is C:\ProgramData\Microsoft\Windows\Hyper-V by default. However, the smart paging file should be stored on a non-system disk—in other words, a different disk from the one holding the \Windows directory.

Virtual Processor Settings   You can adjust how many **virtual processors** are assigned to the virtual machine, up to the total number of physical processors or processor cores installed on the host computer (see Figure 12-28). For example, if you're running a Hyper-V server on a quad-core Xeon, you can assign up to four virtual processors to each VM. However, if your VMs handle substantial processing workloads, the recommended method is to assign one or more virtual processors to each VM and reserve one physical processor (or processor core) for the host

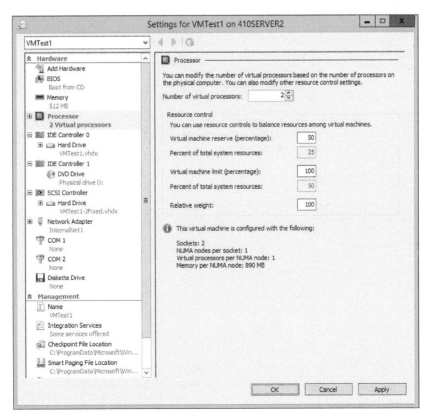

Figure 12-28   Virtual processor settings

computer. For example, if the host computer has a quad-core processor and you're running three VMs on the host, allocate each VM one virtual processor, and reserve one for the host computer. If your VMs aren't carrying substantial processing workloads, you can use more virtual processors than there are physical processors, such as allocating one virtual processor for each of six VMs when the host has only four physical processor cores.

The "Resource control" section specifies how host resources are allocated to the VM. In this example, the host has four processors and the VM has been assigned two:

- *Virtual machine reserve (percentage)*—This setting specifies what percentage of the total processing resources allocated to the VM is guaranteed to be available. The default setting is 0. If you change this setting, the "Percentage of total system resources" value changes to reflect what percentage of the total host processing power is in reserve for the VM. For example, if the VM has been assigned two virtual processors on a host with four processors, and you reserve 50% for the VM, 25% of the total host system resources are held in reserve for the VM.

- *Virtual machine limit (percentage)*—This value specifies what percentage of the assigned processing power the VM can use. The default value is 100. If you assign two processors to the VM on a host with four processors, the VM can use 100% of the processing power of two processors, which sets "Percent of total system resources" at 50. That leaves 50% of the total processing power available for other workloads.

- *Relative weight*—This setting assigns a priority to the VM's access to processing resources when more than one VM is competing for the same resource. The value can be from 1 to 10000; the higher the value, the higher the VM's priority. The default value is 100. If multiple VMs have the same relative weight value, they get an equal share of the available resources.

Integration Services

The Integration Services section of a VM's settings (see Figure 12-29) indicates whether this feature is installed on a VM. Integration Services is installed on a VM after OS installation

Figure 12-29   Integration Services settings

by clicking Action, Insert Integration Services Setup Disk from the menu. You need to install Integration Services manually only on VMs running OSs before Windows Server 2008/Vista or non-Windows OSs.

 You might want to reinstall Integration Services on an OS that automatically installs them in case the guest OS's built-in Integration Services isn't the most recent version.

Integration Services provides enhanced drivers for the guest OS and improves performance and functionality for IDE and SCSI storage devices, network interfaces, and mouse and video devices. The storage controller and network interface drivers included in Integration Services are called **synthetic drivers**, and they're optimized for use in the Hyper-V environment. **Emulated drivers**, which are used when Integration Services isn't installed, are also referred to as "legacy drivers."

Enhanced video and mouse drivers in Integration Services make using a guest OS's user interface easier. Without Integration Services installed, the VM captures the mouse when you click inside the VM window, and you must press Ctrl+Alt+left arrow to release the mouse back to the host OS. With Integration Services installed, however, you can move the mouse from guest to host freely. Furthermore, if you access the guest OS through Remote Desktop, the mouse isn't functional in the guest OS at all unless Integration Services is installed.

Aside from enhanced drivers, Integration Services offers these additional services that you can enable or disable in the VM's settings:

- *Operating system shutdown*—Allows you to shut down the VM by clicking the Shutdown button in the Virtual Machine Connection console or in Hyper-V Manager.

- *Time synchronization*—Allows you to synchronize the VM's time with the host. If the VM is a Windows domain controller, however, you shouldn't use this option because domain controllers have their own time synchronization mechanism.

- *Data Exchange*—Allows the VM and host to exchange information by using Registry keys.

- *Heartbeat*—Allows the host machine to detect when the VM has locked up or crashed. The host sends heartbeat messages to the guest VM periodically, and the heartbeat service on the guest VM responds. If it fails to respond, the host machine logs an event.

- *Backup(volume checkpoint)*—Allows host backup programs to use Volume Shadow Copy Service (VSS) to back up VM hard disk files.

- *Guest services*—New in Windows Server 2012 R2, guest services allow copying files to a running VM "out of band," meaning without using a virtual network connection. Guest services use the Hyper-V virtual machine bus (VMBus) that all VMs are connected to internally through Hyper-V. By default, guest services are disabled, but after they're enabled, you can use the PowerShell cmdlet `Copy-VMFile` to copy files from the host to the VM.

Automatic Start and Stop Actions

You use automatic start actions and automatic stop actions to specify how a VM should behave when the host computer starts and shuts down. The options for automatic start actions are as follows (see Figure 12-30):

- *Nothing*—The VM doesn't start when the host computer starts.

- *Automatically start if it was running when the service stopped*—If the VM was running when the host machine (or Hyper-V service) was last running, it starts when the host starts. If the VM wasn't running previously, it's not started. This option is the default start action and should be used with production VMs.

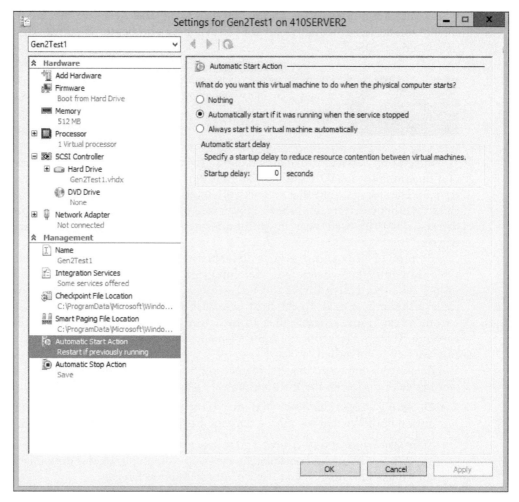

Figure 12-30   Automatic start action settings

- *Always start this virtual machine automatically*—The VM always starts when the host starts.
- *Startup delay*—If multiple VMs are set to start when the host starts, you might want to set a startup delay of different amounts for each VM to prevent resource contention. Also, if the services of one VM depend on another VM, you can set the delay time to ensure that the VMs start in the correct order.

The options for automatic stop actions are as follows (see Figure 12-31):

- *Save the virtual machine state*—The VM's state is saved when the host is shut down, which is similar to hibernate mode for a desktop computer. When the VM restarts, it picks up where it left off. This option is the default stop action, but it's not recommended for domain controllers. Be aware that the same amount of disk space is reserved as the amount of memory the VM uses.
- *Turn off the virtual machine*—This option powers down the VM, which is like pulling the power cord on a physical machine. It's not recommended unless the VM doesn't support shutdown, but even then, the save option is preferable.
- *Shut down the guest operating system*—The VM's OS undergoes a normal shutdown procedure as long as Integration Services is installed and shutdown is supported by the guest OS. This option is recommended for domain controllers, other VMs that run server roles, and applications that synchronize with other servers.

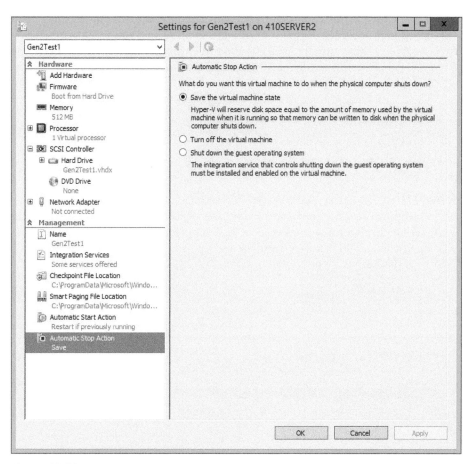

Figure 12-31   Automatic stop action settings

Managing Checkpoints

Checkpoints make working with VMs more flexible than working with physical machines. You can use them to revert a VM to a previous state, which allows you to explore what-if situations and recover from installations and configurations that have gone wrong. You can create up to 50 checkpoints per VM and revert a VM to any saved checkpoint. This feature is particularly useful in testing and lab environments because you can reset a VM to its original state with the click of a button.

Although checkpoints don't take up a lot of disk space because they work much like a differencing disk, you still need to be aware of some issues with checkpoint storage:

- By default, checkpoints are stored in the C:\ProgramData\Microsoft\Windows\Hyper-V folder. Because this location is on the host's system volume (where the C:\Windows folder is stored), however, you might want to relocate the checkpoints folder to a different disk if possible for performance reasons. You can change the checkpoint storage location for each VM in the Hyper-V Manager Settings window.

- After a checkpoint is created for a VM, you can't change the checkpoint location for that VM, but each VM can have a different checkpoint location.

- You should always use Hyper-V Manager to delete checkpoints. Checkpoint files shouldn't be deleted manually because the files must be merged with the original hard disk file.

- If you delete a checkpoint to free up disk space, the actual checkpoint file isn't deleted until the VM is shut down. What actually occurs is that the checkpoint file (which has an .avhd extension) is merged with the original hard disk file (.vhd or .vhdx), and this process can't occur until the VM is shut down. The merge might take some time, depending on the checkpoint file's size. After the files are merged, the system deletes the checkpoint file. Ideally, you should make sure the checkpoint file has been deleted before restarting the VM.

- If you create a checkpoint while a VM is running, the amount of space required for the checkpoint includes the amount of memory allocated to the VM (much like a hibernate file), which substantially increases the total amount of space the checkpoint needs. Ideally, create checkpoints while the VM is shut down to reduce the disk space used.

The cautions mentioned earlier for using checkpoints have been repeated here as a reminder:

- Checkpoints decrease a VM's disk performance.
- Checkpoints must be deleted before expanding a disk.
- Checkpoints can't be used with pass-through or differencing disks.

Reverting to and Applying Checkpoints There are two ways to use a saved checkpoint: revert and apply. Reverting to a checkpoint returns the VM to its state when the *most recent* checkpoint was taken. The Revert option is available in the Actions pane of Hyper-V Manager when a VM is selected and no checkpoints are currently selected. If you click the Revert option in the Actions pane shown in Figure 12-32, VMTest2 reverts to VMTest2-Checkpoint3.

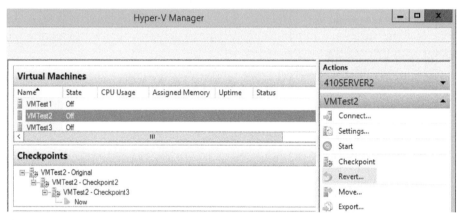

Figure 12-32 The Revert option for checkpoints

The Apply option is available when a checkpoint is selected in the Checkpoints section. Selecting the most recent checkpoint and applying it has the same effect as the Revert option. However, if you select an earlier checkpoint and apply it, a new checkpoint subtree is created, as shown in Figure 12-33. The VMTest2-Checkpoint 2 was applied, and the VM is now in the state it was in when Checkpoint 2 was taken, as indicated by the Now arrow. VMTest2-Checkpoint 3 is still available, but if you create another checkpoint, a new subtree under the Now arrow is started.

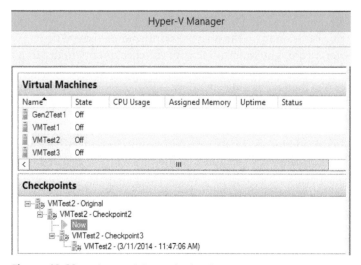

Figure 12-33 After applying a checkpoint

Resource Metering

Resource metering is a Hyper-V feature introduced in Windows Server 2012 that allows vendors of large-scale virtualization to measure customer use of VM resources for billing purposes. Resource metering is enabled and configured by using PowerShell cmdlets on the Hyper-V host and can measure the following resource metrics on a virtual machine:

- Average CPU use

- Incoming and outgoing network traffic per network adapter

- Minimum, maximum, and average physical memory use

- Maximum disk space allocated

To enable resource metering, enter the following command at a PowerShell prompt on the Hyper-V host:

```
Enable-VMResourceMetering -VMName VirtualMachine
```

Resource metering can be enabled on an entire VM with this command, but you might also want to measure use for particular metrics. For example, you might want to measure use of only virtual hard disks, memory, or network. To target specific metrics, you create a resource pool for one or more metrics, and then enable resource metering for the resource pool. You can create resource pools of the following types:

- *Memory*—Measures physical memory use

- *Processor*—Measures CPU use

- *Ethernet*—Measures network traffic

- *VHD*—Measures virtual hard disk use

- *ISO*—Measures CD/DVD usage

- *VFD*—Measures virtual floppy disk use

- *FibreChannelPort*—Measures use of a virtual Fibre Channel port

For example, to create a resource pool named MemoryPool to measure memory use, enter the following command at a PowerShell prompt:

```
New-VMResourcePool MemoryPool -ResourcePoolType Memory
```

Next, you need to configure a VM to use the resource pool. The following command tells VMTest1 to begin using resource pool MemoryPool to measure memory use. The VM must be shut down before entering this command:

```
Set-VMMemory VMTest1 -ResourcePoolName MemoryPool
```

Now enable resource metering for the pool:

```
Enable-VMResourceMetering -ResourcePoolName MemoryPool
```

After resource metering is enabled, you can display resource-metering data. To display all resource-metering data for VMTest1, use the following command to produce the output in Figure 12-34:

```
Measure-VM VMTest1
```

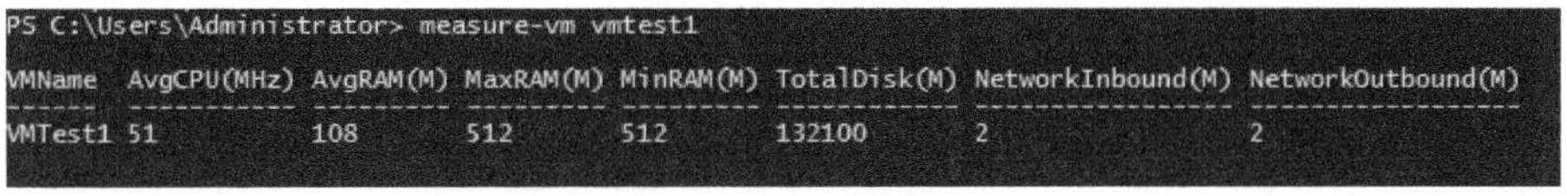

Figure 12-34 Output from the `Measure-VM` cmdlet

To view the data for a resource pool, use the following command to get output similar to Figure 12-35:

```
Measure-VMResourcePool MemoryPool
```

```
PS C:\Users\Administrator> Measure-VMResourcePool MemoryPool

Name          ResourcePoolType AvgCPU(MHz) AvgRAM(M) TotalDisk(M) NetworkInbound(M) NetworkOutbound(M)
----          ---------------- ----------- --------- ------------ ----------------- ------------------
MemoryPool    {Memory}                     166                    0                 0
```

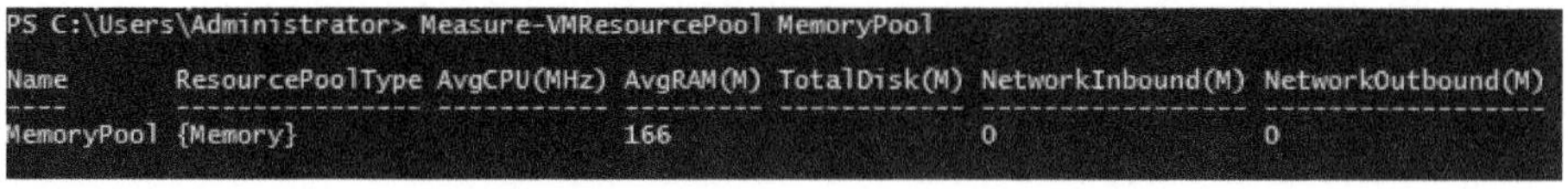

Figure 12-35   Output from the `Measure-VMResourcePool` cmdlet

You can create PowerShell scripts for enabling and disabling resource metering, collecting results, and formatting and saving the results to report files for convenient review.

Enhanced Session Mode

Enhanced Session mode is a feature that improves interaction and device redirection between the host computer and the Virtual Machine Connection console. It's a new feature in Windows Server 2012 R2 and is supported by Windows Server 2012 R2 and Windows 8.1 Pro and Enterprise and later guest OSs. It provides much the same functions as a Remote Desktop connection without the need for a network connection to the guest OS.

A regular session, called a "basic session" in Hyper-V, redirects only screen, mouse, and keyboard I/O from the guest to the Virtual Machine Connection console. An enhanced session offers these additional redirected resources and features:

- Audio redirection
- Printer redirection
- USB devices and smart cards
- Drives
- Some plug-and-play devices
- Display configuration
- Copy and paste of Clipboard data, files, and folders

With Enhanced Session mode enabled, the first thing you notice is that when you try to connect to a Virtual Machine Connection console, a message box prompts you to select the display configuration. If you click the Show Options button, you see the dialog box shown in Figure 12-36.

Figure 12-36   Enhanced Session mode settings

You can click the Local Resources tab to choose which resources from the VM should be redirected to the host computer. For example, you can print to a printer connected to the host computer from the guest OS or play audio files on the guest that play through the host computer's speakers. You also have access to the Clipboard so that you can copy and paste text and files between the host and guest.

To copy and paste files between the host and guest, you must use the copy-and-paste method; you can't drag and drop files between host and guest.

You can also redirect drives so that files on the host computer are available to the VM. If you do, a new drive icon is displayed in File Explorer on the guest OS. For example, if you redirect the C drive on the 410Server2 host, a new icon named "C on 410Server2" is listed under Devices and drives in File Explorer on the guest OS.

Enabling Enhanced Session Mode   To use Enhanced Session mode, you must enable it in Hyper-V Manager and on the guest OS. By default, Enhanced Session mode is enabled on clients that support it. However, verify the following:

- Remote Desktop Services must be running on the guest OS. This service is running by default, but you can verify it or start it, if necessary, in the Services MMC. Selecting the "Allow remote connections to this computer" option in the System Properties dialog box isn't necessary.

- You must log on to the guest OS with an account that's a member of the local Administrators or remote Desktop Users group.

Activity 12-11: Enabling Enhanced Session Mode

12

Time Required: 20 minutes
Objective: Enable Enhanced Session mode in Hyper-V Manager and connect to a VM with this mode.

Required Tools and Equipment: 410Server2
Description: You want your guest OS to have access to files on the host computer and be able to copy and paste files between the host and guest OS, so you enable Enhanced Session mode in Hyper-V Manager.

1. Log on to 410Server2 as **Administrator**, and open Hyper-V Manager, if necessary.

2. Click **Hyper-V Settings** in the Actions pane. In the left pane, under Server, click **Enhanced Session Mode Policy**. By default, this mode is disabled. In the right pane, click **Allow enhanced session mode**.

3. In the left pane, under User, click **Enhanced Session Mode**. In the right pane, click **Use enhanced session mode**, if necessary, and then click **OK**.

4. In Hyper-V Manager, right-click **VMTest1** and click **Connect**. Click the **Start** button in the Virtual Machine Connection console to start VMTest1.

5. The rightmost icon, Session Mode, logs you off the guest OS. You're currently in basic session mode. Click the **Session Mode** icon, and you see the Connect to VMTest1 dialog box shown previously in Figure 12-36. Adjust the display settings, if needed, by using the slider. Click the **Show Options** button to see the Local Resources tab and additional options.

6. Click the **Local Resources** tab, and then click the **More** button. Click to expand **Drives**, click **Local Disk (C:)**, and click **OK**. Click **Connect**.

7. Log on to VMTest1 as **Administrator**. Open File Explorer, and double-click the new **C on 410Server2** icon under Devices and drives. You see the contents of the C drive on 410Server2.

8. On 410Server2, open Notepad, create a text file, and save it on the desktop. Right-click the file and click **Copy**.

9. On VMTest1, right-click the desktop and click **Paste** to copy the file from 410Server2 to VMTest1.

10. Shut down VMTest1, and log off or shut down 410Server2.

Chapter Summary

- Virtualization creates an emulated hardware environment that allows running multiple OSs on the same physical computer simultaneously. Hyper-V is a type 1 hypervisor. Other virtualization software applications, such as Virtual PC and VMware Workstation, are type 2 hypervisors.

- Virtualization can be used in labs and test environments, but type 1 hypervisors, such as Hyper-V, are meant for use in production environments. Some important uses of virtualization in data centers include server consolidation, testing, live migration, and dynamic provisioning.

- Hyper-V is installed as a server role in Windows Server 2012/R2 64-bit versions of Standard, Enterprise, and Datacenter editions. The CPU on the host machine must be 64-bit and support virtualization extensions, such as AMD-V or Intel-VT.

- Standard Edition includes a license for one virtual instance of Windows Server 2012/R2, Enterprise Edition includes four virtual instances, and Datacenter Edition includes unlimited virtual instances.

- VMs are created in Hyper-V Manager. You can specify the amount of RAM allocated to the VM, the name and type of virtual hard disk, and the type of virtual network the VM should connect to. VMs can also be created by importing an exported VM, copying the virtual disk of another VM, and converting a physical machine to a virtual machine.

- There are three types of virtual networks: external, internal, and private. External networks connect the VM to the host's physical network, and internal networks allow VMs to communicate only with one another and the host. Private networks allow communication only between the VMs connected to them. More than one private and internal network can be created on a host.

- Three types of virtual hard disks can be created: dynamically expanding, fixed size, and differencing. A fourth type of hard disk can be attached to a VM, called a pass-through disk, which is an offline physical disk attached to the host. Storage Quality of Service (QoS) is a new feature in Windows Server 2012 R2 that enables administrators to specify minimum and maximum performance values for virtual hard disks.

- Many aspects of a VM's physical environment can be configured, including BIOS settings, memory allocation, and virtual processor settings. A VM's software environment can be enhanced by installing Integration Services, which includes enhanced drivers for disk, network, display, and mouse devices. Automatic start and stop actions can be configured to determine what actions the VM should perform when the host computer is shut down and started. Checkpoints enable you to revert a VM to a previous state. They can't be used with pass-through or differencing disks and shouldn't be used on domain controllers.

- Resource metering allows vendors of large-scale virtualization to measure customer use of VM resources for billing purposes. Enhanced Session mode is a feature that improves interaction and device redirection between the host computer and the Virtual Machine Connection console.

Key Terms

bare-metal virtualization   OS virtualization in which the hypervisor runs directly on the host computer's hardware and controls and monitors guest OSs. Also called a "type 1 hypervisor."

checkpoint   A partial copy of a virtual machine made at a particular moment, used to restore the VM to its state when the checkpoint was taken.

differencing disk   A dynamically expanding virtual disk that uses a parent/child relationship, in which the parent disk is a dynamically expanding or fixed-size disk with an OS installed and possibly some applications and data. The differencing disk is a child of the parent. Changes are made only to the differencing disk; the parent disk remains unaltered.

dynamically expanding disk   A virtual hard disk in which the .vhd file is very small when created but can expand to the maximum size specified for the virtual disk.

Dynamic Memory   A Hyper-V feature that allows an administrator to set startup, minimum, and maximum memory allocation values for each VM.

emulated drivers   Legacy drivers installed on a VM that are used when Integration Services isn't installed; also called "legacy drivers."

Enhanced Session mode   A Hyper-V feature that provides improved interaction and device redirection between the host computer and the guest OS.

external virtual switch   A virtual switch in which one of the host's physical network adapters is bound to the virtual network switch, allowing virtual machines to access a LAN connected to the host.

fixed-size disk   A virtual hard disk in which the disk's full size is allocated on the host system when it's created.

hosted virtualization   OS virtualization in which the hypervisor is installed in a general-purpose host OS, such as Windows 8 or Linux, and the host OS accesses host hardware on behalf of the guest OS. Also called a "type 2 hypervisor."

Integration Services   A software package installed on a VM's guest OS that includes enhanced drivers for the guest OS and improves performance and functionality for IDE and SCSI storage devices, network interfaces, and mouse and video devices. It also integrates the VM with the host OS better to provide services such as data exchange, time synchronization, OS shutdown, and others.

internal virtual switch   A virtual switch that isn't bound to any of the host's physical NICs. However, a host virtual NIC is bound to the internal virtual switch, which allows virtual machines and the host computer to communicate with one another, but VMs can't access the physical network.

pass-through disk   A physical disk attached to the host system that's placed offline so that it can be used by a VM instead of or in addition to a virtual disk.

private virtual switch   A virtual switch with no host connection to the virtual network, thereby allowing VMs to communicate with one another. However, there's no communication between the private virtual network and the host.

resource metering   A Hyper-V feature that allows vendors of large-scale virtualization to measure customer use of VM resources for billing purposes.

single-root I/O virtualization (SR-IOV)   An advanced Hyper-V feature that enhances the virtual network adapter's performance by bypassing the virtual switch software on the parent partition.

smart paging   A Hyper-V feature that uses a file on the host computer for temporary memory storage when a sudden surge in memory requirements exceeds the physical amount of memory available.

synthetic driver   A driver installed on a VM with Integration Services that's optimized for use in the Hyper-V environment.

12

synthetic network adapters   Network adapters that use synthetic drivers in Hyper-V and offer much better performance than legacy network adapters. *See also* synthetic driver.

virtual disk   Files stored on the host computer that represent a virtual machine's hard disk.

virtual instance   An installation of Windows Server 2012/R2 in a Hyper-V virtual machine.

virtual network   A network configuration created by virtualization software and used by virtual machines for network communication.

virtual processor   The virtual representation of a physical processor or processor core residing on the host that can be assigned to a virtual machine.

VLAN identification   A Hyper-V feature that allows creating subnets or broadcast domains on a single external or internal virtual network. Machines sharing a VLAN ID can communicate with one another directly, but those assigned different VLAN IDs must communicate through a router.

Review Questions

1. Which of the following is described as a partial copy of a VM made at a particular moment?

    a. Virtual instance

    b. Differencing disk

    c. Hypervisor

    d. Checkpoint

2. Which Windows Server 2012/R2 edition includes the license for one virtual instance of Windows Server 2012/R2?

    a. Enterprise Edition

    b. Standard Edition

    c. Datacenter Edition

    d. Essentials Edition

3. What type of virtualization environment are you most likely to use for server virtualization in data centers? (Choose all that apply.)

    a. Hosted virtualization

    b. Type 2 hypervisor

    c. Bare-metal virtualization

    d. Type 1 hypervisor

4. You have just purchased a server with Windows Server 2012 R2 Datacenter Edition installed. The server has 4 GB RAM, a 200 GB hard disk, and an Intel 1.6 GHz Xeon processor with Intel-VT. You plan to install the Hyper-V server role on this server and run two Windows Server 2012 R2 VMs, each with a 2 GB RAM allocation. You have found that this server doesn't work for this purpose, however. What should you do?

    a. Install more RAM.

    b. Install a bigger hard disk.

    c. Install Standard Edition.

    d. Upgrade the processor.

5. If you want to run two VMs, each running Windows Server 2012 R2 Standard Edition as the guest OS, on a Windows Server 2012 R2 Standard Edition server, how many Windows Server 2012 R2 licenses must you purchase?

    a. 1

    b. 2

    c. 3

    d. None

6. A virtual switch with the host's physical NIC bound to the Hyper-V Extensible Virtual Switch protocol is called which of the following?

   a. External virtual switch

   b. Private virtual switch

   c. Hosted virtual switch

   d. Internal virtual switch

7. You created a VM running Windows Server 2012 R2 and some applications. You want to create a second VM quickly that has the same configuration options and installed applications as the first one. You plan to use this second VM on the same Hyper-V server as the first. You want good disk performance from both VMs. What should you do?

   a. Create a VM with a differencing disk. Assign the first VM's virtual disk as the parent disk; the first VM will continue to use its original virtual disk.

   b. Export the first VM, and import it with the "Copy the virtual machine" option to create the second VM.

   c. Create a VM. Create a checkpoint of the first VM. Copy and rename the checkpoint file and use it for the second VM's virtual hard disk.

   d. Export the first VM and import it using the "Register the virtual machine in place" option. Use the imported VM as the second virtual server.

8. You have an old server running Windows Server 2012 R2 that has had intermittent hardware failures in the past few months that cause the server to shut down. You haven't been able to isolate the problem, but you suspect the hard disks are beginning to fail, and the server is no longer under warranty. You have been using a Hyper-V server for about a year, with two VMs running on it. This quad-core server has plenty of disk space and ample processing power and memory. Which of the following might be a good solution for the ailing server that requires the least amount of cost and administrative effort?

   a. Purchase a new machine. Remove the hard disk from the old server, and install it in the new server.

   b. Create a VM on your Hyper-V server. Remove the hard disk from the old machine, and install it in the Hyper-V server. Set the disk offline and use it as a pass-through disk for the new VM.

   c. Create a VM on your Hyper-V server. On the old server, run a physical-to-virtual conversion. Use the resulting virtual hard disk file as the virtual disk for the new VM. Take the old server offline.

   d. Create a VM on your Hyper-V server. Install Windows Server 2012 R2 as the guest OS. Carefully configure the guest OS to match the old server's configuration, and take the old server offline.

9. You have three VMs that must communicate with one another and with the host computer but not be able to access the physical network directly. What type of virtual network should you create?

   a. Private

   b. Internal

   c. Hosted

   d. External

12

10. You're installing a new VM in Hyper-V that requires excellent disk performance for the installed applications to perform well. The applications require a virtual disk of about 200 GB. The host has two drives: one used as the Windows system drive and the other as a data drive of 500 GB. It's currently running a VM that uses a virtual disk stored on the host's data drive. This VM requires little disk access, uses only 20 GB of the host's data drive, and will max out at 40 GB. What type of disk should you use for the new VM you're installing?

    a. Differencing disk

    b. Dynamically expanding disk

    c. Pass-through disk

    d. Fixed-size disk

11. Your Hyper-V server has a single disk of 300 GB being used as the system disk and to host a dynamically expanding disk for a Windows Server 2012 R2 VM. The VM's virtual disk has a maximum size of 200 GB and is currently 80 GB and growing. You have only about 30 GB free space on the host disk. You have noticed disk contention with the host OS, and the constant need for the virtual disk to expand is causing performance problems. You also have plans to install at least one more VM. You have installed a new 500 GB hard disk on the host and want to make sure the VM doesn't contend for the host's system disk, and the expansion process doesn't hamper disk performance. What should you do?

    a. Create a new fixed-size disk on the new drive. Use the Disk Management MMC on the VM to extend the current disk to the new fixed-size disk.

    b. Shut down the VM. Convert the dynamically expanding disk to a fixed-size disk, being sure to place the fixed-size disk on the new host drive. Connect the VM to the fixed-size disk in place of the dynamically expanding disk. Delete the old virtual disk.

    c. Shut down the VM. Create a new fixed-size disk on the new drive. Copy the contents of the dynamically expanding disk to the new fixed-size disk. Connect the VM to the fixed-size disk in place of the dynamically expanding disk. Delete the old virtual disk.

    d. Create a new fixed-size disk on the new drive. Add the fixed-size disk to the VM as a new disk. On the VM, create a new volume on the new disk, and begin saving files to the new volume.

12. Your network has had long power outages that have caused Hyper-V servers to shut down after the UPS battery is drained. When power returns, the Hyper-V servers restart automatically, but the VMs don't start. You need to make sure the VMs start when the host starts. What should you do?

    a. Change the VMs' BIOS settings.

    b. Write a script on the host that starts the VMs automatically when the host starts.

    c. Reinstall Integration Services.

    d. Change the automatic start action setting on the VMs.

13. You solved the problem with VMs not starting when the host restarts, but now you notice that VMs take a long time to start when the host starts. On some hosts, you have as many as six VMs. You also find that the VM running an application server can't initialize correctly because the VM running DNS isn't available immediately. What can you do to improve VMs' startup times and solve the application server problem?

    a. Set a virtual machine priority in Hyper-V's Settings window.

    b. Set a startup delay for each VM, making sure the delay for the DNS server is lower than the application server's.

    c. Change the BIOS settings of the DNS server to use the Quick Boot option.

    d. Assign more virtual processors to the VMs you want to start faster.

14. Checkpoints for your test VMs are taking up too much space on the host's system disk. You have two test VMs running, each with one checkpoint to represent the baseline testing environment. You're finished with your current testing and are ready for another round of testing, but you want to make sure your checkpoints are stored on another volume. What should you do?

    a. In Hyper-V Manager, change the checkpoints' path in the Settings window to point to the other volume; the checkpoints are moved automatically.

    b. Use File Explorer to move the checkpoint files from their current location to the other volume.

    c. Shut down the VMs. Apply the checkpoint to each VM, and delete all checkpoints in Hyper-V Manager. Change the path of the checkpoint files to the other volume, and create a new checkpoint for each VM.

    d. In each VM's settings, change the checkpoint path. Apply the checkpoint, and then create a new checkpoint for each VM. Delete the old checkpoints in File Explorer.

15. Which of the following is true about using differencing disks?

    a. Checkpoints can be used with differencing disks, but performance is decreased.

    b. The parent disk must not be changed.

    c. The parent disk must always be connected to a running VM.

    d. Differencing disks are very similar to fixed-size disks.

16. You have four checkpoints of a VM. You want to return the VM to its state when the second checkpoint was taken. Which checkpoint option should you use?

    a. Apply

    b. Save

    c. Select

    d. Revert

17. You're working with a Windows Server 2003 VM in Hyper-V. Every time you click the mouse in the VM window, it's captured, and you have to press Ctrl+Alt+left arrow to use the mouse on the host OS, which is getting annoying. What can you do to make using the VM easier?

    a. Install a new mouse on the host system that supports Hyper-V.

    b. Install Integration Services on the host computer.

    c. Install Integration Services on the VM.

    d. Install emulated mouse drivers on the VM.

18. You want to run four VMs on a Hyper-V server. Two VMs need to be assigned 1 GB RAM, and two need to be assigned 1.5 GB RAM for optimal performance. How much RAM should be installed on the host computer?

    a. 512 MB

    b. 4 GB

    c. 5 GB

    d. 6 GB

19. You want to run three VMs on a Hyper-V server. Two of the VMs should be assigned two virtual processors, and the other requires only one. The host should have at least four processor cores dedicated to it. What configuration should you use on the host?

    a. A quad-core CPU

    b. Two quad-core CPUs

    c. Two dual-core CPUs

    d. One quad-core and one dual-core CPU

12

20. You have just installed a VM named VM5 running an application that requires the best possible network performance when communicating with resources on the physical LAN. The host has four NICs. One NIC is dedicated to the host computer, and the other two are bound to two virtual switches used by four other VMs on the system. One of the NICs is currently unused. What network configuration should you use that wouldn't disturb the current VM's network configuration?

    a. Connect VM5 to an internal network, and run RRAS on the host server.

    b. Connect the four existing VMs to a private network, create a NIC team on the host server, and bind the NIC team to a virtual switch for VM5 to use.

    c. In Virtual Switch Manager, bind the unused NIC to an external virtual switch and enable SR-IOV. Connect VM5's virtual network adapter to that virtual switch and enable SR-IOV on the virtual network adapter.

    d. Create a NIC team in VM5, using all four NICs on the host. Turn on virtual network adapter sharing so that the NICs can be used for both the team and the other two virtual switches.

21. You created a VM and installed Windows Server 2008 R2 over the network, using PXE boot. When you start the VM, it doesn't attempt to boot from the network. What should you do?

    a. Install a legacy virtual network adapter.

    b. Configure the VM as a generation 2 VM.

    c. Install a synthetic virtual network adapter.

    d. Enable PXE boot in the VM's BIOS settings.

22. You currently have four VMs running on a Hyper-V server. You find that VM2 sometimes monopolizes disk I/O. You want to limit the amount of disk resources VM2 can use so that the other VMs have satisfactory disk performance. What should you do?

    a. Enable SR-IOV on VM2's virtual hard disk.

    b. Enable virtual hard disk sharing on VM2.

    c. Configure VM2's disk as a pass-through disk.

    d. Enable storage QoS on VM2's virtual hard disk.

23. You currently have four VMs running on a Hyper-V server. You need to increase the amount of memory to VM4 so that you can install a new application. You're running low on physical memory. You tried to allocate less memory to the other three VMs to free up memory, but after you did so, they wouldn't start. What can you do that doesn't involve installing additional physical memory on the host or changing the configuration of the guest OSs?

    a. Enable Dynamic Memory on all the VMs, and set the startup memory higher than the minimum memory.

    b. Configure resource metering on all four VMs.

    c. Uninstall server roles on the guest OSs until you have enough free memory for VM4.

    d. Enable memory QoS on the other three VMs and set a maximum IOPS for their memory use.

24. You're using a VM with a Windows 8.1 Pro guest OS to run applications that you want isolated from the host computer and the LAN. However, you want to be able to print from the VM to the printer connected to your host and copy files between the host and guest OS. The VM is connected to a private virtual switch. What can you do?

    a. Enable Enhanced Session mode in Hyper-V, and verify that Remote Desktop Services is running on the guest.

    b. Create shares on the host and VM to transfer files back and forth, and install a printer driver on the guest OS.

    c. Connect the VM running Windows 8.1 to an external virtual switch.

    d. Install Integration Services on the Windows 8.1 guest OS and enable the device-sharing and file-sharing options.

Case Projects

Case Project 12-1: Choosing Virtual Disk Configurations

You have two Windows Server 2012 R2 computers with the Hyper-V role installed. Both computers have two hard drives, one for the system volume and the other for data. One server, named HyperVTest, is going to be used mainly for testing and what-if scenarios, and its data drive is 250 GB. You estimate that you might have 8 or 10 VMs configured on HyperVTest with two or three running at the same time. Each test VM has disk requirements ranging from about 10 GB to 30 GB. The other server, named HyperVApp, runs in the data center with production VMs installed. Its data drive is 500 GB. You expect two VMs to run on HyperVApp, each needing about 150 GB to 200 GB of disk space. Both are expected to run fairly disk-intensive applications. Given this environment, describe how you would configure the virtual disks for the VMs on both servers.

Case Project 12-2: Choosing a Virtual Network Configuration

You're setting up a test environment that involves two subnets with three Windows Server 2012 R2 servers on each subnet. The servers are running broadcast-based network services, such as DHCP. The host computer is attached to the production network, so you must prevent any conflicts. You want the two subnets to be able to communicate with one another. The test environment consists of a single Windows Server 2012 R2 machine running Hyper-V. Describe how you plan to configure the virtual network.

Case Project 12-3: Devising a Hyper-V Solution

In this case project, you create three Hyper-V VMs named VM1, VM2, and VM3 and configure virtual switches. VM1 and VM2 are on a private network, and VM3 acts as a router to route traffic between the private network and the physical network. Refer back to Figure 12-13 to see an illustration of this configuration. Create the VMs, and configure the virtual switches suitably. There's no need to install an OS on the VMs unless you want to test the configuration. As documentation of your configuration, give your instructor the following:

Your instructor can add requirements to this project.

- Screenshots of Hyper-V Virtual Network Manager showing each virtual network selected so that its type can be determined
- Screenshots of the Settings window for each VM
- Your IP addressing scheme, showing the IP addresses and default gateways of each NIC on the VMs and the host
- The settings configured on one VM to communicate with the physical network and a statement of which VM you used for these settings

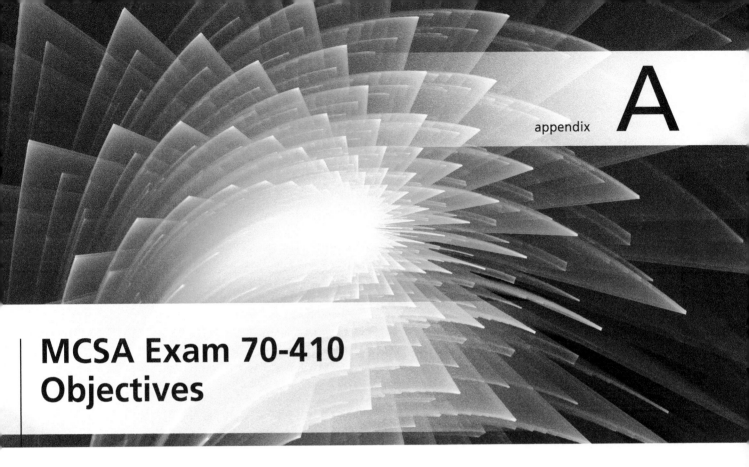

appendix A

MCSA Exam 70-410 Objectives

Table A-1 maps the Installing and Configuring Windows Server 2012 (70-410) exam objectives to the corresponding chapter and section title where the objectives are covered in this book. Major sections are listed after the chapter number, and applicable subsections are shown in parentheses. After each objective, the percentage of the exam that includes the objective is shown in parentheses.

Table A-1 Objectives-to-chapter mapping

Objective	Chapter and section(s)
Install and configure servers (17%)	
Install servers	Chapter 2: Planning a Windows Server 2012/R2 Installation
	Chapter 2: Server Core: Windows That Doesn't Do Windows
	Chapter 2: Using Features on Demand
Configure servers	Chapter 3: Working with Server Roles and Features
	Chapter 3: Configuring Server Modes
	Chapter 3: Configuring Services
	Chapter 3: Configuring NIC Teaming
Configure local storage	Chapter 4: An Overview of Server Storage
	Chapter 4: Configuring Local Disks
	Chapter 4: Working with Virtual Disks
	Chapter 4: Using Storage Spaces
Configure server roles and features (17%)	
Configure file and share access	Chapter 5: An Overview of File and Print Sharing
	Chapter 5: Securing Access to Files with Permissions
	Chapter 5: Creating Windows File Shares
	Chapter 5: Work Folders
Configure print and document services	Chapter 5: Windows Printing
Configure servers for remote management	Chapter 3: Managing Servers Remotely
	Chapter 3: Working with Older Server Operating Systems

585

Objective	Chapter and section(s)
Configure Hyper-V (18%)	
Create and configure virtual machine settings	Chapter 12: Installing Hyper-V
	Chapter 12: Creating Virtual Machines in Hyper-V
	Chapter 12: Managing Virtual Machines
Create and configure virtual machine storage	Chapter 12: Working with Virtual Hard Disks
Create and configure virtual networks	Chapter 12: Hyper-V Virtual Networks
Deploy and configure core network services (17%)	
Configure IPv4 and IPv6 addressing	Chapter 9: An Overview of TCP/IP
	Chapter 9: IPv4 Addresses
	Chapter 9: Configuring IPv4 Addresses
	Chapter 9: Internet Protocol Version 6
	Chapter 9: IP Address Types
	Chapter 9: IPv6 Autoconfiguration
	Chapter 9: Transitioning from IPv4 to IPv6
Deploy and configure Dynamic Host Configuration Protocol (DHCP) service	Chapter 11: An Overview of Dynamic Host Configuration Protocol
	Chapter 11: Installing and Configuring a DHCP Server
	Chapter 11: DHCP Server Configuration
	Chapter 11: DHCP Relay Agents
Deploy and configure DNS service	Chapter 10: Introduction to Domain Name System
	Chapter 10: Installing and Configuring DNS
	Chapter 10: Configuring DNS Zones
	Chapter 10: Advanced DNS Server Settings
	Chapter 10: Monitoring and Troubleshooting DNS
Install and administer Active Directory (15%)	
Install domain controllers	Chapter 6: The Role of a Directory Service
	Chapter 6: Installing Active Directory
	Chapter 6: What's Inside Active Directory
	Chapter 6: Working with Forests, Trees, and Domains
Create and manage Active Directory users and computers	Chapter 7: Managing User Accounts
	Chapter 7: Working with Computer Accounts
	Chapter 7: Automating Account Management
Create and manage Active Directory groups and organizational units (OUs)	Chapter 7: Managing Group Accounts
	Chapter 7: Working with Organizational Units
Create and manage Group Policy (16%)	
Create Group Policy objects (GPOs)	Chapter 6: Introducing Group Policies
	Chapter 8: Group Policy Architecture
Configure security policies	Chapter 8: Group Policy Settings (Security Settings)
	Chapter 8: Using Security Templates
Configure application restriction policies	Chapter 8: Group Policy Settings (Security Settings)
Configure Windows Firewall	Chapter 8: Configuring Windows Firewall with Group Policy

Glossary

6to4 An IPv4-to-IPv6 transition protocol that provides automatic tunneling of IPv6 traffic over an IPv4 network. It can handle host-to-router or router-to-host tunneling but is most often used to create a router-to-router tunnel.

access-based enumeration (ABE) A feature of a file share that shows only file and folders to which a user has at least Read permission.

access control entry (ACE) An entry in a discretionary access control list (DACL); includes a security principal object and the object's assigned permissions. *See also* discretionary access control list (DACL).

Active Directory The Windows directory service that enables administrators to create and manage users and groups, set network-wide user and computer policies, manage security, and organize network resources.

Active Directory–integrated zone A primary or stub zone with the DNS database stored in an Active Directory partition rather than a text file. Because Active Directory zones are replicated to other domain controllers automatically, only primary and stub zones can be Active Directory integrated.

Active Directory replication The transfer of information between all domain controllers to make sure they have consistent and up-to-date information.

administrative shares Hidden shares created by Windows that are available only to members of the Administrators group; they include the root of each volume, the \Windows folder, and IPC$. Hidden shares' names end with a dollar sign.

administrative template files These XML-format text files define policies in the Administrative Templates folder in a GPO. You can create custom ADMX files to create your own policies.

ADMX central store A centralized location for maintaining ADMX files so that when an ADMX file is modified from one domain controller, all DCs receive the updated file.

application directory partition A directory partition that applications and services use to store information that benefits from automatic Active Directory replication and security.

assigned application An application package made available to users via Group Policy and places a shortcut to the application in the Start screen. The application is installed automatically if a user tries to run it or opens a document associated with it. If the assigned application applies to a computer account, the application is installed the next time Windows boots.

attribute value Information stored in each attribute. *See also* schema attributes.

authentication A process that confirms a user's identity, and the account is assigned permissions and rights that authorize the user to access resources and perform certain tasks on the computer or domain.

authoritative server A DNS server that holds a complete copy of a zone's resource records (typically a primary or secondary zone).

Automatic Private IP Addressing (APIPA) A method of automatic IP address assignment that occurs when a computer can't contact a DHCP server; uses the range 169.254.1.0 through 169.254.254.255.

backplane A connection system that uses a printed circuit board instead of traditional cables to carry signals.

bare-metal virtualization OS virtualization in which the hypervisor runs directly on the host computer's hardware and controls and monitors guest OSs. Also called a "type 1 hypervisor."

basic disk A traditional Windows or DOS disk arrangement, in which the disk is partitioned into primary and extended partitions. A basic disk can't hold volumes spanning multiple disks or be part of a RAID.

boot volume The volume where the \Windows folder is located; usually the C drive but doesn't have to be. Also referred to as the "boot partition."

Branch Office Direct Printing A feature available with the Print and Document Services role that allows clients to print directly to a network-attached printer without the job having to go through the print server.

broadcast A packet addressed to all computers on the network.

broadcast domain The bounds of a network that defines which devices must receive a packet that's broadcast by any other device; usually an IP subnet.

built-in user accounts User accounts created by Windows automatically during installation.

caching-only DNS server A DNS server with no zones. Its sole job is to field DNS queries, do recursive lookups to root servers, or send requests to forwarders, and then cache the results.

checkpoint A partial copy of a virtual machine made at a particular moment, used to restore the VM to its state when the checkpoint was taken.

child domains Domains that share at least the top-level and second-level domain name structure as an existing domain in the forest; also called "subdomains."

CIDR notation A method of expressing an IP address in the format A.B.C.D/*n*; *n* is the number of 1 bits in the subnet mask or the number of bits in the network ID. *See also* Classless Interdomain Routing (CIDR).

classful addressing The use of IP addresses with their default subnet masks according to their address class: A, B, or C.

Classless Interdomain Routing (CIDR) The use of IP addresses without requiring the default subnet mask. *See also* subnet mask.

clean installation A Windows OS installation in which the OS is installed on a new disk partition; it's not an upgrade from any previous version of Windows.

client access licenses (CALs) A license required by law for each user who logs on to a Windows Server 2012/R2 Standard or Datacenter Edition server.

cloud computing A collection of technologies for abstracting the details of how applications, storage, network, and other computing resources are delivered to users.

conditional forwarder A DNS server to which other DNS servers send requests targeted for a specific domain.

configuration partition A directory partition that stores configuration information that can affect the entire forest, such as details on how domain controllers should replicate with one another.

conflict detection A DHCP server property that causes the DHCP server to attempt to ping an IP address before it's offered to a client to make sure the address isn't already in use.

contact An Active Directory object that usually represents a person for informational purposes only, much like an address book entry.

Datacenter Edition A Windows Server 2012/R2 edition, intended primarily for organizations using virtualization on a large scale.

delegation of control The process of a user with higher security privileges assigning authority to perform certain tasks to a user with lesser security privileges; usually used to give a user administrative permission for an OU.

destination IP address The IP address of the computer a packet is sent to.

DHCP filter A DHCP server feature that allows administrators to restrict which computers on a network are leased IP addresses.

DHCP policies A new feature in Windows Server 2012 that gives administrators more fine-tuned control over address lease options with conditions based on criteria.

DHCP relay agent A device that listens for broadcast DHCPDISCOVER and DHCPREQUEST messages and forwards them to a DHCP server on another subnet.

DHCP scope A pool of IP addresses and optionally other IP configuration parameters from which a DHCP server leases addresses to DHCP clients.

DHCP server authorization The process of enabling a DHCP server in a domain environment to prevent rogue DHCP servers from operating on the network.

differencing disk A dynamically expanding virtual disk that uses a parent/child relationship, in which the parent disk is a dynamically expanding or fixed-size disk with an OS installed and possibly some applications and data. The differencing disk is a child of the parent. Changes are made only to the differencing disk; the parent disk remains unaltered.

direct-attached storage (DAS) A storage medium directly connected to the server using it but differs from local storage in that it includes externally connected HDDs in an enclosure with a power supply.

directory partition A section of an Active Directory database stored on a domain controller's hard drive. These sections are managed by different processes and replicated to other domain controllers in an Active Directory network.

directory service A database that stores information about a computer network and includes features for retrieving and managing that information.

Directory Services Restore Mode (DSRM) A boot mode used to perform restore operations on Active Directory if it becomes corrupted or parts of it are deleted accidentally.

discretionary access control list (DACL) A list of security principals; each has permissions that define access to an object. *See also* security principal.

disk drive A physical component with a disk interface connector (such as SATA or SCSI) and a power connector.

disk quotas An option on NTFS volumes that enables administrators to limit how much disk space a user can occupy with his or her files.

distribution group A group type used when you want to group users together, mainly for sending e-mails to several people at once with an Active Directory–integrated e-mail application, such as Microsoft Exchange.

DNS namespace Defines the structure of names used to identify resources in Internet domains. It consists of a root name (defined as a period), top-level domains, second-level domains, optionally one or more subdomains, and host-names separated by periods.

domain The core structural unit of Active Directory; contains OUs and represents administrative, security, and policy boundaries.

domain controller A Windows server that has Active Directory installed and is responsible for allowing client computers access to domain resources.

domain directory partition A directory partition that contains all objects in a domain, including users, groups, computers, OUs, and so forth.

domain GPOs Group Policy objects stored in Active Directory on domain controllers. They can be linked to a site, a domain, or an OU and affect users and computers whose accounts are stored in these containers.

domain local group A group scope that's the main security principal recommended for assigning rights and permissions to domain resources.

domain user account A user account created in Active Directory that provides a single logon for users to access all resources in the domain for which they have been authorized.

downlevel server A server running an earlier version of the Windows Server OS; usually in the context of managing that server remotely.

downlevel user logon name The user logon name field defined in a user account object that's used for backward-compatibility with OSs and applications that don't recognize the UPN format.

dual IP layer architecture The current architecture of the IPv6 protocol in Windows, in which both IPv4 and IPv6 share the other components of the stack.

dynamic disk A disk arrangement that can hold up to 128 volumes, including spanned volumes, striped volumes, and RAID volumes.

Dynamic DNS (DDNS) A DNS name-registering process whereby computers in the domain can register or update their own DNS records.

Dynamic Host Configuration Protocol (DHCP) A component of the TCP/IP protocol suite used to assign an IP address to a host automatically from a defined pool of addresses.

Dynamic Memory A Hyper-V feature that allows an administrator to set startup, minimum, and maximum memory allocation values for each VM.

dynamically expanding disk A virtual hard disk in which the .vhd file is very small when created but can expand to the maximum size specified for the virtual disk.

Echo Reply An ICMP message that's the response when a computer receives an Echo Request, generated by the `ping` program.

Echo Request An ICMP message generated by the `ping` program used to test network connectivity and IP configuration. If a computer receives an Echo Request, it responds with an Echo Reply.

effective access The access a security principal has to a file system object when taking sharing permissions, NTFS permissions, and group memberships into account. *See also* security principal.

effective permissions The combination of permissions assigned to an account from explicit and inherited permissions; determines an account's effective access to an object. *See also* effective access.

elevation A process that occurs when a user attempts to perform an action requiring administrative rights and is prompted to enter credentials.

emulated drivers Legacy drivers installed on a VM that are used when Integration Services isn't installed; also called "legacy drivers."

Enhanced Session mode A Hyper-V feature that provides improved interaction and device redirection between the host computer and the guest OS.

Essentials Edition A Windows Server 2012/R2 edition suitable for small businesses with 25 or fewer users. This edition doesn't support Hyper-V, and some services, such as Active Directory and DNS, are installed automatically during OS installation.

exclusion range A range of addresses in the scope that the DHCP server doesn't lease to clients.

explicit permission A permission assigned by adding a user's account to an object's DACL.

extended partition A division of disk space on a basic disk that must be divided into logical drives; can't be marked active and can't hold the Windows system volume.

Extended Unique Identifier (EUI)-64 interface ID An autoconfigured IPv6 host address that uses the MAC address of the host plus an additional 16 bits.

extension An item in a GPO that allows an administrator to configure a policy setting.

external virtual switch A virtual switch in which one of the host's physical network adapters is bound to the virtual network switch, allowing virtual machines to access a LAN connected to the host.

failover A server's capability to recover from network hardware failure by having redundant hardware that can take over immediately for failed hardware.

feature file store A network share containing the files required to install roles, role services, and features on Windows Server 2012/R2 servers. *See also* Features on Demand.

Features on Demand A new feature in Windows Server 2012/R2 that enables you to remove the files used to install roles and features and free up the disk space these files normally consume.

file system The method and format an OS uses to store, locate, and retrieve files from electronic storage media.

fixed provisioning A method of creating virtual disks that allocates all space for the virtual disk from the storage pool immediately.

fixed-size disk A virtual hard disk in which the disk's full size is allocated on the host system when it's created.

Flexible Single Master Operation (FSMO) roles Specialized domain controller tasks that handle operations that can affect the entire domain or forest. Only one domain controller can be assigned a particular FSMO.

forest A collection of one or more Active Directory trees. It can consist of a single tree with a single domain, or it can contain several trees, each with a hierarchy of parent and child domains.

forest root domain The first domain created in a new forest.

formatting The process of preparing a disk with a file system used to organize and store files.

forward lookup zone (FLZ) A DNS zone containing records that translate names to IP addresses, such as A, AAAA, and MX records. It's named after the domain whose resource records it contains.

forwarder A DNS server to which other DNS servers send requests they can't resolve themselves.

Foundation Edition A Windows Server 2012/R2 edition intended as an entry-level server edition. It's an OEM-only version that supports only 15 users and can only be purchased already installed on a server.

fully qualified domain name (FQDN) A domain name that includes all parts of the name, including the top-level domain.

global catalog partition A directory partition that stores the global catalog, which is a partial replica of all objects in the forest. It contains the most commonly accessed object attributes to facilitate object searches and user logons across domains.

global group A group scope used mainly to group users from the same domain who have similar access and rights requirements. A global group's members can be user accounts and other global groups from the same domain. *See also* group scope.

GlobalNames zone (GNZ) A feature that provides a way for IT administrators to add single-label names (computer names that don't use a domain suffix) to DNS, thereby allowing client computers to resolve these names without including a DNS suffix in the query.

glue A record An A record used to resolve the name in an NS record to its IP address.

GPO filtering A method to alter the normal scope of a GPO and exclude certain objects from being affected by its settings. GPO filtering methods include security filtering, which uses GPO permissions, and WMI filtering, which uses Windows Management Instrumentation queries to select objects. *See also* WMI filtering.

GPO scope The objects affected by a GPO linked to a site, domain, or OU.

Group Policy Container (GPC) A GPO component that's an Active Directory object stored in the System\Policies folder. The GPC stores GPO properties and status information but no actual policy settings.

Group Policy object (GPO) A list of settings that administrators use to configure user and computer operating environments remotely through Active Directory.

Group Policy Template (GPT) A GPO component that's stored as a set of files in the SYSVOL share. It contains all the policy settings that make up a GPO as well as related files, such as scripts.

group scope A property of a group that determines the reach of a group's application in a domain or a forest—for example, which security principals in a forest can be group

members and to which forest resources a group can be assigned rights or permissions.

group type A property of a group that defines it as a security group or a distribution group.

guest OS The operating system running in a virtual machine installed on a host computer. *See also* virtual machine (VM).

GUID Partitioning Table (GPT) A disk-partitioning method that supports volume sizes up to 18 exabytes.

host computer The physical computer on which virtualization software is installed and virtual machines run.

hosted virtualization OS virtualization in which the hypervisor is installed in a general-purpose host OS, such as Windows 8 or Linux, and the host OS accesses host hardware on behalf of the guest OS. Also called a "type 2 hypervisor."

hot-add A high-end feature that allows adding hardware (usually memory, processors, or disk drives) to a system while it's running.

hot-replace A high-end feature that allows replacing faulty hardware (usually memory, processors, or disk drives) in a system while it's running.

hypervisor The virtualization software component that creates and monitors the virtual hardware environment, which allows multiple virtual machines to share physical hardware resources.

in-place upgrade An upgrade that replaces the existing OS with the new OS but maintains all the roles and features installed on the existing OS.

inherited permission A permission that comes from an object's parent instead of being assigned explicitly. *See also* explicit permission.

Install from media (IFM) An option when installing a DC in an existing domain; much of the Active Directory database contents are copied to the new DC from media created from an existing DC.

Integrated Scripting Environment (ISE) A PowerShell development environment that helps in creating PowerShell scripts.

Integration Services A software package installed on a VM's guest OS that includes enhanced drivers for the guest OS and improves performance and functionality for IDE and SCSI storage devices, network interfaces, and mouse and video devices. It also improves the VM's integration with the host OS to provide services such as data exchange, time synchronization, OS shutdown, and others.

internal virtual switch A virtual switch that isn't bound to any of the host's physical NICs. However, a host virtual NIC is bound to the internal virtual switch, which allows virtual machines and the host computer to communicate with one another, but VMs can't access the physical network.

intersite replication Active Directory replication that occurs between two or more sites.

Intra-Site Automatic Tunnel Addressing Protocol (ISATAP) An automatic tunneling protocol used to transmit IPv6 packets between dual IP layer hosts across an IPv4 network. *See also* dual IP layer architecture.

intrasite replication Active Directory replication between domain controllers in the same site.

iterative query A type of DNS query to which a DNS server responds with the best information it has to satisfy the query. The DNS server doesn't query additional DNS servers in an attempt to resolve the query.

just a bunch of disks (JBOD) A disk arrangement in which two or more disks are abstracted to appear as a single disk to the OS but aren't arranged in a specific RAID configuration.

Knowledge Consistency Checker (KCC) A process that runs on every domain controller to determine the replication topology.

lease duration A parameter of a DHCP IP address lease that specifies how long a DHCP client can keep an address.

lease renewal The process of a DHCP client renewing its IP address lease by using unicast DHCPREQUEST messages.

Lightweight Directory Access Protocol (LDAP) A protocol that runs over TCP/IP and is designed to facilitate access to directory services and directory objects. It's based on a suite of protocols called X.500, developed by the International Telecommunication Union.

link-local IPv6 address Similar in function to the IPv4 APIPA addresses, link-local IPv6 addresses begin with fe80, are self-configuring, and can't be routed. *See also* Automatic Private IP Addressing (APIPA).

load balancing Distributing traffic between two or more interfaces, thus increasing the overall network throughput a server is capable of maintaining.

load balancing and failover (LBFO) Another term for NIC teaming. *See* NIC teaming.

local GPOs A Group Policy object that's stored on local computers and can be edited by the Group Policy Object Editor snap-in.

local group A group created in the local SAM database on a member server or workstation or a stand-alone computer.

local storage Storage media with a direct and exclusive connection to the computer's system board through a disk controller.

local user account A user account defined on a local computer that's authorized to access resources only on that computer. Local user accounts are mainly used on stand-alone computers or in a workgroup network with computers that aren't part of an Active Directory domain.

localhost A reserved name that corresponds to the loopback address, 127.0.0.1. *See also* loopback address.

logical AND operation A binary operation in which there are two operands; the result is 0 if either operand is 0 and 1 if both operands are 1.

logical unit number (LUN) A logical reference point to a unit of storage that could refer to an entire array of disks, a single disk, or just part of a disk.

loopback address The IP address 127.0.0.1, which always refers to the local computer and is used to test the functioning of TCP/IP.

managed policy setting A type of group policy setting whereby the setting on the user or computer account reverts to its original state when the object is no longer in the scope of the GPO containing the setting.

Master Boot Record (MBR) A disk-partitioning method that supports volume sizes up to 2 TB.

member server A Windows server that's in the management scope of a Windows domain but doesn't have Active Directory installed.

metric A value assigned to the gateway based on the speed of the interface used to access the gateway.

Minimal Server Interface A new feature in Windows Server 2012 that takes up less disk space than the Server with a GUI option but more than the Server Core option. Includes Server Manager, MMCs, and some Control Panel applets.

mirrored volume A volume that uses space from two dynamic disks and provides fault tolerance. Data written to one disk is duplicated, or mirrored, to the second disk. If one disk fails, the other disk has a good copy of the data, and the system can continue to operate until the failed disk is replaced. Also called a "RAID 1 volume."

multicasting A network communication in which a packet is addressed so that more than one destination can receive it.

multimaster replication The process for replicating Active Directory objects; changes to the database can occur on any domain controller and are propagated, or replicated, to all other domain controllers.

Network Address Translation (NAT) A process that translates the source or destination IP address in a packet to a different value; often used to allow using private IP addresses while connected to the Internet.

network-attached storage (NAS) A storage device that has an enclosure, a power supply, slots for multiple HDDs, a network interface, and a built-in OS tailored for managing shared files and folders.

network client The part of the OS that sends requests to a server to access network resources.

network connection A collection of components consisting of a network interface, network protocols, and network client and server software that work together to connect a Windows computer to a network.

Network File System (NFS) The native file-sharing protocol in UNIX and Linux OSs; also supported by Windows Server 2012.

Network Location Awareness A Windows feature for configuring each network connection on your computer with one of three settings, called profiles: Domain Profile, Private Profile, and Public Profile.

network protocol Software that specifies the rules and format of communication between devices on a network.

network server software The part of the OS that receives requests for shared network resources and makes these resources available to a network client.

New Technology File System (NTFS) A file system used on Windows OSs that supports compression, encryption, and fine-tuned permissions.

NIC teaming A feature that allows multiple network interfaces to work in tandem to increase available bandwidth and provide load balancing and fault tolerance.

NTFS permissions Permissions set on folders or files on an NTFS-formatted volume; they protect both network and interactive/local file access.

object A grouping of information that describes a network resource, such as a shared printer, or an organizing structure, such as a domain or OU.

object owner Usually the user account that created the object or a group or user who has been assigned ownership of the object. An object owner has special authority over that object.

octet An 8-bit value; a number from 0 to 255 that's one of the four numbers in a dotted decimal IP address.

offline domain join A feature that allows a running computer or offline virtual disk to join a domain without contacting a domain controller.

offline files A feature of shared folders that allows users to access the contents of shared folders when not connected to the network; also called "client-side caching."

operations master A domain controller with sole responsibility for certain domain or forest-wide functions.

organizational unit (OU) An Active Directory container used to organize a network's users and resources into logical administrative units.

page file A system file in Windows used as virtual memory and to store dump data after a system crash.

partition A logical unit of storage that can be formatted with a file system; similar to a volume but used with basic disks.

pass-through disk A physical disk attached to the host system that's placed offline so that it can be used by a VM instead of or in addition to a virtual disk.

patches Software updates normally intended to fix security vulnerabilities and software bugs.

permission inheritance A method for defining how permissions are transmitted from a parent object to a child object.

permissions A property of the file system that specifies which users can access a file system object (a file or folder) and what users can do with the object if they're granted access.

permissions Settings that define which resources users can access and what level of access they have to resources.

ping A utility used to test network connectivity and IP address configuration.

piping Sending the output of one command as input to another command.

PowerShell A command-line interactive scripting environment that provides the commands needed for most management tasks in a Windows Server 2012/R2 environment.

Preboot Execution Environment (PXE) A network environment built into many NICs that allows a computer to boot from an image stored on a network server.

primary partition A division of disk space on a basic disk used to create a volume. It can be assigned a drive letter, be marked active, and contain the Windows system volume.

primary zone A DNS zone containing a read/write master copy of all resource records for the zone; this zone is authoritative for the zone.

primordial pool A collection of physical disks available to be added to a storage pool.

printer pooling A printer configuration in which a single printer represents two or more print devices. Users can print to a single printer, and the print server sends the job to the print device that's least busy.

printer priority A printer configuration in which two or more printers can represent a single print device. Printers can be assigned different priorities so that jobs sent to the higher priority printer are sent to the print device first.

private cloud A cloud computing service provided by a company's internal IT Department. *See* cloud computing.

private virtual switch A virtual switch with no host connection to the virtual network, thereby allowing VMs to communicate with one another. However, there's no communication between the private virtual network and the host.

public cloud A cloud computing service provided by a third party. *See* cloud computing.

published application An application package made available via Group Policy for users to install by using Programs and Features in Control Panel. The application is installed automatically if a user tries to run it or opens a document associated with it.

RAID 5 volume A volume that uses space from three or more dynamic disks and uses disk striping with parity to provide fault tolerance. When data is written, it's striped across all but one of the disks in the volume. Parity information derived from the data is written to the remaining disk and used to re-create lost data after a disk failure.

read only domain controller (RODC) A domain controller that stores a read-only copy of the Active Directory database but no password information. Changes to the domain must be made on a writeable DC and then replicated to an RODC.

recursive query A query in which the DNS server processes the query until it responds with an address that satisfies the query or with an "I don't know" message. The process might require the DNS server to query several additional DNS servers.

redundant array of independent disks (RAID) A disk configuration that uses space on multiple disks to form a single logical volume. Most RAID configurations provide fault tolerance, and some enhance performance.

referral A response to an iterative query in which the address of another name server is returned to the requester.

relative identifier (RID) The part of a SID that's unique for each Active Directory object. *See also* security identifier (SID).

replication partner A domain controller configured to replicate with another domain controller.

reservation An IP address associated with a DHCP client's MAC address to ensure that when the client requests an IP address, it always gets the same one, along with any configured options.

resilience Another term for fault tolerance; indicates a disk arrangement's capability to maintain data if a disk fails.

resolver A DNS client that sends a recursive query to a DNS server. *See also* recursive query.

resource metering A Hyper-V feature that allows vendors of large-scale virtualization to measure customer use of VM resources for billing purposes.

resource records Data in a DNS database containing information about network resources, such as hostnames, other DNS servers, and services; each record is identified by a letter code.

reverse lookup zone (RLZ) A DNS zone containing PTR records that map IP addresses to names; it's named with the IP network address (IPv4 or IPv6) of the computer whose records it contains.

right A setting that specifies what types of actions a user can perform on a computer or network.

role services Services that can be installed in Server Manager to add functions to the main role. *See also* server role.

root domain controller The first domain controller installed in an Active Directory forest. *See also* domain controller.

root hints A list of name servers preconfigured on Windows DNS servers that point to Internet root servers, which are DNS servers located on the Internet and managed by IANA.

root servers DNS servers that keep a database of addresses of other DNS servers managing top-level domain names.

round robin A method of responding to DNS queries when more than one IP address exists for the queried host. Each IP address is placed first in the list of returned addresses an equal number of times so that hosts are accessed alternately.

schema Information that defines the type, organization, and structure of data stored in the Active Directory database.

schema attributes A category of schema information that defines what type of information is stored in each object.

schema classes A category of schema information that defines the types of objects that can be stored in Active Directory, such as user or computer accounts.

schema directory partition A directory partition containing the information needed to define Active Directory objects and object attributes for all domains in the forest.

secondary zone A DNS zone containing a read-only copy of all resource records for the zone. Changes can't be made directly on a secondary DNS server, but because it contains an exact copy of the primary zone, it's considered authoritative for the zone.

Security Accounts Manager (SAM) database A database on domain member and workgroup computers that holds the users and groups defined on the local computer.

security descriptor A file system object's security settings, composed of the DACL, owner, and SACL. *See also* discretionary access control list (DACL) *and* system access control list (SACL).

security groups A group type that's the main Active Directory object administrators use to manage network resource access and grant rights to users. *See also* group type.

security identifier (SID) A numeric value assigned to each object in a domain that uniquely identifies the object; composed of a domain identifier, which is the same for all objects in a domain, and an RID. *See also* relative identifier (RID).

security principal An object that can be assigned permission to access the file system; includes user, group, and computer accounts.

security templates Text files with an .inf extension that contain information to define policy settings in the Computer Configuration, Policies, Windows Settings, Security Settings node of a local or domain GPO.

Serial ATA (SATA) A common disk interface technology that's inexpensive, fast, and fairly reliable with transfer speeds up to 6 Gb/s; used in both client computers and low-end servers and replaces the older parallel ATA (PATA) technology.

serial attached SCSI (SAS) A newer serial form of SCSI with transfer rates up to 6 Gb/s and higher; the disk technology of choice for servers and high-end workstations. *See also* small computer system interface (SCSI).

Server Core A Windows Server 2012/R2 installation option that doesn't have a traditional GUI.

server features Components you can install that provide functions to enhance or support an installed role or add a stand-alone feature.

Server Message Block (SMB) A client/server Application-layer protocol that provides network file sharing, network printing, and authentication.

server operating systems OSs designed to emphasize network access performance and run background processes rather than desktop applications.

server role A major function or service that a server performs.

server role migration An upgrade in which you perform a clean install of Windows Server 2012/R2 and migrate existing server roles to the new OS.

service A task or process that runs in the background.

service dependencies A service that requires another service or Windows component to function correctly.

service pack A collection of bug fixes, security updates, and new features that can be installed on an OS to bring it up to date.

shadow copies A feature of the Windows file system that allows users to access previous versions of files in shared folders and restore files that have been deleted or corrupted.

share permissions Permissions applied to shared folders that protect files accessed across the network; the only method for protecting files on FAT volumes.

simple volume A volume that resides on a single disk, basic or dynamic.

single-root I/O virtualization (SR-IOV) An advanced Hyper-V feature that enhances the virtual network adapter's performance by bypassing the virtual switch software on the parent partition.

site A physical location in which domain controllers communicate and replicate information regularly.

small computer system interface (SCSI) An older parallel bus disk technology still used on some servers but has reached its performance limits at 640 MB/s transfer rates.

smart paging A Hyper-V feature that uses a file on the host computer for temporary memory storage when a sudden surge in memory requirements exceeds the physical amount of memory available.

solid state drive (SSD) A type of storage medium that uses flash memory, has no moving parts, and requires less power than a traditional HDD. Also faster and more shock resistant than a traditional HDD but costs more per gigabyte and doesn't have as much capacity as an HDD.

source IP address The IP address of a computer that's sending a packet.

spanned volume A volume that extends across two or more physical disks, such as a simple volume that has been extended to a second disk.

special identity group A group whose membership is controlled dynamically by Windows and doesn't appear as an object in Active Directory Users and Computers or Active Directory Administrative Center; can be assigned permissions by adding it to resources' DACLs.

split scope A fault-tolerant DHCP configuration in which two DHCP servers share the same scope information, allowing both servers to offer DHCP services to clients.

stand-alone server A Windows server that isn't a domain controller or a member of a domain.

Standard Edition A Windows Server 2012/R2 edition suitable for most businesses that need a full-featured server and might need to use virtualization on a moderate scale.

standard zone A primary, secondary, or stub zone that isn't Active Directory integrated.

Starter GPO A GPO template that can be used as a baseline for creating new GPOs, much like user account templates.

storage appliance *See* network-attached storage (NAS).

storage area network (SAN) A storage device that uses high-speed networking technologies to give servers fast access to large amounts of shared disk storage. The storage a SAN manages appears to the server OS as though it's physically attached to the server.

storage layout The method used to create a virtual disk with Storage Spaces; includes simple, mirror, and parity. *See also* Storage Spaces.

storage pool A collection of physical disks from which virtual disks and volumes are created and assigned dynamically.

Storage Spaces A new feature in Windows Server 2012/R2 that provides flexible provisioning of virtualized storage.

striped volume A volume that extends across two or more dynamic disks, but data is written to all disks in the volume equally; provides no fault tolerance but does have a performance advantage over simple or spanned volumes.

stub zone A DNS zone containing a read-only copy of only the zone's SOA and NS records and the necessary A records to resolve NS records. A stub zone forwards queries to a primary DNS server for that zone and is not authoritative for the zone.

subnet mask A 32-bit dotted decimal number consisting of an unbroken series of binary 1 digits followed by an unbroken series of binary 0 digits. Used with an IP address to determine the network ID.

subnetting A process that reallocates bits from an IP address's host portion to the network portion, creating multiple smaller address spaces.

supernetting A process that reallocates bits from an IP address's network portion to the host portion, effectively combining smaller subnets into a larger supernet.

superscope A special type of scope consisting of one or more member scopes; it allows a DHCP server to service multiple IP subnets on a single physical network.

synthetic driver A driver installed on a VM with Integration Services that's optimized for use in the Hyper-V environment.

synthetic network adapters Network adapters that use synthetic drivers in Hyper-V and offer much better performance than legacy network adapters. *See also* synthetic driver.

system access control list (SACL) A file system component that defines the settings for auditing access to an object.

system volume A volume containing the files a computer needs to find and load the Windows OS. *See also* volume.

SYSVOL folder A shared folder that stores information from Active Directory that's replicated to other domain controllers.

Teredo An automatic IPv6-over-IPv4 tunneling protocol that solves the problem of 6to4's requirement of a public IPv4 address and the inability to traverse NAT routers. *See also* 6to4.

thin provisioning A method for creating virtual disks, whereby the virtual disk expands dynamically and uses space from the storage pool as needed until it reaches the specified maximum size.

top-level domain (TLD) servers DNS servers that maintain addresses of other DNS servers that are authoritative for second-level domains that use the top-level domain. For example, a TLD server for the com top-level domain contains NS records for authoritative DNS servers for all domains ending in com.

Transmission Control Protocol/Internet Protocol (TCP/IP) A network protocol suite designed to deliver data packets to computers on any scale of network, from a small two-computer LAN to the worldwide Internet.

tree A grouping of domains that share a common naming structure.

trust relationship An arrangement that defines whether and how security principals from one domain can access network resources in another domain.

tunneling A common network protocol technique that allows transmitting a packet in a format that would otherwise be incompatible for the network architecture by encapsulating the packet in a compatible header format.

unicast address An address in a unit of network data intended for a single destination computer.

unique local IPv6 address An address for devices on a private network that can't be routed on the Internet.

universal group A group scope that can contain users from any domain in the forest and be assigned permission to resources in any domain in the forest. *See also* group scope.

universal group membership caching A feature enabled on a domain controller that causes it to keep a local copy of universal group membership after querying a global catalog server.

unmanaged policy setting A type of group policy setting whereby the setting on the user or computer account is persistent, meaning it remains even after the computer or user object falls out of the GPO's scope.

User Account Control policies Policies that determine what happens on a computer when a user attempts to perform an action that requires elevation. *See also* elevation.

User Class A custom value you create on the DHCP server and then configure on a DHCP client; used much like the Vendor Class value.

user principal name (UPN) A user logon name that follows the format *username@domain*. Users can use UPNs to log on to their own domain from a computer that's a member of a different domain.

user template A user account that's copied to create users with common attributes.

Vendor Class A field in the DHCP packet that device manufacturers or OS vendors can use to identify a device model or an OS version.

VHD file The format virtual machines running in Hyper-V use for their virtual disks. VHD files can also be created and mounted with Disk Management and used like physical disks.

virtual desktop infrastructure (VDI) A rapidly growing sector of private cloud computing whereby users access their desktops through a private cloud; the OS and applications run on servers in a corporate data center rather than on the local computer.

virtual disk Files stored on the host computer that represent a virtual machine's hard disk.

virtual instance An installation of Windows Server 2012/R2 in a Hyper-V virtual machine.

virtual machine (VM) The virtual environment that emulates a physical computer's hardware and BIOS.

virtual network A network configuration created by virtualization software and used by virtual machines for network communication.

virtual processor The virtual representation of a physical processor or processor core residing on the host that can be assigned to a virtual machine.

virtualization A technology that uses software to emulate multiple hardware environments, allowing multiple operating systems to run on the same physical server simultaneously.

virtualization software The software for creating and managing virtual machines and creating the virtual environment in which a guest OS is installed.

VLAN identification A Hyper-V feature that allows creating subnets or broadcast domains on a single external or internal virtual network. Machines sharing a VLAN ID can communicate with one another directly, but those assigned different VLAN IDs must communicate through a router.

volume A logical unit of storage that can be formatted with a file system.

Volume Shadow Copy Service (VSS) A Windows service that enables shadow copies and allows copying files that are open, essentially taking a snapshot of the data, which allows making backups of files and applications without taking them offline. *See also* shadow copies.

Windows domain A group of Windows computers that share common management and are subject to rules and policies that an administrator defines.

Windows Remote Management (WinRM) A Windows 2012 feature that provides a command-line interface for performing a variety of remote management tasks.

Windows workgroup Also called a peer-to-peer network, it's a small collection of Windows computers whose users typically have something in common, such as the need to share files or printers with each other. No computer has authority or control over another. Logons, security, and resource sharing are decentralized.

WMI filtering A GPO filtering method that uses Windows Management Instrumentation (WMI), a Windows technology for gathering management information about computers.

Work Folders A role service that's a component of the File and Storage Services role; allows users to synchronize documents between company file servers and mobile devices.

zone A grouping of DNS information that represents one or more domains and possibly subdomains.

zone replication The transfer of zone changes from one DNS server to another.

zone transfer An operation that copies all or part of a zone from one DNS server to another and occurs as a result of a secondary server requesting the transfer from another server.

Index